Praise for  netbooks™

"Thanks to Wolff and friends, the cyber-swamp may just have become a little less murky."—*Entertainment Weekly*

"*NetGuide* is the computer world's online *TV Guide*™."—*Good Morning America*

"*NetGuide* will keep you from wandering around aimlessly on the Internet, and is full of good ideas for where to pull over."—*Forbes FYI*

"*NetGuide* is the liveliest, most readable online guide yet."—*USA Today*

"What you need to connect."—*Worth Magazine*

"*NetGuide* is the *TV Guide*™ to Cyberspace!" —Louis Rossetto, publisher/editor, *Wired*

"One of the more complete, well-organized guides to online topics. From photography to the Church of Elvis, you'll find it here."—*PC Magazine*

"The best attempt yet at categorizing and organizing all the great stuff you can find out there. It's the book people keep stealing off my desk." —Joshua Quittner, *New York Newsday*

"It's changed my online life. Get this book!" —Mike Madson, "Computer Bits," Business Radio Network

"My favorite for finding the cool stuff." —*The Louisville Courier-Journal*

"*NetGuide* focuses on the most important aspect of online information—its content. You name it, it's there—from erotica to religion to politics." —Lawrence J. Magid, *San Jose Mercury News*

"Not only did all the existing Net books ignore Cyberspace's entertaining aspects, but they were process-oriented, not content-oriented. Why hadn't someone made a *TV Guide*™ for the Net? Wolff recognized an opportunity for a new book, and his group wrote *NetGuide*." —Mark Frauenfelder, *Wired*

"Couch potatoes have *TV Guide*™. Now Net surfers have *NetGuide*."—*Orange County Register*

"*NetGuide* is one of the best efforts to provide a hot-spot guide to going online."—*Knoxville News-Sentinel*

"Absolutamente indispensabile!"—*L'Espresso*, Italy

"A valuable guide for anyone interested in the recreational uses of personal computers and modems."—Peter H. Lewis, *The New York Times*

"*NetGames* is a good map of the playing fields of Netdom."—*Newsweek*

"This guide to games people play in the ever-expanding Cyberspace shows you exactly where to go."—*Entertainment Weekly*

"The second book in a very good series from Wolff and Random House."—Bob Schwabach, syndicated columnist

"Hot addresses!"—*USA Weekend*

"Move over Parker Brothers and Nintendo—games are now available online. There's something in *NetGames* for everyone from crossword-puzzle addicts to Dungeons & Dragons fans."—*Reference Books Bulletin*

"Whether you're a hardened game player or a mere newbie, *NetGames* is the definitive directory for gaming on the Internet."—*.net*

"A wide and devoted following."—*The Wall Street Journal*

"*NetMoney* is a superb guide to online business and finance!"—*Hoover's Handbook of American Business*

"[*NetChat*] is…the best surfer's guide out there." —*Entertainment Weekly*

"A product line of guidebooks for explorers of the Internet."—*Inside Media*

Neither *NetGuide* nor Wolff New Media LLC is affiliated with, or sponsored or endorsed by *TV Guide*® or its publishers.

In bookstores now!

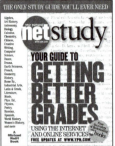

NetStudy

Where can I get help with my algebra homework? My English paper's due tomorrow and the library's closed. I don't understand frog anatomy. From the beginner studying astronomy to the math whiz taking AP calculus, *NetStudy* can help students get an education online. Includes Internet resources for teachers and parents.

ISBN 0-679-77381-9
US: $22.00/Canada: $30.00
400 pages

NetDoctor

NetDoctor offers a powerful cure for medical ignorance—the Internet! Packed with thousands of sites that let you diagnose your own maladies and lead you to the latest research on ailments ranging from AIDS to cancer to the common cold, this is the only book you'll ever need to stay healthy.

ISBN 0-679-77173-5
US: $22.00
Canada: $30.00
400 pages

NetMarketing

NetMarketing is the first book that spells out strategies for how corporate marketers and mom-and-pop businesses can use the Net to powerful advantage. It includes hundreds of successful Web sites, a primer for getting started, and a directory of more than 1,000 marketing sites.

ISBN 0-679-77031-3
US: $22.00
Canada: $30.00
400 pages

Fodor's NetTravel

Fodor's NetTravel—from Fodor's and the creators of *NetGuide* and the NetBooks Series—tells you how to find the best online travel sites. Find your way to brilliant travelogues and wonderful travel secrets—plus subway maps, restaurant and hotel guides, movie listings, and train schedules.

ISBN 0-679-77033-X
US: $22.00
Canada: $30.00
400 pages

NetGames 2

NetGames 2 is the all-new, updated edition of the original bestseller. It covers more than 4,000 games, including *Doom, Marathon, Harpoon II, Myst,* and more than a hundred MUDs, MUSHes, and MOOs, plus demos, tips, and free upgrades!

ISBN 0-679-77034-8
US: $22.00
Canada: $30.00
UK: £20.49 Net
400 pages

NetJobs

NetJobs tells you how to take advantage of the Iway to land the job you've always wanted. It includes the email addresses of over 1,000 companies, special tips for '96 college grads, and a complete directory of online classifieds, help wanted, and job notice boards.

ISBN
0-697-77032-1
US: $12.95
Canada: $17.95
UK: £11.99 Net
200 pages

NetVote

NetVote is a handbook for following the '96 presidential campaign online. *NetVote* takes the user to the places where the political pros hang out. Which party does the NetGeneration align itself with? We'll let you know which cover sells better.

ISBN
0-679-77028-3
  (Democratic cover)
ISBN
0-679-77067-4
  (Republican cover)
US: $12.95
Canada: $17.50
200 pages

Coming soon!

 Become an online sleuth! Now the ordinary computer user can tap into the information and data that credit agencies, lawyers, research companies, government departments, and other investigative and "snooping" firms have used for decades. Leave no relevant Web page unscrolled as you locate lost family members and check out potential employers.

ISBN 0-679-77029-1
US: $12.95/Canada: $17.50
200 pages (9/96)

 Fully revised and updated, this bestseller is the essential resource both for those traversing the Net for the first time and for those who already understand the limitations of search engines. With over 10,000 reviews of Web sites written by experienced netsurfers, *NetGuide* is the essential resource for anyone taking on the Internet.

ISBN 0-679-77384-3
US: $27.95/Canada: $39.00
800 pages (10/96)

 Take a virtual trip through Gotham City! Trade *Seinfeld* anecdotes. Check TV listings and search film databases. Book movie tickets online. Get up close and personal with Sharon Stone. As television and film light up the Web, *NetScreen* is your ticket to the best seats in the house.

ISBN 0-679-77699-0
US: $22.00/Canada: $30.00
400 pages (12/96)

 The first Internet guide written by kids—for kids! What are the best playgrounds in cyberspace? Where are the toothiest shark and dinosaur sites? How can I find a new pen pal? *NetKids* is the first comprehensive guide to age-appropriate activities for kids in cyberspace—from pirates to pop culture. Our junior Web masters rank the sites and tell us where the action is online.

ISBN 0-679-77066-6
US: $22.00 /Canada: $30.00
400 pages (9/96)

 The ultimate guide for science fiction fanatics! *NetSci-Fi* covers everything from *Aliens* to *The X-Files*—and everything in between. Want to work on a *Battlestar Galactica* revival campaign or learn about the value of those old *Star Wars* trading cards? *NetSci-Fi* will unlock a new universe of sci-fi trivia and fandom.

ISBN 0-679-77322-3
US: $22.00 /Canada: $30.00
400 pages (9/96)

Cybercommerce is booming and *NetShopping* will show consumers how to shop big-name retailers and mom-and-pop virtual store fronts from their home computers. Special section on the top 100 FREE products and services in cyberspace.

ISBN 0-679-77700-8
US: $22.00 /Canada: $30.00
400 pages (11/96)

How do I pick the best investments? How should I plan my retirement? How can I get yesterday's market news? *NetMoney* is your complete guide to the thousands of sites in cyberspace that are revolutionizing the way we manage our personal finances.

ISBN 0-679-77382-7
US: $22.00 /Canada: $30.00
400 pages (12/96)

To order call 1-800-NET-1133, ext. 402

Instant

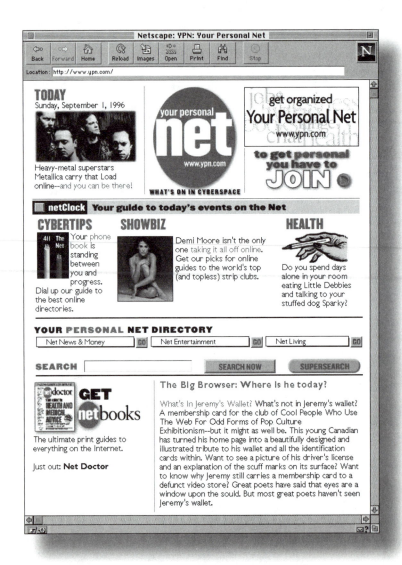

Visit our Web guide at

Updates.

How to Get Into
The School of Your Dreams
Using the Internet and
Online Services

A Michael Wolff Book

For free updates visit our Web site at http://www.ypn.com

WOLFF
NEW
MEDIA

New York

The NetBooks Series is published by Wolff New Media LLC, 520 Madison Avenue, 11th Floor, New York, NY 10022, and distributed by Random House, Inc., 201 East 50th Street, New York, NY 10022, as agent for Wolff New Media LLC.

NetCollege has been wholly created and produced by Wolff New Media LLC. *NetCollege, NetStudy, Net-Doctor, NetMarketing, NetVote, NetJobs, NetGames2, NetTravel, NetTaxes, NetMusic, NetGames, NetChat, NetMoney, NetTech, NetSports,* Your Personal Net, the Your Personal Net Logo, NetBooks, NetHead, Net-Speak, and CyberPower are trademarks of Wolff New Media LLC. The Net Logo, What's On In Cyberspace, and YPN are registered trademarks of Wolff New Media LLC. All design and production has been done by means of desktop-publishing technology. The text is set in the typefaces Garamond, customized Futura, Zapf Dingbats, Franklin Gothic, Eldorado, Century, and Champion.

A portion of the data in this book was provided by Wintergreen/Orchard House, Inc., of New Orleans, Louisiana.

New York

A Michael Wolff Book

Michael Wolff
Publisher and Editor in Chief

Kelly Maloni
Executive Editor

Ben Greenman
Creative Director

Stevan Keane
Editor

Research Editor: Kristin Miller
Senior Editor: Dina Gan
Production Editor: Donna Spivey

Associate Art Director: Eric Hoffsten
Assistant Art Director: Jay Jaffe

Associate Editors: Hylton Jolliffe, Bennett Voyles
Assistant Editors: Deborah Cohn, Rachel Greene
Staff Writers: Wendy Nelson, Stephanie Overby, Wendy Phillips
Editorial Assistants: Jennifer Levy, Vicky Tsolomytis, Eric Zelko
Production Assistants: Amy Gawronski, David Haring
Interns: Riki Markowitz, Sam Pollack

Contributing Writer: Pauline David
Copy Editor: Sonya Donaldson

Vice President, Marketing: Jay Sears
Advertising Director: Michael Domican
Marketing Assistants: Nicholas Bogaty, Amy Winger

Web Producer: Jonathan Bellack
Associate Directory Editor: Richard Egan
Assistant Producer: Alison Grippo

Systems Administrator: Jonathan Chapman
Database Technician: Toby Spinks
Administrative Director: Carol Wyatt

Wolff New Media LLC

Michael Wolff
President

Alison Anthoine
Vice President

Joseph Cohen
Chief Financial Officer

Special thanks:

Random House—Charles Levine, Terry Chisholm, Patricia Damm,
Jennifer Dowling, Susan Lawson, JoAnn Sabatino, Amy Sutton, and Charna West

NetResponse—Tom Feegel, Richard Mintz, Luis Babicek, Bob Bachle, Max Cacas, Cheryl Gnehm, Paul
Hinkle, Larry Kirk, Irene Pappas, Chris Quillian, Jonathan Rouse, and Brent Sleeper

Roger Black Incorporated and the Interactive Bureau

And, as always, Aggy Aed

The editors of *NetCollege* can be reached at Wolff New Media LLC, 520 Madison Avenue, 11th Floor,
New York, NY 10022, or by voice call at 212-308-8100, fax at 212-308-8837, or email at editors@ypn.com.

Contents

Part 1: College Prep

Part 2: Financial Aid

Part 3: Student Life

Part 4: College Directory

Appendices

"Frequently Asked Questions" about NetCollege *and the Internet*

I. How can this book help me use the Internet to get the education I want?

II. What is the Internet and how does it work?

I.

1. First I need to know why *NetCollege* is the only college guide I'll ever need.

Everything you need to know about the best colleges in the country is available on the Internet. Many of the most important online advances in recent years have originated on university campuses—the world's most widely-used browser, Netscape Navigator, evolved from the college work of Marc Andreessen and a few colleagues at the University of Illinois, Urbana-Champaign. In fact, the Internet and higher education are nearly synonymous. Of course, *NetCollege* includes everything you would expect from a traditional college guide: the composition of last year's class, admissions deadlines, required tests, and so on. But in the 1990s, the Net has become essential to your college preparation. With the help of this book, the Net can take you on virtual tours of campuses, fill you in on college life, give you the score on a school's sports teams, let you browse school newspapers, and much more.

2. What can the Internet tell me about the colleges I'm interested in?

The Net can help you identify the schools that match up to your specific interests and needs–for example, an urban school of less than five thousand students with a fine arts department. Then you can virtually meet the current students, and virtually visit clubs, publications, organizations and teams. The Net can also point you to the many grants, scholarships, and financial aid packages for which you might qualify. You can even talk to actual students, admissions officers, and financial aid officers. In many cases, you can learn more online than you could were you to actually visit the school!

3. I'm ready. Talk me through the book.

If you're an experienced surfer and you already know the topic or school you're interested in, then just turn to the *NetCollege* index, where every college, site, and subject covered in the book is listed alphabetically. There again, you may wish to browse the book at a more leisurely pace. What you have in your hands is two books in one. The first is divided into three sections that tell you how to find out everything you need to know about getting into college, getting financial aid, and getting comfortable once you're in. The second is a directory of more than 300 of the country's top colleges and universities rated for their Web presence and computer facilities.

4. How do I prepare for college using the Internet?

You've been inundated with SAT or ACT mailings, plagued by your parents, and tormented by nagging doubts about the whole process. **The ABCs of SATs** can help, whether you're practicing for your first run at the SATs or your last. Try not to feel pressured, but these are the exams that will shape *the rest of your life*. The inside information you'll find can make the difference between success and failure.

5. It's late. I need to study up. Are you saying I can I take a dry run at my SATs?

At the **College Board Home Page** you'll be able to sign up and access test dates for the SAT. You'll be able to find out more about Advanced Placement Exams. You'll also discover tutorials, vocabulary enhancers, even sample questions (some for free, some not). You can scour the various test-taking strategies pioneered by the likes of **The Princeton Review** and **Stanley Kaplan**. A great, if serious-minded, place to start is at **TestPrep.com**. This free service, by Stanford Testing Systems, can help you identify and improve your weak areas.

We follow with something that may seem a long way off right now—college major options and how to choose them. To those of you who have no idea what you'll be spending all your time studying, don't worry. These sites should help you give it some thought. And if you have a major in mind, these sites can help, too.

6. Enough tests already. How do I narrow down the search for the school that's right for me?

There's no rest for the weary. In the midst of all your studying, stressing, and prepping you're also going to have to refine your college hunt. You can't apply to them all, and finding the school that's right for you will be tough. Don't worry—the Internet gives you access to a wealth of information. Whether at home, at school, at your parents' offices, or in your local library, the Net can take you to the college of your choice, introduce you to its students, faculty, and curriculum, guide you through a virtual college tour, and even let you listen in on sporting events and lectures. Prospective students can ask questions of admissions and financial aid personnel, peek into a college's classrooms and libraries, browse through school newspapers, and drop in on campus clubs, groups, and discussions—in some cases even online chat groups. So while it's a tough road, and competition is stiff, take heart: You have the potential to be the most informed freshman ever.

7. Be specific!

If it's details you want, it's details you'll get. **Find the Perfect School** is your guide to the many resources available to help you pick out the perfect school. The most basic site here links to practically every school with a Web presence in the entire world. So if you really must get away from friends and family, look into universities in Chaing Mai, Thailand or La Paz, Bolivia. Chances are you're probably not looking quite so far afield, but even if you are headed clear across the country, the beauty of the Internet is that it brings it all right to you. So, if you happen to be looking for a school of less than 8,000 students in California where you can major in Asian Studies, you will find one, as long as you visit the college databases we review. When fed the state, a maximum enrollment and maximum tuition, **CollegeNet** churns out in-depth profiles from its extensive database. At **FishNet** you can trawl through the list, request information from the schools you're interested in, and even ask questions of the resident admissions guru. The old-timers are here as well: **Princeton Review**, in the business before you could call it a business, provides the usual well-researched low-down on more than 300 schools. And if all you care about is rankings, then the annual **U.S. News and World Report College Edition** is a must; as a bonus there's "Ask the Advisor"—answers supplied by a team of college experts. Finally, if you have specialized interests or requirements, this is where you will find links to technical schools, historically black schools, Jesuit colleges, and any number of other institutions of specific focus.

8. So I've chosen my colleges. How can I use the Net to tell them I'm interested? Can I really apply online?

Indeed you can, and **Desktop Applications** is where we show you how. The days of filling out postcard requests and calling up admissions offices are coming to a close. At most colleges you can simply jump to the admissions offices page for information, and sometimes an application form. While only a small number of schools presently have fully interactive online applications, that number is increasing by the month. At least one school completely waives its application fee if you apply online. Many more have partial applications or forms which allow you to quickly request admissions information and application literature. And almost 200 schools accept the Common Application—only a URL away and yours for the downloading.

9. Neat! Is anyone else offering this kind of help?

Schools aren't the only ones lending a cyberhand. **The Cambridge Essay Service** provides seven tips and a free essay evaluation offer before you're asked to start paying. Another service, **CollegeLink**, provides a disk or an online form for you to answer every possible question a college could throw your way. For $5 a shot, the service will package and send off the relevant application in all its perfectly manicured and fitted glory. Hundreds of schools accept College Link applications; a number of them will even waive or reduce their application fees for CollegeLink applicants.

10. And if I have any other questions?

The resident application expert at **Dear Admissions Guru** should have the answer to most every admissions question ever asked. If you've thought of a new one, fire away. One thing's for sure; by the end of the year it'll all be over. For a little perspective on the whole wonderful process drop in on **Be Real, Get In**. An admissions official who's read some 150,000 applications has contributed this article of helpful hints and down-to-earth advice.

If that doesn't help, and your classmates and family are to busy to sympathize, you can commiserate with total strangers at **soc.college.admissions**. There you'll find an incredibly helpful and friendly crew.

11. I understand that free education is not a constitutional right. How on earth am I going to pay for this?

The **Financial Aid** section should be of particular interest to your parents, although they'd love it if you told them it was none of their business. With tuition healthily outstripping the rise in inflation, the cost of college is quickly becoming absurdly expensive. You and your parents have no choice but to cope; luckily the Internet is a bloodhound when it comes to tracking down financial aid. Businesses, non-profit groups, foundations, even the U.S. government are taking full advantage of the Web, and it's you who reaps the benefits.

We've provided more than 100 of the best financial aid sites; you'll be happy to know there are many more. The section begins with a series of primers, FAQ's, and glossaries of terms, and you can always go to **soc.college.financial-aid**, if you're still stuck. One of your first few stops should definitely be at **Expected Family Contribution** to get a sense of exactly how much your family is going to have to shell out.

Hopefully your parents have been putting away money since the day you were born. If not, there are some excellent resources out there, ranging from Fleet Bank's financial planning advice to **66 Ways to Save Money**, a pamphlet of thrift from the Consumer Information Center.

The government, too, is doing its part to see that its citizens continue to get a decent college education. Your tour starts at the Department of Education's site where you can peek your head in on federal loans, scholarship programs, and helpful pamphlets. Try Easy Access for Students and Institutions (EASI) for an explanation of the complicated financial aid process as it exists. EASI's hard at work trying to shake up the status quo and reengineer the entire ordeal.

12. Okay. Someone else is going to pay... How do I find out who that might be?

Now that you understand the torture that is Financial Aid, it's time to start looking for grants and scholarships, and there are a good number of search services which will do all the work for you. You shouldn't need us to figure this one out, we'll volunteer it anyway: *try the free services first.* One such service, **fastWEB**, boasts that an additional 1,200 awards are added to the database every day. Another free service will even email you daily updates on the latest financial aid offerings.

The Scholarships section profiles a few dozen of the thousands of scholarships available to incoming college students—minorities are well represented, as are the country's best athletes. Regional scholarships number in the tens of thousands; we've provided a cross-country selection. And lastly, we've thrown a large net over the special-interest scholarships, which range from ROTC information to Wal-Mart aid to the Miss America Organization Scholarships.

Another avenue to explore in your quest for financial aid is the one lined with banks and other lenders. PNC Bank, Signet Bank and others are more than happy to part with the greenbacks, provided you give back more than they gave. If you'd rather your hard summer work didn't pad the pockets of bankers try the **Nellie Mae Loan Link**, the nation's largest nonprofit provider of loans to students and their parents.

13. But it's all so unfair. The system is corrupt! What can I do?

At the end of all this you'll surely be a little nuts. So will your parents. The lesson in financial aid concludes with a short section on **Protest & Action**. Here you can find out why it's become so expensive, what's being done about it, and who exactly you should blame—House Democratic Leader Richard Gephardt certainly has his opinion. If you can muster the strength, tune in to **Financial Aid Jokes and Anecdotes** and finish with a laugh.

14. So I'm in. Now what? Can any good come of this?

So your tour has been pretty stressful so far—too many acronyms, too much talk of money and competition. No wonder Bill Gates skipped his last few years of college. In the **Student Life** section you get to see why it is you've been killing yourself to get a place in college. It isn't all work; there is fun to be had. Whether it's on the sports fields, pledging a Greek organization, staging a sit-in or coming together with like-minded coeds, your college years are an incredibly rich time of your life. These sites should help you get a sense of what the years ahead may hold for you.

15. So I know how to get in. I know who's going to pay. I know what to do once I'm there. Tell me everything about the schools.

In the final section we take you to the schools themselves. You'll find the traditional information on tuition costs, application deadlines, and student faculty ratios. More important, however, and for the first time, you will also find comprehensive information on each college's wired status.

The **I need...** section includes the email addresses and URLs for each college's admissions and financial aid offices—many have comprehensive sites that provide admissions requirements, deadlines, statistics on last year's incoming class, and email addresses for individuals within the offices. There are fewer sites for financial aid offices, but those that are available are very helpful. Wondering when your FAFSA form is due at Auburn University? Email the financial aid office and ask away. Want to ensure the soccer coach won't be at an away game when you visit a school? Fire off an inquiring cybermissive to the admissions officer.

We've also included information about each school's relationship to the Internet. **How wired is...?** tells you how much hardware a college has running (the student to computer ratio), whether or not students get home pages (when available we provide the URL for student home page directories), and whether or not the Internet can be accessed from dorms. We've also told you if a school offers IRC servers or other online chat groups.

The usual tour lists the URLs of the more traditional aspects of college life, from student clubs to libraries to college newspapers. You may also find the college calendar, course catalog, student publications, school history, sports teams, departments, a virtual tour, special programs, and fraternities and sororities. All of these should give you a dynamic sense of the school, allowing you to explore the curricular and extracurricular diversions of your prospective alma mater.

Skip the brochure takes you off the beaten path, into the thicket of clubs, 'zines, radio and TV stations, extreme sports teams, humor rags, and the more exotic societies that give a school its real character. You may be surprised by the range of activities online, from the more traditional societies (chess clubs), to the more exotic (an S & M club), to the delightful (one college has its own circus). Among the most popular clubs we found were flying associations, Ayn Rand groups, student activist organizations and, of course, ballroom dancing clubs.

At the bottom of each directory page you will find facts, stats and other need-to-know items. Keep an eye out for the common application information; it appears in the **What You Need to Get In** section. If the school your interested in accepts it, don't forget that you can download the application and relevant information from the site we've provided.

To see expanded and updated listings for all 310 colleges, check out the online version of this book at www.ypn.com/netcollege. You'll find comprehensive financial aid and admissions information, details on campus activities and regulations, as well as a listing of all majors, degrees, and sports offered.

16. Which schools are leading the way?

None of the colleges in this book are failing to compete in cyberspace, but for those who are the best among equals, take a look at our NetCollege Honor Roll on page 414.

II.

1. What is the Net, anyway?

The Net is the electronic medium composed of the millions of computers networked together throughout the world. Also known as cyberspace, the Information Superhighway, or the Infobahn, the Net comprises four types of networks—the Internet, a global, noncommercial system with more than 30 million computers communicating through it; commercial online services, such as America Online and CompuServe; the set of discussion groups known as Usenet; and the thousands of regional and local bulletin board services (BBSs). Although the most common use of the Net is the exchange of email, the past year has seen the development of increasingly sophisticated methods for displaying and sharing information. More and more, the Internet refers to the World Wide Web, and more and more the Web unites all the diverse locations and formats that make up the Net.

2. So what do I need to get around?

You'll need a computer and a modem, and a few tricks to help you navigate.

3. Can you help me decide what computer and modem I'll need?

If you've bought a computer fairly recently, it's likely that it came with everything you need. But let's assume you have only a bare-bones PC. In that case you'll also need to get a modem which will allow your computer to communicate over the phone. So-called 14.4 modems, which transfer data at speeds up to 14,400 bits per second (bps), are standard. You should be able to get one for less than $100. But 28,800 bps modems are fast replacing them, and the prices are dropping rapidly. Next, you'll need a communications program to control the modem. This software will probably come free with your modem, your PC, or—if you're going to sign up somewhere—your online service. Otherwise, you can buy it off the shelf for under $25 or get a friend to download it from the Net. Finally, you'll want a telephone line (although if you plan to use the Net with any regularity, you'll probably want to consider installing a second phone line, because the cost of logging on repeatedly can mount quickly). If that's still not good enough, you can contact your local telephone utility to arrange for installation of an ISDN line, which allows data to be transmitted at even higher speeds. ISDN isn't as expensive as you think.

4. What kind of account should I get?

You'll definitely want to be able to get email; certainly want wide access to the Internet; and possibly want membership to at least one online service. Here are some of your access choices:

Email Gateway

This is the most basic access you can get. It lets you send and receive messages to and from anyone, anywhere, anytime on the Net. Email is quickly becoming a standard way to communicate with friends and colleagues. (Yesterday: "What's your phone number?" Today: "What's your email address?") Email gateways are often available via work, school, or the online services listed here.

Online Services

Priciest but often easiest, these services have a wealth of options for the cyberstudent. Online services are cyber city-states. The large ones have more "residents" (members) than most U.S. cities—enough users, in other words, to support lively discussions and games among their membership, and enough resources to make a visit worthwhile. They generally require their own special start-up software, which you can buy at any local computer store or by calling the numbers listed in this book. (Hint: Look for the frequent starter-kit giveaways.) AOL and CompuServe, the largest online services, both provide access to many of Usenet's more than 10,000 newsgroups, email gateways through which you can subscribe to any Internet mailing lists, and access to the World Wide Web (WWW), although Web access may require use of the service's proprietary software, which have their own eccentricities. America Online is even incorporating links to Web sites in its own forums. The cyberwalls are tumbling and the easy-to-use online services are making the Internet accessible to millions of technophobes.

Internet Providers

There are a growing number of full-service Internet providers (which means they offer email, Usenet, FTP, IRC, telnet, gopher, and WWW access). In practical terms, the Internet will take you to the school of your choice; subscribe to a mailing list that can help you write a better college essay; or locate a newsgroup which can help you find financial aid . Dial-up SLIP (serial line Internet protocol) and PPP (point-to-point protocol) accounts are currently the most popular types of Internet connections, replacing the text-only access of the standard dial-up accounts with significantly faster access and the ability to use point-and-click programs for Windows, Macintosh, and other platforms.

BBSs

BBSs range from mom-and-pop, hobbyist computer bulletin boards to large professional services. What the small ones lack in size they often make up for in affordability and homeyness. In fact, many users prefer these scenic roads to the increasingly commercial information highway. Many of the large BBSs are as rich and diverse as the commercial online services. BBSs are easy to get started with, and if you find one with Internet access or an email gateway, you'll get the best of local color and global reach at once. You can locate local BBSs through the Usenet discussion groups alt.bbs.lists and comp.bbs.misc, the BBS forums of the commercial services, and regional and national BBS lists kept in the file libraries of many BBSs. Many, if not most, local BBSs now offer Internet email, as well as live chat, and file libraries.

Direct Network Connection

Look, Ma Bell: no phone lines! The direct network connection is the fast track of college students, computer scientists, and a growing number of employees of high-tech businesses. It puts the user right on the Net, bypassing phone connections. In other words, it's a heck of a lot faster. If you're downloading hundreds of articles on Shakespeare or trying to follow a Net simulcast of a symposium, you'll need this kind of connection speed.

5. By the way, exactly how do I send email?

With email, you can write to anyone on a commercial service, Internet site, or Internet-linked BBS, as well as to those people connected to the Net via email gateways, SLIPs, and direct-network connections.

Email addresses have a universal syntax called an Internet address. An Internet address is broken down into four parts: the user's name (e.g., wolff), the @ symbol, the computer and/or company name, and what kind of Internet address it is: **net** for network, **com** for a commercial enterprise—as with Your Personal Net (ypn.com) and America Online (aol.com)—**edu** for educational institutions, **gov** for government sites, **mil** for military facilities, and **org** for nonprofit and other private organizations. For instance, the address for the associate editor of this book, the spelling of whose name is repeatedly butchered in company literature, would be jhylton@ypn.com.

6. What about the Web?

The World Wide Web is a hypertext-based information structure that now dominates Internet navigation. The Web is like a house where every room has doors to a number of other rooms, or an electronic magazine where elements on the page are connected to elements on other pages. Words, icons,

ONLINE SERVICES

America Online
- 800-827-6364 (voice)
- Basic Plan: $9.95/month includes 5 hours of access; $2.95 each additional hour
- 20/20 Plan: $19.95/month includes 20 hours of access; $2.95 each additional hour

CompuServe
- 800-848-8199 (voice)
- Basic Plan: $9.95/month includes 5 hours of access; $2.95 each additional hour
- Super Value Plan: $24.95/month includes 20 hours of access; $1.95 each additional hour
- Email: 70001.101@compuserve.com

and pictures on a page link to other pages, not only on the same machine, but anywhere in the world. You have only to click on the appropriate word or phrase or image, and the Web does the rest. In a snap you'll be transported from Stanford's home page to a chat group on admissions or to the home page of the NCAA. All the while you've FTPed, telnetted, gophered, and linked without a thought to case-sensitive Unix commands or addresses.

Your dial-up Internet provider undoubtedly offers programs that allow you to access the Web. Lynx and WWW are pretty much the standard offerings for text-only Web browsing. Usually you choose them by typing **lynx** and **www** and then **<return>**. What you'll get is a "page" with some of the text highlighted. These are the links. Choose a link, hit the return key, and you're off.

If you know exactly where you want to go on the Net and don't want to wade through Net directories and indexes, you can type a Web page's address, known as a URL (uniform resource locator). The URL for Trinity College, for example, is **http://www.trincoll.edu**. On some Web browsers, such as the current version of Netscape, "http://" is not required. In our example, you could simply type **www.trincoll.edu**.

7. What about graphical Web browsers? What are these things?

With the emergence of new and sophisticated software like Netscape Navigator (**http://www.netscape.com**), the Web looks and sounds the way its architects imagined—pictures, icons, appetizing layouts, download-able sound clips, and even animation. Some commercial services, most notably America Online, have developed customized Web browsers for their subscribers, and CompuServe allows for access with any browser; if you sub-scribe to one of these services, head to the service's Internet forum for instructions on how to get on the Web. Web browsers are more than just pre-sentation tools. Most of them allow Netsurfers to see all kinds of sites through a single interface. Want to read newsgroups? Need to send email? Interested in participating in real-time chat? You can do it all with your browser. And many Internet providers, including America Online, allow subscribers to build their own Web pages, which then reside semi-permanently in cyberspace.

8. And these newsgroups?

There are many places in cyberspace where netsurfers can post their opinions, questions, and comments, but the most widely read bulletin boards are a group of some 10,000-plus "newsgroups" collectively known as Usenet. Usenet newsgroups traverse the Internet, collecting thousands of messages a day from whomever wants to "post" to them. More than anything, the newsgroups are the collective, if sometimes babel-like voice of the Net—everything is discussed here. And we mean *everything*. On the alt.college .fraternities newsgroup, you'll see the old boys dropping in to catch up and argue the merits of Sigma Nu over Psi Upsilon. That won't be the debate for some; they'll be contesting the merits of fraternities in general. At soc .college.financial-aid you just may find the answer to financial aid woes. While delivered over the Internet, Usenet newsgroups are not technically part of the Internet. Smaller BBSs that have news feeds sometimes store only a couple dozen newsgroups, while most Internet providers and online services offer thousands. (If there's a group missing that you really want, ask your Internet provider to add the newsgroup back to the subscription list.)

The messages in a newsgroup, called "posts," are listed and numbered chronologically—in other words, in the order in which they were posted. You can scan a list of messages before deciding to read a particular message. If someone posts a message that prompts responses, the original and all follow-up messages are called a thread. The subject line of subsequent posts in the thread refers to the subject of the original message. For example, were you to post a message with the subject "Did Miami Choke or What?" to rec.sport.baseball.college, all responses would read "Re: Did Miami Choke or What?" In practice, however, topics wander in many directions. Popular newsgroups generate hundreds of messages daily. To cut back on repetitive questions, newsgroup members often compile extensive lists of answers to frequently asked questions (FAQs). Many FAQs have grown so large and so comprehensive that they are valuable resources in their own right, informal encyclopedias (complete with hypertext links) dedicated to the newsgroup's topic. For example, the alt.usage.english FAQ not only addresses the basics of words usage and grammar, but also focuses on specific topics like usage disputes and the origins of clichés.

9. Mailing lists?

Mailing lists are like newsgroups, except that they are distributed by Internet email. The fact that messages show up in your mailbox tends to make the discussion group more intimate, as does the proactive act of subscribing. Mailing lists are often more focused, and they're less vulnerable to irreverent and irrelevant contributions. For instance, students and teachers interested in the practicalities of campus life can discuss race relations, handicap access, and safety recommendations on the CAMPCLIM mailing list.

To subscribe to a mailing list, send an email to the mailing list's subscription address. Often you will need to include very specific information, which you will find in this book. To unsubscribe, send another message to that same address. If the mailing list is of the listserv, listproc, or majordomo variety, you can usually unsubscribe by sending the command **unsubscribe <listname>** or **signoff <listname>** in the message body. If the mailing list instructs you to "write a request" to subscribe ("Dear list owner, please subscribe me to…"), you will probably need to write a request to unsubscribe.

Once you have subscribed, messages are almost always sent to a different address than the subscription address. Most lists will send you the address when you subscribe. If not, send another message to the subscription address and ask the owner.

10. And telnet, FTP, gopher? Can you explain?

Telnet:

When you telnet, you're logging on to another computer somewhere else on the Internet. You then have access to the programs running on the remote computer. If the site is running a library catalog, for example, you can search the catalog. If it's running a live chat room, you can communicate with others logged on. Telnet addresses are listed as URLs, in the form **telnet://domain.name:port number**. A port number is not always required, but when listed it must be used.

FTP:

FTP (file transfer protocol) is a method of copying a file from another Internet-connected computer to your own. Hundreds of computers on the Internet allow "anonymous FTP." In other words, you don't need a unique password to access them. Just type "anonymous" at the user prompt and type your email address at the password prompt. The range of material available is extraordinary—from archives of journal articles to collections of anatomical images. Since the advent of Web browsers, netsurfers can transfer files without using a separate FTP program. In this book, FTP addresses are listed as URLs, in the form **ftp://domain.name/directory/filename.txt**. And here's a bonus—logins and passwords aren't required with Web browsers.

Gopher:

A gopher is a program that turns Internet addresses into menu options. Gophers can perform many Internet functions, including telnetting and downloading files. Gopher addresses throughout this book are listed as URLs, with all necessary steps chained together as pieces of a URL.

11. So the addresses will look how exactly?

All entries in *NetCollege* have a name, description, and address. The site name appears first in boldface, followed by the description of the site. After the description, complete address information is provided. The name of the network appears first, in red—**WEB** to designate the World Wide Web, **AMERICA ONLINE** to designate America Online, and so on. When you see an arrow (→), this means that you have another step ahead of you, such as typing a command, searching for a file, or subscribing to a mailing list. Red bullets separate multiple addresses, which indicate that the site is accessible through other networks.

If the item is a Web site, FTP site, telnet, or gopher, it will be displayed in the form of a URL, which can be typed in the command line of your Web browser. FTP and gopher sites will be preceded by **URL**, while telnet sites, which cannot be launched directly through a browser, will be preceded by **TELNET**. If the item is a mailing list, the address will include an email address and instructions on how to subscribe (remember—the address given is usually the subscription address; in order to post to the mailing list, you will use another address that will be emailed to you upon subscribing). IRC addresses indicate what you must type to get to the channel you want once you've connected to the IRC server. Entries about newsgroups are always followed by the names of the newsgroups.

In an online service address, the name of the service is followed by the keyword (also called "go word"). Additional steps are listed where necessary.

In addition, there are a few special terms used in addresses. *Info* indicates a supplementary informational address. *Archives* is used to mark collections of past postings for newsgroups and mailings lists. And *FAQ* designates the location of a "frequently asked questions" file for a newsgroup.

12. College, college, college. I'm sick of it all. Take me away.

Try *NetChat*, *NetGames*, *NetTrek*, *NetSports*, *NetMusic*, *Fodor's NetTravel*, *NetVote*, *NetJobs*, *NetMarketing*, *NetTech*, *NetTaxes*, and the best-selling *NetGuide* (a new edition is due out in November). Getting back to school: check out *NetStudy*, your guide to the how and the where of online studying. And to finish with something light keep your eye out for the forthcoming *NetSpy* and *NetSci-Fi*.

Part 1

College Prep

The ABCs of SATs

The air is tense in the dim light of the oppressively hot gymnasium. Immobile wooden

desks are in martial occupation of the floor usually reserved for running and jumping. There is an almost palpable sense of malice in the air as students eye teachers warily, and friends look through each other as if seeing strangers. Today, traditional high school hierarchies will be usurped—the football captain will bow down to the teacher's pet, the prom queen to the chess king. Today, pencils will regain dominance over their felt-tipped compatriots, and coloring skills learned in kindergarten will be called upon once again. For today is SAT day, and before you can even think about choosing a college, you have to prove you can think. Online test-prep sites are the great equalizers. And once you're into college, online resources can help with the small matter of a major.

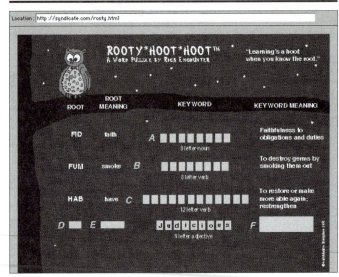

The owls are not what they seem, even if the answers to the questions are
http://syndicate.com/rooty.html

Testing/Admissions

College Board Online Advanced Placement Program

The College Board's Advanced Placement page is all about information: When, where and why to take the exams that strike terror into the hearts of teachers' pets and slackers alike. The page's FAQ addresses such fear-based questions as "How difficult are AP courses?" and "Why should I take a more difficult course and risk getting a lower grade?" with comic predictability. The Board's transparent ploy is to encourage students to imagine educational challenge as a joy to be experienced and relished.
WEB http://www.collegeboard.org/ap/math/html/indx001.html

The College Board Online (America Online)
Like its Internet counterpart, America Online's College Board service allows students to register for the SAT. The Ask the College Board section invites specific testing and college-related questions.
AMERICA ONLINE *keyword* student center→college and beyond→ college board online

The College Board Online Home Page
No, this isn't a clever trap, nor does entrance to the site require knowledge of 1950s television trivia; the enemy really has rolled out the red carpet for its impending torture victims. The College Board Home Page welcomes high and middle schoolers with open arms in a vain attempt to curry favor with those for whom their very name is anathema. The sentiment is appreciated, but there are no secrets to be learned here; no cheat sheets or recipes for a perfect score. However, along with the public relations gloss, visitors to the College Board Home Page can do the following: register for the SAT online, access test dates, and even try their hand at the Test Question of the Day. There is also specific in-

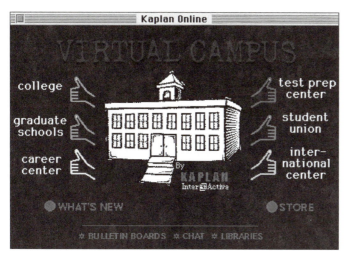

Thumbs up for a virtual campus that puts its hand out for your thirty dollars

America Online *keyword* kaplan

formation on Advanced Placement Exams and the PSAT.
WEB http://www.collegeboard.org

Kaplan The Kaplan Web site is almost daunting in scope, offering a wide range of services, including the opportunity to take a sample SAT or GRE online, free of charge. Kaplan's services don't end with test preparation, however. The College Simulator invites postmatriculators to tour a virtual campus and face day-to-day scenarios, while the Hot Seat simulates a nerve-racking job interview. A new package, SAT RoadTrip Multimedia, promises to prepare students for the test via an in-depth software package. The cost: $30.00. A visit to the test center of America Online's virtual campus yields SAT FAQs that answer baffling questions like "What is the purpose of the PSAT?" An article sings the praises of the Kaplan course, and message boards act as a conduit through which college hopefuls can vent—and Kaplan workers can recruit.
AMERICA ONLINE *keyword* kaplan
WEB http://www.kaplan.com

One-on-One with the S.A.T.
In yet another desperate move to negate the influence of those costly SAT classes, the College Board has designed its own brand of online SAT preparation software. And, of course, they do have one very real claim to fame: One-on-One "is the only program with hundreds of real SAT questions." This may seem akin to accepting aspirin from a flu bug, but there is something to be said for test vérité. The program includes an advisor from the hallowed halls of the College Board, who promises to guide students through the painful process. The program requires an IBM-compatible personal computer, and costs $49.00.
WEB http://www.collegeboard.org /library/html/oneonone.html

The Princeton Review Its name a nod to ETS territory, the Princeton Review debunks the SAT mystique through utter mockery of its writers, Jim and Pam, and all they represent. Process of elimination techniques focus on wiping out the worst answers rather than find-ing the best ones. A character named "Joe Bloggs" teaches students how to avoid falling into pitfalls designed for average-scoring students. The company's Web site includes information on courses, books, and software for anxious college hopefuls. Jump into America Online to learn about the preparation course, browse the message boards, or shop till you drop at the Princeton Review store. The company's America Online presence does not differ substantially from that of its Web site.
AMERICA ONLINE *keyword* Princeton
WEB http://www.review.com

Resource Pathways There's a glut of information on the market to help you make your college decisions, but how do you know what resources are right for you? Resource Pathways has gone down that road for you, reviewing books, CD-ROMs, videotapes, software, Web sites, and other online resources that can lead you on the best path. Provided here are the one-to-four star ratings of each resource's breadth of content, added value, and ease of use, as well as an overall evaluation.
WEB http://www.sourcepath.com

The Study Hall "'You senile dotard!' Dr. Clark grumbled loudly to himself as he bashed his thigh against the corner of his desk. Still not habituated to his new office, the old professor brushed back a few of the sparse wisps of gray hair from his round face and squinted as he peered through his thick eyeglasses trying to identify the amorphous shapes that he perceived…" This mystery novella excerpt is peppered with polysyllabic SAT words for a reason. It's an example of the test prep services offered by this Dallas, Texas company. This Study

Hall site also introduces you to their products, some test-taking tips, and links to recommended sites.

WEB http://rampages.onramp.net /~studyhal

Syndicate.com You can receive tutoring from Einstein's ghost and sell your little sister into servitude to the president of the College Board, but nothing's going to raise your SAT score if you don't study vocabulary. Twelve synonyms for "terse" and a billion ways to call someone a tightwad are required just to get a registration form. Fortunately, syndicate.com is tapped into the needs of monosylabically-inclined teens, featuring puzzles, contests, comic strips and other wordplay designed to make learning less excruciating, if not exactly extracurricular fun.

WEB http://syndicate.com

TestPrep.com The questions are culturally biased and the preparation classes are wallet-biased, but Stanford Testing Systems, Inc. negates the influence of the status quo with its absolutely free and complete online test preparation resources. Simply register following the directions provided at the site, and the WebWare system will diagnose and work to improve weak areas. The experts at Stanford Testing mean business; no cartoons and "fun SAT games" detract from the learning process. WebWare may be free, but it's not lightweight.

WEB http://www.testprep.com /wwmain.sat.html

Choosing a major

Choosing a Major: Factors to Consider This test/worksheet from the University of Pennsylvania helps students prioritize their goals when choosing a major. The test is divided along fiscal and personal interest lines, and is fairly basic.

WEB http://www.sas.upenn.edu /college/major/factors_to _consider.html

College Majors: Complete Guide from Accounting to Zoology Are the liberal arts a bit too liberal? As you lug your books back and forth between Magic in the Middle Ages and Advanced Economics, do you yearn for a little guidance? Choosing the right major may not mean the difference between a lucrative career and a life of misery but it can sure feel that way. Grandma wants a doctor in the family. Your parents just want you to be happy—and off the family payroll. What's a conflicted undergraduate to do? For a mere $40.00, Perfect Data guarantees answers. Shamelessly exploiting the undergrad's already substantial anxiety over this decision ("Before you make a fatal commitment, pick up a copy of College Majors"), Perfect Data includes software with "concise descriptions of each and every major, needed abilities, and resulting career positions." Are these people omniscient? Nope. They're just painstaking data analysts with an eye on the undergraduate market.

WEB http://www.acm.org /~yannone/maj

The Major Resource Kit So you're thinking of majoring in animal science? What types of jobs will you be qualified for? What can you do to enhance your employability? This kit includes tip sheets designed for undergraduates studying a variety of disciplines at the University of Delaware. Each sheet lists job titles that former students held after graduation, describes the

work, and offers suggestions for internships or field experience that make job seekers more desirable.

URL gopher://gopher.udel.edu/11 /.dept/carserv/MRkit

Myer-Briggs Personality Test It's not cheap, but it's one of the most well-respected personality tests available. Misunderstand your strengths, weaknesses, and interests, and your professional life will be unhappy, if not agonizing. Understand them, on the other hand, and you're bound to be more successful. At least, that's the theory. The test recommends occupations that fit your style and talents. For more information, download the file called "Discover your personality style." The cost of the test and written evaluation is $104.00. If you want a 30-minute live online interview included with your evaluation, the cost is $154.00.

AMERICA ONLINE *keyword* career→ career resource mall→featured products→personality testing

Things to Think about before Choosing a Major "College is basically a bunch of rooms where you sit for roughly two thousand hours and try to memorize things," begins this candid, opinionated treatise. "Be sure to choose a major that does not involve Known Facts and Right Answers," it continues, suggesting English or Philosophy over Math and Science due to their subjective natures. While this site may not be particularly good for someone genuinely struggling with the college major dilemma, humanities junkies with overbearing parents should check it out, if only to arm themselves with rhetoric in defense of their chosen path.

WEB http://www.student.uu.se/utk /Annat/Texter/major.html

Find the perfect school

You've tried every online search engine there is, and still you are lost. The best

college for you remains painfully hard to find. But the search must go on, so save your time and energy for the applications (and essays!), and let us sort your cyberoptions for you. If you're looking to take cyber-tours of specific campuses, try **College Xpress**, **College and University Home Pages**, or **Colleges and Universities**. If you're not yet quite focused on your investigation of institutions of higher education, **ExPAN College Search, Internet College Exchange**, and **CollegeNET** will help you match your criteria to the colleges out there. Skeptical about the objectivity of the countless glossy brochures that have been piling up in your bedroom? **The Princeton Review: The Best Colleges** lets you take a peek at the real life behind the promotional gloss of the office of admissions pamphlets and into the realm of parties and dorm life. And the ever popular and polemical *U.S. News and World Report*'s college rankings are online in all their glory in the form of the **U.S. News College Fair**.

College: the final frontier
http://www.collegexpress.com

Starting points

College and University Home Pages MIT provides access to alphabetical and geographical listings of college and university sites worldwide, with several mirror sites from Austria to Australia available for faster access. An FAQ details how schools come to be included on the list and where to go for information not contained here.
WEB http://www.mit.edu:8001 /people/cdemello/univ.html

Colleges and Universities Search this database of more than 3,000 entries for links to institutes of higher learning by entering your keywords of choice.
WEB http://www.universities.com

CollegeXpress Register for free at CollegeXpress and you can search for info on private colleges

by profile, geographic location, or alphabetically. Run by the Howard Greene Group, this site gets you in the mood for higher education by operating on the backpack system—you cram all the schools you're interested in into your cyberschool bag, and you'll get more information directly from the institutions. Also accessible are articles on the college search ("How About a Women's College?", "Private Colleges: The Significant Advantages"), admissions ("Writing the Essay," "The Application as a Reflection of You"), and financial aid ("Scholarships You Can Win," "FAFSA Express").
WEB http://www.collegexpress .com

FishNet In the sea of online college search resources, FishNet is a real catch. Without paying a penny, you can request informa-

Location: http://www.jayi.com/sbi/Open.html

Give the fish a "high-fin"
http://www.jayi.com/jayi

tion from selected schools, build your own profile, seek electronic guidance from an admissions guru, or access an array of articles on the admissions process. Fish-Net also has its own ezine, *Edge*.
WEB http://www.jayi.com/jayi

Higher Ed Home Page A hodgepodge of higher education links. If you're willing to wade through the rather long list, you'll find over 200 sites somehow related to college, from EDUCOM and CollegeNet to Higher Education Gophers and the Syllabus Top 20 Education Sites.
WEB http://128.250.89.9/highered.html

Preparing Your Child for College "American colleges and universities are the 'jewels' of education worldwide. The U.S. boasts a higher education system so excellent that studying abroad is an option—not a necessity—for students in America." Sprinkled amid the braggadocio and oversimplification of this Department of Education publication are some useful career-choice exercises.
WEB http://www.ed.gov/pubs/Prepare

The search

Alumni and Alumnae No one knows a place quite the way someone does who's been there. In college, these insiders would be the alums. This page provides access to hundreds of alumni associations across the country that you may wish to contact for another perspective on your prospective alma mater.
WEB http://www.halcyon.com/investor/alumni.htm

College Assist Utilize the college database, search functions, college Web sites, and get helpful tips about the admissions and financial aid processes as a guest, or become a member (for 39 bucks), and College Assist will personalize the planning process with college matching, a personal organizer, and connections to college admissions offices.
WEB http://www.edworks.com/index.htm

College Quest A cyberad for College Quest's *The College Student's Handbook*.
WEB http://www.aros.net/~create/college/college.htm

College View College recruiting goes high-tech. For those interested in conducting their college searches from the comfort of their computer desks, College View offers multimedia presentations on nearly 100 U.S. colleges and universities. Each desktop display features graphics, audio clips, and a link to the school's Web page.
WEB http://www.collegeview.com

CollegeEdge Even if you have no intention of purchasing the CollegeEdge Software, a trip to this site can be worthwhile. You can tour college home pages, link to financial aid resources, or access tips and information on majors and careers. Or, if the whole college search procedure has got you a little stressed out, take a break at the art gallery, play some games, and enjoy a joke or two.
WEB http://www.collegeedge.com

CollegeNET Your father wants you to go to Sacred Heart; your mother prefers Wellesley; and you want to head south to Mardi Gras and Tulane. Who's going to win? This online database may help you find a school that's right for the whole family. Simply choose the state, a maximum enrollment and maximum tuition, and you'll be rewarded with in-depth profiles on a number of schools. Financial aid info and other academic resources are currently being added.
WEB http://www.collegenet.com

Colleges That Admit Home-schoolers FAQ An alphabetical listing of nearly 200 institutions of higher learning that accept the home-schooled, from Akron University to York College. Also included are reviews of the most popular college guides in publication.
WEB http://198.83.19.39/School_is_dead/colleges_4_hmsc.html

ExPAN College Search The sovereigns of standardized testing are out to help you find the school that suits you best. Using the College Board's ExPAN database of schools, you can search for two- or four-year institutions with specific geographic locations, enrollment sizes, majors offered, admissions or aid policies, student activities, etc. ExPAN will return a list of matching schools with expanded information on enrollment, financial aid, admissions policies, student life, and academic offerings at each institution.
WEB http://www.collegeboard.org /csearch/bin/ch01.cgi

Internet College Exchange
Ideally, you'd like to attend a small liberal arts college in the Southwest, and you can spend up to $20,000 per year. Or maybe you'd rather go to a large, public school in the Midwest for under $10,000? What are your options? Just plug in the pertinent criteria and search a database of college info compiled by the U.S. Department of Education. There's also practical information for parents, students, and guidance coun-

selors—all designed to make the process of choosing a college a little less daunting.
WEB http://www.usmall.com /college

Peterson's Education Center
Peterson's brings together educational opportunities of all levels, from camps to colleges, grade school to graduate study. Links to 4,000 schools and summer programs, as well as language study and study abroad options. Also included is information on educational financing, testing and assessment, and career and vocational information.
WEB http://www.petersons.com

The Princeton Review: The Best Colleges A guide to the best 309 colleges in the U.S. What do they mean by "the best"? Well, yes, the editors took all the usual statistics, but they also gathered responses from at least 100 students at every college for a behind-the-brochures look at campus life. Here you'll find out which schools' professors bring the study material to life and which ones suck all the life out of the material, where

things run smoothly and where there is red tape, where students are almost always studying and where students almost never study. For each school, you'll find quotes from students, quality of life ratings, demographics info, and a list of what's hot and what's not.
WEB http://www.review.com /undergr/best_colleges.html

Resource Pathways There's a glut of information on the market to help you make your college decisions, but how do you know which resources are right for you? Resource Pathways has gone down that road for you, reviewing books, CD-ROMs, videotapes, software, Web sites, and other online resources. They've assigned one- to four-star ratings to each resource's breadth of content, added value, and ease of use, as well as overall effectiveness.
WEB http://www.sourcepath.com

soc.college.admissions Learn what's more important—good grades, good standardized test scores, a good essay, or a long list of extracurricular achievements. And find out how many AP exams you should take. The helpful advice just keeps coming and, amazingly enough, there are plenty of people around who stop by just to offer helpful tidbits of wisdom. Just remember—no matter how much you learn, there's still plenty of work to do off line; in the words of one message writer, "The colleges certainly aren't going to read a stupid newsgroup to find good students!"
USENET soc.college.admissions

Fee–based

Academic Counseling Services, Inc. The staff of ACS claims to be able to "fit students' strengths, weaknesses, needs, in-

College search: the next generation
http://www.collegenet.com

terests, and financial resources to appropriate college opportunities… in a careful, organized manner, while understanding the importance of this decision in relation to personal satisfaction and career development." Nowhere in the site does ACS publicize the price of its professional help, but if you're truly interested in hearing more, you can fill out an email information request form.
WEB http://www2.interaccess.com /nichenet/acs

College Guidance Services
Which schools are generous with financial aid, offer the strongest programs in your major area, or have a team in a specific sport? You won't find answers to these questions (and many more) at the College Guidance Services Web site. That's right—won't. What you will find is information on ordering College Guidance Services' financial aid guide or college-search-assistance service, and the number for their college-information hotline ($1.99 a minute).
WEB http://ultimate.org/2569

College Solutions
Attention, college shoppers! At College Solutions, they refer to the college-search process as shopping, and they want to be one of your purchases. But, even if you choose not to shell out for the services of the well-rounded staff (which can include a college-search consultant, an essay critique specialist, a tax-and-financial planning consultant, and a needs-analysis consultant), this site may offer some helpful free hints. Take their self-test in college shopping know-how, check out the college-bound calendar, or brush up on four fatal errors to avoid when searching for a school.
WEB http://college-solutions.com

Search by Video For weeks, attorney Shelly Spiegel had been helping her younger brother Brad with the confusing and expensive business of searching for the right college. Over kung pao chicken at a Chinese restaurant in Washington, D.C., she found her fortune, and it wasn't in a cookie. The idea hit her: Create a national clearinghouse for college recruitment videos to streamline the search process. At Search by Video you can purchase the available merchandise—videos from schools like Alabama's Auburn University or the University of Wyoming. Besides ordering info, the site also features hot links to certain colleges, as well as search aids, and "Been there, wish they'd known that" quotes from folks who were once in your shoes.
WEB http://www.searchbyvideo .com

Specific study

The Academic South Hey, y'all, it's a list of institutions of higher learning in the South—from Abilene Christian University in Texas to Winthrop University in South Carolina. Some may find ceaseless sunshine distracting, but if you like your weather mild and your cafeteria stocked with grits, this may be the place to start your cybercollege hunt.
WEB http://sunsite.unc.edu/doug _m/pages/south/academic.html

alt.art.colleges Perpetrating the tradition of the "starving artist" and the "starving student," the alt.art.colleges newsgroup, whose audience is a monetarily disadvantaged mixture of the two, is littered with get-rich-quick email. But scattered amid the scams, you'll find some discussion on the merits of specific art schools.
USENET alt.art.colleges

The Alternative Higher Education Network Grades got you down? Want the opportunity to study woodworking, solar energy, or poverty instead of accounting? Head to this Web site for the nontraditional approach to higher education. You can link to the home pages of schools like Antioch, Hampshire, Marlboro, Oberlin, Bard, or the New School, all famous for their innovative programs.
WEB http://hampshire.edu/html/cs /ahen/ahen.html

Associated Western Universities Incorporated If you have that pioneering spirit, attending an AWU member school may be for you. Associated Western Universities Incorporated is a consortium of 62 universities that work toward the advancement of scientific knowledge by promoting partnerships and collaboration among academic institutions, research facilities, government, and industry and by providing opportunities for faculty and students to participate in research at non-academic facilities. Check out the map of member institutions and access AWU contacts and university home pages from Texas A&M to Lewis and Clark.
WEB http://online.awu.org /homepage.html

Association of Jesuit Colleges and Universities Links to the 28 Jesuit schools in the U.S., including Boston College, Holy Cross, Georgetown, and Marquette.
WEB http://www.ajcunet.edu

BSA's Community College Link From sea to shining sea, community colleges are everywhere, including here, in BSA Advertising's CareerMart.
WEB http://www.careermart.com /MMM/communitycolleges.html

Community College Web No longer the Rodney Dangerfields of higher learning, community colleges are starting to gain respect as something more than stepping stones to bigger, better four-year colleges. Not only does CC Web have a searchable list of links to over 450 of these 2-year institutions, it also contains a compilation of related resources like the *Community College Review*, the COMMCOLL mailing list, and the Community College Leadership Program.
WEB http://www.mcli.dist.maricopa .edu/cc

Ivy League Universities If you're truly interested in getting into the Ivies, you've probably already got this list of the conventional cream of the college crop memorized and ranked. For everyone else, this provides links to Brown, Columbia, Cornell, Dartmouth, Harvard, Penn, Princeton, and Yale.
WEB http://www.artsci.wustl.edu /~jrdorkin/ivy.html

Military Academies & Colleges of the United States A top-rated education, a guaranteed job upon graduation, no tuition, and even a paycheck each month—why would anyone pass up the opportunity to go to a military academy? Well, for starters, there are the uniforms and all those pesky rules…. To find out if the pros outweigh the cons, you can link to any academy here— Army, Navy, Air Force, Marines.
WEB http://www.artsci.wustl.edu /~jrdorkin/military.html

Minority Colleges and Institutions by State An interactive map of HBCUs (Historically Black Colleges and Universities) and HSIs (Hispanic-Serving Institutions). Pick a school, any school,

and link to institution information, research centers, and financial advice.
WEB http://web.fie.com/web/mol /schlmap.htm

National Liberal Arts Colleges A list of schools fitting the Carnegie Foundation for the Advancement of Teaching's definition of "national liberal arts college." Here, you're a click away from the home pages of hundreds of sources of a liberal arts education, from Albion College to Wofford.
WEB http://www.aavc.vassar.edu /libarts.colleges.html

SDBP Historically Black Colleges and Universities From Clark University in Georgia to Xavier University in Louisiana, you can find all of the historically black institutions of higher learning here. Related resources like the Black Collegian, the United Negro College Fund, and Black Excel are accessible as well.
WEB http://www.webcom.com /~cjcook/SDBP/hbcu.html

U.S. Two-Year College Touting itself as the most complete list of two-year colleges available, this University of Toledo Community and Technical College index links to over 500 community colleges, technical colleges, junior colleges, branches of four-year colleges focusing on associate degree education, and accredited two-year proprietary schools. UT's index also connects to other CC indexes, associations, and programs.
WEB http://www.sp.utoledo.edu /twoyrcol.html

Web U.S. Community Colleges Search community colleges alphabetically, by state, or by degree of newness on the Web.
WEB http://www.utexas.edu/world /comcol.html

Publications

Chronicle of Higher Education: Academe This Week For those interested in the highbrow aspect of higher education (in other words, not the frat parties and playing field shenanigans that occupy the thoughts of so many other students), this site provides a guide to the latest edition of the weekly *Chronicle of Higher Education*. Although you won't be able to access entire articles from the dead-tree version, there are exclusive stories about notable Internet sites for academics as well as facts, deadlines, and information on events.
WEB http://www.chronicle.merit .edu

High School Senior Magazine The monthly mag for and by those who rule the school—high school seniors. The traditional publication covers everything from social trauma to prom drama. Unfortunately, its cyber-counterpart provides only the first few paragraphs of each story, followed by a frustrating, "For more, pick up the latest issue of *High School Senior Magazine*."
WEB http://www.hssm.com

U.S. News College Fair The much-hyped and oft-contested college rankings from *U.S. News and World Report* are now available online. Also included are features from the best-selling perennial, like "Grad School Best Buys," "Studying Abroad: Not the Same Old Trip," and a series on new cyberjobs. Unique to the College Fair is Ask the Advisor—submit your college queries to the managing editor of the *U.S. News* guides, and he and his team of experts will answer you electronically.
WEB http://www.usnews.com /usnews/fair/home.htm

Desktop applications

You've done it. After months of stressful research, you've narrowed your college search

to five or so possibilities. Unfortunately, the process doesn't end there, and you've still got to apply to the schools. Now those applications are piling up on the coffee table, and the one essay you have worked on sounds like it was written by a warped sixth-grader. Despair and its cousin inertia are swooping down on you like a pair of jaded admissions officers. How do you set yourself apart? Can't you just fill out one application and send it by email? Isn't everybody supposed to be using the Internet? Well, some people are. These questions and more could be answered if you write to **Dear Admissions Guru**. Don't forget while you **Build Your Profile** to **Be Real**, **Get In**. **XAP.com** or **Peterson's Undergraduate Applications** are free, and **CollegeLink**, although it'll cost you, is a great way to reduce your application aggravation. Good luck!

The process

Be Real, Get In Applying to college makes most students feel like nothing more than a nameless, faceless number and statistic.

Location: http://www.jayi.com/ACG/articles/Be_Real.html

Be Real, Get In
Presenting yourself in the college application

by Ron Moss

Mrs. Isbel's third-grade class was an academic coming of age for me in many ways, but in retrospect one particular assignment turned out to be analogous to the college application process. Not to suggest that little of academic or personal significance has occurred in my life since third grade, but the assignment and its satisfactory completion come to me as if it were yesterday.

"Class," Mrs. Isbel barked, "before Christmas you will have completed one of the most valuable experiences of your primary career." I was excited by this prospect, but that excitement was put in check when Mrs. Isbel explained that this opportunity to achieve the academic equivalent of winning Olympic gold was to complete a research paper about a country other than our own.

With ample lead time of almost three months, my enthusiasm for the project waned. And on late Sunday afternoon of Thanksgiving break, the afternoon before the research paper was due, I finally found value in the encyclopedias my family had recently purchased.

Or get real and be in—preferably more real than this charming yet unconvincing cyberguide
http://www.jayi.com/ACG/articles/Be_Real.html

SATs, GPAs, AP Tests, class rank… this article has much to say about just being yourself and gives advice about presenting the true you to colleges, which often do make admissions decisions entirely subjectively. It's written by a true authority—an admissions official who estimates he has read 150,000 applications by people just like you.
WEB http://www.jayi.com/ACG /articles/Be_Real.html

Cambridge Essay Service Did cranking out that first draft make you long for a cool breeze? Welcome to Cambridge Essay Service. They're editors. They will help you find your voice so that the person

you present to that admissions staff is the best possible version of yourself. Check out the seven tips for writing an essay and the free evaluation offer for your first draft. **WEB** http://world.std.com/~edit

Dear Admissions Guru "There is a rumor going around my school that if you get accepted to Yale you won't get accepted to Harvard and vice versa. Is it true that these two schools share admissions information?" is the question one desperate student asks the Admissions Guru (actually several senior admissions officers). Admissions Guru responds: "No way." Anyone with a specific question or problem regarding the

admissions process should read here, and if the question's not already answered, ask away.
WEB http://www.jayi.com/jayi /ACG/ques.html

U.S. News CollegeFair Forum

Why do they call it a Personal Statement, anyway? (By the time you're done with it, it sounds pretty stilted and impersonal!) Should you write one of those cute "human interest" essays, or a more serious one conveying your intention to save the world? The folks using this forum have a lot to ask about the most dreaded part of the college application. Fortunately, there are experts here to answer the questions.
AMERICA ONLINE *keyword* college →College Search→US News CollegeFair Forum→Browse Messages→College Essay

Absolutely free

ApplyWeb CollegeNet is the sponsor of this program, which provides online applications and information about dozens of schools. (The schools pay for the privilege of being listed.) View the schools here, then establish an account and get to it.
WEB http://www.collegenet.com /apply

Build Your Profile The best things in life are free, of course, and, while college applications are never any fun, FishNet has provided an easy way to go about them. Building a profile of yourself doesn't count as an official application, but it does make a good introduction. Write brief essays about academic honors, school sports, and activities and clubs, update it as often as you like, and email it to as many colleges as you want.
WEB http://www.jayi.com/jayi /ACG/profile.html

Electronic Common Application Do any of the schools you're applying to accept the Electronic Common Application? Many probably do. Wesleyan University provides an electronic, downloadable version of the application here for Macintosh, DOS, or Windows.
WEB http://www.admiss.wesleyan .edu/ecommon.html

Peterson's Undergraduate Applications That gentle giant Peterson's has 220 colleges' downloadable applications to choose from, right here on its Web site (though most are just the standard application). They run the gamut from Adirondack Community College to Worcester Polytechnic Institute, and often include admissions tours, and other information.
WEB http://www.petersons.com /features/ugapp.html

The Presidents' Network Fifty for the price of one: That's what you'll get at the Presidents' Network. More than four dozen educational institutions have adopted a common application process that allows each student to make a single application and have his/her qualifications evaluated by every school applied to. The PresNet site contains lists and maps of the universities, liberal arts colleges, engineering schools, and two-year institutions that belong to the group, along with the appropriate application forms.
WEB http://www.studyusa.com /factshts/presbroc.htm

Undergraduate Admissions E-Apps* Plenty of schools have online applications, *if* you can find them in the maze of the college's Web site. E-Apps* makes it easy. At this site, find the college in the alphabetical list, and click on the appropriate icon to go straight to that school's email application. Plus, visit the college's home page, downloadable application, printable application, and tuition information. Very helpful stuff, huh? Yes, except that the number of colleges is pretty small.
WEB http://www.eapp.com/UNIV /UGLIST.HTM

XAP.com Pick a college, any college. Then download the college's

---

Xap that app!
http://www.xap.com

CYBERNOTES

Q: "I'm a student who is taking all the college prep courses in high school that I can. My grades are sometimes very good and sometimes awful. I sometimes get Ds. But I'm involved in almost every club in our school, and I volunteer a lot. So what I'm asking is if my extracurricular activities will make a difference in how the college will look at my application?"

A: "Extracurricular activities matter. Whether they can overcome Ds is doubtful. You need to do better in those classes, and if you can't do better, get out of them. My dad used to tell this joke about the kid who brought home three Fs and and a D on his report card, and when his father asked him what the problem was, the kid says, 'I think I'm spending too much time on one subject.' The point is that maybe you can spend less time on the subjects you do very well in, and more time on the subjects that are kicking your butt. Also, when you get around to applying to college, make sure you select schools that match up favorably with the work you have done. Put some thought into it."

—from **Dear Admissions Guru**

application in any computer format. Also visit the college home page from here. Starting in the fall, students will actually be able to apply by email to a few colleges from this site. All for free (not counting those admissions fees, of course).
WEB http://www.xap.com

This will cost you

ACADEM Planning on applying to at least 25 schools? Maybe 50? Does the guidance department of your school dread more requests for your transcript? Are they working overtime to fill them? If this sounds like you, then ACADEM is where you want to turn. All your school has to do is send them one copy of your transcript and ACADEM will (for a price) send out as many official copies as you need.
WEB http://members.aol.com/academ/academ.html

Collegeapps.com Shannon Barth and Sue Berescik, the two

former English teachers behind Collegeapps.com, claim to be able to motivate you to get started on those college applications, take the fear out of the process, show you how to perform a self-assessment and identify your unique qualities and experiences, and give you a surefire method of writing essays that leap off the page. If you buy their book for $19.95, that is. For $34.95, you can get their video as well, and for a mere $500 you get the deluxe package, which includes advice on school selection, financial assistance information, and help with essay- and resumé-editing. On their home page, see if you can get a free email evaluation of your college essay.
WEB http://www.collegeapps.com

CollegeLink Avoid college application-induced writer's cramp or carpal tunnel syndrome and download the free CollegeLink software. You can apply to as many colleges as you wish while entering your vital stats only once, and each application is cus-

tomized to fit the institution's forms and requirements. Although the software and first application are on the house, it's $5 for each additional school. But the convenience may be worth the cost. Check and see if your colleges of choice are on the list of hundreds of schools that accepting the applications that use CollegeLink. The current list of participants includes colleges from Adelphi to Xavier, with several lowering or waiving their fees for CollegeLink applicants.
WEB http://www.collegelink.com

ENTA For $50, this Australian company will allow you to use their common application to send to ten schools worldwide. If your application is successful, you get your money back. (Seems like it should work the other way....) There are 1,500 schools participating in this service, and you can test it out as a demo user for free.
WEB http://WebTrax.com.au/ENTA

Part 2

Financial Aid

Free money 101

Once upon a time, about six months before you were born, your parents began to wonder

how the heck they were going to send you to college. If you're lucky, they have studied the process ever since, won the lottery, or earned a fortune selling goat cheese out of the back of the family minivan. But, if they're like most American parents, they're clueless. If you're tempted to put the book down now, "work study" may be your destiny. So, do we have everybody's attention? The Internet is a great place to go for the basic information you'll need to arm yourself against the Financial Aid dragon. Don't miss **Financing College** or **FinAid: The Financial Aid Information Page** for starters. When the acronyms grow overwhelming, clear your head and increase your vocabulary at the Glossary of **Financial Aid Terms**. What's your EFC IQ? Zero? Join Mensa with **Expected Family Contribution**. When you've got questions or just want to vent your spleen, hop on down **The Money Trail** or seek out some advice on **College Planning**. OK, now you have permission to panic.

Location: http://www.collegebound.com/

Why Send Your Money To College?

If all you really want to send is your kids.

C O L L E G E   B O U N D   Aid Eligibility
Educational Counseling

PHONE: (800)-962-2713 / (302) 478-4411
EMAIL: fireston@collegebound.com

Looking for dead presidents?
http://www.collegebound.com

Starting points

College Bound "Why send your money to college?" begins this Web ad for an aid eligibility counseling service. Why indeed, when you can send your money to College Bound? For an undisclosed fee, the company says it will provide strategies to maximize financial aid eligibility, a college selection service to match the student with the appropriate school, and comprehensive admissions counseling—what they refer to as "marketing the child to the school."
WEB http://www.collegebound .com

College Funding Company A simpler, user-friendly approach that explains options for financing a college education, this site does a good job of introducing the topic without inducing shell shock. Probably a good place to start be-

fore tackling the more detailed sites.
WEB http://www.collegefundingco .com

FinAid: The Financial Aid Information Page Just remember that time is money: you'll have to allot yourself plenty of the former while checking out this site if you want to score lots of the latter in terms of financial aid for college. Some of the many resources available here are: a form for electronically submitting questions to financial aid advisors; a glossary of financial aid terms; calculation tools for determining how much your family will be asked to contribute to college expenses; and how much aid you'll need. This site also links to other financial aid resources on the Web, including sources of scholarships/fellowships, grants, loans, and tuition payment plans. Links are further cataloged according to special in-

CYBERNOTES

"Helpful Tips to Receive Financial Aid

As you prepare to apply for financial aid, keep these things in mind to make the process go smoothly:

- Start looking for scholarships at least one year before you need them. Even small dollar amounts can add up. See our FASTWEB link for national scholarships.

- Complete the FAFSA each year in January or February in order to meet the college's priority deadline. If you need to apply for education loans, apply for them 8 to 10 weeks before the start of school, and keep the same lender every time you borrow. That will make keeping track of and repaying your loans much easier.

- DO NOT borrow more than you need. Student loans must be repaid shortly after graduation or dropping below half-time status. Many parent loans must be repaid immediately after receiving the funds. Make sure you know what your monthly payment will be before you borrow. See our Loan Repay section."

—from **College Funding Company**

terest groups (i.e., students with disabilities, students from minority backgrounds, older students). A good place to start at this extensive site would probably be Mark's Picks, a selection of the best/most popular financial aid sites.
WEB http://www.cs.cmu.edu/afs /cs/user/mkant/Public/FinAid /finaid.html

Financing College A primer from the renowned Princeton Review, starting with a comprehensive explanation of the financial aid process. Also included: general information on grants and scholarships, explanations of state and federal loan and grant programs,

and a Q&A covering such queries as "Will applying for aid jeopardize my chance of admission?" and "Should I hire a professional to help me fill out the forms?" Plus, this site allows you to search TPR's college database for even more information on the college thing.
AMERICA ONLINE *keyword* princeton →College→Financing College
WEB http://www.review.com/faid /college_faid.html

Paying for College Seven articles authored by AOL's Career Center covering only the most basic of financial aid frets like "How is Financial Aid Determined?", "What If I Do Not Qualify?", and

"I Only Want a Loan."
AMERICA ONLINE *keyword* career center→College Planning→Paying for College

Peterson's Education Center: Financing Education All right, face it: you're stressed. Being a high school junior or senior isn't easy—you figure it's time to enjoy the privileges of being an upperclassman, like unqualified respect and a better locker, but everyone's bugging you about this college thing, and how you're going to afford it. Luckily, Peterson's has gotten the financial aid scene down to a science. Besides a general description of types of aid and a glossary of useful terms, there's a month-by-month college admissions calendar for both high school juniors and seniors to make sure you're not so consumed worrying about the prom and yearbook that you can't remember to file your FAFSA. At this site you can also read up on other financial aid sources—including, of course, Peterson's own *Paying Less for College.*
WEB http://www.petersons.com /resources/finance.html

Start Your Homework Now If You Will Be Applying for Financial Aid in The Spring Maybe Hawaiian Electric Industries wasn't the first place you thought of when you started needing financial aid information, but lucky for you, they thought of you. This Web page gives a brief overview of financial aid issues with some gentle, parental admonitions. Keep in mind that this is a site with advice but no concrete answers (they're not handing out money here, OK?)—the last pointer they offer is "Get help," meaning somewhere else.
WEB http://www.hei.com/asb /finaid.html

Glossaries & FAQs

College Center FAQs Kaplan helps you keep on top of financial assistance with articles like "The Financial Aid Process in Ten Steps," "Negotiating Your Financial Aid Award," (apparently it can be done) and "Tips for Comparing Financial Aid Awards."
AMERICA ONLINE *keyword* kaplan →College→FAQs

Finaid FAQ Rather than waiting around for it to be reposted on the college and education newsgroups, you can come here to read the latest update of the FAQ on Financial Aid, Scholarships, and Fellowships. The questions and answers provided here give the lowdown on getting—or not getting—money for school. You might not yet understand how PC = (EPC + (n-1) x $500) / n, or what that means about financing your college education, but you will soon: just let the FAQ demystify the process for you. The FAQ offers advice and warnings, and also has sections for foreign students and the issue of the taxability of financial aid.
WEB http://www.cs.cmu.edu/afs /cs.cmu.edu/user/mkant/ftp /finaid/finaid.faq
URL ftp://rtfm.mit.edu/pub /usenet/news.answers/college /financial-aid-faq

Glossary of Financial Aid Terms "Collection agency" is one term in this glossary that no family paying for college wants to learn. Fortunately, there are other more pleasant words like "Gift aid" that families won't want to miss. Confused about the difference between Stafford and Pell or unsure what repayment options are all about? Try looking here first: it's a super list of just about everything that might come up. Noticeably absent—"trust fund." Sigh.
WEB http://www.collegeboard.org /css/html/gloss.html

Peterson's Education Center: Glossary of FA Terms Indirect Costs? Self-Help Expectation? Default and Collateral? Yikes! Get thee to this glossary.
WEB http://www.petersons.com /resources/gloss.html

Your first homework

ABACI's College Financial Aid Software Normal suspicion of people trying to make a buck off of naive newbies is suspended as this guy has a daughter in college—so we give him empathy points. Anyway, he's written a downloadable shareware program containing some financial aid worksheets and calculations, in a not-too-scary format. (The full version costs $39.50 and is for PCs only.)
WEB http://users.aol.com /abacifaw/faw.htm

Expected Family Contribution What's the magic number? For college applicants, it's the EFC. Parents dread it, knowing that all grants, loans, and even many private scholarships are based on this unrealistic-seeming number. Fill out the simple forms (have that financial data ready), cross your fingers and all your toes, and submit to find out the damage. And you wanted a car for your birthday—HA!
WEB http://www.collegeboard.org /efc/bin/efc-init.cgi

Paying for College The College Board—those friendly folks who bring you the SAT—aren't just out to make your senior year of high school standardized test hell. They're on your side, really. Here they help you deal with the cost of college with a student expenses worksheet, a financial aid checklist, and a financial assistance glossary of sorts.
AMERICA ONLINE *keyword* college board→Paying for College

Discussion & advice

College Planning Who is Dr. Richard Andrea? Well, he's the guy who's about to give you some straight talk about financial aid. Scroll down to the Paying for College section and he'll tell you what kinds of financial aid exist and

---

If FinAid gets to you, there are places to get help
America Online *keyword* Career Center

If you have quick "college-related" question, one that can be answered with a brief response, you are invited to email your question to Dr. Andrea at screen name "DrCollege." Dr. Andrea will respond to your question within 48 hours.

Please ...

* keep your question brief and to the point.
* only forward questions that are related to the subject of college planning.

Chat With Dr. Andrea

Dr. Andrea can be reached via email at screen name "DrCollege".

CYBERNOTES

"Here's my situation:

I'm a twenty-eight year old student returning from two years in Mexico. I've been accepted by UC Berkeley but have only twenty-five pesos to my name. I'm currently mooching from friends and family while trying to find the cash to get to school in August.

My question is this: How do I access ACTUAL scholarship information on the Net? I'm looking for names and addresses of fools who will give me money so that I can put off a real life for another two years or so.

I've been to the library and been through all the books. It seems to me that the Net should offer me access to most of the information I'm looking for, but I don't know how to find it. The best tools thus far have been Yahoo! and Altavista, though I haven't been able to find the actual scholarship sources, and this is what I want.

Can anyone point me in the right direction?

I'd also be interested in talking with any students on the UC Berkeley campus for other information unrelated to money.

REWARD: Anyone who provides me with useful information will be invited over to my place for molé and tequila and a few cheap laughs."

—from **soc.college.financial-aid**

---

how to apply for them. He also delivers some advice and warnings regarding scholarship-search services.
AMERICA ONLINE *keyword* Career Center→College Planning

College/Adult Students Forum The Messages section of this forum is almost entirely in Q&A format. Apparently, you and your parents aren't the only ones baffled and mystified by the range of advice and options for financial aid out there. But good news! The government has come to your rescue! All questions on Admissions/Financing are answered by real honest-to-goodness U.S. Department of Education representatives. Plus, the Libraries are filled with goodies, from specific information relating to getting into the particular college of your choice (almost 200 are listed here) to Financial Aid Myths.
COMPUSERVE *go* stufob→Browse Libraries→Admission/Financing

The Money Trail Byron wants to know if filling out the FAFSA is worthwhile. Twins in California are trying to figure out how to finance their double education. Cass is looking for advice on whether she should shell out $100 for a scholarship-search service. This is the place where would-be college students share their problems and solutions, questions and answers, and successes and failures as they make their forays into the financial aid arena. Some folders of discussion include the High School Student Forum, Looking for Scholarships, and Financial Aid War Stories.
AMERICA ONLINE *keyword* rsp→The Money Trail

Real Life and Education According to Real Life, for those students who entered college this fall, the four-year cost including tuition, room and board, a few books, and other incidentals will average almost $95,000 at a private school and $45,000 at a public university. That said, this online financial forum wants to help you take the bite out of that bill with a newsletter, testimonials, and suggestions.
AMERICA ONLINE *keyword* real life→Education

soc.college.financial-aid One subject line reads, "Help the poor boy," and that's basically the type of plea you'll see in the messages being posted to this newsgroup. Be forewarned, however, that questions greatly outnumber answers here (just as in life). Other postings include recommendations for other points of interest regarding financial aid on the Internet.
USENET soc.college.financial-aid

Start saving yesterday

Moms, Dads, we know you're out there. And we know that, unfair as it may seem, while

little Jennifer and Jimmy are working late at the Save 'n' Shop to earn money for designer clothes and used-but-oh-so-cool cars, you are tearing your hair out around the kitchen table. Why are you worrying, when you could be contemplating the golden years of your retirement? Because college costs a lot of money. Even if you haven't begun to plan, it's not too late. Surf over to **College Savings Adviser** or **College Cost Calculator** for a reality check. Quell the ensuing panic at **The Tuition Challenge** and **Adventures in Education.** Bring a big piggy bank to the **Scholarship Consultants of North America** and crack it over your own head for the entertainment of others at **misc.invest**. P.S., To Jennifer and Jimmy: Working at the dining hall is pretty much like Save 'n Shop. In other words, maybe you should read this, too.

Investments

College Savings Bank Everyone's heard the statistics. Everyone's speculated on what a college education will cost in the year 2000. With costs rising so rapidly,

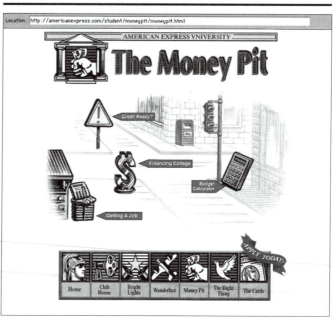

Location: http://americanexpress.com/student/moneypit/moneypit.html

AMERICAN EXPRESS VNIVERSITY

The Money Pit

Credit Ready?

Financing College

Budget Calculator

Getting A Job

APPLY TODAY!

Home | Club House | Bright Lights | Wanderlust | Money Pit | The Right Thing | The Cards

When you're overcome with financing questions, fall into the Money Pit
http://americanexpress.com/student/moneypit/moneypit.html

how can you possibly save enough money now to finance a college education ten years, five years, or even one year down the road? College Savings Bank has come up with an answer: the CollegeSure® CD, which is sold in units equivalent to one full year's average, current college tuition. It is guaranteed to earn enough to pay one full year's tuition at current prices upon maturity. More detailed information about the CD is available at the site, including a college-cost calculator (not for the faint hearted), where you can estimate how much you'll need to save between now and convocation.
WEB http://www.collegesavings .com

Galaxy College Investment Program Fleet Bank's Galaxy mutual funds offer this special program for college investments. But be warned—most experts don't advise mutual funds unless the kids are still pretty young. If they are? Check this out.
WEB http://www.fleet.com /persbank/invstmnt/mutfun /galfun/galcol.html

Goal Star—College Investment Mortgage The old sage said that if it sounds too good to be true, it is. Reconfigure your mortgage, pay less than $205 a month, and save hundreds of thousands of dollars in mortgage payments while still having plenty

`Location:` http://wwwp.exis.net/~goalstr/goalpgm2.htm

When you read something like this, all you want to do is believe
http://wwwp.exis.net/~goalstr/goalpgm2.htm

for college educations? And it's tax-free? Sounds great. Get the pamphlet, take it directly to your financial advisor and see if the old sage is right.
WEB http://wwwp.exis.net/~goalstr/goalpgm2.htm

Investment Strategies—Education and Retirement: Ouch!
Education costs have been rising at twice the rate of the economy for a long time now. And for many families who are having kids later in life, retirement comes all too quickly after college costs. The subtitle of this intelligent and well-written advice article is absolutely on target. *Ouch!* is right.
WEB http://www.gnn.com/meta/finance/feat/21st/ch20/ch20.html

misc.invest You are concerned solely with the best way to raise money for that college education. Investment seems to be the answer. This group examines general investment topics, including stocks and bonds and mutual funds. If you want to discuss your retirement plans or complain about the mistreatment of the to-

bacco industry—"Congress and the anti-smoking lobby are driving the tobacco industry out of business in the U.S."—put your two cents in, and see what the yields are. A few committed newsgroup participants upload market reports—the same data that you're paying for on other services.
USENET misc.invest

Planning Takes Financial Sting Out of College Tuition
As if we didn't already know this! This article is an introductory paragraph, shall we say, to the huge book about college investing you should have read ten years ago.
WEB http://www.ag.ohio-state.edu/~ohioline/lifetime/lt3-4b.html

Scholarship Consultants of North America With the rising cost of postsecondary education, it sometimes seems impossible to imagine saving enough money. The Education Savings Plans described here offer tax-sheltered methods of investing money for your child or grandchild's future for a $100 enrollment fee.
WEB http://www.resp-usc.com

Wall Street Financial, Inc. College Investment Planner
Technically, this is just another numbers-cruncher, but since you have to give 'em your name, we'll call it an investment. Just round up the usual suspects (child's age, years until college, etc.), and these guys will get back to you with your options and, no doubt, a sales pitch. Could be helpful.
WEB http://www.wallstreetfinancial.com/college.htm

Number-crunching

College Cost Calculator Having recently celebrated sweet young Sarah's first birthday, you

are casually wondering what her college fees are going to cost seventeen years from now. Brace yourself. A four-year education at a private college will cost $264,598.50. That's $59,595.02 per year.
WEB http://www.merrill-lynch.ml.com/personal/college/collegecalc.html

College Savings Adviser So it's August, your little girl is starting to pack her bunny slippers and her brand new notebooks and is talking about meal plans, and you haven't figured out how you're going to pay for college yet? Sorry, it's too late! OK, so if that scenario didn't apply but the prospect haunts your every sleepless night, head straight for this site. Plug in some numbers about your savings (e.g., how much you're able to save, and the time until your child enters college), and this engine will spit out how much money you'll have. If it's not enough, you may need to rethink your financial plans.
WEB http://www.collegeboard.org/css/html/save.html

DCB&T Financial Planning Calculator College Savings Planner This amazing little program calculates any missing variable in the usual college savings scenario. Enter information in all fields except the one you need to know (e.g., Amount to Invest Towards College Savings Per Year), and receive a full assessment of the vital numbers.
WEB http://www.dcbt.com/FinCalc/College.html

Education Funding Calculator
"They will be going to college sooner than you think," say the good folks at Waddell & Reed, a big ol' company that would love to do your financial planning.

"Thanks for the news flash," you say as you plug in the magic numbers in their calculator. They suggest that you try different scenarios (like changing the age of your child, perhaps?), and to consider some different strategies (like running away from home?). If the numbers don't seem to add up, or you just like free stuff, fill out another screen for a free financial planning session at Waddell & Reed.

WEB http://www.waddell.com /edu_ill.html

Life-Plan Software: Education Funding The Brady bunch, the Bobbsey Twins, or that family in *Cheaper By the Dozen* would love this software. It can compute and coordinate savings needs for the college careers of up to 15 children of all ages, although it doesn't provide any emotional support for their unfortunate parents. The bad news is that, far from actually providing the parent with the investments it recommends, the software costs money, although a demo is free. Then again, perhaps having all the cal-

culations for Jan, Marcia, Cindy, and the rest all on one piece of paper is worth it.

WEB http://life-plan.com /educ-d.html

Saving money

66 Ways to Save Money Wear your socks twice before washing them. Take cold showers. What? You already do these things. Then why not check out some of these tips on household economy—they might actually be useful. This Consumer Information Center pamphlet covers insurance, cars, groceries, funeral arrangements, and more.

URL gopher://gopher.gsa.gov:70 /00/staff/pa/cic/money /save$.txt

$tarving $hirley's $avings Page "I promise to take coupons wherever I go," begins the $tarving $hirley oath. She also suggests shopping at thrift and consignment stores, holding yard sales, eating cheap (she's got recipes), and lots of other stuff that the typical middle-class family would

sniff at. (To its cost!) Shirley provides shareware, too, for organizing those coupons and rebates. Remember that a penny saved is 1/100 of a dollar.

WEB http://www.shirl.com

> ## " Wear socks twice before washing them. "

Services

College Board Financial Aid Services for Students and Parents "Some of the best things in life may be free; unfortunately, college isn't one of them." If you didn't know that already, you have a lot of studying ahead of you. The College Board is a good resouce for some hard lessons. For free, it will give you an overview of the costs of college and the ins and outs of financial aid, including detailed tips for parents and students (such as how to check on your credit report and stick to a budget once you're on the college campus). For a fee, it will analyze your finances and tell you exactly what to do and how to do it so that you can make your college dreams come true.

WEB http://www.collegeboard.org /css/html/indx001.html

College Money Planner Form $14.95 for 18 personalized pages. It's from the College Board, so it ought to be good, and of course, it's strictly confidential.

WEB http://www.collegeboard.org /css/html/planform.htmll

Step-by-step

Adventures in Education If you're truly up for the adventure, this will guide you through life—

Saving for college can be a pig
http://www.collegeboard.org/css/html/planform.html

from eighth grade to the real world—with outlines of steps to take in planning for standardized tests, choosing and applying to college, funding your education, deciding upon a career, and preparing for your first job hunt. With such helpful guidance, you might be tempted to believe that real life is actually simple. Moms and dads get tips on how to set their kids on the right track (i.e., when exactly to nag them to study for the SAT), and there are sections devoted to information for high school counselors and teachers, financial aid officers, lenders, services, and secondary markets.
WEB http://www.tgslc.org

American Express University: The Money Pit This section of American Express University specifically deals with financial issues surrounding pre-, at-, and post-college students. The Credit Ready? section will prepare you for thinking about all the money you have—and don't have. Financing College will connect you with FASTWeb. Budget Calculator offers a handy tool for getting your finances under control, and Getting a Job will coach you through your resumé, getting an internship, and surviving without allowance.
WEB http://americanexpress.com /student/moneypit/moneypit.html

Don't Miss Out The handbook, entitled *The Ambitious Student's Guide to Financial Aid*, from Signet Bank takes would-be students step-by-step through the quest for college funding, from defining their monetary need through successful financing. Included are tricks of the trade for tilting the financial aid process in your favor, like reducing the family contribution or increasing the cost of education in order to up

CYBERNOTES

"'Advanced planning is critical when considering college,' said Carolyn McKinney, state specialist in family resource management for Ohio State University Extension. 'People easily get discouraged when they see college-expense projections of about $120,000 for four years by the year 2010,' McKinney said. That often-quoted figure assumes tuition and other related costs will rise by 7 percent annually.

'The good news in this picture is that today's $45,000 annual salary will rise to about $119,000 in the same period, assuming a 5 percent annual wage increase,' said McKinney, an assistant professor. Still, people who plan ahead should find financing a college education less painful than those who do nothing until the last minute."

—from **Planning Takes Financial Sting Out of College Tuition**

your award.
WEB http://jerome.signet.com /collegemoney/toc1.html

How Are You Going to Pay for College? It's the question that precollege panic attacks are made of. This Nellie Mae site aims to soothe even the most harried high school senior. The lending leaders talk you through your financial aid options, important deadlines, and discussions you should have with the folks; they also provide a college planning checklist perfect for printing out and posting on your bulletin board.
WEB http://jerome.signet.com /collegemoney

Parent Soup: College Planning One of the best guides to financial planning of a college education, whether you have six years or six months to go. It answers questions like, "What if You Come Up Short?" and provides

both detailed and general advice about investment strategies, including Scholarships and Grants, Setting Up an Investment Plan Now!, and How Can My Children Help Pay for College?
WEB http://www.parentsoup.com /cgi-bin/genobject/gtsx000

The Tuition Challenge The kindly bunch at Fleet Bank have prepared this excellent article with advice and comfort for parents attempting to fathom the cost of college. It follows the basic strategy of all investment planning documents: it scares readers to death and then tells them not to panic. If Junior is going to college just a few months from now and you're already in a state of terror, skip the fear tactics and long-term advice and scroll down to: Help! We waited too long to start saving!
WEB http://www.fleet.com/abtyou /inveduc/tuition.html

Ask Uncle Sam

Believe it or not, the U.S. government occasionally works smoothly. Take financial aid, for

example (completely at random, of course): The student fills out one form, and the government responds with an aid package consisting of grants, loans, and Work-Study plans. Does it get any simpler? Well, yes. The Department of Education is making it simpler on the World Wide Web by providing free explanatory pamphlets like **Funding Your Education** and **The Student Guide** online. Could it possibly be any easier? It certainly could. The student, fully informed by the didactic pamphlets, can now submit the FAFSA (Free Application for Federal Student Aid) without ever picking up a pencil at the **Office of Post-secondary Education.** But oh, does life get any closer to true nirvana? No. And you still have to pay the loans back.

Assistance

American Student Assistance Home Page Extremely helpful and thorough information about federal student loan programs. AMSA offers detailed advice about making reasonable estimates regarding how much you'll need to

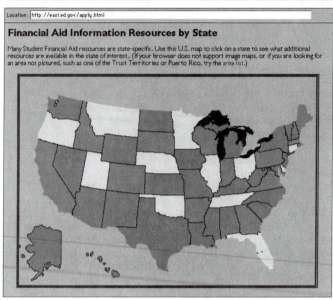

Financial Aid Information Resources by State

Many Student Financial Aid resources are state-specific. Use this U.S. map to click on a state to see what additional resources are available in the state of interest.. (If your browser does not support image maps, or if you are looking for an area not pictured, such as one of the Trust Territories or Puerto Rico, try the area list.)

You are here... and somewhere so is your money
http://easi.ed.gov

pay and how much you can afford to pay. There's also a section called Tips and Tricks, which guides even the most loan-phobic student through the application process.
WEB http://www.amsa.com/welcome.html

Catalogue of Federal Domestic Assistance Almost every government agency, from the Department of Transportation to the Department of Energy, funds scholarships. No matter what your academic interest (mining, nursing, international business, or dance) or personal background (minority student, first-generation citizen, disabled, or returning student), the federal government more than likely has a scholarship up your alley. The Catalogue of

Federal Domestic Assistance provides detailed information on requirements, application procedures, and contacts for scholarships.
URL gopher://solar.rtd.utk.edu:70/11/Federal/CFDA

EASI: Easy Access for Students and Institutions Imagine a world where applying for federal aid was free from complicated forms to fill in, long lines to stand in, and running around to find answers to your questions. Project EASI is a collaborative effort among government, business, and education leaders initiated by the U.S. Department of Education to reengineer the country's post-secondary financial aid delivery system. But since you

can't just wait for their federal dream to become reality (you've got an FAFSA to fill out, an appointment with the financial aid counselor, and a trip to make to the bank), you can visit the EASI site now for an explanation of the entire financial aid process as it exists now, from applying to repaying.
WEB http://easi.ed.gov

ED Office of Postsecondary Education Ask not what your Department of Education can do for you... oh, all right, go ahead and ask. As it turns out, the Office of Postsecondary Education, part of the Department of Education, offers both money and advice on how to get your hands on it. Some highlights include information on completing the Free Application for Federal Student Aid (FAFSA) and FAFSA Express, from which you can download free software for Windows which allows you to submit the FAFSA forms electronically.
WEB http://www.ed.gov/offices/OPE/index.html

Funding Your Education This DOE pamphlet is sort of the baby brother of the exhaustive Student Guide, and as such is a great way to start reading about Pell, Perkins, and their sidekick Stafford. Plus, you'll find out how to apply for aid, how to reduce the cost of school so you're not saddled with debt, and the best question of them all, "How will I receive my FSEOG?" Indeed. That is, the Federal Supplemental Educational Opportunity Grant.
WEB http://www.ed.gov/prog_info/SFA/FYE/

Paying for College Here's another of those government pamphlets, written by (we assume) government pamphleteers forced

---

CYBERNOTES

"What criteria do I have to meet to get federal student aid?

Basically, to receive aid from our programs, you must--

- have financial need (not part of the criteria for some loans),
- have a high school diploma or a General Equivalency Diploma (GED) certificate or pass a test approved by the Department of Education,
- be enrolled as a regular student (that is, you have to be working toward a degree or certificate) in an eligible program,
- be a U.S. citizen or eligible noncitizen,
- have a valid Social Security Number,
- register with the Selective Service if required, and
- maintain satisfactory academic progress once in school.

If you have a question about your citizenship status, contact the financial aid office at the college or career school you plan to attend."

—from **Funding Your Education**

---

to reside in basement cubicles. It's a good one, though, full of information about, well, paying for college. And it's pretty ugly, too.
URL gopher://gopher.gsa.gov:70/00/staff/pa/cic/fed_prog/paycollg.txt

The Student Guide from ED Got questions about how you're going to finance your education? Ask your Uncle Sam. This is the official guide from the U.S. Department of Education's Office of Postsecondary Education, updated each academic year. General information on student eligibility for federal aid, the application process, and borrower rights and responsibilities are available. You'll also find specifics on Pell Grants,

Stafford Loans, PLUS Loans, and other federal assistance programs. A glossary helps future freshmen interpret the financial aid lingo.
WEB http://www.ed.gov/prog_info/SFA/StudentGuide

William D. Ford Federal Direct Loan Program Has your friend Bill Ford called on you recently? Have you heard that he's a great guy to meet? The Department of Education (where Bill lives) has archived some information about him, like how to write to him and how to borrow money from him. (Bill's uncle, Sam has deep pockets.) Plus, there are newsletters about what Bill's up to.
WEB http://www.ed.gov/offices/OPE/DirectLoan

Following the money

Shopping for financial aid is a lot like being a rat in a maze. When you get to the end of

the labyrinth, you never know if you're going to get a pellet or a zap of electricity. The Internet is the biggest maze of all, of course, but luckily for small rats like you, **fastWeb!** is one of the tastiest morsels imaginable. It's free and it's meaty. Those who have already been accepted to a few colleges might want to visit **University Financial Aid Office Web Pages** for comparison shopping. Lucky rats with money to lose may want to check out the commercial search services like **The Grantseeker's Resource Center**, but beware, the costs can be quite shocking.

Free services

Collegiate Connections Funding and Finance If you see just one thing here, make sure it's that unobtrusive little entry marked NC Help. This takes you to the CommonLine network, which is a CompuServe supported automated student loan application and disbursement process created through the National Council of Higher Education Loan Programs. There's a searchable database of participants and regular updates. Also in the Funding and Finance section are links to *Money Magazine*, *Fortune Magazine*, and a page called Information USA.
COMPUSERVE *go* college→Funding and Finances

If I had a dollar for every one of the more than 180,000 scholarships, grants, fellowships, and loans collected here...
http://www.studentservices.com

fastWEB! (Financial Aid Search Through the Web) Fast it's not. This financial aid search requires you to give up screen after screen of personal details before providing you with information about scholarships and loans. However, it pays off with a personally tailored search which you can check for updates (according to the site, approximately 1,200 awards are added to the database each day, and additions matching your profile are added to your 'mailbox'). Best of all, it's free.
WEB http://www.fastweb.com

Money for Undergraduate Study A searchable database of scholarships, loans, grants, awards, and internships to help the under-funded undergrad. The programs posted are sponsored by professional organization, federal, state, and foreign governments, foundations, educational associations, military and veterans' groups, sororities and fraternities, religious groups, and big corporations. All areas of the sciences, social sciences, and humanities are covered and special folders are available for

women, minorities, veterans, and the disabled.
AMERICA ONLINE *keyword* rsp→ Money for Study→Undergraduate

Nerd World: Financial Assistance An index of online outlets of financial aid facts and sources ranging from AlphaMega Scholarship Resources to Whitaker Financial Solutions, with brief descriptions of each link.
WEB http://www.nerdworld.com /nw1178.html

RSP Funding Focus Basically, if you want money for anything you should check here. That's a very simplistic way of describing this sophisticated financial aid resource. It's an enormous compilation of scholarships, grants, fellowships, internships, and other sources of free money for undergraduates, graduates, and professionals. A special section of RSP alerts you to programs with imminent deadlines. After you've browsed to your heart's content, go to RSP's financial aid library and check out listings of financial aid directories, along with publica-

CYBERNOTES

Spend $ to get $

Chinook College Funding Service Although the beginning of this site looks like just another place to read about the difference between SEOG and Stafford, Pell and Perkins, don't be surprised when you scroll down and realize that the site's major thrust is to discuss the Chinook College Funding Service itself. What exactly is it? Go to the Chinook FAQ and learn about how Chinook will search its scholarship database for you by keyword, for a fee. (Hey, you've got to spend money to make money, right?) Online search results are $15; Express Mail results cost $44. An online preliminary assessment, where you can get an idea of Chinook's usefulness for your specific needs, is free.
WEB http://home.chinook.com /chinook

tion and ordering information. Or, go to the state-agency address book in order to track down your options in receiving state-based financial aid. The Money Trail, the message board component, allows you to communicate with like-minded money-seekers.
AMERICA ONLINE *keyword* RSP

Scholarship Listings Directory (UC Irvine) Although best for students heading to University of California at Irvine, this directory is certainly worth a look for others. It's comprehensive and annotated; and of course the amount of the award is listed right on top, for quickly scanning the scholarship wish list.
WEB http://www.honors.uci.edu /~honors/SOP/listing.html

Student Services Student Services maintains a database of 180,000 scholarships, grants, fel-

lowships, and loans collected from thousands of universities, private companies, and financial houses nationwide. Enter your intended major, interests, and heritage, and the fastWEB server will match you up with programs for which you qualify. In addition, you'll be provided with your own personal mailbox and updated nightly with the latest financial aid offerings.
WEB http://www.studentservices .com

University Financial Aid Office Web Pages This subsection of FinAid: The Financial Aid Information Page is worth noting for students with specific college destinations. Search by college/university name to be connected to institution-specific pages dealing with financial aid for students.
WEB http://almond.srv.cs.cmu.edu /afs/cs/user/mkant/Public/FinAid /html/univ.html

Grant Master Free money—it's the stuff that dreams are made of, especially financial aid fantasies. Email Grant Master and they'll send you a list of grant-givers like private corporations, universities, foundations, and charitable organizations that may have money set aside to help send you to the school of your dreams.
WEB http://www.f1.wa.com /planner/grantm.htm

The Grantseeker's Resource Center If you think the words "gift aid" have a nice ring to them, join the club. Everyone wants grants for school, but locating the assistance you qualify for can be difficult. The Grantseeker's Resource Center wants to be your guide. However, unlike the grants they may help you find, GRC's services are not free.
WEB http://www.pcwin.com /grants/tuition_seekers.html

More fee-based services

Academic Scholarship Consultants
www.webcreations.com/asc

Academic Scholarship Services
www.itsnet.com/home/vtechad
/public_html/money.html

Aid For College
pages.prodigy.com/jose

Americana Funding
www.eden.com/~mainlink
/scholar/american

Birchwood Scholarship Services
www.birchwood.com
/index.html

Cash for Class
www.cashforclass.com

College Connection
users.aol.com/scholarshp

College Edge
www.collegeedge.com

College Fund Finders
apollo.co.uk/a/cff

College Money
pages.prodigy.com/TX/mafc03a
/college.html

Color Charter Company
www.earthlink.com/~wwweber
/cs/precs.html

Daedalus Company
www.daedco.com

DiMin Enterprises
apollo.co.uk/a/dimin

EDP Enterprises
www.apc.net/edp/college.htm

Financial Aid for College
www.he.net/~accucomm
/fafc.htm

Financial Aid for College
www.cw2.com/BCS
/fafc.htm

Financial Aid for College —Executive Search
www.skraam.com/fafc.htm

Free Money for College Information
www.webpres.com
/vanvleck

Free Money for College Information/Free Scholar- ships and Grants
virtumall.com/VanVleck

Free Personal Grants
spider.lloyd.com/~grants

Info-Center: The Scholarship Source
www.admazing.com
/info-center

Jordan Concepts
www.jordanconcepts.com

Leo Financial Aid Services
www.olywa.net/ikaika
/lfas.htm

Miranda Educational Consultants
www.kern.com/miranda

Scholarship Aid for Education
www.studentaid.holowww
.com

Scholarship Bank
www.idyllmtn.com
/scholarbank

Scholarship Fund Finders
www.dallasweb.com
/scholarship

Scholarship Locator Services
www.pinn.net/Scholarship

Scholarship Resources—Jody Schneider, Consultant
www.connecti.com/%7Ehomecom
/schneidr.htm

Scholarship Search Services
www2.msstate.edu/%7Etmt1
/schweb.html

Scholarship Searches
www.iea.com/~garyw
/college

Student Financial Aid Consultants
www.financeaid.com

Student Financial Aid Software
www.tpsoftware.com

Student Scholarship Assistance Center
www.novakint.com/SSAC

Student Services, Inc.
web.studentservices.com

Thompson Scholarship Services
www.calweb.com/~tss
/tss2.html

Winning Scholarship Searches!
pages.prodigy.com/mikep
/scholar.htm

Your Scholar Ship
www.webcom.com/~excelle

Scholarships

Look in the mirror. It may just be that you have a marketable heritage and that a world of

minority scholarships awaits you. That being the case, your first step might be to visit **Money for Minorities and Women**, followed by a little fishing in the **Minority Scholarships and Fellowships** pond. Perhaps you're happiest when there's a ball, bat, stick, puck, pool or goal post in your life. That being the case, you may well be entitled to **Money Because You're an Athlete**. Could the providers of this service be any clearer? Simultaneously, don't miss scoring with **Allsport's Free College Sports Recruiting and Scholarship Service**, or **Sport A.S.I.S.T**. Perhaps you felt an affinity for Dorothy when she observed that there was no place like home. But did you know that you might get money just for staying there? Check out regional scholarships and more at **Connecticut Scholarships A-Z**. Face it, we all have a special interest in something, and that special interest could take us places, whether via routes traditional, the **Air Force ROTC**, or fabulous, the **Donna Reed Foundation**.

Location: http://www.missamerica.com/miss_gal.htm

The foundation of a good education: foundation
http://www.missamerica.com/schola03.htm

Ethnic & minority

Armenian Students' Association of America This organization, widely represented on college campuses around the country, sponsor several scholarships for both college students and high school seniors of appropriate ethnic descent, and often requires active commitment to both ASA and the Armenian community.
WEB http://www.asainc.org

Black Excel: The College Help Network This is no cozy, big-brother-helping-little-brother site. It's a business, and wants to sell you something. Specifically, Black Excel is a college-counseling service that has helped students get into over a hundred different colleges. They've also compiled a list of scholarships. A long list of links and several sample articles are free.

Who knows, you may want to opt for the paid services.
WEB http://cnct.com/home/ijblack/BlackExcel.shtml

Hispanic Educational Foundation HEF, as they call themselves, provides many scholarships on the local level to eligible Hispanic students. Success stories, addresses, and several hot lines are among the items available here.
WEB http://www.nmt.edu/~larranag/hef/hef.html

Minority Scholarships and Fellowships No matter what kind of program you're headed for, there's probably financial aid for which you are eligible. Search financial aid opportunities by school, state, degree program, or sponsoring institution.
WEB http://web.fie.com/htbin/cashe.pl

Money for Minorities and Women

This chapter of the wonderful *Don't Miss Out* pamphlet lists dozens of specific and general sources of information about minority and women's scholarships. Most of them involve the dreaded SASE instead of something more wired, but that does not at all diminish this article's value. Of special interest are the sources for Native American scholarships—there are lots out there, and they're often overlooked.

WEB http://jerome.signet.com /collegemoney/ch22.html

Athletic

Allsport's Free College Sports Recruiting and Scholarship Service

This excellent site is the only free recruiting service in the country. Jump, surf, field, or make an end run straight to the Allsport stadium for introductory information, including the all-important Playbook. Post your resumé, update it as often as you like, and receive feedback from coaches. Allsport actively markets its database, and will soon be a commercial service, so your participation will always be free. If you only see one site between practice sessions, this should be the one.

WEB http://www.irc-coordinator .com

College Athletic Consulting Services

So many people to take your money, and so little time! This is another athlete-marketing service, and while there is little substantive information here, they mention that they specialize in foreign students. So if you're reading this in England but are dying to play "football" for the Big Ten, give 'em a call. A phone call can't hurt—it's not even a 900 number.

WEB http://members.aol.com /cacs96/private/index.htm

College Prospects of America

This is the world's largest athletic-recruiting service. It markets all sports, which means that whether you play soccer, field hockey, basketball, or just run really fast, it might be able to help you. CPOA does mailings, has a hot line, produces videos, and provides other services that, despite their price, could be of assistance in tracking down that elusive sports scholarship.

WEB http://www.jette.com/cpoa

Cyberdive

For some people, the biggest thrill in the world is to stand 20 feet in the air, jump backwards and upside down, turn various aerial somersaults, and land in a large concrete tub of chemically treated water. OK, whatever! If you like to dive and are interested in doing it in exchange for a college education, check out this page. Post your dive resumé for college coaches to read. Then find out about diving camps, dive difficulties, financial aid, and more. Geronimo!

WEB http://www.igateway.net /sano/cyberdive

Getting a Shot at College Sports

Only the first chapter of this book is available for cyberperusal, but if chapter titles such as "Are you training in the right place?" and "Is video recommended for your sport to showcase your skills?" are of interest, you may want to order this book.

WEB http://www.iwsc.com/sports /scholarships/index.html

Graphic Sports Marketing

Don't kid yourself, baseball players. NCAA recruiting is big business. And apparently, just popping one over the fence in your local vacant lot ain't gonna cut it. Graphic Sports Marketing is a company devoted to helping high school baseball players market themselves effectively to the best schools—for a price. But for shortstops who wouldn't know a recruiter from a fly ball, they just may be the answer to a prayer.

WEB http://www.opennet.com /ww/gsm.htm

International Society of Student Athletes

For $35, high school and junior-college athletes

Jock till you drop with Allsport

http://www.irc-coordinator.com

Location: http://www.irc-coordinator.com/

ALLSPORT RECRUITING

Helping High School Athletes Achieve Their Athletic Dreams

 WHAT IS ALLSPORT?

Allsport is a FREE college sports scholarship recruiting tool for high school athletes and college coaches. This is the only place where high school student athletes and college coaches can **build and update** profiles FREE!

can receive a year's membership in this nonprofit association devoted to college-bound athletes. Membership includes the *College Bound Sport Report*, a bimonthly newsletter, as well as subscription to an email hot line and an online sports resumé. Plus, a membership card gets discounts on sports paraphernalia. Well, at least it's nonprofit.
WEB http://www.aces.org/issa.htm

Money Because You are an Athlete "All-star athletes don't need this book," states this chapter of *Don't Miss Out*. So who does? Those better-than-average student athletes who are either less visible than those pesky all-stars, or those who may be looking for hidden sports scholarships in less common sports like fencing. Don't miss this helpful introduction to the recruiting process, especially the step-by-step guide to marketing yourself instead of paying somebody else to do it.
WEB http://jerome.signet.com /collegemoney/ch19.html

Sport A.S.I.S.T "Do not overestimate your athletic ability" is just some of the advice from this practical and useful guide to the recruiting process. (In other words, don't hold out for Division I if Division III is more your level.) This book is available for order here, but a little bit of the content is free and online, including a Challenge Quiz, Facts and Information, and a Parents' Guide. Good stuff.
WEB http://www.athletes.com/asist .html

Regional

Amarillo's ACE Scholarship Program The lucky kids of Palo Duro High School in Amarillo, Texas, are given a free college edu-

Location: http://info.utas.edu.au/docs/scholarships/scholarships.html

Tasmania National Undergraduate Scholarships

Between the Tasmanian Devils and the deep blue sea
http://info.utas.edu.au/docs/scholarships/scholarships.html

cation if they meet certain requirements throughout their high school and college years. If you're from Palo Duro, you surely know this already. If you're not, come here and be envious. If you're a parent of young children, doesn't Amarillo sound like a nice place for kids to grow up?
WEB http://www.tbp.com/ace /acehome.htm

California Student Aid Commission Residents of California are lucky enough to be provided with this helpful guide to financial aid in the land of stars and sunshine. While specific scholarships aren't listed, the suggestions for finding them are plentiful and helpful for residents of any state.
WEB http://www.csac.ca.gov

Canadian Merit Scholarship Foundation College-bound students in Canada should definitely check out this home page for the Canadian Merit Scholarship Foundation to find out about the national, regional, and provincial awards offered by the foundation.

WEB http://sciborg.uwaterloo.ca /~slkeith/cmsf.html

Connecticut Scholarships A-Z Connecticut high schoolers, rejoice! But first, travel to this ugly but encyclopedic listing of scholarships for every geographic location and interest under the Greater Hartford sun. Note that some of the scholarships are not restricted by geographic residence.
WEB http://emporium.turnpike.net /R/Rodnet/htfd

Frank H. Buck Scholarships Few specific scholarships have their own Web presence, complete with an illustrated deer logo. But then, the Frank H. Buck Scholarships do. They're only for residents of certain California counties, but they are full scholarships to the institution of the Buck Scholar's choice.
WEB http://coos.dartmouth.edu /~phuoc/buck.html

Georgia Student Finance Commission One-stop shopping for Georgia residents trying to fig-

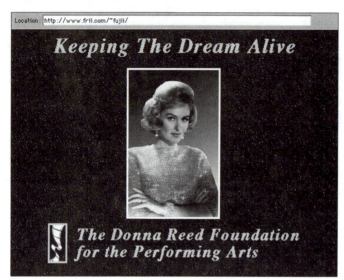

Location: http://www.frii.com/~fujii/

Keeping The Dream Alive

The Donna Reed Foundation for the Performing Arts

She has a foundation. It gives away money. It wants to give you some of that money. Any questions?
http://www.frii.com/~fujii

ure out who to call. Only state aid is covered here, but the people behind these phone numbers could probably point you to private sources.
WEB http://www.gsfc.org

Higher Education Services Corporation Do you love New York? More to the point, do you live there? Here's the place to go if you said yes, or if you merely need a large image of Governor Pataki for your desktop wallpaper.
WEB http://www.hesc.state.ny.us

Illinois State Tuition Waiver Simple, but to the point. Does your state have one of these?
WEB http://www.iit.edu/~afrotc /istw.html

Money in Your Community "Just about every community offers scholarship assistance to its young citizens," begins this fantastic article, yet another of the chapters in *Don't Miss Out*. There are enough hints, tips, and suggested

resources here to get any regional scholarship hunt underway.
WEB http://jerome.signet.com /collegemoney/ch15.html

Moonlight Graham Scholarship Fund If you are a Chisolm, Minn., high school student or a baseball fan, you'll want to read about the scholarship fund commemorating Doc "Moonlight" Graham, immortalized in the movie *Field of Dreams*. The scholarship is awarded to two graduating Chisholm seniors each year; everyone else is invited to visit the site and look at photographs of Doc.
WEB http://www.cardmall.com /moonlight-graham

Ohio Board of Regents Financial Aid Ohio residents should read this informational sheet regarding financial aid programs administered by the Ohio Board of Regents. A variety of grants and scholarships is available, with eligibility requirements

ranging from special interest groups to high academic achievement.http://www.bor.ohio.gov/pro gs/obrprog3.html
WEB http://www.bor.ohio.gov /progs/obrprog3.html

Scholarships Info While some of your classmates might be dreaming of heading off to Cambridge, New Haven, or Palo Alto for college, why not buck the trend and set your sights on Tasmania? This site describes the various scholarships available for study at the University of Tasmania; one of them is an undergraduate scholarship which provides financial assistance for tuition, a living allowance, air travel "if required," and an academic mentor.
WEB http://info.utas.edu.au/docs /scholarships/scholarships.html

University of Maine Directory of Restricted Scholarships Students who live in tiny Maine towns have a good chance of qualifying for random scholarships. For example, if your last name is Sawyer or Gray and you grew up in Castine, Maine, today's your lucky day. Many other lucky days here.
WEB http://cardinal.umeais.maine .edu/~stuaid/resident.html

Special-interest

Air Force ROTC Not only can you get a big fat scholarship from Uncle Sam, but you get cool combat boots as well. Reserve Officer Training Corps programs, in all branches of the military, are some of the best-known and best-loved government scholarship programs. They include tuition scholarships and cash stipends, in exchange for a certain amount of active duty commitment.
WEB http://www.coe.uncc.edu/rotc _www/det592.html

Donna Reed Foundation Can you bake a perfect batch of cookies while wearing pearls? Then you might be perfect… just joking. The Donna Reed Foundation awards scholarships in all areas of the performing arts at the Donna Reed Festival of Workshops, which all scholarship finalists attend for free. The big prize is a $10,000 scholarship and there are lots of smaller awards. Shine those tap shoes, start singing those scales, practice your piano and read more here.
WEB http://www.frii.com/~fujii

The Elks National Foundation The men in cool hats give away more than $2 million in scholarships and grants every year. Doesn't the Great Heart of Elkdom suddenly make yours go pitter-patter?
WEB http://www.elks.org/enf /default.htm

FRED Scholarship Fund So, the town you grew up in is miles from a stoplight, the local pastime is survival, and the chickens outnumber people 300 to 1? And, what's more, you love it? You sound like a candidate for a Fund for Rural Education and Development (FRED) Scholarship, awarded each year to rural students pursuing careers in telecommunications, rural education, or rural development.
WEB http://www.assocdata.com /opastco/fd_attb.html

MENSA Education and Research Foundation (MERF) Five thousand students apply for 60 MENSA scholarships every year. Winners don't have to be Marilyn vos Savant or Albert Einstein to win one of the genius club's scholarships, but it helps. They're particularly awarded to those in some way studying—what else?—the intellectually gifted.
WEB http://www.miracle.com /mensa/merf.html

Miss America Organization Scholarships If the words "There she is, Miss America!" just make you think about butt padding, bouffant hairdos and horrible beaded evening gowns, then you're missing the big picture. While only 50 young women get to wear a swimsuit down the runway at the big show in Atlantic City, over $29 million in scholarship money is distributed at the local, state, and national level each year. The winner gets not only Bert Parks's scatterbrained singing and national adulation, but $40,000 in cash. Try to earn that flipping burgers.
WEB http://www.missamerica.com /schola03.htm

MTU Army ROTC Frequently Asked Questions This brief FAQ offers information about the Reserve Officer Training Corps and its scholarship opportunities, which include two-, three-, and four-year, and athletic scholarships.
WEB http://www.yth.mtu.edu /armyrotc/faq.html

National Science Foundation A searchable database of the National Science Foundation. Listings include scholarship information, application deadlines, contacts, and requirements.
URL gopher://stis.nsf.gov

Phi Theta Kappa Scholarships A state-by-state description of college/university scholarships sponsored by Phi Theta Kappa. Note, though, that these scholarships are intended for students already enrolled at the institution, not for incoming freshmen.
WEB http://www.phithetakappa .jackson.ms.us/dir95.htm

CYBERNOTES

"Did you know that in 1995 alone, there are nearly one million football players and about one half of that playing basketball nationally. Of these numbers only about 150 make it to the NFL and about 50 make it to the NBA. Less than 3% of college seniors will play one year of pro basketball and the odds of playing pro football are 6,000 to 1. So you must ask yourself, can I make it to the pros?

"There are several prerequisites that you must meet:

1. Do I have the physical ability?
2. Do I have the mental ability?
3. Do I have the commitment and desire to make it happen?"

—from **Sport A.S.I.S.T.**

Wal-Mart Community Involvement Save money in more ways than one with Wal-Mart. Now, in addition to providing low-cost dorm-room supplies, Wal-Mart offers inexpensive ways of ending up in that dorm room. This section of the Wal-Mart Stores home page describes the various scholarships available for Wal-Mart employees and their children, as well as for those who merely live near a Wal-Mart.
WEB http://sam.wal-mart.com /cgi-bin/htmldisp?in:2

Student loans

What do loans, troubled ghosts, and spicy food have in common? They're all guaranteed

to come back to haunt you. Especially loans. College students and their parents are advised (by those who are in the know and in debt, possibly for the rest of their lives) to limit the amount of money they borrow. All the same, loans are an important part of any financial aid package, and some of the terms for private and government-supported education loans are more than reasonable. Shopping around is the key, of course, and the Internet makes it easier than ever before. (No more schlepping to nine different banks to meet nine rude branch managers.) Go play around at the **Crestar Student Loan Web Site**, visit **The Loan Counselor**, or have a chat with **Sallie Mae**. With enough advance research, the words "You've been approved!" will actually turn out to be good news.

Commercial faces for a commercial service
http://www.student-loans.com

Info

The Loan Counselor All the benefits of a trip to the financial aid office without the impertinent student receptionists, long lines, and curt counselors. Purdue provides prospective students with loan counseling, ways to manage

educational loan debt before your payments begin, a list of lenders, and alternative financing options. And you don't have to go to the Indiana school for the information to be applicable.
URL gopher://oasis.cc.purdue .edu:2525/11/student/cnslr

Institutions

The Complete Source for Financing Education Looking into loans to finance your college education? Worried about how you'll manage to afford a Mac once you're there? The United Student Services site offers information on federal loan programs and applications, the U.S.S. Education Loan, P.L.A.T.O. (The Classic Student Loan), and the Apple Computer Loan. An FAQ for each borrowing option and a free on-line pre-approval request form is

provided, too.
WEB http://www.uss.org

Crestar Student Loan Web Site From a Financial Aid Planning Calendar to the Order-a-Loan Kit, this site is so helpful you'll soon be drawn right under the Crestar wing. Financial Aid zombies (those who have been at this for a couple of hours) might go to the dorkily-named Chillin' section for "games, 'zines, and toys," or try to win a $1,000 scholarship by answering very hard trivia questions.
WEB http://www.student-loans.com

Nellie Mae Loan Link Loan Link's helpful hints about preparing to pay for college come from the nation's largest nonprofit provider of educational loans to students and parents. Explore loan options, check your progress

against the college-planning timetable, find out about interest rates and repayment options, or email Nellie Mae for more information.
WEB http://www.nelliemae.org

PNC Bank Corp. A near comprehensive guide to financial aid and, specifically, loans, PNC, not shy about wanting you as a customer, offers Services, Tutorials, and Reference Materials, including a mention of PNC's academic scholarships.
WEB http://www.eduloans .pncbank.com

Sallie Mae Having trouble distinguishing your SAR from your EFC? A presentation of one of the leading providers of higher-education loans, Sallie Mae will help you straighten out your financial aid confusion. (And just so you're not left hanging, SAR refers to your Student-Aid Report, while EFC is your Expected Family Contribution.) Their glossary contains such commonly tossed-about financial aid acronyms as FAFSA and PLUS. The interactive calculators will help you plan for college or estimate loan repayments. There's even a page designed specifically for financial aid administrators who may get a little discombobulated every now and then.
WEB http://www.salliemae.com

Signet Bank Student Loan Home Page Who better to give advice on money matters than a bank? Besides general information about types of student loans and when and how to apply, Signet offers the very thorough "A Student's Guide to Financial Aid," as well as a discussion of loan repayment options. You can also order applications and financial aid guides here.
WEB http://jerome.signet.com /collegemoney

CYBERNOTES

"**How to Find the Right Lender**

'Aren't all of these loans the same, no matter who you borrow from?'

'Yes and no. Federal guidelines regulate the primary features of the student loan programs such as interest rates and repayment terms. However, all banks are not alike. You will find differences in customer service, as well as in some of the products and services provided.'

'Do I have to have an account at a bank in order to borrow from them?'

'Not at all. In fact, this can be a good time in your life to establish a relationship with a bank. More importantly, however, even if you already have a savings or checking account, it may be best to find a lender who is a specialist in educational lending to provide you with the best information now and the best service later.'

'Won't I find exactly the same loan programs at every lender?'

'Not necessarily. While some lenders participate in only the Federal Stafford Loan Program, others, such as Crestar, offer a wider range of programs, which include Unsubsidized Stafford Loan, the Plus Loan Program for parents, and even Federal Consolidation Loans for those who already have multiple loans in place with different lenders.'"

—from **The Crestar Student Loan Web Site**

Southwest Student Services Corporation Finally, a site that offers you money... more or less. The Southwest SaverLoan and the CollegeCard are two financial aid resources available through Southwest Student Services Corporation. The SaverLoan is a loan with a lower-than-usual origination fee (this site even explains what that means!), and the CollegeCard is essentially a credit card for charging your educational expenses. Southwest also offers general financial aid information (including data on loan consolidation), a Parent's Page, a link to University Tours, and answers to the all-consuming question, "How much is a college education worth?"
WEB http://www.sssc.com/index .html

Protest & action

Why does college cost so much anyway? Just thinking about the strain and drain on a

family's resources is enough to frost a parent's precollege cake. Students everywhere who hold down a full-time job, take out loans, and still can't pay tuition bills are furious. Mothers and fathers of very young children are terrified of the looming college specter, although it's some 15 years away. What's a desperately in debt soul to do? Well, while evil forces aren't exactly responsible in this instance (unless you count technology or the economy), there are still opportunities for protest and action on the Internet. Several excellent analytical articles like **College Education: Is it Worth the Cost?** will provide food for thought. Write a letter to Congress or storm a barricade with the folks at **The Alliance to Save Student Aid**. Find out what trouble the Establishment is causing at **Democratic Leadership: For Students**. And then—what the heck!—find some humor in it all, if you can, at **Financial Aid Jokes and Anecdotes**.

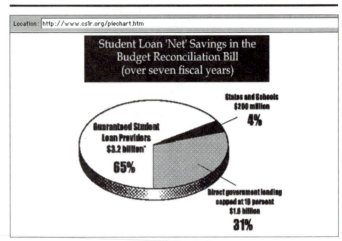

How big is your slice of pie?
http://www.cslr.org

Protest

College Education: Is it Worth the Cost? Wade through the complex mathematical calculations in this article and be rewarded with the final answer to the posed question: "So in a world that demands ever-more mental skills and abilities, for most people, a college degree is the surest way to economic success." A fascinating approach to a problem that most people don't question, and if they did, wouldn't know how to quantify. Is it a relief to know that it's all worth it?
WEB http://sorrel.humboldt.edu /~ty1/topics/college

The Rising Costs of Education
A kid and his dad have written this paper to find out if future kids and dads are going to be able to afford college. It's simplistically written but does a good job tracing the causes of the cost inflation,

along with links to related sites and information. Their conclusion? "Other countries will surpass the U.S. and it will no longer be the superpower it is today" if costs don't stop inflating. Yikes!
WEB http://jeffco.k12.co.us /dist_ed/onlinea/abrown

Why College Costs are Rising
Why should you need financial aid for college, anyway? Why isn't college more affordable? John Hood's article, "Why College Costs are Rising," is reprinted here from *The Freeman* and seeks to explain why you're paying too much for your education.
WEB http://www.self-gov.org /freeman/8811hood.htm

Action

The Alliance to Save Student Aid If financial aid has become not only your pursuit but your passion, you'll probably want to

read about The Alliance To Save Student Aid. After all, "college is the best investment in America's future," and the Alliance would like to tell you why. Included here is information about congressional legislation that threatens financial aid, as well as tips on what you can do as a financial aid activist, both on and off the Web.
WEB http://student-aid.nche.edu

Coalition for Student Loan Reform Beware—while this organization is nonprofit, it is made up of guarantors and secondary markets who want to get a piece of the federal loan program. Are they sincere about helping students? Who knows? But there are dozens of articles linked to this page about government activity with an impact on student loans. Plus, there's a newsletter, surveys, and a legislative action hot line.
WEB http://www.cslr.org

Democratic Leadership: For Students Find out what the liberals are up to in the world of financial aid. House Democratic Leader Richard Gephardt sponsors this excellent if quite partisan guide to the budget's effect on student loans. Don't miss the links at the bottom, there's even one inviting visitors to apply for an internship in Gephardt's office. If he can't get you aid, he'll work you hard for no pay!
WEB http://www.house.gov /democrats/student.html

The Student Financial Aid Crisis in America! After a few minutes of surfing this site you too will begin to speak in exclamations! This is because the current status of federal financial aid is so perilous that it will make you extremely mad! It affects not only college students but graduate and professional students as well! Read

CYBERNOTES

"With the cost of tuition a rate increasing at roughly twice that of salaries, higher learning will, in the future, no longer be an affordable option. Colleges will put themselves out of business by raising costs so high that only a minority of people will be able to afford to attend; not enough people to support the university.

As the cost of college continues to increase at rates exceeding the rest of the economy, there will eventually come a time when it does not make economic sense to attend the "school of your choice". The above calculated ratios were an attempt to demonstrate this. No attempt was made to forecast when this would occur, that would be a good topic for a doctorial thesis. However, the time is coming when a person chooses to attend a university, they will be in serious trouble with college debts that they will have to spend the rest of their lives paying for. Not only would people lose money by spending four years and countless dollars at an institution, but they would never be able to make up for that lost time.

When more and more high school students reach graduation and discover that college is too expensive, the educational level per capita will go down. With fewer educated people in the United States work force, the economy will decline, and lower the United States in economic standing. Other countries will surpass the US and it will no longer be the superpower it is today."

—from The **Rising Costs of Education**

all about it and then join the grassroots crusade!
WEB http://nagps.varesearch.com /Student_Aid/student-aid.html

Financial Aid Jokes and Anecdotes Proving that there really is humor in everything, this collection of financial aid jokes and anecdotes is probably best to look at when you've been contemplating financial aid for so long

that the FAFSA and SAR seem nothing less than an incomprehensible alphabet soup. Particularly entertaining are the top ten lists for entering the financial aid field. From "Top Ten Reasons to Work in Financial Aid"—"No. 9: Sometimes, you get to make people cry."
WEB http://www.cs.cmu.edu/afs /cs/user/mkant/Public/FinAid /html/jokes.html

Part 3

Student Life

The sporting life

College sports have always been a big deal on campuses, whipping up patriotic fervor,

entertaining the masses, attracting participants. In the age of television, they've also become big business, creating a billion-dollar industry that guarantees coaches up to ten times what university presidents earn. Stupid jocks, huh? To be fair, they do bring the schools, coaches, and players substantial monies that allow them to beef up their facilities and academic departments, thus attracting IQs as well as track and field stars. But while national attention is focused on just a few dozen teams, for most colleges, smaller teams and crowds constitute the athletic experience. So whether you're a battleworn D-I star, an untelevised but still talented athlete, or a more sedentary but no less fervent fan, these sites should tell you a bit about the sporting life in college.

Team players

College Nicknames You've probably heard of the Big Green, but who are the Black Flies? Over 20 colleges use the nickname Bulldogs, but which college has the distinctive nickname Geoducks? For tidbits about collegiate sports monikers nationwide, this is the site to beat. Adam Joshua Smar-

Location: http://www.ncaa.org/

Official Web Site of the NCAA

NCAA *Online*

Welcome to NCAA. Online.

The fast track to a sports scholarship and much more
http://www.ncaa.org

gon has neatly compiled this HTML-formatted list of nicknames for colleges in the U.S. An FTP version will soon be available. Schools from all athletic divisions are listed, and links are offered.
WEB http://www.ssc.org /~recycler/sports.html

Gender Equity One of the more interesting sports-related phenomena of the past 25 years has been the battle of the sexes, which, at times, has been less than sporting. The contest hasn't been on the field but in the courtroom, and the issue is an historically uneven playing field—the lack of parity in funds and resources. A section of the 1972 education amendments, Title IX, guarantees equal treatment under the law; this site takes a stab at serving as the on-line watchdog and historical record of note on the subject.
WEB http://www.arcade.uiowa .edu/proj/ge

NCAA The National Collegiate Athletics Association page is the place to start for anything and everything to do with college sports. Its coverage spans the sports spectrum with a seemingly endless battery of statistics, current records, and championship information. Of particular interest to the high school student is the College Bound section, which details eligibility requirements for Division I and II schools, and features an FAQ on recruiting, advice on how to approach schools, and a suggested list of questions to ask coaches. Sports covered include football, soccer, baseball, softball, hockey, and more.
WEB http://www.ncaa.org

The Sports Campus While the presentation starts with a boom and tapers off some, this site is establishing itself as a useful resource for updates and general information on the most popular

college sports around. The folks here are hard at work building up their reportage on the usual sports as well as track, wrestling, field hockey, swimming, and squash.
WEB http://www.btb.com /sportscampus

t@p College Sports How's the lacrosse team doing at your university? Here are links to countless pages of baseball, gymnastics, hockey, swimming, soccer, track and field, wrestling, ultimate Frisbee—you get the idea—clubs and organizations nationwide. There's plenty of stuff to keep you fit: lists of college sports events, team standings, championship predictions, and a viewpoint column. If that's not enough, lose yourself in the wonders of the Division I Collegiate Volleyball Update, or the remarkable section devoted to Australian Rules football.
WEB http://www.taponline.com /tap/csports.html

WomenSports No doubt women will find many of the sports sites and newsgroups dominated by men. Thankfully, there's a place to go to get away from the testosterone-mad teams and fans. WomenSports is an excellent resource, with coverage of women's college, amateur, and professional sports including basketball, volleyball, softball, tennis, and soccer.
WEB http://www.womensports.com

Baseball

College Baseball Just a plain old list of Web site locations neatly alphabetized by school name. If you're dying to know how University of Pennsylvania's hitting this season, or who won the game at the alma mater on Saturday, check out College Baseball—a handy (if bland) and unassuming reference page.

WEB http://stimpy.ame.nd.edu /gross/baseball/other.html

rec.sport.baseball.college Passionate, not to mention well informed, about college baseball, the fans here critique the games played by teams like Clemson, Rice, and Northwestern the same way other baseball fans obsess about the Red Sox and the Dodgers. Game summaries, conference predictions, standings, and discussions about players keep the newsgroup active during baseball season.
USENET rec.sport.baseball.college

Basketball

ALD College Basketball Site Bookmark this address for information on college basketball. There's not a lot of original content, but the minimal graphics and large number of good working links make it a fast-loading source for college hoops info. The wood-grained ball court background and sharp layout obscure the fact that the page is actually just one fan's well chosen links.
WEB http://www.azstarnet.com /~alexeo/sports/collegeb.htm

College Basketball Page If you are looking for random info on college basketball, this is a good place to start—in fact, maybe the best place on the Net. Nothing fancy here, just a list of links, but very good ones, including connections to individual team and conference home pages. This page is constantly expanding. Right now, you can find links to such diverse sites as the Division III basketball home page, the ESPN College Hoops Schedule, and the Usenet group rec.sports .basketball.college. You can also access a list of all college sports teams' nicknames, from the Aggies

(Texas A&M) to the Zips (University of Akron).
WEB http://www.cs.cmu.edu/afs /cs.cmu.edu/user/wsr/Web/bball

GNN College Basketball This page has standings and schedules for every men's Division I team and links to other basketball servers around the world. It also has a frequently updated features section, such items as a summary of the action in the ACC, and previews for the NCAA. It's a little dry on presentation, but the information is all here.
WEB http://gnn.com/gnn/meta /sports/basketball/ncaa/index.html

NandoX-NCAA College Basketball Nando-X (a server run by the Raleigh, N.C. *News and Observer*) has daily updates of scores and highlights for men's and women's hoops, along with up-to-date polls, schedules, and feature stories. The articles (about five new ones each day off the Associated Press wire) are great for the serious fan. This page also links to the pro basketball server on Nando, which is equally outstanding.
WEB http://www.nando.net /SportServer/basketball/col.html

Women's hoops

GNN Women's Basketball News, scores, stats, a game of the week, and links to other Internet resources on women's hoops.
WEB http://gnn.com/gnn/meta /sports/basketball/women/index .html

Women's College Basketball Presented simply, with text on a plain gray background, this fast-loading links page takes you to women's college basketball sites. But unless its current lack of maintenance is rectified, the list will soon become overrun with dead links and access-denied pages. Still, as a starting point for basic information on the sport, you could do worse.

WEB http://www.auburn.edu /~poperic/wbb/wbb.html

Crew

The Rower's Resource Crew can look rather strange at times—hulking men or women towering over a lone diminutive soul, the coxswain. Though you may never have seen this sport before, the concept is certainly familiar and there's a good chance your school will have at least a club team. Although the Ivy Leagues and a smattering of other universities around the country tend to dominate, many more schools are hard at work refining their strokes. The Rower's Resource will bring you up to date as well as link you to the long list of the college teams that have found Web-homes. Pay particular attention if you are tall—crew coaches do their best to beat even basketball coaches to the door, and could potentially lend a hand in the application process.

WEB http://www.rowersresource .com

Football

College Football Hall of Fame

There are two kinds of Web museums: the interactive, involving, exciting, and educational virtual museums; and the illustrated virtual pamphlets that give you driving directions and museum hours. The College Football Hall of Fame, which once belonged to the latter group, has obviously touched things up since we last visited. You can see exactly who has been honored, answer trivia questions, even have your say on running debates. Soon, you'll also be able to vote for players and coaches you'd like to see inducted. And the Hall of Fame has its own adjoining field if you're just dying to toss around the pigskin.

WEB http://collegefootball.org

Nando X-College Football

Page As it stands, Nando is already one of the best sites in cyberspace for fans of college football and it's getting better all the time. With summaries from virtually every game, a handful of polls, season statistics, conference news and notes, and even a visual roundup of last week's action—AP

pictures of quarterbacks rolling, fullbacks plunging, and tackles pouncing—there's enough to keep any NCAA gridiron fan happy for quarters and quarters.

WEB http://www.nando.net /SportServer/football

rec.sport.football.college

Usenet's premier college football chat site occasionally veers off-topic, with threads about the Chicago Bulls or a taunt from an Iowa State tennis fan. But for the most part, this is college football as we have come to expect it—straight down the middle, with heaping servings of ill-informed opinion, senseless number-crunching, and shameless boosterism. Between ongoing conversations about traditional Big Ten rivalries and rising stars, you can find interesting comments about fringe aspects of the game, such as this plaintive post about the fate of gridiron mascots: "I am just replying to a posting about mascots. I am not sure what happened at Nebraska, but we lost Harry Husker a couple of years back. This makes me a little upset. Personally, I liked Harry. There's nothing wrong with tradition, but I also like Herbie, and this other new guy 'Lil' Red'... (I don't name them, I'm just a fan). If anybody out there knows what happened to Harry, please let me know. I would hate to think that he might have been kidnapped and lost forever in an Orange Bowl, and nobody ever tried to rescue him. That would suck!"

USENET rec.sport.football.college

Hockey

Central Collegiate Hockey Association This is the place to get the scoop on Division I hockey teams from Alaska to Ohio, including the 1996 NCAA champion University of Michigan

It's over here! No, it's over here! No, I think it's here!
http://www.auburn.edu/~poperic/wbb/wbb.html

Location: http://www.shu.edu/life/athletic/sports/wbasket/

Wolverines. In addition to statistics, standings, and awards, there's an interesting note about of how CCHA alumni are faring in the professional leagues.
WEB http://web.ccha.com

Hockey East Report Updated every Monday morning during the collegiate hockey season, this well maintained site releases the current Hockey East standings. Each week a Player of the Week and a Rookie of the Week are chosen and the stats for scoring, goaltending, power play efficiency, and penalty-killing are charted.
WEB http://www.tiac.net/users/spickett/hea.html

Western Collegiate Hockey Association Comprised of ten teams from Minnesota, Colorado, North Dakota, and Wisconsin, the WCHA offers one of the more eye-catching sites for college hockey. Besides keeping up on all the statistics, standings, and awards, this page will also tell you about the WCHA Player of the Week. The most appealing feature, however, is the full-color graphic display of team uniforms that connects you to each team's site.
WEB http://www.up.net/~wcha

Women's University Hockey Andria Hunter was captain of an Eastern College Athletic Conference championship team and a member of Team Canada's 1994 World Championship team. She's now a computer science grad student who operates a comprehensive and lively page that provides everything you want to know about women's collegiate hockey in the U.S. and Canada, from the varsity to the intramural level.
WEB http://www.cs.utoronto.ca/~andria/University_Hockey.html

Soccer

College Soccer Web With the popularity of the World Cup and the apparent success of the new professional soccer league, the world's most popular sport seems finally to have found a permanent home in America. The aptly titled College Soccer Web—apparently compiled and maintained by one person—has links to all of the top college teams as well as rankings and tournament updates. CSW also features the men's and women's leagues in all divisions. If you love soccer you'll get a kick out of this excellent resource.
WEB http://teton.ucs.indiana.edu/cbrenner/ncaa/ncaa.html

US College Soccer In the soccer heaven created by Mark Wheeler you'll find this section devoted to men's and women's college soccer teams. Everything a player or fan would want is here. Wheeler has also set up links to high school soccer teams, as well as rankings and a list of all-Americans dating back to 1985. High school players, take note; there's even a link to a recruiting page where college coaches can check up on rising stars. You can submit your own name and accomplishments (if you're so inclined, and willing to pony up $39.95).
WEB http://www.cs.cmu.edu/~mdwheel/us-soccer/ncaa/ncaa.html

Volleyball

Volleyball Worldwide Once the domain of West Coast schools, volleyball has snowballed in popularity and taken hold across the country. Not that you're as fanatical about the sport as this service; Volleyball Worldwide seems to have every conceivable link possible, from Gabrielle Reece to teams in Australia to the men's Olympic team. If you just can't get enough, this is the place to start, with links to college polls, profiles, local junior programs, the rule book, and even high school teams.
WEB http://www.volleyball.org

Brothers & sisters

There was a time when a person could not attend college without meeting at least one

John Belushi-esque frat boy for whom the *sine qua non* of comedy was to impersonate a zit while you ate your lunch. But if the days of Animal House parties are largely over, togas, permanent inebriation, and extreme youthful high spirits can be easily enough found at just about every school. You need scarcely join a fraternity or a sorority for that. Greeks have lately had to undergo '90s-style restructuring; some fraternities and sororities have been forced completely to disband or turn coed, although most have carried on unscathed if a bit more delicate in their bearing. Irrefutable is the fact that Greeks play a prominent social role at the great majority of American colleges and universities. So if it is months of rush and years of siblinghood you're after, or if you'd rather see them all just disappear, here's a brief introduction to the object of your desire or derision, as the case may be.

Taking the pledge

alt.college.fraternities In addition to old-boy greetings and meetings, this newsgroup hosts debates on the institution itself. Haz-

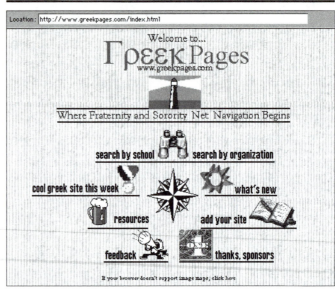

Modern-day classics
http://www.greekpages.com

ing, the single-sex policy, and date rape are consistently hot topics up for discussion and contention.
USENET alt.college.fraternities

alt.college.sororities Less controversial than the fraternities newsgroup, the distaff half of the Greek newsgroups usually consists of friendly contact between "sisters" (and the "brothers" who love them)—both present students and alums.
USENET alt.college.sororities

alt.fraternity.sorority
Question: What do you get when you put fraternities and sororities together in one newsgroup? Answer: Complete degeneration. If you have anything intelligent to say about Greek life, go elsewhere. This is mostly the arena for one-

line messages announcing which frat boys are the coolest and which sorority sisters the cutest.
USENET alt.fraternity.sorority

Greek.com This site likes to see itself as one-stop shopping for Greek life on the Internet, with fraternity and sorority directories, merchandise purchasing information, and links to Greek resources in cyberspace.
WEB http://www.greek.com

Greek Link Dozens of links to fraternity and sorority pages are here supplemented by connections to organizations that promote responsible drinking, Bacchus, and Mothers Against Drunk Driving.
WEB http://pages.prodigy.com/KS /lounges/GREEKLINK.html

Greek Pages Frat boys can do more than tap a keg, and a sorority sister's skills extend beyond the serenade. Between toga parties, they donate their time to worthwhile causes, help each other find jobs, and maintain some pretty cool Web sites. The Greek Pages site honors the cool site of the week, links to more than 750 chapters, and maintains a chat room and library. It's all Greek on the search page—enter your letters and locate sites of chapters and nationwide and abroad.
WEB http://www.greekpages.com

Greek Sites Yet another directory of fraternities and sororities with Web presences.
WEB http://weatherhead.cwru.edu /student/greek

GreekSource GreekSource offers a set of Idea Books where fraternity and sorority members can exchange ideas regarding rushing,

parties, philanthropy and fundraising with their cyberbrothers and sisters. A brief perusal of the descriptions of favorite theme parties is enough to induce instantaneous projectile vomiting. From party themes that are simply in bad taste (such as a Hawaiian party called "comeoniwannaleiya") to ones that are truly too misogynistic and revolting to print here, this collection of ideas appears to exist solely to prove that every stereotype of Greek life is based on fact. Luckily, not all of the content at GreekSource is quite so horrifying. A series of essays provides a refreshingly intellectual look at aspects of fraternity and sorority life. A section called GreekPals allows you to increase your circle of brothers and sisters via correspondence. And GreekAnnounce helps you to keep in touch with the goings-on of other chapters.
WEB http://www.greeksource .com

The University of Georgia's *Sororities OnLine* (from Greek Pages)
http://www.greekpages.com

Location : http://www.grady.uga.edu/ugasororities/ugasororities.html

Benefits
Rush
Individual Sororities
Greek Life
'96 Events
Game

Round 1

NerdWorld Fraternities & Sororities Because of recent stoner, riot-grrl, and nerd chic trends, frat boys and sorority girls have suffered a lapse in popularity, often confined to the outskirts of campuses. Even so, they still keg with reckless abandon. Many a student will happily (stupidly?) volunteer for the trials and tribulations of rushing. This index of Greeks is useful for checking out rites and rituals from around the country. But don't worry: no secret handshakes are required.
WEB http://www.nerdworld.com /nw665.html

Activism '90s-style

So you're feeling like you were born in the wrong generation. There just aren't any burn-

your-bra, destroy-your-draft-card, boycott-the-buses, stand-up, sit-in causes like your parents had when they packed up their tie-dyes and headed off to Berkeley. So where to go with your inclination to change the world? Well, it may not be the sixties, but there are still plenty of causes today looking for spirited students. Find your calling at **alt.activism.d** or **Web-Active.** Help your fellow human at **Amnesty International Online** and **Habitat for Humanity** Homepages Around the World or your fellow mammal at **PETA On-line.** There are swarms of sites for tree huggers, feminists, gay and lesbian activists, and those on either side of the abortion debate. And there's plenty for students with a political penchant, as well. Left-leaning students will want to check out **College Democrats of America**. Right-of-center students will appreciate the **College Republican National Committee**. And libertarians will feel right at home at the **Professors of Liberty Home Page**.

Location: http://www.democrats.org/college_democrats/rally

Dangerous radicals demonstrate their alliance with extremist politics
http://www.democrats.org/college_democrats

Starting points

alt.activism.d A gathering place for activists of all stripes—hence the many discussions that seem to be parties of one. But there are plenty of topics that blossom into interesting discussions, such as a long and compelling explanation of the ins and outs of Vietnam draft dodging, or the debate over a daunting report, complete with "actual statistics," that claims capitalism does not benefit the American worker ("The U.S. is becoming a polarized society—the rich are getting richer; the workers are getting less and less of what they produce"). There's even a 200-plus message thread on the Senate's treatment of the NEA.
USENET alt.activism.d

WebActive It might appear to be an oxymoron that you could be

active while sitting at your computer, but WebActive makes this a distinct possibility. Featured activism sites and the WebActive Directory allow you to keep track of cyberactivists, while the Hot Activist Projects section features information on ways you can become involved as an activist from the privacy of your own Internet connection: "because surfing ain't enough." Get plugged into Real-Audio to experience HearNow, real-time audio programs with a progressive/activist bent.
WEB http://www.webactive.com

Organizations

Amnesty International On-line If poli-sci classes are getting you all riled up about the state of the world, don't just get mad, get active. Known for its letter writing campaigns, Amnesty International

works to combat human rights violations the world over. Publications and country reports are available here, and it's also possible to get in touch with an Amnesty branch on a campus near you.
WEB http://www.amnesty.org

Circle K International Part of the larger Kiwanis organization, Circle K seeks to get college students involved in community service. What this means in terms of specific activities depends largely on the decisions made locally at the different campus clubs and districts. Links to the various off-shoots make it possible to track what's going on where.
WEB http://www.clark.net/pub/jwolff/cki

COOL (Campus Outreach Opportunity League) If you've got an idea for community service that doesn't fit into a pre-existing organization's mission, perhaps you should check out the Campus Outreach Opportunity League, which "helps college students start, strengthen, and expand their community service programs." COOL sponsors a national conference for students involved in community service and also organizes a program model for jump-starting community service activities on college campuses. COOL also provides a list of links to campus-based community service programs that have their own Web pages so you can find out how active your school is on the altruism front.
WEB http://www.cool2serve.org/homeofc/home.html

Habitat for Humanity Stop complaining about the cramped quarters of your dorm room and help provide housing for those who are truly in need. Habitat for Humanity helps to build both

houses and communities. Maintained at the University of Illinois, this page links to the home pages of all Habitat for Humanity chapters around the world.
WEB http://www.students.uiuc.edu/~jwyckoff/HfH.html

PETA On-Line While it's garnered support from such celebrities as Michael Stipe and Ricki Lake, People for the Ethical Treatment for Animals (PETA) is more than just a fashionable cause for Hollywood luminaries. In fact, it's the world's largest animal-rights group, with more than half-a-million members. This site includes news, fact sheets, action alerts, and a cruelty-free shopping guide that lists vegan cosmetics, personal-care items, and household products.
WEB http://www.envirolink.org/arrs/peta

Environment

Environmental Forum This green forum divides environmental issues into national and global topics. The former helps explain what ordinary citizens like Donna ("I try to recycle but sometimes my neighborhood doesn't help me with regular pickups") and Saul ("Are there any environmental harms to email?") can do to improve their environment. As for the latter, the Global Action and Information Network uses the Internet as a base for publishing regular news releases and updates on environmental breakthroughs, and for encouraging all kinds of green activism. Live conferencing happens in the Environmental Chat room.
AMERICA ONLINE *keyword* eforum

Public Interest Research Groups (The PIRGs) PIRG activists canvass neighborhoods in an effort to promote environmental concerns. The Public Interest

Research Groups, a Ralph Nader creation, attack social problems with a vengeance on both a national and a state-by-state level, and college students are crucial to their efforts. Get busy and find out how you can purge social ills with PIRG.
WEB http://www.igc.apc.org/pirg/homepage.htm

Feminist

Feminist Activist Resources on the Net Mad as hell about the glass ceiling or the casting couch? Review the battle for equal rights with this terrific collection of links to sites devoted to a wide range of women's issues. Link from here to the Department of Labor's equal pay information, Congressional gophers, or The Global Fund for Women. Don't miss the Activist Calendar or the Feminist Fun and Games section.
WEB http://www.igc.apc.org/women/feminist.html

Progressive Directory—Women's Resources A multitude of links designed to help women make it in a man's world. Head to the Abortion & Reproductive Rights page to keep track of the ongoing battle. The Domestic Violence gopher empowers women by providing them with relevant information and preventative measures. And the Women's Health Resources gopher reports on breast cancer and other health issues.
WEB http://www.igc.apc.org/womensnet/wom.issues.html

Homelessness

National Coalition for the Homeless "I know there are people out there who look at the homeless as outcasts, but that is not true," says Carolyn, a 27-year-

old homeless woman, in one of several audio files at this site. "We are worth the same." A great spot for resources related to homelessness, with a directory of advocacy organizations and conferences, information on legislative and policy initiatives, and a rundown of the coalition's current projects.
WEB http://nch.ari.net

Political groups

College Democrats of America If you're a bona fide, card-carrying, college-age member of the Democratic party, the CDA wants YOU to assist with reelection campaigns, voter registration drives, and the like. The site features general Democratic information, links to campus branches of the CDA, and an up-to-the-minute news service called CDA Alert, because "[with] the Republican Revolution threatening students at every turn, now more than ever we have to be prepared." It's a war zone out there, kids.
WEB http://www.democrats.org /college_democrats

College Republican National Committee You might think the CRNC is just the kiddie branch of the GOP, but it's much more: "The College Republicans are the real conservative grassroots campaign, everyday facing a battle of ideas in liberal academia." Carry the conservative torch across campus.
WEB http://www.dash.com/netro /gov/crnc/index.html

Professors of Liberty Home Page Remain true to the principles of libertarianism by assuming responsibility for your actions and choosing to study with professors who share your political leanings. This site is a who's who of libertarian professors, the courses they teach, and the lessons they preach.

Also available here are links to other libertarian sites on the Web.
URL ftp://lumina.ucsd.edu/pub /.../libuniv_dir/libprofs.html

SAVE (Students Advocating Valid Education) Free yourself from the shackles of PC enslavement! Escape the tyranny of political harassment on campus! In other words, SAVE yourself with a little bit of help from this bastion of campus conservatism.
WEB http://www.kansas.net /~ttuttle

Reproductive rights

Abortion and Reproduction Rights Internet Resources Links to resources on both sides of the abortion debate, including the *ChoiceNet Report* and *The ProLife News*. Read the pronouncements of the Supreme Court in *Roe v. Wade*, or the Pope in *Humanae Vitae*.
WEB http://www.caral.org/abortion.html

Lifelinks The right-to-life movement is online making its case against abortion. The site links to the Feminists for Life publication, *Abortion does not Liberate Women*, with statements from public personalities such as *Village Voice* writer Nat Hentoff on third-trimester abortions, and Mother Teresa on abortion and peace. Statistics linked to this site allege a relationship between legalized abortion and welfare mothers, juvenile violent crime, teen pregnancy, and child abuse.
WEB http://copper.ucs.indiana.edu /~ljray/lifelink.html

talk.abortion "We've been subjected to 21 years of being told that a woman has a right to do with her body as she wishes," writes one exasperated man. "Can

you present any compelling reasons why she should not be allowed to control her own body?" queries an equally annoyed man. Count on it. The abortion debate here is not pretty, and some of it can be quite volatile. On the other hand, its obnoxiousness is not entirely unentertaining either. Day in, day out, these gladiators sling rhetoric at each other.
USENET talk.abortion

Sexual identity

BiAct-L Elaine, the "list dominatrix," leads her troops in the fight against bi-ignorance. Add your two cents to *Coming Out Bi*, a pamphlet under development; sign up for Fox-TV's open auditions for a real-life bisexual couple; or find out how to enroll your local queer activist group in your state's Adopt-a-Highway program. Recent campaigns have included telephoning support for Visa, which is under attack from the religious right for contributing to Gay Games IV.
EMAIL listserv@brownvm.brown.edu
✍ *Type in message body:* subscribe biact-l <your full name>

Digital Queers What Act Up and Queer Nation were to the '80s, Digital Queers is to the '90s. If the talk of the times is technology, then DQ want to get the queer community wired. DQ's aim is to provide anything, from a state-of-the-art modem or printer to a "complete computer beauty makeover," to gay, lesbian, bisexual, and transgender organizations across America. The DQ site also carries announcements about upcoming queer events, press clippings covering DQ activities, a list of chapters, and instructions on starting a local chapter in your area.
WEB http://www.dq.org/dq

A world of difference

If high school is a time when everyone is expected to be identical, then college should

be a time to throw off those shackles of adolescent conformity and celebrate difference. Getting in touch with one's ethnic identity, sexual orientation, or gender will never be easier than it is on a college campus; simultaneously, many identity groups have found a home in the putatively pale male world of cyberspace, as well. African-American students can find career information at **The Black Collegian**. Gay, lesbian, and bisexual collegians can find relief at **Oasis**. Students concerned about gender and equity will want to visit the **American Association of University Women** site. The **CLNET Student Center** keeps track of the latest Latino and Chicano happenings. Asian-Americans can stop by the **Asian-American Clubs** for links to media sites, commercial organizations, events, FAQs, individual home pages, and newsgroups. And those who want to get in touch with their multicultural side can do so at **ITI's Multi-Cultural Network**.

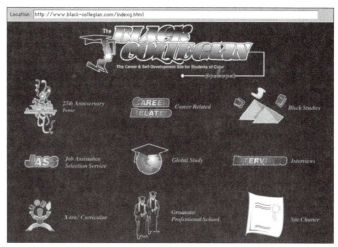

How to get ahead in college with the Black Collegian
http://www.black-collegian.com

Multicultural

ITI's Multi-Cultural Network
Art, books, business, and education links for the African-American, Irish-American, Jewish-American, Puerto-Rican-American, and Native American communities. More ethnicities to come.
WEB http://www.fcg.com/iti /iti_cultnet.html

Multicultural Home Page For those interested in delving into cultures other than their own, this Purdue University site is a simple way to start. Discover cultures and countries from India to Israel, France to the Philippines.
WEB http://pasture.ecn.purdue.edu /~agenhtml/agenmc

African American

AFAM-L This scholarly list for students of African-American cul-

ture has evolved into a very active place to discuss the here and now of African-American life. A news release about the firing of the head of the NAACP sparked immediate debate about the specific incident, the history of the organization, and its current direction. When the Fox Network canceled five black-oriented shows, a week-long discussion of media images and media power ensued. AFAM-L is an essential gathering place for scholars, activists, and anyone else interested in the African-American experience.
EMAIL listserv@mizzou 1.missouri .edu ✍ *Type in message body:* subscribe afam-l <your full name>

Afro-American Culture & Arts Forum The Salon, a general chitchat board, is the most active section in this forum. It's where parents discuss how to deal with a teen "indefinitely homebound" (a

euphemism for "grounded") and where everyone picks apart the media image of the single black mother. Recent immigrants go to Caribbean Meeting to talk about the islands. The forum also includes serious political talk about Rush and O.J., occasional accusations of "blacker than thou" posturing, and a group that periodically shares its favorite items from *Weekly World News*—like the one about the 50-foot Jesus terrorizing a small town. The big draws here are the cultural topics—art, history, film, theater, and music.
COMPUSERVE *go* afro

AFRONET Junior Posse A junior version of the AFRONET site for the younger set. Junior Posse provides all the pertinent 411 with links to historically black colleges, fraternities, and sororities as well as general scholarship, grant, and job-tracking information.
WEB http://www2.earthlink.net /~afronet/JP_files/Junior_Posse .html

ASA-L Provides an opportunity for African-American students worldwide to share ideas, strategies, and humor. Predictably much more active during the school year than the summer months, the list members are young, smart, and impassioned. Keeping abreast of international developments, the ASA-L often creates networks for relief work and political action. Students can form friendships with their counterparts in other countries and check out opportunities for travel (for example, Mark from the U.S. discusses the Egyptian club scene with a new friend in Cairo). The chat is often fun—how about a re-evaluation of fairy tales from a modern perspective?
EMAIL listserv@tamvm1.tamu.edu ✍
Type in message body: subscribe asa-l <your full name>

The Black Collegian This is the cybercousin to the print magazine targeting African-American students seeking information on career and personal development. The site contains career and industry reports, job search guides, motivational readings, black history articles, a Dear Campus Advisor advice column, health and fitness stories, book reviews, a bulletin board, and a calendar of events.
WEB http://www.black-collegian .com

Black Voices The *Orlando Sentinel*'s Black Voices is a good place to go for the latest news affecting the African-American community and topical discussion of the issues. When we visited, there were special folders for the black church fires, the '96 election, and the O.J. Simpson civil trial. For a look at the lighter side of black life, there are special areas like For Lovers Only, Sports Rap, and Brothers and Sisters.
AMERICA ONLINE *keyword* black voices

National Council for Black Studies Founded primarily to institutionalize and perpetuate the discipline of Africana Studies, NCBS subscribes to the philosophy that education should "engender academic excellence and social responsibility by integrating both." Here you'll find a brief history of the council; news of upcoming conferences, colloquia, and lectures; and links to specific schools' Africana studies programs.
WEB http://www.afrinet.net/~griot /ncbs

soc.culture.african.american The African Americans here can be more insightful critics of black politics than any talk-show right-winger, but politics takes a back seat to the mother of all topics—

relationships between men and women. In a recent discussion about love and marriage—"What is it about marriage that women want so desperately?"—more than 100 people weighed in on the subject. Stay around the group long enough, and you'll grow accustomed to the monthly "What is racism?" and its sibling discussion "Is that really racism?" After one participant (not an African American) asked, "Could it be that the funny looks you get in the elevator are more about being male?" an exasperated regular wrote back: "I really think you need a vacation from this group."
USENET soc.culture.african.american

Asian American

A. Magazine A. Magazine takes you inside the Asian-American community, through highlighted features and special supplements. Although you won't be able to get the meat of the 'zine, you will get a taste of what's inside. If it's Japanese animation you want, or hard-to-find classics in Asian-American literature, the @Mall is the place to go, offering one-stop Net shopping for must-have, pop-culture Asian items. There's also the @Mall video box, where you can get a glimpse of the latest Asian animation, complete with thematic descriptions; and @Mall music has… what else? Take a virtual tour of Asian-American resources, or weigh in on the ruling topics of the discussion area, if you're so inspired.
WEB http://www.amagazine.com

Asian Student Connection A mailing list for discussing the specific concerns of the Asian-American collegian—most active during the school year.
EMAIL majordomo@lists.umbc.edu ✍ *Type in message body:* subscribe asc

Asian-American Clubs Links to cyberactive Asian-American clubs from AAA at Indiana University to Williams College Asian-American Students in Action. If you're willing to go for a scroll, the list also includes Asian-American media sites, commercial organizations, events, FAQs, individual home pages, and newsgroups.
WEB http://www.mit.edu:8001/afs /athena.mit.edu/user/i/r/irie /www/aar.html#clubs

Asian-American Studies Center Founded in 1969, the UCLA Asian-American Studies Center has active programs in research, teaching, publications, archival collections, and public educational programs focusing on Asian Pacific Americans in Southern California and the nation. The Center has the largest faculty in Asian-American Studies in the U.S., and the site links to online AA studies resources.
WEB http://www.sscnet.ucla.edu /aasc

Chinese CyberWorld The land of Mao and Deng meets the homeland of hypertext. The library houses Chinese magazines and newspapers with a cyberpresence. The arts and entertainment page links to sites like the Chinese Zodiac, the Asian Electronic Magazines & CD Center, and the Chinese Television Network. Life in the USA connects to employment and financial assistance resources. Other pages include Community Organizations, The Youth Center, Religion, Homeland, and Opinion. For enhanced viewing, you'll want to download the Chinese software.
WEB http://www.aan.net/chinese .htm

soc.culture.asian.american Believed to be the granddaddy of identity newsgroups, soc.culture

The first port of call at Chinese CyberWorld
http://www.aan.net/chinese.htm

.asian.american has survived years of flame wars to become one of the most exciting newsgroups on the Net. Topics include English-only legislation, immigration issues, the media portrayal of Asian Americans (any recent movie, TV series, or, for that matter, comic book with Asian-American characters is likely to get a thorough going-over), issues of violence and cooperation among races, and interracial dating. Sometimes these discussions function as mere triggers for flame wars between the two armed camps that dominate the group. The primary factional breakdown is simple: Non-Asians, who consider the group to be a place for all who admire or concern themselves with Asian-American issues, versus Asian Americans who consider the group to be a haven for intra-Asian discussion and bonding. Most people are truly concerned with the issues here, and they post what they feel and think with passion. They're also pretty regular about it: a few hundred new posts a night are not uncommon. Regional real life get-togethers by soc.culture.asia .american members in the Bay Area, Boston, and New York are common. Students in these areas will be well served.
USENET soc.culture.asian.american

Hispanic/Latino

CiberCentro Recognizing the incredible diversity of Latin countries, Ciber Centro hosts a customized newspaper index for each one. If you want newsgroups for Argentinians or a map of Peru, you can get exactly that. You can also find people who are online (and might be able to answer your college questions) at the "Ciber Citizens" page for each country. Although the main menu of the site is in English, knowledge of elementary Spanish is advised.
WEB http://www.cibercentro.com

CLNET Student Center From a sit-in at Princeton's president's office demanding increased course offerings for Latino studies to a special Chicano graduation at UT Austin, the Chicano-Latino Net-Student Center, maintained at UCLA, has information on Latino student organizations, activities, protests, and other items.
URL gopher://latino.sscnet.ucla .edu:70/11/Student

Frontera What does *tripiar* mean? To bug out. How about a *slackería*? It's a *taquería* that caters to a mostly white (mostly unemployed) clientele. And what would it mean

Location: http://www.mercado.com/queonda/frontera/current/current.htm

Is this guy a *chongista*? Don't *tripiar* about it, just check out *Frontera*

http://www.mercado.com/queonda/frontera/current/current.htm.com

if you called a guy a *chongista*? Probably that he was an avant-garde Latino with a pony tail, dressed all in black (most likely sporting a goatee and reciting poetry). It's all covered in *Frontera*'s glossary of the latest lingo. This monthly Latino ezine also includes features like an interview with Frost, the godfather of Latino hip-hop, a look at the lack of Latinos on network TV, and an assortment of reviews and short articles, on the Refried Nation page.
WEB http://www.mercado.com /queonda/frontera/current /current.htm

Hispanic Heritage Connect to countries of origin here—virtual Spain, Argentina, Peru, and Mexico—or read brief biographies of famous Hispanics like Gabriela Mistral, Salvador Dalí, and Carlos Fuentes. A primer on bullfighting explains the sport and gives current bullfighter rankings (scored in numbers of ears held).
WEB http://www.clark.net/pub /jgbustam/heritage/heritage.html

Hispanic Online Of interest to the college-age Hispanic: the Top 25 Colleges for Hispanics, the Top 10 Hispanic Bars, and the Top 50 Hispanic Restaurants. Beyond the lists, Hispanic Online includes departments like Mundo, Mercado, Ritmo, and Vida, each with message boards and chatrooms. Note: You don't have to be Hispanic to enjoy this online magazine, but it helps if you're fluent in Spanglish.
AMERICA ONLINE *keyword* latino

La Unidad Latina, Lambda Upsilon Lambda Fraternity, Inc. La Fraternidad was established in 1982 to celebrate Latin pride, dignity, and equality. This page from the chapter at Brown University puts the ideals of LUL on the Internet and gives email addresses for the chapter.
WEB http://www.brown.edu /Administration/Dean_of_the _College/TWC/LUL.html

Latino-L This list's purpose is to foster communication among Latino students (as well as other

interested people) across the country. People have used it to share information about social/academic events held on college campuses, scholarship and research opportunities for Latino/Hispanic students, and current events connected to Latinos, in both the United States and Latin America. The intended focus is on issues of concern to Latino students, but anyone's input or participation is welcome. The membership is diverse and includes people of many different nationalities and occupations. Several members have connections with other Latino organizations and computer networks, so this list can give its membership access to a wide range of quick, reliable information.
EMAIL latino-l-request@amherst.edu
✍ *Type in message body:* subscribe latino-l <your full name>

LatinoWeb: Education & History Material on university organizations, fraternities, educational projects, cultural resources, and related articles are woven into this Web site. Some assorted Latino links include Día de los Muertos (Day of the Dead), Electric Mercado: Literature (highlighted works of Latino authors), and Hispanics in the American Revolution.
WEB http://www.catalog.com /favision/history.html

soc.culture.latin-america A cacophony of voices and topics, this newsgroup is lacking in focus but always interesting. Threads are often carried in both English and Spanish (posters even switch in the middle of sentences) and rarely bear any connection to their specified topic. But, hey, it's fun. One woman is seeking ways to say "I Love You" in all languages, and one thread begins, "USA=The Absolute Worst Country."
USENET soc.culture.latin-america

Native American

American Indian College Fund

It's a Lummi belief that a person's wealth is measured by what he gives away, not by what he keeps. The American Indian College Fund is founded on that kind of tradition. You can access the organization's annual report highlighting the year in review and the efforts made in the areas of cultural preservation, language, elders, tribal values and beliefs, archives, tribal arts, research, and scholarship.

WEB http://hanksville.phast.umass .edu/defs/independent/AICF.html

Index of Native American Resources on the Internet

Deceptively simple, this site holds hundreds of pointers on cultural, art, educational, and political resources. Well worth a visit is the collection of electronic Native American texts, which holds everything from turn-of-the-century *Atlantic Monthly* stories to the current issue of the ezine *Red Ink On-line*. Other pointers lead to language lessons, archeological dig sites, and museums. The selection of U.S. and tribal government sites collected is among the best on the Web.

WEB http://hanksville.phast.umass .edu/misc/NAresources.html

Native American Student Organizations

The University of Michigan's NASO is a campus organization designed to increase cultural, political, and social awareness of Native American peoples. Although the site focuses on local activities, it also includes links to other Native American pages on the Net.

WEB http://www.glrain.net/glrain /laura/links.htm

Native American Tribes: Information Virtually Everywhere

Lists are the form of choice here—useful lists of contact information for Native American organizations like Incorporated Americans for Restitution and Rightings of Old Wrongs, and lists of federally recognized tribes like the Barona Capitan Grande Band of Diegueno Mission Indians in California. There are also lists of radio stations with Native American programs and films and videos. The slew of electronic mailing lists and Net links are of great assistance in making further connections.

WEB http://www.afn.org/~native

Native Web This site is one of the most complete Native American resources in cyberspace. Much is available here—learn to speak Cree, read the original story of Hiawatha, apply for a small-business grant, or meet another Mohawk. Native Web provides much more than a terrific collection of links: The site's administrators have compiled a wealth of online information— read about the Navajo/Hopi controversy, or follow the Huaorani protest in Ecuador against petroleum exploration.

WEB http://web.maxwell.syr.edu /nativeweb

Anglo American

Center for the Study of White American Culture

This is not a group for people who like to wear bed sheets and dunce caps. Instead, it is a multiracial organization operating on the premise that knowledge of one's racial heritage (even if it is the so-called mainstream) is essential to establishing understanding among races. The CSWAC also believes that people of all races are required in a group to foster a balanced knowledge of a particular race. Follow links to other resources on white culture, and be surprised at how politically correct a group like this can be.

WEB http://www.euroamerican.org /index.htm

Ancient teachings, modern technology, and nativism—learn to speak Cree, meet a Mohawk, and read the story of Hiawatha
http://web.maxwell.syr.edu/nativeweb

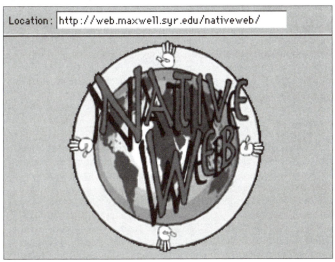

Location: http://web.maxwell.syr.edu/nativeweb/

Jewish

Hillel: The Foundation for Jewish Campus Life Since its inception in 1923, Hillel has grown into the largest Jewish campus organization in the world, with foundations and affiliates in the U.S., Canada, Israel, Australia, Europe, and South America. The site is as comprehensive as the organization itself, including instructions on signing up for several Hillel mailing lists discussing everything from general Jewish issues on campus to feminism and Judaism to political issues in Israel. There are campus profiles for every school with a chapter, and links to sources of news and events affecting the Jewish community. Happenin' Hillel members can click their way to the Jewish Singles Connection.
WEB http://hillel.org
EMAIL listproc@shamash.nysernet .org ✍ *Type in message body:* sub scribe hillel, hillel-women, hillel -shoc, hillel-grad, eco-zionism, zion line, hillel-announce, public-policy <your full name>

Jewish Community What is reform Judaism's viewpoint on homosexuality? Is it permissible to get a tattoo? How can Judaism help one set standards for dating? Where's an observant Jew away at school gonna go with questions like these? Well, he can try the "Ask A Rabbi" forum here. AOL's Jewish Community also contains sections covering arts and culture, family and personal matters, food, holidays and spirituality, and Israel. Active message boards and chat rooms keep the area lively.
AMERICA ONLINE *keyword* jewish

Kesher Reform Students on Campus Kesher is the Hebrew word for "connection." Kesher, the organization, connects Kesher Reform Chavurot (student groups)

on college campuses by providing them with resources on national and international events, an Internet mailing list, grant opportunities, organized trips to Israel, and this Web page, where you'll find a list of all of the Kesher-kosher campuses, with email addresses to contact for each chapter.
WEB http://www.netspace.org /~mharvey/kesher
EMAIL listserv@shamash.nysernet .org ✍ *Type in message body:* sub scribe uahcampus <your full name>

KOACH KOACH is a branch of the United Synagogue of Conservative Judaism that makes its home on college campuses worldwide, helping students maintain their religious identities as they make their way in the university world. KOACH's page provides links to conservative campus communities, the KOACH email listserver and archives, a grant program, and a calendar of events.
WEB http://israel.nysernet.org/uscj /koach
EMAIL listproc@shamash.nysernet .org ✍ *Type in message body:* subscribe KOACH <your full name>

Gay, lesbian, bisexual

Gaynet A mailing list about lesbian and gay concerns on college campuses including, but not limited to, outreach programs, political action, AIDS education, dealing with school administrations and social programs. Items of general gay and lesbian interest are also welcome. The list is not moderated; messages are sent in digest format. Archives are being kept, but are not easily available.
EMAIL majordomo@queernet.org ✍ *Type in message body:* subscribe gaynet

Oasis A welcome site in the relative desert of cyberspace for self-

identifying gay, lesbian, bisexual, and questioning youth. Created by the volunteer organization Youth Action Online, each monthly issue features a cover story on a prominent person in the gay and lesbian community, like writer Camille Paglia or Extra Fancy lead singer Brian Grillo, along with the departments Profiles in Courage, Letters & Opinion, Feature Columns, News & Reviews, and Stories & Poetry.
WEB http://www.cyberspaces.com /outproud/oasis

Queer Campus List A discussion list covering a broad range of topics for lesbian, bi, and gay college students—from confronting campus homophobia to mastering student organization politics, including attempts to remove ROTC from campuses.
EMAIL majordomo@vector.casti.com ✍ *Type in message body:* subscribe queercampus

Queer Infoservers: Colleges and Universities Members of the Multicultural Bisexual Gay Lesbian Alliance and Queer Resource Center at UC Berkeley have surfed the sea of university Internet sites, and, if it's queer, it's here. Links to college bisexual, lesbian, and gay organizations across the country and abroad from the Acadia University Coming Out page to the Yale Lesbian, Gay, Bisexual Cooperative.
WEB http://server.berkeley.edu /queer/qis/college.html

Stanford Queer Resources According to Jason P. Lorber, the worst place for gay people to attend business school is Purdue University, while the most gay-friendly campus is Harvard. You'll find more detailed information in Lorber's report, published as part of Stanford's Queer Resources di-

rectory (Stanford ranks second-best for gay people, by the way). In addition to information aimed specifically at queer Stanford students, there are links to most major queer online directories and a Queer Guide to the Bay Area.
WEB http://www.leland.stanford.edu/group/QR

Women

American Association of University Women The members of AAUW push for a strong public education system that promotes gender fairness, equity, and diversity. In their corner of the Web, you can read about relevant research, resources, fellowships and grants, and the Voter Education Campaign and also find out how to get involved in each aspect of the association.
WEB http://www.aauw.org

soc.women If you ignore the cross-postings from those groups with the dreaded word "feminism" in their title, soc.women is a very different, casual, and warm place to be. The group has fewer lurking male malcontents, and the men who do post are as likely to query why they have to go to the drugstore to buy tampons as they are to leave sexist jokes that die without a response. There are no crusaders. This is down-home chat with the girls (no disrespect intended) about the "business" of being women, with a good deal of joking about leg-shaving, the ordeal of housework (Jeanne from Oregon says she doesn't find it demeaning, just "utterly unnecessary"), and the other "species"—with animosity toward none.
USENET soc.women

Women Homepage Women here, women there, women absolutely everywhere. Jesse Stick-gold-Sarah presents links to a phenomenal number of women-oriented sites. Start by experiencing the intellectual joys of the Women's Resource Project. Broaden your horizons with a trip to the Sexuality and Gender home page. If it's out there, it's probably listed here.
WEB http://www.mit.edu:8001/people/sorokin/women/index.html

Women's Studies Roadmap Admit it. You're lost in cyberspace. If you're looking for women's resources, this meta-index is huge and easy to use. Each entry is carefully annotated and gives a brief sampling of the resource it describes. If it's what you want, just click and go. Mailing lists, Usenet newsgroups, Web pages, and gophers are all part of this reference guide.
WEB http://reks.uia.ac.be/women/roadmap/women/w0000000.html

Women Studies Gopher This catch-all gopher lets intrepid parties visit the electronic resources of women's studies departments worldwide—from Gettysburg College in Pennsylvania to the Chicana-Latina Studies department at UCLA. Gather information on women's studies syllabii, or feminist film reviews.
URL gopher://peg.cwis.uci.edu:7000/11/gopher.welcome/peg/women

Women's Resources on the Net This attractive site is a great place to start exploring women's resources online. Links to NOW, *Ms.*, women's health sites, bisexual and lesbian resources, bibliographies, biographies, legal resources, support groups, and women's colleges. Stay onsite for an online collection of paintings by women artists or sound clips of famous women writers like Maya Angelou, and a calendar of links to women's events ranging from a martial arts training camp for women to WisCon 20: The World's Foremost Feminist Science Fiction Convention.
WEB http://sunsite.unc.edu/cheryb/women/wresources.html

> **"Down-home chat with the girls about the 'business' of being women, with a good deal of joking."**

Women's Studies Issues on the Net Academic resources for the study of women's issues. Gather bibliographies from the Library of Congress or York University in England, or link to women's studies programs worldwide.
URL gopher://marvel.loc.gov/11/global/socsci/area/womens

Older students

Adult Student Survival Guide Heading off to college is a big transition for anyone. But for adult students, the college experience brings with it a unique set of challenges. This guide, sponsored by the Academia Group, is devoted to the 42 percent of all college students who are over the age of 24, providing financial aid tips for the older student, and a look at available Internet resources, covering test preparation, college admissions, and scholarship info.
WEB http://www.mindspring.com/~academia/start.htm

Your mother warned you

Ah, the idyllic college life. Ivy-covered buildings. Professors strolling through quads,

talking intently with bright young students. Coeds cheerily munching on delicacies—served by an exemplary catering service—before retiring to their not-so-elegant, but truly personal dorm rooms for a few hours of post-prandial study. Life in the ivory tower is indeed protected, but the "real world" has a habit of poking its head onto campus and disrupting the collegiate serenity. Whether it's the fact that crime is so high that Congress passed a law requiring colleges and universities to publish campus crime statistics, or the dangers that come with sex, drugs, and alcohol, students too frequently end up with honorary degrees from the school of hard knocks. How not to get sexually transmitted diseases, how to avoid being involved in acquaintance rape, how to spot and address addictions, how to tell when your anxieties are treatable, are the kinds of things the über-resource of the Net can teach you before you even leave the family home. Go ahead, do your digital homework.

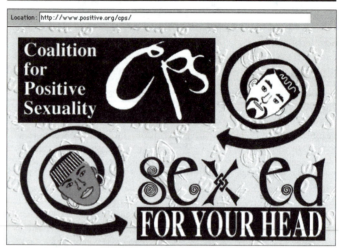

Fresh advice on how to have a healthy sex life
http://www.positive.org/cps

Sex

alt.sex.first-time Many people will arrive at college untainted by physical love. But alt.sex.first-time would quickly bring a smile to the face of even the most embarrassed virgin, as so many of the postings are hilarious. Invaded by professionals, pornographers, phone sexers, masseuses, and prostitutes, this is not, strictly speaking, a place for the inexperienced. Some honest-to-goodness virgins do post, looking for support, or looking to be deflowered.
USENET alt.sex.first-time

Coalition for Positive Sexuality Advocating a positive attitude toward sexuality, this pro-sex Web site was developed from *Just Say Yes: A Pro-Sex, Safer Sex Guide for Teens*, a pamphlet written by the Coalition for Positive Sexuality in Chicago. Topics include myths and realities: "masturbation will not make you blind"; how to talk about sex, safe sex, and birth control; a brief glossary; and links to more safe-sex resources. There's plenty of practical information, such as the chart on the symptoms and treatments of common STDs. The basics of sexuality are explained in terms teens probably wish their high school Sex-Ed teachers would use.
WEB http://www.positive.org/cps
• http://www.actwin.com/aids /jsyIndex.html

Condom Country Prophylactic Pete, the "Condom Cowboy," introduces visitors to a variety of must-have safe-sex devices they can rustle up online. The site also provides fun and facts and the most recent Surgeon General's report on AIDS. It links to a plethora of other below-the-belt sites.
WEB http://www.condom.com

CYBERNOTES

"Why do you encourage sex without Love?

'Learning about love is important; and for most people, learning about love and relationships provides the context for sexual expression. But teaching about love is beyond the scope of what we do. We try to provide the information that teenagers need to make the sexual encounters that they do have free from serious consequences (pregnancy, STDs, AIDS, etc.). We try to give them the tools they need to make informed choices within the relationships they have. We think that if we can help do that, we've done something worthwhile.'"

—from **Coalition for Positive Sexuality**

Condoms and Latex Everything you need to know about old-fashioned rubbers, plus the skinny on the new plastic condoms. This site dishes out the real deal on dental dams, including how to fashion them from latex gloves, condoms, and plastic wrap. Did you know Saran Wrap has been FDA-tested for its ability to block transmission of viruses? Step-by-step instructions on how to use all manner of barrier contraceptives are explained via text, cartoons, and video clips. A section on condom effectiveness tells all about leaks, breaks, and safety ratings.
WEB http://www.cmpharm.ucsf.edu /~troyer/safesex/condoms.html

Guide to Women's Health Issues Some guides to Net-wide resources simply offer pointers to lots of links, without any sense of what you can expect once you get there. Not this guide to women's health. It provides detailed information, including contact names, authors, and useful descriptions of a wide variety of women's resources. Divided into areas focused on emotional, physical, and sexual-health issues, the guide provides links to resources on topics such as body image, eating disorders, stress management, breast cancer, and HIV. Well-organized and thoughtfully presented.
WEB http://asa.ugl.lib.umich.edu /chdocs/womenhealth/womens _health.html

Nature's Method Nonprofit organization Family of the Americas advocates the "ovulation method" of birth control, otherwise known as the "rhythm method" (even though it insists it's not the same thing). The ovulation method is "100 percent natural," as underscored by the site's analogy of female fertility to crop cycles. It includes a link to the full text of Mother Teresa's address to the Fourth Conference on Women in Beijing, which was read by a Family of the Americas representative.
WEB http://upbeat.com/family/om .html

Planned Parenthood Online Reminiscent of a trip to one of the clinics decked out with cartoonish decor, this Web site gives the Planned Parenthood rap on abortion, birth control, and sexually transmitted infections, plus a public affairs section on reproductive-health issues and links to other Web sites. The site's online women's health newsletter has tips on managing PMS, shopping for condoms, and doing a breast self-exam.
WEB http://www.ppca.org

The Safer Sex Page Comprehensive info on safe sex, condoms, health issues, and counseling. The Quickie Roundup of Birth Control Options describes what works and what doesn't. The site's multimedia gallery also features video clips on how to put on a condom, how condoms are made, and safer-sex techniques for lesbians.
WEB http://www.safersex.org

Sex The opening page of this excellent Williams College site briefly addresses the cultural impulse to moralize about sexual pleasure. It then goes on to touch on sexual identity, quoting the famous sexologist Alfred Kinsey's finding that few people experience sexuality as being exclusively heterosexual or exclusively homosexual. Other links include Sexually Transmitted Diseases, Enjoying Safe Sex, and Problems With Male and Female Sexual Functioning.
WEB http://wso.williams.edu/peerh /sex

SHAPE Not the magazine, but the Sexual Health Advocate Peer Education program of the University of Missouri (Columbia) student-health center. The site covers a variety of sexuality topics directed at the campus community, ranging from what to do if you get a sexually transmitted infection to how to decide whether or not to have sex in the first place. There's also a Question of the Week feature, which solicits answers to quandaries like: "What's the most romantic way to ask your partner to

put on a condom?"
WEB http://www.missouri.edu
/~shape

Society for Human Sexuality

Birds do it, bees do it. But they don't do it with as much variety, mythology, or self-importance as humans, who write books, sing songs, paint paintings, and even set up institutions, associations, and societies to study their own pleasure. Curious about the sexual claims of your new friends? Need pointers on tantric-orgasm etiquette? With dozens of articles on such topics as body modification, massage, fetishes, and prostitution, this site serves as a clearinghouse for all things libidinal.
WEB http://weber.u.washington
.edu/~sfpse

STD Forum

"I am a 17-year-old college student and recently found out I contracted genital warts, the doctor said they were very minor and has begun to remove them with some kind of acid, but I still haven't told my boyfriend who I

love very much—I'm afraid of what he'll say. I don't sleep around, but I feel so violated and dirty for having this. Anyone have some comforting advice, please respond!" There are Web links to sites on every STD imaginable, but the greatest strength of this AOL site is its message board. Topics include anger, multiple afflictions, and gender specific conditions. Come with honest emotions and questions, leave with support and answers.
AMERICA ONLINE *keyword* std

The STD Home Page

Created for Boston-area teens, this Web site serves up the facts on AIDS, chancroids, chlamydia, gonorrhea, hepatitis B, herpes simplex, pubic lice and scabies, syphilis, trichomona, and venereal warts. Take the STD Quiz, find out which are low-risk and high-risk behaviors, browse a glossary of STD terms, and cruise through links to other related sites.
WEB http://med-www.bu.edu
/people/sycamore/std/std.htm

True Love Pages

A good number of students will fall in love in college. Along with office hours, roommates, dining services, and eating disorders, its just part of college culture. Love can be the best of times. And the worst of times. Pickup true love's spirit at this page, which collects a wide range of links dedicated to the steadfast heart.
WEB http://seidel.ncsa.uiuc.edu
/romance

Alchohol & drugs

Alcohol, Drugs, Cigarettes & Recovery

If you are going to use, be aware and enlightened. Informative articles on the effects of alcohol on creativity, alcohol and depression, quitting smoking and acupuncture.
AMERICA ONLINE *keyword* pen→
Women's Health→Alcohol, Drugs, Cigarettes & Recovery • *keyword* pen→Men's Health→Alcohol, Drugs, Cigarettes & Recovery

Bacchus

"To guide these efforts, the BACCHUS Peer Education Network operates on the philosophy that students can play a uniquely effective role, unmatched by professional educators, in encouraging their peers to consider, talk honestly about, and develop responsible habits, attitudes and lifestyles regarding alcohol and related issues."
WEB http://www.linkmag.com
/bacchus

National Clearinghouse for Alcohol and Drug Information

Affiliated with the U.S. Department of Health and Human Services, this site offers information aimed at preventing alcohol and drug abuse. It includes Prevention Primer, a reference for prevention practitioners; a variety of studies about drug use; and a

---

Part of a rolling curriculum of sexual advice from the Condoms and Latex page
http://www.cmpharm.ucsf.edu/~troyer/safesex/condoms.html

Location: http://www.cmpharm.ucsf.edu/~troyer/safesex/focus/howto.dunn.html

How to Put on a Condom

Dr. Marian E. Dunn demonstrates the correct way to put on a condom. *This video clip shows a realistic plastic model of a penis.*

Location: http://www.health.org/

The National Clearinghouse for Alcohol and Drug Information

PREVLINE
Prevention Online

A kilobyte of prevention is worth a gigabyte of cure
http://www.health.org

series of publications about prevention. The site includes a telnet link to PREVline, a system designed to allow people to share information about preventing drug and alcohol abuse.
WEB http://www.health.org

talk.politics.drugs This is a college-educated drug crowd; talk of illegal searches and seizures gets lots of airplay, as do concerns about wiretaps and attempts to find constitutional justification for legalization. By far the most common topic is marijuana laws—National Organization for the Reform of Marijuana Laws has a presence on the newsgroup, and most of the subscribers seem outraged that the government hasn't at least acknowledged its relatively minor effects: "Should our laws be such that an adult should go to prison for consuming marijuana at home? Should the users be exposed to brutal, profiteering drug dealers? Should the users have their houses broken into by SWAT teams with

faulty warrants, looking for a few joints?"
USENET talk.politics.drugs

Web of Addictions Dedicated to providing accurate information about alcohol and other drug addictions, this site attempts to counter the pro-drug stances often found in Usenet newsgroups and other Web pages. It includes an excellent section of facts about addictions, with lots of substances covered—everything from amyl-nitrite to steroids—and a varied collection of articles on issues such as How to Help Your Friend and Making Decisions About Substance Abuse Treatment. Other areas of the site focus specifically on help for addictions and related resources across the Net.
WEB http://www.well.com/user/woa

Campus safety

A Woman Scorned University of Pennsylvania professor Peggy

Sanday's readable book on the anthropology of acquaintance rape is excerpted here. Beginning with a famous case of date rape at St. John's University, this book investigates some of the historical and cultural themes of contemporary sexual culture.
WEB http://www.bdd.com/newrl/bddnewrl.cgi/03-01-96/rape_exrt

Acquaintance Rape An important site addressing some of the more uncommon dimensions of acquaintance rape, such as male victims and rape in relationships. Also provided are suggestions for further reading.
URL gopher://gopher.uchicago.edu:70/11/ustudent/sexab/AcquaintanceRape

Friends Raping Friends Sometimes sexual situations can be rather murky. Women are confused; men are confused. Learn how these situations come to be, how to diffuse them, and how to understand them.
WEB http://www.cs.utk.edu/%7Ebartley/acquaint/acquaiRape.html

Guarding Against Rape and Sexual Assault You will learn here that only 3 percent of rapists are diagnosed as psychotic. That being so, how is it that a woman is raped in America every six minutes? On college campuses, drugs, alcohol, and miscommunications factor heavily. This Mount Holyoke resource page has tips for women on how to protect themselves and full explanations about legal definitions of rape.
WEB http://www.mtholyoke.edu/offices/dps/sexasst.htm

Myths and Facts About Rape This excellent document addresses a number of those myths that could cause a person to have doubts about the average level of

national intelligence. It nevertheless illuminates some of the cultural assumptions that circulate around rape. For example: "There is no such thing as a 'typical rape.' Both men and women are raped by both male and female assailants. Victims have ranged in age from two months to 97 years." That should be enough to get even the dullest American thinking.
WEB http://www.cs.utk.edu/%7Ebartley/sa/mythsfacts.html

Slain Student's Mom Fights for Campus Security Campuses are still fraught with concerns for women. In this interview, Constance Clery discusses her daughter's torture and murder at Lehigh, and the changes, or lack thereof, in campus security. Mrs. Clery still maintains that sexual assault and rape are not reported accurately and responsibly by school administrators.
WEB http://www.s-t.com/daily/09-95/09-10-95/0910connie.HTML

Mental health

Eating Disorders Resources on the Internet Cathy, a Norwegian journalist who has suffered for years from anorexia and low-body image, assembled this collection of Internet resources for anorexia and bulimia sufferers.
WEB http://www.stud.unit.no/studorg/ikstrh/ed/ed.html

Go Ask Alice Named for the anonymous '60s-style cult book chronicling the drug addiction of a bright teenage girl, this resource is nothing if not reassuring and competent. Topics fall under the headings of Sexual Health and Relationships, Drug and Alcohol Concerns, Fitness and Nutrition, Emotional Being, and General Health. No question is too big or too small, from coping with

postabortion trauma, to compulsive zit-popping.
WEB http://www.columbia.edu/cu/healthwise/alice.html

Madness Experiencing anxiety, mood swings, visions? Do you hear voices? Are you afraid of people you used to trust? Those in need of support can turn to this discussion group for comfort. It's the home page of the Madness mailing list, which addresses general topics in mental health, and includes masses of links to numerous of psychiatric resources, including the PIE Web Server, the Mental Health Info Database, and the valiantly named Crazy and Proud BBS.
WEB http://www.io.org/~madness
EMAIL listserv@sjuvm.stjohns.edu ✎
Type in message body: subscribe madness <your full name>

Melissa's Therapy FAQ Operating on the principle that psychologists are often more troubled than their patients, Melissa Miles's therapy FAQ is written from the enlightened perspective of a former patient. If you're not interested in technical jargon, let Melissa soothe you with her simple—sometimes simplistic—words of semi-wisdom. Melissa defines her site as the "why, what, where, and how of going to a therapist."
WEB http://abulafia.st.hmc.edu/~mmiles/faq.html

Montreaux Counseling Centre Extreme and emergency cases of eating disorders are treated with 24-hour care at this Canadian clinic recently featured on ABC's *20/20*. Its Web site outlines a program of "facilitated reorientation" for those who have found no success with other clinics and specialists. A multimedia gallery displays sketches and paintings done by a few of the Centre's residents.

WEB http://www.riverhope.org/montrx

Psych Corner Share the special secrets of your relationship. Complain about your ingrate friends. Confess the details of your messy childhood. Blame your parents. And do it all at AOL's Mental Health area. The message boards are divided into broad categories—Relationships, Attention Deficit Disorder, Depression—allowing participants to gripe in a more directed fashion. There is a special area for the deluge of angst-ridden young adult manifestos denouncing parents, society, and school. The chat rooms allow some of the unhappy and disenfranchised to join together for a collective moan.
AMERICA ONLINE *keyword* online psych

Something Fishy: Eating Disorders Page Insomnia, hyperactivity, irregular heartbeat, vomiting blood—just a handful of the adverse effects of striving for the perfect body in a fat-phobic culture. The page delves deeply into the social and biological causes of eating disorders. Essays such as "What You Can Do" and "Remember It Hurts" offer sympathetic advice for victims and their families.
WEB http://www.pb.net/usrwww/w_fishy/ed.htm

Ways to Relax & Manage Stress Commuter stress, relationship stress, parental stress. All are very real and, in large doses, dangerous. Sufferers of stress should practice calming exercises before their problem grows into an anxiety disorder. The articles here offer just that—relaxation techniques, deep breathing, and positive thinking.
AMERICA ONLINE *keyword* pen

After class

College life offers so much: new activities to try out, new indoor and outdoor sports to

learn, new people to meet. So it's a lot like the Net. But if the Net can't offer the sensation of walking across the student union to meet the rest of the film-making club, it at least allows you to encounter other student film-making clubs from around the globe. Drugs, drinking, and sex also have their cybercor-relatives (see the previous chapter), but in the end, cyberspace is all about information. Find out who is doing what where, and read what they think about it all. College chat rooms offer direct access to other students from around the world, and the profusion of college ezines offers another juicy resource. Cybercollege life is very much about extracurricular education: be inspired by the diversity of activities and accomplishments of fellow students. You may even get to meet some of your international brethren if you're lucky enough to study abroad.

Survival skills

CAMPCLIM The CAMPCLIM list provides a forum for discus-

Rollerball **chic for the Rollerblade® generation**
http://www.campusvoice.com

sions pertaining to college campuses' personal, educational, and physical environments. Possible subjects include, but are not limited to: campus race relations, sexual harassment, exterior lighting, fire regulations, handicap access. It is hoped that subscribers will be able to specify how these issues are "handled" at their campus. For example, is there an ombudsman position? How do campus committees with overlapping responsibilities communicate with each other? What are the grievance procedures? Is there a "hate speech" policy? Are athletes treated differently from the rest of the student body?
EMAIL listserv@uafsysb.uark.edu ✍
Type in message body: subscribe campclim <your full name>

Campus Newspapers on the Net The University of Tennessee's *Daily Beacon* shines its searchlight on more than 100 college papers that are online, from *The Hustler* at Vanderbilt University to *OSI-Zeitung* at the Free University of Berlin. Cyberpapers are sorted by frequency of circulation.
WEB http://beacon-www.asa .utk.edu/resources/papers.html

Campus Voice The Serious section at Campus Voice is particularly good for collegers. One wouldn't think that it was possible to write an article on choosing a major without sounding patronizing, but it has been done here. Plus, the feature on cool professors is really interesting. The Culture Vulture section has links to enter-

A flagship online college presence
http://web.linkmag.com

tainment mags, *Lollapalooza*, the ultra kitschy *Hollywood and Vine*, and other au courant sites.
WEB http://www.campusvoice.com

How to Survive College (and still live to tell about it) Top ten tips for college students on topics ranging from how to improve your writing (get to be friends with an English composition major) to what you need to remember when hosting a party (quiet things down a bit after four in the morning).
WEB http://www.skypoint.com /subscribers/jackp/survive.html

Internet University A colorful cybersurvival guide for the college student: 15-minute recipes with ingredients available at the 7-Eleven; how to get free stuff online; and career pointers, with info on where to go to make your dough. Internet University covers the basics and more in the Arts, Entertainment, and Games

departments.
WEB http://www.internetuniv.com

The Link Digital Campus Are colleges still hotbeds of radicalism and sexual experimentation? This site gives you a window on life in the ivy-covered world. Hit the news briefs link for updates on fraternity hazings and affirmative action sit-ins. Or head to the news map and link to hundreds of college newspapers nationwide—for example, *The Missouri Miner*, *The Yale Daily News*, and *The Daily Texan*. Talk to college students from all over the country about date rape or financial aid at the site's bulletin board—or just hang back and discuss music in the Pub.
WEB http://www.linkmag.com

Loci Loci, furnished by the bookstore bigwig Barnes and Noble, is a little mag designed by college students for college students. Features include such goodies as a poll on Olestra and an interview

with an Ivy League stripper. There is also a permanent link to the Princeton Review's online info.
WEB http://www.Loci.com/HO /information/school.html

The Main Quad The Main Quad is not some "corporate fajita." It is not an ezine either. The Main Quad is an 'environment,' and in its charter it stresses its intention to bring students together to start companies, meet, and be political. There's a Dean's List page of links that address hip issues without insulting the intelligence. Here you'll find an emphasis on using the Net for job searches.
WEB http://www.mainquad.com

NerdWorld Student Organizations People seem to have an impulse to band together. Ethnic identity, political affiliation, hobbies, medical conditions, these groups comprise most of this global index. As a stop at the NerdWorld page will demonstrate, people seem to gather around almost any topic, whether it's Modernist Poets or Gene Technologies.
WEB http://challenge.tiac.net /users/dstein/nw840.html

T@P Online T@p is one of the more sophisticated college-targeted ezines. Its biggest unique area is Voyeur, which profiles sites with live cameras, visual manipulations, and CU-SeeMe software. The Style section is especially good, complete with a British correspondent covering the mod trend. Sports, technology, and job sources compose some of the other domains of this pretty site.
WEB http://www.taponline.com

T@P Schools & Money Shopping at thrift stores, buying and freezing day-old bread, and not gambling are just three ways to exhibit financial prudence. This site has articles on financial issues relating to students as well as an online book exchange.

WEB http://www.taponline.com /tap/higher.html

College chat

alt.college.food Some college students post recipes here, others are looking to meet people, and others still are hocking vitamins, or trying to get students to work on their pyramid scheme. But, quickie recipes abound, so if you need to whip together a tuna casserole, and perhaps meet a fellow coed from around the globe, you may want to check in.

USENET alt.college.food

alt.flame.roommate Practical and serious discussions are not the rule. While this newsgroup does occasionally address such real problems as the Roommate Who Will Not Pay Her Share, the Roommate Who Will Not Clean the Bathroom, and the Roommate Who Will Not Spend One Second Without Her Annoying Boyfriend Rick, many of the postings are consumed by hollow rage, filled with the sort of baseless griping that any student knows all too well. Still, roommate bashing is an unavoidable part of college life, and all members of the college set should know about this electronic opportunity to trash a bunkmate mercilessly.

USENET alt.flame.roommate

alt.folklore.college Do you really get a 4.0 if your roommate dies during the term? For answers to this and other myths of college life, dive into this newsgroup. In addition to charting past folklore, the group invites participants to contribute new experiences to the annals of college folklore. Some of them are so extreme (sex in a carillon tower that drowned out the bells) that they sound like lies, but that's the beauty of the Net: epistemologically bankrupt, it makes every story an equal.

USENET alt.folklore.college

alt.society.generation-x The highly touted generation of underachievers, technogeeks, and criminal misfits—"slackers, hackers, and carjackers," as one posting explains with admirable concision—gets yet another media outlet, and uses it to confirm virtually all of its own stereotypes. Gen Xers like pop music and hate literature. Gen Xers like beer and hate their parents. Gen Xers would wear underwear on their head if MTV told them to. Kurt, Kurt, why hast thou foresaken them? How much can you say about a newsgroup that spends much of its energy wondering if its messages should be crossposted to alt.angst?

USENET alt.society.generation-x

Gen-X If the media casts "Generation X" as whiny, apathetic post-baby boomers, the denizens of this list don't want to hear it. Refusing all stereotypes, this diverse and prolific group even debates whether the generation can be limited by age. "Gen-X is a state of mind," insists one list member. There are no boundaries to the unmoderated discussions. Fiery political debates over gun control and hiring quotas mix easily with sillier topics such as "Name the most embarrassing album you own." (One Gen-Xer: "I have the first Tiffany album. Beat that." The response: "Preferably with a large, blunt object to prevent further human suffering!") Get the digest version if you cannot handle 50-200 posts a day.

EMAIL listproc@phantom.com ✍
Type in message body: subscribe gen-x <your full name>

Learn to join the chattering classes
http://web.linkmag.com

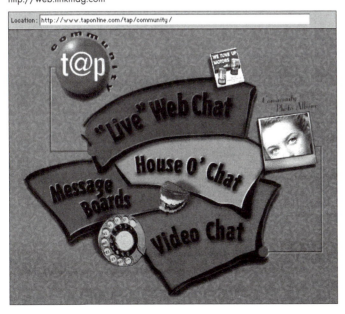

Location: http://www.taponline.com/tap/community/

soc.college There are always hundreds of messages on this newsgroup devoted to "the fine art of procrastination" and other weighty college issues. Despite the slacker veneer, this newsgroup is also useful for guerrilla research: just ask questions about a school of your choice and then lurk in the shadows, listening to the opinions of students who know the answers. Between their alternately jaded and naive insights and the glossy, misleading college brochure you've received in the mail, you may actually start to get a clearer picture of the place. The group's FAQ is a how-to guide to finding student's email addresses.
USENET soc.college
URL ftp://rtfm.mit.edu/pub/usenet-by-group/soc.college

Location: http://www.daad.org/usa.htm

DAAD

New York Office

950 Third Avenue at 57th St.
New York, , NY 10022, , USA
Tel. (212) 758-3223
FAX (212) 755-5780
E-mail:
DAADNY@daad.org

Show a German the big city. And sell him that Bridge!
http://www.daad.org

T@P Online Chat Board
They've got a "live text-based virtual community with social commands and multiple rooms for chatting pleasure" as well as a video chat room, and still more chat rooms. "Twisted" virtual characters are promised, and one can assume the guise of a cartoony figure...
WEB http://www.taponline.com/tap/community

" You don't have to join the Navy to see the world. "

Study abroad

Deutscher Akademischer Austauschdienst Images of Germans abroad evoke fanny packs, brightly colored track suits, and unusual sneakers. Well, this site is

well on the way to dispelling ugly and totally inappropriate stereotypes about the German aesthetic. This simple, clear site describes the DAAD, which in English means the German Academic Exchange Service, an organization dedicated to faculty and student exchanges. Find out about their international programs here.
WEB http://www.daad.org

IBB Home Page How does junior year abroad on the banks of the Seine strike you? This page, sponsored by the University of Oregon, carries information on international study programs and links to important resources like the Electronic Embassy (info on passport requirements) and cheap student travel sites. Homesick international students should also visit the international newsroom, where papers such as *The Irish Times*, *This Week in Germany*, and *The St. Petersburg Press* are available in electronic form.
WEB http://darkwing.uoregon.edu/~oieehome

T@P Online Student Travel
Cool stories from lots of road scholars. Read about eating eel three times a day in Chile, hiking and whining in jalapeno country, or bribing officious bureaucrats to cross a border. Lots of useful tips about student travel: hostels, currency, and subway maps.
WEB http://www.taponline.com/tap/travel.html

Worldwide Classroom You
don't have to join the Navy to see the world. Worldwide Classroom has amassed an impressive compilation of intercultural and educational programs. These courses from educational facilities around the globe include university study, foreign language immersion, adult enrichment programs, internships, volunteer programs, and teen camps. There's also a planning guide to make the passage from one country to another a bit easier, with information on everything from culture shock advice to money matters to global weather.
WEB http://www.worldwide.edu

Programs abroad

American Revolution Summer Study Program at Trinity College in Oxford, England
www.virginia.edu/~contined/oxlet.htm

Amerispan Unlimited (Spanish language and educational travel programs in Latin America)
www.amerispan.com

Baylor in Africa 1996
diogenes.baylor.edu/Courses_Abroad/Africa/welcome.html

Brethren Colleges Abroad
www.studyabroad.com/bca/bcahome.html

British Universities North America Club
www.latoile.com/BUNAC

BYU Travel Study
coned.byu.edu/ts/homepage.htm

CCIS—College Consortium for International Studies
www.studyabroad.com/ccis

Center for International Mobility (CIMO)
www.cimo.fi

Council on International Educational Exchange
www.ciee.org

Experiencing England
www.chapman.edu/animation/EE.html

Florida State University Study Abroad Programs
mailer.fsu.edu/~fsuabrd/phome.html

Institute for American Universities
www.univ-aix.fr/iau/iau.html

Institute of European and Asian Studies
www.mcs.net/~iesiascr/Home/ieshome.html

Institute of Spanish Studies
www.spanish-studies.com

IntelCross Study Abroad
www.study-abroad.org

International Course Guide
www.edunet.com/couridx.html

International Education Service
www.ies-ed.com

Kentucky Institute For International Studies
www.berea.edu/kiis/kiis.html

LEXIA Exchange International
www.stanfordbarn.com/LEXIA

Many Mexicos: Pre-Columbian Cultures to NAFTA
www.maxwell.syr.edu/geo/mexico.htm

MSC L.T. Jordan Institute for International Awareness
wwwmsc.tamu.edu/MSC/Jordan/Jordan.html

National Registration Center for Study Abroad
www.nrcsa.com

Online Study Abroad Directory
www.isp.acad.umn.edu/osad/osadhome.html

Partnership for Service-Learning
www.studyabroad.com/psl

Peterson's Education Center: Studying Abroad
www.petersons.com/stdyabrd/sasector.html

Pont-Aven School of Art
www.pontavensa.org

Semester at Sea
www.pitt.edu/~jjhst13/SemSeahome.html

Study Australia
www.vianet.net.au/~compsolu

studyabroad.com
www.studyabroad.com

U.S. Center for Australian Universities
www.colostate.edu/Depts/IP/AustraL.html

University of Florida Merida Program
www.clas.ufl.edu/anthro/merida/Merida-home.html

University Of Michigan International Center
www.umich.edu/~icenter

University of Oregon—Overseas Study Program
darkwing.uoregon.edu/~oieehome/os

University of Tennessee—Center for International Education
utkvx1.utk.edu/~cie

WISE—Worldwide Internships & Service Education
www.pitt.edu/~wise

Part 4

College Directory

College directory key

(1) School URL The URL for the general home page of the school.

(2) The Wired Rating A rating based on the quality of a school's entire site: its accessibility, design, and ease of use. Generally, the schools with the most facilities and hardware receive the best representation on the Web.

(3) I need... Email addresses and URLs for schools' Admissions and Financial Aid offices. Keep in mind that an email address is an invitation to inquire further.

(4) How wired is...? Here you'll find answers to Web- and tech-related questions.

(5) Online Application Stamp

 You can apply to these schools entirely online. Some will even waive their application fee.

 You can fill out most of the application online at these schools; you'll only need to follow up through snail mail with a few answers and the essay.

 You can download the application from these schools to print and fill out at home.

 If you want more information and an application, these schools let you request them online. They will then send them to you by snail mail.

(6) The usual tour Here you'll find the URLs for any number of college activities, from virtual tours to career centers, academic departments to Greek life.

(7) Skip the brochure The other side of college life: 'zines, humor rags, extreme sports teams, activist groups, radio and TV stations, and more.

(8) What you need to get in Dates, requirements, percentages, and school addresses and telephone numbers. The bare essentials.

(9) Last year's class This gives you an idea of how selective a school is: how many students are accepted out of those who apply; what the average SAT or ACT score is; the percentage of students who graduated at the top of their class; and whether the school accepts early applications.

(10) College Life Here you'll find out whether or not a school has fraternities or sororities, if there's a graduate community, the student to faculty ratio, and so on.

University of Arizona

Tucson, AZ · Est. 1885 · Coed · Public · 22,143 Undergrads · Urban

www.arizona.edu

I need...

Admissions info appinfo@arizona.edu
w3.arizona.edu/admissions
Financial aid info w3.arizona.edu/~finaid
/finaid.html

How wired is University of Arizona?

Do I get email? Yes
Do I get a home page? Yes
Where? ns.arizona.edu
Is my dorm wired? Yes
What is the student to computer ratio? 13:1

FULL APPLICATION ONLINE

The usual tour

DEPARTMENTS www.arizona.edu/academic
/catalog/catalog.html
SPORTS w3.arizona.edu/~athletic/wildcat
STUDENT CLUBS www.asua.arizona.edu/uaclubs
/clublist/main.html
GREEK LIFE www.asua.arizona.edu/UAclubs
/clublist/greek.html
PUBLICATIONS www.arizona.edu/newhome/newsl
.shtml
STUDENT NEWSPAPER wildcat.arizona.edu
/~wildcat
LIBRARY dizzy.library.arizona.edu

Skip the brochure

• **OFF CAMPUS CATS HOME PAGE** Arizona has lots of
wide open spaces, and if you feel lost out
there, fear not. Off-campus students from

Arizona's Wildcats: slamming and jamming their way to a
better future

near and far bond with activities like bowling,
movies, and hiking (not just back to one's
apartment, but the great outdoors).
w3.arizona.edu/~occ

• **STUDENTS FOR THE EXPLORATION AND DEVELOPMENT
OF SPACE, UNIVERSITY OF ARIZONA CHAPTER**
Contrary to popular belief, this organization
does not exist to promote larger dormitory
rooms. Rather, its apparent purpose is to educate the space-fearing, development-loathing
masses. Most students are involved because
of a love of the cause, but "[you] can also use
SEDS as a stepping stone to a space-related
career." **seds.lpl.arizona.edu**

• **CAMP WILDCAT** Students at the University of
Arizona give kids in need the gift of games by
providing a variety of fun activities for Tucson
youth who are financially, mentally, or physical-
ly disadvantaged. **bigdog.engr.arizona.edu/~ieee/cw/**

WHAT YOU NEED TO GET IN **Application Deadline** November 1 for priority consideration; final deadline April 1 **Common
App.** No **Application Fee** $35 (non-residents only) **Tuition Costs** $1,940 ($8,308 out-of-state) **Room & Board**
$4,190 **Need Blind** Yes **Financial Forms Deadline** Priority given to applications received by March 1 **Undergrads
Awarded Aid** 65% **Average Award of Freshman Scholarship Package** $2,248 **Tests Required** SAT1 or ACT
Admissions Address Tucson, AZ 85721-0007 **Admissions Telephone** (520) 621-3237

LAST YEAR'S CLASS **Applied** 16,366 **Accepted** 13,512 **Matriculated** 4,557 **Average SAT M/V** 552/550 **Average
ACT** 23 **In Top Fifth of High School Graduating Class** 50%

COLLEGE LIFE **Gender Breakdown** M 49%, F 51% **Out of State Students** 36% **From Public Schools** 90% **Ethnic
Composition** White & Other 76%, Asian American 5%, Black 3%, Hispanic 14%, Native American 2% **Foreign
Students** 3% **Reside on Campus** 18% **Return as Sophomores** 78% **Total Faculty** 1592 **Student Faculty Ratio**
20:1 **Fraternities (% of men participating)** 25 (15%) **Sororities (% of women participating)** 20 (15%) **Graduate
Students** 8,624

Adelphi University

www.adelphi.edu

Garden City, NY · Est. 1896 · Coed · Private · 3,272 Undergrads · Urban

I need...

Admissions info testemail@adelphi.edu
www.adelphi.edu/admin/admis/admis.html
Financial aid info testfin@adelphi.edu

How wired is Adelphi?

Do I get email? Yes
Do I get a home page? Yes
Where? www.adelphi.edu/adm/People.html
What is the student to computer ratio? 7:1

The usual tour

DEPARTMENTS www.adelphi.edu/acad/Academic
Serv.html
VIRTUAL TOUR www.adelphi.edu/tour/tour.html

Skip the brochure

• **ADELPHI UNIVERSITY STAGECRAFT** Theater and technology merge to bring classic and contemporary shows to the Adelphi campus. Whether

"One site that may yet be worth making a song and dance about."

Adelphi: The oracle of knowledge

you're looking for updates to the slowly evolving FTP site or booking tickets for the new season, this is one site that may yet be worth making a song and dance about. **www.adelphi .edu/~tech**

• **ADELPHI COMPUTER CLUB** Computers can be entertaining, educational, or exasperating. No matter your needs, Adelphi students are here to help. They've got their work cut out for them. **www.adelphi.edu/~compclub**

• **ADELPHI AT-A-GLANCE** There isn't much on site that communicates the personality of Adelphi, but one does learn that the nation's first university-based graduate school in psychotherapy was founded here. This intriguing page of factoids helps characterize an otherwise colorless site. **www.adelphi.edu/admin/info/facts.html**

WHAT YOU NEED TO GET IN **Application Deadline** Rolling admissions; March 1 for priority consideration **Common App.** Yes **Application Fee** $35 **Tuition Costs** $13,360 **Room & Board** $6,300 **Need Blind** Yes **Financial Forms Deadline** June 30 with a priority given to applications received by February 15 **Undergrads Awarded Aid** 76% **Aid That Is Need-Based** 28% **Average Award of Freshman Scholarship Package** $6,954 **Tests Required** SAT1 or ACT **Admissions Address** South Avenue, Garden City, NY 11530 **Admissions Telephone** (516) 877-3050

LAST YEAR'S CLASS **Applied** 2,540 **Accepted** 1,626 **Matriculated** 382 **Average SAT M/V** 540/552 **In Top Fifth of High School Graduating Class** 38%

COLLEGE LIFE **Gender Breakdown** M 32%, F 68% **Out of State Students** 12% **From Public Schools** 71% **Ethnic Composition** White & Other 78%, Asian American 4%, Black 11%, Hispanic 7% **Foreign Students** 4% **Reside on Campus** 18% **Return as Sophomores** 75% **Total Faculty** 561 **Student Faculty Ratio** 12:1 **Fraternities (% of men participating)** 9 (5%) **Sororities (% of women participating)** 9 (10%) **Graduate Students** 3,730

Agnes Scott College

www.scottlan.edu

Decatur, GA · Est. 1889 · Women · Private · 577 Undergrads · Urban

I need...

Admissions info admission@asc.scottlan.edu
www.scottlan.edu/admisson/admiss1.htm
Financial aid info thille@asc.scottlan.edu
www.scottlan.edu/faid.htm

How wired is Agnes Scott?

Do I get a home page? No
What is the student to computer ratio? 5:1

The usual tour

VIRTUAL TOUR www.scottlan.edu/admisson
/campus/camptour.htm
DEPARTMENTS www.scottlan.edu/academic.htm
LIBRARY www.scottlan.edu/library/welcome.htm
CAREER CENTER www.scottlan.edu/jobs.htm

Skip the brochure

• **STUDENT ART GALLERY** The school posts an
impressive collection of student artwork with
commentary by the artists, some of whom
take the opportunity to describe the ideas
behind their work. Others explain their general
philosophies on creative pursuits. **www.scottlan
.edu/academic/art/sgallery/gallery.htm**

• **DEPARTMENT OF PUBLIC SAFETY** If you're worrying
about your security, you're not worrying about
your education: This is the belief of Agnes
Scott's Department of Public Safety, which
seeks to maintain a secure enviroment for students so that they can pour their energies

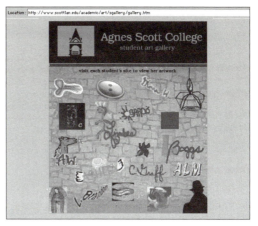

Location: http://www.scottlan.edu/academic/art/sgallery/gallery.htm

Agnes Scott's artists strut their stuff

into their studies. **www.scottlan.edu/pubsaf
/welcome.htm**

• **WOMEN, LEADERSHIP & SOCIAL CHANGE** Called "The
Atlanta Semester," this program combines
coursework with internships in an effort to promote social change in the community. It aims
to develop leadership in students at Agnes
Scott as well as other women in colleges and
universities across the nation. **www.scottlan.edu
/academic/wl&sc/deptpage.htm**

"'The Atlanta Semester' promotes social change in the community."

WHAT YOU NEED TO GET IN Application Deadline Rolling admissions; March 1 for priority consideration **Early Action Deadline** November 15 **Common App.** Yes **Application Fee** $35 **Tuition Costs** $14,325 **Room & Board** $6,020 **Need Blind** Yes **Financial Forms Deadline** Priority given to applications received by February 15 **Undergrads Awarded Aid** 93% **Aid That Is Need-Based** 60% **Average Award of Freshman Scholarship Package** $9,668 **Tests Required** SAT1 or ACT **Admissions Address** 141 East College Avenue, Decatur, GA 30030 **Admissions Telephone** (404) 638-6285

LAST YEAR'S CLASS Applied 423 Accepted 350 Matriculated 125 **Median Range SAT M/V** 480-620/480-620 **In Top Fifth of High School Graduating Class** 70% **Applied Early** 35 **Accepted Early** 31

COLLEGE LIFE Out of State Students 60% **From Public Schools** 78% **Ethnic Composition** White & Other 76%, Asian American 6%, Black 14%, Hispanic 3%, Native American 1% **Foreign Students** 4% **Reside on Campus** 91% **Return as Sophomores** 75% **Total Faculty** 88 **Student Faculty Ratio** 8:1 **Sororities** none **Graduate Students** 21

University of Alabama

www.ua.edu

Tuscaloosa, AL · Est. 1831 · Coed · Public · 14,796 Undergrads · Urban

I need...

Admissions info uaadmit@ualvm.ua.edu
www.ua.edu/admissio.html
Financial aid info www.ua.edu/finaid.html

How wired is University of Alabama?

Do I get email? Yes
Do I get a home page? No
What is the student to computer ratio? 6:1

The usual tour

VIRTUAL TOUR www.ua.edu/tour.html
DEPARTMENTS www.ua.edu/colleges.html
CALENDAR www.ua.edu/calendar.html
SPORTS ua1vm.ua.edu/~uasports/index.html
CAREER CENTER www.sa.ua.edu/SA/UACC/UACC
.HTM
STUDENT CLUBS www.sa.ua.edu/SA/HANDBOOK
/TABLECON.HTM
LIBRARY www.lib.ua.edu

Skip the brochure

• **SPORTS ALUMNI INFORMATION** University of
Alabama alums who made it big in the wide
world of sports are showcased, including

"Future Spielbergs, Siskels and Eberts should consider taking a look."

The mere mention of 'Bama brings ear-to-ear grins to its alums

Olympians and NBA players. Roll Tide! **ualvm
.ua.edu/~uasports/alumni.htm**

• **ALABAMA GYMNASTICS** You'll twist, contort, and
jump for joy when you read about the accomplishments of the women's gymnastic team.
ualvm.ua.edu/~uasports/gymnast/gymindex.htm

• **TUSCALOOSA, ALABAMA** If Tuscaloosa's rich history, active arts community, and many festivals
aren't enough for you, consider this—you're
just a half day's drive away from Florida's Gulf
Coast, Atlanta, New Orleans, and the Great
Smoky Mountains. **www.ua.edu/tuscaloo.html**

• **SCREENSITE: FILM AND TV STUDIES** This Web site is
devoted to the teaching and research of film
and television, maintained by Bama's Tele-
communication and Film Department. Future
Spielbergs, Siskels and Eberts should consider taking a look. **www.sa.ua.edu/tcf/welcome.htm**

WHAT YOU NEED TO GET IN **Application Deadline** March 1 for priority consideration; final deadline August 1 **Common
App.** No **Application Fee** $25 **Tuition Costs** $2,470 ($6,268 out-of-state) **Room & Board** $3,680 **Need Blind**
Yes **Financial Forms Deadline** Priority given to applications received by March 1 **Undergrads Awarded Aid** 50%
Aid That Is Need-Based 64% **Average Award of Freshman Scholarship Package** $3,034 **Tests Required** SAT1
or ACT **Admissions Address** Box 870132, Tuscaloosa, AL 35487-0132 **Admissions Telephone** (800) 933-BAMA

LAST YEAR'S CLASS Applied 6,818 **Accepted** 5,257 **Matriculated** 2,531 **Average ACT** 23 **In Top Quarter of High
School Graduating Class** 61%

COLLEGE LIFE **Gender Breakdown** M 48%, F 52% **Out of State Students** 36% **From Public Schools** 85% **Ethnic
Composition** White & Other 86%, Asian American 1%, Black 12%, Hispanic 0.5%, Native American 0.5% **Foreign
Students** 3% **Reside on Campus** 41% **Return as Sophomores** 83% **Total Faculty** 774 **Student Faculty Ratio**
17:1 **Fraternities (% of men participating)** 27 (16%) **Sororities (% of women participating)** 17 (24%) **Graduate
Students** 3,717

University of Alaska, Fairbanks

zorba.uafadm.alaska.edu

Fairbanks, AK · Est. 1917 · Coed · Public · 6,998 Undergrads · Big Town

I need...

Admissions info fnaws@aurora.alaska.edu

How wired is University of Alaska, Fairbanks?

Do I get email? Yes
What is the student to computer ratio? 46:1

The usual tour

VIRTUAL TOUR zorba.uafadm.alaska.edu
/#Campus
DEPARTMENTS zorba.uafadm.alaska.edu/#Depts
STUDENT CLUBS zorba.uafadm.alaska.edu
/woodctr/activity/clubs.html
ALUMNI ASSOCIATION zorba.uafadm.alaska.edu
/alumni
UNIVERSITY OF ALASKA MUSEUM zorba.uafadm
.alaska.edu/museum/index.html

Skip the brochure

• **UAF WOOD CENTER STUDENT ACTIVITIES** Worried
there will be nothing to do during those long,
cold, dark, Fairbanks winters? The Wood
Center strives to allay such anxieties. There's
the Bust-a-Gut comedy series, screenings of
recent movies, outdoor canoe and hiking trips,
and about a hundred individual student clubs
just for starters. zorba.uafadm.alaska.edu
/woodctr/activity/index.html

Location: http://www.alaska.net/~apu/images/26.jpg

Some students choose to major in Moose

• **THE COFFEEHOUSE** All the hep cats on campus
can surely be found at the Northern Lights
Coffeehouse Series, which features acoustic
acts each week. **zorba.uafadm.alaska.edu/woodctr
/activity/coffee.html**

• **ALASKA VOLCANO OBSERVATORY** The movers and
shakers of the University of Alaska Fairbanks'
Geophysical Institute keep on top of the latest
seismic activity in the state and monitor all the
active volcanoes in the area. Are you ready to
rumble? **www.avo.alaska.edu**

"Ready to rumble: UAF's Geophysical Institute "

WHAT YOU NEED TO GET IN **Application Deadline** August 1 **Common App.** No **Application Fee** $35 **Tuition Costs** $2,100
($6,300 out-of-state) **Room & Board** $3,790 **Financial Forms Deadline** Priority given to applications received by
May 15 **Undergrads Awarded Aid** 70% **Aid That Is Need-Based** 80% **Tests Required** SAT1 or ACT **Admissions
Address** Fairbanks, AK 99775-7480 **Admissions Telephone** (907) 474-7521

LAST YEAR'S CLASS **Applied** 1,764 **Accepted** 1,385 **Matriculated** 869 **Average SAT M/V** 490/463

COLLEGE LIFE **Gender Breakdown** M 44%, F 56% **Out of State Students** 18% **From Public Schools** 90% **Ethnic
Composition** White & Other 80%, Asian American 2%, Black 2%, Hispanic 2%, Native American 14% **Foreign
Students** 3% **Reside on Campus** 20% **Return as Sophomores** 61% **Total Faculty** 717 **Student Faculty Ratio**
14:1 **Fraternities** none **Sororities** none **Graduate Students** 791

Alfred University

www.alfred.edu

Alfred, NY · Est. 1836 · Coed · Private · 1,994 Undergrads · Small Town

I need...

Admissions info admssn@bigvax.alfred.edu
www.alfred.edu/admssn/admssn.html
Financial aid info www.alfred.edu/finaid/finaid
.html

How wired is Alfred?

Do I get email? Yes
Do I get a home page? Yes
Is my dorm wired? No
What is the student to computer ratio? 5:1

The usual tour

DEPARTMENTS www.alfred.edu/college/colgs.html
LIBRARY www.alfred.edu/libr.html
STUDENT CLUBS www.alfred.edu/life/clubs.html
STUDENT NEWSPAPER www.alfred.edu/life/fiat
.html
SPORTS www.alfred.edu/life/athletic.html
GREEK LIFE www.alfred.edu/life/greek.html
CAREER CENTER www.alfred.edu/life/carsvc.html

"Be the Quasimodo of the year with the historic bells of Alfred's carillon!"

Location: http://www.alfred.edu/admssn/admssn.html

Alfred University Admissions

Alfred's Admissions Test: Count the streetlights

Skip the brochure

- **MAJOR WEEKENDS** Start planning early and mark your calendar for the major weekends of the next several school years. After all, you wouldn't want to schedule a conflict with Homecoming Weekend, 1999, now would you? **www.alfred.edu/life/weekend.html**

- **DAVIS MEMORIAL CARILLON** Be the Quasimodo of the year and ring in your college career—every day of it—with the historic bells of Alfred's carillon. **www.alfred.edu/campus/carillon.html**

- **FRIDAY NIGHT LIVE** Live from Alfred, NY, it's... Friday Night Live! Students attempt comedy sketches the night before the cast of SNL shows them what not to do. **www.lsds.com/~turtyl /fnl.html**

WHAT YOU NEED TO GET IN **Application Deadline** February 1 for priority consideration **Early Action Deadline** December 1 **Common App.** Yes **Application Fee** $40 **Tuition Costs** $17,500 **Room & Board** $5,406 **Need Blind** Yes **Financial Forms Deadline** Rolling **Undergrads Awarded Aid** 90% **Aid That Is Need-Based** 75% **Average Award of Freshman Scholarship Package** $10,000 **Tests Required** SAT1 or ACT **Admissions Address** Saxon Drive, Alfred, NY 14802-1205 **Admissions Telephone** (607) 871-2115

LAST YEAR'S CLASS **Applied** 1,648 **Accepted** 1,408 **Matriculated** 495 **Average SAT M/V** 565/565 **In Top Fifth of High School Graduating Class** 40%

COLLEGE LIFE **Gender Breakdown** M 52%, F 48% **Out of State Students** 40% **From Public Schools** 83% **Ethnic Composition** White & Other 89%, Asian American 2%, Black 5%, Hispanic 3%, Native American 1% **Foreign Students** 2% **Reside on Campus** 65% **Return as Sophomores** 82% **Student Faculty Ratio** 12:1 **Fraternities (% of men participating)** 7 (23%) **Sororities (% of women participating)** 5 (16%) **Graduate Students** 411

Allegheny College

www.alleg.edu

Meadville, PA · Est. 1815 · Coed · Private · 1,838 Undergrads · Small Town

I need...

Admissions info admiss@admin.alleg.edu
www.alleg.edu/Admin/Admissions
Financial aid info phart@admin.alleg.edu
www.alleg.edu/Admin/Admissions
/Financial.html

How wired is Allegheny College?

Do I get email? Yes
Do I get a home page? Yes
　Where? ace.alleg.edu
Is my dorm wired? No
What is the student to computer ratio? 6:1

The usual tour

STUDENT CLUBS www.alleg.edu/StudentLife
/StudentLife.html#Organizations
LIBRARY www.alleg.edu/Admin/Library
DEPARTMENTS www.alleg.edu/Info/Departments
.html#Academic
SPORTS www.alleg.edu/Academic/PhysEd
CAREER CENTER www.alleg.edu/Admin
/CareerServices
PUBLICATIONS www.alleg.edu/Admin/Public
Affairs/AllegMonthly.html

Skip the brochure

• **90.3 FM WARC** Roughage for the Soul, Getting
Naked, 2 Tuff Chicks, and Fusion are neither
new bands nor graduate study options. They're
shows featured on Allegheny's alternative

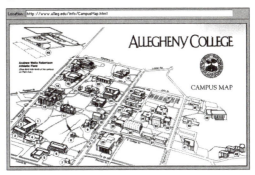

But where are the mountains?

radio station. **ace.alleg.edu/~warc**

• **FRENCH CREEK PROJECT** Perrier it ain't, because
French Creek, a waterway which meanders
through New York and Pennsylvania, is suffering from pollution problems. Luckily, Allegheny
College has banded together with other organizations in an effort to protect French Creek via
public education and a grassroots campaign
against water pollution. **www.alleg.edu/Info
/FrenchCreek**

"Getting Naked and 2 Tuff Chicks are shows on Allegheny's alternative radio station"

WHAT YOU NEED TO GET IN Application Deadline February 15 **Early Action Deadline** November 30 (Plan I) or January 15
(Plan II) **Common App.** Yes **Application Fee** $30 (may be waived in cases of economic hardship) **Tuition Costs**
$18,450 **Room & Board** $4,670 **Need Blind** Yes **Financial Forms Deadline** Priority given to applications received
by February 15 **Undergrads Awarded Aid** 94% **Aid That Is Need-Based** 84% **Average Award of Freshman
Scholarship Package** $10,854 **Tests Required** SAT1 or ACT **Admissions Address** Meadville, PA 16335
Admissions Telephone (814) 332-4351

LAST YEAR'S CLASS Applied 2,811 **Accepted** 2,083 **Matriculated** 565 **Median Range SAT M/V** 520-640/470-570
In Top Fifth of High School Graduating Class 72% **Applied Early** 159 **Accepted Early** 148

COLLEGE LIFE Gender Breakdown M 48%, F 52% **Out of State Students** 45% **From Public Schools** 83% **Ethnic
Composition** White & Other 93.3%, Asian American 2.5%, Black 3.3%, Hispanic 0.6%, Native American 0.3%
Foreign Students 3% **Reside on Campus** 76% **Return as Sophomores** 87% **Total Faculty** 190 **Student Faculty
Ratio** 12:1 **Fraternities (% of men participating)** 6 (30%) **Sororities (% of women participating)** 5 (35%)

The American University

www.american.edu

Washington, DC · Est. 1893 · Coed · Private · 4,982 Undergrads · Urban

How wired is The American University?

Do I get email? Yes
Do I get a home page? Yes
  Where? strauss.cas.american.edu/registry
Are the dorms wired? Yes

The usual tour

DEPARTMENTS www.american.edu/academic
  .depts/index.html#academics
STUDENT NEWSPAPER www.eagle.american.edu
SPORTS www.american.edu/athletics
STUDENT CLUBS www.american.edu/studlife
  /clubs
GREEK LIFE www.american.edu/studlife/clubs
  /#greek
LIBRARY newton.library.american.edu
CAREER CENTER www.american.edu/other.depts
  /career

Skip the brochure

• **THE EAGLE'S WEB** While other schools just put
electronic versions of their newspapers online, American University has made *The*

Location: http://eagle.cas.american.edu/amlit/

american literary
The Journal of Creative Works
at American University

American Literary is an annual journal of art and literature produced by students at
American University in Washington, DC. To aid us in our quest for world domination,
we are currently accepting submissions for our Spring 1996 edition. The deadline for
submissions is February 7.

American's Eagles sink their talons into artistic endeavor.
Watch the creative juices flow

Eagle's Web even better than its print counterpart, *The Eagle*. In addition to the expected
features, there are very cool graphics and
even cooler RealAudio sound clips and
QuickTime videos. **www.eagle.american.edu**

• **STUDENTS FOR HEALTHY DECISIONS** Make your
mom happy and team up with an organization
that exists to make every day worthwhile.
www.american.edu/studlife/clubs/shd

• **BIRD OF PREY** Hunt down the best of the Internet
from the point of view of American University
students. Articles explore various offerings on
the Web, both AU-related and otherwise.
Particularly good for prospective students is
the Virtual Tour of Washington, D.C., which
describes major D.C. attractions and links to
their home pages. **www.eagle.american.edu/bp**

WHAT YOU NEED TO GET IN Application Deadline February 1 for priority consideration **Early Action Deadline** November
15 **Common App.** Yes **Application Fee** $45 **Tuition Costs** $17,514 **Room & Board** $7,008 **Financial Forms
Deadline** Priority given to applications received by March 1 **Undergrads Awarded Aid** 70% **Aid That Is Need-
Based** 35% **Tests Required** SAT1 (preferred) or ACT **Admissions Address** 4400 Massachusetts Avenue, NW,
Washington, DC 20016-8001 **Admissions Telephone** (202) 885-6000

LAST YEAR'S CLASS Applied 5,646 **Accepted** 4,381 **Matriculated** 1,276 **Average SAT M/V** 577/542 **Average ACT**
26 **In Top Fifth of High School Graduating Class** 58% **Applied Early** 322 **Accepted Early** 288

COLLEGE LIFE Gender Breakdown M 41%, F 59% **Out of State Students** 90% **Ethnic Composition** White & Other
83.2%, Asian American 4.6%, Black 7.2%, Hispanic 4.5%, Native American 0.5% **Foreign Students** 12% **Reside
on Campus** 65% **Return as Sophomores** 82% **Student Faculty Ratio** 14:1 **Fraternities (% of men participating)**
7 (20%) **Sororities (% of women participating)** 8 (25%) **Graduate Students** 4,946

Amherst College

Amherst, MA · Est. 1821 · Coed · Private · 1,600 Undergrads · Small Town

I need...

Admissions info www.amherst.edu/~admissio
Financial aid info www.amherst.edu/amherst
/admin/finaid/menu.html

How wired is Amherst College?

Do I get email? Yes
Do I get a home page? Yes
 Where? www.amherst.edu/amherst/personal
 /menu.html
Is my dorm wired? Yes
What is the student to computer ratio? 22:1

The usual tour

DEPARTMENTS www.amherst.edu/amherst
/academ/menu.html
SPORTS www.amherst.edu/amherst/academ
/athletic/menu.html
CALENDAR www.amherst.edu/amherst/events
/listings/menu.html
WRITING CENTER http://www.amherst.edu
/~writing/menu.html
VIRTUAL TOUR www.amherst.edu/Tour
CAREER CENTER www.amherst.edu/amherst/occ
/menu.html

Skip the brochure

• **MEAD ART MUSEUM** Amherst's Mead Museum is
a classy collection of American, Asian, African,
pre-Columbian, and ancient art. **www.amherst
.edu/~mead**

Amherst's excellent ezine: no subject unpoked

• **THE HUNGRY NEWT** Music, big comfy couches, a
fireplace, yummy baked goods, and kegs of
coffee are what you'll find at the Hungry Newt.
And no, the title isn't a clever political jab.
www.amherst.edu/~bcchang/newt

• **CITIZEN POKE** Amherst's humor 'zine is not for
the humorless. With articles like "Where did
you go, Ralph Macchio?" and "Willy Wonka as
Pimp Daddy," your entertainment needs are
well taken care of. And there's more! Be sure
to check out Freaks of the Week.
www.amherst.edu/~poke

• **AMHERST COLLEGE DIVERSITY TASK FORCE**
Frustrated by a course selection that seemed
a whiter shade of pale, Amherst students have
been lobbying since 1994 to diversify the
school's curriculum. **www.amherst.edu/~dtf**

WHAT YOU NEED TO GET IN Application Deadline December 31 **Early Action Deadline** November 15 **Common App.** No
Application Fee $55 **Tuition Costs** $20,710 **Room & Board** $5,600 **Need Blind** Yes **Financial Forms Deadline**
February 15 **Undergrads Awarded Aid** 55% **Aid That Is Need-Based** 100% **Average Award of Freshman
Scholarship Package** $15,146 **Tests Required** SAT1 or ACT **Admissions Address** Amherst, MA 01002
Admissions Telephone (413) 542-2328

LAST YEAR'S CLASS Applied 4,836 **Accepted** 943 **Matriculated** 422 **Average SAT M/V** 677/625 **Average ACT** 29
In Top Fifth of High School Graduating Class 90% **Applied Early** 528 **Accepted Early** 147

COLLEGE LIFE Gender Breakdown M 56%, F 44% **Out of State Students** 87% **From Public Schools** 54% **Ethnic
Composition** White & Other 71%, Asian American 12%, Black 8%, Hispanic 9% **Foreign Students** 3% **Reside on
Campus** 98% **Return as Sophomores** 97% **Total Faculty** 189 **Student Faculty Ratio** 9:1 **Fraternities** none
Sororities none

Antioch University

college.antioch.edu

Yellow Springs, OH · Est. 1852 · Coed · Private · 637 Undergrads · Rural

How wired is Antioch?

Do I get email? Yes
Do I get a home page? Yes
   Where? 192.131.123.121:125/anarcho
   /anarchoantioch.html
What is the student to computer ratio? 6:1

The usual tour

DEPARTMENTS 192.131.123.121:125
   /academic.html
STUDENT NEWSPAPER 192.131.123.121:125
   /record/record.html
LIBRARY 192.131.123.121:125/OKL/index
   .html

Skip the brochure

• **ANARCHOANTIOCH** Students give the scoop on
   Antioch. "Let's face it, this school is intense.
   We are a bunch of college students who are
   enrolled in one of the most intense colleges in
   the country, and we're stuck in the middle of
   rural Southwestern Ohio; we're about to
   burst." All this pent-up energy has yet to find
   an online outlet; in the meantime here are a
   few student home pages and random links.
   192.131.123.121:125/anarcho/anarchoantioch.html

• **SELF, SOCIETY & CULTURE** Coming soon to a college near you: a new interdisciplinary major in

Location: http://college.antioch.edu/~dfriedman/

Antioch's first admissions officers couldn't get it quite right.
We're for diversity and all...

the social sciences. It's perfect if you consider
yourself a people person. **college.antioch.edu
/~dfriedman/ssc.html**

• **STUDENT WORK SHOWCASE** Peaceful and not-so-
   peaceful Antioch students who have taken
   part in the Peace Studies program explain
   their commitment to tranquility. **www.antioch.edu
   /~peace//students/student.central.html**

"Self, Society and Culture: perfect if you consider yourself a people person."

WHAT YOU NEED TO GET IN **Application Deadline** February 1 for priority consideration **Early Action Deadline** November
15 **Common App.** Yes **Application Fee** $35 **Tuition Costs** $16,322 **Room & Board** $3,796 **Need Blind** Yes
Financial Forms Deadline Priority given to applications received by March 1 **Undergrads Awarded Aid** 88% **Aid
That Is Need-Based** 81% **Average Award of Freshman Scholarship Package** $9,127 **Tests Required** SAT1
(preferred) or ACT **Admissions Address** 795 Livermore, Yellow Springs, OH 45387 **Admissions Telephone** (513)
767-6400

LAST YEAR'S CLASS **Applied** 445 **Accepted** 426 **Matriculated** 142 **Average SAT M/V** 520/540 **Average ACT** 25

COLLEGE LIFE **Gender Breakdown** M 40%, F 60% **Out of State Students** 80% **From Public Schools** 62% **Ethnic
Composition** White & Other 85%, Asian American 1%, Black 9%, Hispanic 4%, Native American 1% **Foreign
Students** 1% **Reside on Campus** 95% **Return as Sophomores** 66% **Total Faculty** 61 **Student Faculty Ratio** 9:1
Fraternities none **Sororities** none

University of Arizona

www.arizona.edu

Tucson, AZ · Est. 1885 · Coed · Public· 22,143 Undergrads · Urban

I need...

Admissions info appinfo@arizona.edu
  w3.arizona.edu/admissions
Financial aid info w3.arizona.edu/~finaid
  /finaid.html

How wired is University of Arizona?

Do I get email? Yes
Do I get a home page? Yes
  Where? ns.arizona.edu
Is my dorm wired? Yes
What is the student to computer ratio? 13:1

The usual tour

DEPARTMENTS www.arizona.edu/academic
  /catalog/catalog.html
SPORTS w3.arizona.edu/~athletic/wildcat
STUDENT CLUBS www.asua.arizona.edu/uaclubs
  /clublist/main.html
GREEK LIFE www.asua.arizona.edu/UAclubs
  /clublist/greek.html
PUBLICATIONS www.arizona.edu/newhome/news
  .shtml
STUDENT NEWSPAPER wildcat.arizona.edu
  /~wildcat
LIBRARY dizzy.library.arizona.edu

Skip the brochure

• **OFF CAMPUS CATS HOME PAGE** Arizona has lots of
  wide open spaces, and if you feel lost out
  there, fear not. Off-campus students from

Arizona's Wildcats: slamming and jamming their way to a better future

near and far bond over activities like bowling,
movies, and hiking (not just back to one's
apartment, but the great outdoors).
w3.arizona.edu/~occ

• **STUDENTS FOR THE EXPLORATION AND DEVELOPMENT
OF SPACE, UNIVERSITY OF ARIZONA CHAPTER**
Contrary to popular belief, this organization
does not exist to promote larger dormitory
rooms. Rather, its apparent purpose is to educate the space-fearing, development-loathing
masses. Most students are involved because
of a love of the cause, but "[you] can also use
SEDS as a stepping stone to a space-related
career." **seds.lpl.arizona.edu**

• **CAMP WILDCAT** Students at the University of
Arizona give kids in need the gift of games by
providing a variety of fun activities for Tucson
youth who are financially, mentally, or physical-
ly disadvantaged. **bigdog.engr.arizona.edu/~ieee/cw**

WHAT YOU NEED TO GET IN **Application Deadline** November 1 for priority consideration; final deadline April 1 **Common App.** No **Application Fee** $35 (non-residents only) **Tuition Costs** $1,940 ($8,308 out-of-state) **Room & Board** $4,190 **Need Blind** Yes **Financial Forms Deadline** Priority given to applications received by March 1 **Undergrads Awarded Aid** 65% **Average Award of Freshman Scholarship Package** $2,248 **Tests Required** SAT1 or ACT **Admissions Address** Tucson, AZ 85721-0007 **Admissions Telephone** (520) 621-3237

LAST YEAR'S CLASS **Applied** 16,366 **Accepted** 13,512 **Matriculated** 4,557 **Average SAT M/V** 552/550 **Average ACT** 23 **In Top Fifth of High School Graduating Class** 50%

COLLEGE LIFE **Gender Breakdown** M 49%, F 51% **Out of State Students** 36% **From Public Schools** 90% **Ethnic Composition** White & Other 76%, Asian American 5%, Black 3%, Hispanic 14%, Native American 2% **Foreign Students** 3% **Reside on Campus** 18% **Return as Sophomores** 78% **Total Faculty** 1592 **Student Faculty Ratio** 20:1 **Fraternities (% of men participating)** 25 (15%) **Sororities (% of women participating)** 20 (15%) **Graduate Students** 8,624

University of Arkansas, Fayetteville

www.uark.edu

Fayetteville, AR · Est. 1871 · Coed · Public · 11,937 Undergrads · Big Town

How wired is Fayetteville?

Do I get email? Yes
Do I get a home page? Yes
Where? www.uark.edu/campus/People
/home pages/index.html
Is my dorm wired? Yes
What is the student to computer ratio? 60:1

DOWNLOAD APPLICATION ONLINE

The usual tour

SPORTS www.uark.edu/campus/athletics
LIBRARY www.uark.edu/campus-resources
/libinfo
STUDENT CLUBS www.uark.edu/campus/Student
/studorgs.html
STUDENT NEWSPAPER www.uark.edu/campus
-resources/travinfo
CALENDAR www.uark.edu/calendars/calendar
CAREER CENTER www.uark.edu/campus-resources
/careinfo

Skip the brochure

• **SENIOR WALK** It's an über-alumni directory of
sorts: a walkway which contains the names of

Arkansas percussionists: They got the beat

every Fayetteville graduate, from the first graduating class in 1876 to the present.
pigtrail.uark.edu/info/srwalk

• **UNIVERSITY OF ARKANSAS PERCUSSION WEB PAGE** No
need to worry about moving to the beat of a
different drummer when you're in the company
of these percussionists. Their page includes a
clock that beats perfect Arkansas time.
cavern.uark.edu/~uapercus

• **UNIVERSITY OF ARKANSAS MUSEUM** A museum for
all ages, with exhibits as classic as Ancient
Peruvian Art and Culture and as innovative as
Colorful Kite Tails. A community quilt project
and family workshops make the museum a
Fayetteville favorite. **www.uark.edu/~museinfo**

WHAT YOU NEED TO GET IN **Application Deadline** March 1 for priority consideration; final deadline August 15 **Common App.** No **Application Fee** $15 **Tuition Costs** $2,184 ($5,746 out-of-state) **Room & Board** $1,890 **Need Blind** Yes **Financial Forms Deadline** Priority given to applications received by April 1 **Undergrads Awarded Aid** 56% **Aid That Is Need-Based** 60% **Average Award of Freshman Scholarship Package** $2,368 **Tests Required** SAT1 or ACT **Admissions Address** 200 Silas H. Hunt Hall, Fayetteville, AR 72701 **Admissions Telephone** (501) 575-5346

LAST YEAR'S CLASS **Applied** 4,578 **Accepted** 3,952 **Matriculated** 2,373 **Average ACT** 23

COLLEGE LIFE **Gender Breakdown** M 53%, F 47% **Out of State Students** 13% **From Public Schools** 83% **Ethnic Composition** White & Other 88.5%, Asian American 2.5%, Black 6%, Hispanic 1%, Native American 2% **Foreign Students** 4% **Reside on Campus** 20% **Return as Sophomores** 74% **Total Faculty** 884 **Student Faculty Ratio** 18:1 **Fraternities (% of men participating)** 15 (14%) **Sororities (% of women participating)** 12 (19%) **Graduate Students** 2,355

Assumption College

Worcester, MA · Est. 1904 · Coed · Private · 1,663 Undergrads · Urban

I need...

Admissions info www.assumption.edu/HTML
/Admissions/admiss.html
Financial aid info www.assumption.edu/HTML
/Admissions/admiss.html

How wired is Assumption College?

Do I get email? Yes
Do I get a home page? Yes
   Where? students.assumption.edu
Is my dorm wired? Yes
What is the student to computer ratio? 8:1

The usual tour

DEPARTMENTS www.assumption.edu/HTML
/Academic/deptindex.html
SPORTS www.assumption.edu/HTML/Athletics
/Plourde/home page.html
CALENDAR www.assumption.edu/HTML/Welcome
/college.html
LIBRARY www.assumption.edu/HTML/Library
/libraryindex.html
PUBLICATIONS www.assumption.edu/HTML
/Assumptionists/AssumptionNet.html
CAREER CENTER www.assumption.edu/HTML/SDC
/career.html

Skip the brochure

• **ABOUT THE ASSUMPTIONISTS** Don't assume you
know it all until you've read this discussion of
the venerable Emmanuel d'Alzon and his fol-

We'll make an Assumption that the venerable Emmanuel d'Alzon was not the wildest guy at parties

lowers. The Assumptionists were founded in
1850 and found their way to the United States
by 1895. It is that same tradition which
shapes Assumption College today.
**www.assumption.edu/HTML/Assumptionists
/AssumptionNet.html**

• **DEMETRIUS KANTARELIS** Kantarelis, of the
Department of Economics and Foreign Affairs
collects economist jokes for his students, for
the ghost of Adam Smith, and for you. Here's
one: "Q: What do economists and computers
have in common? A: You have to punch information into both of them." It's so funny you'll
forget to recalculate the prime rate.
**www.assumption.edu/HTML/Faculty/Kantar
/DKANTARI.html**

WHAT YOU NEED TO GET IN **Application Deadline** March 1 **Early Action Deadline** November 1 **Common App.** No
Application Fee $30 **Tuition Costs** $13,700 **Room & Board** $5,980 **Need Blind** Yes **Financial Forms Deadline**
Priority given to applications received by February 1 **Undergrads Awarded Aid** 65% **Aid That Is Need-Based** 100%
Average Award of Freshman Scholarship Package $4,500 **Tests Required** SAT1 or ACT **Admissions
Address** 500 Salisbury Street, Worcester, MA 01615-0005 **Admissions Telephone** (508) 767-7285

LAST YEAR'S CLASS **Applied** 2,200 **Accepted** 1,600 **Matriculated** 453 **Median Range SAT M/V** 450-520/440-510
In Top Fifth of High School Graduating Class 25% **Applied Early** 32 **Accepted Early** 15

COLLEGE LIFE **Gender Breakdown** M 40%, F 60% **Out of State Students** 40% **From Public Schools** 60% **Ethnic
Composition** White & Other 93%, Asian American 3%, Black 1%, Hispanic 3% **Foreign Students** 5% **Reside on
Campus** 85% **Return as Sophomores** 83% **Student Faculty Ratio** 16:1 **Fraternities** none **Sororities** none
Graduate Students 349

Auburn University

mallard.duc.auburn.edu

Auburn University, AL · Est. 1856 · Coed · Public· 18,999 Undergrads · Big Town

I need...

Admissions info fletcjt@mail.auburn.edu
www.auburn.edu/administration/iss
/admissio/admisreq.html
Financial aid info www.auburn.edu
/administration/iss/finaid/sfa1.html

How wired is Auburn University?

Do I get email? Yes
What is the student to computer ratio? 63:1

The usual tour

LIBRARY ralph.lib.auburn.edu
SPORTS www.auburn.edu/athletics/index.html
STUDENT NEWSPAPER www.auburn.edu/~plainsm
DEPARTMENTS www.auburn.edu/academic
/liberal_arts/au_liberal_arts.html
GREEK LIFE www.auburn.edu/student_info/greeks
/au_greeks.html
STUDENT CLUBS www.auburn.edu/student_info
/au_student_orgs.html

Skip the brochure

- **AUBURN FOOTBALL** The Auburn football team is nationally recognized as a perennial front-runner. Illustrious former Tigers include multi-sport superstar Bo Jackson, now felled by injury. Find everything you want to know from last year's stats to the Auburn record books. **www.auburn.edu/athletics/fball/index.html**

- **AUBURN BASEBALL** Auburn baseball has a storied

It's about that time . . .

Subtle eye contact disrupts yet another seemingly innocuous study session

past as well with a handful of players making it to the "show." Frank (The Big Hurt) Thomas, now of the White Sox, is a former Tiger. **www.auburn.edu/athletics/base/index.html**

- **AUBURN'S SPACE POWER INSTITUTE** It's not all fun and games at Auburn. Visit the Diamond Thin Film Lab where a professor is a pioneer in the synthetic diamond construction. Check out the hypervelocity impact facility where particles can be fired at up to 28,000 mph. MPEGs of the collision can be downloaded. **hyperoptic.spi.auburn.edu/index.html**

- **AUBURN UNIVERSITY BAND'S HOME PAGE** Not just one band, but three: marching band, concert band, and basketball pep band. Hear them, see them, join them! **www.auburn.edu/~lauband**

WHAT YOU NEED TO GET IN **Application Deadline** September 1 **Common App.** No **Application Fee** $25 **Tuition Costs** $2,250 ($6,750 out-of-state) **Room & Board** $4,098 **Need Blind** Yes **Financial Forms Deadline** Priority given to applications received by April 17 **Undergrads Awarded Aid** 34% **Average Award of Freshman Scholarship Package** $2,250 **Tests Required** SAT1 or ACT **Admissions Address** Auburn University, AL 36849 **Admissions Telephone** (334) 844-4080

LAST YEAR'S CLASS **Applied** 9,326 **Accepted** 8,281 **Matriculated** 3,592 **Average SAT M/V** 568/498 **Average ACT** 24 **In Top Quarter of High School Graduating Class** 54%

COLLEGE LIFE **Gender Breakdown** M 53%, F 47% **Out of State Students** 41% **From Public Schools** 82% **Ethnic Composition** White & Other 91.3%, Asian American 1.2%, Black 6.2%, Hispanic 0.8%, Native American 0.5% **Reside on Campus** 17% **Return as Sophomores** 80% **Total Faculty** 1,244 **Student Faculty Ratio** 16:1 **Fraternities (% of men participating)** 27 (16%) **Sororities (% of women participating)** 18 (29%) **Graduate Students** 3,123

Austin College

Sherman, TX · Est. 1849 · Coed · Private · 1,057 Undergrads · Big Town

I need...

Admissions info admission@austinc.edu
www.austinc.edu/Admissions/index.html
Financial aid info jtrammell@austinc.edu
www.austinc.edu/Admissions/index.html

How wired is Austin College?

Do I get email? Yes
Do I get a home page? Yes
  Where? www.austinc.edu/Campus_Life/home
  _pages/index.html
What is the student to computer ratio? 10:1

The usual tour

LIBRARY www.austinc.edu/Abell/index.html
DEPARTMENTS www.austinc.edu/Academics
/index.html
CALENDAR www.austinc.edu/Welcome/calendar
.html
STUDENT CLUBS www.austinc.edu/Campus_Life
/activities/organizations/index.html
GREEK LIFE www.austinc.edu/Campus_Life
/activities/organizations/index.html

Skip the brochure

• **JANUARY TERM** Escape the winter doldrums by
taking on a single subject for the January
term. Courses for January term are held both
on and off campus, and include internships
and international research projects. **www.austinc
.edu/Academics/CollegeWide/JanTerm/index.html**

Just what do Admissions and kangaroos have in common?

• **RESIDENCE HALLS** Home is where your heart is...
but what'll it really be like once you're out of
Mom and Dad's nest? Details are the name of
the game at this treatise of sorts on the residence halls. **www.austinc.edu/Campus_Life
/residence/index.html**

• **ACTIVITIES AND ORGANIZATIONS** "Studies have
shown that students who are involved actually
do better in school and are more likely to per-
sist to graduation." Independent research also
notes that citing ill-conceived studies can be
fatuous and a wee bit annoying. Get involved,
if you like. **www.austinc.edu/Campus_Life/activities
/index.html#involved**

WHAT YOU NEED TO GET IN **Application Deadline** December 1 for priority consideration; final deadline February 1 **Early Action Deadline** December 1 **Common App.** Yes **Application Fee** $25 **Tuition Costs** $12,675 **Room & Board** $4,975 **Need Blind** Yes **Financial Forms Deadline** Priority given to applications received by April 1 **Undergrads Awarded Aid** 89% **Aid That Is Need-Based** 49% **Average Award of Freshman Scholarship Package** $6,416 **Tests Required** SAT1 or ACT **Admissions Address** 900 North Grand Avenue, Sherman, TX 75090-4440 **Admissions Telephone** (903) 813-3000

LAST YEAR'S CLASS **Applied** 1,153 **Accepted** 914 **Matriculated** 293 **Average SAT M/V** 584/588 **In Top Fifth of High School Graduating Class** 67%

COLLEGE LIFE **Gender Breakdown** M 47%, F 53% **Out of State Students** 9% **From Public Schools** 92% **Ethnic Composition** White & Other 79%, Asian American 7%, Black 3%, Hispanic 10%, Native American 1% **Foreign Students** 2% **Reside on Campus** 76% **Return as Sophomores** 80% **Total Faculty** 100 **Student Faculty Ratio** 13:1 **Fraternities (% of men participating)** 10 (26%) **Sororities (% of women participating)** 6 (24%) **Graduate Students** 26

Babson College

www.babson.edu

Babson Park, MA · Est. 1919 · Coed · Private · 1,725 Undergrads · Big Town

How wired is Babson College?

Do I get email? Yes
Do I get a home page? No
Is my dorm wired? Yes
What is the student to computer ratio? 7:1

The usual tour

DEPARTMENTS www.babson.edu/ugrad/ucah
/catcibd.html
VIRTUAL TOUR www.babson.edu/campus
GREEK LIFE www.babson.edu/ugrad/osa
/sog.html
CAREER CENTER www.babson.edu/ocs
CALENDAR www.babson.edu/events
LIBRARY www.babson.edu/navigator/index.html

Skip the brochure

• **BABSON PLAYERS** Babson students are acting up both on stage and behind the scenes in crowd-pleasing numbers like *Guys and Dolls* and *Lend Me A Tenor*. **www.babson.edu/student-groups/bplayers**

• **THE BABSON FREE PRESS** Find out what's really important to the Babson community—a new multi-million dollar grant, dorm vandalism,

Bucolic Babson basks in the forests and lakes of Massachusetts

meal plan changes, or special campus events.
info.babson.edu/student-groups/freepress

• **BABSON COLLEGE FACULTY** You know, those people standing at the front of the classroom didn't just spring up overnight—they have stories of their own. Check out the pedigree of the faculty in these profiles. **www.babson.edu/faculty/index.html**

• **CENTER FOR ENTREPRENEURIAL STUDIES** The Center for Entrepreneurial Studies is a base camp at Babson for the study of enterprising and creative individuals and businesses. **www.babson.edu/entrep**

"Act up in crowd-pleasers like *Guys and Dolls*."

WHAT YOU NEED TO GET IN Application Deadline February 1 **Early Action Deadline** November 15 **Common App.** Yes **Application Fee** $50 ($75 for international applicants) **Tuition Costs** $17,430 **Room & Board** $7,275 **Need Blind** Yes **Financial Forms Deadline** Priority given to applications received by February 15 **Undergrads Awarded Aid** 49% **Aid That Is Need-Based** 94% **Average Award of Freshman Scholarship Package** $9,800 **Tests Required** SAT1 or ACT **Admissions Address** Babson Park, MA 02157-0310 **Admissions Telephone** (617) 239-5522

LAST YEAR'S CLASS Applied 2,349 **Accepted** 1,067 **Matriculated** 399 **In Top Fifth of High School Graduating Class** 25% **Applied Early** 74 **Accepted Early** 49

COLLEGE LIFE Gender Breakdown M 63%, F 37% **Out of State Students** 62% **From Public Schools** 58% **Ethnic Composition** White & Other 85%, Asian American 7%, Black 3%, Hispanic 5% **Foreign Students** 21% **Reside on Campus** 78% **Return as Sophomores** 86% **Total Faculty** 173 **Student Faculty Ratio** 11:1 **Fraternities (% of men participating)** 4 (10%) **Sororities (% of women participating)** 2 (8%) **Graduate Students** 1,653

Ball State University

Muncie, IN · Est. 1918 · Coed · Private · 16,961 Undergrads · Big Town

I need...

Admissions info askus@wp.bsu.edu
www.bsu.edu/UP/htmls/02edu02.html
Financial aid info jmcphers@bsu.edu
www.bsu.edu/finaid/home.html

How wired is Ball State University?

Do I get email? Yes
Do I get a home page? Yes
Is my dorm wired? Yes
What is the student to computer ratio? 6:1

The usual tour

DEPARTMENTS www.bsu.edu/UP/htmls/02edu01
.html
CAREER CENTER www.bsu.edu/careers/home.html
LIBRARY www.library.bsu.edu
STUDENT NEWSPAPER www.dailynews.bsu.edu
STUDENT CLUBS www.bsu.edu/UP/htmls/02ap02
.html
SPORTS www.bsu.edu/UP/htmls/01sc.html

Skip the brochure

- **CONNECTIONS TV SHOW** Ball State students take to the airwaves to tell the tale of East Central Indiana on local cable channels. BSU students do all the work here, from field reporting to editing and producing. **www.teleplex.bsu.edu /connect**

- **STUDENT GOVERNMENT ASSOCIATION HOMEPAGE** If you're looking for a student organization that

Study hard at Ball State and maybe you can get a job hosting *The Late Show*

takes itself seriously, look no further. When not voting, debating, legislating, or mediating, the Student Government Association can be found explaining the whole process on its rather extensive home page. **bsuvc.bsu.edu /~d001sga/index.html**

- **SPORTS CORNER** A few years ago Ball State's most famous alum, David Letterman, was downright gushy when the men's basketball team made it to the NCAA basketball tournament. Read all about the Ball State cagers and their sporting siblings. **www.bsu.edu/UP/htmls/01sc.html**

"Ball State's most famous alum is David Letterman."

WHAT YOU NEED TO GET IN **Application Deadline** Rolling admissions; March 1 for priority consideration **Common App.** No **Application Fee** $25 **Tuition Costs** $3,188 ($8,448 out-of-state) **Room & Board** $3,952 **Need Blind** Yes **Financial Forms Deadline** Priority given to applications received by March 1 **Undergrads Awarded Aid** 70% **Aid That Is Need-Based** 40% **Average Award of Freshman Scholarship Package** $3,500 **Tests Required** SAT1 or ACT **Admissions Address** 2000 West University Avenue, Muncie, IN 47306 **Admissions Telephone** (317) 285-8300

LAST YEAR'S CLASS **Applied** 8539 **Accepted** 7560 **Matriculated** 3848 **Average SAT M/V** 497/496 **Average ACT** 21 **In Top Fifth of High School Graduating Class** 24%

COLLEGE LIFE **Gender Breakdown** M 47%, F 53% **Out of State Students** 9% **Ethnic Composition** White & Other 93%, Asian American 1%, Black 4.5%, Hispanic 1%, Native American 0.5% **Foreign Students** 1% **Reside on Campus** 30% **Return as Sophomores** 70% **Student Faculty Ratio** 17:1 **Fraternities (% of men participating)** 18 (13%) **Sororities (% of women participating)** 18 (12%) **Graduate Students** 2,154

Bard College

www.bard.edu

Annandale-on-Hudson, NY · Est. 1860 · Coed · Private · 1,072 Undergrads · Small Town

I need...

Admissions info admission@bard.edu
www.bard.edu/info/adm/adm.htm
Financial aid info g.kelly@bard.edu
www.bard.edu/info/adm/aid.htm

How wired is Bard College?

Do I get email? Yes
What is the student to computer ratio? 9:1

The usual tour

CALENDAR www.bard.edu/events
LIBRARY www.bard.edu/library/index.html
DEPARTMENTS www.bard.edu/resource/division
/index.htm
PUBLICATIONS www.bard.edu/refs/pubs/index
.htm
HISTORY www.bard.edu/info/history.htm
COMPUTER SERVICES www.bard.edu/hcrc/index.htm

Skip the brochure

• **INSTITUTE FOR WRITING AND THINKING** Aspiring
Bards might be interested to know that their
instructors can be students of writing, too.
Bard's Institute for Writing and Thinking provides intensive study in the teaching of writing.
Since its beginnings in 1982, the Institute has
serviced about 30,000 teachers. **wolfpack.bard
.edu/institute/index.htm**

• **THE DISTINGUISHED SCIENTIST LECTURE SERIES** What
has had over eighty-eight participants,

Location: http://www.bard.edu/info/history.htm

Bard, pride of Annandale-on-Hudson, not Stratford-on-Avon,
whose pride is *the* Bard, William Shakespeare

including fourty-four Nobel Laureates? Where
can you go to hear about anti-matter or the
chemistry of sexual selection in insects? It's
all happening at the Distinguished Scientist
Lecture Series since 1979. **www.bard.edu/events
/dss/index.htm**

• **JOURNAL OF THE HISTORY OF SEXUALITY** Still just a
catalog. Let's hope they post such articles as
"Holy Harlots: Prostitute Saints in Medieval
Legend" and "Mother Nature versus the
Amazons: Marina Tsetaeva and Female Same-
Sex Love." **www.bard.edu/refs/pubs/jhs/contvl.htm**

"Where you go to hear about anti-matter"

WHAT YOU NEED TO GET IN **Application Deadline** December 1 for priority consideration; final deadline January 31 **Early
Action Deadline** December 1 **Common App.** Yes **Application Fee** $40 **Tuition Costs** $20,864 **Room & Board**
$6,520 **Need Blind** Yes **Financial Forms Deadline** Priority given to applications received by February 15
Undergrads Awarded Aid 70% **Aid That Is Need-Based** 90% **Average Award of Freshman Scholarship Package**
$13,600 **Tests Required** N/A **Admissions Address** P.O. Box 5000, Annandale-on-Hudson, NY 12504-5000
Admissions Telephone (914) 758-7472

LAST YEAR'S CLASS **Applied** 1,903 **Accepted** 1,014 **Matriculated** 296 **Median Range SAT M/V** 550-680/540-670
In Top Fifth of High School Graduating Class 73% **Applied Early** 308 **Accepted Early** 224

COLLEGE LIFE **Gender Breakdown** M 48%, F 52% **Out of State Students** 74% **From Public Schools** 60% **Ethnic
Composition** White & Other 84%, Asian American 3%, Black 7%, Hispanic 5%, Native American 1% **Foreign
Students** 14% **Reside on Campus** 85% **Return as Sophomores** 91% **Total Faculty** 150 **Student Faculty Ratio**
10:1 **Fraternities** none **Sororities** none **Graduate Students** 177

Barnard College

www.barnard.columbia.edu

New York, NY · Est. 1889 · Women · Private · 2,276 Undergrads · Urban

I need...

Admissions info
admissions@barnard.columbia.edu
www.barnard.columbia.edu/Barnard
/Admission.html

How wired is Barnard College?

Do I get email? Yes
What is the student to computer ratio? 19:1

The usual tour

LIBRARY www.cc.columbia.edu/~met7
STUDY ABROAD www.barnard.columbia.edu
/#degree
STUDENT CLUBS www.barnard.columbia.edu
/#extra
VIRTUAL TOUR www.barnard.columbia.edu
/Barnard/CampusTour/tour.html
SPORTS www.barnard.columbia.edu/#degree

Skip the brochure

• **COLUMBIA UNIVERSITY** Does cyberspace imitate life? Barnard's Web site would be empty but for the rich resources at the Columbia site. In real life, the all-women Barnard enjoys the benefits of an association with Columbia that allows its students to take Columbia classes, play Columbia sports, and more. If you're interested in Barnard, you should be interested in Columbia too. Check out the excellent sites within the Columbia domain, starting with Go Ask Alice... **www.columbia.edu**

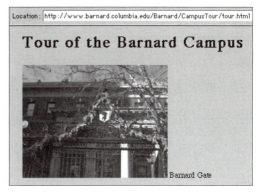

Location: http://www.barnard.columbia.edu/Barnard/CampusTour/tour.html

Tour of the Barnard Campus

Barnard Gate

Barnard's gate, the first line of defense in the big bad city

• **COMMUNITY IMPACT** That Barnard and Columbia are located in Harlem, an economically and socially stressed area, makes a difference. Although the campuses are lovely, and meet the standards of the Ivy League, the surrounding areas are less idyllic. See what students are doing to create an atmosphere of mutual respect in the area. **www.columbia.edu/cu/ci**

"See what students are doing to create an atmosphere of mutual respect in the area."

WHAT YOU NEED TO GET IN **Application Deadline** January 15 **Early Action Deadline** November 15 (Plan I) and January 2 (Plan II) **Common App.** Yes **Application Fee** $45 **Tuition Costs** $19,576 **Room & Board** $8,374 **Need Blind** Yes **Financial Forms Deadline** February 1 **Undergrads Awarded Aid** 60% **Aid That Is Need-Based** 100% **Average Award of Freshman Scholarship Package** $16,300 **Tests Required** SAT1 or ACT **Admissions Address** 3009 Broadway, New York, NY 10027-6598 **Admissions Telephone** (212) 854-2014

LAST YEAR'S CLASS **Applied** 2,973 **Accepted** 1,335 **Matriculated** 531 **Average SAT M/V** 640/600 **In Top Fifth of High School Graduating Class** 89% **Applied Early** 144 **Accepted Early** 85

COLLEGE LIFE **Out of State Students** 62% **From Public Schools** 61% **Ethnic Composition** White & Other 65%, Asian American 25%, Black 4%, Hispanic 5%, Native American 1% **Foreign Students** 4% **Reside on Campus** 90% **Return as Sophomores** 95% **Total Faculty** 284 **Student Faculty Ratio** 12:1 **Sororities** none

Bates College

Lewiston, ME · Est. 1855 · Coed · Private · 1,636 Undergrads · Small Town

I need...

Admissions info admissions@bates.edu
abacus.bates.edu/admissions
Financial aid info finaid@bates.edu
abacus.bates.edu/admissions/FinAidBook

How wired is Bates College?

Do I get email? Yes
Do I get a home page? Yes
Where? abacus.bates.edu/people/folks
Is my dorm wired? Yes
What is the student to computer ratio? 6:1

The usual tour

VIRTUAL TOUR www.bates.edu/CollegeRelations
/Tour
STUDENT CLUBS www.bates.edu/people/orgs
/org-list.html
LIBRARY www.bates.edu/Library
CALENDAR www.bates.edu/CollegeRelations
/calendar
SPORTS abacus.bates.edu/admin/offices/ath
DEPARTMENTS abacus.bates.edu/acad
STUDENT NEWSPAPER abacus.bates.edu/people
/studpubs/BatesStudent

Skip the brochure

- **BATES ART SOCIETY** With a nude modeling session "open to the artist community," who needs anything more? Nevertheless, the BAS also sponsors exhibits of student art each semester. A new offshoot organization, the

Green, clean, and with a crack Ultimate team, Bates also offers nude modeling sessions

Bates Artist Community Connection, links Bates artists with the local community. **www.bates.edu/~amoore/bas.html**

- **BATES AVIATORS HANGAR ON THE WEB** Take off with the high-flyers of Bates. The group is open to "anyone who has an interest in things moving through the air without ground contact." **www.bates.edu/~tmunoz/aviators/aviators.html**

- **BATES COLLEGE ULTIMATE FRISBEE TEAM** The only complaint that can be leveled at these team players is that with a Web page this good, they can't be devoting too much time to their classwork. Team and tournament info is available, as is the lore behind the team's name change from "Crack Babies" to "Discoboles." (Check out the illustrations.) **www.bates.edu/~csantill/disc.html**

WHAT YOU NEED TO GET IN Application Deadline January 15 **Common App.** yes **Application Fee** $50 **Tuition Costs, Room & Board** $27,415 **Need Blind** yes **Financial Forms Deadline** February 10 **Undergrads Awarded Aid** 49% **Aid That Is Need-Based** 100% **Average Award of Freshman Scholarship Package** $12,078 **Tests Required** SAT1 or ACT **Admissions Address** 23 Campus Avenue, Lewiston, 04240 ME **Admissions Telephone** (207) 786-6000

LAST YEAR'S CLASS Applied 3,550 **Accepted** 1,287 **Matriculated** 450 **Average SAT M/V** 650/660 **In Top Fifth of High School Graduating Class** 85%

COLLEGE LIFE Gender Breakdown M 49%, F 51% **Out of State Students** 89% **From Public Schools** 65% **Ethnic Composition** White & Other 92%, Asian American 4%, Black 2%, Hispanic 2% **Foreign Students** 3% **Reside on Campus** 93% **Return as Sophomores** 96% **Total Faculty** 175 **Student Faculty Ratio** 11:1 **Fraternities** none **Sororities** none

Baylor University

www.baylor.edu

Waco, TX · Est. 1845 · Coed · Private · 10,323 Undergrads · Urban

I need...

Admissions info office@baylor.edu
www.baylor.edu/baylor/Departments/admin
/admissions/Welcome_under_adm.html

How wired is Baylor University?

Do I get email? Yes
Do I get a home page? Yes
Is my dorm wired? Yes
What is the student to computer ratio? 13:1

FULL APPLICATION ONLINE

The usual tour

DEPARTMENTS www.baylor.edu/acad/arts
_sciences.html
LIBRARY diogenes.baylor.edu/Library/welcome
.html
GREEK LIFE www.baylor.edu/departments
/Student_Activities/greek.html
STUDENT CLUBS www.baylor.edu/baylor/Student
Org/student_orgs.htm
CALENDAR gopher://gopher.baylor.edu:70/11
/calendar
SPORTS www.baylor.edu/departments/Athletics
STUDENT NEWSPAPER www.baylor.edu/student
_orgs/Lariat

Skip the brochure

• **THE SPIRIT SQUADS** Dying to run around like an idiot in complete anonymity? Like dressing up in someone else's outfit? Sign up to be a Baylor mascot. **www.baylor.edu/departments/Student _Activities/spirit.html#mic**

Location: http://www.baylor.edu/images/bonfire.gif

At the end of each term, Baylor students pass judgment on the school's furnishings

• **MU KAPPA** Where everybody knows your name... Children of missionaries, you've found your home away from home. Missionary kids and other students with multicultural/international backgrounds get together for cultural adjustment, spiritual encouragement, and, of course, the staple of all club gatherings, food. **www.baylor.edu/baylor/StudentOrg/mukappa/mk.html**

• **FACULTY AND STAFF PAGES** Know your teachers. It's worth more than an extended visit. From an art history professor talking about traveling with Paddington Bear, to the wisest of online philosophers, faculty and staff reveal what really makes them tick. **www.baylor.edu/people /emphomes.html**

WHAT YOU NEED TO GET IN **Application Deadline** Rolling admissions; October 1 for priority consideration **Common App.** No **Application Fee** $25 **Tuition Costs** $8,070 **Room & Board** $4,254 **Need Blind** Yes **Financial Forms Deadline** Priority given to applications received by March 1 **Undergrads Awarded Aid** 70% **Aid That Is Need-Based** 60% **Average Award of Freshman Scholarship Package** $3,993 **Tests Required** SAT1 or ACT **Admissions Address** Waco, TX 76798 **Admissions Telephone** (817) 755-1811

LAST YEAR'S CLASS **Matriculated** 2,339 **Median Range SAT M/V** 510-640/440-560 **In Top Quarter of High School Graduating Class** 63%

COLLEGE LIFE **Gender Breakdown** M 44%, F 56% **Out of State Students** 23% **Ethnic Composition** White & Other 80.1%, Asian American 6.4%, Black 4.7%, Hispanic 8.3%, Native American 0.5% **Foreign Students** 4% **Reside on Campus** 26% **Return as Sophomores** 83% **Total Faculty** 674 **Student Faculty Ratio** 18:1 **Fraternities (% of men participating)** 17 (20%) **Sororities (% of women participating)** 13 (25%) **Graduate Students** 1,879

Beloit College

www.beloit.edu

Beloit, WI · Est. 1846 · Coed · Private · 1,249 Undergrads · Big Town

FULL APPLICATION ONLINE

How wired is Beloit College?

Do I get email? Yes
Do I get a home page? Yes
   Where? www.beloit.edu/home/people
Is my dorm wired? Yes
What is the student to computer ratio? 11:1

The usual tour

LIBRARY www.beloit.edu/~libhome
DEPARTMENTS www.beloit.edu/~academic/major
.html
CALENDAR www.beloit.edu/~newspub/eventcal
.html
VIRTUAL TOUR www.beloit.edu/~admiss2
/mentour.html

Skip the brochure

- **THE ROUND TABLE** Beloit's weekly paper is currently shrouded in mystery, thanks to a Spinal Tap-esque black-on-black text design. Luckily the links are highlighted, so you can still reach the latest online op-eds, entertainment, news, and local sports. Be sure to check out their parody issue, *The Hate Monger*. **www.beloit .edu/~rndtable**

Location: http://www.beloit.edu/~newspub/campctr.html

Campus Center

Italianate architecture a stone's throw from Canada

- **FAMOUS BELOITERS** A real-life Indiana Jones and an Olympic team captain are just two of the many who have brought fame and honor to the Beloit name. Look for your bio here too in the future. **www.beloit.edu/~newspub/famous.html**

- **SIGNIFICANT BUILDINGS** Some of these buildings earn their significance by being part of the Near East Side Historic District. Others because they very old. Others still are just cool on their own. **www.beloit.edu/~newspub /build.html**

"One alum is a real-life Indiana Jones."

WHAT YOU NEED TO GET IN Application Deadline Rolling admissions **Early Action Deadline** December 1 **Common App.** Yes **Application Fee** $25 **Tuition Costs** $18,030 **Room & Board** $3,980 **Financial Forms Deadline** Priority given to applications received by April 1 **Undergrads Awarded Aid** 86% **Aid That Is Need-Based** 98% **Average Award of Freshman Scholarship Package** $10,050 **Tests Required** SAT1 or ACT **Admissions Address** 700 College Street, Beloit, WI 53511 **Admissions Telephone** (608) 363-2500

LAST YEAR'S CLASS Applied 1,435 **Accepted** 1,045 **Matriculated** 299 **Average SAT M/V** 583/556 **Average ACT** 26 **In Top Fifth of High School Graduating Class** 48% **Applied Early** 44 **Accepted Early** 32

COLLEGE LIFE Gender Breakdown M 42%, F 58% **Out of State Students** 77% **From Public Schools** 80% **Ethnic Composition** White & Other 91%, Asian American 2%, Black 4%, Hispanic 2%, Native American 1% **Foreign Students** 11% **Reside on Campus** 94% **Return as Sophomores** 92% **Total Faculty** 128 **Student Faculty Ratio** 11:1 **Fraternities (% of men participating)** 4 (10%) **Sororities (% of women participating)** 2 (5%) **Graduate Students** 10

Benedictine College

Atchison, KS · Est. 1858 · Coed · Private · 858 Undergrads · Small Town

I need...

Admissions info mail@benedictine.edu
www.benedictine.edu/bcadview.html
Financial aid info mail@benedictine.edu
www.benedictine.edu/bcadfinaid.html

How wired is Benedictine College?

Do I get email? Yes
Do I get a home page? Yes
Where? www.benedictine.edu/bcdirhomes.html
Is my dorm wired? No
What is the student to computer ratio? 12:1

The usual tour

DEPARTMENTS www.benedictine.edu/bcacad
progs.html
CALENDAR www.benedictine.edu/raven5218.html
STUDENT NEWSPAPER www.benedictine.edu/circuit
/circuit.html
LIBRARY www.benedictine.edu/bcacadlib1.html

Skip the brochure

• **STUDENTS IN FREE ENTERPRISE** Benedictine students play with money in the S.I.F.E. project, designed to develop entrepreneurial drive and create Donald Trump clones (minus the

"Designed to develop Donald Trump clones"

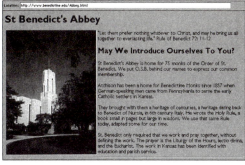

St Benedict's Abbey

"Let them prefer nothing whatever to Christ, and may he bring us all together to everlasting life." Rule of Benedict 72: 11-12

May We Introduce Ourselves To You?

St Benedict's Abbey is home for 75 monks of the Order of St. Benedict. We put O.S.B. behind our names to express our common membership.

Atchison has been a home for Benedictine Monks since 1857 when German-speaking men came from Pennsylvania to serve the early Catholic settlers in Kansas.

They brought with them a heritage of centuries, a heritage dating back to Benedict of Nursia, in 6th century Italy. He wrote the Holy Rule, a book small in pages but large in wisdom. We use that same Rule today, adapted some for our time.

St. Benedict only required that we work and pray together, without defining the work. The prayer is the Liturgy of the Hours, lectio divina, and the Eucharist. The work in Kansas has been identified with education and parish service.

Be sure to catch up on the holy rules of sixth-century Italy

tabloid headlines). **www.benedictine.edu/stu/sife/homepg.html**

• **EDUCATION CLUB** This club for education majors and minors seeks to assist students in the field of education with career preparation by means of educational programs. Ongoing projects include collecting funds to buy books for local children and participating in reading projects in local elementary schools. **www.benedictine.edu/edclub/edclub.html**

• **BENEDICTINE VOLUNTEER PROGRAM** For several months of the year the Benedictine Volunteer Program provides for men and women, in conjunction with the Benedictine Sisters in Atchison, the opportunity to provide general support, tutoring, personal care and hospitality services to the people of northeast Kansas and northwest Missouri. **www.benedictine.edu/volunteer.html**

WHAT YOU NEED TO GET IN Application Deadline March 1 for priority consideration; final deadline August 1 **Common App.** No **Application Fee** $25 **Tuition Costs** $10,020 **Room & Board** $3,990 **Need Blind** Yes **Financial Forms Deadline** July 15 with a priority given to applications received by March 1 **Undergrads Awarded Aid** 96% **Aid That Is Need-Based** 26% **Average Award of Freshman Scholarship Package** $5,350 **Tests Required** SAT or ACT (preferred) **Admissions Address** 1020 North Second Street, Atchison, KS 66002 **Admissions Telephone** (913) 367-5340

LAST YEAR'S CLASS Applied 725 **Accepted** 625 **Matriculated** 256 **Average SAT M/V** 474/442 **Average ACT** 22 **In Top Fifth of High School Graduating Class** 42%

COLLEGE LIFE Gender Breakdown M 51%, F 49% **Out of State Students** 66% **From Public Schools** 49% **Ethnic Composition** White & Other 89%, Asian American 3%, Black 3%, Hispanic 4%, Native American 1% **Foreign Students** 3% **Reside on Campus** 68% **Return as Sophomores** 84% **Total Faculty** 90 **Student Faculty Ratio** 9:1 **Fraternities** none **Sororities** none **Graduate Students** 9

Bennington College

Bennington, VT · Est. 1932 · Coed · Private · 285 Undergrads · Small Town

www.bennington.edu

How wired is Bennington College?

What is the student to computer ratio? 7:1

Skip the brochure

• **BENNINGTON USDAN GALLERY** This art gallery with works by current students includes some excellent sculpture and digital art, and promises to continue to offer superior work. It'd better be good, though—it's the only thing that is up and running at Bennington's site (not

"The Art Gallery had better be good, though—it's the only thing up and running at Bennington's site."

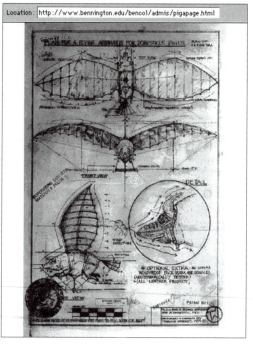

Location: http://www.bennington.edu/bencol/admis/pigapage.html

Leonardo's little-known sketches for the animatronic star of *Babe—The Sequel*

counting the amazingly obtuse "If pigs could fly" admissions section). Go figure. The school with the notoriously expensive tuition is outclassed online by hundreds of other schools. www.bennington.edu/bencol/gallery/usdan/mfal996/intro.html

---

WHAT YOU NEED TO GET IN **Application Deadline** February 1 **Early Action Deadline** December 1 **Common App.** Yes **Application Fee** $45 **Tuition Costs, Room & Board** $25,800 **Need Blind** Yes **Financial Forms Deadline** March 1 with a priority given to applications received by February 1 **Undergrads Awarded Aid** 84% **Aid That Is Need-Based** 91% **Average Award of Freshman Scholarship Package** $17,400 **Tests Required** SAT1 or ACT **Admissions Address** Bennington, VT 05201 **Admissions Telephone** (800) 833-5401

LAST YEAR'S CLASS **Applied** 367 **Accepted** 241 **Matriculated** 78 **Average SAT M/V** 579/553 **Average ACT** 27 **In Top Fifth of High School Graduating Class** 47% **Applied Early** 7 **Accepted Early** 3

COLLEGE LIFE **Gender Breakdown** M 35%, F 65% **Out of State Students** 94% **From Public Schools** 63% **Ethnic Composition** White & Other 94%, Asian American 1%, Black 1%, Hispanic 4% **Foreign Students** 10% **Reside on Campus** 98% **Return as Sophomores** 85% **Total Faculty** 83 **Student Faculty Ratio** 9:1 **Fraternities** none **Sororities** none **Graduate Students** 102

Birmingham-Southern College

Birmingham, AL · Est. 1856 · Coed · Private · 1,501 Undergrads · Urban

www.bsc.edu

I need...

Admissions info www.bsc.edu/cgi-bin/counter
.pl/homelink/admiss.htm
Financial aid info www.bsc.edu/cgi-
bin/counter.pl/catalog/fin_aid.htm

How wired is Birmingham-Southern College?

Do I get email? Yes
Do I get a home page? Yes
  Where? panther.bsc.edu/~netscape
  /personal.html
Is my dorm wired? Yes
What is the student to computer ratio? 114

The usual tour

CALENDAR www.bsc.edu/cgi-bin/counter.pl
  /calendar/comevnt.htm
GREEK LIFE www.bsc.edu/cgi-bin/counter.pl
  /catalog/socia.htm
LIBRARY www.bsc.edu/cgi-bin/counter.pl/library
  /library.htm
VIRTUAL TOUR www.bsc.edu/cgi-bin/counter.pl
  /MAP-TEXT/GERIMAP.HTM

Skip the brochure

• **BSC STUDENT LINK** It's the electronic link to all
  the news and announcements a BSC student
  needs to know. **www.bsc.edu/stdntpub/sl.htm**

Wake up and smell the java at BSC's coffeehouse

• **THE CELLAR COFFEEHOUSE** In the early days, the
coffeehouse existed. Then it didn't, but old
yearbooks attested to its former life. Now the
Cellar Coffeehouse has been reincarnated, as
an actual late-night java joint with its own
entertainment, desserts, and Web page.
www.bsc.edu/cgi-bin/counter.pl/bsc_life/cellar/cellar.htm

• **CENTER FOR LEADERSHIP STUDIES** Learn how to be
a leader, or just look like one. The center
offers a Distinction in Leadership Studies program, a multi-disciplinary course of study
which combines a self-created community project. The center also sponsors a variety of
leadership-related presentations and events
throughout the year. **www.bsc.edu/programs
/cls/leadhome.htm**

WHAT YOU NEED TO GET IN Application Deadline January 5 for priority consideration; final deadline March 1 **Common
App.** Yes **Application Fee** $25 **Tuition Costs** $12,360 **Room & Board** $4,100 **Need Blind** Yes **Financial Forms
Deadline** Priority given to applications received by March 1 **Undergrads Awarded Aid** 84% **Aid That Is Need-
Based** 45% **Average Award of Freshman Scholarship Package** $1,500 **Tests Required** SAT1 or ACT **Admissions
Address** Arkadelphia Road, Birmingham, AL 35254 **Admissions Telephone** (205) 226-4686

LAST YEAR'S CLASS Applied 684 **Accepted** 581 **Matriculated** 247 **Average SAT M/V** 635/605 **Average ACT** 26
In Top Fifth of High School Graduating Class 68%

COLLEGE LIFE Gender Breakdown M 45%, F 55% **Out of State Students** 27% **From Public Schools** 71% **Ethnic
Composition** White & Other 84.5%, Asian American .5%, Black 14%, Hispanic 1% **Foreign Students** 3% **Reside
on Campus** 82% **Return as Sophomores** 91% **Total Faculty** 103 **Student Faculty Ratio** 12:1 **Fraternities (% of
men participating)** 6 (62%) **Sororities (% of women participating)** 7 (70%) **Graduate Students** 82

Boston College

www.bc.edu

Chestnut Hill, MA · Est. 1863 · Coed · Private · 8,896 Undergrads · Big Town

I need...

Admissions info admission@bcvms.bc.edu
infoeagle.bc.edu/bc_org/avp/enmgt/view
book/applying.html
Financial aid info infoeagle.bc.edu/bc_org/avp
/enmgt/viewbook/expenses.html

How wired is Boston College?

Do I get email? Yes
Do I get a home page? Yes
  Where? www.bc.edu/cgi-bin/print_hit_bold
  .pl/bc_org/avp/csom/CS/Students/students
  .html?student+home+page#first_hit
Is my dorm wired? Yes
What is the student to computer ratio? 44:1

The usual tour

DEPARTMENTS infoeagle.bc.edu/cwis/deptdir
/deptdir.html
CALENDAR www.bc.edu/bc_org/svp/odsd/ee.html
LIBRARY www.bc.edu/bc_org/avp/ulib/bclib.html
PUBLICATIONS www.bc.edu/cwis/pub.html

Skip the brochure

- **BC SAILING TEAM** Full of hot air? BC's sailing team has a home here where it posts past results and the team newsletter, and links to the world's tidal charts. **www.bc.edu/bc_org/ath /sail**

- **THE OBSERVER** A school newspaper with an unsurprising conservative bent and an

In Boston, the traditions of the church accompany those of the educators

occasional dose of humor. **www.bc.edu/bc_org /svp/st_org/obsrv**

- **BOSTON COLLEGE ELECTRONIC VIEWBOOK** BC's Electronic Viewbook lets students stroll through sections on financial aid, student life, and off-campus activities. **www.bc.edu/bc_org/avp /enmgt/viewbook/viewbook.html**

- **BOSTON COLLEGE MUSEUM OF ART** BC's small but well-endowed museum has works from six-teenth-century Italy as well as contemporary American art, although you're not likely to see the work of Warhol, Johns, or Stella here. In addition to the permanent collection, there is an admirable catalog of recent and future exhibits. **www.bc.edu/bc_org/avp/cas/artmuseum**

WHAT YOU NEED TO GET IN Application Deadline January 1 (first part) and January 15 (second part) **Early Action Deadline** October 15 (1st part) and November 1 (2nd part) **Common App.** No **Application Fee** $50 **Tuition Costs** $18,820 **Room & Board** $7,530 **Financial Forms Deadline** Priority given to applications received by February 1 **Undergrads Awarded Aid** 49% **Aid That Is Need-Based** 89% **Average Award of Freshman Scholarship Package** $11,449 **Tests Required** SAT1 or ACT **Admissions Address** 140 Commonwealth Avenue, Chestnut Hill, MA 02167 **Admissions Telephone** (617) 552-3100

LAST YEAR'S CLASS Applied 16,680 **Accepted** 6,399 **Matriculated** 2,140 **Median Range SAT M/V** 610-700/ 520-620 **Applied Early** 3,327 **Accepted Early** 1,246

COLLEGE LIFE Gender Breakdown M 47%, F 53% **Out of State Students** 75% **From Public Schools** 58% **Ethnic Composition** White & Other 83%, Asian American 8%, Black 4%, Hispanic 5% **Foreign Students** 4% **Reside on Campus** 69% **Return as Sophomores** 94% **Student Faculty Ratio** 15:1 **Fraternities** none **Sororities** none **Graduate Students** 4,559

Boston University

Boston, MA · Est. 1839 · Coed · Private · 15,097 Undergrads · Urban

I need...

Admissions info admissions@bu.edu
web.bu.edu/ADMISSIONS

How wired is Boston University?

Do I get email? Yes
Do I get a home page? No
What is the student to computer ratio? 30:1

The usual tour

DEPARTMENTS web.bu.edu/#Schools
CALENDAR web.bu.edu/Events.html
DINING SERVICES web.bu.edu/DINING
CHAPLAIN web.bu.edu/CHAPEL

Skip the brochure

• **LOCI WEB LAUNCH** Given the school's rather bland Web presence, the College of Communication is a surprising hotbed of creativity and just plain fun. In 1995, eight of its students were in large part responsible for the launch of one of the more popular online hangouts. Sponsored by Barnes and Noble, it was a combination of commentary and chat called Loci. Read the story, then see the site. It's also definitely worth following the links back to the College of Communication's home page, which features other current multimedia projects. **web.bu.edu/COM/html/loci.html**

• **CHEERLEADING** BU's cheerleaders are a happy, happy crew. You can see and hear them here

Location: http://web.bu.edu/COM/html/bucheer/cheer.html

Get on top with BU's high-spirited cheerleading squad

as well as pick up the latest flips, formations, and cheers. **web.bu.edu/COM/html/bucheer/cheer.html**

• **BOSTON UNIVERSITY STUDENT UNION** Answers to the pressing questions of what the SU is, what it does, and what it's done for its students lately. **web.bu.edu/UNION/main.html**

• **CENTER FOR REMOTE SENSING** Were there really a million men at the Million Man March? Individuals from the CRS were brought in to estimate the number of participants based on scanned color prints of the crowd. They couldn't come up with a hard number but they did spot Elvis—and Waldo, too. **crs-www.bu.edu**

"They did spot Elvis— and Waldo, too."

WHAT YOU NEED TO GET IN Application Deadline January 15 for priority consideration **Early Action Deadline** November 1 **Common App.** Yes **Application Fee** $50 **Tuition Costs** $20,570 **Room & Board** $7,050 **Need Blind** Yes **Financial Forms Deadline** Priority given to applications received by February 15 **Undergrads Awarded Aid** 59% **Aid That Is Need-Based** 77% **Average Award of Freshman Scholarship Package** $12,795 **Tests Required** SAT1 or ACT **Admissions Address** 121 Bay State Road, Boston, MA 02215 **Admissions Telephone** (617) 353-2300

LAST YEAR'S CLASS Applied 23,617 **Accepted** 14,929 **Matriculated** 4,348 **Average SAT M/V** 616/619 **Average ACT** 26 **In Top Fifth of High School Graduating Class** 71% **Applied Early** 409 **Accepted Early** 256

COLLEGE LIFE Gender Breakdown M 44%, F 56% **Out of State Students** 78% **From Public Schools** 71% **Ethnic Composition** White & Other 75%, Asian American 15%, Black 4%, Hispanic 6% **Foreign Students** 12% **Reside on Campus** 60% **Return as Sophomores** 84% **Student Faculty Ratio** 13:1 **Fraternities (% of men participating)** 5 (5%) **Sororities (% of women participating)** 9 (7%) **Graduate Students** 10,532

Bowdoin College

Brunswick, ME · Est. 1794 · Coed · Private · 1,530 Undergrads · Small Town

I need...

Admissions info admissions-lit@polar.bowdoin.edu
www.bowdoin.edu/cwis/admissi/admissi
.html

Financial aid info www.bowdoin.edu/cwis
/admissi/fin_aid.html

How wired is Bowdoin?

Do I get email? Yes

Do I get a home page? Yes

  Where? www.bowdoin.edu/cwis/stud/disclm
.html

What is the student to computer ratio? 17:1

The usual tour

DEPARTMENTS www.bowdoin.edu/cwis/acad/dept
/index.html

STUDENT CLUBS www.bowdoin.edu/cwis/stud
/orgs/index.html

CALENDAR www.bowdoin.edu/cwis/events/cal
/index.html

VIRTUAL TOUR www.bowdoin.edu/cwis/admissi
/tour/index.html

SPORTS www.bowdoin.edu/cwis/events/sports
/index.html

LIBRARY www.bowdoin.edu/cwis/info/lib.html

Skip the brochure

• **BOWDOIN ALUMS** Bowdoin has an impressive roster of graduates including U.S. president Franklin Pierce; classmates Nathaniel Hawthorne and Henry Wadsworth Longfellow;

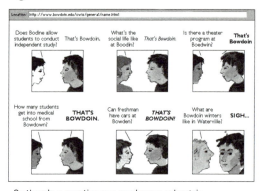

So there's a question you need never ask again

and more recently Alfred C. Kinsey, who conducted the famous contemporary study of human sexuality. **www.bowdoin.edu/cwis/general/almnae.html**

• **WHAT'S IN A NAME?** This site might make you think twice about looking at Bowdoin. One of the dopier pages around, it mocks all those poor uneducated souls who can't pronounce the name of the school. **www.bowdoin.edu/cwis/general/name.html**

• **HISTORICAL SKETCH OF BOWDOIN COLLEGE** Over 200 years of history doth a fairly extensive historical sketch make. Don't say we didn't warn you. **www.bowdoin.edu/cwis/general/histske.html**

"Grads include Hawthorne, Longfellow, and Kinsey."

WHAT YOU NEED TO GET IN Application Deadline January 15 Early Action Deadline November 15 **Common App.** Yes **Application Fee** $50 **Tuition Costs** $21,410 **Room & Board** $6,010 **Need Blind** Yes **Financial Forms Deadline** March 1 with a priority given to applications received by December 1 **Undergrads Awarded Aid** 43% **Aid That Is Need-Based** 100% **Average Award of Freshman Scholarship Package** $14,260 **Tests Required** N/A **Admissions Address** Brunswick, ME 04011 **Admissions Telephone** (207) 725-3100

LAST YEAR'S CLASS Applied 4,122 **Accepted** 1,255 **Matriculated** 449 **Average SAT M/V** 680/610 **In Top Fifth of High School Graduating Class** 91% **Applied Early** 533 **Accepted Early** 184

COLLEGE LIFE Gender Breakdown M 49%, F 51% **Out of State Students** 86% **From Public Schools** 51% **Ethnic Composition** White & Other 86%, Asian American 8%, Black 2%, Hispanic 3%, Native American 1% **Foreign Students** 3% **Reside on Campus** 80% **Return as Sophomores** 94% **Total Faculty** 156 **Student Faculty Ratio** 11:1 **Coed Fraternities (% of students participating)** 8 (28%)

Brandeis University

www.brandeis.edu

Waltham, MA · Est. 1948 · Coed · Private · 2,929 Undergrads · Urban

How wired is Brandeis?

Do I get email? Yes
Do I get a home page? Yes
Where? www.brandeis.edu
/fair/studentpages.html
Is my dorm wired? Yes
What is the student to computer ratio? 29:1

REQUEST APPLICATION ONLINE

The usual tour

CALENDAR www.brandeis.edu/news/reporter
/calendar.html
DEPARTMENTS www.brandeis.edu/departments
/depart2.html
LIBRARY louis.brandeis.edu
VIRTUAL TOUR www.brandeis.edu/tour/a
.start.html
STUDENT NEWSPAPER www.brandeis.edu/news
/reporter/reportertoc.html
CAREER CENTER www.brandeis.edu/hiatt/hiatt
_home.html

Skip the brochure

• **WALTHAM GROUP** The good guys of the Brandeis community, these students participate in a

The cool, clinical lines of the Brandeis campus library

volunteer community service organization in the Waltham, Mass. area. Programs include big/little sibling pairings, blood drives, and soup kitchens. **www.brandeis.edu/campuslife
/waltham.html**

• **WBRS-WALTHAM 100.1 FM** Not just free on-air music, but free live music is also on the agenda for the university's very own radio station. **www.wbrs.org**

• **STUDENT WRITINGS** Hear what some Brandeis students have to say in this sparse collection of student writing. **www.brandeis.edu/news
/writings.html**

• **THE BRANDEIS REPORTER** The student newspaper delivers the expected assortment of news, features, and pics. **www.brandeis.edu/news/reporter
/reportertoc.html**

WHAT YOU NEED TO GET IN **Application Deadline** February 1 **Early Action Deadline** January 1 **Common App.** Yes **Application Fee** $50 **Tuition Costs** $21,440 **Room & Board** $7,080 **Financial Forms Deadline** February 15 **Undergrads Awarded Aid** 50% **Aid That Is Need-Based** 85% **Tests Required** SAT1 (preferred) or ACT **Admissions Address** South Street, P.O. Box 9110, Waltham, MA 02254-9110 **Admissions Telephone** (617) 736-3500

LAST YEAR'S CLASS **Applied** 4,539 **Accepted** 2,998 **Matriculated** 876 **Average SAT M/V** 640/660 **In Top Fifth of High School Graduating Class** 78% **Applied Early** 178 **Accepted Early** 127

COLLEGE LIFE **Gender Breakdown** M 45%, F 55% **Out of State Students** 75% **From Public Schools** 75% **Ethnic Composition** White & Other 86%, Asian American 8%, Black 3%, Hispanic 3% **Foreign Students** 5% **Reside on Campus** 90% **Return as Sophomores** 90% **Student Faculty Ratio** 10:1 **Fraternities** none **Sororities** none

Brigham Young University

www.byu.edu

Provo, UT · Est. 1875 · Coed · Private · 27,507 Undergrads · Urban

I need...

Admissions info admissions@byu.edu
adm5.byu.edu/ar/dept_admission/admiss
_home.html

Financial aid info financial@byu.edu
adm5.byu.edu/ar/dept_financial/financ
_home.html

How wired is BYU?

DOWNLOAD APPLICATION ONLINE

Do I get email? Yes
Do I get a home page? Yes
Is my dorm wired? Yes
What is the student to computer ratio? 18:1

The usual tour

CALENDAR advance.byu.edu/pc/calendars.html
VIRTUAL TOUR visitor.byu.edu/tour/begin.html
LIBRARY www.lib.byu.edu
SPORTS www.byu.edu/univ-services/sports.html

Skip the brochure

- **BYU PROMOTIONAL SPOTS** Watch BYU advertisements from your terminal. These promotional spots highlight some particularly noteworthy and charismatic members of the BYU faculty. **advance.byu.edu/pc/promos.html**

- **KBYU** Not just call letters, but a way of life. Well, almost—KBYU encompasses both radio and TV, and this site gives programming information as well as related features and sports. **kbyuwww.byu.edu**

Academy Square, the original home of Brigham Young University

- **SWIMMING AND DIVING HOMEPAGE** There's some pretty serious stroking going on for the BYU swimmers and divers. Here they publicize their stats and look forward to the coming season of challenges. **acsl.byu.edu/~crumps/byuswm.htm**

- **MUSEUM OF ART** Whatever the current exhibit, there's sure to be a visual and aural feast at the MOA home page in which exhibit pieces are sometimes accompanied by audio clips. **www.byu.edu/tmcbucs/moa/moahome.html**

"Serious stroking for the BYU swimmers"

WHAT YOU NEED TO GET IN **Application Deadline** February 15 **Common App.** No **Application Fee** $25 **Tuition Costs, Room & Board** $4,600 **Financial Forms Deadline** Priority given to applications received by April 15 **Undergrads Awarded Aid** 74% **Tests Required** ACT **Admissions Address** Provo, UT 84602 **Admissions Telephone** (801) 378-2500

LAST YEAR'S CLASS **Applied** 6,988 **Accepted** 5,317 **Matriculated** 4,404 **Average ACT** 27 **In Top Tenth of High School Graduating Class** 55%

COLLEGE LIFE **Gender Breakdown** M 49%, F 51% **Out of State Students** 75% **Ethnic Composition** White & Other 94%, Asian American 3%, Black 0.4%, Hispanic 2%, Native American 0.6% **Foreign Students** 5% **Reside on Campus** 23% **Return as Sophomores** 80% **Total Faculty** 1339 **Student Faculty Ratio** 24:1 **Fraternities** none **Sororities** none **Graduate Students** 2,906

Brown University

Providence, RI · Est. 1764 · Coed · Private · 5,942 Undergrads · Urban

I need...

Admissions info admission_undergraduate
@brown.edu
www.brown.edu/webmaster/tadmission.html
Financial aid info www.brown.edu/Finance
/Financial_Aid

How wired is Brown?

Do I get email? Yes
Do I get a home page? Yes
Where? netspace.students.brown.edu/users.html
Is my dorm wired? Yes
What is the student to computer ratio? 19:1

The usual tour

STUDENT CLUBS www.brown.edu/webmaster
/students.html#sorgs
DEPARTMENTS www.brown.edu/webmaster
/acunits.html
LIBRARY www.brown.edu/Facilities/University
_Library
SPORTS www.brown.edu/Athletics
VIRTUAL TOUR www.brown.edu/Administration
/Photos/photos.html
GREEK LIFE www.brown.edu/Student_Services
/Greek_Council

Skip the brochure

- **DAVID WINTON BELL GALLERY** The Bell gallery ranks as one of the better college art spaces in the country. An online catalog traces the

Peaceful from above, Brown at ground level echoes with heated debate

history of the gallery and its impressive exhibitions. **www.brown.edu/Facilities/David_Winton_Bell
_Gallery/Bell.html**

- **BROWN DAILY HERALD** The school's daily is a great place to acquaint yourself with Brown's ever-raging issues. It includes a searchable archive, dating back to early 1995. **www.netspace.org/herald**

- **BROWN ALUMNI MONTHLY** See the role that Brown graduates and professors have assumed in the world. **www.brown.edu/Administration/Brown
_Alumni_Monthly**

"Acquaint yourself with Brown's ever-raging issues."

WHAT YOU NEED TO GET IN **Application Deadline** January 1 **Early Action Deadline** November 1 **Common App.** No **Application Fee** $55 **Tuition Costs** $21,592 **Room & Board** $6,538 **Need Blind** No **Financial Forms Deadline** January 22 **Undergrads Awarded Aid** 41% **Aid That Is Need-Based** 100% **Average Award of Freshman Scholarship Package** $13,337 **Tests Required** SAT1 (preferred) or ACT **Admissions Address** 45 Prospect Street, Box 1876, Providence, RI 02912 **Admissions Telephone** (401) 863-2378

LAST YEAR'S CLASS **Applied** 13,904 **Accepted** 2,952 **Matriculated** 1,418 **Average SAT M/V** 680/680 **Average ACT** 29 **In Top Quarter of High School Graduating Class** 97% **Applied Early** 2,225 **Accepted Early** 518

COLLEGE LIFE **Gender Breakdown** M 47%, F 53% **Out of State Students** 96% **From Public Schools** 60% **Ethnic Composition** White & Other 73%, Asian American 15%, Black 6%, Hispanic 5%, Native American 1% **Foreign Students** 7% **Reside on Campus** 89% **Return as Sophomores** 97% **Total Faculty** 61 **Student Faculty Ratio** 8:1 **Fraternities (% of men participating)** 10 (10%) **Sororities (% of women participating)** 2 (2%) **Graduate Students** 1,699

Bryn Mawr College

Bryn Mawr, PA · Est. 1885 · Women · Private · 1,143 Undergrads · Suburban

I need...

Admissions info admissions@brynmawr.edu
www.brynmawr.edu/Adm/admissions.html

How wired is Bryn Mawr?

Do I get email? Yes
Do I get a home page? Yes
Is my dorm wired? Yes
What is the student to computer ratio? 8:1

The usual tour

LIBRARY www.brynmawr.edu/library
VIRTUAL TOUR www.brynmawr.edu/Adm/pictures
.html
STUDENT CLUBS www.brynmawr.edu/Adm
/studorgs.html
DEPARTMENTS www.brynmawr.edu/Adm/majors
.html
SPORTS www.brynmawr.edu/Athletics/sports
.html

Skip the brochure

• **SERENDIP** Its mission sounds rather confusing,
given that neurobiologists, computer scientists, educators, and businessmen and women
take part. It's not. Serendip is simply a gathering spot for all to read up on and weigh in on
philosophic matters, particularly as they per-
tain to students. **serendip.brynmawr.edu**

• **BLACKCAT EATS!** Looking for non-traditional (i.e
non-dorm) eating? Searching for that special

In the interconnectedness of all things, let Serendip guide
your journey

place to take Mom and Dad (or have Mom and
Dad take you) over Parents' Weekend? Here's
a collection of restaurant reviews by students
for area establishments. The reviews are generally scanty, but at least the large photos of
the restaurants guarantee you'll know the
place when you see it. **blackcat.brynmawr.edu
/Restaurants**

• **TRICOCHAT!** "Talk" to students at Bryn Mawr,
Haverford, or Swarthmore with this tri-college
Web chat page. The screen refreshes itself
every 25 seconds so you can read the latest
messages. **www.adamar.com/cgi-bin/suid/~adamar
/chat.html**

WHAT YOU NEED TO GET IN **Application Deadline** January 15 **Early Action Deadline** November 15 for fall; January 1 for
winter **Common App.** Yes **Application Fee** $40 (may be waived in cases of economic hardship) **Tuition Costs**
$20,210 **Room & Board** $7,370 **Need Blind** Yes **Financial Forms Deadline** January 15 **Undergrads Awarded Aid**
52% **Aid That Is Need-Based** 100% **Average Award of Freshman Scholarship Package** $13,582 **Tests Required**
SAT1 (preferred) or ACT **Admissions Address** 101 North Merion Avenue, Bryn Mawr, PA 19010-2899 **Admissions
Telephone** (610) 526-5152

LAST YEAR'S CLASS **Applied** 1,719 **Accepted** 997 **Matriculated** 344 **Average SAT M/V** 640/610 **In Top Fifth of High
School Graduating Class** 87% **Applied Early** 157 **Accepted Early** 93

COLLEGE LIFE **Out of State Students** 86% **From Public Schools** 73% **Ethnic Composition** White & Other 73.4%,
Asian American 18%, Black 4.6%, Hispanic 4%, **Foreign Students** 8% **Reside on Campus** 92% **Return as
Sophomores** 94% **Total Faculty** 120 **Student Faculty Ratio** 9:1 **Sororities** none **Graduate Students** 641

Bucknell University

www.bucknell.edu

Lewisburg, PA · Est. 1846 · Coed · Private · 3,413 Undergrads · Small Town

I need...

Admissions info www.bucknell.edu/departments
/admissions/bucknell

How wired is Bucknell?

Do I get email? Yes
Do I get a home page? Yes
   Where? www.bucknell.edu/directory
What is the student to computer ratio? 9:1

DOWNLOAD APPLICATION ONLINE

The usual tour

VIRTUAL TOUR www.bucknell.edu/departments
/admissions/bucknell/tour/tour.html
DEPARTMENTS www.bucknell.edu/Departments
.html
PUBLICATIONS www.bucknell.edu/Publications
.html
STUDENT CLUBS www.bucknell.edu/StudOrg.html
GREEK LIFE www.bucknell.edu/studorg/greek
.html
CALENDAR www.bucknell.edu/cgi-bin/calendars

Skip the brochure

- **TEACHERS** As Bucknell crows about its faculty,
read the fine print to learn about Theatre and
Economy, an interdisciplinary course offering.
**www.bucknell.edu/departments/admissions/bucknell
/teachers.html**

- **DISTINGUISHED ALUMNI** What do Bucknell grads
do all day? These brief profiles show you
where you can go with a Bucknell education:

Lacrosse is one of 14 men's and 12 women's sports at Bucknell. Bucknell plays in NCAA Division I, except football, which is Division IAA, and is a member of the Patriot League with Army, Colgate, Holy Cross, Lehigh, Lafayette, and Navy.

The nearby **Susquehanna River** is a familiar view to members of Bucknell's women's and men's crew teams. The crew teams compete at regattas throughout the nation, and last year the Bucknell men's team won its first national championship and went on to compete in England's prestigious Henley Royal Regatta.

There is no need to become a slacker with the sports offered at Bucknell

become an executive for the NFL, or help
found a new school. **www.bucknell.edu/departments
/admissions/bucknell/alumni.html**

- **THE BUCKNELLIAN** The weekly newspaper offers
articles like "The War over Denim" and opinion
pieces that offer nuggets of insight such as "if
I learned anything here during my four years, it
is that life is really, really short" (especially if
you get caught wearing those pleated, acid-
washed jeans again). **www.bucknell.edu/Bucknellian**

"What do Bucknell grads do all day?"

WHAT YOU NEED TO GET IN **Application Deadline** January 1 **Early Action Deadline** December 1 **Common App.** Yes **Application Fee** $45 **Tuition Costs** $20,230 **Room & Board** $5,075 **Need Blind** No **Financial Forms Deadline** January 15 **Undergrads Awarded Aid** 60% **Aid That Is Need-Based** 100% **Average Award of Freshman Scholarship Package** $11,079 **Tests Required** SAT1 (preferred) or ACT **Admissions Address** Lewisburg, PA 17837 **Admissions Telephone** (717) 524-1101

LAST YEAR'S CLASS **Applied** 6,597 **Accepted** 3,641 **Matriculated** 910 **Median Range SAT M/V** 600-670/510-590 **In Top Fifth of High School Graduating Class** 56% **Applied Early** 413 **Accepted Early** 284

COLLEGE LIFE **Gender Breakdown** M 51%, F 49% **Out of State Students** 73% **From Public Schools** 74% **Ethnic Composition** White & Other 92%, Asian American 3%, Black 3%, Hispanic 2% **Foreign Students** 2% **Reside on Campus** 85% **Return as Sophomores** 94% **Total Faculty** 253 **Student Faculty Ratio** 13:1 **Fraternities (% of men participating)** 12 (47%) **Sororities (% of women participating)** 8 (52%) **Graduate Students** 216

California Institute of Technology

www.caltech.edu

Pasadena, CA · Est. 1891 · Coed · Private · 923 Undergrads · Urban

I need...

Admissions info ugadmissions@caltech.edu
   www.cco.caltech.edu/~ugadm
Financial aid info www.cco.caltech.edu/~citaid

How wired is Caltech?

Do I get email? Yes
Do I get a home page? Yes
   Where? www.ugcs.caltech.edu/beings.html
Is my dorm wired? Yes
What is the student to computer ratio? 2:1

The usual tour

VIRTUAL TOUR www.caltech.edu/~development
   /virt_visit/virtual_visit.html
CALENDAR www.caltech.edu/~development
   /cals_events/cals_events.html
PUBLICATIONS www.caltech.edu/~development
   /news_room/ES_ToC.html
LIBRARY www.caltech.edu/~libraries

Skip the brochure

• **CALTECH CLICKABLE MAP** Click on the map and get a picture of the building. If you just want to get a sense of the campus, this is better and a lot less complicated than the Virtual Visit. **www.caltech.edu/map**

• **CALTECH JAM ROOM** Caltech folks with a few chords and a dream can sign up to practice in

Location: http://www.caltech.edu/pictures/OliveWalk.gif

Unwind along the Olive Walk at Caltech

this room, home to many a local band. And get this—the equipment, including instruments like guitars and drums, is already there! **www.cco.caltech.edu/~jamroom**

• **CALTECH WINDSURFING AND SURFING CLUB** This is California, where even technogeeks know how to surf. Follow a link to the Coastal Marine Forecast for the latest on how they're breaking. **www.cco.caltech.edu/~surfer/surfing.html**

• **FUN AND GAMES AT CALTECH** The students at Caltech don't hang out on the main server. Instead, they're here, along with links to some of the cooler things they've created. **www.ugcs.caltech.edu/fun.html**

WHAT YOU NEED TO GET IN **Application Deadline** January 1 **Early Action Deadline** November 1 **Common App.** No **Application Fee** $40 **Tuition Costs** $18,000 **Room & Board** $5,478 **Need Blind** Yes **Financial Forms Deadline** Priority given to applications received by January 15 **Undergrads Awarded Aid** 69% **Aid That Is Need-Based** 95% **Average Award of Freshman Scholarship Package** $12,532 **Tests Required** SAT1 **Admissions Address** 1201 East California Boulevard, Pasadena, CA 91125 **Admissions Telephone** (818) 395-6341

LAST YEAR'S CLASS **Applied** 1,895 **Accepted** 512 **Matriculated** 218 **Average SAT M/V** 754/651 **In Top Fifth of High School Graduating Class** 81% **Applied Early** 232 **Accepted Early** 85

COLLEGE LIFE **Gender Breakdown** M 75%, F 25% **Out of State Students** 60% **From Public Schools** 79% **Ethnic Composition** White & Other 65.4%, Asian American 29%, Black 0.5%, Hispanic 5%, Native American 0.1% **Foreign Students** 8% **Reside on Campus** 90% **Return as Sophomores** 98% **Total Faculty** 356 **Student Faculty Ratio** 3:1 **Fraternities** none **Sororities** none **Graduate Students** 1,050

California State University, Fresno

www.csufresno.edu

Fresno, CA · Est. 1911 · Coed · Public · 14,461 Undergrads · Urban

How wired is Cal. State Fresno?

Do I get email? Yes
Do I get a home page? Yes
Is my dorm wired? No
What is the student to computer ratio? 24:1

The usual tour

STUDENT NEWSPAPER www.csufresno.edu/CSUF
/CampusPapers.html
LIBRARY duchess.lib.csufresno.edu
PUBLIC INFORMATION/ CALENDAR www.csufresno
.edu/pubinfo/Default.html
HISTORY www.csufresno.edu/avpaa/welcome.html
DEPARTMENTS www.csufresno.edu/CSUF/CSUF
WebSchools.html
FACT SHEET www.csufresno.edu/CSUF/CSUF
Facts.html

Skip the brochure

• **SCIENCE CAREERS OPPORTUNITY PROGRAM** SCOP's
admirable goal is to help steer minorities and
the underprivileged into science and health
careers. They offer not only recruitment but

**MAN/WOMEN
AND THE NATURAL ENVIRONMENT**

Fresno allows students to roam the great outdoors for
credit on the MNE Program

extensive support while the student is in
school. **www.csufresno.edu/SCOP**

• **CENTRAL VALLEY ONLINE** Find out where to play,
eat, shop, and stay while you're visiting or
attending Fresno State. This site is sorted by
topics like arts, business, and parks and
recreation. **www.fresno.com**

• **MAN/WOMAN AND THE NATURAL ENVIRONMENT** If you
were a big fan of field trips, you might be interested in Fresno's 22-year-old MNE program. It's
a one-semester, 21-credit program during which
students spend 40 days in the field. Topics
include biology, geology, and anthropology, and
study takes place in some of California's most
scenic locations. **www.csufresno.edu/avpaa/mne.html**

WHAT YOU NEED TO GET IN **Application Deadline** Rolling admissions; November for priority consideration **Common App.**
No **Application Fee** $55 **Tuition Costs** $7,705 **Room & Board** $4,517 **Financial Forms Deadline** Priority given to
applications received by March 2 **Undergrads Awarded Aid** 38% **Tests Required** SAT1 or ACT **Admissions
Address** 5241 North Maple, Fresno, CA 93740-0057 **Admissions Telephone** (209) 278-6283

LAST YEAR'S CLASS **Applied** 5,244 **Accepted** 3,740 **Matriculated** 1,616 **Average SAT M/V** 472/450 **Average ACT**
19 **In Top Fifth of High School Graduating Class** 39%

COLLEGE LIFE **Gender Breakdown** M 47%, F 53% **Out of State Students** 23% **From Public Schools** 99% **Ethnic
Composition** White & Other 49.1%, Asian American 12.6%, Black 6.7%, Hispanic 30.1%, Native American 1.5%
Foreign Students 4% **Reside on Campus** 6% **Return as Sophomores** 80% **Total Faculty** 654 **Student Faculty
Ratio** 18:1 **Fraternities (% of men participating)** 18 (5%) **Sororities (% of women participating)** 15 (5%)
Graduate Students 2,999

California State University, Hayward

www.csuhayward.edu

Hayward, CA · Est. 1957 · Coed · Public · 9,778 Undergrads · Urban

I need...

Admissions info www.csuhayward.edu/ecat /general/admission.html

How wired is Cal. State Hayward?

Do I get email? Yes

Do I get a home page? Yes

Where? cave.csuhayward.edu/CAVE/HOME /Home.html

What is the student to computer ratio? 65:1

The usual tour

VIRTUAL TOUR imctwo.csuhayward.edu/VR/csuh _vr.html

LIBRARY imctwo.csuhayward.edu/library/www lib.htm

PUBLICATIONS cave.csuhayward.edu

DEPARTMENTS www.csuhayward.edu/acaprogs /academic.html

ON-LINE CATALOG www.csuhayward.edu/ecat /index.html

SPORTS edschool.csuhayward.edu/Departments /KPE/athletics.html

Skip the brochure

• **OCCAM'S RAZOR** Read selections from CSUH's literary journal, which contains contributions from students and alumni. Both poetry and short stories are printed, some with charming titles as

Hayward's home page: students at work and at play

"Mama, don't let your babies grow up to be peaches." cave.csuhayward.edu/CAVE/OCCAMS /occams.html

• **C.E. SMITH MUSEUM OF ANTHROPOLOGY** This museum, founded in 1975, houses "significant collections" of anthropological and archeological specimens. View a recent exhibit, and a tour of local archeological resources. **www.csu hayward.edu/cesmith/acesmith.html**

• **DEPARTMENT OF KINESIOLOGY AND PHYSICAL EDUCATION** Kinesiology is the study of human movement. On this excellent page, interested students can view images of the athletic and lab facilities, and read in-depth descriptions of the department's programs. The CSUH sports links are hiding here, too. **edschool.csuhayward .edu/Departments/KPE/department.HTML**

WHAT YOU NEED TO GET IN **Application Deadline** May 15 for priority consideration; final deadline June 12 **Common App.** No **Application Fee** $55 **Tuition Costs** $7,872 **Room & Board** $2,845 **Financial Forms Deadline** Priority given to applications received by May 2 **Tests Required** SAT1 (preferred) or ACT **Admissions Address** Hayward, CA 94542 **Admissions Telephone** (510) 885-3817

LAST YEAR'S CLASS **Applied** 2,121 **Accepted** 1,126 **Matriculated** 698 **In Top Third of High School Graduating Class** 96%

COLLEGE LIFE **Gender Breakdown** M 39%, F 61% **From Public Schools** 95% **Ethnic Composition** White & Other 52%, Asian American 24%, Black 13%, Hispanic 10%, Native American 1% **Foreign Students** 2% **Reside on Campus** 3% **Total Faculty** 578 **Student Faculty Ratio** 19:1 **Fraternities** 6 **Sororities** 7 **Graduate Students** 3,332

California State University, Long Beach

Long Beach, CA · Est. 1949 · Coed · Public · 21,264 Undergrads · Urban

I need...

Admissions info www.csulb.edu/~eslb/enrll
/admission/adm_index.html

Financial aid info www.csulb.edu/~eslb/enrll
/fin-aid/fa_index.html

How wired is Long Beach?

Do I get email? Yes
Do I get a home page? Yes
Is my dorm wired? No
What is the student to computer ratio? 11:1

REQUEST APPLICATION ONLINE

The usual tour

DEPARTMENTS www.csulb.edu/ua/univ-academics
.html
LIBRARY www.csulb.edu/~libweb
SPORTS www.csulb.edu/~lbsath/lbsath.htm
STUDENT CLUBS grover.cecs.csulb.edu/~palar
STUDENT NEWSPAPER www.csulb.edu/~d49er

Skip the brochure

- **DIGITAL COLLAGE** California State University, Long Beach students plus computing facilities from the Academic Computing Services equals an exciting online presentation of student work. **www.csulb.edu/Collage**

- **STUDENTS FOR OPTIONS** The school's answer to the peer pressure problem, Students for Options seeks to prevent alcohol and drug

Long Beach's home page: a cute exploitation of an awkward acronym

abuse via a number of events which promote "wellness, healthy living, and responsible decision-making." **www.engr.csulb.edu/~palar/stufopts.html**

- **BADMINTON CLUB** A little birdie told us that badminton used to be a varsity sport, with state champion players. It's unclear what has happened since then, but this page offers info on the current doings of this club sport. **www.engr.csulb.edu/~palar/badclub.html**

"Digital Collage offers an exciting presentation of student work."

WHAT YOU NEED TO GET IN **Application Deadline** Rolling admissions; November 1 for priority consideration **Common App.** No **Application Fee** $55 **Tuition Costs** $7,380 **Room & Board** $5,000 **Financial Forms Deadline** March 2 **Undergrads Awarded Aid** 35% **Aid That Is Need-Based** 80% **Average Award of Freshman Scholarship Package** $1,000 **Tests Required** SAT1 or ACT **Admissions Address** 1250 Bellflower Boulevard, Long Beach, CA 90840 **Admissions Telephone** (310) 985-4141

LAST YEAR'S CLASS **Applied** 8,072 **Accepted** 6,586 **Matriculated** 2,212 **Average SAT M/V** 465/447

COLLEGE LIFE **Gender Breakdown** M 46%, F 54% **Out of State Students** 4% **From Public Schools** 78% **Ethnic Composition** White & Other 40%, Asian American 27%, Black 10%, Hispanic 22%, Native American 1% **Foreign Students** 3% **Reside on Campus** 7% **Return as Sophomores** 75% **Total Faculty** 1,362 **Student Faculty Ratio** 20:1 **Fraternities (% of men participating)** 20 (9%) **Sororities (% of women participating)** 12 (5%) **Graduate Students** 5,139

California State University, Los Angeles

Los Angeles, CA · Est. 1947 · Coed · Public · 13,882 Undergrads · Urban

I need...

Admissions info admissions@cslanet.cal-statela.edu
www.calstatela.edu/admiss
Financial aid info kafblgw@oasis.calstatela.edu
www.calstatela.edu/finaid

How wired is Cal. State Los Angeles?

Do I get email? Yes
Do I get a home page? Yes
Where? web.calstatela.edu
/main/directry.htm
What is the student to computer ratio? 17:1

REQUEST APPLICATION ONLINE

The usual tour

BACKGROUND INFORMATION www.calstatela.edu
/calendar/theuniv.htm
VIRTUAL TOUR www.calstatela.edu/ppa/photo
/photo.htm
CALENDAR www.calstatela.edu/calendar
/default.htm
CAMPUS MAP www.calstatela.edu/ppa/campmap
/campmap.htm
LIBRARY web.calstatela.edu/library/index.htm

Skip the brochure

• **NEWS RELEASES** Find out what Cal State's spin doctors want everyone to know. Here are the latest press releases about scholarships,

Put yourself in the middle of Los Angeles at Cal State L.A.

sports events, and other tasty morsels.
www.calstatela.edu/ppa/newsrel

• **THE ABACUS COMPUTER SOCIETY** Almost no student organizations have home pages at Cal State, L.A. So why are these guys trying so hard to get attention? The Abacus site is a truly blinding display containing a newsletter, hot sites, and much more.
www.deltanet.com/users/msangil

• **RECOMMENDED SUMMER READING** Know what the seniors know. This list is handed out to all freshmen and transfer students, and contains dozens of suggested works from the likes of Ralph Ellison and Naomi Wolf. Catch up on the canon before you even enroll.
web.calstatela.edu/library/read.htm

WHAT YOU NEED TO GET IN **Application Deadline** July 1 for priority consideration; final deadline August 7 **Common App.** No **Application Fee** $55 **Tuition Costs, Room & Board** $1,749 ($7,650 out-of-state) **Financial Forms Deadline** March 1 **Undergrads Awarded Aid** 48% **Tests Required** SAT1 or ACT **Admissions Address** 5151 State University Drive, Los Angeles, CA 90032 **Admissions Telephone** (213) 343-3888

LAST YEAR'S CLASS **Applied** 6,491 **Accepted** 3,000 **Matriculated** 1,425

COLLEGE LIFE **Gender Breakdown** M 42%, F 58% **Out of State Students** 3% **From Public Schools** 82% **Ethnic Composition** White & Other 26%, Asian American 27%, Black 9%, Hispanic 38%, **Foreign Students** 8% **Reside on Campus** 4% **Return as Sophomores** 83% **Student Faculty Ratio** 19:1 **Fraternities (% of men participating)** 8 (3%) **Sororities (% of women participating)** 6 (2%) **Graduate Students** 4,342

California State University, Sacramento

www.csus.edu

Sacramento, CA · Est. 1947 · Coed · Public · 18,320 Undergrads · Urban

I need...

Admissions info www.csus.edu/student/admisn.html

Financial aid info www.csus.edu/student/finaid/index.html

How wired is Cal. State Sacramento?

Do I get email? Yes
Do I get a home page? No
What is the student to computer ratio? 30:1

The usual tour

DEPARTMENTS www.csus.edu/academic.html
LIBRARY www.csus.edu/library.html
STUDENT CLUBS www.csus.edu/orgstud.html
INTRAMURAL SPORTS www.csus.edu/student/imweb/IMRecHom.html
STUDENT ACTIVITIES OFFICE www.csus.edu/student/saoweb/SAO_Home.html
GREEK LIFE www.csus.edu/student/saoweb/SAOGreek.html
HISTORY www.csus.edu/history.html

Skip the brochure

- **CSUS MULTI-CULTURAL CENTER** This group wants CSUS to be diverse. It wants to bring in underprivileged and underrepresented ethnic groups and keep them at Cal State. It sponsors various lectures and multicultural events on cam-

Location: http://www.csus.edu/artssci.html

School of Arts & Sciences

One of the several undergraduate schools of Cal State Sacramento

pus. And its Web site is one of the few at CSUS worth looking at. **www.csus.edu/campus/multcult/index.html**

- **INTERNATIONAL BUSINESS ORGANIZATION** Start with the motto: "Global Expansion, Where Leaders Thrive." Then move through the site, which includes a meeting schedule and other international business-related links. **www.csus.edu/ibo/ibo.html**

- **CAMPUS MAP** Find your way around Sacramento with your mouse and your keyboard. **www.csus.edu/map.html**

WHAT YOU NEED TO GET IN **Application Deadline** November 30 for priority consideration; final deadline July 1 **Early Action Deadline** November 30 **Common App.** No **Application Fee** $55 **Tuition Costs** $7,380 **Room & Board** $4650 **Need Blind** Yes **Financial Forms Deadline** Priority given to applications received by March 2 **Undergrads Awarded Aid** 35% **Aid That Is Need-Based** 90% **Tests Required** SAT1 or ACT **Admissions Address** 6000 J Street, Sacramento, CA 95819 **Admissions Telephone** (916) 278-3901

LAST YEAR'S CLASS **Applied** 4,709 **Accepted** 3,200 **Matriculated** 1,330 **Average SAT M/V** 493/475 **Average ACT** 19 **Applied Early** 2,200 **Accepted Early** 2,000

COLLEGE LIFE **Gender Breakdown** M 46%, F 54% **Out of State Students** 3% **From Public Schools** 90% **Ethnic Composition** White & Other 66%, Asian American 15%, Black 6%, Hispanic 12%, Native American 1% **Foreign Students** 3% **Reside on Campus** 4% **Return as Sophomores** 75% **Total Faculty** 1,262 **Student Faculty Ratio** 21:1 **Fraternities** 20 **Sororities** 13 **Graduate Students** 4,476

University of California, Berkeley

Berkeley, CA · Est. 1868 · Coed · Public · 21,138 Undergrads · Urban

I need...

Admissions info ouars@uclink.berkeley.edu
www.uga.berkeley.edu/ouars
Financial aid info garnet.berkeley.edu:4246

How wired is UC Berkeley?

Do I get email? Yes
Do I get a home page? Yes
Is my dorm wired? Yes

The usual tour

LIBRARIES AND MUSEUMS www.berkeley.edu
/libraries
SPORTS ftp://gobears.berkeley.edu/pub
/gobears-archive
DEPARTMENTS www.berkeley.edu/teaching
STUDENT CLUBS server.berkeley.edu/student.html
CALENDAR www.chance.berkeley.edu
/planning/calendar.html
STUDENT NEWSPAPER server.berkeley.edu/DailyCal

Skip the brochure

- **RESOURCE: A GUIDE FOR NEW BERKELEY STUDENTS**
This guide is for anybody who wants to find out about the notoriously politicized student life at Berkeley. And there was that naked guy, too.
www2.uga.berkeley.edu/uga/osl/nsp/R.TOC.HTML

- **MAP OF THE BERKELEY CAMPUS** The rest of the

Berkeley students have many talents. Here one gets arty with Barbie

Berkeley site will leave you hungry for photos. Satisfy your appetite by clicking on the magic map. **server.berkeley.edu/Berkeley/campus.html**

- **ENTERZONE** This cutting edge, liberal, art-obsessed 'zine is more like the Berkeley we've been taught to expect. It's a literary anthology, but don't expect to read it in any particular order, because it's designed for browsers.
ezone.org:1080/enterzone.html

- **ESSIG MUSEUM OF ENTOMOLOGY** "Mommy, Mommy, I want to go to the school with 4.5 million insects!" If this sounds like something you'd say, proceed straight to Berkeley and check out the online version of UCB's bug museum. "Ooh, ooh, aphid parasitoids!"
www.mip.berkeley.edu/essig

WHAT YOU NEED TO GET IN Application Deadline November 30 for priority consideration **Common App.** No **Application Fee** $40 **Tuition Costs** $7,699 **Room & Board** $6,466 **Financial Forms Deadline** Priority given to applications received by March 2 **Undergrads Awarded Aid** 61% **Aid That Is Need-Based** 97% **Average Award of Freshman Scholarship Package** $5,529 **Tests Required** SAT1 or ACT **Admissions Address** Berkeley, CA 94720 **Admissions Telephone** (510) 642-3175

LAST YEAR'S CLASS Applied 20,814 **Accepted** 8,419 **Matriculated** 3,344 **Median Range SAT M/V** 610-730/ 500-640

COLLEGE LIFE Gender Breakdown M 52%, F 48% **Out of State Students** 9% **From Public Schools** 82% **Ethnic Composition** White & Other 40%, Asian American 39%, Black 6%, Hispanic 14%, Native American 1% **Foreign Students** 4% **Reside on Campus** 25% **Return as Sophomores** 94% **Student Faculty Ratio** 17:1 **Fraternities (% of men participating)** 42 (14%) **Sororities (% of women participating)** 17 (13%) **Graduate Students** 8,617

University of California, Davis   www.ucdavis.edu

Davis, CA · Est. 1905 · Coed · Public · 18,001 Undergrads · Big Town

I need...

Admissions info ThinkUCD@ucdavis.edu
lira.ucdavis.edu/admissions.html
Financial aid info undergradfinaid@ucdavis.edu
faoman.ucdavis.edu

How wired is UC Davis?

Do I get email? Yes
Do I get a home page? No
Is my dorm wired? Yes
What is the student to computer ratio? 30:1

The usual tour

DEPARTMENTS lira.ucdavis.edu/schools-colleges
.html
STUDENT NEWSPAPER aggie.ucdavis.edu
FACT SHEET www.ucdavis.edu/factbook
LIBRARY lira.ucdavis.edu/library-exhibit.html
STUDENT CLUBS lira.ucdavis.edu/organizations.html
SPORTS louie.stuaff.ucdavis.edu/ICA/!info.html
CAREER CENTER icc.ucdavis.edu

Skip the brochure

• **THINK. ON-LINE** Getting the Word Out Group,
which publishes *Think.*, is a registered student
organization at Davis which "feels strongly that
everybody deserves to have something interesting to read." To help reach that goal, *Think.*
provides online visual art and literary works by
self-proclaimed thinkers. **think.ucdavis.edu**

• **CALIFORNIA AGGIE MARCHING BAND** The UCD band

UC Davis' anthropology department plumbs man's origins

combines the composure of a regular marching band with the antics of a scatter band. "In
the Aggie Band, you get the best of both
worlds!" And, with the exception of a faculty
advisor/director, it's entirely student-run.
seclab.cs.ucdavis.edu/~wetmore/camb

• **CRAFT CENTER** The closest you'll come to taking
a course in basketweaving at UCD is at the
Craft Center, which offers classes like jewelry-
making, ceramics, glass fusing, and welding.
pubweb.ucdavis.edu/Documents/OA/crafts1.html

• **OUTDOOR ADVENTURES** Clear your mind with an
adventure in the great outdoors. This organization helps members of the UCD community
coordinate trips in a cooperative manner. No
fighting over the kayaks, please. **pubweb.ucdavis
.edu/Documents/OA/oa-ucd.html**

WHAT YOU NEED TO GET IN Application Deadline November 30 for priority consideration **Common App.** No **Application Fee** $40 **Tuition Costs** $4,230 ($12,624 out-of-state) **Room & Board** $5,840 **Need Blind** Yes **Financial Forms Deadline** Priority given to applications received by January 1 **Undergrads Awarded Aid** 52% **Aid That Is Need-Based** 80% **Tests Required** SAT1 or ACT **Admissions Address** Davis, CA 95616-8678 **Admissions Telephone** (916) 752-2971

LAST YEAR'S CLASS Applied 17,722 **Accepted** 12,599 **Matriculated** 3,287 **Average SAT M/V** 585/485 **Average ACT** 24 **In Top Quarter of High School Graduating Class** 100%

COLLEGE LIFE Gender Breakdown M 48%, F 52% **Out of State Students** 4% **From Public Schools** 85% **Ethnic Composition** White & Other 52.5%, Asian American 31.2%, Black 3.7%, Hispanic 11.4%, Native American 1.2% **Foreign Students** 1% **Reside on Campus** 21% **Return as Sophomores** 89% **Student Faculty Ratio** 19:1 **Fraternities (% of men participating)** 29 (10%) **Sororities (% of women participating)** 19 (9%) **Graduate Students** 5,091

University of California, Irvine

Irvine, CA · Est. 1965 · Coed · Public · 13,833 Undergrads · Big Town

I need...

Admissions info oars@uci.edu
www.reg.uci.edu/UCI/ADMISSIONS
Financial aid info finaid@uci.edu
www.fao.uci.edu

How wired is UC Irvine?

Do I get email? Yes
Do I get a home page? Yes
What is the student to computer ratio? 27:1

The usual tour

VIRTUAL TOUR www.reg.uci.edu/UCITOUR/camp
.html
DEPARTMENTS www.uci.edu/academic
LIBRARY www.lib.uci.edu
STUDENT NEWSPAPER www.newu.uci.edu/~newu
CAREER CENTER www.career.uci.edu/~career
STUDY ABROAD www.cie.uci.edu/~cie

Skip the brochure

• **KUCI 88.9 FM HOME PAGE** Read all about the student-run radio station at UCI. KUCI can be heard in most of Orange County and started way back in 1969. This site is great—it contains everything a person could possibly need to know about the station, and more than likely some stuff that no one needs to know, like the fact that baby squirrels and rabbits routinely graze in front of the offices. **www.kuci.uci.edu**

• **SCHOOL OF THE ARTS** The most attractive of the

Student Center
University of California, Irvine

Plantation living at UC Irvine

departmental sites, this page is home to a schedule of performances, a guide to the various schools, and an introduction to the faculty. **www.arts.uci.edu**

• **UCI IN THE NEWS** A handy, clickable guide to all the latest in media coverage of UCI. If it is in print, they'll summarize it here. **www.com munications.uci.edu/~inform/media/96archive.html**

"The student-run radio station at UCI can be heard in most of Orange County."

WHAT YOU NEED TO GET IN **Application Deadline** November 30 **Common App.** No **Application Fee** $40 **Tuition Costs** $4,049 ($11,748 out-of-state) **Room & Board** $5,824 **Need Blind** Yes **Financial Forms Deadline** Priority given to applications received by March 2 **Undergrads Awarded Aid** 63% **Aid That Is Need-Based** 89% **Average Award of Freshman Scholarship Package** $6,083 **Tests Required** SAT1 or ACT **Admissions Address** Irvine, CA 92717 **Admissions Telephone** (714) 824-6703

LAST YEAR'S CLASS **Applied** 15,908 **Accepted** 11,634 **Matriculated** 2,926 **Average SAT M/V** 567/448 **In Top Quarter of High School Graduating Class** 100%

COLLEGE LIFE **Gender Breakdown** M 47%, F 53% **Out of State Students** 4% **From Public Schools** 86% **Ethnic Composition** White & Other 30.1%, Asian American 53.3%, Black 2.6%, Hispanic 13.4%, Native American 0.6% **Foreign Students** 3% **Reside on Campus** 30% **Return as Sophomores** 91% **Student Faculty Ratio** 19:1 **Fraternities** 17 **Sororities** 13 **Graduate Students** 3,448

University of California, Los Angeles

www.ucla.edu

Los Angeles, CA · Est. 1919 · Coed · Public · 23,772 Undergrads · Urban

I need...

Admissions info ugadm@saonet.ucla.edu
www.saonet.ucla.edu/uars.htm
Financial aid info www.ucla.edu/student/library

How wired is UCLA?

Do I get email? Yes
Do I get a home page? No
Is my dorm wired? Yes

The usual tour

STUDENT CLUBS www.asucla.ucla.edu/scl/csp
/orgs9596.htm
DEPARTMENTS www.ucla.edu/people/servers
/academic.html
CALENDAR www.ucla.edu/student/acadinfo
/#calendar
STUDENT NEWSPAPER www.dailybruin.ucla.edu
LIBRARY www.ucla.edu/student/library
CAMPUS MAP www.ucla.edu/welcome/map
CALENDAR www.ucla.edu/current/events
/doc.base.html

Skip the brochure

• **FOWLER MUSEUM OF CULTURAL HISTORY** Few cities
in the U.S. are as culturally diverse as Los
Angeles. In celebration L.A.'s diversity, the
Fowler museum hosts exhibits like the
"Sacred Arts of Haitian Vodou" and "Royal

When UC this home page, UCLA

Tombs of Sipan." **www.fmch.ucla.edu**

• **LOCAL SCENE** What do you see when you stand in
the Hollywood Hills? UCLA. Follow these links,
kindly collected by actual UCLA students, to the
city of the stars. It includes the campus events
pages—as if L.A. doesn't offer enough to do!
www.asucla.ucla.edu/local/local.html

• **DAILY BRUIN PHOTO GALLERY** Ten UCLA student
newspaper photographers have collected their
images of campus life. Check out *A Day in the
Life of UCLA*, too. **www.dailybruin.ucla.edu/db/gallery
/photo/photo.html**

• **NEWSMAGAZINES** *Al-Talib*, *Ha'Am*, *Pacific Ties*,
and *Ten Percent* are just some of the names of
the seven student-run newsmagazines at UCLA.
While *The Daily Bruin* is the "official" voice of
the students, it couldn't possibly represent the
incredible individuality of each student group.
These try. **www.dailybruin.ucla.edu/newsmag/index.html**

WHAT YOU NEED TO GET IN **Application Deadline** November 30 for priority consideration **Common App.** No **Application Fee** $40 **Tuition Costs** $7,699 **Room & Board** $5,859 **Financial Forms Deadline** Priority given to applications received by March 2 **Undergrads Awarded Aid** 84% **Aid That Is Need-Based** 75% **Average Award of Freshman Scholarship Package** $5,000 **Tests Required** SAT1 or ACT **Admissions Address** Box 951436, Los Angeles, CA 90095-1436 **Admissions Telephone** (310) 825-3101

LAST YEAR'S CLASS **Applied** 25,464 **Accepted** 10,740 **Matriculated** 3,702 **Average SAT M/V** 615/521

COLLEGE LIFE **Gender Breakdown** M 49%, F 51% **Out of State Students** 5% **From Public Schools** 83% **Ethnic Composition** White & Other 40.1%, Asian American 34.9%, Black 6.3%, Hispanic 17.6%, Native American 1.1% **Foreign Students** 2% **Reside on Campus** 28% **Return as Sophomores** 94% **Total Faculty** 1,579 **Student Faculty Ratio** 17:1 **Fraternities (% of men participating)** 30 (11%) **Sororities (% of women participating)** 18 (10%) **Graduate Students** 10,944

University of California, Riverside

Riverside, CA · Est. 1954 · Coed · Public · 7,433 Undergrads · Urban

I need...

Admissions info hsro@pop.ucr.edu.
www.students.ucr.edu/admisshome.html
Financial aid info fahelpdesk@regfin.ucr.edu
www.students.ucr.edu/FinancialAid
/financialaid1.html

How wired is UC Riverside?

Do I get email? Yes
Do I get a home page? No
Is my dorm wired? Yes
What is the student to computer ratio? 37:1

The usual tour

VIRTUAL TOUR www.students.ucr.edu/admissions
/UCRView/viewtoc.html
LIBRARY www.ucr.edu/LibMus.html
DEPARTMENTS www.ucr.edu/ListPage.html
PUBLICATIONS www.ucr.edu/Mag.html
CAREER CENTER career333.ucr.edu/CareerHome
.html
COURSE CATALOG www.students.ucr.edu/Catalog
.html

Skip the brochure

- **CALIFORNIA MUSEUM OF PHOTOGRAPHY** Several
hundreds of thousands of prints have accumu-
lated at the renowned California Museum of
Photography since its founding in 1973. This

Lucky Riverside is home to the California Museum of Photography

frames-heavy site is a thorough guide to the
museum, its place at UCR, and the museum's
collection. **www.cmp.ucr.edu/frames**

- **UCR HOUSING** If you, like most potential college
students, would rather eat your own tongue
than get stuck in the campus's worst dorm,
UCR Housing is here to help. Check out all
your options, from residence halls to family
housing. (No, you don't have to bring your parents.) Plenty of pictures, answers, and solutions. **www.housing.ucr.edu/howzine/intro.html**

- **GREETINGS FROM RIVERSIDE!** There's more than
gown to this town. A resident whose family has
lived here for three generations takes you on a
complete tour, including the house she grew
up in. **www.cmp.ucr.edu/exhibitions/helen
/Riverside.html**

WHAT YOU NEED TO GET IN **Application Deadline** November 30 for priority consideration **Common App.** No **Application
Fee** $40 **Tuition Costs** $7,699 **Room & Board** $5,430 **Need Blind** Yes **Financial Forms Deadline** Priority given
to applications received by March 2 **Undergrads Awarded Aid** 55% **Tests Required** SAT1 or ACT **Admissions
Address** 900 University Avenue, Riverside, CA 92521 **Admissions Telephone** (909) 787-4531

LAST YEAR'S CLASS **Applied** 9,885 **Accepted** 7,692 **Matriculated** 1,596 **Average SAT M/V** 540/446 **Average ACT**
22 **In Top Fifth of High School Graduating Class** 95%

COLLEGE LIFE **Gender Breakdown** M 47%, F 53% **Out of State Students** 2% **From Public Schools** 90% **Ethnic
Composition** White & Other 36%, Asian American 39%, Black 5%, Hispanic 19%, Native American 1% **Reside on
Campus** 31% **Return as Sophomores** 86% **Student Faculty Ratio** 16:1 **Fraternities (% of men participating)** 14
(12%) **Sororities (% of women participating)** 12 (13%) **Graduate Students** 1,473

University of California, San Diego

www.uscd.edu

La Jolla, CA · Est. 1959 · Coed · Public · 14,846 Undergrads · Urban

I need...

Admissions info admissionsinfo@ucsd.edu
admissions.ucsd.edu/admissns.html
Financial aid info usdofa@acusd.edu
admissions.ucsd.edu/ofs.html

How wired is UC San Diego?

Do I get email? Yes
What is the student to computer ratio? 56:1

The usual tour

DEPARTMENTS provost.ucsd.edu/main.htm
STUDENT CLUBS www.ucsd.edu/campus/students
/index.html
SPORTS admissions.ucsd.edu/ath-rec.html
CAREER CENTER admissions.ucsd.edu/career.html
VIRTUAL TOUR ucsd.edu/data/campus/general
/visit/index.html

Skip the brochure

- **STUDENT PERSPECTIVES** Meet Amber, who chose
to attend UCSD because of its diverse student
body. Not only does she have a dorm room
with a view of ocean, but as a computer science major, she's confident she won't have to
work at a McJob when she graduates.
admissions.ucsd.edu/ambers.html

- **OPPORTUNITIES FOR DISCOVERY** The word on campus is that learning beyond the lecture hall is

Location: http://infopath.ucsd.edu/data/campus/image/building/APM_West.gif

Have a jolly time at La Jolla

critical, so it's made easy: "This year, over 200
undergraduates were placed as research assistants with a faculty mentor, over 450 studied
abroad, and over 700 interned at professional
organizations in a field related to their major."
This site also describes some of the other interesting opportunities available at UCSD, like an
exchange program with Dartmouth College.
admissions.ucsd.edu/opportun.html

- **PORTER'S PUB** With four simple headings among
its colorful graphics—"beer, food, history, pub-
crew"—one might imagine that folks at UCSD
had limited vocabularies due to overindul-
gence. But maybe they just think of beer as
one of the finer things in life. **www.vidya.com
/porters**

WHAT YOU NEED TO GET IN Application Deadline November 30 **Common App.** No **Application Fee** $40 **Tuition Costs**
$4,198 ($7,699 out-of-state) **Room & Board** $6,627 **Financial Forms Deadline** Priority given to applications
received by March 2 **Undergrads Awarded Aid** 50% **Average Award of Freshman Scholarship Package** $5,000
Tests Required SAT1 or ACT **Admissions Address** 9500 Gilman Drive, La Jolla, CA 92093 **Admissions
Telephone** (619) 534-4831

LAST YEAR'S CLASS Applied 25,769 **Accepted** 15,348 **Matriculated** 4,092 **Average SAT M/V** 623/513

COLLEGE LIFE Gender Breakdown M 51%, F 49% **Out of State Students** 3% **Ethnic Composition** White & Other
50.4%, Asian American 33.6%, Black 3%, Hispanic 12%, Native American 1% **Reside on Campus** 29% **Return as
Sophomores** 91% **Total Faculty** 918 **Student Faculty Ratio** 19:1 **Fraternities (% of men participating)** 14 (12%)
Sororities (% of women participating) 8 (12%)

University of California, Santa Barbara

www.ucsb.edu

Santa Barbara, CA · Est. 1909 · Coed · Public · 15,525 Undergrads · Urban

I need...

Admissions info www.admit.ucsb.edu/sis
Financial aid info www.admit.ucsb.edu/sis/finaid
.html

How wired is UC Santa Barbara?

Do I get email? Yes
Is my dorm wired? No

The usual tour

VIRTUAL TOUR www.admit.ucsb.edu/sis/pics
/pics.html
DEPARTMENTS www.ucsb.edu/academics.shtml
SPORTS www.instadv.ucsb.edu/Athletics/UCSB
Athletics
LIBRARY www.library.ucsb.edu
CALENDAR sis.ucsb.edu/admit/events
/home.html
STUDENT CLUBS www.ucsb.edu/students.shtml
GREEK LIFE sis.ucsb.edu/cac/Fraternities.html
STUDY ABROAD id-www.ucsb.edu/EAP/home.html

Skip the brochure

• **SANTA BARBARA HOME PAGE** The first European
came to Santa Barbara in 1542, but the city
had a rich history centuries before that.
Everything you need to know about Santa
Barbara. **www.internet-cafe.com/sb/sb.html**

Location: http://www.admit.ucsb.edu/sis/pics/26.gif

UCSB students talk of Kafka, Kant, and Kundera

• **ARTS AND LECTURES HOME PAGE** One of the best
things about being in college is all that culture
right under your nose. At UCSB, you can see
The Capitol Steps, listen to the Julliard String
Quartet, attend a lecture by Anna Deavere
Smith, or watch a student film. The schedules
are provided. **www.arts.ucsb.edu/artlec**

• **CENTER FOR RESEARCH IN ELECTRONIC ART
TECHNOLOGY** This is a collection of links to the
various electronic art projects at UCSB, sponsored by the Center for Computer Music
Research and Composition. **www.ccmrc.ucsb.edu**

"All that culture right under your nose"

WHAT YOU NEED TO GET IN **Application Deadline** November 30 **Common App.** No **Application Fee** $40 **Tuition Costs**
$7,699 **Room & Board** $5,900 **Financial Forms Deadline** March 2 **Undergrads Awarded Aid** 49% **Tests
Required** SAT1 or ACT **Admissions Address** Santa Barbara, CA 93106 **Admissions Telephone** (805) 893-2485

LAST YEAR'S CLASS **Applied** 17,060 **Accepted** 14,130 **Matriculated** 2,881 **Average SAT M/V** 544/455

COLLEGE LIFE **Gender Breakdown** M 48%, F 52% **Out of State Students** 4% **From Public Schools** 82% **Ethnic
Composition** White & Other 68%, Asian American 16%, Black 3%, Hispanic 12%, Native American 1% **Foreign
Students** 2% **Reside on Campus** 22% **Return as Sophomores** 85% **Student Faculty Ratio** 18:1 **Fraternities
(% of men participating)** 21 (13%) **Sororities (% of women participating)** 18 (13%) **Graduate Students** 2,309

University of California, Santa Cruz

www.ucsc.edu

Santa Cruz, CA · Est. 1965 · Coed · Public · 8,876 Undergrads · Big Town

How wired is UC Santa Cruz?

Do I get email? Yes
Do I get a home page? Yes
Is my dorm wired? No
What is the student to computer ratio? 39:1

The usual tour

VIRTUAL TOUR www.ucsc.edu/intro/tour/index
.html
DEPARTMENTS www.ucsc.edu/acad/index.html
CALENDAR www.ucsc.edu/ucsc/aci/KeyDates
.html
LIBRARY www.ucsc.edu/library/index.html
STUDY ABROAD www.ucsc.edu/ucsc/student
-affairs/ipo.html
SPORTS www.ucsc.edu/ucsc/opers/sports
/athletics.html
CAREER CENTER www.ucsc.edu/ucsc/careers
/index.html

Skip the brochure

• **RESIDENTIAL COLLEGES** Choice of housing at
UCSC is even more of a nightmare than at

Santa Cruz: incredibly, this is a campus, not a holiday resort

most schools. It's not just a room to keep dirty clothes from taking over the campus—t's a living "experience." Residential colleges are groups of dorms often centered around a theme, and always with a core course and individual events all its own. **www.ucsc.edu/ucsc /housing/oncampus/residential**

• **U.C. SANTA CRUZ BOATING CENTER** Remind yourself why Santa Cruz is a good choice. The Boating Center offers sailing lessons, ocean rowing classes, kayaking, and lots more. **www.ucsc.edu /ucsc/opers/boating/center.html**

• **THE FISH RAP ONLINE** This is the widely-read "underground" UCSC newspaper. It's been published and staffed by students for five years. And its name is an execrable pun. **mail.iuma.com/fishrap**

WHAT YOU NEED TO GET IN **Application Deadline** November 30 **Common App.** No **Application Fee** $40 **Tuition Costs** $4,109 ($11,808 out-of-state) **Room & Board** $6,081 **Financial Forms Deadline** May 2 with a priority given to applications received by March 2 **Undergrads Awarded Aid** 50% **Aid That Is Need-Based** 95% **Average Award of Freshman Scholarship Package** $4,239 **Tests Required** SAT1 or ACT **Admissions Address** Santa Cruz, CA 95064 **Admissions Telephone** (408) 459-4008

LAST YEAR'S CLASS **Applied** 11,440 **Accepted** 9,535 **Matriculated** 1,826 **Average SAT M/V** 550/490

COLLEGE LIFE **Gender Breakdown** M 40%, F 60% **Out of State Students** 8% **From Public Schools** 75% **Ethnic Composition** White & Other 67%, Asian American 10%, Black 4%, Hispanic 18%, Native American 1% **Foreign Students** 1% **Reside on Campus** 48% **Return as Sophomores** 85% **Student Faculty Ratio** 19:1 **Fraternities** none **Sororities** none **Graduate Students** 1,047

Canisius College

www.canisius.edu

Buffalo, NY · Est. 1870 · Coed · Private · 3,409 Undergrads · Urban

I need...

Admissions info inquiry@gort.canisius.edu
www.canisius.edu/canhp/canadmiss/about
.html

Financial aid info www.canisius.edu/canhp/can
admiss/financing.html

How wired is Canisius College?

Do I get email? Yes

Do I get a home page? Yes

Where? www.canisius.edu/canhp/personal
/home pagesstud.html

Is my dorm wired? Yes

What is the student to computer ratio? 25:1

The usual tour

LIBRARY www.canisius.edu/canhp/canlib/index
.html

SPORTS www.canisius.edu/canhp/departments
/athletics

PUBLICATIONS www.canisius.edu/canhp/canpub
/canpubs.htm

DEPARTMENTS gort.canisius.edu/canhp/depart
ments/index.html

STUDENT CLUBS www.canisius.edu/canhp
/studentinfo/studorgs/clubs.html

VIRTUAL TOUR www.canisius.edu/canhp/can
admiss/tour.html

CAREER CENTER www.canisius.edu/canhp
/canadmin/career/career.html

Canisius at the click of a mouse

Skip the brochure

• **WHAT IS A GOLDEN GRIFFIN?** "You can have your Chihuahuas, Piranhas, Horned Frogs and Iguanas. The best all-around athletic mascot in business today has to be the beast adopted by Canisius College—the Golden Griffin." A mascot so memorable it has inspired dithyrambs.
www.canisius.edu/canhp/departments/athletics/griffin.htm

• **ALL-COLLEGE HONORS PROGRAM** Find out what's in store for you if you're a real smarty. If you're in the top 10 percent of entering frosh, you might be able to follow the honors curriculum with small classes and special seminars.
gort.canisius.edu/canhp/canadmiss/majors/honors.html

• **BUFFALO—THE SURROUNDING COMMUNITY** Canisius offers info about the local environs, including major cultural and athletic attractions such as the Albright-Knox Art Gallery and Sabres hockey.
www.canisius.edu/canhp/canadmiss/buffalo.html

WHAT YOU NEED TO GET IN **Application Deadline** Rolling Admissions **Common App.** Yes **Application Fee** $25 **Tuition Costs** $12,600 **Room & Board** $5,825 **Need Blind** Yes **Financial Forms Deadline** Priority given to applications received by February 1 **Undergrads Awarded Aid** 80% **Aid That Is Need-Based** 89% **Average Award of Freshman Scholarship Package** $7,918 **Tests Required** SAT1 (preferred) or ACT **Admissions Address** 2001 Main Street, Buffalo, NY 14208 **Admissions Telephone** 716 888-2200

LAST YEAR'S CLASS **Applied** 2,533 **Accepted** 2,141 **Matriculated** 730 **Average SAT M/V** 526/464 **Average ACT** 24 **In Top Fifth of High School Graduating Class** 38%

COLLEGE LIFE **Gender Breakdown** M 54%, F 46% **Out of State Students** 8% **From Public Schools** 72% **Ethnic Composition** White & Other 89.7%, Asian American 1.4%, Black 5.8%, Hispanic 2.9%, Native American 0.2% **Foreign Students** 3% **Reside on Campus** 30% **Return as Sophomores** 83% **Total Faculty** 421 **Student Faculty Ratio** 17:1 **Fraternities (% of men participating)** 1 (4%) **Sororities (% of women participating)** 2 (4%) **Graduate Students** 1,427

Carleton College

www.carleton.edu

Northfield, MN · Est. 1866 · Coed · Private · 1,777 Undergrads · Small Town

How wired is Carleton College?

Do I get email? Yes
Do I get a home page? Yes
Where? www.carleton.edu/student/pages.html
Is my dorm wired? Yes
What is the student to computer ratio? 7:1

The usual tour

LIBRARY www.library.carleton.edu
DEPARTMENTS www.carleton.edu/campus
/academic.html
STUDENT CLUBS www.carleton.edu/student/orgs
.html
SPORTS www.carleton.edu/curricular/PEAR
/index.html

Skip the brochure

- **EBONY II** Dance the nights and days away with Carleton College's student-run, student-produced, and student-choreographed dance group. Hip-hop and tap are just some of the many offerings. **public.carleton.edu/~rogowskj /ebony.html**

Location: http://www.carleton.edu/admissions/

Ballet/Frisbee fanatics try out some new moves

- **MOVEMENT AGAINST HOMOPHOBIA** The group isn't quite right when it says that it advocates inclusion and tolerance; it is clearly intolerant of people who are homophobic. "Homophobia sucks," this page proclaims. For more detailed information, look at some of their upcoming events, which include workshops and public events. **public.carleton.edu/~leejos/mah/mah_home.html**

- **SCIENCE FICTION HOUSE** If you really, really like science fiction (sometimes referred to here, nerdily enough, as speculative fiction), consider living and breathing it during your stint at Carleton College with a stint in the Science Fiction Interest House. Rumor has it that the television only receives *Star Trek: The Next Generation*, *The X-Files*, and *Battlestar Galactica*. **public.carleton.edu/~TZAVELAC/sfhouse _page.html**

WHAT YOU NEED TO GET IN Application Deadline January 15 for priority consideration **Early Action Deadline** November 15 and January 15 **Common App.** Yes **Application Fee** $30 **Tuition Costs** $20,988 **Room & Board** $4,290 **Need Blind** No **Financial Forms Deadline** Priority given to applications received by February 15 **Undergrads Awarded Aid** 83% **Aid That Is Need-Based** 94% **Average Award of Freshman Scholarship Package** $9,302 **Tests Required** SAT1 or ACT **Admissions Address** One North College Street, Northfield, MN 55057 **Admissions Telephone** (507) 663-4190

LAST YEAR'S CLASS Applied 2,855 **Accepted** 1,444 **Matriculated** 463 **Median Range SAT M/V** 630-720/570-670 **In Top Fifth of High School Graduating Class** 71% **Applied Early** 239 **Accepted Early** 184

COLLEGE LIFE Gender Breakdown M 50%, F 50% **Out of State Students** 76% **From Public Schools** 76% **Ethnic Composition** White & Other 84%, Asian American 9%, Black 3%, Hispanic 4%, **Foreign Students** 1% **Reside on Campus** 92% **Return as Sophomores** 95% **Total Faculty** 198 **Student Faculty Ratio** 11:1 **Fraternities** none **Sororities** none

Carnegie Mellon University

www.cmu.edu

Pittsburgh, PA · Est. 1900 · Coed · Private · 4,572 Undergrads · Urban

I need...

Admissions info undergraduate-admissions+
@CMU.EDU
www.cmu.edu/enrollment/admission
/admission.html
Financial aid info www.cmu.edu/finaid

DOWNLOAD APPLICATION ONLINE

How wired is Carnegie Mellon?

Do I get email? Yes
Do I get a home page? Yes
  Where? www.contrib.andrew.cmu.edu/usr
Is my dorm wired? Yes
What is the student to computer ratio? 12:1

The usual tour

UNDERGRADUATE CATALOG www.cmu.edu/registrar
/catalog.html
DEPARTMENTS www.cmu.edu/cmufront
/department.html
LIBRARY www.library.cmu.edu
SPORTS www.cmu.edu/athletic
FACT BOOKS www.cmu.edu/ba/planning/main.html
STUDENT CLUBS www.contrib.andrew.cmu.edu/org

Skip the brochure

• **CARNEGIE THREADS QUILTING CLUB** Not everyone in
Pittsburgh is into steel. This folksy home page
is owed to one of CMU's more domestic student organizations, and hosts all kinds of
WWW quilting links. It would be a unique club
on any campus. **www.contrib.andrew.cmu.edu/org
/quilt/home.html**

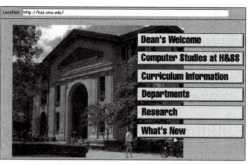

Learn about CMU's famous design, engineering, and acting
programs

• **FIRST CHURCH OF CHRIST, ABORTIONIST** Sometimes
college students are a little angry. And CMU's
campus can get a bit drab during the long,
snowy winters. So some CMU students have
responded to the pro-lifers with this extremist
and satirical page. Apparently, the college
president is not very happy with them. Read
about "A Religion that Believes Abortion is
Good," and be converted. **www.contrib.andrew.cmu
.edu/org/fcca/home page.html**

• **FILM FEST FIVE** You oughta be in pictures, or
maybe your pictures oughta be in here. Film
addicts at Carnegie Mellon submit their artistic treasures each year, and the campus
watches. Download the trailer for this year's
festival, and start that camera rolling for Film
Fest Six. **www.contrib.andrew.cmu.edu/proj/film
/FilmFest/index.html**

WHAT YOU NEED TO GET IN **Application Deadline** February 1 **Early Action Deadline** December 1 **Common App.** No
Application Fee $45 **Tuition Costs** $19,400 **Room & Board** $6,030 **Need Blind** Yes **Financial Forms Deadline**
February 15 **Undergrads Awarded Aid** 71% **Aid That Is Need-Based** 75% **Average Award of Freshman
Scholarship Package** $11,759 **Tests Required** SAT1 or ACT **Admissions Address** 5000 Forbes Avenue,
Pittsburgh, PA 15213 **Admissions Telephone** (412) 268-2082

LAST YEAR'S CLASS **Applied** 10,291 **Accepted** 5,608 **Matriculated** 1,237 **In Top Fifth of High School Graduating
Class** 78%

COLLEGE LIFE **Gender Breakdown** M 68%, F 32% **Out of State Students** 81% **From Public Schools** 66% **Ethnic
Composition** White & Other 76.8%, Asian American 15%, Black 4%, Hispanic 3.2%, Native American 1% **Foreign
Students** 10% **Reside on Campus** 71% **Return as Sophomores** 90% **Total Faculty** 547 **Student Faculty Ratio**
9:1 **Fraternities (% of men participating)** 14 (25%) **Sororities (% of women participating)** 5 (14%) **Graduate
Students** 2,611

Case Western Reserve University

www.cwru.edu

Cleveland, OH · Est. 1967 · Coed · Private · 3,645 Undergrads · Urban

I need...

Admissions info xx329@po.cwru.edu
www.cwru.edu/CWRU/Admin/Provost
/UgAdmiss/ugadmiss.html
Financial aid info www.cwru.edu/CWRU/Admin
/finaid/finaid.htm

How wired is Case Western?

Do I get email? Yes
Do I get a home page? Yes
Where? cnswww.cns.cwru.edu
/net/easy/homes
Is my dorm wired? Yes
What is the student to computer ratio? 18:1

The usual tour

DEPARTMENTS www.cwru.edu/acdepts.html
VIRTUAL TOUR www.cwru.edu/CWRU/Tour/00
_campus_tour.html
STUDENT CLUBS www.cwru.edu/CWRU/student
-organizations.html
LIBRARY www.cwru.edu/uclibraries.html
CALENDAR www.cwru.edu/CWRU/Calendar
/calendar.html

Skip the brochure

- **CWRU ARCHERY CLUB** Visit this site if for no other reason than to see the virtual arrow hit the virtual target again, and again, and... If you manage

Case Western's Archery Club aims to hypnotize you

to snap out of it, you can read more about the club and check out the top scores of its members. **www.cwru.edu/CWRU/Org/archery/archery.html**

- **DESI CLUB** Desi seeks to unite people from all areas of the Indian subcontinent through cultural events and celebrations. **www.cwru.edu/CWRU/Org/desi/sss6/cwdc.html**

- **MAGIC CLUB HOME PAGE** Pity the poor misguided souls who come to this home page in the hopes of reading about the latest David Copperfield exploits. This club is devoted to magic of a different ilk, namely *Magic: The Gathering*, a fantasy card game usually played by pimply adolescent boys (and the occasional girl). **www.cwru.edu/CWRU/Org/magic/magic.html**

WHAT YOU NEED TO GET IN **Application Deadline** Fall for priority consideration; final deadline February 1 **Early Action Deadline** January 1 **Common App.** Yes **Tuition Costs** $17,100 **Room & Board** $4,860 **Need Blind** Yes **Financial Forms Deadline** Priority given to applications received by February 1 **Undergrads Awarded Aid** 84% **Aid That Is Need-Based** 64% **Average Award of Freshman Scholarship Package** $11,550 **Tests Required** SAT1 or ACT **Admissions Address** 10900 Euclid Avenue, Cleveland, OH 44106 **Admissions Telephone** (216) 368-4450

LAST YEAR'S CLASS **Applied** 4,291 **Accepted** 3,289 **Matriculated** 732 **Median Range SAT M/V** 640-740/530-650 **In Top Fifth of High School Graduating Class** 92% **Applied Early** 161 **Accepted Early** 135

COLLEGE LIFE **Gender Breakdown** M 57%, F 43% **Out of State Students** 43% **From Public Schools** 70% **Ethnic Composition** White & Other 80.1%, Asian American 11.7%, Black 6.5%, Hispanic 1.6%, Native American 0.1% **Foreign Students** 7% **Reside on Campus** 75% **Return as Sophomores** 91% **Total Faculty** 1,879 **Student Faculty Ratio** 8:1 **Fraternities (% of men participating)** 17 (33%) **Sororities (% of women participating)** 5 (15%) **Graduate Students** 6,102

The Catholic University of America

www.cua.edu

Washington, DC · Est. 1887 · Coed · Private · 2,417 Undergrads · Urban

I need...

Admissions info cua-admissions@cua.edu
www.cua.edu/www/adms
Financial aid info cua-admissions@cua.edu

How wired is The Catholic University?

Do I get email? Yes
Do I get a home page? Yes
Is my dorm wired? Yes
What is the student to computer ratio? 7:1

The usual tour

LIBRARY www.cua.edu/www/mullen
HISTORY www.cua.edu/www/about_cua
/history.html
VIRTUAL TOUR www.cua.edu/www/adms
STUDENT CLUBS www.cua.edu/www/student-org
.html
SPORTS www.cua.edu/www/adms/viewbook
/Athlet.htm

Skip the brochure

- **AMERICAN SOCIETY FOR INFORMATION SCIENCE AT CUA** Although its mission statement forbodingly says that it is "dedicated to the creation, organization and dissemination, and application of knowledge concerning information and its transfer," this organization is, more simply put, a professional association which covers

CUA Magazine won numerous awards for its Catholic-oriented coverage

library and information science. Or, to put it another way, it exists for librarians with large vocabularies. **www.cua.edu/www/org/asis**

- **GUIDE TO FACULTY EXPERTS** Who you gonna call? No matter what subject you're interested in, there's a CUA faculty member who can guide you and answer questions. The Office of Public Affairs has very conveniently grouped faculty under their respective areas of expertise, so whether it's theology or theater, you're well covered. **www.cua.edu/www/pbaf/main/experts.htm**

- **FACT BOOK** This site offers just the facts. The nitty-gritty of the university is explicated. **www.cua.edu/www/about_cua/fact-book.html**

"Whether it's theology or theater, you're covered."

WHAT YOU NEED TO GET IN Application Deadline February 15 **Early Action Deadline** November 15 **Common App.** Yes **Application Fee** $50 **Tuition Costs** $15,562 **Room & Board** $6,844 **Financial Forms Deadline** Priority given to applications received by January 15 **Undergrads Awarded Aid** 80% **Aid That Is Need-Based** 56% **Average Award of Freshman Scholarship Package** $8,484 **Tests Required** SAT1 (preferred) or ACT **Admissions Address** Cardinal Station Post Office, Washington, DC 20064 **Admissions Telephone** (800)-673-2772

LAST YEAR'S CLASS Applied 2,527 **Accepted** 1,529 **Matriculated** 570 **Median Range SAT M/V** 520-630/540-650 **In Top Fifth of High School Graduating Class** 47% **Applied Early** 248 **Accepted Early** 248

COLLEGE LIFE Gender Breakdown M 44%, F 56% **Out of State Students** 94% **From Public Schools** 37% **Ethnic Composition** White & Other 80.6%, Asian American 4.5%, Black 8.6%, Hispanic 5.9%, Native American 0.4% **Foreign Students** 10% **Reside on Campus** 76% **Return as Sophomores** 85% **Total Faculty** 494 **Student Faculty Ratio** 10:1 **Fraternities (% of men participating)** 1 (1%) **Sororities (% of women participating)** 1 (1%) **Graduate Students** 3,691

Central College

Pella, IA · Est. 1853 · Coed · Private · 1,321 Undergrads · Small Town

I need...

Admissions info sicklere@central.edu
www.central.edu/Admissn/admiss.htm
Financial aid info www.central.edu/finplan
/webpage2.htm

How wired is Central College?

Do I get email? Yes
Do I get a home page? Yes
Where? www.central.edu/Directry/hpages.htm
Is my dorm wired? Yes
What is the student to computer ratio? 11:1

The usual tour

VIRTUAL TOUR www.central.edu/Tour/central.htm
DEPARTMENTS www.central.edu/Majors/index
.htm
STUDY ABROAD www.studyabroad.com/central
/centralhome.html
LIBRARY www.central.edu/Library/libhome.htm

Skip the brochure

• **EDUCATION DEPARTMENT** Central's department of
elementary and secondary education is user-
friendly, as befits a department that teaches
students how to deal with kids. Information is
available about the various programs offered

"Take a trip back in time through Central's past."

Central's '90s students take after their parents' phone booth stuffing antics; one coed couldn't quite get it

through the department; there's even a section devoted to finding a job via the Internet.
www.central.edu/EDUCATION/EDDEPT.htm

• **GEISLER LIBRARY ARCHIVES** Take a break from
wondering what Central College is like now and
take a trip back in time. This site describes
the Archives which, since the 1940s, have
housed a collection of information about
Central College, Pella, and the Reformed
Church of America (which dates back to the
eighteenth century). **www.central.edu/Library
/archives.htm**

• **MISSION OF CENTRAL COLLEGE** Ask not what you
want from your college, but what your college
wants from you. The college describes its
intentions regarding students, faculty, and the
community. **www.central.edu/Profile/mission.htm**

WHAT YOU NEED TO GET IN Application Deadline Rolling admissions; January 1 for priority consideration **Common App.**
No **Application Fee** $25 **Tuition Costs** $12,152 **Room & Board** $3,808 **Need Blind** Yes **Financial Forms
Deadline** Priority given to applications received by January 1 **Undergrads Awarded Aid** 95% **Aid That Is Need-
Based** 51% **Average Award of Freshman Scholarship Package** $7,711 **Tests Required** SAT1 or ACT (preferred)
Admissions Address 812 University Avenue, Pella, IA 50219 **Admissions Telephone** (800) 458-5503

LAST YEAR'S CLASS Applied 1,303 **Accepted** 1,128 **Matriculated** 407 **Average SAT M/V** 546/491 **Average ACT** 24
In Top Fifth of High School Graduating Class 54%

COLLEGE LIFE Gender Breakdown M 44%, F 56% **Out of State Students** 23% **From Public Schools** 98% **Ethnic
Composition** White & Other 93%, Asian American 2%, Black 1%, Hispanic 3%, Native American 1% **Foreign
Students** 4% **Reside on Campus** 86% **Return as Sophomores** 76% **Total Faculty** 130 **Student Faculty Ratio**
13:1 **Fraternities (% of men participating)** 4 (14%) **Sororities (% of women participating)** 2 (5%)

University of Chicago

www.uchicago.edu

Chicago, IL · Est. 1891 · Coed · Private · 3,453 Undergrads · Urban

I need...

Admissions info college-admissions@uchicago.edu
www-college.uchicago.edu/prospective
/default.html
Financial aid info www-college.uchicago.edu
/prospective/Brochures/FinancialAid
/FinancialAid.html

How wired is the University of Chicago?

Do I get email? Yes
Do I get a home page? Yes
  Where? student-www.uchicago.edu/users
What is the student to computer ratio? 3:1

The usual tour

BACKGROUND INFORMATION www.uchicago.edu
/uoc/vi.html
SPORTS www-athletics.uchicago.edu
STUDY ABROAD www-college.uchicago.edu/pros
pective/Brochures/InternationalStudy.html
DEPARTMENTS www.uchicago.edu/uoc/au.html
VIRTUAL TOUR www2.uchicago.edu/grad-adm
/tour.html
STUDENT CLUBS student-www.uchicago.edu/RSOs

"The Chronicle is a great way to discover university life."

Freshmen line up for the most competitive classes at the University of Chicago

Skip the brochure

- **ROOMS WITH A VIEW** The University of Chicago magazine offers this excellent photo essay of dorm life at Chicago. See students doing laundry, studying, laughing, and generally being happy citizens. **www2.uchicago.edu/alumni/alumni .mag//9604/9604Rooms.html**

- **THE ORIENTAL INSTITUTE VIRTUAL MUSEUM** Chicago's museum of the ancient Near East hosts this QuickTime movie virtual tour, which highlights the layout and the collection (which has been around since 1919). **www-oi.uchicago .edu/OI/MUS/QTVR96/QTVR96.html**

- **THE UNIVERSITY OF CHICAGO CHRONICLE ONLINE** *The Chronicle* is UC's "official" (i.e. not student) newspaper. Its online version is a great way to discover life both in and around the university. **unews.uchicago.edu/Chronicle/current/TitlePage.html**

WHAT YOU NEED TO GET IN **Application Deadline** January 1 **Early Action Deadline** November 15 **Common App.** No **Application Fee** $55 **Tuition Costs** $20,970 **Room & Board** $7,275 **Need Blind** Yes **Financial Forms Deadline** Priority given to applications received by February 1 **Undergrads Awarded Aid** 69% **Aid That Is Need-Based** 95% **Average Award of Freshman Scholarship Package** $13,995 **Tests Required** SAT1 or ACT **Admissions Address** 1116 East 59th Street, Chicago, IL 60637 **Admissions Telephone** (312) 702-8650

LAST YEAR'S CLASS **Applied** 5,843 **Accepted** 3,182 **Matriculated** 986 **Average SAT M/V** 640-720/560-690 **In Top Fifth of High School Graduating Class** 89% **Applied Early** 600 **Accepted Early** 350

COLLEGE LIFE **Gender Breakdown** M 54%, F 46% **Out of State Students** 79% **From Public Schools** 70% **Ethnic Composition** White & Other 64%, Asian American 27%, Black 4%, Hispanic 5%, **Foreign Students** 4% **Reside on Campus** 64% **Return as Sophomores** 93% **Student Faculty Ratio** 6:1 **Fraternities (% of men participating)** 9 (14%) **Sororities (% of women participating)** 2 (5%) **Graduate Students** 8,422

University of Cincinnati

Cincinnati, OH · Est. 1819 · Coed · Public · 13,240 Undergrads · Urban

I need...

Admissions info admissions@uc.edu
www.uc.edu/www/admissions/home.html
Financial aid info financeaid@uc.edu
129.137.76.132/pages/sfa/sfa-home.html

How wired is the University of Cincinnati?

Do I get email? Yes
Do I get a home page? Yes
   Where? www.uc.edu/www/users
Is my dorm wired? No
What is the student to computer ratio? 9:1

FULL APPLICATION ONLINE

The usual tour

VIRTUAL TOUR 129.137.76.132/pages/adm /adm-tour.html
STUDENT NEWSPAPER www.uc.edu/www/news record/index.htmlx
STUDENT CLUBS www.uc.edu/www/organizations .html
SPORTS ucunix.san.uc.edu/~zureick/bearcat.html
DEPARTMENTS www.uc.edu/www/college-dept -info.html
LIBRARY www.libraries.uc.edu

Skip the brochure

• **THE GOOSEDOWN GAZETTE** The official publication of the UC Mountaineering Club, this little magazine contains articles about the activities of UCMC. There are links to other outdoor resources, too, and Goosedowners tempt

Herman Schneider Quad

Back to "Virtual Tour"

The quad we are entering is named after Herman Schneider, a former dean of the College of Engineering who "invented" the Co-operative Education (also known as "Professional Practice") program in 1906. This photograph shows Baldwin Hall on the right, and Old Chemistry on the left.

This quad at U Cincinnati is dedicated to the founder of the school's work-study program

visitors with pictures of places they've been. **www.soa.uc.edu/org/UCMC/gd0995.html**

• **PHI KAPPA TAU** The first Greek organization at UC with a home page must have scared the others away, because it looks like a toilet after an all-night frat party. Anyway, look at pictures of some of the young, ripe lads in their scrapbook, and meet the rest of the Gamma Beta bunch. **ucunix.san.uc.edu/~schumarp/phitau.html**

• **STUDENT AFFAIRS LEARNING IMPERATIVE** Read all about the ethical and moral growth you should be undergoing while you're actually partying too hard, cramming for exams, and looking for love in all the wrong places. And enjoy the levelheaded writing and nice pictures while you're there. **soaserver.tuc.uc.edu/sas/imperative2.html**

WHAT YOU NEED TO GET IN Application Deadline December 15 for priority consideration **Common App.** No **Application Fee** $30 **Tuition Costs** $3,732 ($9,405 out-of-state) **Room & Board** $4,698 **Financial Forms Deadline** Rolling **Undergrads Awarded Aid** 68% **Average Award of Freshman Scholarship Package** $1,323 **Tests Required** SAT1 or ACT (preferred) **Admissions Address** Cincinnati, OH 45221-0127 **Admissions Telephone** (513) 556-1100

LAST YEAR'S CLASS Applied 6,498 **Accepted** 5,565 **Matriculated** 2,485 **Average SAT M/V** 535/467 **Average ACT** 24 **In Top Fifth of High School Graduating Class** 46%

COLLEGE LIFE Gender Breakdown M 52%, F 48% **Ethnic Composition** White & Other 88%, Asian American 3%, Black 8%, Hispanic 1%, **Foreign Students** 1% **Reside on Campus** 16% **Return as Sophomores** 76% **Student Faculty Ratio** 19:1 **Fraternities** 22 **Sororities** 11 **Graduate Students** 5,133

City University of New York, Brooklyn College

omni.brooklyn.cuny.edu

Brooklyn, NY · Est. 1930 · Coed · Public · 11,478 Undergrads · Urban

I need...

Admissions info omni.brooklyn.cuny.edu/bc/info /admissug.html

Financial aid info omni.brooklyn.cuny.edu/bc/info /assistug.html

How wired is CUNY Brooklyn?

Do I get email? Yes
Do I get a home page? No
What is the student to computer ratio? 23:1

The usual tour

DEPARTMENTS omni.brooklyn.cuny.edu/bc/depts /ug/ug.html

VIRTUAL TOUR www.brooklyn.cuny.edu/bc/ahp /Campus.html

LIBRARY omni.brooklyn.cuny.edu/bc/fac/bclib .html

STUDENT CLUBS omni.brooklyn.cuny.edu/bc/info /activity.html

STUDY ABROAD omni.brooklyn.cuny.edu/bc/info /special.html#study

GENERAL INFORMATION
omni.brooklyn.cuny.edu/bc/info/general.html

Skip the brochure

• **PRESIDENT CLINTON COMES TO CAMPUS** The Prez needed a photo op, and Brooklyn College needed national coverage. It was a match

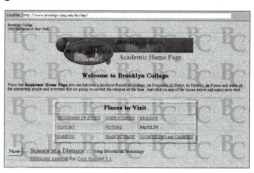

CUNY Brooklyn welcomes prospective students to their Web site.

made in heaven. Read about it, and download extensive sound bites like the ones they played on the evening news. **omni.brooklyn.cuny .edu/bc/news/clinton.html**

• **THE BROOKLYN COLLEGE SEAL** Yeah, it's a seal, but can it clap its flippers, eat a herring, and balance a red ball on its nose all at the same time? **www.brooklyn.cuny.edu/bc/bclogo.html**

• **BROOKLYN COLLEGE MASTER PLAN** They have a master. He has a plan. Find out about the college of tomorrow, and all of the phases of the Master Plan. In short, know which construction sites future students will be forced to walk through. **www.brooklyn.cuny.edu/bc/ahp/Tomorrow.html**

WHAT YOU NEED TO GET IN Application Deadline Rolling admissions; January 16 for priority consideration **Common App.** No **Application Fee** $35 **Tuition Costs** $3,200 ($6,800 out-of-state) **Need Blind** Yes **Financial Forms Deadline** Priority given to applications received by May 1 **Undergrads Awarded Aid** 67% **Aid That Is Need-Based** 99% **Average Award of Freshman Scholarship Package** $500 **Tests Required** SAT1 (preferred) or ACT **Admissions Address** 2900 Bedford Avenue, Brooklyn, NY 11210 **Admissions Telephone** (718) 951-5001

LAST YEAR'S CLASS Applied 3,425 **Accepted** 3,053 **Matriculated** 1,392 **Average SAT M/V** 488/425 **In Top Fifth of High School Graduating Class** 37%

COLLEGE LIFE Gender Breakdown M 41%, F 59% **Out of State Students** 7% **From Public Schools** 58% **Ethnic Composition** White & Other 54%, Asian American 10%, Black 25%, Hispanic 11%, Native American 0.1% **Foreign Students** 4% **Return as Sophomores** 82% **Total Faculty** 939 **Student Faculty Ratio** 16:1 **Fraternities (% of men participating)** 11 (5%) **Sororities (% of women participating)** 12 (5%) **Graduate Students** 4,506

Claremont McKenna College

www.mckenna.edu

Claremont, CA · Est. 1946 · Coed · Private · 959 Undergrads · Small Town

I need...

Admissions info admission@mckenna.edu
www.mckenna.edu/pros-stu
Financial aid info www.mckenna.edu/pros-stu
/finanaid

How wired is Claremont McKenna?

What is the student to computer ratio? 24:1

The usual tour

STUDENT CLUBS www.mckenna.edu/student/orgs
STUDY ABROAD www.mckenna.edu/pros-stu
/majors/abroad/handbook.htm
SPORTS www.mckenna.edu/athletics
VIRTUAL TOUR www.mckenna.edu/tour
LIBRARY voxlibris.claremont.edu
CALENDAR www.mckenna.edu/docs/calendars
/ac-cal.htm

Skip the brochure

- **PLAYBILL** This campus club offers $2 (cheap!
cheap!) movie screenings: As a bonus, the
movies they show are actually recent and fairly
decent. **www.mckenna.edu/colglife/play.htm**

- **SPECIAL ATTRACTONS** As if you needed any con-
vincing that Southern California would be a
prime place to kick back for four years—
Chinatown, Knotts Berry Farm, Disneyland,
Six Flags/Magic Mountain, Farmers Market,
the LA County Arboretum... need we go on?
www.mckenna.edu/colglife/special.htm

Be a valley kid: nestled in the mountains of Claremont,
Calif., is Claremont McKenna

- **PROFESSIONAL SPORTS** So you're a sports fan and
you're worried that, except for the men's volleyball team, the CM Stags and Athenas haven't
exactly kicked too much college butt. Fear not.
Just take your allegiance pro and root for the
Angels, the Dodgers, the Lakers, the Clippers,
the Kings, and of course the Mighty Ducks.
www.mckenna.edu/colglife/sports.htm

"The Claremont McKenna Stags and Athenas haven't kicked too much college butt."

WHAT YOU NEED TO GET IN **Application Deadline** January 15 **Early Action Deadline** November 15 **Common App.** Yes
Application Fee $40 **Tuition Costs** $17,840 **Room & Board** $6,260 **Need Blind** Yes **Financial Forms Deadline**
Priority given to applications received by February 1 **Undergrads Awarded Aid** 72% **Aid That Is Need-Based** 76%
Average Award of Freshman Scholarship Package $9,790 **Tests Required** SAT1 or ACT **Admissions Address**
890 Columbia Avenue, Claremont, CA 91711-6425 **Admissions Telephone** (909) 621-8088

LAST YEAR'S CLASS **Applied** 2,175 **Accepted** 887 **Matriculated** 276 **Average SAT M/V** 690/620 **Average ACT** 30
In Top Fifth of High School Graduating Class 93% **Applied Early** 87 **Accepted Early** 34

COLLEGE LIFE **Gender Breakdown** M 57%, F 43% **Out of State Students** 47% **From Public Schools** 70% **Ethnic**
Composition White & Other 64.2%, Asian American 21%, Black 4.5%, Hispanic 9.6%, Native American 0.7%
Foreign Students 4% **Reside on Campus** 90% **Return as Sophomores** 93% **Student Faculty Ratio** 9:1
Fraternities none **Sororities** none

Clark University

Worcester, MA · Est. 1887 · Coed · Private · 1889 Undergrads · Urban

I need...

Admissions info admissions@clarku.edu
www.clarku.edu/admissions/admission-shello.html

Financial aid info www.clarku.edu/financial-aid/index.html

How wired is Clark?

Do I get email? Yes
Do I get a home page? Yes
Where? www.clarku.edu/students.html
Is my dorm wired? Yes
What is the student to computer ratio? 19:1

The usual tour

HIGHLIGHTS www.clarku.edu/admissions/about/highlights.html
DEPARTMENTS www.clarku.edu/departments/index.html
STUDENT CLUBS www.clarku.edu/stuorgs.html
STUDENT NEWSPAPER www.clarku.edu/~scarlet/index.html
SPORTS www.clarku.edu/~ksalisbu/hello.html

Skip the brochure

• **5TH-YEAR-FREE Q&A** Some college students can't make it out with a bachelor's degree in five

"Get a BA and an MA, and pay for just four years."

Location: http://www.clarku.edu/stuorgs.html

It's neither a bird nor a plane, it's a Clark man

years, let alone a master's and a bachelor's. Clark gives students the chance to get both, and only pay for four years. Ain't that sweet. **www.clarku.edu/admissions/about/5thyear-q-and-a.html**

• **THE IDRISI PROJECT** Geography enthusiasts will be interested in this project, which takes place at Clark Labs for Cartographic Technology and Geographic Analysis. Its aim is to further research in computer-assisted geographical analysis. There are also nice pictures of a tree and a moon. **www.idrisi.clarku.edu**

• **CLARK NEWS** The alumni magazine is full of interesting articles and news about Clark happenings, like new majors, symposia, and sports events. **www.clarku.edu/resources/communications/clarknews/index.html**

WHAT YOU NEED TO GET IN Application Deadline January for priority consideration; final deadline February 1 **Early Action Deadline** December 1 and January 1 **Common App.** Yes **Application Fee** $40 **Tuition Costs** $19,600 **Room & Board** $4,250 **Financial Forms Deadline** Priority given to applications received by February 1 **Undergrads Awarded Aid** 71% **Aid That Is Need-Based** 98% **Average Award of Freshman Scholarship Package** $10595 **Tests Required** SAT1 or ACT **Admissions Address** 950 Main Street, Worcester, MA 01610-1477 **Admissions Telephone** (508) 793-7431

LAST YEAR'S CLASS Applied 2,439 **Accepted** 2,047 **Matriculated** 532 **Median Range SAT M/V** 490-610/450-560 **In Top Fifth of High School Graduating Class** 53%

COLLEGE LIFE Gender Breakdown M 42%, F 58% **Out of State Students** 63% **From Public Schools** 73% **Ethnic Composition** White & Other 90%, Asian American 4%, Black 3%, Hispanic 3% **Foreign Students** 19% **Reside on Campus** 70% **Return as Sophomores** 84% **Total Faculty** 170 **Student Faculty Ratio** 11:1 **Fraternities (% of men participating)** none **Sororities (% of women participating)** none **Graduate Students** 662

Clarkson University

www.clarkson.edu

Potsdam, NY · Est. 1896 · Coed · Private · 2,249 Undergrads · Small Town

I need...

Admissions info heron.tc.clarkson.edu/clarkson/admis/admis.html

How wired is Clarkson University?

Do I get email? Yes
Do I get a home page? Yes
   Where? heron.tc.clarkson.edu/home pages.html
Is my dorm wired? Yes
What is the student to computer ratio? 11:1

The usual tour

GREEK LIFE www.clarkson.edu/~kresskm/ZN/cu-fr.html
DEPARTMENTS www.clarkson.edu/edu/academic.html
VIRTUAL TOUR www.clarkson.edu/deuelpm/ClarksonTour/tour.html
STUDENT CLUBS heron.tc.clarkson.edu/home pages.html
LIBRARY www.clarkson.edu/~libweb/library.html
SPORTS www.clarkson.edu/clarkson/sports

Skip the brochure

• **THE CLARKSON COIL** Feel like you don't fit in anywhere? Well, now you've got a club to call your own. The Community of Independent Living (COIL) is an organization for what are most often termed "non-traditional" students. This can mean students who took time off before beginning college, students with children, or

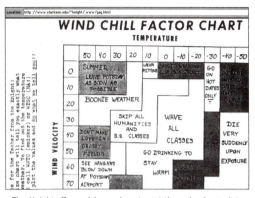

The Knight offers advice on how to get through a long winter

students who just don't fit the typical freshman mold. COIL brings them together for a variety of social events. **www.clarkson.edu/~clabouas/coil/coil.html**

• **THE WINDSOCK** Clarkson University's Flying Club "is devoted to man's passion for flight." **www.clarkson.edu/~vankeuks**

• **THE KNIGHT MAGAZINE** What exactly does *The Knight* cover? Well, you certainly won't find out here, because the editors are too busy with self-deprecation to bother with the periodical itself. Oh, wait: maybe this is a humor magazine? **www.clarkson.edu/~vankeuks**

"COIL is for non-traditional students."

WHAT YOU NEED TO GET IN **Application Deadline** February for priority consideration **Early Action Deadline** December 1 **Common App.** No **Application Fee** $25 **Tuition Costs** $17,500 **Room & Board** $6,064 **Financial Forms Deadline** Priority given to applications received by February 15 **Undergrads Awarded Aid** 85% **Aid That Is Need-Based** 75% **Average Award of Freshman Scholarship Package** $6,300 **Tests Required** SAT1 or ACT **Admissions Address** Box 5605, Potsdam, NY 13699 **Admissions Telephone** (315) 268-6479

LAST YEAR'S CLASS **Applied** 2,334 **Accepted** 2,068 **Matriculated** 645 **Average SAT M/V** 617/535 **In Top Fifth of High School Graduating Class** 66% **Applied Early** 150 **Accepted Early** 124

COLLEGE LIFE **Gender Breakdown** M 76%, F 24% **Out of State Students** 38% **From Public Schools** 88% **Ethnic Composition** White & Other 92.9%, Asian American 2.4%, Black 1.9%, Hispanic 1.6%, Native American 1.2% **Foreign Students** 5% **Reside on Campus** 86% **Return as Sophomores** 83% **Total Faculty** 170 **Student Faculty Ratio** 15:1 **Fraternities (% of men participating)** 16 (25%) **Sororities (% of women participating)** 3 (20%) **Graduate Students** 334

Clemson University

Clemson, SC · Est. 1889 · Coed · Public · 12,557 Undergrads · Small Town

I need...

Admissions info www.clemson.edu/curedesign
/studentinfo/ugrad.admiss.html
Financial aid info FINAID@ars.clemson.edu
hubcap.clemson.edu/~dkr/financial.aid.html

How wired is Clemson?

Do I get email? Yes
Do I get a home page? Yes
  Where? www.clemson.edu/clemweb/personal
  /pppublic.cgi
Is my dorm wired? Yes
What is the student to computer ratio? 13:1

The usual tour

LIBRARY www.lib.clemson.edu
STUDENT CLUBS www.clemson.edu/clemweb
/clubsorgs.html
GREEK LIFE www.clemson.edu/clemweb
/greeklife.html
CALENDAR www.grad.clemson.edu/schedule.htm
HISTORY www.clemson.edu/curedesign
/introducing/history.html

Skip the brochure

• **CLEMSON WATER SKI TEAM** Clemson students
trick, jump, and slalom their way through the
waters of South Carolina. Find out what that
means, and how they're doing at it, at their
home page. **hubcap.clemson.edu/~jhharri/ski_team
/cu_h2O_ski_team.html**

Location: http://hubcap.clemson.edu/~jhharri/ski_team/team_pic.html

Clemson's waterskiers mug for the camera seconds before
they go for a dip

• **SPICMACAY—CLEMSON CHAPTER** This organization
is definitely in the running for the most
unwieldy acronym in existence. However, once
you get past that, you can focus on the activities of the Society for Promotion of Indian
Classical Music and Culture Amongst Youth,
which include concerts, workshops, lectures
and demonstrations. **www.eng.clemson.edu
/~krishns/spicm/spicmacay.html**

• **CLEMSON CRICKET CLUB** If you're looking for little
noisy insects, expect to be disappointed. If
you don't know the lingo behind the game with
the wooden bat, expect to be confused. If,
however, you're a true cricket aficionado,
check out the progress of the Clemson Cricket
Club, complete with stats. Or, skip straight to
the team photo, with the universal language of
smiles and trophies. **hubcap.clemson.edu
/cricket/alt.html**

WHAT YOU NEED TO GET IN Application Deadline June 1 **Common App.** No **Application Fee** $35 **Tuition Costs** $2,922
($8,126 out-of-state) **Room & Board** $3,020 **Need Blind** Yes **Financial Forms Deadline** Priority given to
applications received by April 1 **Undergrads Awarded Aid** 55% **Aid That Is Need-Based** 51% **Average Award of
Freshman Scholarship Package** $3,300 **Tests Required** SAT1 (preferred) or ACT **Admissions Address** 105 Sikes
Hall, Clemson, SC 29634-5124 **Admissions Telephone** (864) 656-2287

LAST YEAR'S CLASS Applied 7,792 **Accepted** 6,217 **Matriculated** 2,575 **Average SAT M/V** 559/483 **Average ACT**
24 **In Top Fifth of High School Graduating Class** 53%

COLLEGE LIFE Gender Breakdown M 55%, F 45% **Out of State Students** 34% **From Public Schools** 80% **Ethnic
Composition** White & Other 89%, Asian American 2%, Black 9% **Reside on Campus** 52% **Return as Sophomores**
85% **Total Faculty** 1,221 **Student Faculty Ratio** 18:1 **Fraternities (% of men participating)** 25 (15%) **Sororities
(% of women participating)** 15 (25%) **Graduate Students** 3,770

Colby College

Waterville, ME · Est. 1813 · Coed · Private · 1,785 Undergrads · Small Town

I need...

Admissions info admissions@colby.edu
  www.colby.edu/admissions
Financial aid info finaid@colby.edu
  www.colby.edu/admissions/finaid.html

How wired is Colby College?

Do I get email? Yes
Do I get a home page? Yes
  Where? www.colby.edu/college/personal.html
Is my dorm wired? Yes
What is the student to computer ratio? 10:1

The usual tour

STUDENT CLUBS www.colby.edu/college/stuorgs
.html
SPORTS www.colby.edu/athletics
PUBLICATIONS www.colby.edu/college/newsevpub
.html
LIBRARY www.colby.edu/librarybase
STUDENT NEWSPAPER www.colby.edu/echo

Skip the brochure

• **COLBY COLLEGE WOODSMEN'S TEAM** Paul Bunyan
would be proud. Colby's Woodsmen "practice
old-time logging skills such as sawing, chop-
ping, log decking, and newer events such as
axe throwing and chainsaw." Hell, Stephen
King would be proud. **www.colby.edu/woodsmen**

• **NEW MOON RISING** Colby's feminist magazine features powerful poetry, fiction, essays and

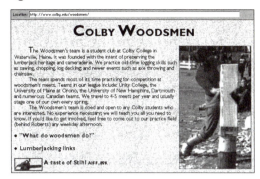

Coeds band together to wield axes and chainsaws

artwork. **www.colby.edu/nmr**

• **F.O.C.U.S.** The goal here is Freeing Our
Community of Unavailing Stereotypes, and the
means to that end is student-produced multimedia productions, some of which can be
viewed via QuickTime movies.
www.colby.edu/focus/index.html

• **COLBY FENCING** Beware of students with sharp,
pointy things. Better yet, let them teach you
how to wield your own weapon. **www.colby.edu/fencing**

> ## "Beware of Colby students with sharp, pointy things."

WHAT YOU NEED TO GET IN **Application Deadline** January 15 **Early Action Deadline** November 15 and January 1
Common App. Yes **Application Fee** $45 **Tuition Costs** $21,260 **Room & Board** $5,710 **Need Blind** No **Financial
Forms Deadline** February 1 **Undergrads Awarded Aid** 41% **Aid That Is Need-Based** 100% **Average Award of
Freshman Scholarship Package** $13,223 **Tests Required** SAT1 or ACT **Admissions Address** Mayflower Hill,
Waterville, ME 04901 **Admissions Telephone** (207) 872-3168

LAST YEAR'S CLASS **Applied** 4,217 **Accepted** 1,605 **Matriculated** 544 **Average SAT M/V** 640/580 **Average ACT** 27
In Top Fifth of High School Graduating Class 92% **Applied Early** 464 **Accepted Early** 213

COLLEGE LIFE **Gender Breakdown** M 45%, F 55% **Out of State Students** 90% **From Public Schools** 62% **Ethnic
Composition** White & Other 91%, Asian American 5%, Black 2%, Hispanic 2%, **Foreign Students** 6% **Reside on
Campus** 89% **Return as Sophomores** 95% **Total Faculty** 155 **Student Faculty Ratio** 11:1 **Fraternities** none
Sororities none

Colgate University

www.colgate.edu

Hamilton, NY · Est. 1819 · Coed · Private · 2,874 Undergrads · Rural

How wired is Colgate?

Do I get email? Yes
Do I get a home page? Yes
   Where? arachnid.colgate.edu/personal
Is my dorm wired? No
What is the student to computer ratio? 11:1

The usual tour

VIRTUAL TOUR www2.colgate.edu/tour
CALENDAR www.colgate.edu/calendar
DEPARTMENTS www2.colgate.edu/offices
STUDENT CLUBS www2.colgate.edu/students
/clublist.html
GREEK LIFE arachnid.colgate.edu/ifc
SPORTS www2.colgate.edu/athletics
LIBRARY exlibris.colgate.edu

Skip the brochure

- **COLGATE ULTIMATE FRISBEE** If you join, they'll tell you what a "scupper" is. After seeing the illustration of one, though, you might have second thoughts. **arachnid.colgate.edu/ultimate**

- **COLGATE 13** Motown! Pop! Barbershop! Humor! Performed at *The Tonight Show*, Super Bowl XIII, and the 1992 Summer Olympics! If that

Location: http://arachnid.colgate.edu/ultimate/layout.gif

Colgate students risk their teeth

doesn't wow you, nothing will. **arachnid.colgate .edu/groups/colgate13**

- **SOCIETY OF FAMILIES** At most schools, parental involvement in their child's college education is limited to filling out the financial aid forms and doing loads of laundry during spring and winter breaks. At Colgate, though, the Society of Families exists to promote family-school interaction. Did someone say Phone-A-Thons? **www2.colgate.edu/offices/sof**

- **THE COLGATE SCENE ON-LINE** This magazine for alumni, students, and parents gives a broad look at life at Colgate, with features on former and current students, school activities, and general school-related news. **www2.colgate.edu /scene**

"What's a scupper?"

WHAT YOU NEED TO GET IN **Application Deadline** January 15 **Early Action Deadline** January 15 **Common App.** Yes **Application Fee** $50 **Tuition Costs** $21,525 **Room & Board** $5,935 **Need Blind** No **Financial Forms Deadline** Priority given to applications received by March 1 **Undergrads Awarded Aid** 66% **Aid That Is Need-Based** 100% **Average Award of Freshman Scholarship Package** $15,861 **Tests Required** SAT1 or ACT **Admissions Address** 13 Oak Drive, Hamilton, NY 13346 **Admissions Telephone** (315) 824-7401

LAST YEAR'S CLASS **Applied** 6,037 **Accepted** 2,465 **Matriculated** 729 **Average SAT M/V** 645/651 **Average ACT** 28 **In Top Quarter of High School Graduating Class** 89% **Applied Early** 343 **Accepted Early** 200

COLLEGE LIFE **Gender Breakdown** M 49%, F 51% **Out of State Students** 70% **From Public Schools** 65% **Ethnic Composition** White & Other 89.7%, Asian American 3.9%, Black 3.5%, Hispanic 2.9% **Foreign Students** 3% **Reside on Campus** 70% **Return as Sophomores** 94% **Total Faculty** 250 **Student Faculty Ratio** 11:1 **Fraternities (% of men participating)** 10 (37%) **Sororities (% of women participating)** 4 (28%)

Colorado College

www.cc.colorado.edu

Colorado Springs, CO · Est. 1874 · Coed · Private · 2,019 Undergrads · Urban

I need...

Admissions info admission@admin.cc.colorado.edu
www.cc.colorado.edu/Admission
Financial aid info finaid@admin.cc.colorado.edu
www.cc.colorado.edu/Admission/Apply
/FinancialAid.html

How wired is Colorado College?

Do I get email? Yes
Do I get a home page? Yes
Where? www.cc.colorado.edu/Students
/Homepages.html
What is the student to computer ratio? 11:1

The usual tour

STUDENT CLUBS www.cc.colorado.edu/Students
PUBLICATIONS www.cc.colorado.edu/NewsAnd
Publications
LIBRARY www.cc.colorado.edu/Library
SPORTS www.cc.colorado.edu/Athletics
DEPARTMENTS www.cc.colorado.edu/Academics
/Departments
GREEK LIFE www.cc.colorado.edu/Students
/Organizations/FraternitiesAndSororities

Skip the brochure

• **COLORADO COLLEGE CHESS CLUB** You'll never do
schoolwork again once you've found this site
and its online chess problem and tactic of the
week. If that's not enough to keep you busy,
check out the archives. Or move offline and

Colorado chess clubbers look for mates

attend one of the weekly meetings. **www.cc
.colorado.edu/Students/Organizations/ChessClub**

• **S.H.A.R.E.** Colorado College students organize to
debunk myths regarding rape and promote
rape prevention. **www.cc.colorado.edu/Students
/Organizations/SHARE**

• **STUDENT INITIATIVE FOR EXCELLENCE IN TEACHING**
As the recipients of all that the faculty has to
offer, Colorado College students have taken it
upon themselves to ensure the quality of the
professoriate (a word which, incidentally,
they've spelled wrong here... but at least
they're concerned with their faculty being
smart). **www.cc.colorado.edu/Students/Excellence
InTeaching**

WHAT YOU NEED TO GET IN Application Deadline January 15 **Common App.** Yes **Application Fee** $40 **Tuition Costs**
$18,084 **Room & Board** $4,562 **Need Blind** Yes **Financial Forms Deadline** Priority given to applications received
by February 15 **Undergrads Awarded Aid** 55% **Aid That Is Need-Based** 90% **Average Award of Freshman
Scholarship Package** $10,300 **Tests Required** SAT1 or ACT **Admissions Address** 14 East Cache La Poudre
Street, Colorado Springs, CO 80903 **Admissions Telephone** (719) 389-6344

LAST YEAR'S CLASS Applied 3,423 **Accepted** 1,951 **Matriculated** 599 **Median Range SAT M/V** 570-670/520-620
In Top Fifth of High School Graduating Class 74%

COLLEGE LIFE Gender Breakdown M 47%, F 53% **Out of State Students** 79% **From Public Schools** 73% **Ethnic
Composition** White & Other 88.8%, Asian American 3.6%, Black 2%, Hispanic 4.6%, Native American 1% **Foreign
Students** 3% **Reside on Campus** 75% **Return as Sophomores** 92% **Student Faculty Ratio** 12:1 **Fraternities
(% of men participating)** 3 (17%) **Sororities (% of women participating)** 3 (20%) **Graduate Students** 22

Colorado School of Mines

gn.mines.colorado.edu

Golden, CO · Est. 1874 · Coed · Public · 2255 Undergrads · Urban

How wired is Colorado School of Mines?

Do I get email? Yes
Do I get a home page? Yes
Where? gn.mines.colorado.edu/students
Is my dorm wired? Yes
What is the student to computer ratio? 9:1

The usual tour

SPORTS gn.mines.colorado.edu/Academic
/athletics
STUDENT CLUBS gn.mines.colorado.edu/Stu_life
/organ
CALENDAR gn.mines.colorado.edu/All_about
/events
HISTORY gn.mines.colorado.edu/All_about/history
STUDENT NEWSPAPER gn.mines.colorado.edu/Stu
_life/pub/csmoredig

Skip the brochure

• **CSM RESEARCH** While it's far from evident here, Colorado's miners must be up to something worthwhile, since the school's research facilities are sponsored in part by the Department of Defense, the Department of Energy, the

What's Mines is yours

Department of the Interior, and the Environmental Protection Agency
gn.mines.colorado.edu/Research/research_dev

• **AISES** The American Indian Science and Engineering Society (AISES) is a private, nonprofit organization founded in 1972 which seeks to nurture the building of community by bridging science and technology with traditional native values. The School of Mines has its own chapter which hopes to equip Native Americans with the ability to help tribal leaders better manage and develop their land and resources.
magma.Mines.EDU/Stu_life/organ/aises/backgnd.shtml

"AISES hopes to help tribal leaders manage and develop resources."

WHAT YOU NEED TO GET IN **Application Deadline** April 1 for priority consideration; final deadline June 1 **Common App.** No **Application Fee** $25 **Tuition Costs** $4,435 ($13,405 out-of-state) **Room & Board** $4,550 **Need Blind** Yes **Financial Forms Deadline** Priority given to applications received by March 1 **Undergrads Awarded Aid** 70% **Aid That Is Need-Based** 70% **Average Award of Freshman Scholarship Package** $3,685 **Tests Required** SAT1 or ACT **Admissions Address** 1500 Illinois Street, Golden, CO 80401-9952 **Admissions Telephone** (303) 273-3220

LAST YEAR'S CLASS **Applied** 1,692 **Accepted** 1,385 **Matriculated** 452 **Average SAT M/V** 650/550 **Average ACT** 28 **In Top Quarter of High School Graduating Class** 92%

COLLEGE LIFE **Gender Breakdown** M 76%, F 24% **Out of State Students** 36% **From Public Schools** 90% **Ethnic Composition** White & Other 86%, Asian American 5%, Black 2%, Hispanic 6%, Native American 1% **Foreign Students** 8% **Reside on Campus** 23% **Return as Sophomores** 85% **Total Faculty** 290 **Student Faculty Ratio** 14:1 **Fraternities (% of men participating)** 6 (20%) **Sororities (% of women participating)** 2 (20%) **Graduate Students** 852

University of Colorado, Boulder

Boulder, CO · Est. 1876 · Coed · Public · 19640 Undergrads · Urban

I need...

Admissions info apply@Colorado.edu
   stripe.colorado.edu/~rai/admissions
Financial aid info finaid@Colorado.edu
   www.colorado.edu/finaid

How wired is UC Boulder?

Do I get email? Yes
Do I get a home page? Yes
   Where? www.colorado.edu/FindPeoplePlaces
   /HomePages.html
Is my dorm wired? No
What is the student to computer ratio? 15:1

The usual tour

DEPARTMENTS www.colorado.edu/AcademicLife
   /DeptListings.html
STUDENT CLUBS www.colorado.edu/StudentLife
   /student_hp.html
SPORTS athl72.colorado.edu/sports/sports.htm
STUDENT NEWSPAPER bcn.boulder.co.us/campus
   press/Presshome.html
PUBLICATIONS www.colorado.edu/Campus
   Resources/Publications.html
CAREER CENTER stripe.colorado.edu/~rai/carserv

Skip the brochure

- **COLORADO CREW** If this beautiful site, with its photos of sunsets over the river and regattas

Boulder guarantees you a colorful Colorado education

nationwide, doesn't make you want to row for Colorado, well, you just don't. The crew team was begun by students in 1992, and is now a competitive fixture. **www.colorado.edu/Student Groups/crew**

- **CAMINOS QUICK REFERENCE GUIDE** Here's the best overall road map to UC-Boulder life. Follow the trail on through... it provides basic information for every aspect on campus life, even those that don't have a Web site. **stripe.Colorado.EDU /~caminos/Home.html**

- **RALPHIE'S GUIDE TO STUDENT LIFE** This is a very specific, hands-on guide to the dos and don'ts that students need to survive at Boulder. Topics include volunteering, cultural events, Boulder hangouts, and campus safety. **www.colorado.edu/sacs/ralphie/home.html**

WHAT YOU NEED TO GET IN Application Deadline February 15 **Common App.** Yes **Application Fee** $40 (may be waived) **Tuition Costs** $ **Room & Board** $4,162 **Need Blind** Yes **Financial Forms Deadline** Priority given to applications received by April 1 **Undergrads Awarded Aid** 48% **Aid That Is Need-Based** 75% **Average Award of Freshman Scholarship Package** $3,500 **Tests Required** SAT1 or ACT **Admissions Address** Campus Box 30, Boulder, CO 80309 **Admissions Telephone** (303) 492-6301

LAST YEAR'S CLASS Applied 15,066 **Accepted** 12,014 **Matriculated** 4,182 **Median Range SAT M/V** 510-640/ 440-550 **In Top Fifth of High School Graduating Class** 48%

COLLEGE LIFE Gender Breakdown M 53%, F 47% **Out of State Students** 46% **From Public Schools** 85% **Ethnic Composition** White & Other 85%, Asian American 6%, Black 2%, Hispanic 6%, Native American 1% **Foreign Students** 2% **Reside on Campus** 25% **Return as Sophomores** 80% **Total Faculty** 1,363 **Student Faculty Ratio** 22:1 **Fraternities (% of men participating)** 17 (15%) **Sororities (% of women participating)** 9 (13%) **Graduate Students** 4,800

Columbia University

New York, NY · Est. 1754 · Coed · Private · 3,573 Undergrads · Urban

I need...

Admissions info ugrad-admiss@columbia.edu
www.columbia.edu/cu/bulletin/apply.html

How wired is Columbia University

Do I get email? Yes
Do I get a home page? Yes
   Where? www.columbia.edu/acis/userlist
Is my dorm wired? Yes
What is the student to computer ratio? 9:1

The usual tour

VIRTUAL TOUR www.columbia.edu/cu/admissions
   /intro
DEPARTMENTS www.columbia.edu/cu/academics
   .html
SPORTS www.columbia.edu/cu/athletics
STUDENT NEWSPAPER www.columbia.edu/cu
   /record/record.html
STUDENT CLUBS www.columbia.edu/cu/groups
   .html

Skip the brochure

- **COLUMBIA TELEVISION—CTV** Any old school can have a student newspaper or a student radio

"See if you want to hang out with these people for four years."

Where to be seen uptown: Columbia's main piazza is a major student hangout

station. But when you pay the big bucks to go to Columbia, you get your own TV station. Not only that, but it's the second oldest in the country. CTV has thirteen active programs now, entirely student-run and produced, which range from news to variety comedy.
www.columbia.edu/cu/ctv

- **THE CLEFHANGERS** Of Columbia's many a cappella singing groups, the Clefhangers site has its head firmly in the clouds. Sample sound clips, hire them for a party, check out their pictures. They even direct you to the home pages of the competition. **www.columbia.edu/cu/clefs/clefs.html**

- **COOLPAGE COMPETITION WINNERS** According to CU's *The Moment*, these are the best student home pages at Columbia. See if you want to hang with these people for four years.
www.columbia.edu/cu/moment/coolpage/winners.html

WHAT YOU NEED TO GET IN **Application Deadline** January 1 **Early Action Deadline** November 1 **Common App.** No **Application Fee** $45 ($60 after December 1 (may be waived for economic hardship) **Tuition Costs** $19,730 **Room & Board** $6,864 **Need Blind** Yes **Financial Forms Deadline** January 1 **Undergrads Awarded Aid** 56% **Aid That Is Need-Based** 100% **Average Award of Freshman Scholarship Package** $14,338 **Tests Required** SAT1 or ACT **Admissions Address** Office of Undergraduate Admissions, 212 Hamilton Hall, New York, NY 10027 **Admissions Telephone** (212) 854-2522

LAST YEAR'S CLASS **Applied** 8,714 **Accepted** 2,045 **Matriculated** 883 **Median Range SAT M/V** 630-730/570-690 **In Top Fifth of High School Graduating Class** 95% **Applied Early** 532 **Accepted Early** 248

COLLEGE LIFE **Gender Breakdown** M 51%, F 49% **Out of State Students** 75% **From Public Schools** 56% **Ethnic Composition** White & Other 59%, Asian American 22.5%, Black 9.2%, Hispanic 9.3% **Reside on Campus** 90% **Return as Sophomores** 96% **Student Faculty Ratio** 7:1 **Fraternities (% of men participating)** 12 (18%) **Sororities (% of women participating)** 7 (8%)

Concordia University

www.concordia.ca

Montreal, Quebec, CN · Est. 1974 · Coed · Public · 21,791 Undergrads · Urban

I need...

Admissions info www.concordia.ca/Academic
_Info/General_Academic_Info/Admissions
.html

Financial aid info www.concordia.ca/Academic
_Info/General_Academic_Info/Financial
_Aid.html

How wired is Concordia University?

Do I get email? Yes
Do I get a home page? Yes
Is my dorm wired? No
What is the student to computer ratio? 79:1

The usual tour

HISTORY www.concordia.ca/Visitor_Centre
/History/History-Concordia.html
DEPARTMENTS www.concordia.ca/Academic_Info
/Fac-Dep.html
STUDENT CLUBS domingo.concordia.ca/clubpages
.html
LIBRARY juno.concordia.ca
STUDENT MEDIA www.concordia.ca/Student
_Centre/Student_Life/Student_media.html

Skip the brochure

• **LOYAL ORDER OF BEER BUFFALO** Were you expecting actual academic advancement in college? How naive. Instead you will join the buffalo, compete in their belching contest, and tour a brewery. Pictures of the above here. "Go have

Did you know that Dick Tracy went to Concordia?

a beer, you Hoser!" Well, they look like they're having fun, anyway. **cug.concordia.ca/~buffalo**

• **MEDIATRIBE** Many college publications with lovely Web presences are for alumni or graduate students only. *Mediatribe*, however, is an undergraduate journal of communication studies that is entirely student-run and published each spring. The articles, like Quebec, are in both French and English. **cug.concordia.ca/~mtribe**

• **CONCORDIA UNIVERSITY PAGAN SOCIETY** About a hundred Concordia students, alumni, and non-students are following one of the Pagan paths. We can't say it better, so we'll quote: "At the eight Sabbats, we provide open worship circles to mark the peaks and transitions of the solar cycle which gives us the four seasons. Once during the lunar month, either at the new or full moon, we meet for esbat rituals which are also open to the public." They have a newsletter, too. **cug.concordia.ca/~cups**

WHAT YOU NEED TO GET IN Application Deadline February 1 for priority consideration; final deadline March 1 **Common App.** No **Application Fee** $30 (Canadian dollars) **Tuition Costs** $1,939 ($7,452 out-of-country) **Room & Board** $4,200 **Undergrads Awarded Aid** 49% **Aid That Is Need-Based** 98% **Tests Required** N/A **Admissions Address** 1455 de Maisonneuve Boulevard, Montreal, Quebec, CN H3G 1M8 **Admissions Telephone** (514) 848-2668

LAST YEAR'S CLASS Applied 10,944 **Accepted** 7,835 **Matriculated** 4,656

COLLEGE LIFE Gender Breakdown M 47%, F 53% **From Public Schools** 90% **Reside on Campus** 2% **Return as Sophomores** 89% **Total Faculty** 1,201 **Student Faculty Ratio** 17:1 **Fraternities** 6 **Sororities** 2 **Graduate Students** 3,275

Connecticut College

camel.conncoll.edu

New London, CT · Est. 1911 · Coed · Private · 1858 Undergrads · Big Town

I need...

Admissions info admit@conncoll.edu
 camel.conncoll.edu/ccadm/home
 page.html
Financial aid info camel.conncoll.edu/ccadm
 /finaid.htm

How wired is Connecticut College?

Do I get email? Yes
Do I get a home page? Yes
 Where? camel.conncoll.edu/menu/students
 .html
Is my dorm wired? Yes
What is the student to computer ratio? 12:1

The usual tour

DEPARTMENTS camel.conncoll.edu/menu
 /departments.html
SPORTS camel.conncoll.edu/ccrec/sports
 /index.html
CALENDAR camel.conncoll.edu/Calendar
 /calendar.html
LIBRARY shain.lib.conncoll.edu
UNIQUE QUALITIES camel.conncoll.edu/menu
 /Signature.html

Skip the brochure

• **WHERE IT'S** @ Connecticut College magazine's
 interactive site is definitely the best one at CC.
 It's the alumni rag, but unlike most similar
 pubs this one does not talk exclusively about

Connecticut College students show their true colors

the college. Instead, faculty and administrators contribute in-depth academic articles in
their discipline, and, well, they talk about the
college, too. **camel.conncoll.edu/Spiff/wia/wia.html**

• **C-GREEN** Environmental activism is big at Connecticut, and C-Green is the clearinghouse for
all such activity. Read about Recycling, the
Inherit the Earth Award, and the Environmental
Studies Program. **camel.conncoll.edu/ccrec/greennet
/c.green.html**

• **DAGHLIAN ION ACCELERATOR LABORATORY** This site
is not for those who think that their ions
already go pretty fast. Others may be interested in this pictorial of the physics department's
pride and joy—a one million volt Pelletron.
Don't forget to "note the charging chain on the
pulley to the right of the ion source."
camel.conncoll.edu/ccacad/physics.web/accel.html

WHAT YOU NEED TO GET IN **Application Deadline** January 15 **Early Action Deadline** November 15 **Common App.** Yes
Application Fee $45 **Tuition Costs, Room & Board** $27,375 **Need Blind** No **Financial Forms Deadline**
February 1 **Undergrads Awarded Aid** 51% **Aid That Is Need-Based** 100% **Average Award of Freshman
Scholarship Package** $14,025 **Tests Required** SAT1 or ACT **Admissions Address** 270 Mohegan Avenue, New
London, CT 06320-4196 **Admissions Telephone** (860) 439-2200

LAST YEAR'S CLASS **Applied** 3,151 **Accepted** 1,571 **Matriculated** 453 **Average SAT M/V** 620/590 **Average ACT** 25
In Top Fifth of High School Graduating Class 71% **Applied Early** 186 **Accepted Early** 112

COLLEGE LIFE **Gender Breakdown** M 43%, F 57% **Out of State Students** 83% **From Public Schools** 52% **Ethnic
Composition** White & Other 89%, Asian American 3%, Black 5%, Hispanic 3% **Foreign Students** 7% **Reside on
Campus** 97% **Return as Sophomores** 91% **Total Faculty** 185 **Student Faculty Ratio** 11:1 **Fraternities** none
Sororities none **Graduate Students** 54

University of Connecticut

www.uconn.edu

Storrs, CT · Est. 1881 · Coed · Public · 11,330 Undergrads · Small Town

I need...

Admissions info beahusky@uconnvm.uconn.edu
www.ucc.uconn.edu/~misadm14
Financial aid info wwwfaid@uconnvm.uconn.edu
www.ucc.uconn.edu/~wwwfaid

How wired is UConn?

Do I get email? Yes
Do I get a home page? Yes
Is my dorm wired? Yes
What is the student to computer ratio? 6:1

The usual tour

SPORTS www.ucc.uconn.edu/~wwwhusky
VIRTUAL TOUR haleh.ucc.uconn.edu/sights
/sights.html
STUDENT CLUBS www.uconn.edu/student
/studorg.html
LIBRARY www.uconn.edu/library.html
DEPARTMENTS www.uconn.edu/academic/dept
list.html
CALENDAR www.uconn.edu/event/evenmenu.html

Skip the brochure

• **WOMEN'S BASKETBALL** If it's UConn athletics, it's
got to be Husky Hoops. Jen Rizzotti's bio is a
dissertation in and of itself, and there's plenty
to say about her teammates as well. **www.ucc
.uconn.edu/~wwwhusky/wbb.html**

• **UCONN'S LOCAL NEWSGROUPS** Although you can't
access the messages in the newsgroups until

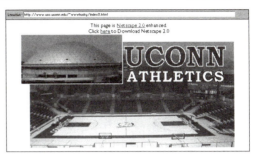

You too may get the Husky feeling

you're part of the uconn.edu domain, you can
get a sense of the scope and variety of newsgroups available by scrolling through the list
and descriptions. **www2.uconn.edu/newsweather
/newsgroups**

• **THE VIRTUAL CLASSROOM** UConn's faculty are running, not walking, into the age of the Internet.
Check out the different ways that professors
are using online resources to supplement their
real-life classes. Read the works for your
English literature class from your screen (no
need to buy books!), or, if you're feeling particularly adventurous, take a few practice exams
in physical chemistry. **yoda.ucc.uconn.edu/Virtual
Class/index.html**

• **WHUS** Sure, other college radio stations offer
alternative rock, jazz, and world music, but
where else are you going to find polkas played
on a regular basis? Sports coverage and news
are also a big part of broadcasts. **www.ucc.uconn
.edu/~whusfm**

WHAT YOU NEED TO GET IN **Application Deadline** April 1 **Common App.** No **Application Fee** $40 **Tuition Costs** $4,036
($12,306 out-of-state) **Room & Board** $5,302 **Need Blind** Yes **Financial Forms Deadline** Priority given to
applications received by March 1 **Undergrads Awarded Aid** 55% **Aid That Is Need-Based** 85% **Tests Required**
SAT1 (preferred) or ACT **Admissions Address** Storrs, CT 06269 **Admissions Telephone** (860) 486-3137

LAST YEAR'S CLASS **Applied** 9,886 **Accepted** 6,884 **Matriculated** 2,021 **Average SAT M/V** 549/479 **In Top Fifth of
High School Graduating Class** 48%

COLLEGE LIFE **Gender Breakdown** M 50%, F 50% **Out of State Students** 22% **Ethnic Composition** White & Other
86%, Asian American 6%, Black 4%, Hispanic 4% **Foreign Students** 1% **Reside on Campus** 65% **Return as
Sophomores** 86% **Total Faculty** 1,203 **Fraternities (% of men participating)** 17 (13%) **Sororities (% of women
participating)** 9 (7%) **Graduate Students** 4,405

Cooper Union

New York, NY · Est. 1859 · Coed · Private · 924 Undergrads · Urban

How wired is Cooper Union?

Do I get email? Yes
Do I get a home page? Yes
   Where? www.cooper.edu/people/people.html
Is my dorm wired? No
What is the student to computer ratio? 6:1

The usual tour

DEPARTMENTS www.cooper.edu/programs.html
CAREER CENTER www.cooper.edu/admin/career
   _services/career_services.html
CALENDAR www.cooper.edu/calendar.html
STUDENT CLUBS www.cooper.edu/organizations
   /organizations.html

Skip the brochure

• **MEDITATION CIRCLE** With a campus located in the heart of the East Village, in the world of skate-boarders, cheap restaurants, dive bars, and 24-hour activity, it is no wonder Cooper Union students have designed a forum where they can drown out the clamor and make peace with themselves. **www.cooper.edu/organizations /clubs/meditation/Welcome.html**

• **THE HISTORY OF COOPER UNION** A legacy of educa-tion and Jello? Cooper Union is the only

Cooper Union architecture students start with the basics

full-scholarship private college in the United States. It's the namesake of Peter Cooper, who not only made his fortune in glue and laid the first Atlantic telegraph cable, but also invented Jello. Still, accomplished as he was, he could not spell, and to provide working class kids with the free education he never had, he founded Cooper Union in 1859. Since then, it has seen the founding of the Red Cross and the NAACP, as well as provided free education to thousands of students. **www.cooper.edu/history.html**

• **THE HERB LUBALIN STUDY CENTER OF DESIGN AND TYPOGRAPHY** The Lubalin Study Center site explains how graphic design is part of visual communication, and how it relates to "verbal and visual literacies." **www.cooper.edu/art/lubalin /LBfront.html**

WHAT YOU NEED TO GET IN **Early Action Deadline** December 1 **Common App.** No **Application Fee** $35 (may be waived in cases of economic hardship) **Tuition Costs** $8,300 **Room & Board** $5,015 **Need Blind** Yes **Financial Forms Deadline** May 15 with a priority given to applications received by February **Undergrads Awarded Aid** 37% **Aid That Is Need-Based** 100% **Average Award of Freshman Scholarship Package** $4,500 **Tests Required** SAT1 (preferred) or ACT **Admissions Address** 41 Cooper Square, New York, NY 10003 **Admissions Telephone** 212 353-4120

LAST YEAR'S CLASS **Applied** 2,244 **Accepted** 281 **Matriculated** 193 **Average SAT M/V** 740/630 **In Top Fifth of High School Graduating Class** 90% **Applied Early** 71 **Accepted Early** 21

COLLEGE LIFE **Gender Breakdown** M 63%, F 37% **Out of State Students** 43% **From Public Schools** 65% **Ethnic Composition** White & Other 56.8%, Asian American 27%, Black 6%, Hispanic 10%, Native American 0.2% **Foreign Students** 8% **Reside on Campus** 19% **Return as Sophomores** 87% **Total Faculty** 192 **Student Faculty Ratio** 7:1 **Fraternities (% of men participating)** 2 (20%) **Sororities (% of women participating)** 2 (10%) **Graduate Students** 80

Cornell University

Ithaca, NY · Est. 1865 · Coed · Public · 13,372 Undergrads · Big Town

I need...

Admissions info admissions@cornell.edu
www.cornell.edu/UAO/Undergrad
_Admissions.html
Financial aid info cornellu_fin_aid@cornell.edu
www.cornell.edu/UAO/finaid.html

How wired is Cornell University?

Do I get email? Yes
Do I get a home page? Yes
   Where? www.cornell.edu/cgi-bin/CUW3_Stud
What is the student to computer ratio? 19:1

The usual tour

VIRTUAL TOUR www.info.cornell.edu/CUHome
Page/PhotoTour.html
DEPARTMENTS www.cornell.edu/Computer/CUW3
_Dept.html
STUDENT CLUBS www.cornell.edu/Computer
/CUW3_Org.html
STUDY ABROAD www.einaudi.cornell.edu/CU
Abroad
LIBRARY www.cornell.edu:3002/library/cul.html
SPORTS www.athletics.cornell.edu

Skip the brochure

• **THE SIERK MEMORIAL MUSEUM OF RANDOM ART** It's
not a major art history research hub. It has yet
to receive a grant. In fact, it's just Apartment
D-34 on Thurston Avenue in Ithaca. View the
Sparks Spaghetti Wall (an installation piece),
the Amazing! Liquid Fire, and much more.

Check out some contemporary sculpture in Cornell's
Engineering Quad

While this site is a dead-on satire of real art
museum sites, it begs the question: "Do
Cornell students have to take any classes?"
www.cheme.cornell.edu/~gwilson/sierk/index.html

• **THE SKITS-O-PHRENICS** Meet the gang from
Cornell's only all-skit comedy troupe on this
sunny page. **www-sunlab.cit.cornell.edu/Info/People
/csaulino/skitsophrenics.html**

• **THE CORNELL REVIEW** The Hall of Great Men
includes Ronald Reagan, Newt Gingrich, Teddy
Roosevelt, and Thomas Jefferson. The
Basement of Filth has Clinton, Gore, and Ted
Kennedy. Willam F. Buckley's house? No! It's
The Cornell Review, the "Conservative Voice of
Cornell." **xanadu.ilr.cornell.edu/cr**

"The Skits-o-Phrenics: an all-skit comedy troupe"

WHAT YOU NEED TO GET IN Application Deadline January 1 **Early Action Deadline** November 10 **Common App.** No
Application Fee $65 **Tuition Costs** $20,000 **Room & Board** $7,035 **Need Blind** Yes **Financial Forms Deadline**
Priority given to applications received by February 15 **Undergrads Awarded Aid** 65% **Aid That Is Need-Based**
100% **Average Award of Freshman Scholarship Package** $10,700 **Tests Required** SAT1 or ACT **Admissions
Address** Ithaca, NY 14853 **Admissions Telephone** (607) 255-5241

LAST YEAR'S CLASS Applied 20,603 **Accepted** 7,050 **Matriculated** 3,204 **Median Range SAT M/V** 640-730
/540-650 **In Top Fifth of High School Graduating Class** 94% **Applied Early** 1,861 **Accepted Early** 752

COLLEGE LIFE Gender Breakdown M 53%, F 47% **Out of State Students** 64% **Ethnic Composition** White & Other
72.5%, Asian American 17%, Black 4%, Hispanic 6%, Native American 0.5% **Foreign Students** 6% **Reside on
Campus** 58% **Return as Sophomores** 95% **Total Faculty** 1,585 **Student Faculty Ratio** 8:1 **Fraternities
(% of men participating)** 45 (32%) **Sororities (% of women participating)** 19 (27%) **Graduate Students** 5,542

Creighton University

Omaha, NE · Est. 1878 · Coed · Private · 3,904 Undergrads · Urban

www.creighton.edu

How wired is Creighton?

Do I get email? Yes
Do I get a home page? Yes
   Where? www.creighton.edu/local/student.html
Is my dorm wired? Yes
What is the student to computer ratio? 16:1

The usual tour

VIRTUAL TOUR www.creighton.edu/tour.html
DEPARTMENTS www.creighton.edu/college.html
SPORTS www.creighton.edu/Athletics
LIBRARY www.creighton.edu/libraries.html
CAREER CENTER gopher://bluejay.creighton.edu
:70/11/employment/career

"St. John's is the literal, figurative, and spiritual center of Creighton."

Creighton's Jesuit Garden is available for classes, socializ-
ing, contemplation, and cheesy college brochure shots

Skip the brochure

- **FELLOWSHIP OF CHRISTIAN ATHLETES** Creighton is a
Jesuit-run college, so organizations like FCA
are really big news. But you don't have to be
Christian or an athlete to join.
bluejay.creighton.edu/~overscot/fca/fca.html

- **BLUE NEWS** What's happening in the movie theater today? What's up at the Skutt Student
Center? This gopher newsletter publishes cal-
endars and schedules for the day. **gopher://www
.creighton.edu/ll/bluenews**

- **UNIVERSITY MINISTRY AND ST. JOHN'S CHURCH** St.
John's is the centerpiece of Creighton, both fig-
uratively and literally. As the campus church, it
serves the college spiritually. And it's nice to
look at, too. **www.creighton.edu/CampusMinistry**

WHAT YOU NEED TO GET IN **Application Deadline** August 1 **Common App.** No **Application Fee** $30 **Tuition Costs**
$11,746 **Room & Board** $4,726 **Need Blind** Yes **Financial Forms Deadline** Priority given to applications received
by April 1 **Undergrads Awarded Aid** 68% **Aid That Is Need-Based** 53% **Average Award of Freshman Scholarship
Package** $3,316 **Tests Required** SAT1 or ACT (preferred) **Admissions Address** 2500 California, Omaha, NE
68178 **Admissions Telephone** (402) 280-2703

LAST YEAR'S CLASS **Applied** 2,558 **Accepted** 2,382 **Matriculated** 786 **Average SAT (combined)** 1057 **Average
ACT** 25 **In Top Tenth of High School Graduating Class** 37%

COLLEGE LIFE **Gender Breakdown** M 40%, F 60% **Out of State Students** 62% **From Public Schools** 65% **Ethnic
Composition** White & Other 86.7%, Asian American 7%, Black 2.8%, Hispanic 3%, Native American 0.5% **Foreign
Students** 3% **Reside on Campus** 27% **Return as Sophomores** 86% **Student Faculty Ratio** 14:1 **Fraternities
(% of men participating)** 7 (33%) **Sororities (% of women participating)** 6 (30%) **Graduate Students** 2,344

University of Dallas

www.udallas.edu

Irving, TX · Est. 1956 · Coed · Private · 1,103 Undergrads · Urban

I need...

Admissions info undadmis@acad.udallas.edu
acad.udallas.edu/www/admiss/bodyaf.html
Financial aid info undadmis@acad.udallas.edu
acad.udallas.edu/www/admiss/bodyf2.html

How wired is University of Dallas?

Do I get email? Yes
Do I get a home page? No
What is the student to computer ratio? 9:1

The usual tour

DEPARTMENTS acad.udallas.edu/www/admiss
/bodya1_c.html
MISSION STATEMENT acad.udallas.edu/www
/constantin/cc_miss.html

Skip the brochure

• **THE UNDERGRADUATE CORE CURRICULUM** The
Constantin College of Liberal Arts spells out
its definition of "liberal" thusly: "The organization and content of the Core are determined by
the premise that these goals can best be

"The road from Rome to Dallas needs no justification..."

Department of Philosophy

Veritatem Justitiam Diligite

General information

About the Department

The Philosophy Program

The Department's Faculty

Internet Resources

Some Ultimate Philosophy Page

Deep thought, Dallas style

achieved through a curriculum founded on the
heritage tradition of liberal education. Within
this heritage, the Christian intellectual tradition is an essential element, and the American
experience merits special consideration."
acad.udallas.edu/www/constantin/cc_core.html

• **THE ROME PROGRAM** Once you're immersed in
the core curriculum and are well on your way
to becoming a model Christian citizen, what
better place for a pilgrimage than Rome? "The
road from Rome to Dallas doubtless needs no
justification... [To] be a student in the Western
World... is to follow the path to Rome." This
semester abroad program is geared toward
sophomores. **acad.udallas.edu/www/constantin
/cc_rome.html**

WHAT YOU NEED TO GET IN **Application Deadline** December 1 for priority consideration; final deadline March 1 **Common App.** No **Application Fee** $30 **Tuition Costs** $12,120 **Room & Board** $4,918 **Need Blind** Yes **Financial Forms Deadline** Priority given to applications received by March 1 **Undergrads Awarded Aid** 89% **Aid That Is Need-Based** 64% **Average Award of Freshman Scholarship Package** $6,933 **Tests Required** SAT1 or ACT **Admissions Address** 1845 East Northgate Drive, Irving, TX 75062-4799 **Admissions Telephone** (214) 721-5266

LAST YEAR'S CLASS **Applied** 722 **Accepted** 655 **Matriculated** 248 **Average SAT M/V** 583/562 **Average ACT** 26 **In Top Fifth of High School Graduating Class** 62%

COLLEGE LIFE **Gender Breakdown** M 46%, F 54% **Out of State Students** 46% **From Public Schools** 59% **Ethnic Composition** White & Other 74.7%, Asian American 10.4%, Black 1.5%, Hispanic 12.9%, Native American 0.5% **Foreign Students** 3% **Reside on Campus** 64% **Return as Sophomores** 85% **Total Faculty** 117 **Student Faculty Ratio** 13:1 **Fraternities** none **Sororities** none **Graduate Students** 1,643

Dartmouth College

Hanover, NH · Est. 1769 · Coed · Private · 3,861 Undergrads · Small Town

I need...

Admissions info www.dartmouth.edu/admin
/admissions/ao/index.html
Financial aid info www.dartmouth.edu/admin
/admissions/fao/index.html

How wired is Dartmouth College?

Do I get email? Yes
Do I get a home page? Yes
   Where? www.dartmouth.edu/index/homes.html
Is my dorm wired? Yes
What is the student to computer ratio? 6:1

The usual tour

DEPARTMENTS www.dartmouth.edu/artsci
STUDENT CLUBS www.dartmouth.edu/student
/sorg/Alphabetical.html
SPORTS www.dartmouth.edu/student/athletics
PUBLICATIONS www.dartmouth.edu/info/pubs
STUDENT NEWSPAPER www.dartmouth.edu
/pages/thed
LIBRARY www.dartmouth.edu/~library
GREEK LIFE www.dartmouth.edu/student/sorg
/Greeks.html

Skip the brochure

• **DARTMOUTH OUTING CLUB** As a Dartmouth student you don't need to be a chemistry major to deal with the elements. Expect a lot of enthusiasm for the outdoors with activities ranging from rock climbing and skiing to environmental studies. **www.dartmouth.edu/student/doc**

Sing-along-a-Dartmouth

• **COALITION FOR LIFE** Dartmouth Republicans often attract national attention; this is just one of several conservatives founts online. The Coalition for Life offers a collection of essays and links on one of the most divisive issues today. **www.dartmouth.edu/student/sorg/life**

• **CREATIVE GAMING** Maybe it's the cold that keeps these folks tucked inside and lost in imaginary worlds. These gamers have certainly been busy with a vast catalog of interactive games for roleplayers, wargamers, and boardgamers. **www.dartmouth.edu/student/sorg/gaming**

"It's the cold that keeps these folks inside."

WHAT YOU NEED TO GET IN **Application Deadline** January **Early Action Deadline** November 1 **Common App.** Yes **Application Fee** $60 **Tuition Costs** $20,805 **Room & Board** $6,135 **Financial Forms Deadline** February 1 **Undergrads Awarded Aid** 40% **Aid That Is Need-Based** 100% **Average Award of Freshman Scholarship Package** $14,660 **Tests Required** SAT1 (preferred) or ACT **Admissions Address** Hanover, NH 03755 **Admissions Telephone** (603) 646-2875

LAST YEAR'S CLASS **Applied** 10,006 **Accepted** 2,281 **Matriculated** 1,048 **Average SAT M/V** 693/635 **In Top Fifth of High School Graduating Class** 97% **Applied Early** 1,303 **Accepted Early** 334

COLLEGE LIFE **Gender Breakdown** M 53%, F 47% **Out of State Students** 97% **From Public Schools** 786% **Ethnic Composition** White & Other 74%, Asian American 10%, Black 7%, Hispanic 5%, Native American 4% **Foreign Students** 7% **Reside on Campus** 92% **Return as Sophomores** 97% **Total Faculty** 339 **Student Faculty Ratio** 11:1 **Fraternities (% of men participating)** 17 (41%) **Sororities (% of women participating)** 7 (28%) **Graduate Students** 1,013

Davidson College

Davidson, NC · Est. 1837 · Coed · Private · 1,616 Undergrads · Urban

I need...

Admissions info admissions@davidson.edu
  www.davidson.edu/administrative
  /admission/admission.html
Financial aid info www.davidson.edu
  /administrative/financial/financial.html

How wired is Davidson College?

PARTIAL APPLICATION ONLINE

Do I get email? Yes
Do I get a home page? No
Is my dorm wired? Yes
What is the student to computer ratio? 12:1

The usual tour

DEPARTMENTS www.davidson.edu/academic
  /academic.html
STUDENT CLUBS www.davidson.edu/student
  /student.html
SPORTS www.davidson.edu/athletics/athletics
  .html
LIBRARY www.davidson.edu/administrative
  /library/library.html
VIRTUAL TOUR www.davidson.edu/introduction
  /tour.html
CAREER CENTER www.davidson.edu/academic
  /academic.html
CAREER CENTER www.davidson.edu/student
  /organizations/davidsonian/davidsonian.html

Skip the brochure

- **DAVIDSON ULTIMATE** The quintessential college
  club sport, Ultimate's found a home at

Location: http://www.davidson.edu/introduction/tour/Library.jpeg

Lake Wylie, Charlotte nightlife, and Doric columns—
Davidson has much to offer

Davidson. Find info on upcoming tournaments
as well as photos of frisbee-hobbled veterans.
**www.davidson.edu/student/organizations/frisbee
/frisbee.html**

- **PROJECT LIFE** Perhaps a little cautious on a college campus but certainly not unappreciated.
  Davidson highlights its own bone marrow drive
  center. **www.davidson.edu/student/organizations
  /project_life/projlife.htm**

- **INVOLUNTARY WITHDRAWAL** Not a new birth-
  control practice, this outlines the rights the
  school has to suspend or expel students for
  underperformance. Which, to think of it in
  other terms, might also be a reason for involuntary withdrawal. **www.davidson.edu/student
  /life/withdraw.html**

WHAT YOU NEED TO GET IN Application Deadline January 15 **Early Action Deadline** November 15 **Common App.** Yes
Application Fee $45 **Tuition Costs** $19,631 **Room & Board** $5,636 **Financial Forms Deadline** February 15
Undergrads Awarded Aid 60% **Aid That Is Need-Based** 75% **Average Award of Freshman Scholarship Package**
$10,273 **Tests Required** SAT1 or ACT **Admissions Address** P.O. Box 1737, Davidson, NC 28036 **Admissions
Telephone** (704) 892-2230

LAST YEAR'S CLASS Applied 3,061 **Accepted** 1,116 **Matriculated** 432 **Average SAT M/V** 659/594 **Average ACT** 29
In Top Tenth of High School Graduating Class 52% **Applied Early** 277 **Accepted Early** 159

COLLEGE LIFE Gender Breakdown M 52%, F 48% **Out of State Students** 79% **From Public Schools** 60% **Ethnic
Composition** White & Other 90.6%, Asian American 3.4%, Black 3.6%, Hispanic 2%, Native American 0.4%
Foreign Students 4% **Reside on Campus** 93% **Return as Sophomores** 97% **Total Faculty** 146 **Student Faculty
Ratio** 12:1 **Fraternities (% of men participating)** 6 (60%) **Sororities** none

University of Delaware

www.udel.edu

Newark, DE · Est. 1743 · Coed · Public · 14,668 Undergrads · Small Town

I need...

Admissions info ask.admissions@mvs.udel.edu
www.udel.edu/eileen/welc/admissions.html
Financial aid info www.udel.edu/admissions
/page53.html

How wired is University of Delaware?

Do I get email? Yes
Do I get a home page? Yes
Is my dorm wired? Yes
What is the student to computer ratio? 26:1

FULL APPLICATION ONLINE

The usual tour

CALENDAR www.udel.edu/eileen/camp
/events.html
LIBRARY www.lib.udel.edu
SPORTS www.udel.edu/lynam/athletics
/athletics.html
DEPARTMENTS www.udel.edu/eileen/lr/college
.html
STUDENT CLUBS www.udel.edu/dcannon/stuorg
.html
GREEK LIFE www.udel.edu/dcannon/greek.html
STUDY ABROAD www.udel.edu/IntlProg/study
abroad/contents.htm

"UD professors would love to probe your mind—literally."

Heed the Blue Hen, she will take you where you need to go

Skip the brochure

- **COGNITIVE SCIENCE PROGRAM** The cognitive science department at UDelaware would love to probe your mind. Trained in linguisitics, neuroscience, mathematics, philosophy, computer science, and psychology, they're bettering our understanding of the brain and hope to create a thinking computer. Eerie, ethereal music and omniscient, omnipotent machines to follow. **www.cis.udel.edu/cogsci**

- **FITNESS CLASSES** When you get to college you may find yourself exercising your mental muscles more than your physical ones. To keep in shape, two-step it to the fitness classes the school offers. **www.udel.edu/lynam/fitness /fitness.html**

WHAT YOU NEED TO GET IN Application Deadline January 1 for priority consideration; final deadline March 1 **Early Action Deadline** November 15 **Common App.** No **Application Fee** $40 **Tuition Costs** $3,860 ($10,730 out-of-state) **Room & Board** $4,420 **Need Blind** Yes **Financial Forms Deadline** May 1 with a priority given to applications received by February 15 **Undergrads Awarded Aid** 58% **Average Award of Freshman Scholarship Package** $4,000 **Tests Required** SAT1 (preferred) or ACT **Admissions Address** Newark, DE 19716 **Admissions Telephone** (302) 831-8123

LAST YEAR'S CLASS Applied 13,860 **Accepted** 10,062 **Matriculated** 3,179 **Median Range SAT M/V** 530-630/530-610 **In Top Fifth of High School Graduating Class** 49% **Applied Early** 620 **Accepted Early** 349

COLLEGE LIFE Gender Breakdown M 43%, F 57% **Out of State Students** 67% **From Public Schools** 76% **Ethnic Composition** White & Other 90%, Asian American 3%, Black 5%, Hispanic 2% **Foreign Students** 1% **Reside on Campus** 53% **Return as Sophomores** 86% **Total Faculty** 1,043 **Student Faculty Ratio** 15:1 **Fraternities (% of men participating)** 25 (18%) **Sororities (% of women participating)** 15 (18%) **Graduate Students** 3,224

Denison University

Granville, OH · Est. 1831 · Coed · Private · 1,995 Undergrads · Rural

I need...

Admissions info www.denison.edu/admissions
Financial aid info www.denison.edu/admissions
   /financial.html

REQUEST APPLICATION ONLINE

How wired is Denison University?

Do I get email? Yes
Do I get a home page? Yes
   Where? www.denison.edu/personal
What is the student to computer ratio? 12:1

The usual tour

LIBRARY www.denison.edu/library
DEPARTMENTS www.denison.edu/depts.shtml
CALENDAR www.denison.edu/calendar
SPORTS www.denison.edu/athletics
VIRTUAL TOUR www.denison.edu/campus
   /map.html
CAREER CENTER www.denison.edu/cdc

"Denison's Women's Studies program has been in place for twenty years."

Location: http://www.denison.edu/campus/burton.html

They build 'em with class in the Buckeye state

Skip the brochure

- **THE DENISONIAN** A frames-enhanced presentation of this weekly newspaper, the school's oldest student-run organization. This site offers politics, philosophy, and local issues in a straight-arrow style **140.141.9.35**

- **WOMEN'S STUDIES** Denison's Women's Studies program has been in place for almost 20 years, offering an impressive array of courses from philosophy to art history. **www.denison.edu/womens_studies/index.shtml**

- **AREA INFORMATION** With Columbus nearby and Cleveland's Rock and Roll Hall of Fame just three hours away, the Denison area is prime Ohio real estate. Not to mention the cows. **www.denison.edu/areainfo/areainfo.html**

WHAT YOU NEED TO GET IN **Application Deadline** January for priority consideration; final deadline February 1 **Early Action Deadline** January 1 **Common App.** Yes **Application Fee** $35 **Tuition Costs** $17,770 **Room & Board** $4,940 **Need Blind** Yes **Financial Forms Deadline** Priority given to applications received by May 1 **Undergrads Awarded Aid** 86% **Aid That Is Need-Based** 77% **Average Award of Freshman Scholarship Package** $11,368 **Tests Required** SAT1 or ACT **Admissions Address** Box H, Granville, OH 43023 **Admissions Telephone** (800) 336-4766

LAST YEAR'S CLASS **Applied** 2,604 **Accepted** 2,193 **Matriculated** 701 **Average SAT M/V** 590/522 **Average ACT** 25 **In Top Fifth of High School Graduating Class** 56% **Applied Early** 98 **Accepted Early** 83

COLLEGE LIFE **Gender Breakdown** M 47%, F 53% **Out of State Students** 57% **From Public Schools** 70% **Ethnic Composition** White & Other 91.1%, Asian American 3.4%, Black 3.9%, Hispanic 1.6% **Foreign Students** 3% **Reside on Campus** 96% **Return as Sophomores** 82% **Total Faculty** 163 **Student Faculty Ratio** 11:1 **Fraternities (% of men participating)** 10 (32%) **Sororities (% of women participating)** 8 (42%)

University of Denver

Denver, CO · Est. 1864 · Coed · Private · 3,347 Undergrads · Urban

I need...

Admissions info admission@du.edu
www.du.edu/admission
Financial aid info fao11@medusa.cair.du.edu
www.du.edu/~jerickso/dept.html

How wired is University of Denver?

Do I get email? Yes
Do I get a home page? Yes
Where? www.du.edu/findit/home pages.html
Is my dorm wired? Yes
What is the student to computer ratio? 7:1

The usual tour

STUDENT CLUBS www.du.edu/sac/organizations
.html
GREEK LIFE www.du.edu/greeklife
LIBRARY www.du.edu/~penrosel
CAREER CENTER www.du.edu/career

Skip the brochure

• **CHEMISTRY CLUB** When not blowing up University of Denver labs, students in the Chemistry Club can be found visiting local schools and helping them create explosions of their own. The peripatetic chemists tutor, organize tours, and set up lectures. www.du.edu/chemistry/club

• **DU RESCUE TEAM** "We staffed another successful event. We gave out many band-aids." Another stressful yet exciting day for members of the University of Denver Rescue Team, an emer-

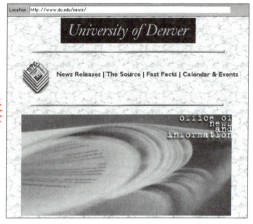

Snow again? Up-to-the-minute information on life around the campus

gency medical care organization for student groups. **www.du.edu/rec/club/rescue**

• **DISABLED PERSONS' RESOURCES** DPR helps students accommodate physical disabilities by providing note-takers, library assistants, adaptive technology, and other resources. DPR also works to increase awareness about the need for accessibility on campus and coordinates Disability Awareness Days each year. www.du.edu/dpr

"We gave out many band-aids."

WHAT YOU NEED TO GET IN Application Deadline February 15 **Early Action Deadline** December 1 **Common App.** Yes **Application Fee** $40 (may be waived in cases of financial need) **Tuition Costs** $16,740 **Room & Board** $5,229 **Financial Forms Deadline** Priority given to applications received by February 20 **Undergrads Awarded Aid** 52% **Aid That Is Need-Based** 65% **Average Award of Freshman Scholarship Package** $7,182 **Tests Required** SAT1 or ACT **Admissions Address** University Park, Denver, CO 80208 **Admissions Telephone** (303) 871-2036

LAST YEAR'S CLASS Applied 2,782 **Accepted** 2,256 **Matriculated** 658 **Average SAT M/V** 542/483 **Average ACT** 24 **In Top Fifth of High School Graduating Class** 51%

COLLEGE LIFE Gender Breakdown M 43%, F 57% **Ethnic Composition** White & Other 85.6%, Asian American 5.5%, Black 3.2%, Hispanic 5.2%, Native American 0.5% **Reside on Campus** 41% **Return as Sophomores** 79% **Total Faculty** 409 **Student Faculty Ratio** 13:1 **Fraternities** 9 **Sororities** 4 **Graduate Students** 5,048

DePaul University

Chicago, IL · Est. 1898 · Coed · Private · 10,450 Undergrads · Urban

I need...

Admissions info admitdpu@wppost.depaul.edu
www.depaul.edu/admission/admission.html
Financial aid info finaid@wppost.depaul.edu
www.depaul.edu/admission/finaid/finaid
.html

How wired is DePaul University?

Do I get email? Yes
Do I get a home page? Yes
  Where? condor.depaul.edu
  /~dpowebpg/home page.html
What is the student to computer ratio? 12:1

REQUEST APPLICATION ONLINE

The usual tour

DEPARTMENTS condor.depaul.edu/~dpulas
/undrprgm.html
LIBRARY www.lib.depaul.edu
GREEK LIFE www.depaul.edu/student/slife/poo
.html#greek
SCHOOL FACTS condor.depaul.edu/~dpulas
/undrprgm.html
CAREER CENTER www.depaul.edu/student/stud
_car_dev.html

"A service bringing you everything you need for the Internet"

A warm welcome to DePaul's corner of the Windy City

Skip the brochure

- **DEPAUL ONLINE** A student service dedicated to bringing you everything you might ever need for the Internet, including home pages, tech help and other goodies. The "nominal" cost comes as a bit of a shock, however, particularly when other schools offer these services for free. condor.depaul.edu/~dpowebpg

- **DEPAUL ALUMNI** Granted, you aren't yet college students, let alone alumni, but it's worth a visit to see what past graduates are up to, and to peruse other DePaul-pertinent information. www.depaul.edu/alumni/alumni.html

- **COLLEGE OF COMMERCE** Most DePaul undergrads attend the College of Liberal Arts and Sciences. But there is another school for undergrads where they can hone in on a straight-and-narrow, business-related education. www.depaul.edu/programs/commerce/intro.html

WHAT YOU NEED TO GET IN **Application Deadline** November 15 for priority consideration; final deadline August 15 **Early Action Deadline** November 15 **Common App.** No **Application Fee** $25 **Tuition Costs** $12,000 **Room & Board** $3,000 **Need Blind** Yes **Financial Forms Deadline** Priority given to applications received by May 1 **Undergrads Awarded Aid** 65% **Average Award of Freshman Scholarship Package** $4,900 **Tests Required** SAT1 or ACT **Admissions Address** 1 East Jackson Boulevard, Chicago, IL 60604-2287 **Admissions Telephone** (312) 362-8300

LAST YEAR'S CLASS **Applied** 5,325 **Accepted** 4,254 **Matriculated** 1,265 **Average SAT M/V** 536/491 **Average ACT** 25 **In Top Quarter of High School Graduating Class** 61% **Applied Early** 2,400 **Accepted Early** 1,500

COLLEGE LIFE **Gender Breakdown** M 41%, F 59% **Out of State Students** 29% **From Public Schools** 69% **Ethnic Composition** White & Other 70.2%, Asian American 6.4%, Black 12.4%, Hispanic 10.7%, Native American 0.3% **Foreign Students** 1% **Return as Sophomores** 84% **Total Faculty** 504 **Student Faculty Ratio** 17:1 **Fraternities (% of men participating)** 3 (3%) **Sororities (% of women participating)** 2 (2%) **Graduate Students** 6,683

DePauw University

www.depauw.edu

Greencastle, IN · Est. 1837 · Coed · Private · 2,102 Undergrads · Small Town

I need...

Admissions info admissions%admin@depauw
.edu
www.depauw.edu/adm/admisshp.htm
Financial aid info www.depauw.edu/adm/finaid
.htm

How wired is DePauw University?

Do I get email? Yes
Do I get a home page? Yes
Is my dorm wired? Yes
What is the student to computer ratio? 13:1

REQUEST APPLICATION ONLINE

The usual tour

LIBRARY www.depauw.edu/lib/homepg.htm
SPORTS www.depauw.edu/ath/athhome.htm
DEPARTMENTS www.depauw.edu/menu
/acdepthp.htm
CALENDAR www.depauw.edu/reg/acadcal.htm
STUDENT CLUBS www.depauw.edu/stulife4/grp
main.htm
CAREER CENTER www.depauw.edu/cpl/career.htm
HISTORY www.depauw.edu/menu/history.htm

Skip the brochure

• **BOULDER RUN** DePauw, steeped in tradition, has
one particularly notable rite of passage: Every
year, with the first snow, students both male
and female streak across campus. So where
are the pictures? **www.depauw.edu/stulife5
/bldrun.htm**

Location: http://www.depauw.edu/dpumag/features.htm

The Amazing Dr. K and his "Home-Brew" Productions

In his 35 years at DePauw,
physics professor Paul Kissinger has
personified the liberal arts
professor – and he has videotapes
to prove it!

FEATURE ARTICLE

Meet your professors-to-be at DePauw's Web site

• **DEPAUWZINE** This online companion to the
DePauw magazine offers the campus news
with particular emphasis on multimedia and
Internet-related features. **www.depauw.edu/dpumag
/features.htm**

• **STUDENT ID'S** This guide helps students look
after one of the most important things in their
wallet, their ID. The tutorial includes stern
advice, such as "Do Not punch holes in your
card." **www.depauw.edu/stulife5/tigerid.htm**

• **THE MONON BELL** Another rich DePauw tradition
is the Monon Bell Rivalry, the annual football
contest between Depauw and Wabash College,
which first took place in 1890. You can even
read the ill-metered ballad written specifically
for the game. **www.depauw.edu/stulife5/mbell.htm**

WHAT YOU NEED TO GET IN **Application Deadline** November 1 for priority consideration; final deadline February 15
Common App. Yes **Application Fee** $30 **Tuition Costs** $15,175 **Room & Board** $5,245 **Need Blind** Yes
Financial Forms Deadline Priority given to applications received by February 15 **Undergrads Awarded Aid** 82%
Aid That Is Need-Based 69% **Average Award of Freshman Scholarship Package** $10,393 **Tests Required** SAT1
or ACT **Admissions Address** 313 South Locust Street, Greencastle, IN 46135 **Admissions Telephone** (800)
447-2495

LAST YEAR'S CLASS **Applied** 2,234 **Accepted** 1,810 **Matriculated** 604 **Median Range SAT M/V** 560-680/490-610
In Top Fifth of High School Graduating Class 71%

COLLEGE LIFE **Gender Breakdown** M 45%, F 55% **Out of State Students** 57% **From Public Schools** 85% **Ethnic
Composition** White & Other 87%, Asian American 2%, Black 7%, Hispanic 4% **Foreign Students** 2% **Reside on
Campus** 95% **Return as Sophomores** 90% **Total Faculty** 207 **Student Faculty Ratio** 12:1 **Fraternities (% of men
participating)** 15 (78%) **Sororities (% of women participating)** 11 (72%)

Dickinson College

Carlisle, PA · Est. 1773 · Coed · Private · 1,859 Undergrads · Small Town

I need...

Admissions info admit@dickinson.edu
www.dickinson.edu/AdmissionsPage
/admitintro.html

Financial aid info www.dickinson.edu/Financial
AidPage/AboutFinAid.html

How wired is Dickinson College?

Do I get email? Yes

What is the student to computer ratio? 6:1

The usual tour

DEPARTMENTS www.dickinson.edu/Academics
Page/Curric.html

STUDENT CLUBS www.dickinson.edu/Student
Organizations/studorgintro.html

LIBRARY www.dickinson.edu/library/Default.html

SPORTS www.dickinson.edu/AthleticPage
/Athleticintro.html

HISTORY www.dickinson.edu/History/HistD.html

STUDY ABROAD www.dickinson.edu/StudyAbroad
/IntlED.html

Skip the brochure

- **OUTING CLUB** On the Web or in the wilderness, Dickinson's Outing Club seems to be one of the most active groups on campus, hiking, biking, caving and kayaking, yet hardly ever breaking a sweat. **www.dickinson.edu/Student Organizations/SPRT-folder/OutingClub/dcoc.html**

Location: http://www.dickinson.edu/images/EastC.jpg

Where Ravens meet Wheels and Chains

- **THE RAVEN'S CLAW** You just might be one of the chosen ones come senior year. Just seven seniors are tapped for overall leadership—but you must be a guy to be a raven. Girls, however, have a group made up of elite seniors, curiously titled Wheel and Chain. **www.dickinson.edu /HonorOrganizations/RavClaw.html** • **www.dickinson.edu /HonorOrganizations/WheelChain.html**

- **DICKINSON FACTS** It's anticipated that Dickinson will at a later date take the opportunity to enhance their site with something other than this list of college facts and stats. **www.dickinson.edu/History/InfoD.html**

"Hiking, biking, caving and kayaking, yet hardly breaking a sweat"

WHAT YOU NEED TO GET IN Application Deadline February 15 **Early Action Deadline** February 1 **Common App.** Yes **Application Fee** $35 **Tuition Costs** $20,600 **Room & Board** $5,660 **Need Blind** Yes **Financial Forms Deadline** Priority given to applications received by February 15 **Undergrads Awarded Aid** 70% **Aid That Is Need-Based** 100% **Average Award of Freshman Scholarship Package** $12,102 **Tests Required** N/A **Admissions Address** P.O. Box 1773, Carlisle, PA 17013-2896 **Admissions Telephone** (717) 245-1231

LAST YEAR'S CLASS Applied 2,920 **Accepted** 2,448 **Matriculated** 534 **Median Range SAT M/V** 520-630/550-640 **In Top Fifth of High School Graduating Class** 39% **Applied Early** 143 **Accepted Early** 109

COLLEGE LIFE Gender Breakdown M 44%, F 56% **Out of State Students** 58% **From Public Schools** 62% **Ethnic Composition** White & Other 94%, Asian American 3%, Black 1%, Hispanic 2% **Foreign Students** 1% **Reside on Campus** 90% **Return as Sophomores** 88% **Total Faculty** 161 **Student Faculty Ratio** 10:1 **Fraternities (% of men participating)** 9 (35%) **Sororities (% of women participating)** 5 (35%)

Drake University

www.drake.edu

Des Moines, IA · Est. 1881 · Coed · Private · 3,802 Undergrads · Urban

I need...

Admissions info admitinfo@acad.drake.edu
www.drake.edu/admissions/admiss.html
Financial aid info www.drake.edu/stulife/finaid
.html

How wired is Drake University?

Do I get email? Yes
Do I get a home page? Yes
Where? www.mac.drake.edu/people
Is my dorm wired? Yes
What is the student to computer ratio? 6:1

The usual tour

LIBRARY www.drake.edu/bgil/www/default.html
STUDENT CLUBS www.drake.edu/stuorgs
/orgs.html
GREEK LIFE www.drake.edu/stuorgs/greek.html
SPORTS www.drake.edu/events/sports.html
CAREER CENTER www.drake.edu/stulife
/careerctr.html
CALENDAR www.drake.edu/events/activities.html

Skip the brochure

• **DRAKE MAGAZINE** This online magazine is an admirable effort to enliven the school's quarterly print magazine for online readabilty. Not your usual college publication fare—it has edgy coverage of the real issues facing students including frank articles on drinking and sex. **mags.drake.edu/drakemag.html**

Newman's Own—not Paul's, but Drake's

• **THE NEWMAN COMMUNITY** At the other end of the spectrum, this community center for followers of the nineteenth century's Cardinal John Henry Newman details its current activity, as well as its history and relevant links. **www.mac.drake.edu/org/Newman**

• **SUBJECT GUIDE** While only a hubsite, this is an excellent place to start in on most all academic fields with links to Drake community resources as well as the wider Web community. **www.drake.edu/bgil/www/disc.html**

"Edgy coverage of the real issues facing students"

WHAT YOU NEED TO GET IN **Application Deadline** March 1 for priority consideration; final deadline August 1 **Common App.** Yes **Application Fee** $25 **Tuition Costs** $14,380 **Room & Board** $5,100 **Need Blind** Yes **Financial Forms Deadline** Priority given to applications received by March 1 **Undergrads Awarded Aid** 85% **Aid That Is Need-Based** 70% **Average Award of Freshman Scholarship Package** $9,000 **Tests Required** SAT1 or ACT **Admissions Address** 2507 University, Des Moines, IA 50311 **Admissions Telephone** (515) 271-3181

LAST YEAR'S CLASS **Applied** 2,705 **Accepted** 2,531 **Matriculated** 742 **Average SAT M/V** 580/570 **Average ACT** 25 **In Top Fifth of High School Graduating Class** 60%

COLLEGE LIFE **Gender Breakdown** M 40%, F 60% **Out of State Students** 75% **From Public Schools** 85% **Ethnic Composition** White & Other 86.7%, Asian American 5.6%, Black 5%, Hispanic 2.5%, Native American 0.2% **Foreign Students** 3% **Reside on Campus** 61% **Return as Sophomores** 80% **Total Faculty** 270 **Student Faculty Ratio** 17:1 **Fraternities (% of men participating)** 11 (34%) **Sororities (% of women participating)** 10 (35%) **Graduate Students** 1,837

Drew University

www.drew.edu

Madison, NJ · Est. 1867 · Coed · Private · 1,421 Undergrads · Urban

I need...

Admissions info www.drew.edu/cla/admissions/info/admissions_main.html

Financial aid info www.drew.edu/admin/finan/financia.html

How wired is Drew University?

Do I get email? Yes

Do I get a home page? Yes

Where? daniel.drew.edu/~emorisse/drewhtml.html

What is the student to computer ratio? 7:1

REQUEST APPLICATION ONLINE

The usual tour

DEPARTMENTS www.drew.edu/cla/depts/depts.html

LIBRARY www.drew.edu/infosys/library/library.html

CAREER CENTER www.drew.edu/admin/career/career-info.html

SPORTS www.drew.edu/sports/sports.html

CALENDAR www.drew.edu/about/events/calendar.html

Skip the brochure

- **UNIVERSITY IN THE FOREST** Since pre-Revolutionary War days, the tract in Madison, N.J. now

"Drew has been known as The Forest."

Take a stroll through the verdant Drew campus

occupied by Drew University has been known as The Forest. Although some 46 buildings today stand among the great oaks and beeches, careful planning has enabled the university to retain thousands of trees on the campus. **www.drew.edu/forest.html**

- **HISTORY** Follow the evolution of Drew through the years, from its inception in 1928 as Drew Theological Seminary with a class of 12 to the coed institution of nearly 1,500 students it is today. **www.drew.edu/about/history.html**

- **DREW UNIVERSITY INTRAMURAL SPORTS** You don't have to be able to play with the big boys and girls to get your organized sports fix at Drew. Even better, you can earn your work study dough supervising or officiating intramurals—now isn't that much better than working the loan desk at the library? **www.drew.edu/sports/intramural/intramural.html**

WHAT YOU NEED TO GET IN Application Deadline February 15 **Early Action Deadline** December 1 and January 15 **Common App.** Yes **Application Fee** $35 **Tuition Costs** $19,128 **Room & Board** $5,834 **Financial Forms Deadline** Priority given to applications received by March 1 **Undergrads Awarded Aid** 80% **Aid That Is Need-Based** 55% **Average Award of Freshman Scholarship Package** $9066 **Tests Required** SAT1 (preferred) or ACT **Admissions Address** 36 Madison Avenue, Madison, NJ 07940 **Admissions Telephone** (201) 408-DREW

LAST YEAR'S CLASS Applied 2,523 **Accepted** 2,032 **Matriculated** 434 **Average SAT M/V** 602/552 **Average ACT** 26 **In Top Fifth of High School Graduating Class** 69% **Applied Early** 60 **Accepted Early** 58

COLLEGE LIFE Gender Breakdown M 40%, F 60% **Out of State Students** 49% **From Public Schools** 66% **Ethnic Composition** White & Other 83%, Asian American 8%, Black 4%, Hispanic 5% **Foreign Students** 2% **Reside on Campus** 87% **Return as Sophomores** 91% **Total Faculty** 110 **Student Faculty Ratio** 12:1 **Fraternities** none **Sororities** none **Graduate Students** 690

Drexel University

www.drexel.edu

Philadelphia, PA · Est. 1891 · Coed · Private · 6,376 Undergrads · Urban

I need...

Admissions info undergrad-admissions@post
.drexel.edu
cmc.www.drexel.edu/adm/admission.html
Financial aid info cmc.www.drexel.edu/adm
/finaid/finaid.html

How wired is Drexel University?

Do I get email? Yes
Do I get a home page? Yes
Where? www.drexel.edu/StudentHomePage
Index.html
Is my dorm wired? Yes
What is the student to computer ratio? 11:1

The usual tour

DEPARTMENTS www.coas.drexel.edu/colldept
.html
GREEK LIFE www.drexel.edu/activities/greek
/greek.html
LIBRARY www.library.drexel.edu
SPORTS www.coas.drexel.edu/colldept.html
STUDENT CLUBS www.drexel.edu/activities
/special_interests.html
HISTORY www.drexel.edu/history.html

Skip the brochure

• **DYSTOPIK SNOMEN** An excellently-drawn cartoon
strip that runs weekly in the school newspaper, "Dystopik Snomen" appears to be the
work of an undergraduate and is already pub-

Location: http://cbis.ece.drexel.edu/SunDragon/SDIV.jpg

Drexel students demonstrate how to cut back on campus
transport costs

lished nationwide. **triangle.student-org.drexel.edu
/docs/Dystopik_Snomen/fav_dystopik.html**

• **WKDU 91.7 FM** Alternative music fans, this is your
mecca, at least at Drexel. The universtiy's student-run radio station posts their playlist as
well as *Communiqué*, a semi-annual publication covering bands such as New Wet Kojak
and the Scissor Girls. **www.punx.com/wkdu.html**

• **SUN DRAGON** While they aren't quite the rage
they were just a few years ago, solar-powered
race cars still attract a passionate following.
Everything you wanted to know about the
Drexel solar racing team. **cbis.ece.drexel.edu
/SunDragon/SunDragon.html**

WHAT YOU NEED TO GET IN **Application Deadline** January 1 for priority consideration; final deadline May 1 **Common App.**
No **Application Fee** $35 (waived if filed on campus) **Tuition Costs** $13,080 **Room & Board** $4,980 **Need Blind**
Yes **Financial Forms Deadline** Priority given to applications received by March 1 **Aid That Is Need-Based** 98%
Average Award of Freshman Scholarship Package $3,367 **Tests Required** SAT1 or ACT **Admissions Address**
3141 Chestnut Street, Philadelphia, PA 19104 **Admissions Telephone** (215) 895-2400

LAST YEAR'S CLASS **Applied** 3,513 **Accepted** 2,819 **Matriculated** 949 **Average SAT M/V** 554/464 **In Top Fifth of
High School Graduating Class** 43%

COLLEGE LIFE **Gender Breakdown** M 68%, F 32% **Out of State Students** 40% **From Public Schools** 60% **Ethnic
Composition** White & Other 76%, Asian American 11%, Black 10%, Hispanic 2%, Native American 1% **Foreign
Students** 9% **Reside on Campus** 45% **Return as Sophomores** 77% **Student Faculty Ratio** 15:1 **Fraternities
(% of men participating)** 13 (17%) **Sororities (% of women participating)** 5 (12%) **Graduate Students** 2,782

Drury College

Springfield, MO · Est. 1873 · Coed · Private · 1,274 Undergrads · Urban

I need...

Admissions info druryad@lib.drury.edu
www.drury.edu/info/admission.html
Financial aid info www.drury.edu/info/admission.html

How wired is Drury College?

REQUEST APPLICATION ONLINE

Do I get email? Yes
Do I get a home page? Yes
Is my dorm wired? Yes
What is the student to computer ratio? 13:1

The usual tour

SPORTS www.drury.edu/info/departments/sports/SPORTHOM.HTM
LIBRARY www.drury.edu/info/departments/lib.html
CALENDAR www.drury.edu/admin/calendar.html
VIRTUAL TOUR www.drury.edu/map/map1.html
DEPARTMENTS www.drury.edu/info/academic/depart.html
STUDENT CLUBS www.drury.edu/info/extra/greeks.html

Skip the brochure

- **THE OZARKS** If you're headed to Drury you may want to know what surprises the area has in store for you. Overdose on the Ozarks and learn about other Missouri pleasures. **www.drury.edu/info/ozarks.html**

- **DRURY HISTORY** Familiarize yourself with the his-

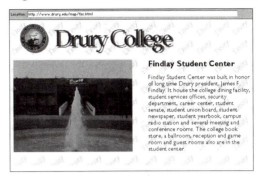

Findlay Student Center

Findlay Student Center was built in honor of long time Drury president, James F. Findlay. It house the college dining facility, student services offices, security department, career center, student senate, student union board, student newspaper, student yearbook, campus radio station and several meeting and conference rooms. The college book store, a ballroom, reception and game room and guest rooms also are in the student center.

There may be a Springifeld in every state, but there's only one Drury

tory of Drury, from its humble beginnings to its present state as multi-disciplined university supporting a graduate business school, and a school of architecture. **www.drury.edu/info/geninfo/DChist.html**

- **STUDENT ORGANIZATIONS** What do Drury students do with themselves? Here's a list with a descriptive sentence or two and contact details for anyone interested in joining a student club, whether it be the College Republicans or the cheerleaders. **www.drury.edu/info/extra/clubs.html**

"At Drury, you can overdose on the Ozarks."

WHAT YOU NEED TO GET IN Application Deadline April 1 for priority consideration; final deadline August 1 **Common App.** No **Application Fee** $20 (may be waived if application filed before October 1) **Tuition Costs** $9,500 **Room & Board** $3,856 **Need Blind** Yes **Financial Forms Deadline** Priority given to applications received by March 15 **Undergrads Awarded Aid** 82% **Aid That Is Need-Based** 80% **Average Award of Freshman Scholarship Package** $3,790 **Tests Required** SAT1 or ACT **Admissions Address** 900 North Benton Avenue, Springfield, MO 65802 **Admissions Telephone** (417) 873-7205

LAST YEAR'S CLASS Applied 920 **Accepted** 860 **Matriculated** 377 **Average ACT** 25 **In Top Fifth of High School Graduating Class** 55%

COLLEGE LIFE Gender Breakdown M 53%, F 47% **Out of State Students** 24% **From Public Schools** 86% **Ethnic Composition** White & Other 97%, Asian American 1%, Black 1%, Hispanic 1% **Foreign Students** 3% **Reside on Campus** 56% **Return as Sophomores** 80% **Total Faculty** 103 **Student Faculty Ratio** 13:1 **Fraternities (% of men participating)** 4 (40%) **Sororities (% of women participating)** 4 (40%) **Graduate Students** 328

Duke University

Durham, NC · Est. 1838 · Coed · Private · 6,264 Undergrads · Urban

I need...

Admissions info www.duke.edu/web/ug
-admissions
Financial aid info www.duke.edu/web/ug
-admissions/finaid.htm

How wired is Duke University?

Do I get email? Yes
Do I get a home page? Yes
  Where? www.duke.edu/people
Is my dorm wired? Yes
What is the student computer ratio? 10:1

The usual tour

DEPARTMENTS aas.duke.edu/departments
LIBRARY www.lib.duke.edu
CALENDAR www.mis.duke.edu/Univ-Calendars
  /Academic-96-97.html
SPORTS www.duke.edu/sports
STUDENT CLUBS www.duke.edu/org
STUDENT NEWSPAPER www.chronicle.duke.edu

Skip the brochure

• **THE DUKE COFFEEHOUSE** Stop here for a taste of
  the local music scene as well as a taste of the
  java-jazzed Duke community. **www.duke.edu
  /~maxehr/coffeehouse.html**

• **EPWORTH/SHARE** Self-proclaimed radicals in all
  matters intellectual and residential, these folks
  don't strike you as your typical Duke
  students. Experimentation and individuality

Duke University, pride of Durham, NC

reign supreme, and scandalous stories simmer
just beneath the surface. **www.duke.edu/epworth**

• **MEN'S BASKETBALL** Think college basketball isn't
  a full-scale business enterprise for these
  schools? Duke offers, for sale of course, a CD-
  ROM of the Blue Devils' accomplishments in
  addition to the yearly stats for these perennial
  March Madness contenders. **www.duke.edu/sports
  /SportsPages/MensBasketball/MensBasketball.html**

"Stop here for a taste of the java-jazzed Duke community."

WHAT YOU NEED TO GET IN **Application Deadline** December 1 for priority consideration; final deadline January 2 **Early Action Deadline** November 1 **Common App.** Yes **Application Fee** $60 **Tuition Costs** $19,995 **Room & Board** $6,605 **Need Blind** Yes **Financial Forms Deadline** Priority given to applications received by February 1 **Undergrads Awarded Aid** 41% **Aid That Is Need-Based** 90% **Average Award of Freshman Scholarship Package** $14,444 **Tests Required** SAT1 or ACT **Admissions Address** 2138 Campus Drive, Box 90586, Durham, NC 27708 **Admissions Telephone** (919) 684-3214

LAST YEAR'S CLASS **Applied** 14,442 **Accepted** 4,137 **Matriculated** 1,639 **Median Range SAT M/V** 650-740/ 640-730 **In Top Fifth of High School Graduating Class** 72% **Applied Early** 1,242 **Accepted Early** 600

COLLEGE LIFE **Gender Breakdown** M 52%, F 48% **Out of State Students** 87% **From Public Schools** 66% **Ethnic Composition** White & Other 76%, Asian American 11%, Black 8%, Hispanic 4%, Native American 1% **Foreign Students** 4% **Reside on Campus** 89% **Return as Sophomores** 98% **Total Faculty** 746 **Student Faculty Ratio** 10:1 **Fraternities (% of men participating)** 21 (29%) **Sororities (% of women participating)** 13 (42%) **Graduate Students** 5,247

Duquesne University

Pittsburgh, PA · Est. 1878 · Coed · Private · 5,716 Undergrads · Urban

www.duq.edu

How wired is Duquesne University?

Do I get email? Yes
Do I get a home page? Yes
  Where? www.duq.edu/Duquesne_Personal
  _Home.html
Is my dorm wired? Yes
What is the student to computer ratio? 14:1

The usual tour

STUDENT CLUBS www.duq.edu/StudentLife
/campusorg.html
LIBRARY www.duq.edu/library/index.html
SPORTS www.duq.edu/StudentLife/student.html
#athletic
GREEK LIFE www.duq.edu/StudentLife/student
.html#greek
CAREER CENTER www.duq.edu/careerservices
/careerse.html
PUBLICATIONS www.duq.edu/newsletter.html

Skip the brochure

- **WDUQ** Home to jazz enthusiasts, WDUQ serves
not just Duquesne's community but all of
Pittsburgh. Comes with a comprehensive guide
to jazz events around Pittsburgh.
www.wduq.duq.edu

Location: http://www.duq.edu/StudentLife/band/pride.html

The oompah-pah of Pittsburgh

- **THE DIGITAL DUKE** This online version of the
school rag has been perked up with a feast of
photographs and cartoons. **the-duke.duq-duke.duq
.edu/dig-duke.htm**

- **DU LITERARY MAGAZINE** Duquesne students with
ample creative juices can now see their
poems, photographs, paintings and short stories online. And so can you. **www.duq.edu
/Publications/lit/Duq.html**

- **DUQUESNE AND PITTSBURGH** Pittsburgh was
recently rated one of America's most livable
cities. Its cultural scene has benefitted from
the philanthropy of many of the city's tycoons,
whether they produced steel (the Carnegies) or
ketchup (the Heinzes). Recent additions to the
city include the Andy Warhol Museum. The city
is also home to the Penguins, Steelers, and
Pirates. **www.duq.edu/setting.html**

- -

WHAT YOU NEED TO GET IN **Application Deadline** December 1 for priority consideration; final deadline July 1 **Early
Action Deadline** December 1 **Common App.** No **Application Fee** $45 **Tuition Costs** $11,662 **Room & Board**
$5,580 **Financial Forms Deadline** May 1 **Undergrads Awarded Aid** 85% **Aid That Is Need-Based** 61% **Average
Award of Freshman Scholarship Package** $6,823 **Tests Required** SAT1 (preferred) or ACT **Admissions Address**
600 Forbes Avenue, Pittsburgh, PA 15282 **Admissions Telephone** (412) 396-6220

LAST YEAR'S CLASS **Applied** 4,125 **Accepted** 3,380 **Matriculated** 1,413 **Average SAT M/V** 520/490 **Average ACT**
24 **Applied Early** 612 **Accepted Early** 406

COLLEGE LIFE **Gender Breakdown** M 43%, F 57% **Out of State Students** 21% **From Public Schools** 65% **Ethnic
Composition** White & Other 90.8%, Asian American 2.5%, Black 5%, Hispanic 1.6%, Native American 0.1%,
Foreign Students 4% **Reside on Campus** 49% **Return as Sophomores** 89% **Total Faculty** 381 **Student Faculty
Ratio** 16:1 **Fraternities (% of men participating)** 3 (14%) **Sororities (% of women participating)** 2 (14%)
Graduate Students 3,569

Earlham College

Richmond, IN · Est. 1847 · Coed · Private · 982 Undergrads · Big Town

www.earlham.edu

How wired is Earlham College?

Do I get email? Yes
Do I get a home page? Yes
  Where? www.earlham.edu/htmldocs/students
  /students.html
Is my dorm wired? Yes
What is the student to computer ratio? 13:1

The usual tour

CAMPUS LIFE www.earlham.edu/htmldocs
  /CampusLife/CampusLife.html
DEPARTMENTS www.earlham.edu/www
  /departments/departments.html
LIBRARY www.earlham.edu/www/library/pages
  /libinfos.htm
VIRTUAL TOUR www.cs.earlham.edu/~roman/links
  /earlham.html
STUDENT CLUBS www.earlham.edu/htmldocs
  /CampusLife/GroupsAndOrganizations
  /GroupsAndOrganizations.html
 HISTORY 205.197.87.231/earlham/essentials
  /quakerid.html

Skip the brochure

• **APPLYING** While Earlham doesn't offer much

Portal to the world of higher learning: Earlham College

more at its Web site than a cursory summary, the content is informative. Particularly useful is the school's admissions advice, including tips on writing college essays. **admis.earlham.edu /earlham/default.html**

• **THE MARKET** Earlham students are busy haggling at their own electronic agora, selling computers, text books, even a 1975 VW Camper. But all that is nothing compared to one particularly desperate student looking to sell his roommate for the one-time-only price of 99¢. **www.earlham.edu/htmldocs/CampusLife/TheMarket /TheMarketMainPage.html**

• **EARLHAM HABITAT** Habitat for Humanity is an ecumenical Christian organization dedicated to providing affordable, decent housing to all people. Earlham's chapter plans to mark the school's 150th anniversary by raising funds and building a house by the summer of 1997. **www.earlham.edu/htmldocs/CampusLife/ehfh/ehfh.html**

WHAT YOU NEED TO GET IN Application Deadline February 15 for priority consideration **Early Action Deadline** December 1 **Common App.** Yes **Application Fee** $30 **Tuition Costs** $17,362 **Room & Board** $4,412 **Need Blind** Yes **Financial Forms Deadline** Priority given to applications received by March 1 **Undergrads Awarded Aid** 62% **Aid That Is Need-Based** 95% **Average Award of Freshman Scholarship Package** $9,595 **Tests Required** SAT1 (preferred) or ACT **Admissions Address** National Road West, Richmond, IN 47374 **Admissions Telephone** (800) 327-5426

LAST YEAR'S CLASS Applied 1,190 **Accepted** 914 **Matriculated** 272 **Average SAT M/V** 550/550 **Average ACT** 25 **In Top Fifth of High School Graduating Class** 47% **Applied Early** 29 **Accepted Early** 27

COLLEGE LIFE Gender Breakdown M 44%, F 56% **Out of State Students** 78% **From Public Schools** 76% **Ethnic Composition** White & Other 84%, Asian American 5%, Black 9%, Hispanic 1%, Native American 1% **Foreign Students** 4% **Reside on Campus** 87% **Return as Sophomores** 83% **Total Faculty** 89 **Student Faculty Ratio** 11:1 **Fraternities** none **Sororities** none **Graduate Students** 49

East Carolina University

ecuvax.cis.ecu.edu

Greenville, NC · Est. 1907 · Coed · Public· 14,342 Undergrads · Big Town

I need...

Admissions info admis@ecuvm.cis.ecu.edu
www.ecu.edu/imagemap/files/undgradm.html
Financial aid info ecuvax.cis.ecu.edu/studlife
/financial/index.htm

How wired is East Carolina?

REQUEST APPLICATION ONLINE

Do I get email? Yes
Do I get a home page? Yes
Is my dorm wired? Yes
What is the student to computer ratio? 10:1

The usual tour

GREEK LIFE ecuvax.cis.ecu.edu/groups/SOCIALF
.HTM - fratsecuvax.cis.ecu.edu/groups
/SOCIALS.HTM - sororities
STUDENT CLUBS www.ecu.edu/imagemap/files
/Studentorg.html
LIBRARY www.ecu.edu/imagemap/files
/Libraries.html
DEPARTMENTS www.artsci.ecu.edu/cas
/academics.html#Dept Anchor
CULTURAL CALENDAR www.ecu.edu/imagemap
/files/Culture.html
SPORTS www.ecu.edu/imagemap/files
/Athletics.html

Skip the brochure

• **NEWS & EVENTS** This is well worth a visit for any
prospective student of ECU with an encyclopedic wealth of tidbits on the university, like a

Location: http://www.news.ecu.edu/Trumple/eight.html

Blown away by yet another graduation

description of the school mascot who goes by
the catchy moniker of Pee-Dee. **150.216.6.18**

• **GAIA** These active ECU students are battling
the environmental baddies. Read up on coming events as well as the local ecological
issues. **ecuvax.cis.ecu.edu/~ugpullin/gaiahome.html**

• **ECU DISTINCTIONS** That EC's School of Nursing
has the only nurse midwifery education program in North Carolina is typical of the trum-
peting at this page. **www.news.ecu.edu
/distinctions.html**

"The school mascot goes by the catchy moniker of Pee-Dee"

WHAT YOU NEED TO GET IN **Application Deadline** December 15 for priority consideration; final deadline March 15
Common App. No **Application Fee** $35 **Tuition Costs** $1,673 ($8,515 out-of-state) **Room & Board** $4,000 **Need
Blind** Yes **Financial Forms Deadline** Priority given to applications received by April 15 **Undergrads Awarded Aid**
50% **Aid That Is Need-Based** 90% **Average Award of Freshman Scholarship Package** $2,553 **Tests Required**
SAT1 or ACT **Admissions Address** East Fifth Street, Greenville, NC 27858-4353 **Admissions Telephone** (919)
328-6640

LAST YEAR'S CLASS **Applied** 8,640 **Accepted** 6,803 **Matriculated** 2,642 **Average SAT M/V** 478/433 **Average ACT**
20 **In Top Fifth of High School Graduating Class** 30%

COLLEGE LIFE **Gender Breakdown** M 43%, F 57% **Out of State Students** 18% **From Public Schools** 90% **Ethnic
Composition** White & Other 87%, Asian American 1%, Black 10%, Hispanic 1%, Native American 1% **Foreign
Students** 1% **Reside on Campus** 26% **Return as Sophomores** 77% **Total Faculty** 792 **Student Faculty Ratio**
18:1 **Fraternities (% of men participating)** 20 (10%) **Sororities (% of women participating)** 13 (15%) **Graduate
Students** 3,103

Emerson College

www.emerson.edu

Boston, MA · Est. 1880 · Coed · Private · 2,410 Undergrads · Urban

I need...

Admissions info admission@emerson.edu
www.emerson.edu/admiss/undergrad
_home.html
Financial aid info finaid@emerson.edu
www.emerson.edu/admiss/finaid/index.html

How wired is Emerson?

Do I get email? Yes
Do I get a home page? No
Is my dorm wired? Yes
What is the student to computer ratio? 17:1

DOWNLOAD APPLICATION ONLINE

The usual tour

DEPARTMENTS www.emerson.edu/acadepts
/academic.htm
LIBRARY www.emerson.edu/lib/thisislib.html
STUDENT CLUBS www.emerson.edu/student_orgs
FILM ARTS SOCIETY www.emerson.edu/acadepts
/academic.htm
CAREER CENTER www.emerson.edu/career
/home.html
SPORTS www.emerson.edu/athletics
/athletics.html

Skip the brochure

• **THE EMERSON COMEDY WORKSHOP** Boasting heavy-weight alums like *The Tonight Show*'s Jay Leno and *No Cure for Cancer*'s Denis Leary, Emerson is no lightweight when it comes to comedy and entertainment.

Emerson lends a hand to the digital revolution

www.emerson.edu/student_orgs/comedy/comedy.html

• **PLOUGHSHARES** While Emerson's better known for its involvement in entertainment media, *Ploughshares* garners a good bit of respect for the school's more literary folk, and is widely regarded as one of the best literary journals in the country. **www.emerson.edu/Ploughshares/Ploughshares.html**

• **EBONI** EBONI has been trying to further the involvement and influence of black students at Emerson since 1969. **www.emerson.edu/student_orgs/EBONI/EBONI.html**

• **MASS COMM ON THE WEB** Emerson has embraced new media in a big way. The mass communication division has here constructed an impressive site highlighting the mission of the school as well as the work of its students. **www.emerson.edu/acadepts/MC/MassComm_Main.HTML**

WHAT YOU NEED TO GET IN **Application Deadline** February 1 for priority consideration **Common App.** No **Application Fee** $45 **Tuition Costs** $16,640 **Room & Board** $8,050 **Need Blind** Yes **Financial Forms Deadline** Priority given to applications received by March 1 **Undergrads Awarded Aid** 73% **Aid That Is Need-Based** 90% **Average Award of Freshman Scholarship Package** $8,973 **Tests Required** SAT1 or ACT **Admissions Address** 100 Beacon Street, Boston, MA 02116 **Admissions Telephone** (617) 824-8600

LAST YEAR'S CLASS **Applied** 2,149 **Accepted** 1,493 **Matriculated** 529 **Average SAT M/V** 522/528 **Average ACT** 24 **In Top Fifth of High School Graduating Class** 41%

COLLEGE LIFE **Gender Breakdown** M 44%, F 56% **Out of State Students** 75% **Ethnic Composition** White & Other 89%, Asian American 2%, Black 3%, Hispanic 5%, Native American 1% **Foreign Students** 9% **Reside on Campus** 50% **Return as Sophomores** 78% **Total Faculty** 245 **Student Faculty Ratio** 15:1 **Fraternities (% of men participating)** 5 (10%) **Sororities (% of women participating)** 5 (10%) **Graduate Students** 888

Emory University

Atlanta, GA · Est. 1836 · Coed · Private · 5,239 Undergrads · Urban

www.emory.edu

I need...

Admissions info admiss@emory.edu
www.emory.edu/ADMISSIONS/admhome.html
Financial aid info www.emory.edu/FINANCIAL_AID
/home page.html

How wired is Emory?

Do I get email? Yes
Do I get a home page? Yes
  Where? www.emory.edu
  /HOMEPAGES/emory.homes.html
Is my dorm wired? Yes
What is the student to computer ratio? 11:1

REQUEST APPLICATION ONLINE

The usual tour

GREEK LIFE www.emory.edu/CAMPUS_LIFE
/HANDBOOK/greeks.htm
DEPARTMENTS www.emory.edu/COLLEGE
/departments.html
VIRTUAL TOUR www.emory.edu/COLLEGE
/departments.html
SPORTS www.emory.edu/SPORTS
STUDENT CLUBS www.emory.edu/STUDENTS
_MAIN/orgs.html
LIBRARY www.emory.edu/MENUS/libraries.html

"*The Fire* tackles the weighty issue of racism."

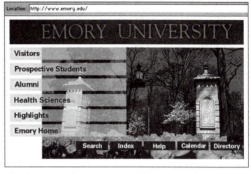

Pearly gates welcome you to enlightened paradise in Atlanta

Skip the brochure

- **THE SPOKE** Emory students have been producing *Spoke* for some twenty years, poking fun at anyone and any publication to chance upon the national stage. Great writing, brilliant visuals, and well worth a stay whether you're interested in Emory or not. **www.emory.edu/SPOKE**

- **THE FIRE** The tone here is decidedly heavier. *The Fire* tackles the weighty issue of racism both at Emory and in the larger American society with discourse and debate on O.J., hate crimes, and Emory's occasional apathy. **www.emory.edu/FIRE**

- **EMORY POLITICS** Election year has Emory politicos in a frenzy. If the Emory Web is any sign, the donkeys are kicking elephant ass. **www.emory.edu/democrats/www.emory.edu/GOP**

WHAT YOU NEED TO GET IN Application Deadline January 15 **Early Action Deadline** November 1 **Common App.** Yes **Application Fee** $40 **Tuition Costs** $19,870 **Room & Board** $6,440 **Need Blind** Yes **Financial Forms Deadline** April 1 with a priority given to applications received by February 15 **Undergrads Awarded Aid** 62% **Aid That Is Need-Based** 73% **Average Award of Freshman Scholarship Package** $10,941 **Tests Required** SAT1 or ACT **Admissions Address** 1380 Oxford Road, NE, Atlanta, GA 30322 **Admissions Telephone** (404) 727-6036

LAST YEAR'S CLASS Applied 9,508 **Accepted** 4,805 **Matriculated** 1,260 **Average SAT M/V** 669/657 **Average ACT** 28 **In Top Quarter of High School Graduating Class** 98% **Applied Early** 475 **Accepted Early** 317

COLLEGE LIFE Gender Breakdown M 44%, F 56% **Out of State Students** 81% **From Public Schools** 63% **Ethnic Composition** White & Other 74%, Asian American 12%, Black 10%, Hispanic 4% **Foreign Students** 2% **Reside on Campus** 65% **Return as Sophomores** 92% **Total Faculty** 59 **Student Faculty Ratio** 10:1 **Fraternities (% of men participating)** 10 (33%) **Sororities (% of women participating)** 10 (33%) **Graduate Students** 5,587

Eugene Lang College of The New School for Social Research

www.newschool.edu

New York, NY · Est. 1978 · Coed · Private · 350 Undergrads · Urban

I need...

Admissions info lang@newschool.edu
www.newschool.edu/academic/lang.htm

How wired is Eugene Lang?

Do I get email? Yes
Do I get a home page? No
What is the student to computer ratio? 5:1

The usual tour

DEPARTMENTS www.newschool.edu/academic
LIBRARY www.newschool.edu/library

Skip the brochure

• **HISTORY OF THE NEW SCHOOL** Just how "new" is
The New School, the parent institution of
Eugene Lang? In 1919, a group of distin-
guished scholars, John Dewey, Thorstein
Veblen, Charles Beard, and others, established
a school for "unfettered inquiry in research and

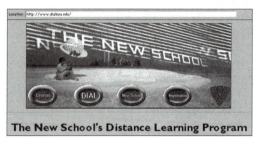

The New School's Distance Learning Program

Via the Web, and the New School, lots of learning gets done

the arts." Today this educational experiment
supports students of fashion design and
Marxism alike. Without conventional funding,
The New School has managed to host some of
the biggest and brightest minds of the century.
Eugene Lang is its major undergraduate institution, although Parsons School of Design and
the Mannes School of Music attract more
undergrads every year. **www.newschool.edu/intro
/history/index.htm**

• **NEW SCHOOL DISCUSSION PAPERS** Via the Web, the
New School community takes part in admin-
strative and academic discussions. These
papers offer insights into the various concerns
facing the school, including the faculty appoint-
ments process, student services, and technology. **www.newschool.edu/admin/discpapr/index.htm**

"Before there was The New School, there was a vision."

WHAT YOU NEED TO GET IN **Application Deadline** February 1 **Early Action Deadline** November 15 **Common App.** Yes
Application Fee $30 (College Board waiver accepted) **Tuition Costs** $16,580 **Room & Board** $8,862 **Need Blind**
Yes **Financial Forms Deadline** Priority given to applications received by April 1 **Aid That Is Need-Based** 85%
Average Award of Freshman Scholarship Package $7,749 **Tests Required** SAT1 or ACT **Admissions Address**
65 West 11th Street, New York, NY 10011 **Admissions Telephone** (212) 229-5665

LAST YEAR'S CLASS **Applied** 306 **Accepted** 225 **Matriculated** 80 **Average SAT M/V** 520/530 **Average ACT** 28
In Top Tenth of High School Graduating Class 48% **Applied Early** 18 **Accepted Early** 15

COLLEGE LIFE **Gender Breakdown** M 31%, F 69% **Out of State Students** 58% **From Public Schools** 60% **Ethnic
Composition** White & Other 79%, Asian American 3%, Black 9%, Hispanic 9% **Foreign Students** 8% **Reside on
Campus** 40% **Return as Sophomores** 77% **Student Faculty Ratio** 9:1 **Fraternities** none **Sororities** none

University of Evansville

www.evansville.edu

Evansville, IN · Est. 1854 · Coed · Private · 3,197 Undergrads · Urban

How wired is University of Evansville?

Do I get email? Yes
Do I get a home page? Yes
Where? cedar.evansville.edu
/search/pages.html
Is my dorm wired? Yes
What is the student to computer ratio? 10:1

REQUEST APPLICATION ONLINE

The usual tour

LIBRARY cedar.evansville.edu/~libweb
STUDENT CLUBS www.evansville.edu/information
/studorgs.html
SPORTS cedar.evansville.edu/~athleweb
DEPARTMENTS www.evansville.edu/academics
/depts.html
COURSE CATALOG cedar.evansville.edu/catalog
GREEK LIFE www.evansville.edu/profiles
/community/studlife/greek.html

Skip the brochure

- **GAMER'S GUILD** Games are supposed to be fun,
and yet so many gamers seem such a somber
lot. One thing these Evansville folk are quite
serious about is their site—the perfect spot
for procrastination. **cedar.evansville.edu/~guildweb**

Evansville, a veritable fountain of knowledge

- **ANCIENT WORLD CULTURES** You might not think
that in the heartland of the United States
you'd find one of the better resources for information on the ancient cultures of Egypt, India,
and the Near East. But then again it's all possible these days. Anthony Beavers, an assistant professor at Evansville, will tell you why.
cedar.evansville.edu/~wcweb/wc101

- **PROFILES** As comprehensive, engaging and
enlightening as our Usual Tour is, we can't
match up to Evansville's own "Profiles."
Details on everyone and everything you need
to know about the school. **cedar.evansville.edu
/profiles**

"Evansville gamers are serious about their site."

WHAT YOU NEED TO GET IN **Application Deadline** December 1 for priority consideration; final deadline February 15
Common App. No **Application Fee** $30 **Tuition Costs** $12,400 **Room & Board** $4,230 **Need Blind** Yes **Financial
Forms Deadline** Priority given to applications received by February 15 **Undergrads Awarded Aid** 93% **Aid That Is
Need-Based** 77% **Average Award of Freshman Scholarship Package** $6,719 **Tests Required** SAT1 or ACT
Admissions Address 1800 Lincoln Avenue, Evansville, IN 47722 **Admissions Telephone** (812) 479-2468

LAST YEAR'S CLASS **Applied** 2,874 **Accepted** 2,467 **Matriculated** 785 **Average SAT M/V** 570/569 **Average ACT** 25
In Top Fifth of High School Graduating Class 65%

COLLEGE LIFE **Gender Breakdown** M 41%, F 59% **Out of State Students** 49% **Ethnic Composition** White & Other
95.6%, Asian American 1%, Black 2.6%, Hispanic 0.8% **Foreign Students** 7% **Reside on Campus** 71% **Return as
Sophomores** 85% **Total Faculty** 179 **Student Faculty Ratio** 13:1 **Fraternities (% of men participating)** 5 (30%)
Sororities (% of women participating) 4 (23%) **Graduate Students** 94

Evergreen State College

Olympia, WA · Est. 1967 · Coed · Public · 3,773 Undergrads · Big Town

I need...

Admissions info rodriga@elwha.evergreen.edu
www.evergreen.edu/admissions.html
Financial aid info www.evergreen.edu/faid
/index.html

How wired is Evergreen State College?

Do I get email? Yes
Do I get a home page? Yes
Where? 192.211.16.13/individuals/home.html
Is my dorm wired? No
What is the student to computer ratio? 27:1

The usual tour

SPORTS www.evergreen.edu/crcstuff
/athhome.html
STUDENT CLUBS www.evergreen.edu/student
_groups/index.html
LIBRARY www.evergreen.edu/library/library.html
HOUSING www.evergreen.edu/housing
/index.html
COURSE CATALOG 192.211.16.13/Katlinks/coll
_rltns/maincat96/a1-contents-hyper

Skip the brochure

• **ENVIRONMENTAL RESOURCE CENTER** Working to protect Evergreen's beautiful and threatened environs, the ERC is active in a mess of green
causes. **www.evergreen.edu/student_groups/ERC
/ERC.html**

Location: http://www.evergreen.edu/student_groups/ERC/ERC.html

Evergreen's swim team gets some tips from wild salmon

• **SODA POP** Do you prefer Dr. Pepper, Fresca, and
Tab to alcohol and drugs? Soda Pop is an active
campus organization aiding in abuse
prevention and recovery. **www.evergreen.edu
/student_groups/sodapop.html**

• **RESEARCH PROJECTS** Undergraduates, as evi-
denced here, are able to work on an impressive range of research projects, from infrared
spectroscopy to puppetry. **www.evergreen.edu
/serv_res/research/home.html**

• **HEALTH CENTER** When a school's best site is its
health center you get to thinking a bit about
why that is. undoubtedly there is a healthy reason for this. **www.evergreen.edu/health_center
/home.html**

"The school's best site is its health center."

WHAT YOU NEED TO GET IN **Application Deadline** March 1 **Common App.** No **Application Fee** $35 **Tuition Costs** $2,439
($8,625 out-of-state) **Room & Board** $5,000 **Need Blind** Yes **Financial Forms Deadline** Priority given to
applications received by February 15 **Undergrads Awarded Aid** 47% **Aid That Is Need-Based** 77% **Tests
Required** SAT1 or ACT **Admissions Address** Olympia, WA 98505 **Admissions Telephone** (206) 866-6000

LAST YEAR'S CLASS **Applied** 3,498 **Accepted** 2,855 **Matriculated** 1,285 **Average SAT M/V** 518/502 **Average ACT** 24

COLLEGE LIFE **Gender Breakdown** M 43%, F 57% **Out of State Students** 39% **From Public Schools** 95% **Ethnic
Composition** White & Other 86%, Asian American 5%, Black 3%, Hispanic 3%, Native American 3% **Foreign
Students** 1% **Reside on Campus** 33% **Return as Sophomores** 74% **Student Faculty Ratio** 22:1 **Fraternities**
none **Sororities** none **Graduate Students** 27

Fairleigh Dickinson University

www.fdu.edu

Teaneck, NJ · Est. 1942 · Coed · Private · 4,331 Undergrads · Small Town

I need...

Admissions info www.fdu.edu/admissions.html
Financial aid info www.fdu.edu/admissions.html

How wired is Fairleigh Dickinson?

REQUEST APPLICATION ONLINE

Do I get email? Yes
Do I get a home page? Yes
Is my dorm wired? Yes
What is the student to computer ratio? 10:1

The usual tour

CALENDAR www.fdu.edu/fdu_news/calendar.html
SPORTS www.fdu.edu/vc/facts/athletics.html
DEPARTMENTS www.fdu.edu/academic_programs
  /undergraduate.html
HISTORY www.fdu.edu/vc/history.html
SPECIAL PROGRAMS www.fdu.edu/vc/facts
  /special.html
PUBLICATIONS www.fdu.edu/vc/facts
  /publications.html

Skip the brochure

- **THE LITERARY REVIEW** Fine literary magazines often sprout from the ivied walls of academia. First appearing in 1957, Fairleigh Dickinson's *Literary Review* has distinguished itself by devoting entire issues to global, contemporary writing. **www.fdu.edu/fdu_news/literary_review.html**

- **COMMUNITY PROGRAMS** Those prone to complacency can join the throngs of other students. For those looking to contribute to the commu-

Welcome to Fairleigh Dickinson University!

Visitor's Center · FDU News · Admissions · Academic Programs · Student / Campus Life · Library / Information Services · People at FDU · Alumni · Help / Comments · Hotlinks to Other Places

Do GREAT Things

Do great things in the Garden State at Fairleigh Dickinson

nity, Fairleigh Dickinson lists some of its stronger initiatives. **www.fdu.edu/fdu_news /community.html**

- **PRESIDENT'S WELCOME** Read Fairleigh Dickinson's president's gushing welcome to visitors and see if he can whip you into a frenzy about FDU. **www.fdu.edu/vc/pres_welcome.html**

"Fine literary magazines often sprout from the ivied walls of academia."

WHAT YOU NEED TO GET IN Application Deadline Rolling admissions; December 1 for priority consideration **Early Action Deadline** December 1 **Common App.** Yes **Application Fee** $35 **Tuition Costs** $11,610 **Room & Board** $5,550 **Need Blind** Yes **Financial Forms Deadline** Priority given to applications received by March 15 **Undergrads Awarded Aid** 57% **Aid That Is Need-Based** 79% **Average Award of Freshman Scholarship Package** $12,264 **Tests Required** SAT1 (preferred) or ACT **Admissions Address** 1000 River Road, Teaneck, NJ 07666 **Admissions Telephone** (201) 692-2553 (Teaneck)

LAST YEAR'S CLASS Applied 3,216 **Accepted** 1,844 **Matriculated** 526 **Average SAT M/V** 499/436 **In Top Fifth of High School Graduating Class** 22% **Applied Early** 41 **Accepted Early** 25

COLLEGE LIFE Gender Breakdown M 46%, F 54% **Out of State Students** 16% **Ethnic Composition** White & Other 78%, Asian American 4%, Black 12%, Hispanic 6% **Foreign Students** 9% **Reside on Campus** 43% **Return as Sophomores** 77% **Total Faculty** 572 **Student Faculty Ratio** 11:1 **Fraternities (% of men participating)** 10 (10%) **Sororities (% of women participating)** 11 (10%) **Graduate Students** 3,483

Fisk University

Nashville, TN · Est. 1867 · Coed · Private · 840 Undergrads · Urban

www.fisk.edu

How wired is Fisk University?

Do I get email? Yes
Do I get a home page? Yes
   Where? www.fisk.edu/students.html
Is my dorm wired? No

The usual tour

LIBRARY www.fisk.edu/~ghawk/gwen.html
DEPARTMENTS www.fisk.edu/programs.html
HISTORY www.fisk.edu/~ghawk/gwen.html
VIRTUAL TOUR www.fisk.edu/buildings.html
ALUMNI www.fisk.edu/alumni.html

Skip the brochure

• **SPECIAL COLLECTIONS** Listed are some of the school's impressive holdings, with over 100 paintings from the collection of Georgia O'Keefe, including works by Picasso, Cezanne, Renoir, and O'Keefe herself. Fisk's collection also contains varied memorabilia, clippings, and journals from W.E.B. Dubois, and even *The Lincoln Bible*, presented to Abraham Lincoln in 1864 by ex-slaves from Maryland and given to the school by the president's son in 1916. www.fisk.edu/collections.html

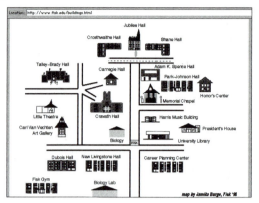

The Fisk campus map—rendered by a minimalist

• **CAMPUS MAP** It's unsophisticated and it's not going to win any design or tech awards, but this map will at least point visitors in the right directions. **www.fisk.edu/buildings.html**

"Paintings by Picasso, Cézanne, Renoir, and O'Keefe herself, among others"

WHAT YOU NEED TO GET IN **Application Deadline** June 15 **Common App.** Yes **Application Fee** $25 **Tuition Costs** $7,212 **Room & Board** $4,224 **Financial Forms Deadline** April 20 **Undergrads Awarded Aid** 82% **Aid That Is Need-Based** 95% **Average Award of Freshman Scholarship Package** $2,000 **Tests Required** SAT1 or ACT **Admissions Address** 1000 17th Avenue North, Nashville, TN 37208 **Admissions Telephone** (615) 329-8666

LAST YEAR'S CLASS **Applied** 1,025 **Accepted** 825 **Matriculated** 204 **In Top Fifth of High School Graduating Class** 27%

COLLEGE LIFE **Gender Breakdown** M 30%, F 70% **Out of State Students** 76% **From Public Schools** 91% **Ethnic Composition** Black 100% **Reside on Campus** 65% **Return as Sophomores** 75% **Total Faculty** 59 **Student Faculty Ratio** 12:1 **Fraternities** 4 **Sororities** 4 **Graduate Students** 39

Florida International University

North Miami, FL · Est. 1965 · Coed · Public · 22,478 Undergrads · Urban

www.fiu.edu

How wired is FIU?

REQUEST APPLICATION ONLINE

Do I get email? Yes

Do I get a home page? Yes

Where? www.fiu.edu/personal

Is my dorm wired? No

What is the student to computer ratio? 13:1

The usual tour

SPORTS www.fiu.edu/orgs/athletics

LIBRARY www.fiu.edu/~library

STUDENT CLUBS www.fiu.edu/~gc104dev/clbs-org .html

CAREER CENTER www.fiu.edu/~career

NEWS www.fiu.edu/fiunews.html

CALENDAR www.fiu.edu/orgs/student/96-97 /shortcal.html

Skip the brochure

• **INSTITUTE FOR PUBLIC OPINION RESEARCH** *USA Today* led the charge to statistics and polls and other media outlets have been playing catch-up since. Sometimes telling, sometimes distracting, public polling is playing a major role in American politics. Learn how to hone

Location: http://www.fiu.edu/picturenm.html

North Miami Campus

[FIU WWW Home]

Who has time to study on a campus like this?

your questions and grill the everyman. **www.fiu.edu/orgs/ipor**

• **FIU NEWS** A visit here will give you a sense of all that's brewing at Florida International—from coming games and weekly events to the wave of hurricanes that annually threaten the state of Florida. **www.fiu.edu/fiunews.html**

• **UNIVERSITY STATISTICS** Stressed out by all this college stuff? Enter the zone of FIU statistics. You'll be dozing in no time. **www.fiu.edu/~instires**

"Learn how to hone your questions and grill the everyman."

WHAT YOU NEED TO GET IN **Application Deadline** Rolling admissions; February 1 for priority consideration **Common App.** No **Application Fee** $20 **Tuition Costs** $1,813 ($7,182 out-of-state) **Room & Board** $6,256 **Need Blind** Yes **Financial Forms Deadline** March 15 with a priority given to applications received by February 1 **Undergrads Awarded Aid** 35% **Aid That Is Need-Based** 45% **Average Award of Freshman Scholarship Package** $3,026 **Tests Required** SAT1 (preferred) or ACT **Admissions Address** University Park, Miami, FL 33199 **Admissions Telephone** (305) 348-2363

LAST YEAR'S CLASS **Applied** 3,786 **Accepted** 2,469 **Matriculated** 1,166 **Average SAT M/V** 609/548 **Average ACT** 23 **In Top Fifth of High School Graduating Class** 74%

COLLEGE LIFE **Gender Breakdown** M 43%, F 57% **Out of State Students** 12% **From Public Schools** 52% **Ethnic Composition** White & Other 31%, Asian American 3%, Black 14%, Hispanic 52% **Foreign Students** 6% **Reside on Campus** 5% **Return as Sophomores** 87% **Total Faculty** 1,177 **Student Faculty Ratio** 16:1 **Fraternities (% of men participating)** 9 (8%) **Sororities (% of women participating)** 8 (9%) **Graduate Students** 5,693

Florida State University

Tallahassee, FL · Est. 1857 · Coed · Public · 22,554 Undergrads · Urban

I need...

Admissions info admissions@mailer.fsu.edu
128.186.180.152/admissions/wel-001
.html

Financial aid info finaid@admin.fsu.edu
www.fsu.edu/~finaidpg/finaid.htm

How wired is FSU?

Do I get email? Yes
Do I get a home page? Yes
Is my dorm wired? Yes
What is the student to computer ratio? 34:1

The usual tour

STUDENT CLUBS www.fsu.edu/Students/Activities
.html
SPORTS www.fsu.edu/~athletic
LIBRARY www.fsu.edu/Library.html
GREEK LIFE www.fsu.edu/Campus/Frat+Sor.html
DEPARTMENTS www.fsu.edu/Links/FSU.html
COURSE CATALOG www.fsu.edu/Class-Schedules

Skip the brochure

• **MARCHING CHIEFS** Who needs a football team?
FSU's marching band could beat the majority

"As you might imagine, FSU is strong in oceanographic studies."

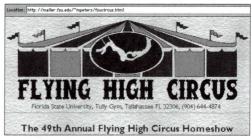

FLYING HIGH CIRCUS

Florida State University, Tully Gym, Tallahassee FL 32306, (904) 644-4874

The 49th Annual Flying High Circus Homeshow

The alma mater of the Flying Wallendas?

of football teams in the country. Numbering some 450 men and women a year, they perform often at home, travel internationally and are the only marching band ever to be featured in *Sports Illustrated*. You're free to see many of their field formations and download a handful of their best fight songs. **www.hcs.eng
.fsu.edu/~todd/Chiefs.html**

• **FLYING HIGH CIRCUS** Talk about feeder school.
FSU has its own circus, the perfect stepping stone to the big tops of Ringling Brothers, Barnum & Bailey. All students are welcome to try their hand at juggling, the flying trapeze, and the irresistibly named Mexican cloudswing in shows that take place across the southeast and occasionally in the Bahamas.
mailer.fsu.edu/~mpeters/fsucircus.html

• **OCEANOGRAPHY** Nothing fishy here. As you might imagine FSU is strong in oceanographic studies. Read up on present research, coming events and major breakthroughs in the department newsletter. **ocean.fsu.edu**

WHAT YOU NEED TO GET IN **Application Deadline** December for priority consideration; final deadline March 3 **Common App.** No **Application Fee** $20 **Tuition Costs** $1,925 ($7,170 out-of-state) **Room & Board** $4,472 **Need Blind** Yes **Financial Forms Deadline** Priority given to applications received by March 1 **Undergrads Awarded Aid** 54% **Aid That Is Need-Based** 56% **Average Award of Freshman Scholarship Package** $2,697 **Tests Required** SAT1 or ACT **Admissions Address** Tallahassee, FL 32306-1009 **Admissions Telephone** (904) 644-6200

LAST YEAR'S CLASS **Applied** 13,801 **Accepted** 10,538 **Matriculated** 3,175 **Median Range SAT M/V** 540-630/ 540-640 **Average ACT** 24 **In Top Fifth of High School Graduating Class** 67%

COLLEGE LIFE **Gender Breakdown** M 45%, F 55% **Out of State Students** 22% **From Public Schools** 69% **Ethnic Composition** White & Other 81.1%, Asian American 2.4%, Black 10%, Hispanic 6.2%, Native American 0.3% **Foreign Students** 1% **Reside on Campus** 18% **Return as Sophomores** 86% **Fraternities (% of men participating)** 26 (19%) **Sororities (% of women participating)** 20 (20%) **Graduate Students** 7,119

University of Florida

www.ufl.edu

Gainesville, FL · Est. 1853 · Coed · Public · 29,859 Undergrads · Urban

I need...

Admissions info spritz@nw.mail.ufl.edu
www.reg.ufl.edu/admissions.html
Financial aid info www.ufsa.ufl.edu/SFA/SFA.html

How wired is University of Florida?

Do I get email? Yes
Do I get a home page? Yes
What is the student to computer ratio? 49:1

DOWNLOAD APPLICATION ONLINE

The usual tour

DEPARTMENTS www.ufl.edu/uf-active.html
VIRTUAL TOUR www.reg.ufl.edu/vtour
LIBRARY www.uflib.ufl.edu/uflib.html
COURSE CATALOG www.reg.ufl.edu/catalog
/catalog.html
SPORTS www.uaa.ufl.edu
STUDY ABROAD nervm.nerdc.ufl.edu/~oisp2
/oisp.htm

Skip the brochure

• **GATOR GROWL** In its first incarnation in 1906, when the school numbered just 102 young men, "Gator Growl" was known as "Dad's Day." In its present form it is one of the centerpieces of Homecoming; takes some 500 students to produce; is hosted by celebs such as Bill Cosby and Robin Williams; and is billed as the world's largest student-run pep rally. nersp.nerdc.ufl.edu/~growl/index.html

• **FOOTBALL TEAM** The Florida Gators football team

Location: http://nersp.nerdc.ufl.edu/~growl/gg-logo.jpg

Rule of thumb: never wrestle with a Gator in a space suit

is an institution unto itself with a site as comprehensive as that of many professional teams. **www.uaa.ufl.edu/sports/Football/football.htm**

• **PEOPLE AWARENESS WEEK** The University of Florida would like to make a political correction: PC does not Rest In Peace, is a thriving institution, and is celebrated in all its colors and sexual flavors here. **www.ufsa.ufl.edu/paw /purpose.htm**

"The Florida Gators football team is an institution unto itself."

WHAT YOU NEED TO GET IN **Application Deadline** November 1 for priority consideration; final deadline February 1 **Early Action Deadline** October 1 **Common App.** Yes **Application Fee** $20 **Tuition Costs** $1,830 ($7,100 out-of-state) **Room & Board** $4,500 **Need Blind** Yes **Financial Forms Deadline** Priority given to applications received by April 15 **Undergrads Awarded Aid** 64% **Aid That Is Need-Based** 58% **Average Award of Freshman Scholarship Package** $3,000 **Tests Required** SAT1 (preferred) or ACT **Admissions Address** Gainesville, FL 32611 **Admissions Telephone** (352) 392-1365

LAST YEAR'S CLASS **Applied** 12,724 **Accepted** 8,479 **Matriculated** 3,699 **Median Range SAT M/V** 590-680/ 570-670 **In Top Fifth of High School Graduating Class** 83% **Applied Early** 11 **Accepted Early** 5

COLLEGE LIFE **Gender Breakdown** M 52%, F 48% **Out of State Students** 9% **Ethnic Composition** White & Other 78%, Asian American 6%, Black 6%, Hispanic 10% **Reside on Campus** 21% **Return as Sophomores** 90% **Total Faculty** 2225 **Student Faculty Ratio** 17:1 **Fraternities (% of men participating)** 28 (15%) **Sororities (% of women participating)** 18 (15%) **Graduate Students** 9,554

Fordham University

Bronx, NY · Est. 1841 · Coed · Private · 5,796 Undergrads · Urban

www.fordham.edu

I need...

Admissions info AD_KOREVEC@lars.fordham.edu
www.fordham.edu/main/unadmin.html
Financial aid info www.fordham.edu/main/finaid
/cover.html

How wired is Fordham University?

Do I get email? Yes
Do I get a home page? Yes
Is my dorm wired? Yes
What is the student to computer ratio? 25:1

The usual tour

CALENDAR gopher://sueann.fordham.edu:70
/00gopher_root%3a%5b_public_affairs%5d
_events.txt
DEPARTMENTS www.fordham.edu/main
/acopps.html
ALUMNI www.fordham.edu/main/Alumni.html
LOCAL INFO www.fordham.edu/main/nyc.html
LIBRARY gopher://rhoda.fordham.edu:70
/11gopher_root%3A%5B_library%5D
VIRTUAL TOUR www.fordham.edu/photos

Skip the brochure

- **WFUV 90.7 FM** Fordham's own public radio station is home to Mountain Stage, World Cafe, and an eclectic mix of artists from Ani DiFranco to Leonard Cohen to Morphine. Musical highlights aside, the station is also home to NPR and a series of radio documentaries. With additional information on upcom-

WFUV—where Fordham students launch broadcasting careers

ing musical festivals and a bevy of links, WFUV sounds like an excellent place to tune your dial and maybe get a start in the radio biz. **www.users.interport.net/~stoner3/wfuva.html**

- **RESIDENTIAL LIVING** With more than 8 million people living in the five boroughs, student housing is a big issue. Here, Fordham supplies info on housing, campus resources, events and meal plans. **www.fordham.edu /main/residence/catalog1996_97/res_main.html**

- **JESUIT TRADITION** While Fordham defers to Lemoyne with an off-site link, it's still worth a stop to acquaint oneself with the Jesuit foundation upon which Fordham is built. **maple.lemoyne.edu/~bucko/Jesuit.html**

"WFUV—an excellent place to tune your dial"

WHAT YOU NEED TO GET IN **Application Deadline** February 1 **Early Action Deadline** November 1 **Common App.** Yes **Application Fee** $50 **Tuition Costs** $15,800 **Room & Board** $7,063 **Need Blind** Yes **Financial Forms Deadline** Priority given to applications received by February 1 **Undergrads Awarded Aid** 72% **Aid That Is Need-Based** 96% **Average Award of Freshman Scholarship Package** $9,065 **Tests Required** SAT1 or ACT **Admissions Address** East Fordham Road, Bronx, NY 10458 **Admissions Telephone** (718) 817-4000

LAST YEAR'S CLASS **Applied** 4,680 **Accepted** 3,259 **Matriculated** 1,098 **Average SAT M/V** 553/512 **Average ACT** 25 **In Top Fifth of High School Graduating Class** 52% **Applied Early** 71 **Accepted Early** 53

COLLEGE LIFE **Gender Breakdown** M 42%, F 58% **Out of State Students** 36% **From Public Schools** 35% **Ethnic Composition** White & Other 74%, Asian American 5%, Black 6%, Hispanic 15% **Foreign Students** 2% **Reside on Campus** 70% **Return as Sophomores** 92% **Total Faculty** 184 **Student Faculty Ratio** 17:1 **Fraternities** none **Sororities** none **Graduate Students** 8,299

Franklin & Marshall College   www.fandm.edu

Lancaster, PA · Est. 1787 · Coed · Private · 1,866 Undergrads · Big Town

I need...

Admissions info admission@FandM.edu
www.fandm.edu/Departments/Admission
/Admission.html
Financial aid info www.fandm.edu/Departments
/Admission/financialaid.html

How wired is Franklin & Marshall College?

Do I get a home page? No
Is my dorm wired? Yes
What is the student to computer ratio? 27:1

The usual tour

STUDENT CLUBS 155.68.3.11/CampusLife
/Organizations/Organizations.html
CALENDAR admin.fandm.edu/Calendar/Calendar
DEPARTMENTS www.fandm.edu/Departments
/Academic.html
LIBRARY www.fandm.edu/Departments/Library
/Library_home.html
VIRTUAL TOUR www.fandm.edu/Departments
/Admission/CampusTour/tour.html
SPORTS www.fandm.edu/Departments
/Athletic.html
PUBLICATIONS www.fandm.edu/departments
/CollegeRelations/NewsandPubs/Newsand
Pubs.html

Skip the brochure

- **LGB & A** At many schools the local Lesbian, Gay,
Bisexual and Allies alliance is one of the better and more informative sites. Franklin &

This wittily named *a cappella* group has a large following on
the Franklin & Marshall campus

Marshall is no exception, with a strong presence for its resident BGLAD chapter.
**www.fandm.edu/CampusLife/Organizations/Allies
/Allies_Home.html**

- **CONUNDRUM—HUMOR SOCIETY** Franklin &
Marshall's humor group couldn't be more in
love with themselves; they just can't stop
cracking each other up. And while they don't
let us in on the jokes, they do post a thing or
two on their activities. **www.fandm.edu/CampusLife
/Organizations/HumorSociety/socks.au**

- **THE POOR RICHARDS** *A cappella* groups are huge
at some schools and F & M has its share with
several having their own sites where you can
tune in and listen to the songs their singing.
This coed crew has even cut an album.
**www.fandm.edu/CampusLife/Organizations/PoorRichards
/PoorRichards.html**

WHAT YOU NEED TO GET IN **Application Deadline** February 1 **Early Action Deadline** January 15 **Common App.** Yes
Application Fee $50 **Tuition Costs** $21,940 **Room & Board** $4,460 **Financial Forms Deadline** Priority given to
applications received by February 1 **Undergrads Awarded Aid** 58% **Aid That Is Need-Based** 95% **Average Award
of Freshman Scholarship Package** $12,242 **Tests Required** SAT1 or ACT **Admissions Address** P.O. Box 3003,
Lancaster, PA 17604-3003 **Admissions Telephone** (717) 291-3951

LAST YEAR'S CLASS **Applied** 3,430 **Accepted** 2,366 **Matriculated** 500 **Median Range SAT M/V** 580-680/500-620
Average ACT 26 **In Top Fifth of High School Graduating Class** 71% **Applied Early** 149 **Accepted Early** 117

COLLEGE LIFE **Gender Breakdown** M 54%, F 46% **Out of State Students** 68% **From Public Schools** 59% **Ethnic
Composition** White & Other 82%, Asian American 11%, Black 3%, Hispanic 4% **Foreign Students** 7% **Reside on
Campus** 74% **Return as Sophomores** 96% **Total Faculty** 152 **Student Faculty Ratio** 11:1 **Fraternities (% of men
participating)** 9 (45%) **Sororities (% of women participating)** 3 (30%)

Furman University

www.furman.edu

Greenville, SC · Est. 1826 · Coed · Private · 2,417 Undergrads · Urban

I need...

Admissions info Admissions/furman@furman.edu
www.furman.edu/admin/admissions
/viewbook/Fa_Admissions.html
Financial aid info sayer_lynda/furman@furman
.edu
www.furman.edu/admin/admissions
/viewbook/Fa_Admissions.html

How wired is Furman?

Do I get email? Yes
Do I get a home page? Yes
    Where? www.furman.edu/people/student.html
Is my dorm wired? Yes
What is the student to computer ratio? 11:1

The usual tour

DEPARTMENTS www.furman.edu/academics/dept
/index.htm
LIBRARY carolus.furman.edu/library/index.html
VIRTUAL TOUR www.furman.edu/campus
/index.html
STUDENT CLUBS www.furman.edu/life
/organizations
GREEK LIFE www.furman.edu/life/organizations
/greek

Skip the brochure

• **THE PALADIN** The school newspaper has been
published weekly for the last 80 years. While
its been up on the Web for less than a year,
The Paladin's editors aren't missing the oppor-

Nothing could be finer in Greenville, S.C.

tunity to tune the world into Furman.
www-student.furman.edu/Paladin

• **UNIVERSITY CHAPLAINCY** Founded by Baptists,
Furman still takes the church seriously. But
don't be put off—Sunday attendance is not
required. **www.furman.edu/life/chaplaincy**

• **FURMAN FACTS** Interested in the study of health
and exercise? Looking for a pre-med program
with a liberal arts feel? Feel strongly about
accounting? Find out if Furman can can deliver
the goods. **www.furman.edu/admin/admissions
/viewbook/Facts.html**

"Looking for a pre-med program with a liberal arts feel?"

WHAT YOU NEED TO GET IN **Application Deadline** February 1 **Early Action Deadline** December 1 **Common App.** Yes
Application Fee $30 **Tuition Costs** $15,360 **Room & Board** $4,304 **Need Blind** Yes **Financial Forms Deadline**
February 1 **Undergrads Awarded Aid** 69% **Aid That Is Need-Based** 60% **Average Award of Freshman
Scholarship Package** $8,500 **Tests Required** SAT1 or ACT **Admissions Address** 3300 Poinsett Highway,
Greenville, SC 29613 **Admissions Telephone** (864) 294-2034

LAST YEAR'S CLASS **Applied** 2,896 **Accepted** 2,318 **Matriculated** 703 **Average SAT M/V** 613/545 **Average ACT** 26
In Top Fifth of High School Graduating Class 77% **Applied Early** 487 **Accepted Early** 416

COLLEGE LIFE **Gender Breakdown** M 46%, F 54% **Out of State Students** 71% **From Public Schools** 75% **Ethnic
Composition** White & Other 93%, Asian American 2%, Black 4%, Hispanic 1% **Foreign Students** 1% **Reside on
Campus** 60% **Return as Sophomores** 88% **Total Faculty** 196 **Student Faculty Ratio** 12:1 **Fraternities (% of men
participating)** 8 (35%) **Sororities (% of women participating)** 7 (35%) **Graduate Students** 256

George Mason University

www.gmu.edu

Fairfax, VA · Est. 1957 · Coed · Public · 13,777 Undergrads · Urban

I need...

Admissions info adm@gmu.edu
www.admissions.gmu.edu
Financial aid info apollo.gmu.edu/finaid

How wired is George Mason?

Do I get email? Yes
Do I get a home page? Yes
Is my dorm wired? Yes
What is the student to computer ratio? 28:1

FULL APPLICATION ONLINE

The usual tour

STUDENT CLUBS www.gmu.edu/student/uusa
/organ.htm
SPORTS www.pubs.gmu.edu/sports
CAREER CENTER www.gmu.edu/student/uusa
/greek.htm
DEPARTMENTS www.gmu.edu/academic
/departments.html
LIBRARY www.gmu.edu/library
CALENDAR www.gmu.edu/academic/calendars

Skip the brochure

• **GEORGE MASON SOCIETY** Staunch defenders of
the Constitution and passionate supporters of

"GMU students sustain the tradition of the school's namesake"

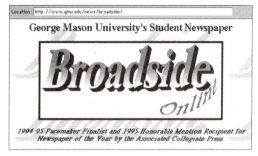

George Mason University's Student Newspaper

Broadside *Online*

*1994-95 Pacemaker Finalist and 1995 Honorable Mention Recipient for
Newspaper of the Year by the Associated Collegiate Press*

GMU's news lifeline, *Broadside*, comes out twice a week
during the school year

every citizen's right to say what he or she
chooses, GMU students sustain the tradition
of the school's namesake, a player in the
development of both the Constitution and the
Bill of Rights. Online, this makes for a diverse
and fascinating collection of links.
www.gmu.edu/org/freedom/#glb

• **GMU TELEVISION** Join up with the production
team for George Mason's own TV station
which delivers several area programs including
The Mason Report. There's also the opportunity to produce, and perhaps even star in your
own step, low-impact, and seniors' aerobics TV
show. **www.gmu.edu/departments/tvstudio**

• **WRESTLING TEAM** Before Hulk Hogan there was
the sport of Greco-Roman warriors and the
novelist John Irving. Check it out here.
129.174.32.216/sports/Wrestling/wrestle.html

WHAT YOU NEED TO GET IN **Application Deadline** December 1 for priority consideration; final deadline February 1 **Early
Action Deadline** December 1 **Common App.** Yes **Application Fee** $30 **Tuition Costs** $4,212 ($11,604 out-of-
state) **Room & Board** $4,930 **Need Blind** Yes **Financial Forms Deadline** Priority given to applications received by
March 1 **Undergrads Awarded Aid** 45% **Aid That Is Need-Based** 72% **Average Award of Freshman Scholarship
Package** $3,626 **Tests Required** SAT1 or ACT **Admissions Address** 4400 University Drive, Fairfax, VA 22030
Admissions Telephone (703) 993-2400

LAST YEAR'S CLASS **Applied** 5,497 **Accepted** 4,536 **Matriculated** 1,918 **Average SAT M/V** 530/500 **Applied Early**
1,600 **Accepted Early** 800

COLLEGE LIFE **Gender Breakdown** M 44%, F 56% **Out of State Students** 20% **From Public Schools** 95% **Ethnic
Composition** White & Other 77%, Asian American 14%, Black 7.8%, Hispanic 5.8%, Native American 0.5%
Foreign Students 3% **Reside on Campus** 12% **Return as Sophomores** 72% **Total Faculty** 1,205 **Student Faculty
Ratio** 17:1 **Fraternities (% of men participating)** 18 (15%) **Sororities (% of women participating)** 10 (12%)
Graduate Students 10,396

Georgetown University

www.georgetown.edu

Washington, DC · Est. 1789 · Coed · Private · 6,374 Undergrads · Urban

How wired is Georgetown?

Do I get email? Yes
Do I get a home page? Yes
Is my dorm wired? Yes
What is the student to computer ratio? 16:1

The usual tour

STUDENT CLUBS www.georgetown.edu/student
-programs/organizations/organizations.html
CALENDAR www.georgetown.edu/calendars
DEPARTMENTS www.georgetown.edu
/departments/departments.html
LIBRARY gulib.lausun.georgetown.edu
SPORTS www.georgetown.edu/athletics
PUBLICATIONS www.georgetown.edu
/#publications

Skip the brochure

- **GEORGETOWN MEN'S BASKETBALL** Patrick Ewing, Alonzo Mourning, and Allen Iverson are just a few of the many Hoya players to grace the NBA over the years. With stats, team records, and frequent updates you won't miss any of the action. **www.georgetown.edu/athletics/bball**

- **GEORGETOWN ALUMS** It's likely you'll drink some

The Hoyas lay out the welcome mat

in college. If you want to see who else has drunk from the Georgetown fountain, check out this listing. You'll recognize many of the names, including Bill Clinton. **guweb.georgetown .edu/oaur/about/alumfame.htm**

- **NOMADIC THEATRE** These undergrads are tackling some of the most intelligent theater of the past ten years, including plays by A.R. Gurney, Tom Stoppard, and John Guare. **www.georgetown .edu/student-programs/organizations/nomadic/index.html**

- **WHAT'S A HOYA?** Curious about the Georgetown nickname? Greek and Latin somehow fractured, fused and eventually evolved into the present day "Hoya." **guweb.georgetown.edu/oaur /about/hoya-def.htm**

WHAT YOU NEED TO GET IN **Application Deadline** January 10 **Early Action Deadline** November 1 **Common App.** No **Application Fee** $50 **Tuition Costs** $20,208 **Room & Board** $7,462 **Need Blind** Yes **Financial Forms Deadline** Priority given to applications received by February 1 **Undergrads Awarded Aid** 52% **Aid That Is Need-Based** 97% **Average Award of Freshman Scholarship Package** $12,171 **Tests Required** SAT1 or ACT **Admissions Address** 37th and O Streets, NW, Washington, DC 20057 **Admissions Telephone** (202) 687-3600

LAST YEAR'S CLASS **Applied** 12,832 **Accepted** 2,860 **Matriculated** 1,467 **Median Range SAT M/V** 620-710/ 550-660 **In Top Fifth of High School Graduating Class** 90% **Applied Early** 3,038 **Accepted Early** 990

COLLEGE LIFE **Gender Breakdown** M 48%, F 52% **Out of State Students** 98% **From Public Schools** 41% **Ethnic Composition** White & Other 79%, Asian American 8%, Black 7%, Hispanic 6%, **Foreign Students** 11% **Reside on Campus** 80% **Return as Sophomores** 95% **Total Faculty** 966 **Student Faculty Ratio** 12:1 **Fraternities** none **Sororities** none **Graduate Students** 6,244

George Washington University

Washington, DC · Est. 1821 · Coed · Private · 6,378 Undergrads · Urban

www.gwu.edu

I need...

Admissions info gwadm@gwis.circ.gwu.edu
www.gwu.edu/~gwadm

How wired is George Washington University?

Do I get email? Yes
Do I get a home page? Yes
   Where? gwis2.circ.gwu.edu/~www/student.html
Is my dorm wired? No
What is the student to computer ratio? 12:1

The usual tour

CALENDAR www.gwu.edu/events.html
DEPARTMENTS www.gwu.edu/acad.html
LIBRARY www.gwu.edu/libraries.html
SPORTS www.gwu.edu/athletics.html

Skip the brochure

• **FROM STRENGTH TO STRENGTH: A PICTORIAL HISTORY OF GWU, 1821-1996** You probably know all about George Washington—the man, myth, and legend. Now learn all there is to know about George Washington, the university, with this illustrated school history. **www.gwu.edu/~info/history**

• **INDEPENDENCE MAGAZINE** Subtitled "The Voice of Reason for The George Washington University," this campus magazine reveals its capital-city origins with news and in-depth analyses. A variety of opinion pieces round out

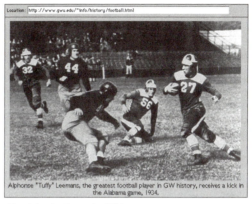

Alphonse "Tuffy" Leemans, the greatest football player in GW history, receives a kick in the Alabama game, 1934.

Breakdancing began in 1934

the magazine, and the title for one column, "The Token Liberal," speaks volumes about the entire D.C. scene. **www.gwu.edu/~auth**

• **THE COMMUTER STUDENTS ASSOCIATION HOME PAGE** As if dealing with D.C. traffic wasn't bad enough, commuter students must cope with finding a social place without the advantage of late-night bonding sessions. The Commuter Students Association seeks to bring these students together. **www.gwu.edu/~gwucc**

• **FORENSIC SCIENCES STUDENT ORGANIZATION** A program for budding J. Edgar Hoovers, it's also a feeder program of sorts for the F.B.I. Just make sure you have a clean record before you apply. **www.gwu.edu/~forensic**

WHAT YOU NEED TO GET IN **Application Deadline** Rolling admissions; Febuary 1 for priority consideration **Early Action Deadline** November 1 (Part I), December 1 (Part II) **Common App.** Yes **Application Fee** $50 **Tuition Costs** $19,065 **Room & Board** $6,910 **Need Blind** Yes **Financial Forms Deadline** Priority given to applications received by February 1 **Undergrads Awarded Aid** 65% **Aid That Is Need-Based** 66% **Average Award of Freshman Scholarship Package** $10,372 **Tests Required** SAT1 or ACT **Admissions Address** 2121 Eye (I) Street, NW, Washington, DC 20052 **Admissions Telephone** (800) 447-3765

LAST YEAR'S CLASS **Applied** 10,469 **Accepted** 5,738 **Matriculated** 1,395 **Median Range SAT M/V** 570-660/ 580-670 **In Top Fifth of High School Graduating Class** 72% **Applied Early** 449 **Accepted Early** 220

COLLEGE LIFE **Gender Breakdown** M 47%, F 53% **Out of State Students** 96% **From Public Schools** 70% **Ethnic Composition** White & Other 77%, Asian American 12%, Black 7%, Hispanic 4% **Foreign Students** 11% **Reside on Campus** 54% **Return as Sophomores** 91% **Total Faculty** 1,232 **Student Faculty Ratio** 15:1 **Fraternities (% of men participating)** 12 (19%) **Sororities (% of women participating)** 7 (12%) **Graduate Students** 10,845

University of Georgia

Athens, GA · Est. 1785 · Coed · Public · 23,572 Undergrads · Suburban

I need...

Admissions info undergrad@admissions.uga.edu
www.uga.edu/admit/undergrad.html
Financial aid info www.uga.edu/~osfa

How wired is University of Georgia?

Do I get email? Yes
Do I get a home page? Yes
  Where? www.uga.edu/uga-participants.html
Is my dorm wired? Yes
What is the student to computer ratio? 25:1

The usual tour

DEPARTMENTS www.uga.edu/acad/sch-col.html
LIBRARY www.libs.uga.edu
STUDENT CLUBS www.uga.edu/student
SPORTS www.sports.uga.edu
VIRTUAL TOUR www.uga.edu/uga/photo-tour
CALENDAR www.uga.edu/cgi-bin/ca2html.sh

Skip the brochure

• **UGA V** Being born to a rich and honored blood-line can be a burden to some, but not to Uga the Fifth. Though his father appeared in such magazines as *Sports Illustrated*, *Time*, and *Newsweek*, Uga V has stayed true to himself, carrying on the rich tradition as the school's bulldog mascot. His forebears lie buried within the stadium beneath marble headstones; he too permanently resides there in a different sort of heaven, an air-conditioned suite

Location: http://www.sports.uga.edu/uga_v.html

Uga V says, "Bark if you love Georgia"

abutting the cheerleaders' platform.
www.sports.uga.edu/uga_v.html

• **GEORGIA MUSEUM OF ART** The Georgia Museum of Art has made considerable progress since its humble beginnings in 1945. It became such the envy of the area that in 1982 the state designated it the official museum of Georgia. **www.budgets.uga.edu/gma**

• **WUOG, 90.5 FM** It'd be irresponsible not to mention the local music scene. Athens is legendary home to the grandpappies of college radio programming, R.E.M., and has become one of the music capitals of the South, if not the country. **www.uga.edu/~wuog**

WHAT YOU NEED TO GET IN **Application Deadline** February 1 **Common App.** No **Application Fee** $25 **Tuition Costs** $2,115 ($5,181 out-of-state) **Room & Board** $3,820 **Need Blind** Yes **Undergrads Awarded Aid** 50% **Average Award of Freshman Scholarship Package** $1,200 **Tests Required** SAT1 (preferred) or ACT **Admissions Address** Athens, GA 30602 **Admissions Telephone** (706) 542-8776

LAST YEAR'S CLASS **Applied** 13,401 **Accepted** 7,935 **Matriculated** 5,695 **Average SAT M/V** 581/528 **Average ACT** 25 **In Top Quarter of High School Graduating Class** 85%

COLLEGE LIFE **Gender Breakdown** M 47%, F 53% **Out of State Students** 14% **From Public Schools** 87% **Ethnic Composition** White & Other 89%, Asian American 2%, Black 7%, Hispanic 1%, Native American 1% **Foreign Students** 2% **Reside on Campus** 29% **Return as Sophomores** 85% **Student Faculty Ratio** 17:1 **Fraternities (% of men participating)** 26 (16%) **Sororities (% of women participating)** 22 (21%) **Graduate Students** 6,577

Georgia Institute of Technology

www.gatech.edu

Atlanta, GA · Est. 1885 · Coed · Private · 9,473 Undergrads · Urban

I need...

Admissions info admissions@success.gatech
.edu
www.gatech.edu/admissions/undergrad
/index.html
Financial aid info www.gatech.edu/admissions
/undergrad/index.html#Financial

How wired is Georgia Tech?

Do I get email? Yes
Do I get a home page? Yes
   Where? www.gatech.edu/individuals
Is my dorm wired? Yes
What is the student to computer ratio? 7:1

The usual tour

STUDENT CLUBS www.gatech.edu/studlife/soh
   /soh.html
SPORTS www.gatech.edu/techhome
   /Athletics.html
LIBRARY www.library.gatech.edu
GREEK LIFE www.library.gatech.edu
DEPARTMENTS www.gatech.edu/techhome
   /Colleges.html

Skip the brochure

- **ERATO** In a sea of techies a creative heart does beat. Georgia Tech's writers and poets have found a voice at *Erato*, the school's recently

Georgia Tech: Yellow Jackets take to the air

resurrected literary magazine. **www.prism.gatech
.edu/~gt799lc/erato.html**

- **YELLOW JACKET FLYING CLUB** Now here's a club worth joining. These folks not only convene to talk about flying—they also, from the looks of it, own four of their own planes. Buzz off with the Yellow Jacket Flying Club. **www.gcatt.gatech
.edu/~ian/yjfc/yjfc.html**

- **MARKSMANSHIP CLUB** Need to blow off a little steam? Doom no longer hitting the spot? Join this club and have an excuse for firing off a few rounds every week. **www.prism.gatech.edu
/~dsadmmc**

- **WOMEN'S VARSITY VOLLEYBALL** Georgia Tech's women's volleyball team has risen from an unspectacular past to national prominence and top 25 rankings. You can even download video clips of the Lady Jackets in action. **www.ce
.gatech.edu/Students/M.Bertz/Vball/Varsity/varsity.html**

WHAT YOU NEED TO GET IN **Application Deadline** February 1 for priority consideration **Common App.** No **Application Fee** $25 (waived if application is completed electronically) **Tuition Costs** $2,115 ($8,019 out-of-state) **Room & Board** $5,900 **Financial Forms Deadline** March 1 **Undergrads Awarded Aid** 55% **Aid That Is Need-Based** 56% **Tests Required** SAT1 (preferred) or ACT **Admissions Address** 225 North Avenue, NW, Atlanta, GA 30332 **Telephone** (404) 894-4154

LAST YEAR'S CLASS **Applied** 7,405 **Accepted** 4,625 **Matriculated** 1,850 **Average SAT M/V** 672/560 **In Top Fifth of High School Graduating Class** 89%

COLLEGE LIFE **Gender Breakdown** M 73%, F 27% **Out of State Students** 35% **From Public Schools** 85% **Ethnic Composition** White & Other 75.5%, Asian American 11%, Black 10%, Hispanic 3%, Native American 0.5% **Foreign Students** 3% **Reside on Campus** 43% **Return as Sophomores** 85% **Total Faculty** 644 **Student Faculty Ratio** 20:1 **Fraternities (% of men participating)** 31 (30%) **Sororities (% of women participating)** 8 (27%) **Graduate Students** 3,563

Georgia State University

www.gsu.edu

Atlanta, GA · Est. 1913 · Coed · Public · 16,849 Undergrads · Urban

I need...

Admissions info admissions@GSU.EDU
www.gsu.edu/dept/admin/adm
/admissions.html
Financial aid info www.gsu.edu/student.html

How wired is Georgia State University?

Do I get a home page? No
What is the student to computer ratio? 14:1

The usual tour

LIBRARY wwwlib.gsu.edu
STUDENT CLUBS www.gsu.edu/organizations.html
DEPARTMENTS www.gsu.edu/dept/admin/adm
/admissions.html#Programs Of Study
COMPUTER RESOURCES www.gsu.edu/computer
.html
VIRTUAL TOUR glacier.gsu.edu/CS/Campus
/campus3d.html
OVERVIEW www.gsu.edu/overview.html

Skip the brochure

• **THE CENTER FOR ETHICS** Georgia State has a size-
able department devoted solely to the discussion and dissemination of ethical theory. In
addition to its focus on the history of ethics
and applied ethics, the center sponsors a wide
variety of lectures and workshops in the
greater Atlanta area. **www.gsu.edu/~phlgwr
/cntrhome.html**

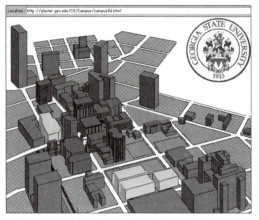

Enjoy a virtual fly-by of the Georgia State campus

• **COMMUNICATIONS** If you're interested in film,
video, journalism, and multimedia, Georgia
State's Communications site is a must visit.
Check out the new Digital Arts and Entertainment Laboratory and see what Kodak and SGI
have to offer. **www.gsu.edu/~jougcl/welcome.html**

• **GEOLOGY DEPARTMENT** Rock and roll with the
suitably granite-like structure of this cheerful
introduction to the world of geology.
www2.Gsu.EDU/~geocxr/mainmenu.html

• **GSU STATUTES** Think it's easy to run a school?
It's certainly not easy to read about all the
don'ts, can'ts, and why nots. **www.gsu.edu/doc
/govern/attacha.html**

WHAT YOU NEED TO GET IN **Application Deadline** July 1 **Common App.** No **Application Fee** $10 **Tuition Costs** $2,124
($6,255 out-of-state) **Room & Board** $4,800 **Need Blind** Yes **Financial Forms Deadline** Priority given to
applications received by May 1 **Undergrads Awarded Aid** 45% **Aid That Is Need-Based** 80% **Average Award of
Freshman Scholarship Package** $2,000 **Tests Required** SAT1 or ACT **Admissions Address** University Plaza,
Atlanta, GA 30303 **Admissions Telephone** (404) 651-2365

LAST YEAR'S CLASS **Applied** 2,758 **Accepted** 1,714 **Matriculated** 851 **Average SAT M/V** 517/461 **Average ACT** 22

COLLEGE LIFE **Gender Breakdown** M 41%, F 59% **Out of State Students** 9% **Ethnic Composition** White & Other 66%,
Asian American 7%, Black 23%, Hispanic 3%, Native American 1% **Foreign Students** 4% **Total Faculty** 1,381
Fraternities (% of men participating) 11 (6%) **Sororities (% of women participating)** 9 (3%) **Graduate Students**
7,467

Gettysburg College

Gettysburg, PA · Est. 1832 · Coed · Private · 1,992 Undergrads · Small Town

I need...

Admissions info admissions@gettysburg.edu
www.gettysburg.edu/admissions
Financial aid info www.gettysburg.edu/admissions
/html/info/topical/financially.html

How wired is Gettysburg?

Do I get email? Yes
Do I get a home page? Yes
Is my dorm wired? Yes
What is the student to computer ratio? 3:1

DOWNLOAD APPLICATION ONLINE

The usual tour

STUDENT CLUBS www.gettysburg.edu/project
/studentorgs.html
STUDY ABROAD www.gettysburg.edu/project
/abroad/top.html
DEPARTMENTS www.gettysburg.edu/project
/academics.html
GREEK LIFE www.gettysburg.edu/project
/greekorgs.html
SCHOOL FACTS www.gettysburg.edu/home_page
_items/gburg.facts.html
AREA GUIDE www.gettysburg.edu/~kthomas
/book.html

Skip the brochure

- **DINING HALL** Wondering what scrumptious cafeteria fare is for dinner? Check the daily postings of each day's goodies. Better yet, go
straight to the source and take a look.

What's the recipe today, Gettysburg?

Gettysburg has a permanently fixed camera in
the dining hall so you can see how long the
line is for ice cream. Hilarious—and useful.
dining.www.gettysburg.edu

- **RESIDENTIAL COLLEGE PROJECTS** Gettysburg offers
an innovative academic program, linking a different course every semester with one of three
residential colleges. Students have worked on
such projects as "Confucius, Footbinding, and
Spitting, Culture Revolution in China."
www.gettysburg.edu/~s275250/rescol/islands.html

- **CIVIL WAR CLUB** Situated in the town whose
address most everyone learned in elementary
school, Gettysburg has a club devoted to
studying the history and impact of the War
Between the States. **www.gettysburg.edu/project
/clubs/cwc.html**

WHAT YOU NEED TO GET IN **Application Deadline** Fall for priority consideration; final deadline February 15 **Early Action Deadline** February 1 **Common App.** Yes **Application Fee** $35 **Tuition Costs** $20,744 **Room & Board** $4,522 **Need Blind** Yes **Financial Forms Deadline** February 15 **Undergrads Awarded Aid** 52% **Aid That Is Need-Based** 95% **Average Award of Freshman Scholarship Package** $12,875 **Tests Required** SAT1 or ACT **Admissions Address** Gettysburg, PA 17325-1484 **Admissions Telephone** (717) 337-6100

LAST YEAR'S CLASS **Applied** 3,680 **Accepted** 2,495 **Matriculated** 605 **Median Range SAT M/V** 550-640/500-580 **In Top Fifth of High School Graduating Class** 70% **Applied Early** 175 **Accepted Early** 132

COLLEGE LIFE **Gender Breakdown** M 49%, F 51% **Out of State Students** 75% **From Public Schools** 77% **Ethnic Composition** White & Other 91%, Asian American 4%, Black 3%, Hispanic 2% **Foreign Students** 3% **Reside on Campus** 85% **Return as Sophomores** 90% **Total Faculty** 221 **Student Faculty Ratio** 11:1 **Fraternities (% of men participating)** 11 (55%) **Sororities (% of women participating)** 5 (45%)

Grinnell College

Grinnell, IA · Est. 1846 · Coed · Private · 1,304 Undergrads · Small Town

www.grin.edu

I need...

Admissions info askgrin@admin.grin.edu
www.ioweb.com/grin150/admission
Financial aid info www.ioweb.com/grin150
/admission/#finance

How wired is Grinnell College?

REQUEST APPLICATION ONLINE

Do I get email? Yes
Do I get a home page? Yes
Is my dorm wired? No
What is the student to computer ratio? 5:1

The usual tour

DEPARTMENTS www.ioweb.com/grin150
/admission/#programs
LIBRARY www.lib.grin.edu
CALENDAR www.grin.edu/~sesqui/calendar.html
SPORTS www.grin.edu/www/sports.html
VIRTUAL TOUR www.grin.edu/~sesqui/camptour
.html

Skip the brochure

- **SWIMMING & DIVING** Dive in and get wet with the Grinnellian water bugs from the swimming and diving teams. ac.grin.edu/~hurley/index.html
- **SCARLET & BLACK** The campus rag has been coming out weekly since 1894. No doubt its current content is a bit meatier. A recent article, "The Link Between Meat-eating and Misogyny," clearly demonstrates as much. **www.math.grin.edu/~andersos/sandb**

Location: http://www.grin.edu/~sesqui/

CELEBRATING GRINNELL AND GRINNELLIANS
GRINNELL COLLEGE
SESQUICENTENNIAL 1846-1996

Grinnell is celebrating 150 years, but can grads spell "sesquicentennial"?

- **SESQUICENTENNIAL MERCHANDISE** Good to see Grinnell's got no compunction about following the lead of more commmercial sites. The school is hawking any and everything they can. Stay tuned to see if it starts taking ads. **www.grin.edu/~sesqui/merchan.html**
- **GRINNELL'S SESQUICENTENNIAL** Welcome to the anniversary party (read fundraising drive) that never ends—18 months of celebrating the school's birthday. **www.grin.edu/~sesqui**

"Dive in and get wet with the Grinnellian water bugs."

WHAT YOU NEED TO GET IN **Application Deadline** February 1 for priority consideration **Early Action Deadline** November 20 **Common App.** Yes **Application Fee** $25 **Tuition Costs** $16,724 **Room & Board** $4,926 **Need Blind** Yes **Financial Forms Deadline** Priority given to applications received by February 1 **Undergrads Awarded Aid** 83% **Aid That Is Need-Based** 83% **Average Award of Freshman Scholarship Package** $9,757 **Tests Required** SAT1 or ACT **Admissions Address** P.O. Box 805, Grinnell, IA 50112 **Admissions Telephone** (515) 269-3600

LAST YEAR'S CLASS **Applied** 1,809 **Accepted** 1,346 **Matriculated** 307 **Average SAT M/V** 642/606 **Average ACT** 30 **In Top Fifth of High School Graduating Class** 83% **Applied Early** 105 **Accepted Early** 76

COLLEGE LIFE **Gender Breakdown** M 45%, F 55% **Out of State Students** 86% **From Public Schools** 76% **Ethnic Composition** White & Other 86%, Asian American 4%, Black 5%, Hispanic 4%, Native American 1% **Foreign Students** 10% **Reside on Campus** 85% **Return as Sophomores** 93% **Total Faculty** 157 **Student Faculty Ratio** 10:1 **Fraternities** none **Sororities** none

Guilford College

Greensboro, NC · Est. 1837 · Coed · Private · 1,093 Undergrads · Urban

I need...

Admissions info admission@rascal.guilford.edu
www.guilford.edu/admissionfolder
/admission.html
Financial aid info www.guilford.edu/admission
folder/financial.html

How wired is Guilford College?

Do I get email? Yes
Do I get a home page? Yes
Is my dorm wired? Yes
What is the student to computer ratio? 7:1

The usual tour

STUDY ABROAD www.guilford.edu/StudyAbroad
/mainstudy.html
LIBRARY www.guilford.edu/LibraryArt/Hege.html
DEPARTMENTS www.guilford.edu/Academic
/Academic.html
CURRENT EVENTS www.guilford.edu/College
Relations/college_front.html
PUBLICATIONS www.guilford.edu/publications
/publications.html
GENERAL INFO www.guilford.edu/info2.html

Skip the brochure

• **GUILFORD SPORTS** While Guilford isn't the largest
of schools it does have an active set of both
intercollegiate and intramural teams participating in golf, soccer, kickball, and free throw
shooting. **www.guilford.edu/StudentLife/Sports
/SportsIntroduction.html**

Hang out with some Friends on the lawns of Guilford

• **WEB CLASS '95** The Quakers have their own way
of approaching the Web, or so the ones who
designed the Guilford site claim. Meet them
and their professors. **www.guilford.edu/Web_Class
_95/Webclass.html**

• **QUAKERISM** If you're headed to Guilford you better know a bit about the guiding light of the
school: Quakerism. The school provides suggested readings in addition to an informative
introduction and an interview with happy-to-
expound faculty members. **www.guilford.edu
/Quakerlife/Quaker.html**

"Guilford provides suggested readings on the guiding light of the school: Quakerism."

WHAT YOU NEED TO GET IN **Application Deadline** February 1 **Early Action Deadline** December 1 **Common App.** Yes
Application Fee $25 **Tuition Costs** $14,180 **Room & Board** $5,270 **Need Blind** Yes **Financial Forms Deadline**
March 1 **Undergrads Awarded Aid** 79% **Aid That Is Need-Based** 81% **Average Award of Freshman Scholarship
Package** $8,795 **Tests Required** SAT1 or ACT **Admissions Address** 5800 West Friendly Avenue, Greensboro, NC
27410 **Admissions Telephone** (800) 992-7759

LAST YEAR'S CLASS **Applied** 1,204 **Accepted** 983 **Matriculated** 290 **Average SAT M/V** 538/515 **Average ACT** 25
In Top Fifth of High School Graduating Class 45% **Applied Early** 56 **Accepted Early** 49

COLLEGE LIFE **Gender Breakdown** M 49%, F 51% **Out of State Students** 77% **From Public Schools** 70% **Ethnic
Composition** White & Other 89%, Asian American 1%, Black 7%, Hispanic 2%, Native American 1% **Foreign
Students** 4% **Reside on Campus** 83% **Return as Sophomores** 73% **Total Faculty** 132 **Student Faculty Ratio**
14:1 **Fraternities** none **Sororities** none

Hamilton College

Clinton, NY · Est. 1812 · Coed · Private · 1,684 Undergrads · Rural

www.hamilton.edu

I need...

Admissions info www.hamilton.edu/html
/admissions

Financial aid info www.hamilton.edu/html
/admissions

How wired is Hamilton?

Do I get email? Yes

Do I get a home page? Yes

Where? www.hamilton.edu/html/studentlife
/studentp.html

Is my dorm wired? Yes

What is the student to computer ratio? 5:1

The usual tour

CALENDAR www.hamilton.edu/html/news
/calendar/calendar.html

SPORTS www.hamilton.edu/html/news
/athletic/varsity/teamindex.html

LIBRARY www.hamilton.edu/html/library
/home1.htm

MEDIA www.hamilton.edu/html/news/student
media

VIRTUAL TOUR www.hamilton.edu/html/campus
/campus.html

STUDENT CLUBS www.hamilton.edu/html/student
life/studentact/StudentOrganizations/Student
Organizations.html

Skip the brochure

• **PANORAMA: LIFE ON THE HILL** Once a week
Hamilton students put together what looks like

It's a banner day at Hamilton College

an informative and entertaining show on the
local public access channel. Check out a clip
or two. **www.hamilton.edu/html/news/studentmedia
/panorama/panorama.home.html**

• **OFFICE OF MULTICULTURAL AFFAIRS** Small Northern
campuses can seem a bit homogenous, so it's
good that Hamilton's Office of Multicultural
Affairs is as active as it appears, helping anyone even a step out of the mainstream.
www.hamilton.edu/html/studentlife/mca

• **THE SPECTATOR** Check out *The Spectator*, the
weekly campus newspaper, which also looks
beyond Hamilton's confines to the greater
geopolitical spectrum. **www.hamilton.edu/html
/news/studentmedia/spectator**

WHAT YOU NEED TO GET IN **Application Deadline** January 15 **Early Action Deadline** November 15 for Plan I; January 10 for Plan II **Common App.** Yes **Application Fee** $50 **Tuition Costs** $20,700 **Room & Board** $5,250 **Need Blind** Yes **Financial Forms Deadline** February 1 **Undergrads Awarded Aid** 60% **Aid That Is Need-Based** 100% **Average Award of Freshman Scholarship Package** $11,700 **Tests Required** SAT1 or ACT **Admissions Address** Clinton, NY 13323 **Admissions Telephone** (315) 859-4421

LAST YEAR'S CLASS **Applied** 3,475 **Accepted** 1,889 **Matriculated** 481 **Average SAT M/V** 603/536 **In Top Fifth of High School Graduating Class** 68% **Applied Early** 239 **Accepted Early** 132

COLLEGE LIFE **Gender Breakdown** M 54%, F 46% **Out of State Students** 59% **From Public Schools** 60% **Ethnic Composition** White & Other 90%, Asian American 4%, Black 3%, Hispanic 3% **Foreign Students** 6% **Reside on Campus** 98% **Return as Sophomores** 98% **Total Faculty** 195 **Student Faculty Ratio** 10:1 **Fraternities (% of men participating)** 7 (32%) **Sororities (% of women participating)** 4 (18%)

Hampden-Sydney College

lion.hsc.edu

Hampden-Sydney, VA · Est. 1776 · Men · Private · 971 Undergrads · Small Town

How wired is Hampden-Sydney?

Do I get email? Yes
Do I get a home page? Yes
   Where? www.hsc.edu/student/pages.html
Is my dorm wired? Yes
What is the student to computer ratio? 5:1

The usual tour

STUDENT CLUBS www.hsc.edu/student/org.html
SPORTS lion.hsc.edu/athletics/index.html
CALENDAR lion.hsc.edu/calendar/index.html
DEPARTMENTS lion.hsc.edu/acad/departments
.html
VIRTUAL TOUR lion.hsc.edu/pictures/index.html

Skip the brochure

• **GHOST STORY** Good PR? Not the school's
strongest selling point, but nonetheless interesting, this factoid is one that has the ghouls
a-dancing. In 1857 one student murdered

"Ghosts are said to still roam the halls."

Hampden-Sydney, where honorable young men dare to tread

another over the honor of a young lady and
was later acquitted when his lawyer invoked
the school's storied honor code in his
defense. Their ghosts are said to still roam
the halls. **www.hsc.edu/admiss/facil/ghosts.html**

• **SOCCER** These young men take themselves a
bit too seriously, dubbing themselves ambassadors for Hampden-Sydney College and the
sport of soccer as a whole. **www.hsc.edu/athletics
/sports/soccer/soccer1.html**

• **GOOD MEN & GOOD CITIZENS** Who needs four
years? Ten minutes at the Hampden-Sydney
site will drub the school's mission into you,
with constant allusions to its men of character,
honor, and leadership. GM & GC is but another
reminder of this, albeit, of course, an honorable one. **www.hsc.edu/student/org/gmgcinfo.html**

WHAT YOU NEED TO GET IN **Application Deadline** Fall for priority consideration; final deadline March 1 **Early Action
Deadline** November 15 **Common App.** Yes **Application Fee** $30 **Tuition Costs** $13,878 **Room & Board** $4,942
Need Blind Yes **Financial Forms Deadline** March 1 **Undergrads Awarded Aid** 79% **Aid That Is Need-Based** 80%
Average Award of Freshman Scholarship Package $5,300 **Tests Required** SAT1 or ACT **Admissions Address**
Hampden-Sydney, VA 23943 **Admissions Telephone** (804) 223-6120

LAST YEAR'S CLASS **Applied** 817 **Accepted** 680 **Matriculated** 285 **Average SAT M/V** 550/507 **Average ACT** 24
In Top Fifth of High School Graduating Class 25% **Applied Early** 120 **Accepted Early** 91

COLLEGE LIFE **Out of State Students** 47% **From Public Schools** 57% **Ethnic Composition** White & Other 94%, Asian
American 2%, Black 3%, Hispanic 1% **Foreign Students** 1% **Reside on Campus** 97% **Return as Sophomores** 78%
Total Faculty 92 **Student Faculty Ratio** 13:1 **Fraternities (% of men participating)** 11 (37%)

Hampshire College

Amherst, MA · Est. 1965 · Coed · Private · 1,073 Undergrads · Small Town

I need...

Admissions info admissions@hampshire.edu
www.hampshire.edu/Hampshire/adm/html
/admissions.html
Financial aid info admissions@hampshire.edu

How wired is Hampshire?

REQUEST APPLICATION ONLINE

Do I get email? Yes
Do I get a home page? Yes
Where? hamp.hampshire.edu/html
/directories/students_by_last_name.html
What is the student to computer ratio? 17:1

The usual tour

VIRTUAL TOUR www.hampshire.edu/Hampshire
/toplevel/html/HampMap.html
HISTORY www.hampshire.edu/Hampshire/lo
/html/archives/AATBL.CON.html
STUDENT CLUBS www.hampshire.edu/Hampshire
/lo/html/library/menu.html
PUBLICATIONS www.hampshire.edu/Hampshire
/students/html/student.info.html
SPECIAL PROGRAMS www.hampshire.edu
/Hampshire/toplevel/html/programs.html

Skip the brochure

- **LEMELSON PROGRAM** In 1993, Jerome and
Dorothy Lemelson founded the Lemelson
National Program in Invention, Innovation, and
Creativity to propel students into careers as
entrepreneurs and inventors. Here they

Hampshire: home to sheep, dogs, cows, and the occasional student

include the catalog of innovative courses offered, including "Inventing the Post-Human Body." **hamp.hampshire.edu/html/Lemelson**

- **HAMPSHIRE COLLEGE FARM CENTER** Hampshire students, if they choose, can study at the school's own farm center, noted for its research in sustainable agriculture and the behavior of livestock guard dogs.
www.hampshire.edu/Hampshire/farm/html/farm.html

- **BOARD OF TRUSTEES** Hampshire's trustees are yet another sign of its less than orthodox approach. They include filmmaker Ken Burns; Judith Berry Griffin, president of A Better Chance; and Bennett Cohen, "Ben" of Ben & Jerry's Ice Cream. **www.hampshire.edu/Hampshire/toplevel/html/trustees.html**

WHAT YOU NEED TO GET IN Application Deadline February 1 for priority consideration; final deadline February 1 **Early Action Deadline** November 15 **Common App.** Yes **Application Fee** $45 **Tuition Costs** $21,645 **Room & Board** $5,740 **Need Blind** Yes **Financial Forms Deadline** Priority given to applications received by February 15 **Undergrads Awarded Aid** 62% **Aid That Is Need-Based** 99% **Average Award of Freshman Scholarship Package** $13,000 **Tests Required** N/A **Admissions Address** Amherst, MA 01002 **Admissions Telephone** (413) 582-5471

LAST YEAR'S CLASS Applied 1,637 **Accepted** 1,118 **Matriculated** 314 **Average SAT M/V** 568/571 **In Top Fifth of High School Graduating Class** 21% **Applied Early** 50 **Accepted Early** 41

COLLEGE LIFE Gender Breakdown M 42%, F 58% **Out of State Students** 83% **From Public Schools** 72% **Ethnic Composition** White & Other 89%, Asian American 3%, Black 4%, Hispanic 3%, Native American 1% **Foreign Students** 4% **Reside on Campus** 95% **Return as Sophomores** 83% **Total Faculty** 98 **Student Faculty Ratio** 12:1 **Fraternities** none **Sororities** none

Hanover College

Hanover, IN · Est. 1827 · Coed · Private · 1,086 Undergrads · Rural

I need...

Admissions info spinner@hanover.edu
www.hanover.edu/admission
Financial aid info allmon@hanover.edu
www.hanover.edu/admission

How wired is Hanover?

Do I get email? Yes
Do I get a home page? Yes
Where? mars.hanover.edu/student
Is my dorm wired? Yes
Is there an online student hangout? Yes (IRC)
What is the student to computer ratio? 12:1

The usual tour

VIRTUAL TOUR www.hanover.edu/about.html
DEPARTMENTS www.hanover.edu/acad.html
LIBRARY www.hanover.edu/Library
PUBLICATIONS www.hanover.edu/publications
/pub.html
SPORTS www.hanover.edu/publications
/sports.html

"Hanover's students, alumni, and faculty are no strangers to the creative impulse."

Smile, and Hanover smiles with you

Skip the brochure

- **HISTORY DEPARTMENT** Hanover's historians are working hard to sell undergraduates on their major. They're doing a good job of it with essays, helpful hints, and informative links for the prospective history buff. **history.hanover.edu**

- **THE HANOVER QUARTERLY** Hanover's students, alumni, and faculty are no strangers to the creative impulse: *The Quarterly* attests to the varied and impressive accomplishments of Hanover's stars. **www.hanover.edu/publications /HQ.html**

- **THE HANOVERIAN** As the general Hanover site is fairly spotty, it'd be a shame to miss *The Hanoverian*. It's not what you would call thrilling reading, but it will tell you a tad more about the school. **www.hanover.edu/publications/backhans.html**

WHAT YOU NEED TO GET IN **Application Deadline** March 1 for priority consideration **Common App.** Yes **Application Fee** $25 **Tuition Costs** $9,250 **Room & Board** $3,915 **Need Blind** Yes **Financial Forms Deadline** March 1 with a priority given to applications received by February 15 **Undergrads Awarded Aid** 83% **Aid That Is Need-Based** 80% **Average Award of Freshman Scholarship Package** $4,000 **Tests Required** SAT1 or ACT **Admissions Address** P.O. Box 108, Hanover, IN 47243 **Admissions Telephone** (812) 866-7021

LAST YEAR'S CLASS **Applied** 1,068 **Accepted** 828 **Matriculated** 321 **Average SAT M/V** 580/580 **Average ACT** 25 **In Top Fifth of High School Graduating Class** 63%

COLLEGE LIFE **Gender Breakdown** M 48%, F 52% **Out of State Students** 46% **From Public Schools** 80% **Ethnic Composition** White & Other 98.2%, Asian American 0.5%, Black 0.7%, Hispanic 0.6% **Foreign Students** 3% **Reside on Campus** 98% **Return as Sophomores** 83% **Total Faculty** 108 **Student Faculty Ratio** 11:1 **Fraternities (% of men participating)** 5 (44%) **Sororities (% of women participating)** 4 (45%)

Hartwick College

www.hartwick.edu

Oneonta, NY · Est. 1797 · Coed · Private · 1,522 Undergrads · Small Town

How wired is Hartwick?

Do I get email? Yes
Do I get a home page? Yes
Is my dorm wired? Yes
What is the student to computer ratio? 19:1

The usual tour

DEPARTMENTS www.hartwick.edu/academic.html
LIBRARY www.hartwick.edu/library
/home page.html
STUDENT CLUBS www.hartwick.edu/student.html
#organizations
CALENDAR 147.205.15.81/osp/sphotlin.html
GREEK LIFE www.hartwick.edu/student.html
#greek_life
CAREER CENTER www.hartwick.edu/tcpd
SCHOOL FACTS www.hartwick.edu/welcome.html

"Hartwick allows students to study in such far-flung places as Costa Rica and India"

Have a heart-to-heart with Hartwick

Skip the brochure

- **JANUARY TERM OFF CAMPUS** One of a handful of schools to offer an entire course crammed into the month of January, Hartwick allows students to study abroad in this time in such far-flung places as Costa Rica, Austria, and India. **www.hartwick.edu/offcamp.html#january**

- **HARTWICK SPORTS** If you're considering continuing your athletic career, it's worth it to drop by here and get a sense if Hartwick's teams are any good. **witten.hartwick.edu/students/picabo/skeds.html**

- **HOPE UNLIMITED** Don't know if this is a good sign. One of the more active groups, at least in regards to Web presence, is the alcohol and drug prevention group HOPE (Hartwick Offers Perspective Through Empowerment). **witten.hartwick.edu/hope**

WHAT YOU NEED TO GET IN Application Deadline February 15 **Early Action Deadline** December 1 or January 15 **Common App.** Yes **Application Fee** $35 **Tuition Costs** $20,480 **Room & Board** $5,570 **Need Blind** Yes **Financial Forms Deadline** February 15 **Undergrads Awarded Aid** 67% **Aid That Is Need-Based** 68% **Average Award of Freshman Scholarship Package** $7,621 **Tests Required** SAT1 or ACT **Admissions Address** Oneonta, NY 13820-4020 **Admissions Telephone** (607) 431-4150

LAST YEAR'S CLASS Applied 2,631 **Accepted** 2,311 **Matriculated** 451 **Average SAT M/V** 527/469 **Average ACT** 23 **In Top Fifth of High School Graduating Class** 42% **Applied Early** 110 **Accepted Early** 96

COLLEGE LIFE Gender Breakdown M 47%, F 53% **Out of State Students** 44% **From Public Schools** 85% **Ethnic Composition** White & Other 91.8%, Asian American 2%, Black 3%, Hispanic 3%, Native American 0.2% **Foreign Students** 2% **Reside on Campus** 81% **Return as Sophomores** 80% **Total Faculty** 144 **Student Faculty Ratio** 13:1 **Fraternities (% of men participating)** 5 (20%) **Sororities (% of women participating)** 4 (13%)

Harvard University

www.harvard.edu

Cambridge, MA · Est. 1636 · Coed · Private · 7,098 Undergrads · Urban

I need...

Admissions info college@harvard.edu
www.harvard.edu/home/admissions.html

How wired is Harvard?

Do I get email? Yes
Do I get a home page? Yes
  Where? hcs.harvard.edu/harvard/personal
  bytype.html
Is my dorm wired? Yes

The usual tour

STUDENT CLUBS www.harvard.edu/home
  /student.html
CALENDAR gopher://gopher.harvard.edu:70/hh
  /.vine/mainmenu/calendars_and_events
VIRTUAL TOUR www.fas.harvard.edu/map
LIBRARY www.harvard.edu/home/library.html
NEWSGROUPS www.harvard.ewww.harvard.edu
  /home/harvard_newsgroups.htmldu/home
  /course_catalogs.html
PUBLICATIONS hcs.harvard.edu/harvard
  /pubs.html
COURSE CATALOG www.harvard.edu/home/course
  _catalogs.html

Skip the brochure

• **THE HARVARD LAMPOON** Although the *Lampoon*
  has been boot camp for TV's comedic glit-
  terati, including Conan O'Brien and a raft of
  Simpsons writers, its Web site is as amusing
  as an afternoon spent looking at your aunt's

Good to know Harvard brainiacs can hang ten: Harvard's Snowboarding Club

holiday pics. Perhaps "the Best of the Best"
defies electronic transmission, or perhaps the
site needs more work. **hcs.harvard.edu/~lampoon**

• **ELEKTRA** While this online magazine is still
evolving, it will surely be an invaluable
resource for Harvard students interested in all
things technological. Digitas, the club that publishes *Elektra*, hosts lectures as well as meetings both in person and virtually. **www.digitas.org**

• **CHESS CLUB** If you know Harvard Square, you
know the prominent role chess gurus play
there. The question is who's schooling whom.
Drop in on the Harvard students as they flex
their chess muscles. **hcs.harvard.edu/~hcc**

"Boot camp for TV's comedic glitterati"

WHAT YOU NEED TO GET IN **Application Deadline** December 15 for priority consideration; final deadline January 1 **Early Action Deadline** October 15 (priority), November 1 (final) **Common App.** Yes **Application Fee** $60 **Tuition Costs** $19,770 **Room & Board** $6,995 **Need Blind** Yes **Financial Forms Deadline** Priority given to applications received by February 1 **Undergrads Awarded Aid** 66% **Aid That Is Need-Based** 100% **Average Award of Freshman Scholarship Package** $14,174 **Tests Required** SAT1 or ACT **Admissions Address** Byerly Hall, 8 Garden Street, Cambridge, MA 02138 **Admissions Telephone** (617) 495-1551

LAST YEAR'S CLASS **Applied** 17,852 **Accepted** 2,150 **Matriculated** 1,618 **Median Range SAT M/V** 690-760/630-720 **In Top Fifth of High School Graduating Class** 98% **Applied Early** 2,990 **Accepted Early** 728

COLLEGE LIFE **Gender Breakdown** M 56%, F 44% **Out of State Students** 85% **From Public Schools** 68% **Ethnic Composition** White & Other 65%, Asian American 19%, Black 8%, Hispanic 7%, Native American 1% **Foreign Students** 7% **Reside on Campus** 96% **Return as Sophomores** 95% **Total Faculty** 1182 **Student Faculty Ratio** 8:1 **Fraternities** none **Sororities** none **Graduate Students** 11,454

Harvey Mudd College

www.hmc.edu

Claremont, CA · Est. 1955 · Coed · Private · 631 Undergrads · Small Town

I need...

Admissions info www.hmc.edu/admin/admission
Financial aid info www.hmc.edu/admin
/admission/aid.html

REQUEST APPLICATION ONLINE

How wired is Harvey Mudd?

Do I get email? Yes
Do I get a home page? Yes
Where? www.hmc.edu/dir/personal
/student-home-pages.html
Is my dorm wired? Yes
What is the student to computer ratio? 6:1

The usual tour

CATALOG www.hmc.edu/admin/colrel/catalogue
DEPARTMENTS www.hmc.edu/acad
LIBRARY www.hmc.edu/library
STUDENT CLUBS www.hmc.edu/org
VIRTUAL TOUR www.hmc.edu/campus
/campus-map

Skip the brochure

• **GONZO UNICYCLE MADNESS** The members of this 40-strong club are determined to ride on one wheel not two and take part in such sports as unicycle hockey and unicycle jousting, as well as the yearly highlight, Foster's Run, an 8.7 mile ride to Foster's Donut Man.
www.pitzer.edu/~jfrinier/gonzo

• **SHADES** The only *a cappella* group whose members hail from all five of the Claremont

20 unicyclists before the run

No Gonzos are ever caught spinning their wheels

Colleges. You can see and hear them as they harmoniously mix pop, jazz, rap and barbershop tunes. **thumper.pomona.edu/~harmony**

• **DORM RIVALRY** Drop in to see which Harvey Mudd dorm qualifies as the odder place to be; here they rant and rave about the annual pepper fest or vie for the title of most apathetic dorm. **www3.hmc.edu/~rcagleywww.pitzer.edu/~jfrinier
/south**

"An *a cappella* group harmoniously mixes pop, jazz, rap, and barbershop tunes."

WHAT YOU NEED TO GET IN Application Deadline January 15 **Early Action Deadline** November 15 **Common App.** No **Application Fee** $50 **Tuition Costs** $18,900 **Room & Board** $7,197 **Financial Forms Deadline** Priority given to applications received by February 1 **Undergrads Awarded Aid** 75% **Aid That Is Need-Based** 100% **Average Award of Freshman Scholarship Package** $9,927 **Tests Required** SAT1 **Admissions Address** 301 East 12th Street, Claremont, CA 91711-5990 **Admissions Telephone** (909) 621-8011

LAST YEAR'S CLASS Applied 1,394 **Accepted** 576 **Matriculated** 174 **Median Range SAT M/V** 720-760/590-690 **In Top Fifth of High School Graduating Class** 100% **Applied Early** 106 **Accepted Early** 45

COLLEGE LIFE Gender Breakdown M 74%, F 26% **Out of State Students** 63% **From Public Schools** 80% **Ethnic Composition** White & Other 69%, Asian American 24%, Black 1%, Hispanic 5%, Native American 1% **Foreign Students** 2% **Reside on Campus** 97% **Return as Sophomores** 89% **Total Faculty** 73 **Student Faculty Ratio** 8:1 **Fraternities** none **Sororities** none **Graduate Students** 8

Haverford College

www.haverford.edu

Haverford, PA · Est. 1833 · Coed · Private · 1,115 Undergrads · Suburban

I need...

Admissions info admitme@haverford.edu
www.haverford.edu/admissions/hcadmis
.html
Financial aid info finaid@haverford.edu
www.haverford.edu/admindepthome:Finaid
:A.overview.html

REQUEST APPLICATION ONLINE

How wired is Haverford?

Do I get email? Yes
Do I get a home page? Yes
Where? www.students.haverford.edu
Is my dorm wired? Yes
What is the student to computer ratio? 6:1

The usual tour

STUDENT CLUBS www.haverford.edu/hcextra.html
DEPARTMENTS www.haverford.edu/hccurric2.html
CAREER CENTER www.haverford.edu/hcadmi.html
SPORTS www.haverford.edu/athletics
/hcathl.html
LIBRARY www.haverford.edu/library/web
/library.html

Skip the brochure

- **FOETID** Bragging about its overly pretentious,
poorly written, angst-ridden prose and photography, *Foetid* delivers in full on its promise.
Good gag, kids. **blackcat.brynmawr.edu/~apeterse
/foetid**

- **HONOR CODE** Quakerism is Haverford's spiritual

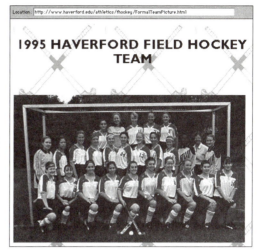

Location: http://www.haverford.edu/athletics/fhockey/FormalTeamPicture.html

1995 HAVERFORD FIELD HOCKEY TEAM

Haverford's field hockey players—net heads one and all

and moral rudder. The school's honor code is
the school's other moral steering mechanism.
Get it straight from the source. **www.haverford
.edu/hchonor.html**

"Foetid brags about its overly pretentious, poorly written, angst-ridden prose."

WHAT YOU NEED TO GET IN Application Deadline January 15 **Early Action Deadline** November 15 **Common App.** Yes
Application Fee $45 **Tuition Costs** $20,692 **Room & Board** $6,810 **Need Blind** Yes **Financial Forms Deadline**
January 31 **Undergrads Awarded Aid** 45% **Aid That Is Need-Based** 100% **Average Award of Freshman
Scholarship Package** $13,518 **Tests Required** SAT1 or ACT **Admissions Address** 370 Lancaster Avenue,
Haverford, PA 19041-1392 **Admissions Telephone** (610) 896-1350

LAST YEAR'S CLASS Applied 2,622 **Accepted** 975 **Matriculated** 306 **Median Range SAT M/V** 640-720/580-670
In Top Fifth of High School Graduating Class 92% **Applied Early** 136 **Accepted Early** 75

COLLEGE LIFE Gender Breakdown M 50%, F 50% **Out of State Students** 89% **From Public Schools** 61% **Ethnic
Composition** White & Other 82.6%, Asian American 7.8%, Black 4.3%, Hispanic 5.2%, Native American 0.1%
Foreign Students 5% **Reside on Campus** 96% **Return as Sophomores** 97% **Total Faculty** 110 **Student Faculty
Ratio** 10:1 **Fraternities** none **Sororities** none

University of Hawaii, Manoa

www.hawaii.edu/uhinfo.html

Honolulu, HI · Est. 1907 · Coed · Public · 13,357 Undergrads · Urban

I need...

Admissions info www.hawaii.edu/welcome/#admission
Financial aid info www.hawaii.edu/catalog/tuition.html

How wired is UH, Manoa?

Do I get email? Yes
Do I get a home page? Yes
   Where? www.hawaii.edu/leisure/personal.html
Is my dorm wired? Yes
What is the student to computer ratio? 13:1

The usual tour

DEPARTMENTS www.hawaii.edu/links/manoa-h.html
STUDENT CLUBS www.hawaii.edu/student/#orgs
SPORTS student-www.eng.hawaii.edu/yogi/Uh/Home/uhath.html
VIRTUAL TOUR www2.hawaii.edu/walktour/walking.tour.html
LIBRARY www2.hawaii.edu/lib

Skip the brochure

• **BALLROOM DANCING** Is this a resurgent fad or one that just never really died? Yet another club which vies competitively on the ballroom dance floor. **www2.hawaii.edu/dsc**

Location: http://www2.hawaii.edu:80/walktour/images/hawaii.hall.jpeg

Storm clouds loom over the Manoa campus. Surfers rejoice

• **WEATHER AND SURF** All surfers are closet meteorologists, but only in Hawaii would the state university supply hourly forecasts and surf reports. Satellite links even allow students to plan ahead for distant storm systems. **www.hawaii.edu/news/weather.html**

• **UH WAHINE VOLLEYBALL** Volleyball is a religion not a sport in Hawaii. The UH Wahines women's team show their spikes, their stats and more. **student-www.eng.hawaii.edu/yogi/Uh/WVball/wvball.html**

"All surfers are closet meteorologists."

WHAT YOU NEED TO GET IN Application Deadline May 1 **Common App.** No **Application Fee** $25 (out-of-state applicants only) **Tuition Costs** $2,304 ($7,752 out-of-state) **Room & Board** $4,700 **Need Blind** Yes **Financial Forms Deadline** Priority given to applications received by March 1 **Undergrads Awarded Aid** 13% **Aid That Is Need-Based** 90% **Average Award of Freshman Scholarship Package** $2,000 **Tests Required** SAT1 (preferred) or ACT **Admissions Address** 2600 Campus Road, Room 001, Honolulu, HI 96822 **Admissions Telephone** (808) 956-8975

LAST YEAR'S CLASS Applied 4,560 **Accepted** 2,972 **Matriculated** 1,774 **Average SAT M/V** 541/443 **In Top Fifth of High School Graduating Class** 57%

COLLEGE LIFE Gender Breakdown M 46%, F 54% **Out of State Students** 7% **From Public Schools** 69% **Ethnic Composition** White & Other 25%, Asian American 72%, Black 1%, Hispanic 1%, Native American 1% **Foreign Students** 3% **Reside on Campus** 16% **Return as Sophomores** 81% **Fraternities (% of men participating)** 8 (3%) **Sororities (% of women participating)** 7 (3%) **Graduate Students** 6,368

Hendrix College

www.hendrix.edu

Conway, AR · Est. 1876 · Coed · Private · 959 Undergrads · Big Town

How wired is Hendrix?

Do I get email? Yes
Do I get a home page? Yes
   Where? www.hendrix.edu/Homes/stufac.html
Is my dorm wired? Yes
What is the student to computer ratio? 5:1

The usual tour

STUDENT CLUBS www.hendrix.edu/Activ
DEPARTMENTS www.hendrix.edu/dept/Departmental.html
LIBRARY www.hendrix.edu/Library
VIRTUAL TOUR www.hendrix.edu/tours/scenery.html
SPORTS www.hendrix.edu/Ath
CAREER CENTER www.hendrix.edu/studev/careercenter.html

Skip the brochure

• **HENDRIX CHOIR** Hendrix's choral achievements are impressive; they've performed at the National Cathedral and traveled to Western and Eastern Europe to croon their hearts out. **www.hendrix.edu/homes/org/choir/choir.html**

Location: http://www.hendrix.edu/tours/scenery/beach.gif

It's green, but they call it a beach, Veasey Beach!

• **RIGHT TO LIFE** These right-to-lifers are a ragtag but committed team of undergraduates; among them you'll find an anarchist, a Democrat, and even someone who loves alternative music. **www.hendrix.edu/homes/org/life/life.html**

• **THE PROFILE** This biweekly has been published for more than 80 years on paper and more than two online. Billed as the first electronic newspaper in Arkansas, this student publication is a forum for news, reviews, and opinions on the wonderful world of Hendrix. **www.hendrix.edu/profile/onlinehome page.html**

"Hendrix's choral achievements are impressive."

WHAT YOU NEED TO GET IN Application Deadline Rolling admissions; April 1 for priority consideration **Common App.** Yes **Application Fee** $25 (may be waived) **Tuition Costs** $9,790 **Room & Board** $3,807 **Need Blind** Yes **Financial Forms Deadline** Priority given to applications received by February 15 **Undergrads Awarded Aid** 81% **Aid That Is Need-Based** 61% **Average Award of Freshman Scholarship Package** $4,883 **Tests Required** SAT1 or ACT **Admissions Address** 1601 Harkrider Street, Conway, AR 72032-3080 **Admissions Telephone** (800) 277-9017

LAST YEAR'S CLASS Applied 699 **Accepted** 631 **Matriculated** 273 **Average SAT M/V** 572/542 **Average ACT** 26 **In Top Fifth of High School Graduating Class** 40%

COLLEGE LIFE Gender Breakdown M 45%, F 55% **Out of State Students** 25% **From Public Schools** 87% **Ethnic Composition** White & Other 91.5%, Asian American 2%, Black 5%, Hispanic 0.7%, Native American 0.8% **Foreign Students** 2% **Reside on Campus** 78% **Return as Sophomores** 84% **Total Faculty** 68 **Student Faculty Ratio** 12:1 **Fraternities** none **Sororities** none

Hillsdale College

Hillsdale, MI · Est. 1844 · Coed · Private · 1,162 Undergrads · Small Town

I need...

Admissions info admissions@ac.hillsdale.edu
www.hillsdale.edu/Admissions/hc
.admissions.html
Financial aid info www.hillsdale.edu/GeneralInfo
.html

How wired is Hillsdale?

Do I get email? Yes
What is the student to computer ratio? 8:1

REQUEST APPLICATION ONLINE

The usual tour

STUDY ABROAD www.hillsdale.edu
/Oxford.html
DEPARTMENTS www.hillsdale.edu/Departmental
HomePages.html
PUBLICATIONS www.hillsdale.edu/imprimis
/imprimis.html
GENERAL INFO www.hillsdale.edu/General
Info.html

Skip the brochure

- **IMPRIMIS** Hillsdale refuses government funding for fear it will affect its independence and

"Tune in to *Imprimis* to hear Ralph Reed and others preach."

Hillsdale College Home Page

Location: http://www.hillsdale.edu/

Brand yourself with the Hillsdale crest

imprimatur to examine modern moral issues from its own prescribed high ground. *Imprimis* embodies this charge and claims over 640,000 readers of its print and Web publication. Tune in to hear Ralph Reed and others preach. **www.hillsdale.edu/imprimis/imprimis.html**

- **WASHINGTON-HILLSDALE INTERN PROGRAM** The Washington/Hillsdale Intern Program provides students the unique opportunity to spend a semester in Washington D.C. in a Congressional or Executive Branch Office and to attend a university in the area for course credit. **www.hillsdale.edu/WHIP.html**

- **MISSION** Hillsdale College stands by its belief in the importance of a traditional liberal arts program for the development of hard working and moral-minded individuals. **www.hillsdale.edu /GeneralInfo.html**

WHAT YOU NEED TO GET IN **Application Deadline** January 15 for priority consideration; final deadline June 15 **Common App.** Yes **Application Fee** $15 **Tuition Costs** $12,110 **Room & Board** $5,180 **Need Blind** Yes **Financial Forms Deadline** Priority given to applications received by March 15 **Undergrads Awarded Aid** 75% **Aid That Is Need-Based** 80% **Average Award of Freshman Scholarship Package** $5,500 **Tests Required** SAT1 or ACT **Admissions Address** Hillsdale, MI 49242 **Admissions Telephone** (517) 437-7341

LAST YEAR'S CLASS **Applied** 1,063 **Accepted** 803 **Matriculated** 358 **Average SAT M/V** 610/550 **Average ACT** 26 **In Top Quarter of High School Graduating Class** 74%

COLLEGE LIFE **Gender Breakdown** M 49%, F 51% **Out of State Students** 53% **From Public Schools** 65% **Foreign Students** 1% **Reside on Campus** 80% **Return as Sophomores** 93% **Total Faculty** 118 **Student Faculty Ratio** 12:1 **Fraternities (% of men participating)** 4 (40%) **Sororities (% of women participating)** 4 (50%)

Hobart and William Smith Colleges

www.hws.edu

Geneva, NY · Est. 1908 · Coed · Private · 1,770 Undergrads · Small Town

I need...

Admissions info hoadm@hws.edu *OR*
 wsadm@hws.edu
 hws3.hws.edu:9000/www/admis
 /admisform.html
Financial aid info freeman@hws.edu

How wired is Hobart and William Smith?

Do I get email? Yes
Do I get a home page? Yes
 Where? hws3.hws.edu:9000
 /www/HomePages.html
What is the student to computer ratio? 12:1

REQUEST APPLICATION ONLINE

The usual tour

VIRTUAL TOUR hws3.hws.edu:9000/www
 /postcards/mapOfCampus.html
SPORTS hws3.hws.edu:9000/info/sports
 /sports.html
KIOSK hws3.hws.edu:9000/htbin/kiosk
 _view.com
SCHOOL FACTS hws3.hws.edu:9000/www/info
 /QuickFacts.html
HISTORY hws3.hws.edu:9000/www/info
 /hws_history.html

Skip the brochure

- **WEOS** Never mind that listening to this station must be a bit jarring given that it's a mix of

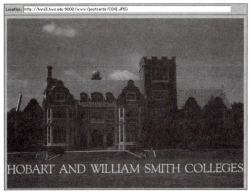

Hobart and William Smith, a veritable country estate

alternative music and NPR broadcasting, WEOS must still be a great place to get a start. If nothing else, your resume will reflect one of the broader ranges of programming possible. **HWS3.HWS.EDU:9000/weos/index.html**

- **SAILING TEAM** According to one team member sailing is a near-religious experience: "I empty my mind and I concentrate only on the wind and the feel of the boat." **hws3.hws.edu:9000 /~sailing/www/index.html**

- **SPEAKERS BOX** Whether you slept through a campus lecture or are just a curious outsider, you're in luck. The full texts of recent talks is online. **hws3.hws.edu:9000/info/speakers.html**

WHAT YOU NEED TO GET IN Application Deadline February 1 **Early Action Deadline** November 15 and January 1 **Common App.** Yes **Application Fee** $45 **Tuition Costs** $19,962 **Room & Board** $6,075 **Need Blind** Yes **Financial Forms Deadline** Priority given to applications received by February 15 **Undergrads Awarded Aid** 68% **Aid That Is Need-Based** 99% **Average Award of Freshman Scholarship Package** $12,000 **Tests Required** SAT1 (preferred) or ACT **Admissions Address** Geneva, NY 14456 **Admissions Telephone** (800) 852-2256 (Hobart)

LAST YEAR'S CLASS Applied 2,786 **Accepted** 2,117 **Matriculated** 460 **Median Range SAT M/V** 530-610/530-620 **In Top Fifth of High School Graduating Class** 51% **Applied Early** 123 **Accepted Early** 101

COLLEGE LIFE Gender Breakdown M 49%, F 51% **Out of State Students** 51% **From Public Schools** 63% **Ethnic Composition** White & Other 89%, Asian American 1%, Black 5%, Hispanic 4%, Native American 1% **Foreign Students** 3% **Reside on Campus** 82% **Return as Sophomores** 86% **Total Faculty** 128 **Student Faculty Ratio** 13:1 **Fraternities (% of men participating)** 7 (30%) **Sororities** none

Hofstra University

www.hofstra.edu

Hempstead, NY · Est. 1935 · Coed · Private · 7,846 Undergrads · Urban

I need...

Admissions info hofstra@hofstra.edu
www.hofstra.edu/where.html

How wired is Hofstra?

Do I get email? Yes
What is the student to computer ratio? 31:1

The usual tour

VIRTUAL TOUR www.hofstra.edu/map.html
SPORTS gopher://vaxc.hofstra.edu:70
  /11gopher_root%3A%5B000000.vaxc
  .athletics%5D
LIBRARY gopher://vaxc.hofstra.edu:70
  /11gopher_root%3A%5B000000.vaxc
  .library_dir%5D
CALENDAR gopher://vaxc.hofstra.edu:70
  /11gopher_root%3A%5B000000.vaxc
  .calendar%5D
PUBLICATIONS gopher://vaxc.hofstra.edu:70
  /11gopher_root%3A%5B000000.vaxc
  .publications.hofstra_pride%5D
DEPARTMENTS gopher://vaxc.hofstra.edu:70
  /11gopher_root%3A%5B000000.vaxc
  .schools_dir%5D

Skip the brochure

• CONFERENCES ON THE AMERICAN PRESIDENCY
Hofstra began its series on modern American presidencies in 1982. The format of the conferences includes three days of panels and

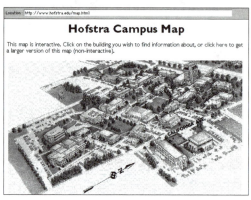

As the crow flies: the Hofstra campus

special presentations which bring together scholars amd journalists. Notable guests throughout the years have included: Margaret Truman, Susan Eisenhower, Gerald Ford, Rosalynn and Jimmy Carter, and Maureen Reagan. **www.hofstra.edu/bushconf97/short-hist.html**

"Notable guests of Hofstra have included Rosalynn and Jimmy Carter."

WHAT YOU NEED TO GET IN Application Deadline Rolling admissions; February 15 for priority consideration **Early Action Deadline** December 1 **Common App.** Yes **Application Fee** $40 **Tuition Costs** $12,255 **Room & Board** $6,370 **Need Blind** Yes **Financial Forms Deadline** Priority given to applications received by March 1 **Undergrads Awarded Aid** 72% **Aid That Is Need-Based** 74% **Average Award of Freshman Scholarship Package** $3,825 **Tests Required** SAT1 or ACT **Admissions Address** Hempstead, NY 11550 **Admissions Telephone** (516) 463-6700

LAST YEAR'S CLASS Applied 7,610 **Accepted** 6,210 **Matriculated** 1,547 **Average SAT M/V** 530/460 **Average ACT** 23 **In Top Fifth of High School Graduating Class** 50%

COLLEGE LIFE Gender Breakdown M 47%, F 53% **Out of State Students** 21% **From Public Schools** 70% **Ethnic Composition** White & Other 84%, Asian American 5%, Black 5%, Hispanic 5%, Native American 1% **Foreign Students** 4% **Reside on Campus** 50% **Return as Sophomores** 80% **Total Faculty** 978 **Student Faculty Ratio** 15:1 **Fraternities (% of men participating)** 19 (16%) **Sororities (% of women participating)** 13 (16%) **Graduate Students** 3,931

College of the Holy Cross

Worcester, MA · Est. 1843 · Coed · Private · 2,738 Undergrads · Urban

I need...

Admissions info admissions@holycross.edu
www.holycross.edu/www_html/admissions
/admissionsgate.html

How wired is Holy Cross?

Do I get email? Yes
Do I get a home page? Yes
Is my dorm wired? Yes
What is the student to computer ratio? 21:1

The usual tour

STUDENT CLUBS www.holycross.edu/www_html
/studentinfo/organization.html
LIBRARY www.holycross.edu/www_html/library
/libhome.html
SPORTS www.holycross.edu/www_html
/departments/athletics/athleticdept.html
DEPARTMENTS
www.holycross.edu/www_html/departments
/collegedept.html
VIRTUAL TOUR www.holycross.edu/www_html
/admissions/tour/main.html
CALENDAR www.holycross.edu/www_html
/schedules/calevent.html

Skip the brochure

• **WORCESTER** You should know what Worcester's
about if you're headed to Holy Cross. This site
has info on museums, getaways, local organizations and everything else you need to round out
your Worcester experience. **worcester.lm.com**

Location: http://www.holycross.edu/

The College of the Holy Cross
Worcester, Massachusetts

Holy Cross, the jewel in Worcester's crown

• **WCHC** Tune your dial to WCHC, the station
"more alternative than Newt." That can't be
hard. They seem to play everything here from
jazz and the blues to metal and punk. **www.holy
cross.edu/www_html/departments/wchc/current.htm**

• **THE FENWICK REVIEW** This student journal hopes
to "disturb you and provoke discontent." The
conservative *Fenwick Review* is a forum for
many of the day's hotly contested issues.
**www.holycross.edu/www_html/studentinfo/fenrev
/Fenwick_Review.html**

"WCHC is 'more alternative than Newt.'"

WHAT YOU NEED TO GET IN Application Deadline February 1 **Early Action Deadline** January 15 **Common App.** Yes
Application Fee $50 **Tuition Costs** $19,700 **Room & Board** $6,750 **Need Blind** Yes **Financial Forms Deadline**
Priority given to applications received by February 1 **Undergrads Awarded Aid** 64% **Aid That Is Need-Based** 99%
Average Award of Freshman Scholarship Package $10,621 **Tests Required** SAT1 (preferred) or ACT
Admissions Address College Street, Worcester, MA 01610-2395 **Admissions Telephone** (508) 793-2443

LAST YEAR'S CLASS Applied 3,536 **Accepted** 1,774 **Matriculated** 712 **Average SAT M/V** 613/560 **In Top Fifth of
High School Graduating Class** 84% **Applied Early** 283 **Accepted Early** 176

COLLEGE LIFE Gender Breakdown M 47%, F 53% **Out of State Students** 64% **From Public Schools** 45% **Ethnic
Composition** White & Other 92%, Asian American 3%, Black 2%, Hispanic 2%, Native American 1% **Foreign
Students** 1% **Reside on Campus** 86% **Return as Sophomores** 94% **Total Faculty** 259 **Student Faculty Ratio**
13:1 **Fraternities** none **Sororities** none

University of Houston

Houston, TX · Est. 1927 · Coed · Public · 23,721 Undergrads · Urban

www.uh.edu

I need...

Admissions info admissions@uh.edu
www.uh.edu/admissions/admissions
.welcome.html
Financial aid info rsheridan@uh.edu
www.uh.edu/admissions/admissions
_financialaid.html

How wired is the University of Houston?

Do I get email? Yes
Do I get a home page? No
Is my dorm wired? Yes
What is the student to computer ratio? 59:1

The usual tour

STUDENT CLUBS www.studev.uh.edu/dos/hdbk
/campuslife/stuorglist.html
DEPARTMENTS www.uh.edu/colleges.html
GREEK LIFE www.studev.uh.edu/CA/GreekLife
/Default.html
LIBRARY www.uh.edu/libraries.html
CAREER CENTER www.uh.edu/libraries.html
SPORTS www.uh.edu/campus/athletics.html

Skip the brochure

• **SUCCESS STORIES** While they haven't excelled at
presenting themselves on the Web, the
University of Houston, one of the country's
best research universities, has accomplished
much, as they're happy to tell you here.
www.uh.edu/welcome/uhsuccess.html

Welcome to the jungle

• **RESEARCH PROJECTS** While you may have to wait
until you're a graduate student to get in on
these projects, it would be a shame to miss
them. UH is the leader in many fields of
research, particularly in the arena of space,
which makes sense given that NASA is nearby
and turns to them for a significant part of its
research. www.uh.edu/research.html

• **CHRISTIAN SCIENCE ORGANIZATION** Religious institutions were expert recruiters long before any
academic or business institutions. The
University of Houston's Christian Scientists
carry on the tradition. www.studev.uh.edu/CA
/StuOrgs/ChristianScience.html

"One of the country's best research Universities"

WHAT YOU NEED TO GET IN **Application Deadline** August 1 **Common App.** No **Application Fee** $25 **Tuition Costs** $900
($6,660 out-of-state) **Room & Board** $4,405 **Need Blind** Yes **Financial Forms Deadline** April 1 **Undergrads
Awarded Aid** 33% **Aid That Is Need-Based** 75% **Average Award of Freshman Scholarship Package** $2,102
Tests Required SAT1 or ACT **Admissions Address** 4800 Calhoun, Houston, TX 77004 **Admissions Telephone**
(713) 743-1010

LAST YEAR'S CLASS **Applied** 5,009 **Accepted** 3,783 **Matriculated** 2,218 **Average SAT M/V** 546/529 **Average ACT**
22 **In Top Fifth of High School Graduating Class** 45%

COLLEGE LIFE **Gender Breakdown** M 48%, F 52% **Out of State Students** 4% **Ethnic Composition** White & Other
55.8%, Asian American 17%, Black 10.6%, Hispanic 16.1%, Native American 0.5% **Foreign Students** 5% **Reside
on Campus** 7% **Return as Sophomores** 73% **Total Faculty** 1,318 **Student Faculty Ratio** 18:1 **Fraternities (% of
men participating)** 17 (4%) **Sororities (% of women participating)** 10 (3%) **Graduate Students** 7,036

Howard University

www.howard.edu

Washington, DC · Est. 1867 · Coed · Private · 7,300 Undergrads · Urban

I need...

Admissions info www.howard.edu/hupage
/admissions.html

Financial aid info www.howard.edu/facts/aid
.html

How wired is Howard?

Do I get email? Yes
Do I get a home page? Yes
Is my dorm wired? No
What is the student to computer ratio? 24:1

The usual tour

VIRTUAL TOUR www.howard.edu/hupage
/photos.html
STUDENT CLUBS www.howard.edu/hupage
/websites.html#org
DEPARTMENTS www.howard.edu/hupage/schools
.html
LIBRARY 138.238.41.254
CALENDAR www.howard.edu/hupage/calendar
.html
DEPARTMENTS www.howard.edu/hupage/schools
.html

Skip the brochure

• **CSTEA** The Center for the Study of Terrestrial &
Extraterrestrial Atmospheres was established
at Howard in 1992. Funded by NASA, the center is an interdisciplinary research unit with
special emphasis on the training of African

Let Howard show you the way

Americans in space-based sciences and engineering. **www.cstea.howard.edu**

• **MILLION MAN MARCH SURVEY** Political Science professors, students, and researchers conducted
this enlightening survey on the day of the
march. There are many interesting, disturbing
responses, including one which put at 34 percent the number of attendees who believed
that America would be a better place in 10
years. **www.cldc.howard.edu/~blkpol/mmmrep.htm**

"The center puts special emphasis on the training of Americans in space-based sciences."

WHAT YOU NEED TO GET IN **Application Deadline** November 1 for priority consideration; final deadline April 15 **Common App.** No **Application Fee** $25 **Tuition Costs** $8,320 **Room & Board** $4,268 **Financial Forms Deadline** Priority given to applications received by April 1 **Undergrads Awarded Aid** 63% **Tests Required** SAT1 or ACT **Admissions Address** 2400 Sixth Street, NW, Washington, DC 20059 **Admissions Telephone** (202) 806-2752

LAST YEAR'S CLASS **Applied** 6,532 **Accepted** 1,743 **Matriculated** 1,549 **Average SAT M/V** 452/426 **Average ACT** 20

COLLEGE LIFE **Gender Breakdown** M 37%, F 63% **Out of State Students** 84% **From Public Schools** 80% **Ethnic Composition** White & Other 10%, Asian American 2%, Black 87%, Hispanic 1% **Foreign Students** 5% **Reside on Campus** 32% **Return as Sophomores** 75% **Total Faculty** 2171 **Student Faculty Ratio** 6:1 **Fraternities of men participating)** 4 (1%) **Sororities (% of women participating)** 4 (1%) **Graduate Students** 5,369

Humboldt State University

www.humboldt.edu

Arcata, CA · Est. 1913 · Coed · Public · 6,666 Undergrads · Small Town

I need...

Admissions info hsuinfo@laurel.humboldt.edu
  sorrel.humboldt.edu/~admrec
Financial aid info sorrel.humboldt.edu/~finaid

How wired is Humboldt State?

Do I get email? Yes
**What is the student to computer
  ratio?** 22:1

DOWNLOAD APPLICATION ONLINE

The usual tour

COURSE CATALOG www.humboldt.edu/~oaa
  /catalog/index.html
STUDENT CLUBS sorrel.humboldt.edu/~humboldt
  /activities.html
CALENDAR www.humboldt.edu/~humboldt
  /cen.html
SPORTS sorrel.humboldt.edu/~hsujacks
LIBRARY library.humboldt.edu
DEPARTMENTS www.humboldt.edu/~humboldt
  /acadinfo.html#college

Skip the brochure

• **ASTRONOMY CLUB** Stargazers at Humboldt have
their heads in the clouds as much as they can.
It seems to be keeping them away from this
site, which is fairly light and consists mostly of
links. **sorrel.humboldt.edu/~hsuastro**

• **FORENSICS CLUB** If you're thinking of Jack
Klugman's "Quincy," Sherlock Holmes and
other detectives, you're wrong. Forensics is

Humboldt State University

Set between redwood groves and the Pacific Ocean 270 miles north of San Francisco, Humboldt State University is the northernmost, westernmost campus in the 22-campus California State University system. This spring, Humboldt's enrollment was about 7,300 students. Like Alexander von Humboldt, the university's namesake, our students tend to be adventurous, self-reliant, drawn to nature and socially conscientious. This fact is borne out by Humboldt's continual ranking as one of the greatest sources, if not the greatest source per capita, of Peace Corps representatives.

Humbolt, alma mater to many a Peace Corps volunteer

the study of debate and presentation;
Humboldt's team, armed with expert coaches,
competes locally, and on occasion takes their
argumentative skills abroad. **www.humboldt.edu
/~speech/forensics.html**

• **ALTRUISM** This center has a noble goal. The
Altruistic Personality and Prosocial Behavior
Institute studies what makes do-gooders click
and how they might make good works conta-
gious. **www.humboldt.edu/~spol/altru.htm**

• **TIDES** If you're headed to Humboldt for a visit,
check the tides, and don't forget your board,
dude. **ceob-g30.nos.noaa.gov/pub/mosaic/tides
/westHB.html**

"Don't forget your board, dude."

WHAT YOU NEED TO GET IN Application Deadline Rolling admissions; November 30 for priority consideration **Common
App.** No **Application Fee** $55 **Tuition Costs** $1,858 ($7,762 out-of-state) **Room & Board** $4,934 **Need Blind**
Yes **Financial Forms Deadline** March 1 **Undergrads Awarded Aid** 49% **Average Award of Freshman Scholarship
Package** $1,192 **Tests Required** SAT1 or ACT **Admissions Address** Arcata, CA 95521 **Admissions Telephone**
(707) 826-4402

LAST YEAR'S CLASS Applied 4,146 **Accepted** 3,198 **Matriculated** 927 **Average SAT M/V** 529/538 **Average ACT** 22

COLLEGE LIFE Gender Breakdown M 50%, F 50% **Out of State Students** 38% **From Public Schools** 88% **Ethnic
Composition** White & Other 84%, Asian American 3%, Black 2%, Hispanic 8%, Native American 3% **Foreign
Students** 1% **Reside on Campus** 20% **Return as Sophomores** 84% **Total Faculty** 562 **Student Faculty Ratio**
18:1 **Fraternities (% of men participating)** 3 (1%) **Sororities (% of women participating)** 4 (1%) **Graduate
Students** 761

Illinois College

www.ic.edu

Jacksonville, IL · Est. 1829 · Coed · Private · 965 Undergrads · Big Town

How wired is Illinois College?

Do I get email? Yes
Do I get a home page? Yes
   Where? www.ic.edu/students/students.html
Is my dorm wired? No
What is the student to computer ratio? 15:1

The usual tour

VIRTUAL TOUR www.ic.edu/vttour
SPORTS www.ic.edu/pr/sports/prsports.htm
HISTORY www.ic.edu/admis/college.html
STUDENT CLUBS www.ic.edu/studlife/actorg/actorg.html
STUDENT NEWSPAPER www.ic.edu/studlife/actorg/rambler.html
RELIGIOUS LIFE www.ic.edu/studlife/religlife/religlife.html
CALENDAR www.ic.edu/events/calendar.htm
LIBRARY www.ic.edu/library/libindx.htm

Skip the brochure

- **CONVOCATIONS** A unique feature of IC life is the convocation, or the traditional "calling together" of the entire campus community. Illinois students are required to attend 60 before they graduate. Meeting the requirement shouldn't be too painful; they take the form of literary

Welcome to Illinois College

Illinois College...
...a selective, four year, co-educational, liberal arts college located in the downstate Illinois community of Jacksonville. Founded in 1829, Illinois College was the first college in the state to confer a degree.

Come and be convocated

discussions, plays, and concerts. **www.ic.edu/studlife/convos/convos.html**

- **MODEL U.N.** What do Illinois students have to say about international affairs? The papers of students participating in the nationwide Model U.N. are online. **www.ic.edu/studlife/actorg/modelun.html**

- **I.C. NEWS** "Dr. Evans injured in bicycle accident." "Music Ensemble plans tour of East Coast." This is the source for the latest headlines from student life in Jacksonville. **www.ic.edu/pr/news/prnews.htm**

- **LITERARY SOCIETIES** From Chi Beta to Sigma Pi, the six IC literary societies play a big role in student life: Several of them occupy entire floors of campus buildings. Milton and Shakespeare get their due, but these clubs also participate in service projects and social activities. **www.ic.edu/studlife/actorg/societies.html**

WHAT YOU NEED TO GET IN **Application Deadline** April 1 for priority consideration; final deadline August 15 **Common App.** No **Application Fee** $10 **Tuition Costs** $9,150 **Room & Board** $4,150 **Need Blind** Yes **Financial Forms Deadline** May 1 with a priority given to applications received by April 15 **Undergrads Awarded Aid** 93% **Aid That Is Need-Based** 72% **Average Award of Freshman Scholarship Package** $4,220 **Tests Required** SAT1 or ACT **Admissions Address** 1101 West College Avenue, Jacksonville, IL 62650 **Admissions Telephone** (217) 245-3030

LAST YEAR'S CLASS **Applied** 823 **Accepted** 719 **Matriculated** 223 **Average SAT M/V** 556/493 **Average ACT** 24 **In Top Fifth of High School Graduating Class** 46%

COLLEGE LIFE **Gender Breakdown** M 46%, F 54% **Out of State Students** 6% **From Public Schools** 88% **Ethnic Composition** White & Other 96.9%, Asian American 2%, Black 1%, Native American 0.1% **Foreign Students** 1% **Reside on Campus** 75% **Return as Sophomores** 71% **Total Faculty** 63 **Student Faculty Ratio** 15:1 **Fraternities (% of men participating)** 4 (29%) **Sororities (% of women participating)** 3 (28%)

Illinois Institute of Technology

Chicago, IL · Est. 1890 · Coed · Private · 2,262 Undergrads · Urban

I need...

Admissions info admission@charlie.acc.iit.edu
www.iit.edu/~admission
Financial aid info www.iit.edu/~admission/adm
.html

How wired is Illinois Tech?

Do I get email? Yes
Do I get a home page? Yes
   Where? www.iit.edu/people/students
What is the student to computer ratio? 5:1

The usual tour

VIRTUAL TOUR www.iit.edu/iit/map
DEPARTMENTS www.iit.edu/academics
/departments.html
RESEARCH www.iit.edu/academics/research.html
STUDENT CLUBS www.iit.edu/student
/organizations.html
CAREER CENTER www.iit.edu/~cdc
CALENDAR www.iit.edu/~calendar
GREEK LIFE www.iit.edu/~ifc

Skip the brochure

• **GAY, LESBIAN, AND BISEXUAL STUDENT ALLIANCE** At a
school as diverse as IIT, every member of
every group can find a niche, as this friendly
site demonstrates. Links to queer resources
on the Web, specifically in Chicago and on
campus, are here. **www.iit.edu/~glbsa**

• **SOME FACTS ABOUT IIT** From its beginnings in

IIT's campus was designed by the great architect, Mies van
der Rohe

1893 as Armour Institute, to its addition of a
law school in 1969, to the merger with its
most recent campus in 1986, IIT has continued to grow at a healthy clip. The school now
hosts some 5,000 students from over 70
countries and boasts dozens of degree programs. Get these facts and more at this in-
depth guide. **www.iit.edu/~pr/factbook**

• **WOUI 88.9 CHICAGO** What is it about campus
radio that inspires such cool Web sites?
Actually, despite first appearances, this is
basically just a pretty face. But head to
"People" and visit Medusa and her show
Deathdanse. She also hosted the Iron
Butterfly tribute "In-A-Gadda-Da-Vida"
Marathon. **www.iit.edu/~woui**

WHAT YOU NEED TO GET IN **Application Deadline** Rolling admissions **Common App.** No **Application Fee** $30 **Tuition Costs** $15,840 **Room & Board** $4,620 **Need Blind** Yes **Financial Forms Deadline** Priority given to applications received by March 15 **Undergrads Awarded Aid** 85% **Aid That Is Need-Based** 84% **Average Award of Freshman Scholarship Package** $8,764 **Tests Required** SAT1 or ACT **Admissions Address** 3300 South Federal Street, Chicago, IL 60616 **Admissions Telephone** (312) 567-3025

LAST YEAR'S CLASS **Applied** 1,448 **Accepted** 927 **Matriculated** 229 **Average SAT M/V** 646/524 **Average ACT** 26 **In Top Quarter of High School Graduating Class** 80%

COLLEGE LIFE **Gender Breakdown** M 77%, F 23% **Out of State Students** 34% **From Public Schools** 90% **Ethnic Composition** White & Other 67%, Asian American 12%, Black 12%, Hispanic 9% **Foreign Students** 13% **Reside on Campus** 53% **Return as Sophomores** 77% **Student Faculty Ratio** 7:1 **Fraternities (% of men participating)** 9 (15%) **Sororities (% of women participating)** 2 (10%)

University of Illinois, Chicago

www.uic.edu

Chicago, IL · Est. 1946 · Coed · Public · 16,142 Undergrads · Urban

I need...

Admissions info cqadmit@uicvmc.aiss.uic.edu
www.uic.edu/depts/oar

REQUEST APPLICATION ONLINE

How wired is UI, Chicago?

Do I get email? Yes
Do I get a home page? Yes
Is my dorm wired? No
What is the student to computer ratio? 32:1

The usual tour

STUDENT NEWSPAPER www.uic.edu/depts
/paff/uicnews
LIBRARY www.uic.edu/depts/lib
CAREER CENTER www.uic.edu/depts/ocs/ocs.htm
STUDENT CLUBS, SERVICES, AND SPORTS www.uic
.edu/studserv.html
DEPARTMENTS www.uic.edu/acdepts.html
CALENDAR gopher://gopher.uic.edu/11
/campus/mse00000
RESEARCH RESOURCES CENTER www.rrc.uic.edu

Skip the brochure

• **CAMPUS UNIONS** The UIC Campus Unions (there
are two) make up the third largest union complex in the USA. If you can't make it there in
person before you pick your college, take a virtual visit. **www.uic.edu/depts/chcc/home.html**

Location: http://www.uic.edu/depts/chcc/ciu.html

Get a little perspective on the college life at UI, Chicago

• **CAMPUS MAPS** Inexplicably buried in the home
page of the Student Development Services,
these helpful maps illustrate exactly how
sprawling the UIC campus is. Print out the
East side of campus and the West side of
campus and tape 'em together to get the
whole picture! **www.uic.edu/depts/sada/MAP/map.htm**

• **FLAMES RADIO AT U OF I** Here's where the whole
wacky WUIC 89.5 radio gang hangs out, and
it's entirely student-run. They only broadcast to
the East side of campus, but hey, you can see
a picture of a graffiti-covered space shuttle or
a promo for WUIC by Bill Clinton and Al Gore.
Plus, follow other links to radio-related sites
around the Web. **www.eecs.uic.edu/~pday/wuic.html**

WHAT YOU NEED TO GET IN **Application Deadline** February 28 for priority consideration; final deadline June 7 **Common
App.** No **Application Fee** $30 ($40 for international applicants) **Tuition Costs** $2,870 ($8,214 out-of-state)
Room & Board $5,394 **Need Blind** Yes **Financial Forms Deadline** Priority given to applications received by
March 1 **Undergrads Awarded Aid** 63% **Aid That Is Need-Based** 70% **Tests Required** SAT1 or ACT (preferred)
Admissions Address Chicago, IL 60680 **Admissions Telephone** (312) 996-4350

LAST YEAR'S CLASS **Applied** 8,568 **Accepted** 5,615 **Matriculated** 2,533 **Average SAT M/V** 528/431 **Average ACT**
22 **In Top Fifth of High School Graduating Class** 43%

COLLEGE LIFE **Gender Breakdown** M 47%, F 53% **Out of State Students** 5% **From Public Schools** 75% **Ethnic
Composition** White & Other 59%, Asian American 17%, Black 10%, Hispanic 13%, Native American 1% **Foreign
Students** 2% **Reside on Campus** 10% **Return as Sophomores** 68% **Total Faculty** 1539 **Student Faculty Ratio**
10:1 **Fraternities (% of men participating)** 8 (2%) **Sororities (% of women participating)** 4 (2%)

University of Illinois, Urbana-Champaign

Urbana, IL · Est. 1867 · Coed · Public · 26,673 Undergrads · Urban

I need...

Admissions info admssion@uiuc.edu
www.uiuc.edu/providers/oar/home
page.html
Financial aid info www.odos.uiuc.edu/osfa

How wired is UI, Urbana-Champaign?

Do I get email? Yes
Do I get a home page? Yes
  Where? www.acm.uiuc.edu/webmonkeys
uiuc-people
Is my dorm wired? Yes
What is the student to computer ratio? 9:1

The usual tour

LIBRARY www.grainger.uiuc.edu
PUBLICATIONS www.uiuc.edu/providers/uipress
STUDENT CLUBS www.cen.uiuc.edu/org.html
GREEK LIFE ux1.cso.uiuc.edu/~efantis/hellenic
STUDENT NEWSPAPER gopher://gopher.uiuc.edu
  /11/News/Dl
DEPARTMENTS www.uiuc.edu/academics.html
SPORTS www.uiuc.edu/athletics.html
VIRTUAL TOUR www.uiuc.edu/navigation/walk

Skip the brochure

• **UIUC ARTS AND CULTURE** UIUC is huge, hence, the
equally huge opportunities for absorbing

WELCOME

The Illini Union draws together all members of the University of Illinois community. It is the shared possession of students, faculty, staff, alumni and guests. While each of these groups is important, it is students who are at the heart of what the Illini Union is all about.

UI's Union: one big happy family

culture. Find out what's going on at the Krannert Center for the Performing Arts, or in any one of a dozen or so campus performing arts organizations. **www.uiuc.edu/fun/art.html**

• **NCSA** Chances are that the browser you're using to view this page is the one descended from Mosaic, which was born here in the Supercomputer department. See how Illinois is keeping up with its illustrious alum, Marc Andreessen. **ncsa.uiuc.edu**

• **HOUSING AND DINING SERVICES** "I don't want to live in THAT dorm!" is commonly heard the summer before freshman year starts, when those all-important housing papers arrive. Get the inside scoop on good campus (or off-campus) housing here, by going on the introductory tour, "The Best Place to Be." **www.urh.uiuc.edu**

WHAT YOU NEED TO GET IN **Application Deadline** November 15 for priority consideration; final deadline January 1 **Common App.** No **Application Fee** $30 **Tuition Costs** $3,150 ($8,580 out-of-state) **Room & Board** $4,916 **Need Blind** Yes **Financial Forms Deadline** Priority given to applications received by March 15 **Undergrads Awarded Aid** 82% **Aid That Is Need-Based** 60% **Average Award of Freshman Scholarship Package** $1,830 **Tests Required** SAT1 or ACT **Admissions Address** 506 South Wright Street, Urbana, IL 61801 **Admissions Telephone** (217) 333-0302

LAST YEAR'S CLASS **Applied** 17,173 **Accepted** 12,320 **Matriculated** 6,108 **Average ACT** 27 **In Top Fifth of High School Graduating Class** 77%

COLLEGE LIFE **Gender Breakdown** M 55%, F 45% **Out of State Students** 9% **From Public Schools** 83% **Ethnic Composition** White & Other 74.8%, Asian American 12.5%, Black 7%, Hispanic 5.5%, Native American 0.2% **Foreign Students** 2% **Reside on Campus** 30% **Return as Sophomores** 91% **Total Faculty** 1,739 **Student Faculty Ratio** 15:1 **Fraternities (% of men participating)** 56 (20%) **Sororities (% of women participating)** 27 (24%) **Graduate Students** 9,792

Indiana University, Bloomington

Bloomington, IN · Est. 1820 · Coed · Public · 25,773 Undergrads · Big Town

I need...

Admissions info iuadmit@indiana.edu
www.indiana.edu/iub/attend/admit.html
Financial aid info rsvposfa@wpo.franklin.indiana
.edu
www.indiana.edu/~sfa

DOWNLOAD APPLICATION ONLINE

How wired is IU, Bloomington?

Do I get email? Yes
Do I get a home page? Yes
Where? www.indiana.edu/~hyplan/hyplans
.html
Is my dorm wired? Yes
What is the student to computer ratio? 11:1

The usual tour

LIBRARY www.indiana.edu/~libweb/index.html
DEPARTMENTS www.indiana.edu/iub/academic
/departments_schools.html
STUDENT CLUBS www.indiana.edu/iub/people
/groups.html
SPORTS www.indiana.edu/iub/recreate
/athletic.html
CALENDAR www.indiana.edu/~iuevents/iub.html
VIRTUAL TOUR www.indiana.edu/~iuadmit
/tourl.html
GREEK LIFE www.indiana.edu/iub/people
/greek.html

Indiana University: hug your way to success

Skip the brochure

• **EXPOSURE—THE IU PHOTO CLUB** This photography club sponsors guest speakers, photography trips, and competitions, and also has an electronic gallery where you can view the work of some of the club's members. All that in an aesthetically pleasing and extremely well-developed Web site. **www.indiana.edu/~exposure**

• **STUDENT LEGAL SERVICES** Your landlord won't fix the toilet. Your student organization wants to hold a bachelor auction. Your roommate used your towel, again. Whether it's debt counseling, contract disputes, or criminal proceedings, help is available in the form of Student Legal Services. **www.indiana.edu/~sls**

• **IU UNDERGRADUATE FINANCE CLUB** If you like money, you'll love the Finance Club. Surprisingly enough, in addition to monetary games like Investment Challenge, the club is also active in community service projects. **www.indiana.edu/~finance**

WHAT YOU NEED TO GET IN **Application Deadline** Rolling admissions; February 15 for priority consideration **Common App.** No **Application Fee** $35 **Tuition Costs** $3,570 ($10,700 out-of-state) **Room & Board** $3,863 **Need Blind** Yes **Financial Forms Deadline** Priority given to applications received by March 1 **Undergrads Awarded Aid** 80% **Aid That Is Need-Based** 90% **Average Award of Freshman Scholarship Package** $1,100 **Tests Required** SAT1 or ACT **Admissions Address** 300 North Jordan Avenue, Bloomington, IN 47405 **Admissions Telephone** (812) 855-0661

LAST YEAR'S CLASS **Applied** 17,372 **Accepted** 13,870 **Matriculated** 5,751 **Average SAT M/V** 533/467 **Average ACT** 24 **In Top Fifth of High School Graduating Class** 49%

COLLEGE LIFE **Gender Breakdown** M 47%, F 53% **Out of State Students** 29% **Ethnic Composition** White & Other 91%, Asian American 3%, Black 4%, Hispanic 2% **Foreign Students** 3% **Reside on Campus** 37% **Return as Sophomores** 79% **Total Faculty** 1,626 **Student Faculty Ratio** 19:1 **Fraternities (% of men participating)** 32 (12%) **Sororities (% of women participating)** 18 (11%) **Graduate Students** 7,449

Iowa State University

www.iastate.edu

Ames, IA · Est. 1858 · Coed · Public · 20,208 Undergrads · Big Town

How wired is Iowa State University?

Do I get email? Yes
Do I get a home page? Yes
   Where? www.public.iastate.edu/directory.html
Is my dorm wired? Yes
What is the student to computer ratio? 13:1

The usual tour

DEPARTMENTS www.iastate.edu/academics
/depts.html
SPORTS www.public.iastate.edu/~athletics_info
CALENDAR www.iastate.edu/cal/cal.html
STUDENT CLUBS www.public.iastate.edu/~stu_org
CAREER CENTER www.public.iastate.edu/~career
_info
STUDY ABROAD www.iastate.edu/~study-abroad
LIBRARY www.lib.iastate.edu
PUBLICATIONS www.iastate.edu/news/news.html

Skip the brochure

• **ISU MEAT LAB** Vegetarians beware! ISU is actively engaged in the science of animal husbandry. It even hosts a fancy, Java-enhanced Web site for its meat lab, with detailed descriptions of the slaughtering, cutting, and processing

Location: http://www.public.iastate.edu/~adm_info/homepage.html

Iowa State: the next step in your academic career

involved. The results of lecture and class experiments are sold in a retail sales outlet. From bratwurst to lamb liver, if it was formerly on the hoof, you can order it online. **www.ag.iastate.edu/centers/meatlab**

• **HOW THE CYCLONES GOT THEIR NAME** You could yell "Go Cyclones!" for four years straight and never hear this story. Be the most informed in the stadium by reading the background of the name that has matched that spinning cardinal since 1895. **www.public.iastate.edu/~athletics_info/color/cyclones.html**

• **ISU POP QUIZ** Your first college test begins with this question: "What did Iowa State professor John Vincent Atanasoff start with his 1939 invention?" Stumped? The answer: the computer revolution. The president's office sponsors this interesting, trivia-filled page. **www.public.iastate.edu/~pres_info/popquiz/questions.html**

WHAT YOU NEED TO GET IN **Application Deadline** August 26 **Common App.** No **Application Fee** $20 **Tuition Costs** $2,470 ($8,284 out-of-state) **Room & Board** $3,508 **Need Blind** Yes **Financial Forms Deadline** Priority given to applications received by March 1 **Undergrads Awarded Aid** 48% **Aid That Is Need-Based** 61% **Average Award of Freshman Scholarship Package** $1,720 **Tests Required** SAT1 or ACT (preferred) **Admissions Address** 314 Alumni Hall, Ames, IA 50011-2010 **Admissions Telephone** (515) 294-5836

LAST YEAR'S CLASS **Applied** 9,088 **Accepted** 8,226 **Matriculated** 3,412 **In Top Fifth of High School Graduating Class** 49%

COLLEGE LIFE **Gender Breakdown** M 57%, F 43% **Out of State Students** 24% **From Public Schools** 92% **Ethnic Composition** White & Other 93.3%, Asian American 2.2%, Black 2.7%, Hispanic 1.6%, Native American 0.2% **Foreign Students** 6% **Reside on Campus** 42% **Return as Sophomores** 82% **Total Faculty** 1,781 **Student Faculty Ratio** 17:1 **Fraternities (% of men participating)** 35 (14%) **Sororities (% of women participating)** 20 (14%) **Graduate Students** 4,223

University of Iowa

Iowa City, IA · Est. 1847 · Coed · Public · 18,740 Undergrads · Big Town

I need...

Admissions info admissions@uiowa.edu
www.uiowa.edu/~admit/index.html
Financial aid info financial-aid@uiowa.edu
www.uiowa.edu/~finaid

How wired is University of Iowa?

Do I get email? Yes
Do I get a home page? No
Is my dorm wired? No
What is the student to computer ratio? 14:1

The usual tour

VIRTUAL TOUR www.uiowa.edu/~admit/Campus
/Slideshow/index.html
LIBRARY www.lib.uiowa.edu
SPORTS www.biz.uiowa.edu/hawkeyes
/index.html
STUDY ABROAD www.uiowa.edu/~oies
PUBLICATIONS www.uiowa.edu/~uipress
FACT BOOK www.uiowa.edu/~our/fact.book
STUDENT NEWSPAPER www.uiowa.edu/~dlyiowan

Skip the brochure

• **HONORS PROGRAM** So, smarty pants, you think
you're better than just a regular old Hawkeye?
Seriously, though, applying to an Honors
Program (and completing it) is one of the best
ways to set yourself apart from the thousands
of other graduates of a big state school. But
that's not all, of course: You also get ping-

The University of Iowa sits atop a hill

pong and darts privileges in the rec room of
the Honors Building. **www.uiowa.edu/~honorpgm
/index.html**

• **HANCHER AUDITORIUM** If your name's in lights
somewhere at U of I, you'll probably want it to
be at Hancher, Iowa's Broadway-caliber performing arts complex. Recent performances
include *Stomp* and the Alvin Ailey American
Dance Theater. A cultural treasure in the land
of cornfields. **www.uiowa.edu/~hancher**

• **UNIVERSITY OF IOWA NEWS SERVICES** Follow the
news at all the colleges that compose the
University of Iowa with this campus-wide wire
service. It's a great way to track grants and
internship announcements. **www.uiowa.edu
/~ournews/index.html**

WHAT YOU NEED TO GET IN **Application Deadline** Rolling admissions **Common App.** No **Application Fee** $20 **Tuition Costs** $2,470 ($9,068 out-of-state) **Room & Board** $3,688 **Need Blind** Yes **Financial Forms Deadline** Priority given to applications received by January 1 **Undergrads Awarded Aid** 65% **Aid That Is Need-Based** 65% **Average Award of Freshman Scholarship Package** $1,450 **Tests Required** SAT1 or ACT **Admissions Address** 107 Calvin Hall, Iowa City, IA 52242-1396 **Admissions Telephone** (319) 335-3847

LAST YEAR'S CLASS **Applied** 9,940 **Accepted** 8,544 **Matriculated** 3,578 **Median Range SAT M/V** 510-640/440-570 **In Top Fifth of High School Graduating Class** 42%

COLLEGE LIFE **Gender Breakdown** M 47%, F 53% **Out of State Students** 38% **From Public Schools** 88% **Ethnic Composition** White & Other 91.6%, Asian American 3.7%, Black 2.4%, Hispanic 1.9%, Native American 0.4% **Foreign Students** 3% **Reside on Campus** 29% **Return as Sophomores** 81% **Total Faculty** 1,803 **Student Faculty Ratio** 15:1 **Fraternities (% of men participating)** 24 (14%) **Sororities (% of women participating)** 18 (15%) **Graduate Students** 8,857

James Madison University

www.jmu.edu

Harrisonburg, VA · Est. 1908 · Coed · Public · 10,503 Undergrads · Big Town

I need...

Admissions info gotojmu@jmu.edu
   www.jmu.edu/admissions
Financial aid info sellerjh@jmu.edu
   www.jmu.edu/finaid/index.html

How wired is James Madison?

Do I get email? Yes
Do I get a home page? Yes
   Where? www.jmu.edu/edir/people
Is my dorm wired? Yes
What is the student to computer ratio? 21:1

The usual tour

CALENDAR www.jmu.edu/catalog/95/9-calend
   .html
DEPARTMENTS www.jmu.edu/cwis/colleges.htm
SPORTS www.jmu.edu/sportsinfo/index.html
STUDENT CLUBS www.jmu.edu/cwis/admin.htm
LIBRARY www.jmu.edu/library
CAREER CENTER www.jmu.edu/career
STUDY ABROAD www.jmu.edu/intl-ed
STUDENT NEWSPAPER breeze.jmu.edu
VIRTUAL TOUR www.jmu.edu/publications
   /Admtour1.html

Skip the brochure

• **THE MARCHING ROYAL DUKES** Slightly more popular than the football team, JMU's 375-member marching band recently won the Sudler Trophy for the best college band in the nation. Check

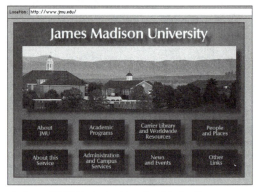

Is James Madison on your educational horizon?

out the sound files of the Royal Dukes.
www.jmu.edu/music/mrd/index.html

• **WXJM—STUDENT RADIO AT JMU** Future Howard Sterns flock to WXJM, one of Harrisonburg's few decent radio stations. Competition for airtime is fierce. Find out what's on and check out *Oxencrotch*, WXJM's 'zine. **www.jmu.edu /wxjm/index.html**

• **SURF THE 'BURG** This isn't part of the JMU home page, although it's linked. Find out why JM's Bar and Grill is one of the most popular campus hangouts. (Hint: The Dave Matthews Band and others played here frequently before you heard of them, the beer is cheap, and most importantly, it's right across the street from campus!) Other highlights include Luigi's (good pizza) and Town & Campus Records (good albums). **www.uconnect.com/Harrison.htm**

WHAT YOU NEED TO GET IN Application Deadline December 1 for priority consideration; final deadline January 15 **Early Action Deadline** December 1 **Common App.** No **Application Fee** $25 **Tuition Costs** $1,401 ($8,580 out-of-state) **Room & Board** $4,666 **Need Blind** Yes **Financial Forms Deadline** Priority given to applications received by February 15 **Undergrads Awarded Aid** 59% **Aid That Is Need-Based** 35% **Average Award of Freshman Scholarship Package** $2,535 **Tests Required** SAT1 (preferred) or ACT **Admissions Address** Harrisonburg, VA 22807 **Admissions Telephone** (540) 568-6147

LAST YEAR'S CLASS Applied 12,314 **Accepted** 6,989 **Matriculated** 2,539 **Average SAT M/V** 589/590 **In Top Fifth of High School Graduating Class** 63% **Applied Early** 4,702 **Accepted Early** 1,224

COLLEGE LIFE Gender Breakdown M 46%, F 54% **Out of State Students** 35% **From Public Schools** 95% **Ethnic Composition** White & Other 88%, Asian American 3.7%, Black 6.5%, Hispanic 1.5%, Native American 0.3% **Foreign Students** 1% **Reside on Campus** 49% **Return as Sophomores** 92% **Total Faculty** 716 **Student Faculty Ratio** 19:1 **Fraternities (% of men participating)** 18 (20%) **Sororities (% of women participating)** 12 (18%) **Graduate Students** 859

Johns Hopkins University

www.jhu.edu

Baltimore, MD · Est. 1876 · Coed · Private · 3,444 Undergrads · Urban

I need...

Admissions info www.jhu.edu/~admis
/admissions/contact.html
www.jhu.edu/www/students/admiss.html
Financial aid info fin_aid@jhunix.hcf.jhu.edu
www.jhu.edu/~finaid

How wired is Johns Hopkins?

Do I get email? Yes
Do I get a home page? Yes
Where? infonet.welch.jhu.edu/people
/personal.html
What is the student to computer ratio? 16:1

The usual tour

STUDENT CLUBS www.jhu.edu/~sacexec
DEPARTMENTS www.jhu.edu/www/schools
LIBRARY www.jhu.edu/www/library
PUBLICATIONS www.jhu.edu/www/newspubs
SPORTS www.jhu.edu/www/newspub
/athlete.html

Skip the brochure

- **JHU STUDENT PUGWASH** Student Pugwash is a national student organization "dedicated to exploring the ways in which scientific and technological progress affect our society and lives." Join and discuss **www.jhu.edu/~pugwash**

- **CAVEAT LECTOR** Should you judge a digital book by its cover? The online version of the *Caveat Lector* rivals most professional ezines. The

Take a peek at Johns Hopkins University

graphics are clean and pleasant, if a bit staid, but the organization of this forum for fiction, poetry, and commentary is exceptional. Discover what academics are loading the canon with these days. **www.jhu.edu/~caveat/h.html**

- **THE BUTTERED NIBLETS** Want to see a man dressed as a buttered niblet? It is now possible at the home page of this student comedy troupe. There isn't an enormous amount of substance at this site, but the picture of the human niblet is fairly impressive, as is the interactive "Hamster Lovin' Homepage." **www.jhu.edu/~nibs/niblets.html**

- **THINGS TO DO AT JHU** How fun is life at Johns Hopkins? Well, you can visit the nearby Lacrosse Hall of Fame, head into D.C. for the weekend, catch a movie in Baltimore, and attend the Johns Hopkins theater. Visit this site for more details. **www.jhu.edu/~nibs/niblets.html**

"The picture of the human niblet is impressive."

WHAT YOU NEED TO GET IN Application Deadline January 1 **Early Action Deadline** November 15 **Common App.** Yes **Application Fee** $50 **Tuition Costs** $20,740 **Room & Board** $8,100 **Need Blind** No **Financial Forms Deadline** January 15 **Undergrads Awarded Aid** 58% **Aid That Is Need-Based** 95% **Average Award of Freshman Scholarship Package** $13,749 **Tests Required** SAT1 (preferred) or ACT **Admissions Address** 3400 North Charles Street, Baltimore, MD 21218 **Admissions Telephone** (410) 516-8171

LAST YEAR'S CLASS Applied 7,877 **Accepted** 3,313 **Matriculated** 876 **Average SAT M/V** 690/670 **Average ACT** 31 **In Top Fifth of High School Graduating Class** 93% **Applied Early** 476 **Accepted Early** 246

COLLEGE LIFE Gender Breakdown M 62%, F 38% **Out of State Students** 87% **From Public Schools** 59% **Ethnic Composition** White & Other 72%, Asian American 21%, Black 5%, Hispanic 2% **Foreign Students** 5% **Reside on Campus** 65% **Return as Sophomores** 94% **Student Faculty Ratio** 10:1 **Fraternities (% of men participating)** 13 (30%) **Sororities (% of women participating)** 5 (25%) **Graduate Students** 1,403

Kalamazoo College

www.kzoo.edu

Kalamazoo, MI · Est. 1833 · Coed · Private · 1,272 Undergrads · Urban

I need...

Admissions info admissions@hobbes.kzoo.edu
www.kzoo.edu/~admst/applying.html
Financial aid info www.kzoo.edu/~admst
/scholarships.html

How wired is Kalamazoo College?

Do I get email? Yes
Do I get a home page? Yes
Is my dorm wired? No
What is the student to computer ratio? 9:1

The usual tour

SPORTS www.kzoo.edu/~admst/sports.html
STUDENT CLUBS www.kzoo.edu/stu_orgs/index
.html
DEPARTMENTS www.kzoo.edu/acad_depts/index
.html
LIBRARY www.kzoo.edu/~library/LibInfoCat.html
VIRTUAL TOUR www.kzoo.edu/~admst/finalcopy
.mov
PUBLICATIONS www.kzoo.edu/campusnews/index
.html

Skip the brochure

- **WJMD 90.1** "It's not Jelly... It's THE JAM!" Michigan's oldest college radio station boasts some of Michigan's oldest radio equipment as well (and WJMD is damn proud of it). Becoming a DJ is perhaps just an email missive away. **www.kzoo.edu/~wjmd**

Waterbugs abound at the 'zoo

- **CITY OF KALAMAZOO HOME PAGE** Where in the world is Kalamazoo? Get a grasp of where it's located (and what the weather will be like once you get there) with this collection of "K" info. **kalamazoo.inetmi.com/cities/kazoo/kazoo.htm**

- **THE LAND SEA EXPERIENCE** What better way to bond with your future classmates than to place your life in their hands (and vice versa) during this Outward Bound-esque orientation program? The land part of the program features hiking, climbing, and backpacking, while the sea part takes place either on a brigantine or in canoes. **www.kzoo.edu/~admst/landSea.html**

- **K-HANDBELLS OF KALAMAZOO COLLEGE** Since 1987, this Kalamazoo student group has been ringing in the school year with the melodious sound of handbells. **www.kzoo.edu/~cooper /khandbells.html**

WHAT YOU NEED TO GET IN **Application Deadline** Rolling admissions; February 15 for priority consideration **Common App.** Yes **Application Fee** $45 **Tuition Costs** $17,214 **Room & Board** $5,738 **Need Blind** Yes **Financial Forms Deadline** Priority given to applications received by February 15 **Undergrads Awarded Aid** 90% **Aid That Is Need-Based** 51% **Average Award of Freshman Scholarship Package** $8,300 **Tests Required** SAT1 or ACT **Admissions Address** 1200 Academy Street, Kalamazoo, MI 49006-3295 **Admissions Telephone** (616) 337-7166

LAST YEAR'S CLASS **Applied** 1,358 **Accepted** 1,252 **Matriculated** 350 **Average SAT M/V** 618/567 **Average ACT** 27 **In Top Quarter of High School Graduating Class** 85%

COLLEGE LIFE **Gender Breakdown** M 42%, F 58% **Out of State Students** 27% **From Public Schools** 78% **Ethnic Composition** White & Other 90%, Asian American 5%, Black 3%, Hispanic 1%, Native American 1% **Foreign Students** 3% **Reside on Campus** 95% **Return as Sophomores** 83% **Total Faculty** 108 **Student Faculty Ratio** 11:1 **Fraternities** none **Sororities** none

Kansas State University

www.ksu.edu

Manhattan, KS · Est. 1863 · Coed · Public · 17,014 Undergrads · Big Town

I need...

Admissions info kstate@ksuvm.ksu.edu
www.ksu.edu/Consider/applynow/admiss.pdf
Financial aid info ksusfa@ksuvm.ksu.edu
www.ksu.edu/Consider/applynow/finaid.pdf

How wired is Kansas State?

FULL APPLICATION ONLINE

Do I get email? Yes
Do I get a home page? Yes
Is my dorm wired? Yes
What is the student to computer ratio? 42:1

The usual tour

DEPARTMENTS www.ksu.edu/Directories
SPORTS www.ksu.edu/sportsinfo
VIRTUAL TOUR www.cis.ksu.edu/tour/about.ksu.html
STUDENT NEWSPAPER www.spub.ksu.edu
CALENDAR www.ksu.edu/calendar
LIBRARY www.lib.ksu.edu

Skip the brochure

• **CLASSES USING THE WEB** Having trouble making it to class? That's OK. Class now comes to you. Syllabi and course info online mean you might never have to leave your computer again. www.ksu.edu/courses/web-classes.html

• **K-STATE ALUMNI ASSOCIATION** Yeah, but what about after I graduate? Check out the goodies in store for KSU alums, which include the traditional alumni clubs, magazine, and reunions,

What we do:

- Alumni clubs
- K-Stater magazine
- Homecoming
- Family Weekend
- Traveling Wildcats alumni tours
- Class reunions and special reunions
- Constituent group activities
- Multicultural programs
- Alumni awards
- College Nights and student recruitment activities
- Scholarships
- Student Ambassadors
- Student Alumni Board
- Catbacker clubs
- Junior Wildcat club
- Pregame events
- Watch parties
- Tradition Founders Fund
- Maintain alumni records

Fall in step with the KSU faithful

as well as the less traditional "Traveling Wildcats" tours and cruises to exciting locales like Switzerland, Alaska, and Greece. **www.ksu.edu/alumni**

• **KANSAS CROP PERFORMANCE TESTS** 1995: A corn-popping good year? Find out for yourself. **www.ksu.edu/~kscpt**

• **MANHATTAN MOVIE LISTINGS** Looking for a diversion from your studies? Thanks to a selfless volunteer, the movie listings for the local movie theaters are posted. **www.ksu.edu/jl57**

"Goodies in store for alums include tours to locales like Greece"

WHAT YOU NEED TO GET IN Application Deadline Rolling admissions **Common App.** No **Application Fee** $15 **Tuition Costs** $1,890 ($7,950 out-of-state) **Room & Board** $3,490 **Need Blind** Yes **Financial Forms Deadline** February 1 **Undergrads Awarded Aid** 70% **Aid That Is Need-Based** 60% **Average Award of Freshman Scholarship Package** $1,600 **Tests Required** SAT1 or ACT (preferred) **Admissions Address** Manhattan, KS 66506 **Admissions Telephone** (913) 532-6250

LAST YEAR'S CLASS Applied 6,552 **Accepted** 4,599 **Matriculated** 3,267 **Average ACT** 23 **In Top Quarter of High School Graduating Class** 57%

COLLEGE LIFE Gender Breakdown M 54%, F 46% **Out of State Students** 12% **From Public Schools** 90% **Ethnic Composition** White & Other 91%, Asian American 2%, Black 4%, Hispanic 2%, Native American 1% **Foreign Students** 2% **Reside on Campus** 20% **Return as Sophomores** 75% **Total Faculty** 215 **Student Faculty Ratio** 16:1 **Fraternities (% of men participating)** 26 (20%) **Sororities (% of women participating)** 12 (21%) **Graduate Students** 3,462

University of Kansas

www.ukans.edu

Lawrence, KS · Est. 1866 · Coed · Public · 18,657 Undergrads · Big Town

How wired is Kansas?

Do I get email? Yes
Do I get a home page? Yes
   Where? www.cc.ukans.edu/cwis
   /organizations/kucia/zoo/zoo_kucia.html
Is my dorm wired? Yes
What is the student to computer ratio? 34:1

The usual tour

VIRTUAL TOUR www.sped.ukans.edu/campus
/ku.html
SPORTS falcon.cc.ukans.edu/~kusports
DEPARTMENTS kufacts.cc.ukans.edu/cwis/units
/acadept.html
STUDENT CLUBS kufacts.cc.ukans.edu/cwis
/organizations/org_main.html
LIBRARY kufacts.cc.ukans.edu/cwis/reference
/Libraries.html

"KU Jayhawks are hell on wheels."

REQUEST APPLICATION ONLINE

Prepare to cheer for the Jayhawks

◀))) Listen to the Fight Song

Skip the brochure

- **KU ROLLER HOCKEY** These KU Jayhawks are hell on wheels. Watch out, Kansas State, it's Wildcat hunting season. **www.cc.ukans.edu /cwis/organizations/dmoscato/hockey.html**

- **SUNFLOWER HOUSE COOPERATIVE** KU students escape the stress of college life by living the cooperative way. **www.cc.ukans.edu/~sunflowr /sunflow.htm**

- **FEMINIST COLLECTIVE FORCE** The FCF supports "equality, meaningful choices, welfare rights, environmental protection, guaranteed and safe health care for all, affordable and safe child care," and, let's not forget, "the empower-ment of all people." With an agenda so large, it's a good thing they meet every week. **www.ukans.edu/~fcf**

WHAT YOU NEED TO GET IN **Application Deadline** February 1 for priority consideration; final deadline April 1 **Common App.** No **Application Fee** $15 **Tuition Costs** $1,890 ($7,950 out-of-state) **Room & Board** $3,640 **Need Blind** Yes **Financial Forms Deadline** May 1 with a priority given to applications received by March 1 **Undergrads Award-ed Aid** 37% **Tests Required** SAT1 or ACT **Admissions Address** Lawrence, KS 66045 **Admissions Telephone** (913) 864-3911

LAST YEAR'S CLASS **Applied** 8,234 **Accepted** 5,569 **Matriculated** 3,555 **Average ACT** 23 **In Top Quarter of High School Graduating Class** 55%

COLLEGE LIFE **Gender Breakdown** M 49%, F 51% **Out of State Students** 37% **Ethnic Composition** White & Other 91%, Asian American 3%, Black 3%, Hispanic 2%, Native American 1% **Foreign Students** 6% **Reside on Campus** 20% **Return as Sophomores** 75% **Total Faculty** 1,312 **Student Faculty Ratio** 15:1 **Fraternities (% of men participating)** 27 (21%) **Sororities (% of women participating)** 18 (23%) **Graduate Students** 8,982

Kent State University

Kent, OH · Est. 1910 · Coed · Public · 16,222 Undergrads · Urban

www.kent.edu

I need...

Admissions info www.ba.kent.edu
Financial aid info www.kent.edu/viewbook/faid
.html

How wired is Kent State?

Do I get email? Yes
Do I get a home page? Yes
Is my dorm wired? Yes
What is the student to computer ratio? 5:1

The usual tour

DEPARTMENTS www.kent.edu/viewbook
/majors.html
CALENDAR www.kent.edu/viewbook/calendar
.html
STUDENT NEWSPAPER www.saed.kent.edu/Stater
LIBRARY www.library.kent.edu
VIEWBOOK www.ba.kent.edu/admissions/nvb-text
-pics.html
VIRTUAL TOUR www.kent.edu/flashpoint/Campus
_Map.html
STUDENT NEWSPAPER www.saed.kent.edu/Stater

Skip the brochure

• **MAY 4, 1970** You have probably seen the photograph of a young woman screaming, leaning over the lifeless body of a fellow student. In the spring of 1970 the student anti-war movement slammed into government brutality at Kent State when the National Guard opened

If you're not familiar with Kent State, you should be. It figures prominently in the history of student protest

fire—leaving four dead, one paralyzed—and eight injured. This site features the school's official memorial and links to discussions on the cultural and political significance of the tragedy. **www.kent.edu/May4/welcome.html**

• **DOC WHIZ HOME PAGE** With the passing of Jerry Garcia, sightings of bearded 50-ish men with thick glasses against a tie-dyed background have waned. Well, this Kent State prof is one. It doesn't even matter that his advice about "succeeding" at college sucks. Check out the pictures of him with antennae and *Planet of the Apes* T-shirts. **monster.educ.kent.edu/docwhiz**

• **WKSU-FM RADIO** The sounds of classical music and Ohio Light Opera fill the air. National Public Radio favorites like *Morning Edition* and *All Things Considered* are also broadcast. **www.wksu.kent.edu**

WHAT YOU NEED TO GET IN Application Deadline Fall for priority consideration; final deadline March 15 **Common App.** No **Application Fee** $25 **Tuition Costs** $3,927 ($7,854 out-of-state) **Room & Board** $3,666 **Need Blind** Yes **Financial Forms Deadline** Priority given to applications received by February 15 **Undergrads Awarded Aid** 77% **Aid That Is Need-Based** 84% **Average Award of Freshman Scholarship Package** $3,500 **Tests Required** SAT1 or ACT **Admissions Address** P.O. Box 5190, Kent, OH 44242-0001 **Admissions Telephone** (216) 672-2444

LAST YEAR'S CLASS Applied 8,725 **Accepted** 7,675 **Matriculated** 2,782 **Average SAT M/V** 458/420 **Average ACT** 21 **In Top Quarter of High School Graduating Class** 38%

COLLEGE LIFE Gender Breakdown M 43%, F 57% **Out of State Students** 7% **Ethnic Composition** White & Other 91%, Asian American 1%, Black 6%, Hispanic 1%, Native American 1% **Foreign Students** 1% **Reside on Campus** 33% **Return as Sophomores** 72% **Student Faculty Ratio** 21:1 **Fraternities (% of men participating)** 19 (7%) **Sororities (% of women participating)** 11 (6%)

University of Kentucky

www.uky.edu

Lexington, KY · Est. 1865 · Coed · Public · 17,384 Undergrads · Urban

I need...

Admissions info www.uky.edu/Undergraduate
Studies/admissions
Financial aid info www.uky.edu/FinancialAid

How wired is University of Kentucky?

Do I get a home page? No
What is the student to computer ratio? 21:1

The usual tour

VIRTUAL TOUR www.uky.edu/Undergraduate
Studies/admissions/tour.html
STUDENT CLUBS www.uky.edu/StudentOrgs
SPORTS www.uky.edu/Alumni/athletic
/sports.htm
LIBRARY www.uky.edu/Libraries
CAREER CENTER www.uky.edu/CareerCenter
CALENDAR www.uky.edu/Registrar/calendar.html

Skip the brochure

- **BLUEGRASS WATER WATCH** Water: it's not just for washing anymore. For environmentally-minded University of Kentucky students, water is definitely worth watching and studying. **www.uky.edu/StudentOrgs/BWW/bww.html**

- **HARRISON GARMAN ENTOMOLOGY CLUB** Who cares about the birds and the bees? These students are definitely more interested in bugs. **www.uky.edu/StudentOrgs/HGEC**

- **WUKY** A public university needs a public radio affiliate. UKY students and alumni (NPR's

Kentucky's Wildcats experience a rare snowy day

Noah Adams was a Wildcat) turn it up on the airwaves. **www.npr.org/members/WUKY/wuky.html**

- **UK ATHLETICS** You'd think a school that won the NCAA basketball championship and pays its coach at least a million dollars would have a more high-tech Web site. The Wildcats, however, have learned the value of economy. Students can check in for schedules, coach profiles, and pictures of their teams. **www.uky.edu/Alumni/athletic/sports.htm**

"Who cares about the birds and bees? These students are more interested in bugs."

WHAT YOU NEED TO GET IN **Application Deadline** February 15 for priority consideration; final deadline June 1 **Common App.** No **Application Fee** $15 **Tuition Costs** $2,340 ($7,020 out-of-state) **Room & Board** $3,198 **Tests Required** SAT1 or ACT (preferred) **Admissions Address** 100 W.D. Funkhouser Building, Lexington, KY 40506 **Admissions Telephone** (606) 257-2000

LAST YEAR'S CLASS **Applied** 7,974 **Accepted** 6,045 **Matriculated** 2,610 **Average SAT** 1040 (combined average) **Average ACT** 25 **In Top Quarter of High School Graduating Class** 63%

COLLEGE LIFE **Gender Breakdown** M 50%, F 50% **Out of State Students** 21% **Ethnic Composition** White & Other 92.1%, Asian American 1.8%, Black 5.2%, Hispanic 0.7%, Native American 0.2% **Foreign Students** 4% **Reside on Campus** 25% **Return as Sophomores** 78% **Total Faculty** 2,158 **Student Faculty Ratio** 16:1 **Fraternities (% of men participating)** 22 (16%) **Sororities (% of women participating)** 17 (16%) **Graduate Students** 6,410

Kenyon College

Gambier, OH · Est. 1824 · Coed · Private · 1,522 Undergrads · Rural

I need...

Admissions info admissions@kenyon.edu
www.kenyon.edu/admiss

Financial aid info www.kenyon.edu/admiss
/finanaid.htm

DOWNLOAD APPLICATION ONLINE

How wired is Kenyon College?

Do I get email? Yes
Do I get a home page? Yes
Is my dorm wired? Yes
What is the student to computer ratio? 13:1

The usual tour

VIRTUAL TOUR www.kenyon.edu/vc/vctour.htm
CALENDAR www.kenyon.edu/calendar
DEPARTMENTS www.kenyon.edu/acad
/acaddept.htm
SPORTS www.kenyon.edu/athletic
PUBLICATIONS www.kenyon.edu/pubs
STUDENT CLUBS www.kenyon.edu/vc/activity.htm
LIBRARY www.kenyon.edu/depts/library

Skip the brochure

- **KENYON COLLEGE BOOKSTORE HOME PAGE** Some people are writing at Kenyon. Some people are writing about Kenyon. Some people are selling what they write at Kenyon. The bookstore's home page gives the low-down. www.kenyon.edu/bookstor/bookstor.htm

- **KENYON PUBLIC AFFAIRS FORTNIGHTLY** The Office of Public Affairs keeps you abreast of what's

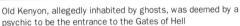

Visitors' Center

Location: http://www.kenyon.edu/vc/

- Brief Introduction to the College
- Brief Overview of Kenyon
- Campus Guide
- Campus Map
- Virtual Campus Tour
- Guest Book - Please sign!
- Office Hours
- Transportation
- Lodging
- Local Weather
- Dining
- Gambier and Knox County
- Prospective Student Information

Old Kenyon, allegedly inhabited by ghosts, was deemed by a psychic to be the entrance to the Gates of Hell

going on around campus, from lectures and sporting events to coming concerts. www.kenyon.edu/depts/college_relations/pubaff/fortcurr/fortnite.htm

- **FIVE COLLEGE CONSORTIUM** Five schools for the price of one: Kenyon is part of the Five College Consortium, along with Denison University, Oberlin College, Ohio Wesleyan University, and the University of Wooster. www.denison.edu/ohio5

- **GAMBIER AND KNOX COUNTY** Information about Kenyon's endearing environs with pictures that look more Bavarian than middle American. www.kenyon.edu/vc/gambknox.htm

"Five schools for the price of one: The Five College Consortium"

WHAT YOU NEED TO GET IN **Application Deadline** February 15 **Early Action Deadline** December 1 or February 1 **Common App.** Yes **Application Fee** $45 (may be waived) **Tuition Costs** $21,370 **Room & Board** $3,820 **Need Blind** Yes **Financial Forms Deadline** February 15 **Undergrads Awarded Aid** 40% **Aid That Is Need-Based** 82% **Average Award of Freshman Scholarship Package** $12,032 **Tests Required** SAT1 or ACT **Admissions Address** Gambier, OH 43022-9623 **Admissions Telephone** (614) 427-5776

LAST YEAR'S CLASS **Applied** 2,303 **Accepted** 1,654 **Matriculated** 441 **Average SAT M/V** 619/646 **Average ACT** 28 **In Top Fifth of High School Graduating Class** 65% **Applied Early** 125 **Accepted Early** 86

COLLEGE LIFE **Gender Breakdown** M 48%, F 52% **Out of State Students** 78% **From Public Schools** 68% **Ethnic Composition** White & Other 88.7%, Asian American 4.2%, Black 4.1%, Hispanic 2.6%, Native American 0.4% **Foreign Students** 3% **Reside on Campus** 100% **Return as Sophomores** 90% **Total Faculty** 145 **Student Faculty Ratio** 10:1 **Fraternities (% of men participating)** 8 (25%) **Sororities (% of women participating)** 2 (3%)

Lafayette College

Easton, PA · Est. 1826 · Coed · Private · 2,190 Undergrads · Big Town

www.lafayette.edu

How wired is Lafayette?

Do I get email? Yes

Do I get a home page? Yes

Where? www.lafayette.edu/faccipop
/studpers.htm

Is my dorm wired? Yes

What is the student to computer ratio? 9:1

The usual tour

CALENDAR www.lafayette.edu/faccipop
/calendar.htm

DEPARTMENTS www.lafayette.edu/faccipop
/depts.htm

SPORTS www.lafayette.edu/faccipop/sports.htm

STUDENT CLUBS www.lafayette.edu/faccipop
/studorg.htm

STUDENT NEWSPAPER www.lafayette.edu/~paper

LIBRARY www.lafayette.edu/library/home
page.html

Skip the brochure

- **ALTERNATIVE SCHOOL BREAK CLUB** Selfless
Lafayette students spend school breaks work-
ing on volunteer projects instead of their tans.
Recent trips took students to Kentucky and

You ain't seen nothing 'Yette

Arizona as well as to Honduras to lend a hand
in the local community. **www.lafayette.edu/millerg
/asb.html**

- **LAFAYETTE ULTIMATE FRISBEE HOME PAGE** A regula-
tion Ultimate Frisbee field measures 70 yards
by 40 yards, with 25-yard deep end zones.
Now, there's something they don't teach you
in school. Go disc crazy. **www.lafayette.edu/~ultfris**

- **WJRH RADIO 104.9** From witty banter to psyche-
delic mind trips, WJRH has it all covered.
www.lafayette.edu/~wjrh/wjrh.html

- **LAFAYETTE COLLEGE SONGS** Sound like an alum
before you even set foot on campus: practice
the college songs in the privacy of your own
shower. **www.lafayette.edu/faccipop/songs.htm**

WHAT YOU NEED TO GET IN **Application Deadline** January 15 for priority consideration **Early Action Deadline** January 15
Common App. Yes **Application Fee** $40 **Tuition Costs** $20,308 **Room & Board** $6,335 **Need Blind** Yes
Financial Forms Deadline Priority given to applications received by February 15 **Undergrads Awarded Aid** 60%
Aid That Is Need-Based 99% **Average Award of Freshman Scholarship Package** $13,812 **Tests Required** SAT1
(preferred) or ACT **Admissions Address** Easton, PA 18042-1770 **Admissions Telephone** (610) 250-5100

LAST YEAR'S CLASS **Applied** 4,060 **Accepted** 2,423 **Matriculated** 526 **Average SAT M/V** 600/590 **In Top Fifth of
High School Graduating Class** 60% **Applied Early** 163 **Accepted Early** 105

COLLEGE LIFE **Gender Breakdown** M 55%, F 45% **Out of State Students** 74% **From Public Schools** 68% **Ethnic
Composition** White & Other 92.3%, Asian American 3.1%, Black 3.2%, Hispanic 1.3%, Native American 0.1%
Foreign Students 4% **Reside on Campus** 98% **Return as Sophomores** 89% **Total Faculty** 182 **Student Faculty
Ratio** 11:1 **Fraternities (% of men participating)** 11 (11%) **Sororities (% of women participating)** 6 (67%)

Lake Forest College

www.lfc.edu

Lake Forest, IL · Est. 1857 · Coed · Private · 1,011 Undergrads · Urban

I need...

Admissions info www.lfc.edu/www/lfcweb
/catalog/admission.html
Financial aid info www.lfc.edu/www/lfcweb
/catalog/finaid.html

How wired is Lake Forest?

Do I get email? Yes
Do I get a home page? Yes
   Where? www.lfc.edu/www/who/people.html
Is my dorm wired? Yes
What is the student to computer ratio? 5:1

The usual tour

CALENDAR GOPHER://GOPHER.LFC.EDU:70
/11GOPHER_ROOT:[000000.cwis.calendar]
DEPARTMENTS www.lfc.edu/www/lfcweb
/academic/academic.html
LIBRARY www.lfc.edu/www/lfcweb/library
/welcome.html

Skip the brochure

• **INTERNET CONSORTIUM HOMEPAGE** The Internet
Consortium Initiative connects you to the world
around Lake Forest via the Web. Check out the

"Spread your wings, academically speaking."

Well, there's a lake and a forest—what should we call this town?

home pages of other schools and organizations
in the area, including elementary and high
schools **www.lfc.edu/www/lfcweb/icinet/icinet.html**

• **INDEPENDENT SCHOLAR PROGRAM** Spread your
wings, academically speaking. Second-semes-
ter sophomores and first-semester juniors can
apply to be independent scholars and design
their own multidisciplinary degree programs.
**www.lfc.edu/www/lfcweb/catalog/undergrad
/indepscholar.html**

• **PROGRAMS FOR FRESHMEN** No, Freshman Studies
isn't a curricular program where you sit around
talking about what it's like to live away from
home and do your own laundry. Instead, it's a
program that combines advising and instruction for first-year students. Lake Forest also
offers special freshman courses and the
Richter Apprentice Scholar Program which
combines an interdisciplinary seminar with
summer research experience. **www.lfc.edu/www
/lfcweb/catalog/undergrad/progfresh.html**

WHAT YOU NEED TO GET IN **Application Deadline** March 1 for priority consideration **Early Action Deadline** January 1
Common App. Yes **Application Fee** $35 **Tuition Costs** $18,750 **Room & Board** $4,400 **Need Blind** Yes
Financial Forms Deadline Priority given to applications received by March 1 **Undergrads Awarded Aid** 76% **Aid
That Is Need-Based** 94% **Average Award of Freshman Scholarship Package** $13,049 **Tests Required** SAT1 or
ACT **Admissions Address** 555 North Sheridan Road, Lake Forest, IL 60045 **Admissions Telephone** (847)
735-5000

LAST YEAR'S CLASS **Applied** 1,055 **Accepted** 734 **Matriculated** 266 **In Top Fifth of High School Graduating Class**
53% **Applied Early** 117 **Accepted Early** 90

COLLEGE LIFE **Gender Breakdown** M 45%, F 55% **Out of State Students** 67% **From Public Schools** 65% **Ethnic
Composition** White & Other 84%, Asian American 5%, Black 6%, Hispanic 5% **Foreign Students** 5% **Reside on
Campus** 83% **Return as Sophomores** 74% **Total Faculty** 113 **Student Faculty Ratio** 11:1 **Fraternities (% of men
participating)** 4 (21%) **Sororities (% of women participating)** 3 (19%) **Graduate Students** 11

LaSalle University

www.lasalle.edu

Philadelphia, PA · Est. 1863 · Coed · Private · 4,068 Undergrads · Urban

How wired is LaSalle?

Do I get email? Yes
Do I get a home page? Yes
Where? www.lasalle.edu/hpgs/hpgs.htm
Is my dorm wired? Yes
What is the student to computer ratio? 18:1

The usual tour

SPORTS www.lasalle.edu/athletic/athletic.htm
CALENDAR www.lasalle.edu/bboard/bboard.htm
LIBRARY www.lasalle.edu/library/home.htm
STUDENT CLUBS www.lasalle.edu/gen-info
/stulif.htm
DEPARTMENTS www.lasalle.edu/gen-info
/acdchoic.htm

Skip the brochure

- **CRIMINAL JUSTICE PROGRAM** The LaSalle faculty thinks it would be criminal if you didn't learn about the justice system. www.lasalle.edu/academ/original/cjustbro.htm

- **HIGH-POWERED CONNECTIONS AND OUTCOMES** It's not just what you study, but who you meet. Learn that secret handshake and watch your career take off. www.lasalle.edu/gen-info/hpowco.htm

Go to college and major in collage at LaSalle

- **THE CHRISTIAN BROTHERS** They're not just teachers, but brothers, too, with a commitment to providing a value-centered education grounded in practicality, and the church, of course. www.lasalle.edu/gen-info/brothers.htm

- **SPECIAL COLLECTIONS** A special library collection entitled "Imaginative Representations of the Vietnam War" offers an in-depth look at the way in which the events of the Vietnam War were interpreted in creative media. www.lasalle.edu/library/vietnam.htm

"It's not just what you study, but who you meet."

Lawrence Technological University

Southfield, MI · Est. 1932 · Coed · Private · 3,651 Undergrads · Urban

I need...

Admissions info www.ltu.edu/htm/adm.htm
Financial aid info www.ltu.edu/htm/adm.htm

How wired is Lawrence Tech?

Do I get a home page? No
Is my dorm wired? No
What is the student to computer ratio? 9:1

The usual tour

STUDENT CLUBS www.ltu.edu/htm/other.htm
CAMPUS MAP www.ltu.edu/images/campus.gif

Skip the brochure

- **FUTURECAR AND THE HYBRID ELECTRIC VEHICLE**
Lawrence Tech students are motoring into the future with Response II, a hybrid auto with both an internal combustion engine and an electric motor. Will they meet the challenge of developing an electric vehicle that gets 80 miles to the gallon? Watch this space.
www.ltu.edu/htm/hev.htm

- **FRANK LLOYD WRIGHT AFFLECK HOUSE** If you thought there was no important modern architecture in Southfield, Michigan, you were wrong. Have you ever heard of a little architectural tinkerer named Frank Lloyd Wright? Explore the house that Wright built for Gregor

Location: http://www.ltu.edu/htm/aff.htm

The Gregor S. and Elizabeth B. Affleck House, designed by **Frank Lloyd Wright** and completed in 1941, was donated to the University in 1978 by the late Afflecks' children. The home has been restored by the University and is located in the nearby City of Bloomfield Hills. It is considered an outstanding example of Wright's efforts to design an innovative, highly livable home affordable by the "middle class" and situated in harmony with its natural surroundings.

Visit a Frank Lloyd Wright house in Southfield

S. and Elizabeth B. Affleck, which was donated to the University in 1978. This site has only one measly photo, and yet there's still a distinctive Wright vibe. **www.ltu.edu/htm/aff.htm**

"Will they meet the challenge of developing a vehicle that gets 80 miles to the gallon?"

WHAT YOU NEED TO GET IN Application Deadline August 1 **Common App.** Yes **Application Fee** $30 **Tuition Costs** $8,992 **Room & Board** $2,457 **Financial Forms Deadline** Priority given to applications received by March 1 **Undergrads Awarded Aid** 60% **Aid That Is Need-Based** 85% **Average Award of Freshman Scholarship Package** $3,100 **Tests Required** SAT1 or ACT (preferred) **Admissions Address** 21000 West Ten Mile Road, Southfield, MI 48075 **Admissions Telephone** (810) 204-3160

LAST YEAR'S CLASS Applied 1,951 **Accepted** 1,726 **Matriculated** 928 **Average ACT** 22 **In Top Quarter of High School Graduating Class** 51%

COLLEGE LIFE Gender Breakdown M 77%, F 23% **Ethnic Composition** White & Other 86%, Asian American 3%, Black 9%, Hispanic 1%, Native American 1% **Reside on Campus** 7% **Return as Sophomores** 60% **Student Faculty Ratio** 20:1 **Fraternities (% of men participating)** 5 (1%) **Sororities (% of women participating)** 3 (1%) **Graduate Students** 502.

Lehigh University

Bethlehem, PA · Est. 1865 · Coed · Private · 4,357 Undergrads · Urban

www.lehigh.edu

I need...

Admissions info inado@lehigh.edu
www.lehigh.edu/~innmr/view/view.html
Financial aid info www.lehigh.edu/~innmr/view
/glance.html#finances

REQUEST APPLICATION ONLINE

How wired is Lehigh?

Do I get a home page? Yes
Is my dorm wired? Yes
What is the student to computer ratio? 9:1

The usual tour

VIRTUAL TOUR www.lehigh.edu/~inclass/tour
/tour.html
DEPARTMENTS www.lehigh.edu/~innmr/view
/major1.html
STUDY ABROAD www.lehigh.edu/~innmr/view
/glance.html#abroad
SPORTS www.lehigh.edu/~www/sports
/welcome.html
STUDENT CLUBS www.lehigh.edu/~www/people
/student_center/student_orgs.html
STUDENT NEWSPAPER www.lehigh.edu/~inbrw
/inbrw.html
CALENDAR luna.cc.lehigh.edu/EVENTS

Skip the brochure

• **THE SPIRIT OF LEHIGH** A feast of sights, sounds,
and speech celebrates Lehigh University: an
1891 text entitled "Walls in Ivy Dressed" by
John J. Gibson is accompanied by photo-

Mustard & Cheese Drama Society

No doubt the ideal condiments for a stage full of hams

graphs and college songs. www.lehigh.edu
/~innmr/leaf/page1.html

• **THE LEHIGH MOUNTAIN HAWK** It took 130 years of
careful deliberation to come up with Lehigh's
official mascot. See the hawk in all its splen-
dor. www.lehigh.edu/inlab/public/hawkdir/mhawk.html

• **CREDIBLE JOURNEYS** The *Alumni Bulletin* chronicles the adventures and accomplishments of
Lehigh's alumni and its 25 years of coeduca-
tional history. www.lehigh.edu/inlab/public/www-data
/s96/feature2.html

• **MUSTARD & CHEESE DRAMA SOCIETY** Serving up
dramatic fare and flair since 1884, it's
Lehigh's Mustard & Cheese Society. www.lehigh
.edu/~inmac/m&c.html

"It took 130 years to come up with Lehigh's offical mascot."

WHAT YOU NEED TO GET IN **Application Deadline** January 1 for priority consideration; final deadline February 15 **Early Action Deadline** December 1 or January 15 **Common App.** Yes **Application Fee** $40 **Tuition Costs** $20,500 **Room & Board** $6,020 **Need Blind** No **Financial Forms Deadline** Priority given to applications received by February 15 **Undergrads Awarded Aid** 58% **Aid That Is Need-Based** 98% **Average Award of Freshman Scholarship Package** $11,625 **Tests Required** SAT1 or ACT **Admissions Address** Bethlehem, PA 18015-3035 **Admissions Telephone** (610) 758-3100

LAST YEAR'S CLASS **Applied** 6,483 **Accepted** 3,870 **Matriculated** 1,046 **Median Range SAT M/V** 590-680/550-640 **In Top Fifth of High School Graduating Class** 75% **Applied Early** 360 **Accepted Early** 244

COLLEGE LIFE **Gender Breakdown** M 63%, F 37% **Out of State Students** 70% **From Public Schools** 70% **Ethnic Composition** White & Other 89.4%, Asian American 5.2%, Black 3.1%, Hispanic 2.2%, Native American 0.1% **Foreign Students** 3% **Reside on Campus** 75% **Return as Sophomores** 90% **Total Faculty** 413 **Student Faculty Ratio** 11:1 **Fraternities (% of men participating)** 28 (42%) **Sororities (% of women participating)** 7 (37%) **Graduate Students** 1,898

LeMoyne College

Syracuse, NY · Est. 1946 · Coed · Private · 2,177 Undergrads · Urban

 www.lemoyne.edu

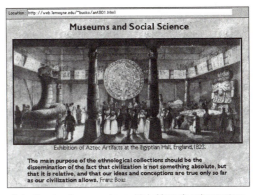

Museums and Social Science

Exhibition of Aztec Artifacts at the Egyptian Hall, England, 1823.

The main purpose of the ethnological collections should be the dissemination of the fact that civilization is not something absolute, but that it is relative, and that our ideas and conceptions are true only so far as our civilization allows. Franz Boas

Take the grand museum tour with LeMoyne's cybercurators

I need...

Admissions info www.lemoyne.edu/admiss.html

How wired is LeMoyne?

Do I get email? Yes
Do I get a home page? Yes
  Where? web.lemoyne.edu/www/local
  _home_pages.html
Is my dorm wired? Yes
What is the student to computer ratio? 15:1

The usual tour

DEPARTMENTS www.lemoyne.edu/services.html
CALENDAR www.lemoyne.edu/calendars
  _menu.html
CAREER CENTER www.lemoyne.edu/career.html

Skip the brochure

- **VIRTUAL MUSEUMS PAGE** An impressive and eclectic collection of nine virtual museums created by LeMoyne students for a Museums and Social Science course during Fall 1995. Exhibits teach about Syracuse's role in the manufacture of typewriters, the social history of *Archie* comics, and much more. **web.lemoyne.edu/~bucko/ant301.html**
- **CAMPUS MINISTRY HOME PAGE** Whether holding mass, organizing retreats, or offering pastoral counseling, the LeMoyne ministry is a guiding force at the school. **maple.lemoyne.edu/~xgreerdj/index.html**

- **NARRATIVE PSYCHOLOGY** A collection of material for LeMoyne's Narrative Psychology Proseminar, this is also an in-depth source of information about the field of narrative psychology, with an annotated guide to bibliographical resources. **maple.lemoyne.edu/~hevern/narpsych.html**
- **DEPARTMENT OF PHYSICS** A professional baseball player and a commodities trader number among LeMoyne graduates who majored in physics/engineering. Maybe viewing the variety of professions now held will pique your interest in reading an overview of the program. **web.lemoyne.edu/www_root/documents/cwis/academic_affairs/academic_departments/physics/physics.htm**

"An impressive collection of virtual museums"

WHAT YOU NEED TO GET IN Application Deadline February 1 for priority consideration; final deadline March 15 **Early Action Deadline** December 1 **Common App.** No **Application Fee** $25 **Tuition Costs** $12,390 **Room & Board** $5,390 **Financial Forms Deadline** April 15 with a priority given to applications received by February 15 **Undergrads Awarded Aid** 90% **Aid That Is Need-Based** 80% **Average Award of Freshman Scholarship Package** $8,000 **Tests Required** SAT1 or ACT **Admissions Address** Syracuse, NY 13214 **Admissions Telephone** (315) 445-4300

LAST YEAR'S CLASS Applied 1,719 **Accepted** 1,344 **Matriculated** 403 **Median Range SAT M/V** 490-590/490-590 **In Top Fifth of High School Graduating Class** 50% **Applied Early** 122 **Accepted Early** 100

COLLEGE LIFE Gender Breakdown M 41%, F 59% **Out of State Students** 13% **From Public Schools** 73% **Ethnic Composition** White & Other 90%, Asian American 1%, Black 4%, Hispanic 4%, Native American 1% **Foreign Students** 1% **Reside on Campus** 74% **Return as Sophomores** 88% **Total Faculty** 212 **Student Faculty Ratio** 13:1 **Fraternities** none **Sororities** none **Graduate Students** 616

Lenoir-Rhyne College

www.lrc.edu

Hickory, NC · Est. 1891 · Coed · Private · 1,429 Undergrads · Big Town

I need...

Admissions info www.lrc.edu/www/home/admis
.html

How wired is Lenoir-Rhyne?

Do I get email? Yes
Do I get a home page? No
Is my dorm wired? No
What is the student to computer ratio? 11:1

The usual tour

STUDENT CLUBS www.lrc.edu/www/home
/organs.html
SPORTS www.lrc.edu/www/home/Sports.html
DEPARTMENTS www.lrc.edu/www/departments
/departments.html
CALENDAR www.lrc.edu/www/home/news.html
LIBRARY www.lrc.edu/www/library/library3.htm
GREEK LIFE www.lrc.edu/www/home/organs.html

Skip the brochure

• **ADMINISTRATION** Meet the president at this site.
It appears that the estimable Dr. LaHurd has
his elbow jammed between the T and the U
volumes of the *World Book Encyclopedia.*
www.lrc.edu/www/home/admin.html

• **SPORTS** What can be deduced from this essay
page describing the latest athletic news from
Hickory? Not much, but, there are baseball,
softball, basketball and soccer teams at
Lenoir-Rhyne. If other sports are played, they

Lenoir-Rhyne, located in the furniture capital of N.C., is a
comfortable place to be

aren't mentioned in this cybernewsletter.
www.lrc.edu/www/home/Sports.html

• **STUDENT ORGANIZATIONS** The blasé roster of
student organizations at Lenoir-Rhyne isn't
exactly bursting at the seams with information
or innovation. It plainly lists the standard clubs,
like SEAC (Student Environmental Action
Coalition), Amnesty International, and Circle K.
One does sound a bit different—the Bear-
tracking Club—although what it is and what it
does remains a mystery. **www.lrc.edu/www/home
/organs.html**

"The Beartracking Club remains a total mystery."

WHAT YOU NEED TO GET IN **Application Deadline** January 1 for priority consideration; final deadline August 1 **Common App.** No **Application Fee** $25 (may be waived in cases of economic hardship) **Tuition Costs** $10,980 **Room & Board** $4,324 **Need Blind** Yes **Financial Forms Deadline** Priority given to applications received by March 1 **Undergrads Awarded Aid** 100% **Aid That Is Need-Based** 60% **Average Award of Freshman Scholarship Package** $2,400 **Tests Required** SAT1 (preferred) or ACT **Admissions Address** Hickory, NC 28603 **Admissions Telephone** (704) 328-7300

LAST YEAR'S CLASS **Applied** 1,064 **Accepted** 910 **Matriculated** 292 **Average SAT M/V** 475/428 **Average ACT** 21 **In Top Fifth of High School Graduating Class** 37%

COLLEGE LIFE **Gender Breakdown** M 39%, F 61% **Out of State Students** 49% **From Public Schools** 89% **Ethnic Composition** White & Other 91%, Asian American 2%, Black 5%, Hispanic 2% **Foreign Students** 1% **Reside on Campus** 70% **Return as Sophomores** 88% **Total Faculty** 111 **Student Faculty Ratio** 12:1 **Fraternities (% of men participating)** 4 (30%) **Sororities (% of women participating)** 4 (35%) **Graduate Students** 126

Lewis & Clark College

www.lclark.edu

Portland, OR · Est. 1867 · Coed · Private · 1,837 Undergrads · Urban

I need...

Admissions info admissions@lclark.edu
www.lclark.edu/COLLEGE/ADMIS/index.html
Financial aid info sfs@lclark.edu
www.lclark.edu/COLLEGE/FINAN/index.html

How wired is Lewis & Clark?

Do I get email? Yes
Do I get a home page? Yes
Where? www.lclark.edu/GENERAL/PERSO
/U.student.html
Is my dorm wired? Yes
What is the student to computer ratio? 13:1

The usual tour

VIRTUAL TOUR www.lclark.edu/VISIT/index.html
CALENDAR www.lclark.edu/~public/CALENDAR
/events/calendar.html
DEPARTMENTS www.lclark.edu/COLLEGE/DEPAR
/index.html
SPORTS www.lclark.edu/COLLEGE/DEPAR
/ATHB/index.html
LIBRARY www.lclark.edu/~refdesk
STUDENT CLUBS www.lclark.edu/GENERAL/PERSO
/U.org.html
STUDENT NEWSPAPER www.lclark.edu/~piolog

Skip the brochure

• **WHERE ARE THEY NOW?** They used to be athletes
at Lewis & Clark. Where are they now? See for
yourself. **www.lclark.edu/COLLEGE/DEPAR
/ATHB/athbroc6.html**

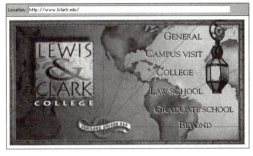

Map out your future at Lewis & Clark

• **INSTITUTE FOR PHILOSOPHICAL PLEASURE** "The
Institute for Philosophical Pleasure (a.k.a. The
Philosophy Club) exists to provide an arena for
stimulating discussion, socialization, and
uhhhh, well, a place to have fun." Just don't
forget your thinking cap. **www.lclark.edu/~ipp**

• **SKI TEAM AND CLUB** Explore the slopes of the
Pacific Northwest with fellow undergrads and
graduate students from Lewis & Clark.
www.lclark.edu/~skiteam

• **PHILLIS YES** View a lace-covered Porsche and
other works of art by Phillis Yes, Lewis &
Clark's Dean of Arts and Humanities and
Professor of Art. **www.lclark.edu/~art/phyllis.html**

"Explore the slopes of the Pacific Northwest with fellow undergrads."

WHAT YOU NEED TO GET IN **Application Deadline** February 1 for priority consideration **Early Action Deadline** November
15 **Common App.** Yes **Application Fee** $45 (may be waived) **Tuition Costs** $17,560 **Room & Board** $5,780
Need Blind Yes **Financial Forms Deadline** Priority given to applications received by March 1 **Undergrads
Awarded Aid** 64% **Aid That Is Need-Based** 85% **Average Award of Freshman Scholarship Package** $9,734
Tests Required SAT1 or ACT **Admissions Address** 0615 S.W. Palatine Hill Road, Portland, OR 97219-7899
Admissions Telephone (503) 768-7040

LAST YEAR'S CLASS **Applied** 3,011 **Accepted** 2,317 **Matriculated** 458 **Median Range SAT M/V** 550-650/560-670
In Top Fifth of High School Graduating Class 59% **Applied Early** 42 **Accepted Early** 38

COLLEGE LIFE **Gender Breakdown** M 43%, F 57% **Out of State Students** 79% **From Public Schools** 73% **Ethnic
Composition** White & Other 84%, Asian American 10%, Black 2%, Hispanic 3%, Native American 1% **Foreign
Students** 6% **Reside on Campus** 55% **Return as Sophomores** 76% **Total Faculty** 151 **Student Faculty Ratio**
13:1 **Fraternities** none **Sororities** none **Graduate Students** 1,466

Long Island University, C.W. Post Campus

www.liunet.edu/cwis/post.html

Brookville, NY · Est. 1954 · Coed · Private · 4,447 Undergrads · Big Town

I need...

Admissions info admissions@collegehall.liunet.edu
www.liunet.edu/../cwis/cwp/cwpphone.html

How wired is Long Island U?

Do I get email? Yes
Do I get a home page? No
What is the student to computer ratio? 11:1

The usual tour

LIBRARY www.liunet.edu/../cwis/cwp/library
/libhome.htm
STUDY ABROAD www.liunet.edu/cwis
/international/intindex.html
GREEK LIFE www.liunet.edu/studentact/grek.htm
STUDENT CLUBS www.liunet.edu/studentact
/cl.htm
DEPARTMENTS www.liunet.edu/cwis/post.html

Skip the brochure

• **CULTURAL ORGANIZATIONS** Though most of the clubs' pages listed are under construction, one can at least get a sense of the diversity quotient at Long Island University. Africans, Indo-Pakistanis, Caribbeans, Japanese, and many more have contact info for their own respective associations.
www.liunet.edu/studentact/cult.htm

The C.W. Post page is straightforward and informative, with Tudor flair

• **ARTS ORGANIZATIONS** It's not clear why there's a photograph of three Long Island University women here, but this index of Arts Organizations lists a Graphic Design Association, a radio station, a theater troupe, a jazz club, and a number of singing groups. **www.liunet.edu /studentact/arts.htm**

"Africans, Indo-Pakistanis, Caribbeans, Japanese, and more have their own cultural entities here."

WHAT YOU NEED TO GET IN **Application Deadline** Rolling admissions **Early Action Deadline** rolling **Common App.** No **Application Fee** $30 **Tuition Costs** $12,430 **Room & Board** $5,880 **Financial Forms Deadline** Priority given to applications received by May 15 **Undergrads Awarded Aid** 75% **Aid That Is Need-Based** 55% **Average Award of Freshman Scholarship Package** $3,500 **Tests Required** SAT1 (preferred) or ACT **Admissions Address** 720 Northern Boulevard, Brookville, NY 11548-1300 **Admissions Telephone** (516) 299-2413

LAST YEAR'S CLASS **Applied** 3,500 **Accepted** 2,964 **Matriculated** 680 **Average SAT M/V** 505/458 **In Top Fifth of High School Graduating Class** 20%

COLLEGE LIFE **Gender Breakdown** M 42%, F 58% **Out of State Students** 10% **From Public Schools** 81% **Ethnic Composition** White & Other 81.1%, Asian American 4%, Black 7.9%, Hispanic 5.8%, Native American 1.2% **Foreign Students** 2% **Reside on Campus** 30% **Return as Sophomores** 69% **Total Faculty** 100 **Student Faculty Ratio** 10:1 **Fraternities (% of men participating)** 10 (6%) **Sororities (% of women participating)** 10 (4%) **Graduate Students** 3,413

Louisiana State University

www.lsu.edu

Baton Rouge, LA · Est. 1860 · Coed · Public · 20,374 Undergrads · Urban

I need...

Admissions info unix1.sncc.lsu.edu/prospective
/requirements.html

How wired is LSU?

Do I get email? Yes
Do I get a home page? No
Is my dorm wired? No
What is the student to computer ratio? 4:1

The usual tour

DEPARTMENTS unix1.sncc.lsu.edu/prospective
/majors.html
CALENDAR gopher://lsumvs.sncc.lsu.edu
/1GOPHER.LSUMVS.MENU%28UCE%29
STUDENT CLUBS unix1.sncc.lsu.edu/students
/index.html
LIBRARY www.lib.lsu.edu/index.html
STUDENT NEWSPAPER www.lsu.edu/guests
/revedit/public_html
HISTORY AND GENERAL INFORMATION unix1
.sncc.lsu.edu/visitor/LSU/index.html

Skip the brochure

- **ANIME & CULTURE SOCIETY @ LSU** *Metal Skin Panic
2* up your alley? Seen *Fist of the Northstar*? Or
perhaps you just want *Street Fighter II: The
Movie*. This is only a small selection of the
society's frequent film screenings. **www.lsu.edu
/guests/anime**

- **LSU KARATE CLUB HOME PAGE** Get rid of your

LSU's one and only anime organization needs a summer
vacation, just like everyone else

aggression with a few quick moves, illustrated
for your convenience. **www.phys.lsu.edu/dept
/lsukarate/karateb.html**

- **LSU STUDENT GOVERNMENT HOME PAGE** Take me to
your leaders! Student government at LSU is
serious stuff, complete with executive, legislative, and judicial branches. Perfect for students with gripes, this home page provides
lists of who's who in the student government,
so you'll always know where to direct your
complaints. **www.lsu.edu/guests/emonday/public_html**

- **HIGHLIGHTS ABOUT LSU** Subtitled "Things to brag
about," this compilation of information is perfect for anyone who says "LS Who?" when you
mention your school of choice. **unixl.sncc.lsu
.edu/visitor/LSU/brag94.html**

WHAT YOU NEED TO GET IN **Application Deadline** June 1 **Common App.** No **Application Fee** $25 **Tuition Costs** $2,663
($5,963 out-of-state) **Room & Board** $3,610 **Need Blind** Yes **Undergrads Awarded Aid** 60% **Aid That Is Need-
Based** 39% **Average Award of Freshman Scholarship Package** $3,325 **Tests Required** SAT1 or ACT (preferred)
Admissions Address Baton Rouge, LA 70803-2750 **Admissions Telephone** (504) 388-1175

LAST YEAR'S CLASS **Applied** 6,886 **Accepted** 5,536 **Matriculated** 3,428 **Average ACT** 23 **In Top Fifth of High School
Graduating Class** 45%

COLLEGE LIFE **Gender Breakdown** M 49%, F 51% **Out of State Students** 13% **Ethnic Composition** White & Other
85%, Asian American 4%, Black 9%, Hispanic 2% **Foreign Students** 3% **Reside on Campus** 22% **Return as
Sophomores** 78% **Total Faculty** 1,435 **Student Faculty Ratio** 18:1 **Fraternities (% of men participating)** 20
(14%) **Sororities (% of women participating)** 15 (15%) **Graduate Students** 5,523

University of Louisville

www.louisville.edu

Louisville, KY · Est. 1798 · Coed · Public · 15,189 Undergrads · Urban

I need...

Admissions info admitme@ulkyvm.louisville.edu
   www.louisville.edu/groups/admis-ao-www
Financial aid info www.louisville.edu/financial.aid
   .html

How wired is University of Louisville?

Do I get email? Yes
Do I get a home page? Yes
Is my dorm wired? Yes
What is the student to computer ratio? 15:1

The usual tour

DEPARTMENTS www.louisville.edu/home/schools
   -depts.html
LIBRARY www.louisville.edu/library
CALENDAR gopher://ULKYVM.LOUISVILLE.EDU
   :70/11/uofl/ulinfo/cap
SPORTS www.louisville.edu/athletics
VIRTUAL TOUR www.louisville.edu/ur/onpi
   /tourmenu.html
CAREER CENTER gopher://ULKYVM.LOUISVILLE
   .EDU:70/11/uofl/ulinfo/co

Skip the brochure

• **RAUCH MEMORIAL PLANETARIUM** See what's in the stars for you at the Rauch site, which has a monthly celestial guide and history of the planetarium. **www.louisville.edu/~jsmill01**

• **A BRIEF HISTORY** The steam engine and medical education have played a significant role in this

Enjoy bluegrass culture, deep thought, and a burgeoning arts scene at the U of L

school's history. This site tells the story of the University of Louisville from the B.Y. (Before You) era. **www.louisville.edu/home/temp/history.html**

• **WUOL 90.5 FM** Thanks to the Public Radio Partnership and the University of Louisville, you can set your dial for classical music. Remember, studies have shown that listening to classical music increases academic performance. **www.wuol.org**

• **LOUISVILLE** If all you know about Kentucky has to do with a certain bearded colonel and lots of pieces of deep-fried poultry, you have a lot to learn. Louisville is the largest city in Kentucky, and its historic inhabitants include Cherokees and a concentrated German population. Explore it at this cute site replete with Southern charm. **www.iglou.com/lou**

WHAT YOU NEED TO GET IN **Application Deadline** Rolling admissions **Common App.** No **Application Fee** $25 **Tuition Costs** $2,340 ($7,020 out-of-state) **Room & Board** $3800 **Need Blind** Yes **Financial Forms Deadline** Priority given to applications received by April 15 **Undergrads Awarded Aid** 55% **Aid That Is Need-Based** 60% **Average Award of Freshman Scholarship Package** $800 **Tests Required** SAT1 or ACT (preferred) **Admissions Address** Houchens Building, Louisville, KY 40292 **Admissions Telephone** (502) 852-6531

LAST YEAR'S CLASS **Applied** 5,136 **Accepted** 3,335 **Matriculated** 1,893 **Average ACT** 22 **In Top Quarter of High School Graduating Class** 41%

COLLEGE LIFE **Gender Breakdown** M 47%, F 53% **Out of State Students** 7% **Ethnic Composition** White & Other 82.8%, Asian American 2.6%, Black 13.1%, Hispanic 1.2%, Native American 0.3% **Foreign Students** 2% **Reside on Campus** 10% **Return as Sophomores** 70% **Total Faculty** 1,763 **Student Faculty Ratio** 11:1 **Fraternities** 16 **Sororities** 10 **Graduate Students** 4,152

Loyola University, Chicago

www.luc.edu

Chicago, IL · Est. 1870 · Coed · Private · 7,978 Undergrads · Urban

I need...

Admissions info admission@luc.edu
www.luc.edu/depts/undadmis

How wired is Loyola?

Do I get email? Yes
Do I get a home page? Yes
Is my dorm wired? Yes
What is the student to computer ratio? 25:1

The usual tour

VIRTUAL TOUR www.luc.edu/photos
DEPARTMENTS www.luc.edu/depts
STUDENT CLUBS www.luc.edu/orgs/student.html
SPORTS www.luc.edu/depts/athletics
STUDENT NEWSPAPER www.luc.edu/orgs/phoenix
LIBRARY www.luc.edu/libraries

Skip the brochure

• **THE LOYOLA FRESHMAN EXPERIENCE** Getting to know all about you means getting to know all about the freshman orientation experience. **www.luc.edu/depts/fe**

• **CHICAGO INFORMATION** Loyola links you to information about your new hometown. Chicago happenings, weather, and public transportation are all covered. **www.luc.edu/info/chicago.html**

• **THE LUCKI CLUB HOMEPAGE** Loyola University's Circle K International Homepage promotes the activities of Circle K International, "the largest collegiate community service organization in

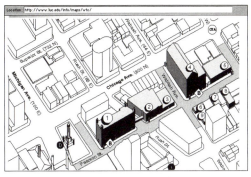

Get a VR flavor of Loyola via a number of cool maps

the world." **www.luc.edu/orgs/circlek/index2.html**

• **SOLO CHALLENGER** On Jan. 8, 1996, Steve Fossett became the first man to attempt to circumnavigate the earth non-stop in a balloon. The Solo Challenger, Loyola's flight information Web site, provides details, photos, flight updates, and an Ask the Pilot section. **www.luc.edu/solo/index.html**

"Learn what awaits you in the freshman orientation experience."

WHAT YOU NEED TO GET IN **Application Deadline** April 1 for priority consideration; final deadline July 9 **Common App.** No **Application Fee** $25 **Tuition Costs** $14,400 **Room & Board** $6,500 **Need Blind** Yes **Financial Forms Deadline** Priority given to applications received by March 1 **Undergrads Awarded Aid** 75% **Aid That Is Need-Based** 65% **Average Award of Freshman Scholarship Package** $7,525 **Tests Required** SAT1 or ACT **Admissions Address** 820 North Michigan Avenue, Chicago, IL 60611 **Admissions Telephone** (312) 915-6500

LAST YEAR'S CLASS **Applied** 3,812 **Accepted** 3,285 **Matriculated** 1,186 **Average SAT M/V** 557/502 **Average ACT** 24 **In Top Fifth of High School Graduating Class** 53%

COLLEGE LIFE **Gender Breakdown** M 37%, F 63% **Out of State Students** 26% **From Public Schools** 60% **Ethnic Composition** White & Other 73.6%, Asian American 14.4%, Black 4.5%, Hispanic 7.3%, Native American 0.2% **Foreign Students** 1% **Reside on Campus** 30% **Return as Sophomores** 82% **Student Faculty Ratio** 13:1 **Fraternities (% of men participating)** 6 (8%) **Sororities (% of women participating)** 9 (7%) **Graduate Students** 6,023

Macalester College

St. Paul, MN · Est. 1874 · Coed · Private · 1,768 Undergrads · Urban

I need...

Admissions info admissions@macalstr.edu
www.macalester.edu/~admissns
Financial aid info admissions@macalstr.edu
www.macalester.edu/~admissns/finaid
/finaid.htm

How wired is Macalester?

Do I get email? Yes
Do I get a home page? Yes
  Where? www.macalester.edu
  /~admissns/collaborations
Is my dorm wired? Yes
What is the student to computer ratio? 5:1

REQUEST APPLICATION ONLINE

The usual tour

SPORTS www.macalester.edu/~athletic
/home page.html
CAREER CENTER www.macalester.edu/~cdc
LIBRARY www.macalester.edu /~library
COMPUTER AND TECHNOLOGY CENTER www
.macalester.edu/~cit

Skip the brochure

• **THE NEIGHBORHOOD AND THE CITIES** Macalester
lies between St. Paul and Minneapolis. St.
Paul is famous for beer brewing; in 1995 it
was also rated the third best American city to
live in. Minneapolis, home of the Artist
Formerly Known as Prince, has a glowing reputation for diversity and safety. Check out how

Macalester counts among its alums National Book Award winner Tim O'Brien

the school fits between these two towns.
**www.macalester.edu/~admissns/twin_cities
/twincit.htm**

• **PORTRAITS** Meet Macalester faculty and students like American Book Award Winner Diane
Glancy, who teaches Native-American literature
and creative writing. **www.macalester.edu/~admissns
/collaborations**

• **MACALESTER ALUMNI ACHIEVERS** National Book
Award winner Tim O'Brien went to Macalester.
So did lots of other people; find out who,
when, and where they are now. **www.macalester
.edu/~admissns/graduates/alumni.htm**

"St. Paul is famous for beer brewing."

WHAT YOU NEED TO GET IN **Application Deadline** January 15 **Early Action Deadline** November 15 and January 1
Common App. Yes **Application Fee** $40 **Tuition Costs** $17,580 **Room & Board** $5,275 **Need Blind** Yes
Financial Forms Deadline March 1 with a priority given to applications received by February 1 **Undergrads
Awarded Aid** 79% **Aid That Is Need-Based** 97% **Average Award of Freshman Scholarship Package** $10,793
Tests Required SAT1 or ACT **Admissions Address** 1600 Grand Avenue, St. Paul, MN 55105 **Admissions
Telephone** (612) 696-6357

LAST YEAR'S CLASS **Applied** 2,880 **Accepted** 1,562 **Matriculated** 437 **Median Range SAT M/V** 620-700/550-660
In Top Fifth of High School Graduating Class 83% **Applied Early** 167 **Accepted Early** 118

COLLEGE LIFE **Gender Breakdown** M 45%, F 55% **Out of State Students** 77% **From Public Schools** 71% **Ethnic
Composition** White & Other 86%, Asian American 5%, Black 4%, Hispanic 4%, Native American 1% **Foreign
Students** 13% **Reside on Campus** 66% **Return as Sophomores** 88% **Total Faculty** 208 **Student Faculty Ratio**
11:1 **Fraternities** none **Sororities** none

University of Maine

Orono, ME · Est. 1865 · Coed · Public · 6,843 Undergrads · Big Town

I need...

Admissions info um_admit@maine.maine.edu
www.ume.maine.edu/~umadmit
Financial aid info cardinal.umeais.maine.edu
/~stuaid/main.html

How wired is the University of Maine?

Do I get email? Yes
Do I get a home page? Yes
Where? maine.maine.edu/hp.html
Is my dorm wired? Yes
What is the student to computer ratio? 27:1

The usual tour

DEPARTMENTS www.ume.maine.edu/~umadmit
/collmaj.html#18
CAREER CENTER www.umeais.maine.edu/~career
LIBRARY libinfo.ume.maine.edu
STUDENT CLUBS www.ume.maine.edu/studentlife
.html
VIRTUAL TOUR www.ume.maine.edu/~paffairs
/maptour/UMaineMap.html
CALENDAR www.ume.maine.edu/newsevents
.html

"Maine has an overabundance of natural beauty."

The Maine Center for the Arts

Take a look at "the cultural focus of the University of Maine"

Skip the brochure

- **MAINE CENTER FOR THE ARTS** What is the art scene like in Orono, Maine? Explore the MCA, "the cultural focus of the University of Maine campus and the surrounding region." With a Concert Hall, Museum, and Gallery, the MCA is well-equipped to keep the campus artistically satiated. **www.ume.maine.edu/~mca**

- **CAMPUS LIVING TELEVISION** The University of Maine has its own television cable system, and of course its own channel where student programs are broadcast. **www.ume.maine.edu/~clvs/cltvn/clvshmel.htm**

- **ACADIA NATIONAL PARK** Maine has an overabundance of natural beauty; Acadia National Park is just one of the stunning places to go. With one of the few sandy beaches in Northern Maine, and a series of granite cliffs and fjords, Acadia offers particularly spectacular camping venues. **www.state.me.us/decd/tour/newacad.html**

WHAT YOU NEED TO GET IN **Application Deadline** December 1 for priority consideration; final deadline February 1 **Common App.** No **Application Fee** $25 **Tuition Costs** $4,146 ($10,686 out-of-state) **Room & Board** $4,820 **Financial Forms Deadline** Priority given to applications received by March 1 **Undergrads Awarded Aid** 75% **Aid That Is Need-Based** 60% **Average Award of Freshman Scholarship Package** $3,043 **Tests Required** SAT1 (preferred) or ACT **Admissions Address** Orono, ME 04469 **Admissions Telephone** (207) 581-1561

LAST YEAR'S CLASS **Applied** 3,602 **Accepted** 3,024 **Matriculated** 1,152 **Average SAT M/V** 530/470 **In Top Fifth of High School Graduating Class** 43%

COLLEGE LIFE **Gender Breakdown** M 52%, F 48% **Out of State Students** 26% **Ethnic Composition** White & Other 96%, Asian American 1.5%, Black 0.7%, Hispanic 0.4%, Native American 1.4% **Foreign Students** 2% **Reside on Campus** 52% **Return as Sophomores** 76% **Total Faculty** 647 **Student Faculty Ratio** 14:1 **Fraternities (% of men participating)** 12 (6%) **Sororities (% of women participating)** 7 (4%) **Graduate Students** 2,266

Marlboro College

www.marlboro.edu

Marlboro, VT · Est. 1946 · Coed · Private · 262 Undergrads · Rural

How wired is Marlboro?

Do I get email? Yes
Do I get a home page? Yes
   Where? www.marlboro.edu/pages/individuals.html
Is my dorm wired? Yes
What is the student to computer ratio? 9:1

REQUEST APPLICATION ONLINE

The usual tour

DEPARTMENTS www.marlboro.edu/pages/AreasOfStudy.html
LIBRARY www.marlboro.edu/#library
PUBLICATIONS www.marlboro.edu/pr/news/pubs.html
CALENDAR www.marlboro.edu/pr/news/events.html

Skip the brochure

- **THE OUTDOOR PROGRAM** Spelunkers, pull on your helmets. With Marlboro's Outdoor Program you can delight in potholes and caves, that is, if you have time between rock climbing, cross-country skiing, canoeing, white water rafting, backpacking, snowshoeing, mountain biking,

If you get tired of Marboro's pretty campus, go under-gound—or abroad

hang gliding, kayaking, skydiving, downhill skiing, ice climbing, scuba diving, and animal tracking. **www.marlboro.edu/pr/op.html**

- **THE WORLD STUDIES PROGRAM** If Marlboro starts to feel a bit too small, leave. The World Studies Program is a four-year course of study that allows students to concentrate on their particular international interests, and also encourages a six- to eight-month working internship overseas. **www.marlboro.edu/pr/wsp.html**

- **THE FRED PICKER PHOTOGRAPHY WORKSHOP** Marlboro, Vt. is pretty enough to inspire the inner photographer in everyone. Plus, with all the spelunking going on, you might as well keep a camera handy to catch the natural beauty of Vermont's caves. **www.marlboro.edu/pr/PhotoHomePage.html**

WHAT YOU NEED TO GET IN **Application Deadline** Rolling admissions; March 1 for priority consideration **Early Action Deadline** December 1 **Common App.** Yes **Application Fee** $30 **Tuition Costs** $19,100 **Room & Board** $6,400 **Need Blind** Yes **Financial Forms Deadline** Priority given to applications received by March 1 **Undergrads Awarded Aid** 83% **Aid That Is Need-Based** 100% **Average Award of Freshman Scholarship Package** $8,500 **Tests Required** SAT1 or ACT **Admissions Address** Marlboro, VT 05344 **Admissions Telephone** (802) 257-4333

LAST YEAR'S CLASS **Applied** 275 **Accepted** 191 **Matriculated** 72 **Average SAT M/V** 600/610 **In Top Quarter of High School Graduating Class** 43%

COLLEGE LIFE **Gender Breakdown** M 52%, F 48% **Out of State Students** 83% **From Public Schools** 70% **Ethnic Composition** White & Other 96%, Asian American 1%, Black 1%, Hispanic 2% **Foreign Students** 3% **Reside on Campus** 75% **Return as Sophomores** 80% **Total Faculty** 34 **Student Faculty Ratio** 8:1 **Fraternities** none **Sororities** none **Graduate Students** 1

Marquette University

Milwaukee, WI · Est. 1881 · Coed · Private · 7,664 Undergrads · Urban

www.mu.edu

Admissions info 9240uadd@vms.csd.mu.edu

How wired is Marquette?

Do I get email? Yes
Do I get a home page? Yes
Is my dorm wired? Yes
What is the student to computer ratio? 10:1

The usual tour

DEPARTMENTS www.mu.edu/academic.html
CALENDAR www.mu.edu/acad-calendar.html
VIRTUAL TOUR www.mu.edu/campus/index.html
SPORTS www.mu.edu/athletics/index.html
STUDENT CLUBS www.mu.edu/dept/saffairs
/osl/orgs/studorg.html

Skip the brochure

- **MEN'S BASKETBALL** Want to see a man dribble? Meet some of the NCAA's darlings and their coaches. The skinny on the team, recruits, and all the stats a person could need are available. Games are soon to be broadcast live on the Net, but in the meantime, watch some videos and check out the snaps. **www.mu.edu/athletics/mbball/index.html**

- **JESUITS** A Jesuit school whose focus goes beyond academics to include the spiritual, Marquette requires that undergrads study philosophy and theology. This commitment to the "whole" person clearly allows room for

6'7" Faisal Abraham plays on Marquette's celebrated basketball team

athletic achievement, hence the celebrated Golden Eagles of the NCAA (who apparently have God on their side). Although there is a strong Jesuit presence intellectually and spiritually, Marquette does have a relatively diverse student body and faculty. **www.mu.edu/jesuits.html**

- **MARQUEE** Get the campus pulse by reading film and music reviews from Marquette's student newspaper. **gopher://sunny.csd.mu.edu:70/II/camp info/campserv/Marquette%20Tribune/lateissue/Marquee**

"Want to see a man dribble? Meet some NCAA b-ball darlings."

WHAT YOU NEED TO GET IN **Application Deadline** Rolling admissions; Fall for priority consideration **Common App.** Yes **Application Fee** $30 **Tuition Costs** $13,230 **Room & Board** $5,350 **Need Blind** Yes **Financial Forms Deadline** Priority given to applications received by March **Undergrads Awarded Aid** 80% **Aid That Is Need-Based** 80% **Average Award of Freshman Scholarship Package** $7,400 **Tests Required** SAT1 or ACT **Admissions Address** 517 North 14th Street, Milwaukee, WI 53233 **Admissions Telephone** (414) 288-7302

LAST YEAR'S CLASS **Applied** 5,487 **Matriculated** 1,616 **Average SAT M/V** 563/495 **Average ACT** 25 **In Top Fifth of High School Graduating Class** 52%

COLLEGE LIFE **Gender Breakdown** M 48%, F 52% **Out of State Students** 62% **From Public Schools** 55% **Ethnic Composition** White & Other 88%, Asian American 4%, Black 4%, Hispanic 3.6%, Native American 0.4% **Foreign Students** 2% **Reside on Campus** 45% **Return as Sophomores** 88% **Total Faculty** 709 **Student Faculty Ratio** 25:1 **Fraternities (% of men participating)** 11 (7%) **Sororities (% of women participating)** 9 (7%) **Graduate Students** 3,102

Mary Washington College

Fredericksburg, VA · Est. 1908 · Coed · Public · 3,690 Undergrads · Small Town

I need...

Admissions info admit@mwc.edu
 www.mwc.edu/jblair
Financial aid info www.mwc.edu/jblair/costs.html

How wired is Mary Washington?

Do I get email? Yes
Do I get a home page? Yes
 Where? www.mwc.edu/rmacmich/personal
 .html
Is my dorm wired? Yes
What is the student to computer ratio? 24:1

The usual tour

CALENDAR www.mwc.edu/~mmcclure
DEPARTMENTS www.mwc.edu/#depts
LIBRARY www.mwc.edu/~jperkins
SPORTS www.mwc.edu/~vbenigni

Skip the brochure

• **STEVE GRIFFIN RETROSPECTIVE** Who is Steve
Griffin? If you attend Mary Washington he
could be your advisor, but the sight of his face
bent into a number of artistic ways on his
home page could affect your college career in
ways that you can only begin to
understand.This virtual retrospective showcas-
es some of the work of this MWC Art
Professor. **www.mwc.edu/ernie/sg/virtexhibit.html**

• **HISPANIC STUDENTS ASSOCIATION** Organizing
speakers and programs to educate about

Critique the art of one of your professors

Hispanic people and culture, the HSA is a terrific voice for diversity at MWC. **www.mwc.edu
/~ogaithe/hsa**

• **THE ECOLOGY CLUB** The MWC Ecology Club is saving paper by sponsoring a terrific Web site,
and river clean-ups, petitioning drives, and
environmental education programs. **www.mwc
.edu/~rcour69c/ecoclub.html**

• **WMWC RADIO STATION** Want to get your band
played? Plug into MWC's college radio station.
www.mwc.edu/rmacmich/wmwc/wmwc.html

• **SPEAKING INTENSIVES** MWC students speak thier
minds. Classes on oral communication are
requisites, but not everyone speaks at once—
listening skills are taught, too. **www.mwc.edu
/~jmorello/speakint.html**

WHAT YOU NEED TO GET IN Application Deadline January 15 for priority consideration; final deadline February 1 **Early
Action Deadline** November 1 **Common App.** No **Application Fee** $25 **Tuition Costs** $2,086 ($6,976 out-of-state)
Room & Board $6,024 **Need Blind** Yes **Financial Forms Deadline** Priority given to applications received by
March 1 **Undergrads Awarded Aid** 60% **Aid That Is Need-Based** 63% **Average Award of Freshman Scholarship
Package** $1,800 **Tests Required** SAT1 or ACT **Admissions Address** 1301 College Avenue, Fredericksburg, VA
22401-5358 **Admissions Telephone** (540) 654-2000

LAST YEAR'S CLASS Applied 4,035 **Accepted** 2,298 **Matriculated** 766 **Median Range SAT M/V** 530-620/560-660
In Top Fifth of High School Graduating Class 69% **Applied Early** 179 **Accepted Early** 108

COLLEGE LIFE Gender Breakdown M 34%, F 66% **Out of State Students** 35% **From Public Schools** 84% **Ethnic
Composition** White & Other 89.5%, Asian American 3%, Black 5%, Hispanic 2%, Native American 0.5% **Foreign
Students** 1% **Reside on Campus** 70% **Return as Sophomores** 87% **Total Faculty** 235 **Student Faculty Ratio**
17:1 **Fraternities** none **Sororities** none **Graduate Students** 65

University of Maryland, College Park

inform.umd.edu

College Park, MD · Est. 1859 · Coed · Private · 22,925 Undergrads · Urban

I need...

Admissions info umadmit@uga.umd.edu
www.uga.umd.edu
Financial aid info www.uga.umd.edu/costs.html

How wired is College Park?

Do I get email? Yes
Do I get a home page? Yes
Is my dorm wired? Yes
What is the student to computer ratio? 13:1

DOWNLOAD APPLICATION ONLINE

The usual tour

DEPARTMENTS www.umcp.umd.edu/servers.html
CALENDAR www.inform.umd.edu:8080/Campus Info/Calendars
STUDENT CLUBS www.inform.umd.edu:8080 /Student/Campus_Activities
GREEK LIFE www.inform.umd.edu:8080 /Student/Campus_Activities/Greek_Life
STUDY ABROAD www.inform.umd.edu:8080 /EdRes/Intl

Skip the brochure

• **MARYLAND ELECTRONIC CAPITOL** It looks small, but it has quite a history. Maryland, that is. Everything you wanted to know about the state but were afraid to ask. **www.mec.state.md.us/mec**

• **FIRST YEAR FOCUS** Forget hazing, University of Maryland students bond over books. Every

Maryland's Gymkana Troupe, founded in 1946, travels the country promoting gymnastics and drug-free lifestyles

year, first year students read the same book, presumably so they have something to talk about while waiting in line at the keg. **www.inform.umd.edu:8080/EdRes/UgradInfo/Ugrad Studies/FirstBook/.WWW/firstbook.html**

• **DIVERSITY RESOURCES** Want to go to a school where everyone looks the same, talks the same? Then forget University of Maryland—sexual identity, ethnicity, religion, a wide range is covered—check out the mix of students. **www.inform.umd.edu:8080/Student/Diversity _Resources Venus**

"Forget hazing. University of Maryland students bond over books."

WHAT YOU NEED TO GET IN **Application Deadline** December 1 for priority consideration; final deadline April 30 **Common App.** No **Application Fee** $30 **Tuition Costs** $3,494 ($9,553 out-of-state) **Room & Board** $5,442 **Need Blind** Yes **Financial Forms Deadline** May 31 with a priority given to applications received by February 15 **Undergrads Awarded Aid** 57% **Aid That Is Need-Based** 84% **Average Award of Freshman Scholarship Package** $3,891 **Tests Required** SAT1 or ACT **Admissions Address** College Park, MD 20742 **Admissions Telephone** (301) 314-8385

LAST YEAR'S CLASS **Applied** 14,956 **Accepted** 10,143 **Matriculated** 3,632 **Median Range SAT M/V** 520-650/ 440-560 **In Top Fifth of High School Graduating Class** 53%

COLLEGE LIFE **Gender Breakdown** M 53%, F 47% **Out of State Students** 37% **Ethnic Composition** White & Other 67.9%, Asian American 14.4%, Black 13.2%, Hispanic 4.3%, Native American 0.2% **Foreign Students** 8% **Reside on Campus** 35% **Return as Sophomores** 85% **Total Faculty** 1,374 **Student Faculty Ratio** 14:1 **Fraternities (% of men participating)** 26 (13%) **Sororities (% of women participating)** 20 (14%) **Graduate Students** 7,724

Massachusetts Institute of Technology

web.mit.edu

Cambridge, MA · Est. 1861 · Coed · Private · 4,495 Undergrads · Urban

I need...

Admissions info mitfrosh@mit.edu *OR*
mitintl@mit.edu
web.mit.edu/admissions/www
Financial aid info finaid@mitvmc.mit.edu
web.mit.edu/seo/www/finaid.html

How wired is MIT?

Do I get email? Yes
Do I get a home page? Yes
Is my dorm wired? Yes
What is the student to computer ratio? 6:1

The usual tour

DEPARTMENTS web.mit.edu/admissions/www
/gen/summaries.html
LIBRARY nimrod.mit.edu
SPORTS www.mit.edu:8001/activities
/sports.html
STUDENT CLUBS www.mit.edu:8001/activities
GREEK LIFE www.mit.edu:8001/activities
/living_groups.html

Skip the brochure

• **MEDIA LAB** MIT's Media Lab was famous even
before the digital revolution took over the world.
The center is devoted to the theory and practice
of digital technologies. **www.media.mit.edu**

Location: http://web.mit.edu/

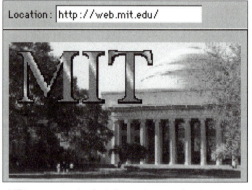

MIT has a reputation for being at the cusp of technology.
Check out the cybergoods

• **ROADKILL BUFFET** is a "guerilla revolutionary
movement disguised as an improvisational
comedy troupe." Performers don't plan, prepare, rehearse, or use scripts. If they don't get
laughs, they blame the audience. **www.mit.edu
:8001/activities/roadkill/home.html**

• **THE SHAKESPEARE ENSEMBLE** If you can't imagine
Romeo and Juliet set at MIT, think again: the
Bard rears his head here every term. **www.mit
.edu:8001/activities/ensemble/home.html**

• **THE CAPOEIRA CLUB** The zany Brazilian exercise
that blends martial art, dance, music, ritual,
singing, and playing into one is big at MIT.
www.mit.edu:8001/activities/capoeira/capoeira.html

WHAT YOU NEED TO GET IN Application Deadline January 1 **Early Action Deadline** November 1 **Common App.** No
Application Fee $50 **Tuition Costs** $22,000 **Room & Board** $6,350 **Need Blind** Yes **Financial Forms Deadline**
Priority given to applications received by January 19 **Undergrads Awarded Aid** 59% **Aid That Is Need-Based**
100% **Average Award of Freshman Scholarship Package** $12,428 **Tests Required** SAT1 or ACT **Admissions
Address** 77 Massachusetts Avenue, Cambridge, MA 02139 **Admissions Telephone** (617) 253-4791

LAST YEAR'S CLASS Applied 7,958 **Accepted** 2,113 **Matriculated** 1,116 **Median Range SAT M/V** 720-790/660-750
In Top Fifth of High School Graduating Class 100% **Applied Early** 1,672 **Accepted Early** 557

COLLEGE LIFE Gender Breakdown M 62%, F 38% **Out of State Students** 92% **From Public Schools** 79% **Ethnic
Composition** White & Other 55%, Asian American 29%, Black 6%, Hispanic 9%, Native American 1% **Foreign
Students** 8% **Reside on Campus** 94% **Return as Sophomores** 97% **Total Faculty** 960 **Student Faculty Ratio** 5:1
Fraternities (% of men participating) 30 (50%) **Sororities (% of women participating)** 5 (26%) **Graduate
Students** 5,465

University of Massachusetts, Amherst

Amherst, MA · Est. 1863 · Coed · Public · 18,021 Undergrads · Big Town

I need...

Admissions info amh.admis@dpc.umassp.edu
www.umass.edu/cwis/admissions/index.html
Financial aid info www-vms.oit.umass.edu
/~umfa/home page.html

DOWNLOAD APPLICATION ONLINE

How wired is UMass, Amherst?

Do I get email? Yes
What is the student to computer ratio? 18:1

The usual tour

DEPARTMENTS www.umass.edu/cwis/acad_info
/alpha_list.html
LIBRARY www.library.umass.edu
STUDENT CLUBS www.umass.edu/cwis/stud_org
CALENDAR www-ureg.admin.umass.edu/Student
/AcCalend.htm
PUBLICATIONS www.vyne.com/umasspress

Skip the brochure

- **THE STONEWALL CENTER** Following a series of homophobic incidents in the mid-80's, the Stonewall Center, a Lesbian, Bisexual, Gay, and Transgender resource, was created, and has since become a model for other schools. www.umass.edu/stonewall

- **THE FINE ARTS CENTER** Check out this arty community for performing and visual artists. www.umass.edu/fac/fac.html

One stopping point on Amherst's student clubs list

- **ASIAN DANCE** Want to boogie? Asian Cultures explored and represented through dance. Catch that Bhangra beat. www.umass.edu/fac/AsianDanceAndMusic.html

- **AUGUSTA SAVAGE GALLERY** UMass has a thriving arts community. At this gallery, you'll find social and political art by artists of color from all over. www.umass.edu/fac/AugustaSavage Gallery.html

- **THE GRENADIERS** If you think *Dungeons and Dragons* is a thing of the past, think again. The Grenadiers are into games, serious games. www-unix.oit.umass.edu/~dunkelza /grenadiers.html

WHAT YOU NEED TO GET IN **Application Deadline** February 15 **Common App.** No **Application Fee** $25 ($40 for out-of-state applicants) **Tuition Costs** $2,220 ($8,566 out-of-state) **Room & Board** $4,228 **Need Blind** Yes **Financial Forms Deadline** March 1 with a priority given to applications received by February 15 **Undergrads Awarded Aid** 57% **Aid That Is Need-Based** 95% **Average Award of Freshman Scholarship Package** $2,300 **Tests Required** SAT1 (preferred) or ACT **Admissions Address** Whitmore Building, Amherst, MA 01003 **Admissions Telephone** (413) 545-0222

LAST YEAR'S CLASS **Applied** 17,562 **Accepted** 13,780 **Matriculated** 3,861 **Average SAT M/V** 541/479 **In Top Fifth of High School Graduating Class** 22%

COLLEGE LIFE **Gender Breakdown** M 52%, F 48% **Out of State Students** 33% **From Public Schools** 84% **Ethnic Composition** White & Other 85.6%, Asian American 6%, Black 4.3%, Hispanic 3.8%, Native American 0.3% **Foreign Students** 3% **Reside on Campus** 58% **Return as Sophomores** 76% **Total Faculty** 1,273 **Student Faculty Ratio** 18:1 **Fraternities (% of men participating)** 22 (8%) **Sororities (% of women participating)** 13 (6%) **Graduate Students** 6,104

University of Massachusetts, Boston

www.umb.edu

Boston, MA · Est. 1964 · Coed · Public · 8,997 Undergrads · Urban

I need...

Admissions info adminfo@umbsky.cc.umb.edu
www.umb.edu/learn-more.html
Financial aid info www.umb.edu/learn-more.html

How wired is UMass, Boston?

Do I get email? Yes
Do I get a home page? Yes
   Where? www.umb.edu/personal-pages.html
What is the student to computer ratio? 36:1

The usual tour

LIBRARY www.lib.umb.edu
DEPARTMENTS www.umb.edu/programs-and
-people.html
CAREER CENTER www-saris.admin.umass.edu
/uccweb/index.htm

Skip the brochure

• **THE BLUESTOCKING ARCHIVE** For the Romantic in
all of you: Women's intellectual achievements
from the Romantic period are compiled and
hyperlinked at this site. **www.umb.edu/pages
/efay/toc.html**

• **VISION REHABILITATION** Take a look at what is
going on in the field of visual rehab. University
of Massachusetts, Boston has a special
program in this field. In conjunction with

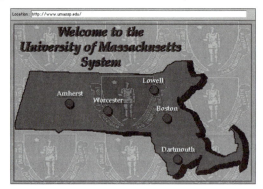

Boston is just one of the five UMass campuses

several hospitals and foundations, the
program teaches students to help the visually
impaired. **hydra.cc.umb.edu/pages/v**

• **PLAYWRITING AND PERFORMANCE IN NANTUCKET**
Actors and actresses: This UMass summer
program allows students to learn play
analysis, performance techniques, and design.
"Participants have the opportunity to examine
and develop their own scripts, translate
dialogue into character development, and
integrate elements of performance preparation
and production design into their work." As
deep a trawl of dramatic art as you could wish
for, all while living in the quaint historic town of
Nantucket. **www.conted.umb.edu/theater.html**

WHAT YOU NEED TO GET IN **Application Deadline** Rolling admissions; March 1 for priority consideration **Common App.**
No **Application Fee** $20 ($35 for out-of-state applicants) **Tuition Costs** $2,109 ($8,842 out-of-state) **Need Blind**
Yes **Financial Forms Deadline** Priority given to applications received by March 1 **Undergrads Awarded Aid** 55%
Aid That Is Need-Based 90% **Average Award of Freshman Scholarship Package** $3,000 **Tests Required** SAT1
(preferred) or ACT **Admissions Address** 100 Morrissey Boulevard, Boston, MA 02125-3393 **Admissions
Telephone** (617) 287-6000

LAST YEAR'S CLASS **Applied** 2,110 **Accepted** 1,363 **Matriculated** 691 **Average SAT M/V** 479/427 **In Top Fifth of
High School Graduating Class** 23%

COLLEGE LIFE **Gender Breakdown** M 46%, F 54% **Out of State Students** 7% **From Public Schools** 71% **Ethnic
Composition** White & Other 68.6%, Asian American 9.9%, Black 15.4%, Hispanic 5.6%, Native American 0.5%
Foreign Students 2% **Reside on Campus** 0% **Return as Sophomores** 74% **Total Faculty** 835 **Student Faculty
Ratio** 16:1 **Fraternities** none **Sororities** none **Graduate Students** 2,605

McGill University

Montreal, Quebec, CAN · Est. 1821 · Coed · Public · 23,999 Undergrads · Urban

I need...

Admissions info admissions@arnold.lan.mcgill.ca
www.is.McGill.ca/admissions
Financial aid info www.is.McGill.ca/admissions
/sa0406.htm

How wired is McGill?

Do I get email? Yes
Do I get a home page? Yes
Is my dorm wired? Yes
What is the student to computer ratio? 5:1

The usual tour

STUDENT CLUBS www.mcgill.ca/Stud.html
SPORTS www.mcgill.ca/Athletics.html
LIBRARY www.library.mcgill.ca
CALENDAR gopher://vm1.mcgill.ca:70/1-BBS
/CW99%3A@INF.UR.CAL
VIRTUAL TOUR gopher://vm1.mcgill.ca:70/1-BBS
/CW99%3A@INF.UR.CAL

Skip the brochure

• **MCGILL BIOLOGY STUDENT UNION** Great graphics decorate this page devoted to those who love protozoans. The Biology Student Union goes beyond academics to the recreational—play Ultimate frisbee with your lab partner while discussing the facts of life. **www.mcgill.ca/Biology /mbsu.htm**

• **POLISH STUDENTS UNION** Witamy! McGill's Polish students have created a friendly Internet pres-

Location: http://www.mcgill.ca/famfeb.htm

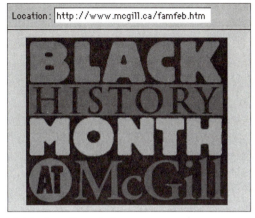

Celebrating online and off

ence for the exchange of Polish news, gossip, and other information. **www-acaps.cs.mcgill.ca /~lapkow/PSA/welcome.html**

• **MCGILL QPIRG** The Quebec People's Interest Research Group is one of the many activist groups at McGill. Students can get involved with organic food co-ops, monitor natural resources, audit business ethics, or participate in feminist and anti-racist collectives. **www.vub.mcgill.ca/clubs/qpirg**

• **THE QUEER SCENE IN MONTREAL** Want to find a queer-friendly greasy spoon? The Queer Scene is bound to guide anyone to the hippest clubs, restaurants, and bars in Montreal. **www.vub.mcgill.ca/clubs/lbgtm/glb-mtl.html**

WHAT YOU NEED TO GET IN Application Deadline January 15 for priority consideration **Common App.** No **Application Fee** $60 (CND$) **Tuition Costs** $1,700 (CND$) ($7,460 (CND$) out-of-country) **Room & Board** $4,461 (CND$) **Financial Forms Deadline** Rolling **Undergrads Awarded Aid** 35% **Aid That Is Need-Based** 100% **Average Award of Freshman Scholarship Package** $2,000 **Tests Required** SAT1 (preferred) or ACT **Admissions Address** 845 Sherbrooke Street West, Montreal, Quebec, CAN H3A 2T5 **Admissions Telephone** (514) 398-3910

LAST YEAR'S CLASS Applied 15,221 **Accepted** 8,252 **Matriculated** 4,530

COLLEGE LIFE Gender Breakdown M 43%, F 57% **Out of State Students** 5% **Reside on Campus** 9% **Return as Sophomores** 85% **Student Faculty Ratio** 22:1 **Fraternities (% of men participating)** 13 (4%) **Sororities (% of women participating)** 4 (2%) **Graduate Students** 5,025

Mercer University

Macon, GA · Est. 1833 · Coed · Private · 4,203 Undergrads · Urban

www.mercer.edu

How wired is Mercer University?

Is my dorm wired? No
What is the student to computer ratio? 30:1

The usual tour

DEPARTMENTS www.mercer.edu/www/atlinfo.html
LIBRARY www.mercer.edu/www/main/mainhome
.html
VIRTUAL TOUR falcon.mercer.peachnet.edu/web
team95/students/douglas/map1.html
CALENDAR gopher://atl1.mercer.edu:70/11
gopher_root%3A%5Bnews.calendar%5D
CAREER CENTER Atl1.Mercer.PeachNet.Edu
/~career
GREEK LIFE falcon.mercer.peachnet.edu/~Muah
_s/aphia1.html

Skip the brochure

• **HISTORY OF ALPHA PHI ALPHA** Read about the first
fraternity established for African Americans.
Founded at Cornell in 1906 this frat has since
gone multiracial and international. **falcon.mer-
cer.peachnet.edu/~Muah_s/frathist.html**

• **MEDIA WEB** It might be in Macon, but Mercer
College gets its news hot off the cyberpress.
Folks at Mercer keep up with the daily news
through major news resources linked here.
mumc.mercer.peachnet.edu/center/daily.html

Location: http://www.mercer.edu/www/atlinfo.html

Mercer's virtual students compare notes online

• **HEALTH ADMINISTRATION RESOURCES** This joint pro-
ject with Georgia State University's Institute of
Health Administration consists of links to
Hospitals, Health Data Sources, Health
Administration listservs and academic
programs. **www.mercer.edu/www/health/health.html**

• **FOOD SERVICES** Never, ever underestimate the
importance of campus grub. Check out the
selection of eats at Mercer, which isn't
exclusively Southern: there is a Wok and
Waffle buffet. **gopher://atl1.mercer.edu:70
/11gopher_root%3A%5Bnews.food%5D**

"Never underestimate the importance of grub."

WHAT YOU NEED TO GET IN **Application Deadline** Rolling admissions; winter for priority consideration **Early Action
Deadline** December 1 **Common App.** No **Application Fee** $25 **Tuition Costs** $13,896 **Room & Board** $4,740
Financial Forms Deadline May 1 **Undergrads Awarded Aid** 93% **Aid That Is Need-Based** 68% **Average Award of
Freshman Scholarship Package** $7,740 **Tests Required** SAT1 or ACT **Admissions Address** 1400 Coleman
Avenue, Macon, GA 31207 **Admissions Telephone** (912) 752-2650

LAST YEAR'S CLASS **Applied** 2,029 **Accepted** 1,699 **Matriculated** 571 **Average SAT M/V** 529/473 **Average ACT** 25
In Top Fifth of High School Graduating Class 37% **Applied Early** 42 **Accepted Early** 39

COLLEGE LIFE **Gender Breakdown** M 47%, F 53% **Out of State Students** 40% **From Public Schools** 78% **Ethnic
Composition** White & Other 83%, Asian American 2%, Black 13%, Hispanic 1%, Native American 1% **Foreign
Students** 2% **Reside on Campus** 58% **Return as Sophomores** 82% **Total Faculty** 174 **Student Faculty Ratio**
12:1 **Fraternities (% of men participating)** 9 (30%) **Sororities (% of women participating)** 6 (30%) **Graduate
Students** 1,433

Miami University

Oxford, OH · Est. 1809 · Coed · Public · 14,119 Undergrads · Small Town

I need...

Admissions info admissions@muohio.edu
www.muohio.edu/Admission/1MUHome
.htmlx

Financial aid info www.muohio.edu/Admission
/1GeneralInfo.html#RTFToC5

How wired is Miami University?

Do I get email? Yes
Do I get a home page? Yes
Is my dorm wired? Yes
What is the student to computer ratio? 20:1

REQUEST APPLICATION ONLINE

The usual tour

DEPARTMENTS www.muohio.edu/Admission
/1Majors.html
LIBRARY www.muohio.edu/Admission
/1Academiclife.html#RTFToC5
SPORTS www.muohio.edu/Admission/1Campus
Life.html#RTFToC2
STUDENT CLUBS www.muohio.Edu/~CWIS/Sources
/Sources_Organizations_Student.htmlx
CALENDAR www.muohio.edu/~CWIS
/Events.htmlx

"Want to feel the earth move?"

Active Tectonics

Miami's Tectonics experts show you the faults of the world

Skip the brochure

- **THE MIAMI STUDENT ONLINE** All the news thats fit to print, digitally! **MiaVXI.MUOhio.Edu/~MUStudent**

- **MIAMI UNIVERITY IN LUXEMBOURG** Miami runs a number of international programs; study European languages and culture at its campus overseas. **www.muohio.edu/Luxembourg**

- **BIOSPHERE 2000** Two tree-hugging Miami faculty members have written an environmental science textbook that focuses on the impact of human activities on natural systems. The book and a grant opportunity for students are described here. **MiaVXI.MUOhio.Edu/~ZOOCWIS /faculty/kaufman/Biospl.html**

- **ACTIVE TECTONICS** Want to feel the earth move? The Active Tectonics server, hosted by Miami University, should pull the floor out from under you. **MiaVXI.MUOhio.Edu/~Tectonics/Active Tectonics.html**

WHAT YOU NEED TO GET IN **Application Deadline** January 31 **Early Action Deadline** November 1 **Common App.** No **Application Fee** $30 **Tuition Costs** $5,098 ($10,854 out-of-state) **Room & Board** $4,440 **Need Blind** Yes **Financial Forms Deadline** Priority given to applications received by February 15 **Undergrads Awarded Aid** 51% **Aid That Is Need-Based** 66% **Average Award of Freshman Scholarship Package** $3,274 **Tests Required** SAT1 or ACT **Admissions Address** Oxford, OH 45056 **Admissions Telephone** (513) 529-2531

LAST YEAR'S CLASS **Applied** 10,723 **Accepted** 7,927 **Matriculated** 3,244 **Median Range SAT M/V** 560-660/ 470-560 **In Top Fifth of High School Graduating Class** 71% **Applied Early** 767 **Accepted Early** 544

COLLEGE LIFE **Gender Breakdown** M 46%, F 54% **Out of State Students** 30% **Ethnic Composition** White & Other 93%, Asian American 2%, Black 3%, Hispanic 1%, Native American 1% **Foreign Students** 1% **Reside on Campus** 45% **Return as Sophomores** 92% **Total Faculty** 944 **Student Faculty Ratio** 17:1 **Fraternities (% of men participating)** 27 (35%) **Sororities (% of women participating)** 21 (43%) **Graduate Students** 1,482

University of Miami

www.miami.edu

Coral Gables, FL · Est. 1925 · Coed · Private · 7,923 Undergrads · Big Town

I need...

Admissions info admission@admiss.msmail
.miami.edu
www.miami.edu/home/admission.html
Financial aid info www.miami.edu

How wired is Miami?

Do I get email? Yes
What is the student to computer ratio? 4:1

The usual tour

DEPARTMENTS www.miami.edu/home/colleges
-schools.html
LIBRARY www.miami.edu/home/libraries.html
STUDENT CLUBS www.miami.edu/home/org.html
SPORTS www.miami.edu/canes
GREEK LIFE www.bus.miami.edu/~slife/so
/orgs/greeks

Skip the brochure

• **THE MIAMI HURRICANE ONLINE** Whether you follow
the football team, the Miami Hurricanes, or
not, this student newspaper stirs up the latest
news from Florida. **www.miami.edu/hurricane**

• **THE RATHSKELLAR** Located on Lake Osceola, the
Rathskellar is a gathering place for University

"As if the water and the sun weren't enough..."

Welcome to the University of Miami

Coral Gables

UNIVERSITY OF Miami

RSMAS   School of Medicine

The Miami Hurricanes have touched down in Coral Gables

of Miami students. As if the water and the sun
weren't enough, comedians, bands, and other
performers are scheduled to keep students
entertained. **www.bus.miami.edu/~slife/rat**

• **WVUM RADIO STATION** Listen up! The "Voice of
the University of Miami" features jazz, rock,
news, and public affairs as well as live
Hurricane football and basketball coverage.
www.bus.miami.edu/~wvum

• **ALTERNATIVE SPRING BREAK** This is not a new
music festival, it's actually an "alternative" to
cheesy holidays spent in hedonistic pursuit.
Students help out the needy across the country. **www.bus.miami.edu/~slife/vsc/asb.html**

WHAT YOU NEED TO GET IN Application Deadline November 15 for priority consideration; final deadline March 1 **Early Action Deadline** November 15 **Common App.** Yes **Application Fee** $35 **Tuition Costs** $18,580 **Room & Board** $7,000 **Need Blind** Yes **Financial Forms Deadline** Priority given to applications received by February 15 **Undergrads Awarded Aid** 77% **Aid That Is Need-Based** 50% **Average Award of Freshman Scholarship Package** $14,919 **Tests Required** SAT1 or ACT **Admissions Address** Coral Gables, FL 33124 **Admissions Telephone** (305) 284-4323

LAST YEAR'S CLASS Applied 10,564 **Accepted** 6,109 **Matriculated** 1,701 **Median Range SAT M/V** 940-1180 (combined) **In Top Fifth of High School Graduating Class** 65% **Applied Early** 1,878 **Accepted Early** 633

COLLEGE LIFE Gender Breakdown M 49%, F 51% **Out of State Students** 51% **Ethnic Composition** White & Other 52%, Asian American 7%, Black 11%, Hispanic 30% **Foreign Students** 10% **Reside on Campus** 43% **Student Faculty Ratio** 8:1 **Fraternities (% of men participating)** 15 (15%) **Sororities (% of women participating)** 10 (13%) **Graduate Students** 5,252

Michigan State University

www.msu.edu

East Lansing, MI · Est. 1855 · Coed · Public · 31,329 Undergrads · Urban

I need...

Admissions info www.msu.edu/admfin/admissions.html

Financial aid info deptwww.msu.edu/personal/finaid

How wired is Michigan State?

Do I get email? Yes
Do I get a home page? Yes
Is my dorm wired? Yes
What is the student to computer ratio? 6:1

DOWNLOAD APPLICATION ONLINE

The usual tour

DEPARTMENTS www.msu.edu/academics/academics2.html

CALENDAR deptwww.msu.edu/dept/registr/regdocs/calendar/index.htm

CAREER CENTER web.msu.edu/csp

STUDENT CLUBS gopher://burrow.cl.msu.edu:70/11/msu/students/rso

SPORTS www.msu.edu/athletics/spartanathletics.html

STUDY ABROAD www.egr.msu.edu/ISP

Skip the brochure

• **OVERSEAS STUDY** Michigan State has numerous programs for overseas study that can take you

"Listen to the roar of the crowd via Audionet."

Preview those East Lansing winters at the MSU home page

from the Bahamas and the Baltics, to Tobago and the West Indies. **www.egr.msu.edu/ISP/overseas**

• **THE HONORS COLLEGE** Bypass prerequisites. Plan your own course of study, and graduate with honors. It's available to incoming freshmen, sophomores, and juniors. **wxweb.msu.edu/~honcoll**

• **SPARTAN FOOTBALL** Check out the Big 10 team, order merchandise, check the play schedule, and listen to the roar of the crowd via Audionet. **web.msu.edu/sports/teams/football.html**

• **G. ROBERT VINCENT VOICE LIBRARY** A sound engineer from the Nuremburg Trials and the United Nations donated his tapes to start the Vincent Voice Library. Get an earful. **gopher://burrow.cl.msu.edu:70/00/about_msu/collect/libvoice**

WHAT YOU NEED TO GET IN **Application Deadline** July 30 **Common App.** No **Application Fee** $30 **Tuition Costs** $3,983 ($10,838 out-of-state) **Room & Board** $3,828 **Financial Forms Deadline** Rolling **Undergrads Awarded Aid** 67% **Aid That Is Need-Based** 45% **Average Award of Freshman Scholarship Package** $2,782 **Tests Required** SAT1 or ACT **Admissions Address** East Lansing, MI 48824-0590 **Admissions Telephone** (517) 355-8332

LAST YEAR'S CLASS **Applied** 19,663 **Accepted** 16,111 **Matriculated** 6,420 **Average SAT M/V** 540/468 **Average ACT** 23 **In Top Fifth of High School Graduating Class** 42%

COLLEGE LIFE **Gender Breakdown** M 48%, F 52% **Out of State Students** 10% **Ethnic Composition** White & Other 85%, Asian American 4%, Black 8%, Hispanic 2%, Native American 1% **Reside on Campus** 46% **Return as Sophomores** 84% **Total Faculty** 2614 **Student Faculty Ratio** 16:1 **Fraternities (% of men participating)** 35 (8%) **Sororities (% of women participating)** 19 (8%) **Graduate Students** 9,318

Michigan Technological University

Houghton, MI · Est. 1885 · Coed · Public · 5,699 Undergrads · Small Town

I need...

Admissions info mtu4u@mtu.edu
www.sas.it.mtu.edu/em/stumarket
/Admissions.html

How wired is Michigan Tech?

Do I get email? Yes
Do I get a home page? Yes
What is the student to computer ratio? 6:1

REQUEST APPLICATION ONLINE

The usual tour

DEPARTMENTS www.sas.it.mtu.edu/em/stumarket
/Viewbook/pages/programslist.html
CAREER CENTER www.ucc.mtu.edu
STUDY ABROAD www.sas.it.mtu.edu/intlprog
STUDENT CLUBS www.mtu.edu/under/allorg.html
SPORTS www.mtu.edu/sports/sports.html
LIBRARY www.lib.mtu.edu
PUBLICATIONS www.hu.mtu.edu/~bull2

Skip the brochure

- **MTU CABLE TV** If you're a cable guy or gal, check out MTU's cable system. Plan programming, film-a-thons, and make life better for couch potatoes on campus. **www.ets.mtu.edu/catv.html**

- **THE BAWDY BULL** With articles on how to get girls, and spoofs on *Playboy*, the Bawdy Bull communicates the message that Michigan

Be sure to check out *Playtoy* courtesy of the Bawdy Bull

Tech men aren't just brainy, they are playful, too. **www.hu.mtu.edu/~bull2/bawdy**

- **THE ONLINE LODE** This digital newspaper ensures you'll never have to leave the dorm, and considering the online snow thermometer, that may be a really good option. **pacemaker.cts.mtu .edu/lode/issue/96/05/10/current051096.html**

- **STUDENT PUGWASH CHAPTER** Ah, the happy union of techies and social concerns: "Student Pugwash educates young people on the relevance of science and technology to their own lives and its ability to shape the future of the global community." **www.grp.mtu.edu/pugwash**

WHAT YOU NEED TO GET IN **Application Deadline** August 1 **Common App.** No **Application Fee** $30 **Tuition Costs** $3,829 ($8,865 out-of-state) **Room & Board** $4,284 **Need Blind** Yes **Financial Forms Deadline** February 15 with a priority given to applications received by January 1 **Undergrads Awarded Aid** 68% **Aid That Is Need-Based** 66% **Average Award of Freshman Scholarship Package** $3,768 **Tests Required** SAT1 or ACT (preferred) **Admissions Address** 1400 Townsend Drive, Houghton, MI 49931-1295 **Admissions Telephone** (906) 487-2335

LAST YEAR'S CLASS **Applied** 2,577 **Accepted** 2,422 **Matriculated** 1,074 **Average SAT M/V** 630/583 **Average ACT** 26 **In Top Fifth of High School Graduating Class** 63%

COLLEGE LIFE **Gender Breakdown** M 74%, F 26% **Out of State Students** 24% **Ethnic Composition** White & Other 95%, Asian American 1%, Black 2%, Hispanic 1%, Native American 1% **Foreign Students** 4% **Return as Sophomores** 81% **Total Faculty** 407 **Student Faculty Ratio** 16:1 **Fraternities (% of men participating)** 16 (13%) **Sororities (% of women participating)** 8 (16%) **Graduate Students** 691

University of Michigan, Ann Arbor

www.umich.edu

Ann Arbor, MI · Est. 1817 · Coed · Public · 23,575 Undergrads · Urban

I need...

Admissions info www.umich.edu/~info
   /admissfront.html
Financial aid info www.umich.edu/~info
   /admissfront.html

How wired is University of Michigan?

Do I get email? Yes
Do I get a home page? Yes
   Where? www.umich.edu/hpgw
Is my dorm wired? Yes
What is the student to computer ratio? 5:1

The usual tour

LIBRARY www.umich.edu/contents/UM
   -Libraries.html
PUBLICATIONS www.pub.umich.edu/daily
STUDENT CLUBS www.umich.edu/contents
   /UM-Clubs.html
CAREER CENTER www.umich.edu/~cpp

Skip the brochure

• **GARGOYLE MAGAZINE** Is the *Gargoyle* supposed to inspire amusement or fear? It does neither. This humor magazine includes dirty jokes, inane commentary on absurd topics, and wacky cartoons. **www.pub.umich.edu/garg**

• **ONLINE WRITING LAB** Too bad you can't submit

The University of Michigan is huge. Let its Web site make sense of it all for you

college essays for help, because the Online Writing Lab allows students to access online writing resources and submit papers for feedback and advice. **www.umich.edu/~cpp**

• **DESCENDANTS OF THE MONKEY GOD** Film clips, photos, sounds, and music are available from this Asian performance group. **www.umich.edu/~actors**

• **THE CONTINUUM** Humans are highly illogical. These University of Michigan Trekkies live by Spock's dictum as they plan recreational activities based on *Star Trek* and related matters. They boldly provide "a common atmosphere" away from studies. **www.umich.edu/~trekclub**

WHAT YOU NEED TO GET IN **Application Deadline** February 1 **Common App.** No **Application Fee** $40 **Tuition Costs** $5,550 ($16,776 out-of-state) **Room & Board** $4,659 **Need Blind** Yes **Financial Forms Deadline** September 30 with a priority given to applications received by February 1 **Undergrads Awarded Aid** 46% **Aid That Is Need-Based** 95% **Average Award of Freshman Scholarship Package** $3,600 **Tests Required** SAT1 or ACT **Admissions Address** Ann Arbor, MI 48109 **Admissions Telephone** (313) 764-7433

LAST YEAR'S CLASS **Applied** 18,993 **Accepted** 13,180 **Matriculated** 5,149 **Average SAT M/V** 642/543 **Average ACT** 27 **In Top Fifth of High School Graduating Class** 86%

COLLEGE LIFE **Gender Breakdown** M 51%, F 49% **Out of State Students** 38% **From Public Schools** 80% **Ethnic Composition** White & Other 74.4%, Asian American 11.3%, Black 8.9%, Hispanic 4.6%, Native American 0.8% **Foreign Students** 3% **Reside on Campus** 32% **Return as Sophomores** 93% **Total Faculty** 3,923 **Student Faculty Ratio** 11:1 **Fraternities (% of men participating)** 37 (20%) **Sororities (% of women participating)** 23 (20%) **Graduate Students** 13,112

Middlebury College

Middlebury, VT · Est. 1800 · Coed · Private · 2,046 Undergrads · Small Town

I need...

Admissions info www.middlebury.edu/~admit
/index.html
Financial aid info www.middlebury.edu/~admit
/cost.html

How wired is Middlebury?

Do I get email? Yes
Do I get a home page? Yes
Is my dorm wired? Yes
What is the student to computer ratio? 12:1

DOWNLOAD APPLICATION ONLINE

The usual tour

DEPARTMENTS www.middlebury.edu/DirAcad.html
STUDY ABROAD www.middlebury.edu/~sap
CALENDAR www.middlebury.edu/MiddEvents.html
STUDENT CLUBS www.middlebury.edu/~sa
/stud-org-list.html
PUBLICATIONS www.middlebury.edu/~campus
/05081996/home.shtml
SPORTS www.middlebury.edu/~sports
CAREER CENTER www.middlebury.edu/~ccp
/index.html

"If you want to be immersed in a language 24-7, explore this renowned program."

These Ultimate afficianados lay it out online

Skip the brochure

- **MIDDLEBURY COLLEGE LANGUAGE SCHOOL** Speak globally, live locally. Known for its rigorous language instruction, Middlebury is currently offering Arabic, Chinese, French, Italian, Japanese, Russian, and Spanish. If you want to be immersed in a language 24-7, explore this renowned program. **www.middlebury.edu/~ls**

- **CHELLIS HOUSE** Associated with the Coalition for Feminist Consciousness, the campus feminist center, Chellis House, may appear quaint from the outside, but inside, women are serious about feminist issues. Images of their women's studies library and their infamous bathroom are available. **www.middlebury.edu/~cffc/tour.html**

- **ULTIMATE FRISBEE CLUB** These people are having fun! Very cool graphics form the background of this page which offers links to other Ultimate spots and to the home pages of Middlebury players. **www.middlebury.edu/~uf**

WHAT YOU NEED TO GET IN Application Deadline November 15 for priority consideration; final deadline January 1 **Early Action Deadline** November 15 (Part I), December 15 (Part II) **Common App.** Yes **Application Fee** $50 (may be waived) **Tuition Costs, Room & Board** $27,020 **Need Blind** Yes **Financial Forms Deadline** January 15 with a priority given to applications received by November 15 **Undergrads Awarded Aid** 41% **Aid That Is Need-Based** 100% **Average Award of Freshman Scholarship Package** $15,648 **Tests Required** SAT1 or ACT **Admissions Address** Middlebury, VT 05753-6002 **Admissions Telephone** (802) 388-3711

LAST YEAR'S CLASS Applied 3,871 **Accepted** 1,224 **Matriculated** 493 **Median Range SAT M/V** 600-690/540-650 **In Top Fifth of High School Graduating Class** 83% **Applied Early** 334 **Accepted Early** 149

COLLEGE LIFE Gender Breakdown M 51%, F 49% **Out of State Students** 95% **From Public Schools** 57% **Ethnic Composition** White & Other 88%, Asian American 4%, Black 3%, Hispanic 4%, Native American 1% **Foreign Students** 11% **Reside on Campus** 98% **Return as Sophomores** 97% **Total Faculty** 206 **Student Faculty Ratio** 11:1 **Fraternities** none **Sororities** none

Mills College

www.mills.edu

Oakland, CA · Est. 1852 · Women · Private · 870 Undergrads · Urban

How wired is Mills College?

Do I get email? Yes
Do I get a home page? Yes
Is my dorm wired? Yes
What is the student to computer ratio? 11:1

The usual tour

DEPARTMENTS www.mills.edu/ACAD_INFO/UG
_PROGS/UGProgs.html
LIBRARY www.mills.edu/LIBRARY/library
.home page.html
CALENDAR www.mills.edu/CALENDARS
/calendars.home page.html
PUBLICATIONS www.mills.edu/PUBS/pubs
.home page.html
SPORTS www.mills.edu/LIFE/ATHLETICS
/athletics.home page.html

Skip the brochure

• **TO PIERCE OR NOT TO PIERCE** In the '90s, piercings
have become *de rigeuer*: noses, eyebrows,
belly buttons, even below the belt. The whole
body is fair game, and ear piercing has fallen
into the gratuitous category. It hasn't always

One of the recreational athletic options at Mills

been so, something to which this letter from a
1965 Mills student attests. See how times
have changed, using piercing as an index.
www.mills.edu/LIFE/TIDBITS/pierce.html

• **RECREATIONAL SPORTS** Lip sync contests,
karaoke, and a litany of more conventional
recreational activities are offered. **www.mills.edu
/LIFE/ATHLETICS/REC.SPORTS/spr96.rec.cal.html**

• **MILLS COLLEGE CHILDREN'S SCHOOL** Concerned that
your college peers might be a little too mature
and serious? There is a way out. More than 90
kids, from infants to 10 year-olds, are waiting
for you. This program, run by the Department of
Education, is a learning environment for Mills
students interested in education. **www.mills.edu
/LIFE/CSCHOOL/cschool.home page.html**

WHAT YOU NEED TO GET IN Application Deadline February 15 for priority consideration; final deadline August 1 **Common App.** Yes **Application Fee** $35 **Tuition Costs** $15,260 **Room & Board** $6,480 **Need Blind** Yes **Financial Forms Deadline** July 15 with a priority given to applications received by February 15 **Undergrads Awarded Aid** 78% **Aid That Is Need-Based** 71% **Average Award of Freshman Scholarship Package** $9,000 **Tests Required** SAT1 (preferred) or ACT **Admissions Address** 5000 MacArthur Boulevard, Oakland, CA 94613 **Admissions Telephone** (510) 430-2135

LAST YEAR'S CLASS Applied 568 **Accepted** 465 **Matriculated** 133 **Median Range SAT M/V** 520-610/540-660 **Average ACT** 23 **In Top Fifth of High School Graduating Class** 50%

COLLEGE LIFE Out of State Students 33% **From Public Schools** 76% **Ethnic Composition** White & Other 75%, Asian American 11%, Black 7%, Hispanic 6%, Native American 1% **Foreign Students** 2% **Reside on Campus** 57% **Return as Sophomores** 78% **Student Faculty Ratio** 12:1 **Sororities** none **Graduate Students** 298

Millsaps College

Jackson, MS · Est. 1892 · Coed · Private · 1,294 Undergrads · Urban

www.millsaps.edu

How wired is Millsaps College?

Do I get email? Yes
Do I get a home page? Yes
  Where? www.millsaps.edu/www/upages-name
  .html
Is my dorm wired? Yes
What is the student to computer ratio? 26:1

The usual tour

DEPARTMENTS www.cs.millsaps.edu/catalog
  /index.html#DEPARTMENTS
CALENDAR gopher://gopher2.millsaps.edu:70/11
  GOPHER_ROOT_CWIS%3a%5bcalendar%5d
CAREER CENTER www.millsaps.edu/www/stuafr
  /career.html
SPORTS gopher://gopher2.millsaps.edu:70/11
  GOPHER_ROOT_ATHLETIC%3a%5b000000%5d
GREEK LIFE www.millsaps.edu/www/frt_srt.html
LIBRARY www.millsaps.edu/www/library
  /index.html

Skip the brochure

• **JACKSON, MISS** A Millsaps student has put
together a page on Jackson, introducing some
of the town's highlights, like the International
Ballet Competition, and the three day long
Jubilee. **www.millsaps.edu/~crajat/jackson.html**

• **THE ELSE SCHOOL OF MANAGMENT** Business school

Frat boys stick together

for undergraduate and graduate students.
Undergrads can study accounting, business
administrations, or economics. **www.cs
.millsaps.edu/catalog/Departments/ElseSchool.html**

• **RECIPES FROM MILLSAPS** The dining service at
Millsaps is hip and cyberfriendly; not only does
it have the funkiest graphics at the entire site,
it also posts recipes. So, if you're homesick
for Mom's (or Dad's) cooking, whip up your
own blueberry cobbler or spinach fantastic.
www.millsaps.edu/~kingst/recipes/recipes.html

• **ACY'S PLACE** "PICK UP ON THAT HAM AND
CHEESE!" That is what Acy says. Acy has
worked at Millsaps, feeding its students and
teachers since the 1950s. So they named a
cafe after her. **www.millsaps.edu/~kingst/acys-place
/acy.html**

WHAT YOU NEED TO GET IN **Application Deadline** February 1 for priority consideration; final deadline March 1 **Early
Action Deadline** November 15 **Common App.** Yes **Application Fee** $25 **Tuition Costs** $12,448 **Room & Board**
$4,902 **Need Blind** Yes **Financial Forms Deadline** Priority given to applications received by March 1 **Undergrads
Awarded Aid** 83% **Aid That Is Need-Based** 60% **Average Award of Freshman Scholarship Package** $8,087
Tests Required SAT1 or ACT **Admissions Address** Jackson, MS 39210 **Admissions Telephone** (601) 974-1050

LAST YEAR'S CLASS **Applied** 988 **Accepted** 845 **Matriculated** 260 **Average SAT M/V** 605/605 **Average ACT** 26
In Top Quarter of High School Graduating Class 67% **Applied Early** 35 **Accepted Early** 28

COLLEGE LIFE **Gender Breakdown** M 48%, F 52% **Out of State Students** 55% **From Public Schools** 57% **Ethnic
Composition** White & Other 92%, Asian American 2.7%, Black 5%, Hispanic 0.3% **Foreign Students** 1% **Reside
on Campus** 73% **Return as Sophomores** 84% **Total Faculty** 109 **Student Faculty Ratio** 14:1 **Fraternities
(% of men participating)** 6 (62%) **Sororities (% of women participating)** 4 (60%) **Graduate Students** 136

University of Minnesota, Twin Cities

www.umn.edu/tc

Minneapolis, MN · Est. 1851 · Coed · Public · 23,715 Undergrads · Urban

I need...

Admissions info admissions@tc.umn.edu
admissions.tc.umn.edu

Financial aid info admissions.tc.umn.edu/info
/financialaid.html

How wired is Minnesota - Twin Cities?

Do I get email? Yes
Do I get a home page? Yes
Is my dorm wired? Yes
What is the student to computer ratio? 1:1

FULL APPLICATION ONLINE

The usual tour

LIBRARY www.lib.umn.edu
PUBLICATIONS www.umn.edu/info/publications
.html
DEPARTMENTS www.umn.edu/info/colleges.html
#Departments
STUDENT CLUBS www.umn.edu/info/colleges.html
#Student

Skip the brochure

• **ROLE-PLAYING SIG CLUB** Role-playing does not just happen at sketchy clubs in seedy parts of town. Really. This student club is dedicated to a brand of improvisation called "role-playing." Scenes unfold, characters interact, and no one wins— it's just for the experience. www.tc.umn.edu /nlhome/m043/bras0023/rpsig.html

Location: http://hudson.acad.umn.edu/building/Daytime38K.jpg

Check out the Weisman Museum by Frank Gehry

• **THE FREDERICK R. WEISMAN MUSEUM** The new part of the Weisman museum, designed by Frank Gehry, was completed in 1993. Gehry was asked not to build another "brick lump"; his answer: a convoluted and contorted steel facade that attracted international attention and acclaim. If you can find the door you'll find a renowned collection of American art inside. **hudson.acad.umn.edu/WAMbldg.html**

• **THE EGYPTIAN CLUB** This club aims to introduce Arabic culture to UMinn and provide support for Egyptian students. **www.tc.umn.edu/nlhome/g077 /egyptian**

WHAT YOU NEED TO GET IN Application Deadline December 15 for priority consideration; final deadline June 1 **Common App.** No **Application Fee** $25 **Tuition Costs** $3,420 ($9,905 out-of-state) **Room & Board** $4,085 **Need Blind** Yes **Tests Required** SAT1 or ACT (preferred) **Admissions Address** 231 Pillsbury Drive, SE, Minneapolis, MN 55455-0213 **Admissions Telephone** (612) 625-2008

LAST YEAR'S CLASS Applied 13,271 **Accepted** 8,247 **Matriculated** 4,356 **Average SAT M/V** 593/508 **Average ACT** 24 **In Top Fifth of High School Graduating Class** 46%

COLLEGE LIFE Gender Breakdown M 50%, F 50% **Out of State Students** 35% **Ethnic Composition** White & Other 85.8%, Asian American 8.3%, Black 3.5%, Hispanic 1.8%, Native American 0.6% **Foreign Students** 3% **Reside on Campus** 12% **Return as Sophomores** 81% **Total Faculty** 2,828 **Student Faculty Ratio** 15:1 **Fraternities (% of men participating)** 27 (6%) **Sororities (% of women participating)** 15 (5%) **Graduate Students** 9,202

University of Mississippi

University, MS · Est. 1844 · Coed · Public · 7,946 Undergrads · Small Town

I need...

Admissions info A&RMAIL@Lyceuml.Reg.olemiss.edu
sunset.backbone.olemiss.edu/admissions/instructions
Financial aid info sunset.backbone.olemiss.edu/admissions/instructions/schol.html

How wired is Ole Miss?

Do I get email? Yes
Do I get a home page? Yes
   Where? sunset.backbone.olemiss.edu/userdir
What is the student to computer ratio? 2:1

FULL APPLICATION ONLINE

The usual tour

DEPARTMENTS sunset.backbone.olemiss.edu/depts/vc_academic_affairs/schools.html
SPORTS sunset.backbone.olemiss.edu/sports.a.html
LIBRARY sunset.backbone.olemiss.edu/depts/general_library
STUDY ABROAD sunset.backbone.olemiss.edu/depts/international_programs
STUDENT CLUBS sunset.backbone.olemiss.edu/student_life/orgs.html

Skip the brochure

- **OLE MISS** "Ole Miss." What does it mean? Obviously, it is derived from "Old Mississippi," but what is it meant to evoke? Semantically, it

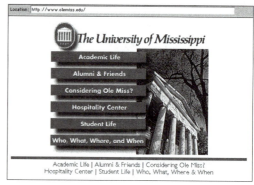

Academic Life | Alumni & Friends | Considering Ole Miss?
Hospitality Center | Student Life | Who, What, Where & When

Demystify the 'Ole Miss' mystique

recalls an old nanny or mother figure, and "Ole Miss" is all about feeling nostalgiac, evoking for many an alum the ineffable mood, emotion, and spirit of the University of Mississippi. **sunset.backbone.olemiss.edu/hospitality/olemiss.html**

- **ARNOLD AIR SOCIETY** When hit with the dilemma of how to pay for college, some students take out loans, some work at McJobs, and others begin training with the military hoping to get a ROTC scholarship. The Arnold Air Society helps bridge the gap between military and civilians. **sunset.backbone.olemiss.edu/orgs/alkey**

- **KELVIN'S CAMERA** The Rebels have a beautiful site with a big emphasis on publicizing the team. Kelvin, an Ole Miss cameraman, is responsible for these Rebel film clips. **www.olemiss.edu/depts/teleproductions/kt.html**

WHAT YOU NEED TO GET IN **Application Deadline** April 1 for priority consideration; final deadline August 1 **Common App.** No **Application Fee** $0 **Tuition Costs** $2,546 ($5,006 out-of-state) **Room & Board** $1,600 **Need Blind** Yes **Financial Forms Deadline** Priority given to applications received by April 1 **Undergrads Awarded Aid** 66% **Average Award of Freshman Scholarship Package** $2,367 **Tests Required** SAT1 or ACT **Admissions Address** University, MS 38677 **Admissions Telephone** (601) 232-7226

LAST YEAR'S CLASS **Applied** 3,600 **Accepted** 3,114 **Matriculated** 1,645 **In Top Quarter of High School Graduating Class** 48%

COLLEGE LIFE **Gender Breakdown** M 48%, F 52% **Out of State Students** 48% **Ethnic Composition** White & Other 90%, Asian American 1%, Black 9% **Foreign Students** 5% **Reside on Campus** 44% **Return as Sophomores** 77% **Student Faculty Ratio** 17:1 **Fraternities (% of men participating)** 19 (35%) **Sororities (% of women participating)** 14 (40%) **Graduate Students** 1,774

Mississippi State University

Mississippi State, MS · Est. 1878 · Coed · Public · 11,115 Undergrads · Small Town

I need...

Admissions info sharron@admissions.msstate
.edu
msuinfo.ur.msstate.edu/admissions
/admiss_d.htm
Financial aid info sanjana@SFA.msstate.edu
www.msstate.edu/Dept/SFA/sfa.htm

How wired is Mississippi State?

Do I get email? Yes
What is the student to computer ratio? 4:1

FULL APPLICATION ONLINE

The usual tour

DEPARTMENTS www.msstate.edu/web/acad.htm
SPORTS www.msstate.edu/web/athletic.htm
STUDENT CLUBS www.msstate.edu/web
/students.htm
LIBRARY www.msstate.edu/web/library.htm

Skip the brochure

- **STARKVILLE AND OKTIBBEHA COUNTY** The New South, and the new Mississippi in particular, have been made famous by the novels of William Faulkner and their setting of Yoknapatawpha County. Starkville and Oktibbeha are of the same ilk. This site presents the setting of Mississippi State with a surreal tone and lots of photos of its beautiful, lush landscape. **www.eda.co.oktibbeha.ms.us**

Ring in the new academic year at Mississippi State's Carillon Tower

- **THE BUDO CLUB** Meet some karate kids... Check out the judo syllabus, and see when throws, hold-downs, chokes, and joint-locks will be taught. This group studies aikido, hapkido/tae-kwon-do, jodo, judo, and jujitsu. **www.msstate.edu/org/ubc**

- **HIGHTOWER HALL** Some of the more academically minded students might be found living in Hightower Hall, which houses many a university honors program member. **www.msstate.edu/org/hightower**

"Meet some Mississippi State karate kids."

WHAT YOU NEED TO GET IN **Application Deadline** Rolling admissions; August 1 for priority consideration **Common App.** No **Application Fee** $15 (out-of-state applicants only) **Tuition Costs** $1,996 ($4,816 out-of-state) **Room & Board** $4100 **Need Blind** Yes **Financial Forms Deadline** Priority given to applications received by April 1 **Undergrads Awarded Aid** 73% **Aid That Is Need-Based** 63% **Average Award of Freshman Scholarship Package** $1,796 **Tests Required** SAT1 or ACT (preferred) **Admissions Address** Mississippi State, MS 39762 **Admissions Telephone** (601) 325-2224

LAST YEAR'S CLASS **Applied** 4,908 **Accepted** 4,007 **Matriculated** 1,759 **Average ACT** 23 **In Top Quarter of High School Graduating Class** 62%

COLLEGE LIFE **Gender Breakdown** M 59%, F 41% **Out of State Students** 24% **Ethnic Composition** White & Other 81.8%, Asian American 1.2%, Black 16.1%, Hispanic 0.7%, Native American 0.2% **Foreign Students** 3% **Reside on Campus** 43% **Return as Sophomores** 77% **Total Faculty** 897 **Student Faculty Ratio** 26:1 **Fraternities (% of men participating)** 19 (17%) **Sororities (% of women participating)** 11 (20%) **Graduate Students** 2,462

University of Missouri, Columbia

Columbia, MO · Est. 1839 · Coed · Public · 16,784 Undergrads · Big Town

I need...

Admissions info www.missouri.edu/~regwww
/admission/US/index.html
Financial aid info www.missouri.edu/~mufinaid

How wired is Missouri - Columbia?

Do I get email? Yes
Do I get a home page? Yes
Is my dorm wired? No
What is the student to computer ratio? 20:1

REQUEST APPLICATION ONLINE

The usual tour

CALENDAR www.missouri.edu/~muwww
/calendar/acadcalendars.html
CAREER CENTER www.missouri.edu/~cppcwww
STUDY ABROAD www.missouri.edu/~cipsmary
/abroad.html
LIBRARY www.missouri.edu/~elliswww
STUDENT CLUBS students.missouri.edu/msa
/stuorg.html
DEPARTMENTS www.missouri.edu/homes
/departments.html

Skip the brochure

• **STUDENT TIPS** Written by students for prospective students. Get the inside track on which classes don't go well back-to-back. Find out the best places on campus to study, or not to study. Whatever your concern, those who have been

Campus Peaceworks, STIR, and other groups keep the Columbia campus active

there share their experiences. **www.missouri.edu/CAFNR/StudentMisc/sttips.html**

• **CAMPUS PEACEWORKS** Even if you're not keeping the peace yourself, the Campus Peaceworks site is a rich source of good-times, good-deeds, and eco-minded news. **students.missouri.edu/~peace**

• **STIR MAGAZINE** Founded by the English department, *STIR* is the only creative arts magazine on campus which provides a forum for works of fiction, poetry, and reviews. Text-only versions of *STIR*'s archives are published online. **students.missouri.edu/~stir**

• **93FM** "If you don't like it, come down and play it your damn self!" They mean it too. So either get with the program, or change it. **www.missouri.edu/~c620751/93fm.html**

WHAT YOU NEED TO GET IN **Application Deadline** May 1 **Common App.** No **Application Fee** $25 **Tuition Costs** $3,388 ($10,128 out-of-state) **Room & Board** $4,125 **Need Blind** Yes **Financial Forms Deadline** Priority given to applications received by March 1 **Undergrads Awarded Aid** 51% **Aid That Is Need-Based** 88% **Average Award of Freshman Scholarship Package** $4,434 **Tests Required** SAT1 or ACT (preferred) **Admissions Address** Columbia, MO 65211 **Admissions Telephone** (573) 882-2456

LAST YEAR'S CLASS **Applied** 8,441 **Accepted** 7,568 **Matriculated** 3,845 **Average SAT M/V** 578/520 **Average ACT** 25 **In Top Fifth of High School Graduating Class** 54%

COLLEGE LIFE **Gender Breakdown** M 48%, F 52% **Out of State Students** 17% **Ethnic Composition** White & Other 90.4%, Asian American 2.4%, Black 5.5%, Hispanic 1.3%, Native American 0.4% **Foreign Students** 7% **Reside on Campus** 47% **Return as Sophomores** 82% **Total Faculty** 1,599 **Student Faculty Ratio** 14:1 **Fraternities (% of men participating)** 32 (24%) **Sororities (% of women participating)** 18 (24%) **Graduate Students** 4,441

University of Missouri, Rolla

www.umr.edu

Rolla, MO · Est. 1870 · Coed · Public · 4,386 Undergrads · Small Town

I need...

Admissions info egghead@umrvmb.umr.edu
www.umr.edu/~enrol
Financial aid info www.umr.edu/enrol/finap.html

How wired is Missouri - Rolla?

Do I get email? Yes
Do I get a home page? Yes
Is my dorm wired? Yes
What is the student to computer ratio? 7:1

DOWNLOAD APPLICATION ONLINE

The usual tour

DEPARTMENTS www.umr.edu/tour/academic.html
LIBRARY www.umr.edu/~library
STUDENT CLUBS www.umr.edu/~stuco
/campusorg.html
CALENDAR www.umr.edu/events/index.html
VIRTUAL TOUR www.umr.edu/tour

Skip the brochure

- **ALL FOR LOVE** All for Love maintains that "not everyone is doing it", and provides a forum to

"At All for Love, students discuss reasons for abstaining from sex."

Learn how engineering students build speedy formula race cars

discuss the health, cultural, or religious reasons for abstaining from sex. **www.umr.edu/~afl**

- **THE DAVINCI SOCIETY** Like many of the world's finest artists, Leonardo DaVinci is widely thought to have been homosexual; the group bearing his name attempts to educate others about alternative sexualities. **www.umr.edu/~davinci**

- **FORMULA SAE AT UMR** Go speedracer! Learn how engineering students build formula race cars, and listen to one of the cars in action at this very cool student activity home page. **www.umr.edu/~formula**

WHAT YOU NEED TO GET IN **Application Deadline** November 1 for priority consideration; final deadline May 1 **Common App.** No **Application Fee** $20 (waived for applications via World Wide Web) **Tuition Costs** $3,630 ($10,851 out-of-state) **Room & Board** $3,422 **Need Blind** Yes **Financial Forms Deadline** July 15 with a priority given to applications received by November 1 **Undergrads Awarded Aid** 78% **Aid That Is Need-Based** 34% **Average Award of Freshman Scholarship Package** $2,750 **Tests Required** SAT1 or ACT (preferred) **Admissions Address** 1890 Miner Circle, Rolla, MO 65401-0910 **Admissions Telephone** (314) 341-4164

LAST YEAR'S CLASS **Applied** 2,242 **Accepted** 2,177 **Matriculated** 828 **Average SAT M/V** 651/542 **Average ACT** 28 **In Top Fifth of High School Graduating Class** 70%

COLLEGE LIFE **Gender Breakdown** M 76%, F 24% **Out of State Students** 36% **From Public Schools** 88% **Ethnic Composition** White & Other 92%, Asian American 3%, Black 3%, Hispanic 2% **Foreign Students** 3% **Reside on Campus** 50% **Return as Sophomores** 78% **Total Faculty** 386 **Student Faculty Ratio** 14:1 **Fraternities (% of men participating)** 21 (25%) **Sororities (% of women participating)** 5 (20%) **Graduate Students** 1,040

University of Montana

www.umt.edu

Missoula, MT · Est. 1893 · Coed · Public · 9,675 Undergrads · Urban

I need...

Admissions info admiss@selway.umt.edu
www.umt.edu/home page/admiss.htm
Financial aid info grizzly.umt.edu/fin-aid

How wired is Montana?

Do I get email? Yes
Do I get a home page? No
Is my dorm wired? Yes
What is the student to computer ratio? 32:1

REQUEST APPLICATION ONLINE

The usual tour

DEPARTMENTS www.umt.edu/home page
/academic.htm
PUBLICATIONS www.umt.edu/home page
/news.htm
CALENDAR gopher://wilcox.umt.edu:70/00
/UofM/calendar
LIBRARY www.lib.umt.edu
VIRTUAL TOUR www.umt.edu/home page/pic-tour
.htm
STUDY ABROAD www.umt.edu/home page
/pic-tour.htm

Skip the brochure

• **THE KAIMIN** University of Montana students
have done a great job of digitizing their newspaper. Read an issue and get the latest scoop
from Missoula. **grizzly.umt.edu/kaimin/stories**

• **THE MONTANAN ONLINE** Another terrific digital
publication: this one covers more general

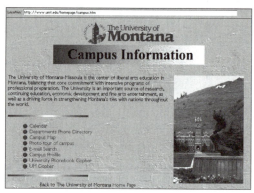

Beautiful Missoula is home to the University of Montana

social and cultural topics. **grizzly.umt.edu/comm**

• **RECREATE** Work and play hard: Missoula is an
ideal place for outdoor recreation. The possibilities are numerous: "Hiking and biking trails
start at the edge of campus. You might try
kayaking the Clark Fork River, or fly fishing in
the Blackfoot. When winter arrives, you're minutes away from two ski areas and hundreds of
miles of groomed cross-country trails." If this
isn't enough, Yellowstone is five hours away,
and Glacier National Park a mere three hours.
grizzly.umt.edu/nss/viewbook/recreate.htm

"Work and play hard: Missoula is ideal for outdoor recreation."

WHAT YOU NEED TO GET IN **Application Deadline** March 1 for priority consideration; final deadline July 1 **Common App.**
No **Application Fee** $30 **Tuition Costs** $2,400 ($6,600 out-of-state) **Room & Board** $4,000 **Need Blind** Yes
Financial Forms Deadline Priority given to applications received by March 1 **Undergrads Awarded Aid** 60% **Aid
That Is Need-Based** 75% **Average Award of Freshman Scholarship Package** $1,500 **Tests Required** SAT1 or
ACT (preferred) **Admissions Address** Missoula, MT 59812 **Admissions Telephone** (406) 243-6266

LAST YEAR'S CLASS **Applied** 3,900 **Accepted** 3,161 **Matriculated** 1,670 **Average SAT M/V** 534/460 **Average ACT**
23 **In Top Fifth of High School Graduating Class** 63%

COLLEGE LIFE **Gender Breakdown** M 48%, F 52% **Out of State Students** 35% **Ethnic Composition** White & Other
92%, Asian American 3%, Black 1%, Hispanic 1%, Native American 3% **Foreign Students** 7% **Reside on Campus**
30% **Total Faculty** 668 **Student Faculty Ratio** 19:1 **Fraternities (% of men participating)** 11 (9%) **Sororities
(% of women participating)** 4 (7%) **Graduate Students** 1,357

Morehouse College

144.125.128.1/frames.html

Atlanta, GA · Est. 1867 · Men · Private · 3,005 Undergrads · Urban

I need...

Admissions info 144.125.128.1/applyinfo.html

How wired is Morehouse?

Do I get a home page? No
Is my dorm wired? No
What is the student to computer ratio? 12:1

REQUEST APPLICATION ONLINE

The usual tour

DEPARTMENTS www.morehouse.auc.edu
/departments.html

Skip the brochure

• **MOREHOUSE'S PRESIDENT** Symbolically, Morehouse is very important. Founded in 1867, the historically black liberal arts institution can boast of alumni such as the Reverend Martin Luther King Jr. and Edwin Moses. Meet its latest president here. The former president of the National Science Foundation and also a

"President Walter E. Massey outlines his goals and hopes for Morehouse College."

Martin Luther King, Jr. is an alumnus of Morehouse College

Morehouse alum, Walter E. Massey became president of Morehouse in August of 1995. Here, he outlines his goals and hopes for the college. **www.the-scientist.library.upenn.edu/yrl995 /august/massey_950821.html**

• **ATLANTA** What's happening off campus? It's not just the home of the Atlantic Braves, the '96 Olympics, and Coca Cola; Atlanta is one of America's hottest cities. Explore the setting of Morehouse College. **www.america.net/com/waga /links.html**

• **MOREHOUSE SCHOOL OF MEDICINE** Although it's just a baby, less than 20 years old, Morehouse School of Medicine has quickly earned an admirable reputation. Founded to help redress the shortage of minority physicians and their under-representation in the higher sciences, the school is thriving—check out the latest research projects at their friendly site. **www.msm.edu**

WHAT YOU NEED TO GET IN **Application Deadline** November 1 for priority consideration; final deadline February 15 **Early Action Deadline** December 15 **Common App.** Yes **Application Fee** $35 **Tuition Costs** $7,430 **Room & Board** $5,770 **Financial Forms Deadline** Priority given to applications received by February 15 **Undergrads Awarded Aid** 71% **Aid That Is Need-Based** 65% **Average Award of Freshman Scholarship Package** $3,000 **Tests Required** SAT1 (preferred) or ACT **Admissions Address** 830 Westview Drive, SW, Atlanta, GA 30314 **Admissions Telephone** (800) 851-1254

LAST YEAR'S CLASS **Applied** 3,708 **Accepted** 1,678 **Matriculated** 722 **In Top Fifth of High School Graduating Class** 28%

COLLEGE LIFE **Out of State Students** 80% **From Public Schools** 74% **Ethnic Composition** White & Other 2%, Black 98% **Foreign Students** 2% **Reside on Campus** 55% **Return as Sophomores** 80% **Student Faculty Ratio** 17:1 **Fraternities (% of men participating)** 6 (3%) **Graduate Students** 3,005

Mount Holyoke College

www.mtholyoke.edu

South Hadley, MA · Est. 1837 · Women · Private · 1,884 Undergrads · Big Town

How wired is Mount Holyoke?

Do I get email? Yes
Do I get a home page? Yes
 Where? www.mtholyoke.edu/dir
Is my dorm wired? No
What is the student to computer ratio? 8:1

The usual tour

DEPARTMENTS www.mtholyoke.edu/acad
LIBRARY www.mtholyoke.edu/offices/library
 /libhome.html
CALENDAR www.mtholyoke.edu/cic/news
 _events.html
VIRTUAL CAMPUS TOUR www.mtholyoke.edu/visit
 /map.html

Skip the brochure

- **PROFILE OF JOANNE CREIGHTON** Noted as a
 preeminent women's college, Mt. Holyoke has
 recently welcomed a new president, Joanne
 Creighton, a respected Joyce Carol Oates
 scholar. Get to know your future prez.
 www.mtholyoke.edu/offices/comm/profile/creighton.html

- **OTHER FACILITIES AND PROGRAMS** Mount Holyoke
 might look like a country club with its own golf
 course and equestrian center, traditional
 Japanese meditation garden and hand-crafted

Find out what the women of South Hadley, Mass. are up to

 teahouse, as well as arboretum, but as you
 will find at this site, it is not. **www.mtholyoke.edu
 /visit/other.html**

- **FIVE COLLEGES CONSORTIUM** Mount Holyoke,
 Amherst, Smith, Hampshire, and UMass
 Amherst have forged a general purpose consortium. More than 5,000 students from the
 schools take courses within the consortium,
 but the links go well beyond the academic.
 Students frequently collaborate on activities,
 productions, and of course lots of social interaction takes place. **www.fivecolleges.edu**

- **THE MHC EQUESTRIAN CENTER** Offering one of the
 most competitive college riding programs in
 the country, Mount Holyoke lets students participate in varsity competitions or take horse-
 back riding to fulfill their physical education
 requirements. **www.mtholyoke.edu/offices/equest
 /index.htm**

WHAT YOU NEED TO GET IN **Application Deadline** January 15 **Early Action Deadline** December 1 and January 1
Common App. Yes **Application Fee** $50 **Tuition Costs** $21,250 **Room & Board** $6,250 **Financial Forms Dead-
line** Priority given to applications received by February 1 **Undergrads Awarded Aid** 73% **Aid That Is Need-Based**
100% **Average Award of Freshman Scholarship Package** $17,467 **Tests Required** ACT **Admissions Address**
College Street, South Hadley, MA 01075-1488 **Admissions Telephone** (413) 538-2023

LAST YEAR'S CLASS **Applied** 2,033 **Accepted** 1,328 **Matriculated** 493 **Average SAT M/V** 588/553 **In Top Fifth of
High School Graduating Class** 84% **Applied Early** 141 **Accepted Early** 97

COLLEGE LIFE **Out of State Students** 80% **From Public Schools** 72% **Ethnic Composition** White & Other 84%,
Asian American 8%, Black 4%, Hispanic 3.5%, Native American 0.5% **Foreign Students** 12% **Reside on Campus**
99% **Return as Sophomores** 96% **Student Faculty Ratio** 10:1 **Sororities** none

Nazareth College of Rochester

Rochester, NY · Est. 1924 · Coed · Private · 1,755 Undergrads · Urban

www.naz.edu

I need...

Admissions info www.naz.edu/admissn.htm
Financial aid info www.naz.edu/admissn.htm#aid

How wired is Nazareth College?

Do I get email? Yes
Do I get a home page? Yes
Is my dorm wired? Yes
What is the student to computer ratio? 15:1

FULL APPLICATION ONLINE

The usual tour

DEPARTMENTS www.naz.edu/academ.htm
STUDENT CLUBS www.naz.edu/student.htm#clubs
LIBRARY www.naz.edu/fastfact.htm#facil

Skip the brochure

- **GEORGE EASTMAN HOUSE** George Eastman, founder of Eastman Kodak, was a major industrialist and philanthropist. The museum at his former estate has exhibits on the

"Explore the integral role photography played in the development of modernism."

The gospel according to Nazareth

cultural importance of photography and the integral role it played in the development of modernism. **www.it.rit.edu/~gehouse/index.html**

- **THE GEVA THEATER** The Geva is obviously trying to provoke its Net visitors, claiming that theater is the only true interactive entertainment experience. Check out this local theater, and see if its staged bark is bigger than its acted bite. **www.roccplex.com/atroch/geva**

- **ROCHESTER** There is a Nazareth in Israel, but this one's in Rochester. This site can keep you up to date on the latest weather forecast, the political climate, and can connect you to local stores such as the Glorious Goat. **www.rochester.ny.us**

WHAT YOU NEED TO GET IN **Application Deadline** February 15 for priority consideration; final deadline March 1 **Early Action Deadline** December 1 **Common App.** Yes **Application Fee** $30 **Tuition Costs** $11,926 **Room & Board** $5,690 **Need Blind** Yes **Financial Forms Deadline** Priority given to applications received by March 1 **Undergrads Awarded Aid** 95% **Aid That Is Need-Based** 90% **Average Award of Freshman Scholarship Package** $7,442 **Tests Required** SAT1 or ACT **Admissions Address** 4245 East Avenue, Rochester, NY 14618 **Admissions Telephone** (800) 462-3944

LAST YEAR'S CLASS **Applied** 1,174 **Accepted** 904 **Matriculated** 304 **Average SAT M/V** 547/495 **Average ACT** 24 **In Top Quarter of High School Graduating Class** 30%

COLLEGE LIFE **Gender Breakdown** M 24%, F 76% **Out of State Students** 5% **From Public Schools** 88% **Ethnic Composition** White & Other 95%, Asian American 1%, Black 2%, Hispanic 1%, Native American 1% **Foreign Students** 1% **Reside on Campus** 63% **Return as Sophomores** 85% **Total Faculty** 111 **Student Faculty Ratio** 14:1 **Fraternities** none **Sororities** none **Graduate Students** 1,047

University of Nebraska, Lincoln

www.unl.edu

Lincoln, NE · Est. 1869 · Coed · Public · 19,186 Undergrads · Urban

I need...
Admissions info lschmidt@ccmail.unl.edu

How wired is University of Nebraska, Lincoln?
Do I get email? Yes
What is the student to computer ratio? 20:1

The usual tour
DEPARTMENTS www.unl.edu/unlpub/academics .html
SPORTS nusports.unl.edu
LIBRARY www.unl.edu/lovers/home.html
PUBLICATIONS www.unl.edu/DailyNe

Skip the brochure
• **LINCOLN LIVE** View Lincoln Nebraska Live. OK, it may not be the Bulls/Sonics playoffs, or the reading of the O.J. verdict, but this live video link is fascinating, particularly if you have never been to the great Midwest. **www.starcitymall.com/webcam**

• **NEBRASKA FOOTBALL** Where else could you hear "Sirius" by the Alan Parsons Project? Here, at the Cornhuskers site. (The song is also played as the team leaves the field). The Huskers were the 1995 NCAA Division I champions and have a huge following online. There is a mailing list here, lots of information on players and coaches, schedules, a photo gallery, and links to

University of Nebraska: an icon for every occasion

other Husker sites. **www.huskers.com/husker_toc**

• **IANR COMMUNICATIONS AND INFORMATION TECHNOLOGY MULTIMEDIA SERVER** Feel as if you really are in Lincoln. If you missed the commencement address, no problem. Listen to it here, as well as the installation of the chancellor. Just click your mouse, close your eyes, and listen. **citv.unl.edu**

"Where else could you hear 'Sirius' by the Alan Parsons Project?"

WHAT YOU NEED TO GET IN Application Deadline June 30 **Common App.** no **Application Fee** $25 **Tuition Costs** $2,248 ($6,118 out-of-state) **Room & Board** $3,450 **Need Blind** Yes **Financial Forms Deadline** Rolling **Undergrads Awarded Aid** 47% **Aid That Is Need-Based** 80% **Average Award of Freshman Scholarship Package** $1,260 **Tests Required** SAT1 or ACT (preferred) **Admissions Address** 14th and R Streets, Lincoln, NE 68588 **Admissions Telephone** (402) 472-2023

LAST YEAR'S CLASS Applied 7,318 **Accepted** 6,158 **Matriculated** 3,984 **Average SAT M/V** 499/453 **Average ACT** 22 **In Top Fifth of High School Graduating Class** 37%

COLLEGE LIFE Gender Breakdown M 54%, F 46% **Out of State Students** 12% **Ethnic Composition** White & Other 94.4%, Asian American 1.8%, Black 1.9%, Hispanic 1.6%, Native American 0.3% **Foreign Students** 3% **Reside on Campus** 23% **Return as Sophomores** 75% **Total Faculty** 1,516 **Student Faculty Ratio** 16:1 **Fraternities (% of men participating)** 28 (20%) **Sororities (% of women participating)** 16 (17%) **Graduate Students** 5,134

University of Nevada, Las Vegas

www.unlv.edu

Las Vegas, NV · Est. 1957 · Coed · Public · 15,635 Undergrads · Urban

I need...

Admissions info www.nscee.edu/unlv/UNLV
_Home_Page/ThirdLevel/Admissions.html
Financial aid info sfssc@ccmail.nevada.edu

How wired is UNLV?

Do I get email? Yes
Do I get a home page? Yes
Is my dorm wired? Yes
What is the student to computer ratio? 20:1

REQUEST APPLICATION ONLINE

The usual tour

VIRTUAL TOUR www.nscee.edu/unlv/UNLV_News
_and_Publications/ViewBook
DEPARTMENTS www.nscee.edu/unlv/UNLV
_Home_Page/ThirdLevel/Colleges.html
LIBRARY www.nscee.edu/unlv/Libraries
CALENDAR www.nscee.edu/unlv/UNLV
_News_and_Publications/Calendars
SPORTS tmc.nevada.edu

Skip the brochure

• **ROBIN AND DAVE'S WAY COOL ROCK CALENDAR** To find
out what is happening in the Vegas music
scene, check here. Robin and Dave know the
latest and have hyperlinks to home pages of
some of the coming acts. **www.unlv.edu/~daveg
/home.html**

• **THE WOMEN'S CENTER** Who says Las Vegas isn't

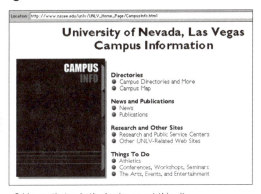

Odds are that only the basics are at this site

a good place to be a woman? The Women's
Center provides mentoring programs, scholarships, support groups, and plans special
events, all with the needs of women in mind.
www.unlv.edu/WC

• **POINTS OF INTERESTS** Keeping it green in the middle of the desert; UNLV has a drought-tolerant
garden, arboretums, atriums, and pools. And
those are only some of the points of interest.
**www.nscee.edu/unlv/UNLV_News_and_Publications/Points
_of_Interest**

"UNLV has drought-tolerant arboretums."

WHAT YOU NEED TO GET IN **Application Deadline** July 15 for priority consideration; final deadline August 15 **Early Action Deadline** March 1 **Common App.** no **Application Fee** $40 ($95 for international applicants) **Tuition Costs** $1,920 ($7,020 out-of-state) **Room & Board** $5,016 **Need Blind** Yes **Financial Forms Deadline** Priority given to applications received by February 15 **Undergrads Awarded Aid** 53% **Aid That Is Need-Based** 45% **Average Award of Freshman Scholarship Package** $1,500 **Tests Required** SAT1 or ACT (preferred) **Admissions Address** 4505 South Maryland Parkway, Las Vegas, NV 89154 **Admissions Telephone** (702) 895-3443

LAST YEAR'S CLASS **Applied** 7,836 **Accepted** 5,774 **Matriculated** 3,348 **Average SAT M/V** 508/485 **Average ACT** 21 **Applied Early** 409 **Accepted Early** 291

COLLEGE LIFE **Gender Breakdown** M 48%, F 52% **Out of State Students** 31% **Ethnic Composition** White & Other 79.5%, Asian American 6.4%, Black 6.5%, Hispanic 6.8%, Native American 0.8% **Foreign Students** 2% **Reside on Campus** 5% **Return as Sophomores** 71% **Total Faculty** 979 **Student Faculty Ratio** 18:1 **Fraternities (% of men participating)** 14 (15%) **Sororities (% of women participating)** 7 (11%) **Graduate Students** 4,134

New College of the University of South Florida

www.sar.usf.edu/NC

Sarasota, FL · Est. 1960 · Coed · Public · 586 Undergrads · Big Town

I need...

Admissions info www.sar.usf.edu/~computin
/html/departments/admissions.html
Financial aid info www.sar.usf.edu/new_college
/paying.html#financialaid

How wired is New College?

Do I get email? Yes
Do I get a home page? Yes
Is my dorm wired? No
What is the student to computer ratio? 12:1

The usual tour

LIBRARY virtu.sar.usf.edu/~library
DEPARTMENTS www.sar.usf.edu/~computin/html
/divisions
CALENDAR www.sar.usf.edu/new_college
/cal2.html
STUDENT CLUBS www.sar.usf.edu/~computin
/html/students
PUBLICATIONS www.sar.usf.edu/~catalyst
/otherpubs.html
VIRTUAL TOUR virtu.sar.usf.edu/~hilderbr/virtual

Skip the brochure

- **NEW COLLEGE FOUR WINDS COFFEEHOUSE HOMEPAGE**
Get involved with the process of building a coffee house at your future college. Ahead of its
time, the Four Winds Coffeehouse Web site

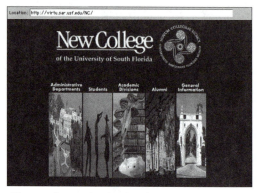

Many a college student heads to Sarasota for spring break.
These coeds live it

chronicles, as it happens, the construction of
your own personal coffeehouse from the
groundbreaking to the clinking of little silver
spoons on china. **www.sar.usf.edu/~ncoffeeh**

- **THE CATALYST** *The Catalyst* is a weekly newspaper serving New College students. News, features, and opinions are published. Current
issues are featured online. **www.sar.usf.edu
/~catalyst/current**

- **NEW COLLEGE BIKE SHOP HOMEPAGE** Find out where
you can get free bike repairs, discount bike
parts, or even become a volunteer bike technician. If your hobby is bicycling through the
tulips, this home page can help you connect
with the right people. **www.sar.usf.edu/~ncbs**

WHAT YOU NEED TO GET IN **Application Deadline** February 1 for priority consideration; final deadline May 1 **Common App.** no **Application Fee** $20 **Tuition Costs** $2,211 ($8,506 out-of-state) **Room & Board** $4,017 **Need Blind** Yes **Financial Forms Deadline** May 15 with a priority given to applications received by February 1 **Undergrads Awarded Aid** 84% **Aid That Is Need-Based** 42% **Average Award of Freshman Scholarship Package** $5,035 **Tests Required** SAT1 or ACT **Admissions Address** 5700 North Tamiami Trail, Sarasota, FL 34243-2197 **Admissions Telephone** (941) 359-4269

LAST YEAR'S CLASS **Applied** 524 **Accepted** 310 **Matriculated** 143 **Average SAT M/V** 650/627 **Average ACT** 29 **In Top Fifth of High School Graduating Class** 86%

COLLEGE LIFE **Gender Breakdown** M 46%, F 54% **Out of State Students** 44% **From Public Schools** 79% **Ethnic Composition** White & Other 85%, Asian American 8%, Black 2%, Hispanic 5% **Foreign Students** 3% **Reside on Campus** 60% **Return as Sophomores** 80% **Total Faculty** 53 **Student Faculty Ratio** 12:1 **Fraternities** none **Sororities** none

University of New Hampshire

unhinfo.unh.edu:70/1/unh

Durham, NH · Est. 1866 · Coed · Public · 10,620 Undergrads · Small Town

I need...

Admissions info admissions@unh.edu
www.unh.edu/admissions/index.html
Financial aid info unhinfo.unh.edu:70/0/unh
/admin/finaid/fin-aid-info.html

How wired is UNH?

Do I get email? Yes
Do I get a home page? Yes
Where? unhinfo.unh.edu:70/0/unh
/personal/pubpages.html
Is my dorm wired? Yes
What is the student to computer ratio? 55:1

The usual tour

DEPARTMENTS unhinfo.unh.edu:70/1/unh/acad
CALENDAR unhinfo.unh.edu:70/1/unh/events
LIBRARY wwwsc.library.unh.edu
STUDENT CLUBS unhinfo.unh.edu:70/1/unh
/student/orgs
CAREER CENTER www.unh.edu/career-services
/index.html

Skip the brochure

• **STUDENT DISCOVERY GROUPS** The nitty gritty of campus issues laid bare. These groups deal with some of the most undiscussed, but real, student issues. Groups deal with sexual identity, eating disorders (for both men and

Location: http://unhinfo.unh.edu:70/0/unh/personal/pubpages.html

Some Personal Home Pages

UNH campus home pages.

Some of these are on our central systems and some are on departmental or private systems.

You can get there from here!

| A - C | D - K | L - O | P - Z |

Check out your typical UNH student

women), post-abortion trauma, and ethnic identity. **unhinfo.unh.edu:70/lm/unh/student /discovery.struc-file**

• **GREAT BAY FOOD COOPERATIVE** Eating can be an educational experience, especially if you get involved with the Great Bay Food Cooperative. Co-ops are non-profit, so their food is sold to members at lower prices, and co-op members volunteer their labor. Read the fascinating history of food co-ops. **unhinfo.unh.edu:70/0/unh /student/orgs/gbfc/index.html**

• **SEAC** Since the early '90s, the Student Environmental Action Committee has become one of the more accomplished student activist groups in the country. Well connected and extremely active, SEACers are exemplary among the new generation of student activists. Get to know this chapter, which works on local UNH issues and participates in national campaigns. **www.unh.edu/seac/index.html**

WHAT YOU NEED TO GET IN **Application Deadline** Fall for priority consideration; final deadline February 1 **Early Action Deadline** December 1 **Common App.** no **Application Fee** $25 ($45 for out-of-state applicants) **Tuition Costs** $4,033 ($13,003 out-of-state) **Room & Board** $4,354 **Need Blind** Yes **Financial Forms Deadline** Priority given to applications received by March 1 **Undergrads Awarded Aid** 76% **Aid That Is Need-Based** 98% **Average Award of Freshman Scholarship Package** $4,602 **Tests Required** SAT1 (preferred) or ACT **Admissions Address** Durham, NH 03824 **Admissions Telephone** (603) 862-1360

LAST YEAR'S CLASS **Applied** 10,026 **Accepted** 7,723 **Matriculated** 2,440 **Average SAT M/V** 553/553 **In Top Fifth of High School Graduating Class** 43% **Applied Early** 1,624 **Accepted Early** 929

COLLEGE LIFE **Gender Breakdown** M 43%, F 57% **Out of State Students** 44% **Ethnic Composition** White & Other 96.5%, Asian American 1.6%, Black 0.6%, Hispanic 1.1%, Native American 0.2% **Reside on Campus** 55% **Return as Sophomores** 83% **Total Faculty** 712 **Student Faculty Ratio** 17:1 **Fraternities (% of men participating)** 11 (12%) **Sororities (% of women participating)** 6 (12%) **Graduate Students** 1,794

New Hampshire College

Manchester, NH · Est. 1932 · Coed · Private · 4,051 Undergrads · Urban

I need...

Admissions info www.nhc.edu/admissio/admitpg
.html

Financial aid info www.nhc.edu/admissio/finaid
.html

How wired is New Hampshire College?

Do I get email? Yes
Do I get a home page? No
Is my dorm wired? Yes
What is the student to computer ratio? 12:1

The usual tour

DEPARTMENTS www.nhc.edu/academic/usdegs
.html
CAMPUS MAP www.nhc.edu/maps/nhcmapsp
.html
CALENDAR www.nhc.edu/calendar/cal.html
SPORTS www.nhc.edu/student/athletic/athletic
.html

Skip the brochure

• **AMERICAN LANGUAGE AND CULTURE CENTER**
Manchester may evoke images of Americana

"What's Happening: a guide to New Hampshire's latest"

Pretty as a picture: New Hampshire College

and New England charm, but New Hampshire
College's American Language and Culture
Center spices things up by inviting the rest of
the world to study language and culture there.
www.nhc.edu/academic/alcc.html

• **TECHNOLOGY INFORMATION CENTER** New
Hampshire is somewhat new to the world of
computers, but has just opened a
Communications/Technology Center to meet
the demands of the '90s. Students now have
Net access, online library catalogs, email
accounts, and can even take classes over the
Web. **www.nhc.edu/alumni/technlgy.html**

• **WHAT'S HAPPENING** This is not the home page of
one of the most important television programs
of the '70s, but a guide to what's on in and
around New Hampshire. **www.nh.com/nhhappen**

WHAT YOU NEED TO GET IN **Application Deadline** Rolling admissions **Common App.** Yes **Tuition Costs** $11,866 **Room & Board** $5,112 **Need Blind** Yes **Financial Forms Deadline** Priority given to applications received by March 15 **Undergrads Awarded Aid** 75% **Aid That Is Need-Based** 46% **Average Award of Freshman Scholarship Package** $2,000 **Tests Required** SAT1 (preferred) or ACT **Admissions Address** 2500 North River Road, Manchester, NH 03106-1045 **Admissions Telephone** (603) 645-9611

LAST YEAR'S CLASS **Applied** 1,457 **Accepted** 1,212 **Matriculated** 314 **Average SAT M/V** 431/386 **In Top Fifth of High School Graduating Class** 9%

COLLEGE LIFE **Gender Breakdown** M 48%, F 52% **Out of State Students** 60% **From Public Schools** 80% **Ethnic Composition** White & Other 95%, Asian American 3%, Black 1%, Hispanic 1% **Foreign Students** 15% **Reside on Campus** 80% **Return as Sophomores** 65% **Total Faculty** 99 **Student Faculty Ratio** 17:1 **Fraternities (% of men participating)** 4 (10%) **Sororities (% of women participating)** 4 (10%) **Graduate Students** 1,794

New Jersey Institute of Technology

Newark, NJ · Est. 1881 · Coed · Public · 5,042 Undergrads · Urban

www.njit.edu

I need...

Admissions info admissions@admin.njit.edu
www.njit.edu/njIT/Directory/Admin
/Admissions/index.html

Financial aid info finaid@admin.njit.edu
www.njit.edu/njIT/Directory/Admin
/Admissions/finaid.html

FULL APPLICATION ONLINE

How wired is NJIT?

Do I get email? Yes

Do I get a home page? Yes
Where? hertz.njit.edu/hertz_home page.html

Is my dorm wired? Yes

What is the student to computer ratio? 4:1

The usual tour

DEPARTMENTS www.njit.edu/njIT/instruct/degree
/bsdeg.html

SPORTS www.njit.edu/njIT/Overview/About
/Students/athletic.html

LIBRARY www.njit.edu/njIT/Library/Welcome.html

STUDENT CLUBS www.njit.edu/njIT/Overview
/About/Students/clubs.html

CAREER CENTER www.njit.edu/njIT/Directory
/Admin/Career/Welcome.html

Skip the brochure

- **WOMEN'S CENTER** Go techie girls! NJIT is not just
interested in increasing the presence of

New Jersey Tech shouts out its accomplishments

women in the science and technology fields,
but also making them comfortable while they
study. In fact, the '90s is the "Decade of the
Woman at NJIT." **www.njit.edu/njIT/Overview/About
/Students/womens.html**

- **ATHLETICS** You can get a trainer at NJIT!
Besides a slew of competitive intercollegiate
teams, NJIT also has three gyms and various
fitness facilities. **www.njit.edu/njIT/Overview/About
/Students/athletic.html**

- **CLASS NOTES** Why wait until you arrive on campus? See what courses are like by perusing syllabi and hyperlinked reading. Make sure the
courses you're checking are for undergrads, as
the grad classes will be indecipherable and difficult. **www.njit.edu/njIT/ClassNotes/index.html**

WHAT YOU NEED TO GET IN **Application Deadline** Rolling admissions; April 1 for priority consideration **Early Action Deadline** December 1 **Common App.** No **Application Fee** $35 **Tuition Costs** $4,500 ($8,844 out-of-state) **Room & Board** $5,600 **Need Blind** Yes **Financial Forms Deadline** Priority given to applications received by March 15 **Undergrads Awarded Aid** 69% **Aid That Is Need-Based** 82% **Average Award of Freshman Scholarship Package** $5,134 **Tests Required** SAT1 (preferred) or ACT **Admissions Address** University Heights, Newark, NJ 07102-1982 **Admissions Telephone** (201) 596-3300

LAST YEAR'S CLASS **Applied** 1,916 **Accepted** 1,277 **Matriculated** 564 **Average SAT M/V** 608/481 **In Top Fifth of High School Graduating Class** 39% **Applied Early** 86 **Accepted Early** 40

COLLEGE LIFE **Gender Breakdown** M 82%, F 18% **Out of State Students** 7% **From Public Schools** 80% **Ethnic Composition** White & Other 55.6%, Asian American 17.7%, Black 13.1%, Hispanic 13.4%, Native American 0.2% **Foreign Students** 5% **Reside on Campus** 25% **Return as Sophomores** 85% **Total Faculty** 530 **Student Faculty Ratio** 13:1 **Fraternities (% of men participating)** 14 (15%) **Sororities (% of women participating)** 9 (8%) **Graduate Students** 2,843

New Mexico Institute of Mining and Technology

www.nmt.edu

Socorro, NM · Est. 1889 · Coed · Public · 1,252 Undergrads · Small Town

I need...

Admissions info admission@admin.nmt.edu
www.nmt.edu/mainpage/uginfo/ugadmis.html

Financial aid info ahansen@admin.nmt.edu
www.nmt.edu/mainpage/catalog/finaid.html

How wired is New Mexico Tech?

Do I get email? Yes
Do I get a home page? Yes
What is the student to computer ratio? 8:1

DOWNLOAD APPLICATION ONLINE

The usual tour

CALENDAR www.nmt.edu/mainpage/calendar/calendars.html
LIBRARY nmt.edu/~nmtlib
STUDENT CLUBS www.nmt.edu/mainpage/stulife/stuclubs.html
CLUB SPORTS www.nmt.edu/mainpage/stulife/clubsports.html
VIRTUAL TOUR www.nmt.edu/mainpage/tour/pubinfo.html
RECENT NEWS STORIES www.nmt.edu/mainpage/news/stories.html

Skip the brochure

- **THE VIRTUAL WORLD CLUB** To Infinity and Beyond... The Virtual World Club focuses on MUDs (Multi-User Dimensions) and operates

Techies bone up on the ol' Taijutstu

an established AberMUD called Infinity.
www.nmt.edu/~vwclub

- **THE LOST AND FOUND** You can tell a lot about a campus from what people lose and find there. When we visited the virtual lost and found, it was empty— so either the students are conscientious and never lose their things or they're devilishly dishonest, and keep whatever they find. OK, so maybe you really can't tell a lot from a campus's lost and found. **www.nmt.edu/mainpage/stulife/lost_and_found.html**

- **SOCORRO, NEW MEXICO** So most of us outside New Mexico probably don't know about Socorro. Apparently, it's abundant with outdoor activity including hiking, camping, rock climbing, fishing, and hunting. **www.nmt.edu/mainpage/tour/socorro.html**

WHAT YOU NEED TO GET IN Application Deadline March 1 for priority consideration; final deadline August 1 **Common App.** no **Application Fee** $15 **Tuition Costs** $1,407 ($5,814 out-of-state) **Room & Board** $3,426 **Need Blind** Yes **Financial Forms Deadline** Priority given to applications received by March 1 **Undergrads Awarded Aid** 73% **Aid That Is Need-Based** 75% **Average Award of Freshman Scholarship Package** $2,915 **Tests Required** ACT **Admissions Address** 801 Leroy Place, Socorro, NM 87801 **Admissions Telephone** (505) 835-5424

LAST YEAR'S CLASS Applied 753 **Accepted** 556 **Matriculated** 235 **Average ACT** 26 **In Top Fifth of High School Graduating Class** 60%

COLLEGE LIFE Gender Breakdown M 64%, F 36% **Ethnic Composition** White & Other 76%, Asian American 3%, Black 1%, Hispanic 17%, Native American 3% **Foreign Students** 4% **Reside on Campus** 45% **Return as Sophomores** 65% **Total Faculty** 103 **Student Faculty Ratio** 11:1 **Fraternities** none **Sororities** none **Graduate Students** 243

University of New Mexico

www.unm.edu

Albuquerque, NM · Est. 1889 · Coed · Public · 19,042 Undergrads · Urban

I need...

Admissions info www.unm.edu/~unmreg
/reghome.html

Financial aid info www.unm.edu/~finaid/finaid
.html

How wired is University of New Mexico?

Do I get email? Yes
Do I get a home page? Yes
   Where? www.unm.edu/stu_home_msg.html
Is my dorm wired? No
What is the student to computer ratio? 55:1

The usual tour

STUDENT CLUBS www.unm.edu/studentorg.html
DEPARTMENTS www.unm.edu/colleges.html
LIBRARY www.unm.edu/~libinfo/newlibraries
   .html
STUDY ABROAD www.unm.edu/~libinfo
   /newlibraries.html

Skip the brochure

• **UNM SNOWBOARDING CLUB** The members of this
group definitely know how to have a good time.
They don't just snowboard—they cross-dress
and clearly have a sense of humor. Beyond
this, they are well-organized, listing all the
stores where UNM snowboarders receive discounts, and outlining the seasonal schedule.
www.unm.edu/~thumpj/unmsc.html

• **ALBUQUERQUE** With less than half a million peo-

Adobe or not adobe? That is the question

ple, Albuquerque is a small city with an incredibly rich culture, not to mention the natural
beauty stretching "from mountains to desert,
volcanic cliffs to ice caves, White Sands to
Carlsbad Caverns, from mountain climbing to
skiing, from old mining towns like Madrid to
art communities like Taos and Sante Fe." If
you've got eyes and want to use them, New
Mexico is a great place to be a student.
www.unm.edu/sneak_preview/alb-nm.html

• **LIVING IT UP ON A BUDGET** Budgeting 101. This
helpful page not only gives the breakdown of
tuition and housing costs, but also estimates
how much a student might spend in the bookstore, and lists lots of local activities and
sites. There are lots of free things to do on the
UNM campus (11 museums alone), and it
seems that Albuquerque has lots of cheap
eats too. **www.unm.edu/sneak_preview/budget.html**

WHAT YOU NEED TO GET IN **Application Deadline** Rolling admissions **Common App.** no **Application Fee** $15 **Tuition
Costs** $2,071 ($7,822 out-of-state) **Room & Board** $4,000 **Financial Forms Deadline** Priority given to
applications received by March 1 **Undergrads Awarded Aid** 50% **Aid That Is Need-Based** 63% **Average Award of
Freshman Scholarship Package** $1,720 **Tests Required** SAT1 or ACT (preferred) **Admissions Address**
Albuquerque, NM 87131 **Admissions Telephone** (505) 277-2446

LAST YEAR'S CLASS **Applied** 3,666 **Accepted** 3,154 **Matriculated** 1,727 **Average SAT M/V** 533/539 **Average ACT**
22 **In Top Fifth of High School Graduating Class** 43%

COLLEGE LIFE **Gender Breakdown** M 43%, F 57% **Out of State Students** 22% **Ethnic Composition** White & Other
61%, Asian American 3%, Black 3%, Hispanic 28%, Native American 5% **Foreign Students** 1% **Reside on Campus**
10% **Return as Sophomores** 69% **Total Faculty** 2,006 **Student Faculty Ratio** 16:1 **Fraternities (% of men
participating)** 10 (7%) **Sororities (% of women participating)** 4 (3%) **Graduate Students** 5,389

University of New Orleans

www.uno.edu

New Orleans, LA · Est. 1958 · Coed · Public · 11,694 Undergrads · Urban

How wired is University of New Orleans?

**What is the student
to computer ratio?** 11:1

FULL APPLICATION ONLINE

The usual tour

DEPARTMENTS www.uno.edu/university
/academic.html
LIBRARY www.uno.edu/~liad
SPORTS www.uno.edu/undercons.html
CALENDAR www.uno.edu/~acse/home page
calendar.html
STUDY ABROAD www.uno.edu/~oiss

Skip the brochure

• **SCHOOL OF HOTEL, RESTAURANT AND TOURISM** With a
booming tourist trade, Cajun history, food and
architecture, New Orleans makes a great "living laboratory" for the study of hospitality and
tourism management. And for those interested
in a less urban, more green field of study, the
surrounding swamps and wetlands offer opportunities for "ecotourism" research.
www.uno.edu/~hrt

• **UNO INTERNATIONAL SUMMER SCHOOL** Innsbruck, in
the heart of the Austrian Alps, is the home of
UNO's Summer School. One of the largest
U.S. university programs abroad, Innsbruck/

Location: http://www.uno.edu/~wmon/

**WELCOME TO THE
UNO WOMEN'S CENTER**

Main Menu | What's New | UNOWC Library | Upcoming Events | Local Links | Other Links

New Orleans women come together online

UNO offers more than 50 courses every year.
www.uno.edu/~inst/innsbcs.html

• **OFFICE OF MULTICULTURAL AFFAIRS** Though the
whole UNO site has a terrific look, this site
may be worth visiting just for its graphics.
There isn't much text here, just the warm and
fuzzy message that ethnic diversity is to be
understood and celebrated. **www.uno.edu/~stlf
/oma.html**

"Office of Multicultural Affairs: full of warm and fuzzy messages"

WHAT YOU NEED TO GET IN **Application Deadline** July 1 for priority consideration; final deadline August 18 **Common App.**
Yes **Application Fee** $20 **Tuition Costs** $2,362 ($5,154 out-of-state) **Room & Board** $3,100 **Need Blind** Yes
Financial Forms Deadline Priority given to applications received by May 1 **Undergrads Awarded Aid** 61% **Aid
That Is Need-Based** 85% **Average Award of Freshman Scholarship Package** $3,500 **Tests Required** SAT1 or
ACT (preferred) **Admissions Address** New Orleans, LA 70148 **Admissions Telephone** (504) 286-6595

LAST YEAR'S CLASS **Applied** 2,912 **Accepted** 2,564 **Matriculated** 1,677 **Average SAT M/V** 515/453 **Average ACT** 21

COLLEGE LIFE **Gender Breakdown** M 45%, F 55% **Out of State Students** 5% **From Public Schools** 60% **Ethnic
Composition** White & Other 73%, Asian American 4%, Black 17%, Hispanic 6% **Foreign Students** 2% **Reside on
Campus** 5% **Return as Sophomores** 65% **Total Faculty** 698 **Student Faculty Ratio** 21:1 **Fraternities (% of men
participating)** 9 (3%) **Sororities (% of women participating)** 7 (3%) **Graduate Students** 3,789

New York University

New York, NY · Est. 1831 · Coed · Private · 15,612 Undergrads · Urban

I need...

Admissions info nyu.admit.eduwww.jayi.com/NYU
Financial aid info www.nyu.edu/finanaid.html

How wired is NYU?

Do I get email? Yes
Do I get a home page? Yes
   Where? pages.nyu.edu
Is my dorm wired? Yes
What is the student to computer ratio? 18:1

The usual tour

DEPARTMENTS www.nyu.edu/dept.html
LIBRARY www.nyu.edu/library
SPORTS www.nyu.edu/coles.html
STUDENT CLUBS pages.nyu.edu/clubs
VIRTUAL TOUR www.nyu.edu/infocenter
   /campus2/ws/index.html

Skip the brochure

• **PAPERLESS GUIDE TO NEW YORK CITY** Bought for less than $25 from the Indians, and once the United States capitol, New York City has always had its appeal. Arguably the most exciting city in the world, New York is a welter of transportation, sightseeing, hotels, restaurants, current events, and shopping. This site can help. **www.mediabridge.com/nyc**

• **SUMMERSTAGE** Summerstage is one of the things that makes hot sticky New York summers bearable. Fantastic artists appear

In NYU's melting pot, the Greeks are actually from Greece

for free (almost always), performing classical, jazz, and funk music. **www.metrobeat.com/nyc/locations/lmc0123.html**

• **GALLATIN SCHOOL OF INDIVIDUALIZED STUDY** And you thought all the funky students went to Tisch. With courses like "Concepts of Morality" and "A Sense of Place," the Gallatin School of Individualized Study is home to NYU's intellectually ambitious undergrads. **www.nyu.edu/gallatin**

• **NYU SOCIETY FOR CREATIVE ANACHRONISM** Lost touch with your inner serf? There is the possibility of acting out and recreating the European Middle Ages. This club is a satellite of the incredibly popular "living history" movement, which studies and reenacts the dance, calligraphy, martial arts, cooking, metalwork, stained glass, and costuming of various historical periods. **www.nyu.edu/pages/nyusca**

WHAT YOU NEED TO GET IN **Application Deadline** January 15 **Early Action Deadline** November 15 **Common App.** Yes **Application Fee** $45 **Tuition Costs** $20,756 **Room & Board** $7,856 **Need Blind** Yes **Financial Forms Deadline** Priority given to applications received by February 15 **Undergrads Awarded Aid** 73% **Aid That Is Need-Based** 90% **Average Award of Freshman Scholarship Package** $8,808 **Tests Required** SAT1 or ACT **Admissions Address** 22 Washington Square North, New York, NY 10011 **Admissions Telephone** (212) 998-4500

LAST YEAR'S CLASS **Applied** 16,491 **Accepted** 7,619 **Matriculated** 2,901 **In Top Fifth of High School Graduating Class** 75% **Applied Early** 1,165 **Accepted Early** 46

COLLEGE LIFE **Gender Breakdown** M 41%, F 59% **Out of State Students** 48% **From Public Schools** 70% **Ethnic Composition** White & Other 60%, Asian American 21%, Black 10%, Hispanic 9% **Foreign Students** 6% **Reside on Campus** 60% **Return as Sophomores** 88% **Student Faculty Ratio** 13:1 **Fraternities (% of men participating)** 11 (7%) **Sororities (% of women participating)** 7 (5%) **Graduate Students** 15,487

University of North Carolina, Chapel Hill

www.unc.edu

Chapel Hill, NC · Est. 1789 · Coed · Public · 15,702 Undergrads · Big Town

I need...

Admissions info UAdm@email.unc.edu
www.adp.unc.edu/sis/admissions/under
grad.html

Financial aid info www.adp.unc.edu/sis/finaid
/finaid.html

How wired is UNC, Chapel Hill?

Do I get email? Yes
Do I get a home page? Yes
Is my dorm wired? Yes
What is the student to computer ratio? 39:1

DOWNLOAD APPLICATION ONLINE

The usual tour

DEPARTMENTS www.unc.edu/depts/arts
/deptlist.html

STUDENT CLUBS www.unc.edu/student/orgs
/recog/all.html

CAREER CENTER www.unc.edu/depts/career

SPORTS www.adp.unc.edu/sis/athletics
/home.html

PUBLICATIONS www.unc.edu/student/orgs/recog
/pubs.html

Skip the brochure

- **THE DAILY TAR HEEL** *The Daily Tar Heel* is a good way to explore UNC campus culture. Catch up on the latest dramas and controversies, check out who is coming to play and perform, and

Dean Smith's boys in blue keep on slamming

take the political temperature by reading the editorial page. **www.unc.edu/dth**

- **TAR HEELS BASKETBALL** For some the Tar Heels men's basketball program is important simply because Michael Jordan was a product of it. Even hoop fans who aren't such NBA groupies, will enjoy catching up with the latest boys in blue. **www.adp.unc.edu/sis/athletics/teams /mbball/home.html**

- **NEWSGROUPS AT CHAPEL HILL** Coffee talk? There are newsgroups for chemistry, geology, physics, student jobs, and more. Just be clear that the newsgroup for coffee is different from the one for Java (the former being for the addictive hot beverage, the latter for a computer language). These groups are for UNC students, but at least you can get a sense of the word on campus. **www.unc.edu/pubs/news.html**

WHAT YOU NEED TO GET IN **Application Deadline** October 15 for priority consideration; final deadline January 15 **Common App.** Yes **Application Fee** $55 **Tuition Costs** $1,386 ($9,918 out-of-state) **Room & Board** $4,500 **Need Blind** Yes **Financial Forms Deadline** Priority given to applications received by March 1 **Undergrads Awarded Aid** 37% **Aid That Is Need-Based** 76% **Average Award of Freshman Scholarship Package** $2,500 **Tests Required** SAT1 (preferred) or ACT **Admissions Address** Chapel Hill, NC 27599-2200 **Admissions Telephone** (919) 966-3621

LAST YEAR'S CLASS **Applied** 15,159 **Accepted** 5,571 **Matriculated** 3,239 **Average SAT M/V** 603/539 **Average ACT** 28 **In Top Fifth of High School Graduating Class** 89%

COLLEGE LIFE **Gender Breakdown** M 40%, F 60% **Out of State Students** 17% **From Public Schools** 87% **Ethnic Composition** White & Other 82.9%, Asian American 4.9%, Black 10.5%, Hispanic 1%, Native American 0.7% **Reside on Campus** 29% **Return as Sophomores** 93% **Total Faculty** 2,369 **Student Faculty Ratio** 6:1 **Fraternities (% of men participating)** 28 (17%) **Sororities (% of women participating)** 17 (17%) **Graduate Students** 8,737

North Carolina State University

Raleigh, NC · Est. 1887 · Coed · Public · 21,338 Undergrads · Urban

I need...

Admissions info Undergrad_Admissions@NCSU
.edu
www2.acs.ncsu.edu/uga/adm
Financial aid info www2.acs.ncsu.edu/uga/adm
/66xpg36.htm

How wired is NC State?

Do I get email? Yes
Do I get a home page? Yes
Is my dorm wired? Yes
What is the student to computer ratio? 6:1

The usual tour

CALENDAR www.acs.ncsu.edu/Calendar
STUDENT CLUBS www.ncsu.edu/stud_orgs.html
LIBRARY www.lib.ncsu.edu
SPORTS www2.ncsu.edu/ncsu/athletics
GREEK LIFE www2.ncsu.edu/ncsu/stud_orgs
/frat_sor
DEPARTMENTS www2.ncsu.edu/ncsu/provost
/info/ugcatalog/programs/idx-coll.html

Skip the brochure

• **SCHOOL OF DESIGN** NC State's Design for Living:
"Design education is more than an attempt to
'teach' a set of technical skills. The environment, including the spaces in which people
live and work, the products they consume, and

From the loom to the Web: NC State's College of Textiles

the messages they receive, have a powerful
impact on how humans function as a society."
www2.ncsu.edu/ncsu/design

• **WINDHOVER** *Windhover* is the literary and visual
arts journal for North Carolina State University.
Poetry, short stories, and artwork from the
NCSU community are showcased. **www2.ncsu
.edu/ncsu/stud_pubs/Windhover**

• **FAN'S CORNER** Fan's Corner has RealAudio
speeches by Jeff Blench, the recently appoint-
ed men's Basketball Coach. There is also an
article titled, modestly, "The Greatest College
Basketball Game," on a 1974 NC State/
Maryland game, and Wolfpackers congregate
at the Wolfpack's Live chatroom. **www.agrafx
.com/pack/fan**

WHAT YOU NEED TO GET IN Application Deadline November 1 for priority consideration; final deadline February 1
Common App. Yes **Application Fee** $55 **Tuition Costs** $1,732 ($9,848 out-of-state) **Room & Board** $3,670
Need Blind Yes **Financial Forms Deadline** Priority given to applications received by March 1 **Undergrads
Awarded Aid** 43% **Aid That Is Need-Based** 76% **Average Award of Freshman Scholarship Package** $2,501
Tests Required SAT1 or ACT **Admissions Address** Box 7103, Raleigh, NC 27695-7103 **Admissions Telephone**
(919) 515-2434

LAST YEAR'S CLASS Applied 10,534 **Accepted** 7,606 **Matriculated** 3,528 **Average SAT M/V** 570/491 **In Top Fifth of
High School Graduating Class** 59%

COLLEGE LIFE Gender Breakdown M 60%, F 40% **Out of State Students** 14% **From Public Schools** 96% **Ethnic
Composition** White & Other 83.7%, Asian American 4.1%, Black 10.3%, Hispanic 1.2%, Native American 0.7%
Foreign Students 1% **Reside on Campus** 40% **Return as Sophomores** 93% **Total Faculty** 1,615 **Student Faculty
Ratio** 13:1 **Fraternities (% of men participating)** 24 (14%) **Sororities (% of women participating)** 10 (14%)
Graduate Students 6,200

University of North Dakota www.und.nodak.edu

Grand Forks, ND · Est. 1883 · Coed · Public · 9,468 Undergrads · Big Town

How wired is University of North Dakota?

Do I get email? Yes
Do I get a home page? Yes
Is my dorm wired? Yes
**What is the student to
computer ratio?** 3:1

REQUEST APPLICATION ONLINE

The usual tour

DEPARTMENTS www.und.nodak.edu/acedem.htm
SPORTS www.und.nodak.edu/athletic.htm
PUBLICATIONS www.und.nodak.edu/pubs.htm
CAREER CENTER www.und.nodak.edu/dept/career
CALENDAR gopher://sage.und.nodak.edu
:70/11/events/calendar/monthly

Skip the brochure

• **NTRY** This ezine has more spunk than anything
else at the University of North Dakota site.

"NTRY: This ezine has more spunk that anything else at the UND site."

Location: http://www.und.nodak.edu/gifs/fountain.gif

UND: in the heart of the beautiful Red River Valley

The editor's note touches on such contemporary buzz-books as Nicholas Negroponte's *Being Digital* and Neil Postman's *Amusing Ourselves to Death*. Hyperlinks to *The Paris Review* reaffirm that indeed, this editor is a bookish sort. **www.und.nodak.edu/org/ntry/ntry.html**

• **CAMPUS MAP** This map is one of the most sophisticated features at the site, which, all told, isn't saying much. **www.und.nodak.edu /maps/index.html**

• **WITMER ART GALLERY** The Witmer Gallery hocks artistic wares like drawings, collages, paintings, stoneware, jewelry, and notecards. This *Twin Peaks*-ish link says something about UND, though it's not clear what. **www.operations .und.nodak.edu/witag**

WHAT YOU NEED TO GET IN **Application Deadline** March 1 for priority consideration; final deadline July 1 **Common App.** no **Application Fee** $25 **Tuition Costs** $2,110 ($5,634 out-of-state) **Room & Board** $2910 **Need Blind** Yes **Financial Forms Deadline** Priority given to applications received by April 15 **Undergrads Awarded Aid** 56% **Aid That Is Need-Based** 64% **Average Award of Freshman Scholarship Package** $992 **Tests Required** SAT1 or ACT (preferred) **Admissions Address** University Station, Grand Forks, ND 58202-8172 **Admissions Telephone** (701) 777-3821

LAST YEAR'S CLASS **Applied** 2,764 **Accepted** 1,989 **Matriculated** 1,649 **Average SAT M/V** 518/461 **Average ACT** 23 **In Top Quarter of High School Graduating Class** 55%

COLLEGE LIFE **Gender Breakdown** M 52%, F 48% **Out of State Students** 48% **Ethnic Composition** White & Other 94%, Asian American 1%, Black 1%, Hispanic 1%, Native American 3% **Foreign Students** 4% **Reside on Campus** 35% **Return as Sophomores** 77% **Total Faculty** 674 **Student Faculty Ratio** 17:1 **Fraternities (% of men participating)** 17 (12%) **Sororities (% of women participating)** 7 (8%) **Graduate Students** 1,571

Northeastern University

www.neu.edu

Boston, MA · Est. 1898 · Coed · Private · 19,737 Undergrads · Urban

I need...

Admissions info www.neu.edu/top/adm-fn.html
Financial aid info www.neu.edu/top/adm-fn.html

How wired is Northeastern?

Do I get email? Yes
Do I get a home page? Yes
Is my dorm wired? Yes
What is the student to computer ratio? 39:1

The usual tour

DEPARTMENTS www.neu.edu/top/academics.html
STUDENT CLUBS www.neu.edu/top/stdact.html
LIBRARY www.neu.edu/top/library.html
CALENDAR www.voice.neu.edu/Voice
/calendar.html
PUBLICATIONS www.voice.neu.edu
SPORTS www.neu.edu/athletics

Skip the brochure

• **NORTHEASTERN UNIVERSITY'S HUS-SKIERS AND
OUTING CLUB** If the graphics are for real, you
should join this club. These folks have their
own lodge in the White Mountain National
Forest, and it looks beautiful. The Hus-skiers
participate in many different outdoor activities
and have lots of equipment and resources
available. **www.dac.neu.edu/SG/NUHOC/nuhoc
_home.html**

• **BOSTON** Though Beantown evokes better visual
imagery, Boston may well be called "Student-

Scientific Diving Program

Explore the Deep at Northeastern's Marine Science Center

town," as it hosts more than 300,000 students every school year. This site touches on
some of the attractions of Boston, from the
Head of the Charles Regatta to Filene's
Basement. **www.neu.edu/top/boston.html**

• **MARINE SCIENCE CENTER** Study seaweed and
learn scientific diving through all the enticing
opportunities at Northeastern's Marine
Science Center. Research is being conducted
on lobster based underwater robots and beach
pollution, to name just a few projects This
aqua blue site is bound to inspire many
marine biology majors. **www.dac.neu.edu/units
/artsSci/MSC/MSCHomePage.html**

"The Hus-skiers have their own lodge."

WHAT YOU NEED TO GET IN **Application Deadline** Rolling admissions; March 1 for priority consideration **Common App.**
no **Application Fee** $40 **Tuition Costs** $15,045 **Room & Board** $8,025 **Need Blind** Yes **Financial Forms
Deadline** Priority given to applications received by April 14 **Undergrads Awarded Aid** 70% **Aid That Is Need-
Based** 88% **Average Award of Freshman Scholarship Package** $7,616 **Tests Required** SAT1 (preferred) or ACT
Admissions Address 360 Huntington Avenue, Boston, MA 02115 **Admissions Telephone** (617) 373-2200

LAST YEAR'S CLASS **Applied** 13,609 **Accepted** 9,960 **Matriculated** 2,783 **Average SAT M/V** 535/473 **Average ACT**
23 **In Top Fifth of High School Graduating Class** 31%

COLLEGE LIFE **Gender Breakdown** M 52%, F 48% **Out of State Students** 49% **Ethnic Composition** White & Other
80.9%, Asian American 7.2%, Black 7.5%, Hispanic 4.1%, Native American 0.3% **Foreign Students** 10% **Reside
on Campus** 65% **Return as Sophomores** 73% **Total Faculty** 754 **Student Faculty Ratio** 13:1 **Fraternities
(% of men participating)** 18 (9%) **Sororities (% of women participating)** 8 (5%) **Graduate Students** 4,868

Northwestern University

www.acns.nwu.edu

Evanston, IL · Est. 1851 · Coed · Private · 7,604 Undergrads · Suburban

I need...

Admissions info ug-admissions@nwu.edu
www.acns.nwu.edu/admissions

How wired is Northwestern?

Do I get email? Yes
Do I get a home page? Yes
Is my dorm wired? Yes

The usual tour

DEPARTMENTS www.acns.nwu.edu/schools
LIBRARY www.acns.nwu.edu/classes/library.html
SPORTS www.acns.nwu.edu/student/athletics.html
STUDENT CLUBS www.nwu.edu/norris/studorg
PUBLICATIONS www.acns.nwu.edu/admin
/publications.html

Skip the brochure

• **THE ELECTRIC ARMADILLO** It's not entirely clear why this page is called the "Electric Armadillo" but it doesn't really matter. Rallying enthusiasm and energy for the annual Mayfest and listing the featured performers is its purpose. www.studorg.nwu.edu/mayfest

"Northwestern is quite the media epicenter."

Location: http://www.studorg.nwu.edu/nucrew/pictures.html

Northwestern towers over many of its collegiate brethren

• **STUDIO 22** This is an important site for anyone interested in student cinema. Studio 22 is a student-run production company that turns out several half-hour animated and documentary films every year, and also organizes the occasional film festival. www.rtvf.nwu.edu
/organizations/Studio22

• **NORTHWESTERN NEWS NETWORK** Thanks to its journalism school and excellent media facilities, Northwestern is quite the media epicenter. If the creative side of film (i.e. Studio 22) doesn't raise your antenna, then NNN may be an activity worth considering: "NNN is a student-run, non-profit television news program which provides a broad-based, hands-on training for students interested in television news. www.nwu.edu/norris/studorg
/docs/nnn.html

WHAT YOU NEED TO GET IN **Application Deadline** January 1 **Early Action Deadline** November 1 **Common App.** no **Application Fee** $50 **Tuition Costs** $18,108 **Room & Board** $6,054 **Need Blind** Yes **Financial Forms Deadline** Priority given to applications received by February 15 **Undergrads Awarded Aid** 60% **Aid That Is Need-Based** 97% **Average Award of Freshman Scholarship Package** $11,300 **Tests Required** SAT1 or ACT **Admissions Address** P.O. Box 3060, 1801 Hinman Avenue, Evanston, IL 60204-3060 **Admissions Telephone** (847) 491-7271

LAST YEAR'S CLASS **Applied** 12,918 **Accepted** 5,125 **Matriculated** 1,950 **Median Range SAT M/V** 610-720/ 610-700 **In Top Fifth of High School Graduating Class** 94% **Applied Early** 553 **Accepted Early** 328

COLLEGE LIFE **Gender Breakdown** M 49%, F 51% **Out of State Students** 73% **From Public Schools** 75% **Ethnic Composition** White & Other 73%, Asian American 18.1%, Black 6.1%, Hispanic 2.7%, Native American 0.1% **Foreign Students** 2% **Reside on Campus** 71% **Return as Sophomores** 96% **Total Faculty** 676 **Student Faculty Ratio** 11:1 **Fraternities (% of men participating)** 21 (40%) **Sororities (% of women participating)** 11 (40%) **Graduate Students** 4,592

University of Notre Dame

www.nd.edu

Notre Dame, IN · Est. 1842 · Coed · Private · 7,600 Undergrads · Urban

I need...

Admissions info www.nd.edu/NDHome
/admissions.html

Financial aid info www.nd.edu/~finaid

DOWNLOAD APPLICATION ONLINE

How wired is Notre Dame?

Do I get email? Yes

Do I get a home page? Yes

Where? www.nd.edu/PersonalPages

What is the student to computer ratio? 15:1

The usual tour

DEPARTMENTS www.nd.edu/NDHome/academics
.html

SPORTS www.nd.edu/~joyceacc

LIBRARY www.nd.edu/~ndlibs

STUDENT CLUBS www.nd.edu/Groups

Skip the brochure

• **THE FIGHTING IRISH FOOTBALL** The Fighting Irish do not mess around. Take for example, the small token of appreciation bestowed on Head Coach Lou Holtz on St. Patrick's Day of 1994—a 50-pound piece of "Authentic Blarney Stone," given by an Irish quarry. The Fighting

"Explore the history that has led to Notre Dame's powerhouse stature."

Our Lady of the Fighting Irish

Irish constitute an intense and heartfelt culture—learn the A-Zs, get the very latest on the current team, and explore the long history that has led to Notre Dame's athletic powerhouse stature. **www.nd.edu/~ndsi**

• **STUDENT FILMS** This is bound to occupy some online time, as there are so many terrific film clips. The film and video-making possibilities at Notre Dame are outlined (they look pretty good), as are production facilities. There's even a page inviting student actors to get involved. **www.nd.edu/~cothweb/wwwstudfilm.html**

• **CHILDREN OF MARY/KNIGHTS OF THE IMMACULATA** "Notre Dame" means "Our Lady." And that means Mary. Get a sense of some of the religious culture at Notre Dame. These groups focus on devotion to Christianity's über-woman, the Virgin Mary. **www.nd.edu/~mary**

WHAT YOU NEED TO GET IN **Application Deadline** November 1 for priority consideration; final deadline January 6 **Early Action Deadline** November 1 **Common App.** no **Application Fee** $40 (may be waived in cases of economic hardship) **Tuition Costs** $18,850 **Room & Board** $4,850 **Need Blind** Yes **Financial Forms Deadline** Priority given to applications received by February 15 **Undergrads Awarded Aid** 74% **Aid That Is Need-Based** 53% **Average Award of Freshman Scholarship Package** $8,850 **Tests Required** SAT1 or ACT **Admissions Address** 113 Main Building, Notre Dame, IN 46556 **Admissions Telephone** (219) 631-7505

LAST YEAR'S CLASS **Applied** 9,999 **Accepted** 3,924 **Matriculated** 1,906 **Median Range SAT M/V** 630-720/530-630 **In Top Fifth of High School Graduating Class** 94% **Applied Early** 1,490 **Accepted Early** 990

COLLEGE LIFE **Gender Breakdown** M 58%, F 42% **Out of State Students** 93% **From Public Schools** 56% **Ethnic Composition** White & Other 86%, Asian American 4%, Black 3%, Hispanic 6%, Native American 1% **Foreign Students** 2% **Reside on Campus** 84% **Return as Sophomores** 97% **Total Faculty** 625 **Student Faculty Ratio** 12:1 **Fraternities** none **Sororities** none **Graduate Students** 2,400

Oberlin College

Oberlin, OH · Est. 1833 · Coed · Private · 2,881 Undergrads · Small Town

How wired is Oberlin College?

Do I get email? Yes
Do I get a home page? Yes
Is my dorm wired? Yes
What is the student to computer ratio? 12:1

The usual tour

STUDENT CLUBS www.oberlin.edu/students
/stuorgs/stuorg.html
SPORTS www.oberlin.edu/~athletic
HISTORY www.oberlin.edu/~welcome
/history.html

Skip the brochure

- **CAT IN THE CREAM COFFEEHOUSE** Excuse me, waiter, there's a cat in my cream. But there's also live music (folk, jazz, and the like) and baked goods, and it's all run by student volunteers. **www.oberlin.edu/students/stuorgs/Cat.html**

- **NEW STUDENT SURVIVAL GUIDE** Find out what you need to know before you even realize quite how much you need to know it. **www.oberlin.edu /~presidnt/NSSG/main.html**

- **ALLEN MEMORIAL ART MUSEUM** Take a virtual tour of some of the offerings of one of the nation's

The lion eats tonight—as he has since 200 B.C.

best college art museums. **www.oberlin .edu/wwwmap/allen_art.html**

- **PLUM CREEK REVIEW HOMEPAGE** Poetry, prose, drama, and art are published both on paper and on the Web by this literary mag, which also sponsors readings and open-mike sessions. **www.oberlin.edu/~plmcreek**

"Excuse me, waiter, there's a cat in my cream. But there's also live music..."

WHAT YOU NEED TO GET IN **Application Deadline** January 15 **Early Action Deadline** November 15 and January 2 **Common App.** Yes **Application Fee** $45 **Tuition Costs** $21,425 **Room & Board** $6,174 **Need Blind** No **Financial Forms Deadline** February 15 **Undergrads Awarded Aid** 60% **Aid That Is Need-Based** 97% **Average Award of Freshman Scholarship Package** $12,618 **Tests Required** SAT1 or ACT **Admissions Address** 101 North Professor Street, Oberlin, OH 44074 **Admissions Telephone** (216) 775-8411

LAST YEAR'S CLASS **Applied** 3,728 **Accepted** 2,694 **Matriculated** 668 **Average SAT M/V** 629/671 **Average ACT** 28 **In Top Fifth of High School Graduating Class** 76% **Applied Early** 142 **Accepted Early** 126

COLLEGE LIFE **Gender Breakdown** M 42%, F 58% **Out of State Students** 91% **From Public Schools** 67% **Ethnic Composition** White & Other 78%, Asian American 10%, Black 8%, Hispanic 4% **Foreign Students** 6% **Reside on Campus** 75% **Return as Sophomores** 94% **Total Faculty** 208 **Student Faculty Ratio** 12:1 **Fraternities** none **Sororities** none **Graduate Students** 21

Occidental College

Los Angeles, CA · Est. 1887 · Coed · Private · 1,580 Undergrads · Urban

I need...

Admissions info admission@oxy.edu
www.oxy.edu/departments/admissions
/home2.htm
Financial aid info www.oxy.edu/departments
/admissions/fees.htm

How wired is Occidental?

Do I get email? Yes
Do I get a home page? Yes
Where? www.oxy.edu/oxy
/oxycomm/students.htm
What is the student to computer ratio? 20:1

The usual tour

DEPARTMENTS www.oxy.edu/oxy/academia
/acadepts/acadepts.htm
CALENDAR www.oxy.edu/oxy/news/marapr.htm
STUDENT NEWSPAPER www.oxy.edu/~suingt
/the-occidental.html
STUDENT CLUBS
www.oxy.edu/oxy/oxycomm/clubs.htm
LIBRARY www.oxy.edu/~libdir/home.html
SPORTS www.oxy.edu/departments/athletics
/home.htm

"Retreat from the stress of college with some role-playing."

Location: http://www.oxy.edu/oxy/welcome/map/greek.htm

Remsen Bird Hillside Theater

It's just a stage Occidental undergraduates go through

Skip the brochure

- **BLYTH FUND** Get some practice for when you're stinking rich with the hands-on experience in financial securities and investments offered via the Blyth Fund. **www.oxy.edu/~mhenning/blyth**

- **THE FOURTH FOUNDATION'S HOME PAGE** Retreat from the stress of college with some role-playing, a "cheesy" Sci-Fi/Fantasy night, or the annual Halloween Dance and *Evil Dead* movie marathon. **www.oxy.edu/~4thfound**

- **OCCIDENTAL COLLEGE BOOKSTORE** Show everyone at home you're interested in attending Occidental with some spanking new paraphernalia. Or maybe you'd like to shop for course books extra early? **www.oxy.edu/oxy/beyond /bookstor/index.htm**

WHAT YOU NEED TO GET IN **Application Deadline** January 15 **Early Action Deadline** November 15 **Common App.** Yes **Application Fee** $40 **Tuition Costs** $18,900 **Room & Board** $5,660 **Need Blind** Yes **Financial Forms Deadline** Priority given to applications received by February 1 **Undergrads Awarded Aid** 74% **Aid That Is Need-Based** 85% **Average Award of Freshman Scholarship Package** $11,000 **Tests Required** SAT1 or ACT **Admissions Address** 1600 Campus Road, Los Angeles, CA 90041 **Admissions Telephone** (213) 259-2700

LAST YEAR'S CLASS **Applied** 2,085 **Accepted** 1,389 **Matriculated** 407 **Average SAT M/V** 600/600 **In Top Fifth of High School Graduating Class** 52% **Applied Early** 30 **Accepted Early** 21

COLLEGE LIFE **Gender Breakdown** M 43%, F 57% **Out of State Students** 34% **From Public Schools** 67% **Ethnic Composition** White & Other 55.7%, Asian American 17.7%, Black 5.8%, Hispanic 19.7%, Native American 1.1% **Foreign Students** 4% **Reside on Campus** 70% **Return as Sophomores** 86% **Total Faculty** 191 **Student Faculty Ratio** 11:1 **Fraternities (% of men participating)** 4 (20%) **Sororities (% of women participating)** 3 (20%) **Graduate Students** 36

Ohio State University

Columbus, OH · Est. 1870 · Coed · Public · 35,475 Undergrads · Urban

I need...

Admissions info www.acs.ohio-state.edu/osu
/admis.html

How wired is Ohio State University?

Do I get email? Yes
Do I get a home page? No
What is the student to computer ratio? 32:1

The usual tour

DEPARTMENTS www.acs.ohio-state.edu/orgosu
.html#Colleges
VIRTUAL TOUR www.acs.ohio-state.edu/units
/ouc/campus_tour.html
STUDENT CLUBS www.osu.edu/osu/organ.html
LIBRARY www.lib.ohio-state.edu
SPORTS www.acs.ohio-state.edu/units/athletics

Skip the brochure

• **UNDERWATER HOCKEY** If you think it's a joke, think again. The home page for underwater hockey at Ohio State University displays the legitimacy of underwater sports, with video

"Underwater hockey: if you think it's a joke, think again."

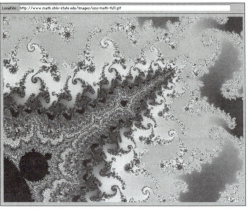

Take a fractal holiday with Ohio State's math department

clips to boot. **www.acs.ohio-state.edu/students
/uwhc/index.html**

• **THE OHIO STATE UNIVERSITY MARCHING BAND** "Hang On, Sloopy," they're playing our song. The marching band elucidates the phenomenon surrounding the McCoys' song, as well as other time-honored band traditions such as the Skull Session and Script Ohio. **www.acs.ohio -state.edu/org/osuband**

• **THE OSU WEATHER SERVICE** Hey, is that a storm-cloud forming above the library? Get online, then go get your umbrella. **aspl.sbs.ohio-state.edu /text/wxascii/osufor/osutext.html**

• **THE OHIO STATE UNIVERSITY CYCLING CLUB** The biking boys and girls of OSU. **www.acs.ohio-state .edu/students/cycle/index.html**

WHAT YOU NEED TO GET IN **Application Deadline** February 15 **Common App.** No **Application Fee** $30 **Tuition Costs** $3,273 ($9,819 out-of-state) **Room & Board** $2,844 **Need Blind** Yes **Financial Forms Deadline** Priority given to applications received by February 15 **Tests Required** SAT1 or ACT **Admissions Address** 3rd Floor Lincoln Tower, 1800 Cannon Drive, Columbus, OH 43210-1200 **Admissions Telephone** (614) 292-3980

LAST YEAR'S CLASS **Applied** 15,887 **Accepted** 14,285 **Matriculated** 5,968 **Average SAT M/V** 550/550 **Average ACT** 23 **In Top Fifth of High School Graduating Class** 38%

COLLEGE LIFE **Gender Breakdown** M 53%, F 47% **Out of State Students** 9% **Ethnic Composition** White & Other 86%, Asian American 4.8%, Black 7.1%, Hispanic 1.8%, Native American 0.3% **Foreign Students** 3% **Reside on Campus** 20% **Return as Sophomores** 77% **Total Faculty** 3,747 **Student Faculty Ratio** 13:1 **Fraternities (% of men participating)** 39 (10%) **Sororities (% of women participating)** 24 (11%) **Graduate Students** 10,494

Ohio University

Athens, OH · Est. 1804 · Coed · Public · 16,271 Undergrads · Small Town

www.ohiou.edu

How wired is Ohio U.?

Do I get email? Yes
Do I get a home page? No
What is the student to computer ratio? 18:1

The usual tour

DEPARTMENTS www.ohiou.edu/departments
VIRTUAL TOUR www.ohiou.edu/ohiou/about/tour
/tour.html
HISTORY www.ohiou.edu/ohiou/about/history
.html
LIBRARY www.library.ohiou.edu
STUDENT CLUBS www.ohiou.edu/sorgs
STUDENT NEWSPAPER thepost.baker.ohiou.edu
/welcome.html

"Whatever you do, don't call it ping-pong."

Location: http://oak.cats.ohiou.edu/~video/archive/fridays/frid.

At Ohio U., sketch comedy show that parodies daytime TV. Watch out, Ben Stiller!

Skip the brochure

• **THE OHIO UNIVERSITY TABLE TENNIS CLUB** Whatever you do, don't call it ping-pong. Ohio University students prove that some of the most vigorous athletic activity around can be obtained at a table. **www.ent.ohiou.edu/~fieno/info.html**

• **AVW PRODUCTIONS ONLINE** This cherry red site is among the sleekest you will find in the realm of college clubs. Take an interactive tour of the building; and get to know some of the original programming. Take, for example, the *Friends/Saved by the Bell:The College Years* derivative, *My New Roomates*, which is tantalizingly described: "Watch the antics of five college kids as they experience life as we know it." Could someone pull a Coen brothers intervention here? **oak.cats.ohiou.edu/~video**

WHAT YOU NEED TO GET IN Application Deadline February 1 **Common App.** No **Application Fee** $30 (may be waived in cases of economic hardship) **Tuition Costs** $3,666 ($7,905 out-of-state) **Room & Board** $3,201 **Need Blind** Yes **Financial Forms Deadline** Priority given to applications received by March 1 **Undergrads Awarded Aid** 60% **Aid That Is Need-Based** 62% **Average Award of Freshman Scholarship Package** $2,085 **Tests Required** SAT1 or ACT (preferred) **Admissions Address** Athens, OH 45701-2979 **Admissions Telephone** (614) 593-4100

LAST YEAR'S CLASS Applied 11,746 **Accepted** 8,452 **Matriculated** 3,415 **Average SAT M/V** 550/556 **Average ACT** 24 **In Top Fifth of High School Graduating Class** 44%

COLLEGE LIFE Gender Breakdown M 46%, F 54% **Out of State Students** 10% **From Public Schools** 86% **Ethnic Composition** White & Other 93%, Asian American 1%, Black 4%, Hispanic 1%, Native American 1% **Foreign Students** 2% **Reside on Campus** 42% **Return as Sophomores** 83% **Total Faculty** 1,109 **Student Faculty Ratio** 18:1 **Fraternities (% of men participating)** 17 (11%) **Sororities (% of women participating)** 11 (16%) **Graduate Students** 2,872

Ohio Wesleyan University

www.owu.edu

Delaware, OH · Est. 1842 · Coed · Private · 1,712 Undergrads · Small Town

How wired is Ohio Wesleyan?

Do I get email? ?
Do I get a home page? No
What is the student to computer ratio? 10:1

The usual tour

DEPARTMENTS www.owu.edu/~acadweb/index
.html
LIBRARY www.owu.edu/~librweb/index.html
SPORTS www.owu.edu/~athlweb/index.html
STUDENT CLUBS www.owu.edu/www/sl.html

Skip the brochure

- **THE HOUSE OF H.O.P.E.** Not quite a house, but rather a small living unit, the House of H.O.P.E. is dedicated to Helping Others Pursue Education through a variety of community tutoring programs. **www.owu.edu/~hopeweb/index.html**

- **OHIO WESLEYAN'S MODEL UNITED NATIONS** OWU students practice the fine art of diplomacy. **192.68.223.4:8000/~apnarain/mun.html**

- **THE OWU OUTDOOR CLUB** "The sworn mission of the OWU Outdoor Club is to break the bonds of our mundane existence and exchange the standard collegiate experience for something

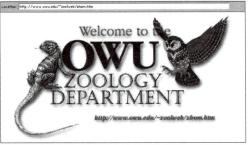

Get a sneak peek at your new roommates in their natural habitat

much greater than us all—the wild outside world..." Be careful, kids—It's a jungle out there. **www.owu.edu/~jlbrown/owu_outdoor.html**

"The sworn mission of Ohio Wesleyan's Outdoor Club is to break the bonds of our mundane existence."

WHAT YOU NEED TO GET IN **Application Deadline** Rolling admissions; March 1 for priority consideration **Early Action Deadline** December 1 **Common App.** Yes **Application Fee** $35 **Tuition Costs** $18,228 **Room & Board** $5,994 **Need Blind** Yes **Financial Forms Deadline** March 15 with a priority given to applications received by February 1 **Undergrads Awarded Aid** 80% **Aid That Is Need-Based** 66% **Average Award of Freshman Scholarship Package** $11,608 **Tests Required** SAT1 or ACT **Admissions Address** 61 South Sandusky Street, Delaware, OH 43015 **Admissions Telephone** (614) 368-3020

LAST YEAR'S CLASS **Applied** 2,234 **Accepted** 1,878 **Matriculated** 480 **Median Range SAT M/V** 510-650/510-660 **In Top Fifth of High School Graduating Class** 45% **Applied Early** 150 **Accepted Early** 140

COLLEGE LIFE **Gender Breakdown** M 49%, F 51% **Out of State Students** 51% **From Public Schools** 75% **Ethnic Composition** White & Other 92%, Asian American 3%, Black 4%, Hispanic 1% **Foreign Students** 8% **Reside on Campus** 97% **Return as Sophomores** 82% **Total Faculty** 161 **Student Faculty Ratio** 13:1 **Fraternities (% of men participating)** 11 (50%) **Sororities (% of women participating)** 7 (30%)

Oklahoma State University

pio.okstate.edu

Stillwater, OK · Est. 1890 · Coed · Public · 14,564 Undergrads · Big Town

I need...

Admissions info bubba.ucc.okstate.edu/registrar
/admiss.html

Financial aid info www.okstate.edu/registrar
/financ.html

How wired is Oklahoma State?

FULL APPLICATION ONLINE

Do I get email? Yes
Do I get a home page? Yes
  Where? www.su.okstate.edu
  /pages/index.html
What is the student to computer ratio? 15:1

The usual tour

DEPARTMENTS www.pio.okstate.edu/academics
  .html#COLLEGE
LIBRARY www.library.okstate.edu
SPORTS www2.okstate.edu/athletics
STUDENT CLUBS bubba.ucc.okstate.edu/skel
  /student.html

Skip the brochure

- **FLYING AGGIES OF OKLAHOMA STATE UNIVERSITY** Up, up, and away with the student aviators at OSU. Join the Flying Aggies and lift off in their very own aircraft. bubba.ucc.okstate.edu/aesp/FlyingAggies

- **DUSTBOWL DIVERS** So Oklahoma isn't the first place you think of when you consider ideal scuba diving locales? Perhaps that's why the group plans trips to Cozumel, Mexico and other exotic locales. bubba.ucc.okstate.edu/osu_orgs/ddasc

It's happy, it's peppy, but that's OK!

- **OSU PISTOL PETE SPORTING CLUB** Hmm, it's a "non-political" club with a link to the National Rifle Association. The purpose of the club is to "promote the shooting sports in a safe and enjoyable manner." bubba.ucc.okstate.edu/gopher-data/Student_Services/ppsc/.www/index.html

- **IN-LINE HOCKEY CLUB** In-line skating is a year-long pursuit, with hockey seasons in the spring, summer, and fall. bubba.ucc.okstate.edu/osu_orgs/oihc

"Hmm, it's a 'non-political' club with a link to the National Rifle Association."

WHAT YOU NEED TO GET IN **Application Deadline** Rolling admissions **Common App.** No **Application Fee** $15 **Tuition Costs** $1,892 ($5,339 out-of-state) **Room & Board** $3,700 **Need Blind** Yes **Financial Forms Deadline** Priority given to applications received by March 1 **Undergrads Awarded Aid** 76% **Aid That Is Need-Based** 50% **Average Award of Freshman Scholarship Package** $2,460 **Tests Required** SAT1 or ACT (preferred) **Admissions Address** Stillwater, OK 74078 **Admissions Telephone** (405) 744-6858

LAST YEAR'S CLASS **Applied** 4,355 **Accepted** 4,180 **Matriculated** 2,479 **Average ACT** 24 **In Top Fifth of High School Graduating Class** 52%

COLLEGE LIFE **Gender Breakdown** M 54%, F 46% **Out of State Students** 18% **From Public Schools** 99% **Ethnic Composition** White & Other 87%, Asian American 2%, Black 2%, Hispanic 2%, Native American 7% **Foreign Students** 7% **Reside on Campus** 21% **Return as Sophomores** 76% **Total Faculty** 691 **Student Faculty Ratio** 23:1 **Fraternities (% of men participating)** 25 (15%) **Sororities (% of women participating)** 13 (17%) **Graduate Students** 4,286

Oregon State University

Corvallis, OR · Est. 1868 · Coed · Public · 13,249 Undergrads · Big Town

I need...

Admissions info www.orst.edu/vc/prostu/freadm
Financial aid info www.orst.edu/vc/prostu
/freadm/frefin.htm

How wired is Oregon State?

Do I get email? Yes
Do I get a home page? Yes
Where? www.orst.edu
/cgi-bin/personalpagesearch
Is my dorm wired? Yes
What is the student to computer ratio? 44:1

REQUEST APPLICATION ONLINE

The outline of what's to come is below the active links. Links to the pages will be put in place as they are created...there are several here now...

Up in the air—it's a bird, it's a plane, it's...a flying Beaver?

The usual tour

SPORTS www.orst.edu/Dept/athletics
CALENDAR www.orst.edu/cu/atheve/calsch.htm
PUBLICATIONS www.orst.edu/cu/newpub
/stumed.htm
STUDENT NEWSPAPER www.orst.edu/dept
/barometer
GREEK LIFE www.orst.edu/dept/activities
/sorfra.htm
STUDENT CLUBS www.orst.edu/dept/activities
/stuorg.htm

"A supportive community for leather afficionados of all proclivities"

Skip the brochure

- **O.S.U. GO CLUB** Neither a society for travelers nor a group of Go Fish players, this is a club of people who play the ancient board game of Go both recreationally and competitively. **www.orst.edu/groups/osugo**

- **OSU FLYING CLUB** Fly the friendly Oregon skies in a variety of crafts. **www.peak.org/~spud/osu.html**

- **EVANGELICAL PERV ASSOCIATION** "We don't recruit; we abduct!" A supportive community for leather afficionados of all stripes, proclivities, and perversions officially recognized by O.S.U. since May 1, 1996. **www.orst.edu/groups/perv**

- **OREGON STATE UNIVERSITY BOTANY & PLANT PATHOLOGY UNDERGRADUATE CLUB** For those who are pathologically consumed with plants. Dilettantes are welcome, too. **www.orst.edu/dept/botany/undergrad/botclub**

WHAT YOU NEED TO GET IN **Application Deadline** March 1 **Common App.** No **Application Fee** $40 **Tuition Costs** $3,312 ($10,116 out-of-state) **Room & Board** $3,315 **Financial Forms Deadline** Priority given to applications received by March 1 **Undergrads Awarded Aid** 65% **Average Award of Freshman Scholarship Package** $1,210 **Tests Required** SAT1 or ACT **Admissions Address** Corvallis, OR 97331 **Admissions Telephone** (503) 737-4411

LAST YEAR'S CLASS **Applied** 5,425 **Accepted** 4,594 **Matriculated** 3,674 **Average SAT M/V** 511/446 **Average ACT** 20

COLLEGE LIFE **Gender Breakdown** M 57%, F 43% **Ethnic Composition** White & Other 89%, Asian American 6%, Black 1%, Hispanic 2%, Native American 2% **Foreign Students** 5% **Reside on Campus** 21% **Return as Sophomores** 76% **Student Faculty Ratio** 17:1 **Fraternities (% of men participating)** 26 (12%) **Sororities (% of women participating)** 15 (7%) **Graduate Students** 2,709

University of Oregon

www.uoregon.edu

Eugene, OR · Est. 1872 · Coed · Private · 13,717 Undergrads · Urban

I need...

Admissions info uoadmit@oregon.uoregon.edu
darkwing.uoregon.edu/~admit/application
.html

Financial aid info www-vms.uoregon.edu/~finaid
/fa.html

How wired is University of Oregon?

Do I get email? Yes

Do I get a home page? Yes

Where? darkwing.uoregon.edu
/~joe/www_authors.html

Is my dorm wired? Yes

What is the student to computer ratio? 6:I

REQUEST APPLICATION ONLINE

The usual tour

DEPARTMENTS darkwing.uoregon.edu/UOcolleges
/cas.html

CALENDAR darkwing.uoregon.edu/~uocomm
/calendar/calndr.html

SPORTS ducks.uoregon.edu

STUDENT CLUBS darkwing.uoregon.edu/~liwang
/asuo/UOstudent-orgs.html

STUDENT NEWSPAPER darkwing.uoregon.edu/~ode

GREEK LIFE darkwing.uoregon.edu/~grklife
/index.html

LIBRARY libweb.uoregon.edu/uo/libhome

"The Survival Center unites activists."

Location: http://oregon.uoregon.edu/~paige/pics.html

Fans go quackers for the Ducks' Marching Band

Skip the brochure

- **UNIVERSITY OF OREGON CAMPUS RECYCLING PROGRAM** Learn how to discourage junk mail and recycle your confidential material without fear. **darkwing.uoregon.edu/~recycle**

- **UNIVERSITY OF OREGON SURVIVAL CENTER HOME PAGE** Feeling active? The Survival Center unites activists no matter the cause, whether Hemp Education or Ancient Forest Issues. **gladstone.uoregon.edu/~survival**

- **DAVE'S SKYDIVING HOME PAGE** The University of Oregon Ducks take to the sky—"for once you have tasted flight, you will walk with your eyes turned skyward." **gladstone.uoregon.edu/~daves**

- **OREGON BALLROOM DANCE CLUB** These Ducks are mighty light on their feet. **gladstone.uoregon.edu/~ballroom**

WHAT YOU NEED TO GET IN **Application Deadline** March 1 **Common App.** Yes **Application Fee** $50 **Tuition Costs** $2,693 ($10,817 out-of-state) **Room & Board** $4,325 **Financial Forms Deadline** Priority given to applications received by February 1 **Undergrads Awarded Aid** 45% **Tests Required** SAT1 or ACT **Admissions Address** Eugene, OR 97403-1217 **Admissions Telephone** (541) 346-3201

LAST YEAR'S CLASS **Applied** 8,348 **Accepted** 7,541 **Matriculated** 2,542 **Median Range SAT M/V** 490-620/500-610

COLLEGE LIFE **Gender Breakdown** M 49%, F 51% **Out of State Students** 39% **From Public Schools** 89% **Ethnic Composition** White & Other 87%, Asian American 7%, Black 2%, Hispanic 3%, Native American 1% **Foreign Students** 9% **Reside on Campus** 25% **Return as Sophomores** 84% **Total Faculty** 834 **Student Faculty Ratio** 19:1 **Fraternities (% of men participating)** 16 (7%) **Sororities (% of women participating)** 11 (7%) **Graduate Students** 3,421

Pennsylvania State University

University Park, PA · Est. 1855 · Coed · Public· 32,790 Undergrads · Big Town

I need...

Admissions info www.psu.edu/psu/admissions
Financial aid info www.psu.edu/students1.html

How wired is Penn State?

Do I get email? Yes
Do I get a home page? Yes
   Where? www.psu.edu/ph/ph.html
Is my dorm wired? Yes
What is the student to computer ratio? 11:1

The usual tour

STUDENT CLUBS www.psu.edu/clubs/orgs.html
GREEK LIFE athens.cac.psu.edu
SPORTS www.psu.edu/sports/home.html
LIBRARY www.libraries.psu.edu
CALENDAR www.psu.edu/calendars.html
CAREER CENTER www.psu.edu/staff/cdps
/cdpshome.html

Skip the brochure

- **THE ASYLUM** No, you're not crazy. It is possible to have fun without alcohol. At least that's the premise behind this Penn State non-alcoholic nightclub, which sponsors bands, comedians, magicians, and other good, clean, sober fun. www.geocities.com/Broadway/1737

"Hitch a ride on a very small railroad."

PSU: light at the end of the admissions tunnel

- **NITTANY GROTTO** A-spelunking we shall go! Join area enthusiasts in the wonderful world of cave exploration. Just remember: "A cave is a dark, cramped, usually damp, and always dirty, hole in the ground." cac.psu.edu/~cjal12

- **PENN STATE MODEL RAILROAD CLUB HOMEPAGE** Want to take a very small trip? Hitch a ride on a very small railroad, courtesy of the Model Railroad Club. All skill levels are welcome. cac.psu.edu/~jhal05/psmrrc.html

- **PENN STATE OBJECTIVISM CLUB** Make friends and influence people the Ayn Rand way. www.math.psu.edu/simpson/PSOC.html

- **FINDING COMMON GROUND HOMEPAGE** There's a lot of ground to cover, since this group aims to achieve racial, sexual, and socio-economic equality while also preserving natural resources. Join the cause. www.envirolink.org/orgs/fcg/index.html

---

WHAT YOU NEED TO GET IN **Application Deadline** Rolling admissions; November 30 for priority consideration **Common App.** No **Application Fee** $40 **Tuition Costs** $5,188 ($11,240 out-of-state) **Room & Board** $4,300 **Need Blind** Yes **Financial Forms Deadline** Priority given to applications received by February 15 **Undergrads Awarded Aid** 80% **Average Award of Freshman Scholarship Package** $2,906 **Tests Required** SAT1 (preferred) or ACT **Admissions Address** University Park, PA 16802 **Admissions Telephone** (814) 865-5471

LAST YEAR'S CLASS **Applied** 22,361 **Accepted** 11,306 **Matriculated** 4,310 **Average SAT M/V** 599/511 **In Top Fifth of High School Graduating Class** 75%

COLLEGE LIFE **Gender Breakdown** M 56%, F 44% **Out of State Students** 19% **Ethnic Composition** White & Other 89%, Asian American 5%, Black 3%, Hispanic 2%, Native American 1% **Foreign Students** 1% **Reside on Campus** 39% **Return as Sophomores** 93% **Total Faculty** 3,008 **Student Faculty Ratio** 19:1 **Fraternities (% of men participating)** 55 (14%) **Sororities (% of women participating)** 25 (17%) **Graduate Students** 6,856

University of Pennsylvania

www.upenn.edu

Philadelphia, PA · Est. 1740 · Coed · Private · 10,195 Undergrads · Urban

I need...

Admissions info www.upenn.edu/admissions
Financial aid info www.upenn.edu/admissions
   /Paying/index.html

How wired is Penn?

Do I get email? Yes
Do I get a home page? Yes
   Where? www.upenn.edu/overview
   /personal_pages.html
Is my dorm wired? Yes
What is the student computer ratio? 18:1

The usual tour

DEPARTMENTS www.upenn.edu/students
   /Undergraduate_Schools.html
LIBRARY www.library.upenn.edu
SPORTS www.upenn.edu/athletics
STUDENT CLUBS dolphin.upenn.edu/~oslaf
   /orgmain.html
STUDY ABROAD pobox.upenn.edu/~oip
PUBLICATIONS dolphin.upenn.edu/~oslaf
   /pubmedia.html

Skip the brochure

- **PENNSYLVANIA SIX-5000** This all male a cappella group sings a version of the Police's "King of Pain" called "It's not easy being Conrad Bain" describing the downfall of the stars of *Diff'rent Strokes*. Even if you don't usually like a cappella, these boys just might win you over. **dolphin.upenn.edu/~pennsix**

Penn students build for the future

- **UNIVERSITY OF PENNSYLVANIA MUSEUM OF ARCHAE-OLOGY AND ANTHROPOLOGY** Ever consider the cultural significance of grass socks? They are just one of many cultural adaptations made by Eskimos to deal with the Arctic environment. The museum is not just home to beautiful collections, but also serves as the base for Penn's anthropologists and archaeologists. Wait until you see what Professor Alan Mann has discovered about human evolution in his work with Neanderthal teeth. **www.upenn.edu /museum**

- **UTV 13** Perhaps your 15 minutes of fame will take place on campus TV. Penn's station, UTV, broadcasts a range of original programs and news shows while serving as an educational environment for students interested in TV, production, and video. The site even has an online course in color bars. **dolphin.upenn.edu/~utv13**

WHAT YOU NEED TO GET IN **Application Deadline** January 1 **Early Action Deadline** November 1 **Common App.** No **Application Fee** $55 **Tuition Costs** $18,964 **Room & Board** $7,500 **Need Blind** Yes **Financial Forms Deadline** Priority given to applications received by January 1 **Undergrads Awarded Aid** 45% **Aid That Is Need-Based** 100% **Average Award of Freshman Scholarship Package** $14,300 **Tests Required** SAT1 or ACT **Admissions Address** Philadelphia, PA 19104 **Admissions Telephone** (215) 898-7507

LAST YEAR'S CLASS **Applied** 15,074 **Accepted** 4,981 **Matriculated** 2,384 **Average SAT M/V** 686/598 **Average ACT** 28 **In Top Fifth of High School Graduating Class** 95% **Applied Early** 1,629 **Accepted Early** 944

COLLEGE LIFE **Gender Breakdown** M 53%, F 47% **Out of State Students** 82% **From Public Schools** 62% **Ethnic Composition** White & Other 67%, Asian American 21%, Black 7%, Hispanic 5% **Foreign Students** 9% **Reside on Campus** 61% **Return as Sophomores** 95% **Total Faculty** 2,239 **Student Faculty Ratio** 5:1 **Fraternities (% of men participating)** 29 (30%) **Sororities (% of women participating)** 14 (30%) **Graduate Students** 8,472

University of Pittsburgh

www.pitt.edu

Pittsburgh, PA · Est. 1787 · Coed · Public · 16,447 Undergrads · Urban

I need...

Admissions info www.pitt.edu/~oafa/reps.htm
Financial aid info www.pitt.edu/~oafa/fin.htm

How wired is Pitt?

Do I get email? Yes
Do I get a home page? Yes
Is my dorm wired? Yes
What is the student to computer ratio? 24:1

The usual tour

SPORTS www.pitt.edu/~sports/l_index.html
DEPARTMENTS www.pitt.edu/~provost/undergr
  .htm
CALENDAR www.pitt.edu/~provost/calendar.html
LIBRARY www.library.pitt.edu
GREEK LIFE www.pitt.edu/~ifcoun/Greek
STUDENT CLUBS www.pitt.edu/~ivan1/studact
  /studact.html

Skip the brochure

- **UNIVERSITY OF PITTSBURGH CHESS CLUB** Chess with and without computer intercession is the pursuit of these Pitt students. **www.pitt.edu /~schach**

- **PITTSBURGH CREW** There's a whole lotta stroking going on for Pittsburgh men and women interested in crew. **www.pitt.edu/~crew**

- **UNIVERSITY OF PITTSBURG PANTHER CYCLING CLUB** Take to the road with all types of cyclists:

The cycle of life: Pitt's bicycling club lines up for the wheel life

recreational or competitive, road or mountain. **www.pitt.edu/~cycling/pcc**

- **PANTHER TABLE TENNIS CLUB** Play for your G.P.A.: square off against President Rich Burnside and faculty advisor John Ramirez, both nationally-ranked ping-pongers and members of the Panther Table Tennis Club. **www.pitt.edu/~kennet /pingpong.html**

> ## "Pittsburgh men and women crew: There's a whole lotta stroking going on."

WHAT YOU NEED TO GET IN **Application Deadline** Rolling Admissions **Common App.** No **Application Fee** $35 **Tuition Costs** $5,184 ($11,270 out-of-state) **Room & Board** $4,834 **Need Blind** Yes **Financial Forms Deadline** Priority given to applications received by March 1 **Undergrads Awarded Aid** 60% **Aid That Is Need-Based** 90% **Average Award of Freshman Scholarship Package** $2,933 **Tests Required** SAT1 or ACT **Admissions Address** 4200 Fifth Avenue, Pittsburgh, PA 15260 **Admissions Telephone** (412) 624-PITT

LAST YEAR'S CLASS **Applied** 7,825 **Accepted** 5,188 **Matriculated** 2,002 **Average SAT M/V** 551/496 **In Top Fifth of High School Graduating Class** 47%

COLLEGE LIFE **Gender Breakdown** M 48%, F 52% **Out of State Students** 19% **Ethnic Composition** White & Other 86%, Asian American 3%, Black 9%, Hispanic 1%, Native American 1% **Foreign Students** 2% **Reside on Campus** 39% **Return as Sophomores** 85% **Total Faculty** 3,410 **Student Faculty Ratio** 15:1 **Fraternities (% of men participating)** 21 (14%) **Sororities (% of women participating)** 15 (11%) **Graduate Students** 9,636

Pitzer College

www.pitzer.edu

Claremont, CA · Est. 1963 · Coed · Private · 732 Undergrads · Small Town

I need...

Admissions info www.pitzer.edu/admissions/#admit

Financial aid info www.pitzer.edu/admissions/#finaid

How wired is Pitzer?

Do I get email? Yes

Do I get a home page? Yes

Where? www.pitzer.edu/internet/students.html

Is my dorm wired? Yes

What is the student to computer ratio? 13:1

The usual tour

VIRTUAL TOUR www.pitzer.edu/admissions/campus/tour.html

CALENDAR www.pitzer.edu/academics/catalog/calendar.html

DEPARTMENTS www.pitzer.edu/academics

SPORTS www.pitzer.edu/students/#athletics

STUDENT CLUBS www.pitzer.edu/internet/organizations.html

CAREER CENTER www.pitzer.edu/departments/Career_Services

"Composting dining hall remnants is a 'rewarding experience.' Really."

Pitzer: college with a California angle

Skip the brochure

- **ECOLOGY CENTER** Composting dining hall remnants is a "rewarding experience." Really. Do your part for the ecology of Claremont. **www.pitzer.edu/~nlampher/Ecology_Center**

- **THE CENTER FOR CAREER AND COMMUNITY SERVICES—COUNSELOR INFO** Help! You haven't even started college and people are already asking you what you want to do with your life! Luckily Pitzer career counselors are super-friendly, with smiling photos of themselves, plus a year-by-year guide to planning your entire future. **www.pitzer.edu/departments/Career_Services/counselor.html**

- **CAMPUS LIFE AND ACTIVITIES** Rent a bike, play with kids, or join one of the dozens of 5-college organizations and hang out with other Claremont College students. **www.pitzer.edu/students/handbook/activities**

WHAT YOU NEED TO GET IN **Application Deadline** February 1 **Early Action Deadline** December 1 **Common App.** Yes **Application Fee** $40 **Tuition Costs** $19,360 **Room & Board** $6,454 **Financial Forms Deadline** Priority given to applications received by February 1 **Undergrads Awarded Aid** 48% **Aid That Is Need-Based** 100% **Average Award of Freshman Scholarship Package** $13,730 **Tests Required** SAT1 or ACT **Admissions Address** 1050 North Mills Avenue, Claremont, CA 91711 **Admissions Telephone** (909) 621-8129

LAST YEAR'S CLASS **Applied** 1,219 **Accepted** 970 **Matriculated** 199 **Average SAT M/V** 590/540 **Average ACT** 23 **In Top Fifth of High School Graduating Class** 54%

COLLEGE LIFE **Gender Breakdown** M 44%, F 56% **Out of State Students** 46% **From Public Schools** 45% **Ethnic Composition** White & Other 68%, Asian American 10%, Black 6%, Hispanic 15%, Native American 1% **Foreign Students** 10% **Reside on Campus** 92% **Return as Sophomores** 66% **Total Faculty** 75 **Student Faculty Ratio** 10:1 **Fraternities** none **Sororities** none

Pomona College

www.pomona.edu

Claremont, CA · Est. 1887 · Coed · Private · 1,402 Undergrads · Small Town

I need...

Admissions info www.pomona.edu/AboutPom
/Prospectives/Admissions/Admissions.html
Financial aid info www.pomona.edu/AboutPom
/Prospectives/FinAid.html

How wired is Pomona?

Do I get email? Yes
Do I get a home page? Yes
   Where? students.pomona.edu
   /pages/links.html
Is my dorm wired? Yes
What is the student to computer ratio? 20:1

REQUEST APPLICATION ONLINE

The usual tour

SPORTS www.pomona.edu/AboutPom/Campus
Life/Athletics.html
LIBRARY www.pomona.edu/AboutPom/Facilities
/Library.html
DEPARTMENTS www.pomona.edu/Academics
/TOC/TOC.html
CALENDAR cuc.claremont.edu/calendar.htm
STUDENT CLUBS students.pomona.edu/pages
/orgs.html

Skip the brochure

• **KSPC 88.7 FM** Escape the regular L.A. basin radio
programming with Pomona's alternative station.
It's 30 years old and still on the cutting edge.
www.pomona.edu/AboutPom/KSPC/Intro.html

• **THE SPIRIT THEME GROUP HOME PAGE** Let's get this

Pomona: the order of things to come

straight... So it's a home page for a group that
no longer exists? A spirited, thematic look at
the end of the Spirit Theme Group.
pages.pomona.edu/~spirit

• **ON THE LOOSE** Based at Pomona but open to students at all of the Claremont Colleges, the On
the Loose Club roams the great outdoors.
pages.pomona.edu/~otl/otl.html

• **THE STUDENT-RUN WEB REVIEW** The indispensable
service of a student course review.... Find out
what students are really saying about courses
at Pomona before you even arrive. **pages.pomona
.edu/~review**

"What students are really saying about courses"

WHAT YOU NEED TO GET IN **Application Deadline** Fall for priority consideration; final deadline January 1 **Early Action Deadline** November 15 **Common App.** Yes **Application Fee** $50 (may be waived in cases of economic hardship) **Tuition Costs** $19,530 **Room & Board** $7,860 **Need Blind** Yes **Financial Forms Deadline** Priority given to applications received by February 11 **Undergrads Awarded Aid** 55% **Aid That Is Need-Based** 100% **Average Award of Freshman Scholarship Package** $14,800 **Tests Required** SAT1 or ACT **Admissions Address** 333 North College Way, Claremont, CA 91711-6312 **Admissions Telephone** (909) 621-8134

LAST YEAR'S CLASS **Applied** 3,586 **Accepted** 1,221 **Matriculated** 392 **Average SAT M/V** 706/703 **Average ACT** 30 **In Top Quarter of High School Graduating Class** 98% **Applied Early** 164 **Accepted Early** 67

COLLEGE LIFE **Gender Breakdown** M 52%, F 48% **Out of State Students** 59% **From Public Schools** 69% **Ethnic Composition** White & Other 60%, Asian American 23%, Black 4%, Hispanic 10%, Native American 3% **Foreign Students** 5% **Reside on Campus** 96% **Return as Sophomores** 93% **Total Faculty** 154 **Student Faculty Ratio** 9:1 **Fraternities (% of men participating)** 3 (4%) **Sororities** none

Princeton University

Princeton, NJ · Est. 1746 · Coed · Private · 4,609 Undergrads · Big Town

I need...

Admissions info www.princeton.edu/Main
/newstudents.html

How wired is Princeton?

Do I get email? Yes
Do I get a home page? Yes
Is my dorm wired? Yes
What is the student to computer ratio? 12:1

REQUEST APPLICATION ONLINE

The usual tour

VIRTUAL TOUR www.princeton.edu/~okkey
DEPARTMENTS www.princeton.edu/Main
/deptacad.html
LIBRARY infoshare1.princeton.edu:2003
PUBLICATIONS www.princeton.edu/Main
/publications.html
CALENDAR www.princeton.edu/Main/events.html
SPORTS www.princeton.edu/Main/athletics.html
STUDENT CLUBS webware.princeton.edu/stulife
/stuorgs/studorg.htm

Skip the brochure

- **PELVIS: PRINCETON FOR ELVIS** An essential organization, "dedicated to spreading the magic of
the King." Advertised here is the chance to be
on the PElvis email mailing list to receive daily
Elvis wisdom and trivia. This hunk-a hunk-a
burning academia sounds too good to be true.
www.princeton.edu/~pelvis

- **THE PRINCETON SPIGOT** Princeton's own ezine is

Location: http://www.princeton.edu/~okkey/page7.html

They don't call it the Ivy-League for nothing

flashy and fun and even offers Web how-tos
for *Spigot* readers who wish they were *Spigot*
writers. Bonus: an archived article called "The
Secrets of Princeton" offers the inside skinny.
www.princeton.edu/~spigot

- **THEATRE INTIME** It started in a dorm room
(how's that for intimate?) and has now expanded to the small stage. A student-run company
produces shows in a 200-person theater.
www.princeton.edu/~intime

- **DISTRACTIONS** In your copious free time as a
student at an Ivy-League university, maybe
you'd like to focus your attention on the completely original (and completely frustrating)
puzzles provided by this magazine. The Web
site contains one of the more recent puzzles.
www.princeton.edu/~distract

WHAT YOU NEED TO GET IN **Application Deadline** January 2 **Early Action Deadline** November 1 **Common App.** No
Application Fee $55 **Tuition Costs** $22,000 **Room & Board** $6,359 **Need Blind** Yes **Financial Forms Deadline**
February 1 **Undergrads Awarded Aid** 44% **Aid That Is Need-Based** 100% **Average Award of Freshman**
Scholarship Package $13,900 **Tests Required** SAT1 (preferred) or ACT **Admissions Address** Princeton, NJ
08544 **Admissions Telephone** (609) 258-3060

LAST YEAR'S CLASS **Applied** 14,311 **Accepted** 2,013 **Matriculated** 1,209 **Average SAT M/V** 725/665 **In Top Fifth of**
High School Graduating Class 96% **Applied Early** 1,455 **Accepted Early** 556

COLLEGE LIFE **Gender Breakdown** M 54%, F 46% **Out of State Students** 87% **From Public Schools** 59% **Ethnic**
Composition White & Other 72%, Asian American 13%, Black 7%, Hispanic 7%, Native American 1% **Foreign**
Students 6% **Reside on Campus** 96% **Return as Sophomores** 96% **Total Faculty** 886 **Student Faculty Ratio** 5:1
Fraternities none **Sororities** none **Graduate Students** 1,810

Providence College

Providence, RI · Est. 1917 · Coed · Private · 4,533 Undergrads · Urban

I need...

Admissions info pcadmiss@providence.edu
www.providence.edu/admiss/pca14.htm
Financial aid info www.providence.edu/admiss
/pca17.htm

How wired is Providence College?

Do I get email? Yes
Do I get a home page? No
Is my dorm wired? Yes
What is the student to computer ratio? 40:1

The usual tour

SPORTS www.providence.edu/admiss/pca09.htm
DEPARTMENTS www.providence.edu/admiss
/pca05.htm
STUDY ABROAD www.providence.edu/admiss
/pca08.htm
COMPUTER SERVICES www.providence.edu
/compserv
CALENDAR www.providence.edu/admiss
/pcac.htm

Skip the brochure

• **FEINSTEIN INSTITUTE FOR PUBLIC SERVICE** Can college make you a better human being? Sure, if you're involved in an interdisciplinary program like the Feinstein Institute for Public Service which combines public and community service with a liberal arts curriculum. **www.providence.edu /admiss/pspl.htm**

Divine Providence: big learning in the country's smallest state

• **LIBERAL ARTS HONORS PROGRAM** Calling all smarty-pants: Study harder and deeper in this honors program which focuses on seminar work. **www.providence.edu/admiss/lah.htm**

• **THE DEVELOPMENT OF WESTERN CIVILIZATION PROGRAM** Providence College is proud of its two-year required program in Western Civilization. "The study of Western civilization, in its moments of majesty and madness, glory and shame, provides a key to self-understanding." **www.providence.edu/admiss/dwc.htm**

"Western civilization, in its moments of glory and shame, provides a key to self-understanding."

WHAT YOU NEED TO GET IN **Application Deadline** December 15 for priority consideration; final deadline January 15 **Early Action Deadline** November 15 **Common App.** No **Application Fee** $40 **Tuition Costs** $15,800 **Room & Board** $6,670 **Need Blind** Yes **Financial Forms Deadline** February 1 **Undergrads Awarded Aid** 69% **Aid That Is Need-Based** 90% **Average Award of Freshman Scholarship Package** $8,000 **Tests Required** SAT1 or ACT **Admissions Address** 549 River Avenue, Providence, RI 02918-0001 **Admissions Telephone** (401) 865-2535

LAST YEAR'S CLASS **Applied** 3,836 **Accepted** 2,879 **Matriculated** 962 **Average SAT M/V** 552/493 **Average ACT** 25 **In Top Fifth of High School Graduating Class** 52% **Applied Early** 336 **Accepted Early** 229

COLLEGE LIFE **Gender Breakdown** M 43%, F 57% **Out of State Students** 86% **From Public Schools** 62% **Ethnic Composition** White & Other 92%, Asian American 2%, Black 4%, Hispanic 2% **Foreign Students** 1% **Reside on Campus** 74% **Return as Sophomores** 96% **Student Faculty Ratio** 13:1 **Fraternities** none **Sororities** none **Graduate Students** 933

Purdue University

www.purdue.edu

West Lafayette, IN · Est. 1869 · Coed · Public · 27,982 Undergrads · Big Town

How wired is Purdue?

Do I get email? Yes
Do I get a home page? No
Is my dorm wired? Yes
What is the student to computer ratio? 3:1

FULL APPLICATION ONLINE

Towering over West Lafayette: Purdue University

The usual tour

DEPARTMENTS www.purdue.edu/Admissions
/Schools_and_Majors
CALENDAR www.cea.purdue.edu/ceafiles
/calendar.htm
LIBRARY thorplus.lib.purdue.edu
SPORTS www.purdue.edu/Purdue/Sports.html
STUDENT CLUBS www.purdue.edu/Purdue
/Activities.html

Skip the brochure

• **KRAZY EIGHTS SQUARE DANCE CLUB** Monday
evenings feature the krazy kombinations of
dosado, acey deucey and cloverleaf with the
Krazy Eights square dancers. Come as you
are, or with a partner. **www.cs.purdue.edu/homes
/man/keights/krazy8s.html**

• **PAGAN ACADEMIC NETWORK** They don't sacrifice
small animals in order to achieve higher

grades. And though they won't seek to convert
you, they're more than willing to explain the
tenets of paganism and extend their community to all people interested in "traditional reli-
gions." **expert.cc.purdue.edu/~pan**

• **PURDUE UNIVERSITY JUGGLING CLUB HOME PAGE**
Some club members can juggle three balls
while standing on a bowling ball. Some can do
a "6-ball lift bounce on rola bola." Others just
throw lots of things in the air and keep them
aloft. **omni.cc.purdue.edu/~bell/Juggle/juggle.html**

• **PURDUE PAINTBALL CLUB HOMEPAGE** Relieve your
stress by pegging your classmates with paint
capsules in this colorful version of Capture the
Flag. **expert.cc.purdue.edu/~pntball**

"Monday evenings feature acey-deucy."

WHAT YOU NEED TO GET IN **Application Deadline** Rolling admissions **Common App.** No **Application Fee** $30 **Tuition Costs** $3,210 ($10,640 out-of-state) **Room & Board** $4,520 **Need Blind** Yes **Financial Forms Deadline** Priority given to applications received by March 1 **Undergrads Awarded Aid** 53% **Aid That Is Need-Based** 91% **Average Award of Freshman Scholarship Package** $3,086 **Tests Required** SAT1 or ACT **Admissions Address** West Lafayette, IN 47907 **Admissions Telephone** (317) 494-1776

LAST YEAR'S CLASS **Applied** 16,714 **Accepted** 15,124 **Matriculated** 6,186 **Average SAT M/V** 545/455 **Average ACT** 24 **In Top Fifth of High School Graduating Class** 46%

COLLEGE LIFE **Gender Breakdown** M 57%, F 43% **Out of State Students** 27% **Ethnic Composition** White & Other 89.5%, Asian American 4%, Black 4%, Hispanic 2%, Native American 0.5% **Foreign Students** 2% **Reside on Campus** 38% **Return as Sophomores** 84% **Total Faculty** 2,220 **Student Faculty Ratio** 17:1 **Fraternities (% of men participating)** 46 (20%) **Sororities (% of women participating)** 24 (18%) **Graduate Students** 6,397

Reed College

www.reed.edu

Portland, OR · Est. 1909 · Coed · Private · 1,276 Undergrads · Urban

How wired is Reed?

Do I get email? Yes
Do I get a home page? Yes
Where? www.reed.edu/reed/users
Is my dorm wired? Yes
What is the student to computer ratio? 2:1

The usual tour

DEPARTMENTS web.reed.edu/academic
/departments/index.html
VIRTUAL TOUR web.reed.edu/life/photos/index
.html
CALENDAR web.reed.edu/life/Calendar.pdf
STUDENT CLUBS web.reed.edu/life/studentorgs
.html
LIBRARY web.reed.edu/resources/library
/lib_menu.html
CAREER CENTER
web.reed.edu/resources/career/career.html

Skip the brochure

• **REED COLLEGE REACTOR FACILITY** Reed College students have a blast with the campus nuclear reactor. Students from any department are welcome to receive an operator's license and

Location: http://web.reed.edu/academic/departments/theatre/durang.html

END MOMENT FROM "A STYE IN THE EYE"

Begin your thespian career with Reed's dramatic society

become the modern-day incarnation of Dr. Strangelove. **www.reed.edu/~reactor**

• **REED THEATRE HOME PAGE** What's playing at Reed, and who's playing in it? Get a piece of the action with performance info and audition announcements. **web.reed.edu/academic/departments/theatre**

• **OLD REED PHOTOS** Reed alumni remember the good ol' days with a smattering of photos dating back to 1921. Be sure to check out the picture from the "Athletics" section of *The Griffin*—an idyllic image. **web.reed.edu/community/alumni/alum7.html**

"Become the modern-day Dr. Strangelove."

WHAT YOU NEED TO GET IN **Application Deadline** December 1 for priority consideration; final deadline February 1 **Early Action Deadline** December 1 **Common App.** Yes **Application Fee** $40 **Tuition Costs** $21,330 **Room & Board** $6,000 **Financial Forms Deadline** March 1 with a priority given to applications received by February 1 **Undergrads Awarded Aid** 45% **Aid That Is Need-Based** 100% **Average Award of Freshman Scholarship Package** $14,200 **Tests Required** SAT1 or ACT **Admissions Address** 3203 S.E. Woodstock Boulevard, Portland, OR 97202-8199 **Admissions Telephone** (503) 777-7511

LAST YEAR'S CLASS **Applied** 2,149 **Accepted** 1,531 **Matriculated** 355 **Average SAT M/V** 651/684 **Average ACT** 29 **Applied Early** 154 **Accepted Early** 105

COLLEGE LIFE **Gender Breakdown** M 48%, F 52% **Out of State Students** 90% **From Public Schools** 72% **Ethnic Composition** White & Other 85%, Asian American 9%, Black 1%, Hispanic 4%, Native American 1% **Foreign Students** 7% **Reside on Campus** 54% **Return as Sophomores** 87% **Total Faculty** 126 **Student Faculty Ratio** 10:1 **Fraternities** none **Sororities** none **Graduate Students** 14

Rensselaer Polytechnic Institute www.rpi.edu

Troy, NY · Est. 1824 · Coed · Private · 4,360 Undergrads · Big Town

I need...

Admissions info admissions@rpi.edu
www.rpi.edu/dept/admissions/www
Financial aid info www.rpi.edu/dept/admissions
/www/financial_aid.html

How wired is RPI?

Do I get email? Yes
Do I get a home page? Yes
Where? www.rpi.edu/homepages/homepages
.html
Is my dorm wired? Yes
What is the student to computer ratio? 7:1

The usual tour

DEPARTMENTS www.rpi.edu/Departments
/Academic.html
STUDENT CLUBS www.union.rpi.edu/Organizations
SPORTS www.rpi.edu/dept/athletics
CALENDAR www.rpi.edu/dept/NewsComm
/Review/calendar.html
PUBLICATIONS www.union.rpi.edu/Organizations
/publications.html
GREEK LIFE www.union.rpi.edu/Organizations
/greek.html
LIBRARY www.rpi.edu/dept/library/html/LibInfo
.html
CAREER CENTER www.rpi.edu/dept/cdc

Skip the brochure

- **FAMOUS GRADS AND GADGETS** What do the REACH
toothbrush, the Ferris wheel, and baking

Practice your swordplay at Rensselaer

powder all have in common? They were all created by minds trained at RPI. Who will be highlighted here in the future? **www.rpi.edu/dept
/admissions/www/student_life/famous_grads.html**

- **SOCIETY FOR CREATIVE ANACHRONISM** Chivalry is
not dead at RPI, at least not with this club,
which seeks to replicate the Middle Ages and
the Renaissance—kingdoms, tournaments,
and all. **www.rpi.edu/dept/union/sca/homepage
/index.html**

- **AMERICA'S PEP BAND** Rumor has it that *Sports
Illustrated* once called the RPI pep band "the
most spirited band in America," and although
no one at RPI can find a copy of the article,
that's OK—they're too busy cheering for the
RPI football and hockey players. **www.rpi.edu
/dept/union/pep/www/index.html**

WHAT YOU NEED TO GET IN **Application Deadline** January 1 **Early Action Deadline** December 1 **Common App.** Yes
Application Fee $45 **Tuition Costs** $19,075 **Room & Board** $6,377 **Need Blind** Yes **Financial Forms Deadline**
Priority given to applications received by February 15 **Undergrads Awarded Aid** 85% **Aid That Is Need-Based** 80%
Average Award of Freshman Scholarship Package $12,138 **Tests Required** SAT1 or ACT **Admissions
Address** Troy, NY 12180 **Admissions Telephone** (518) 276-6216

LAST YEAR'S CLASS **Applied** 4,543 **Accepted** 3,848 **Matriculated** 963 **Average SAT M/V** 664/546 **Average ACT** 30
In Top Fifth of High School Graduating Class 80% **Applied Early** 148 **Accepted Early** 125

COLLEGE LIFE **Gender Breakdown** M 76%, F 24% **Out of State Students** 58% **From Public Schools** 79% **Ethnic
Composition** White & Other 77.2%, Asian American 13.6%, Black 4.1%, Hispanic 4.8%, Native American 0.3%
Foreign Students 6% **Reside on Campus** 54% **Return as Sophomores** 90% **Student Faculty Ratio** 12:1
Fraternities (% of men participating) 30 (40%) **Sororities (% of women participating)** 6 (40%) **Graduate
Students** 2,040

Rhode Island School of Design

Providence, RI · Est. 1877 · Coed · Private · 1,848 Undergrads · Urban

I need...

Admissions info www.risd.edu

How wired is RISD

Do I get email? Yes
Do I get a home page? Yes
Is my dorm wired? Yes
What is the student to computer ratio? 10:1

Skip the brochure

- **SUMMER PROGRAMS HOME PAGE** RISD's Web site might fool you into thinking that there's hardly anything going on in the summer, when actually the school opens its doors to high school students, college students, artists, art educators, and design professionals for intensive summer study. **www.risd.edu/sumrhome.htm**

- **THE COLLEGE HILL INDEPENDENT** *The College Hill Independent* is currently the best RISD-generated resource online, at least while RISD's Web site remains under construction. A joint venture with Brown University, *The College Hill Independent* is what one might expect from these two liberal schools. The digital paper is well-designed and browsable, and articles cover a range of socio-cultural political topics: global warming, leg waxing, and more. There are also arts reviews, though the music reviewed is decidedly less mainstream, and more, to invoke a tired cliché, "alternative." **www.netspace.org/indy**

Academic departments at RISD are more decorative than those at other colleges: jewelry, ceramics, furniture, etc.

- **DEPARTMENTS** RISD elegantly focuses its resources on one beautifully designed page outlining courses of study for areas of concentration (architecture, ceramics, glass, graphic design, painting, sculpture, etc.). Each major has its own online gallery, emphasizing that RISD is a training school for artists. **www.risd.edu/depts1.html**

"RISD elegantly focuses its resources on one beautifully designed page."

WHAT YOU NEED TO GET IN Application Deadline January 21 for priority consideration; final deadline February 15 **Common App.** No **Application Fee** $35 **Tuition Costs** $17,600 **Room & Board** $6,618 **Need Blind** Yes **Financial Forms Deadline** February 15 **Undergrads Awarded Aid** 59% **Average Award of Freshman Scholarship Package** $8,921 **Tests Required** SAT1 (preferred) or ACT **Admissions Address** 2 College Street, Providence, RI 02903 **Admissions Telephone** (401) 454-6300

LAST YEAR'S CLASS Applied 1,407 **Accepted** 837 **Matriculated** 375 **Average SAT M/V** 565/500 **In Top Fifth of High School Graduating Class** 47%

COLLEGE LIFE Gender Breakdown M 44%, F 56% **Out of State Students** 95% **From Public Schools** 56% **Ethnic Composition** White & Other 86%, Asian American 8%, Black 2%, Hispanic 3%, Native American 1% **Foreign Students** 21% **Reside on Campus** 33% **Return as Sophomores** 96% **Total Faculty** 323 **Student Faculty Ratio** 12:1 **Fraternities** none **Sororities** none **Graduate Students** 159

University of Rhode Island

www.uri.edu

Kingston, RI · Est. 1892 · Coed · Public · 10,531 Undergrads · Small Town

I need...

Admissions info www.uri.edu/ugadmis/ug_home.html

How wired is URI?

Do I get a home page? No
What is the student to computer ratio? 21:1

REQUEST APPLICATION ONLINE

The usual tour

LIBRARY www.library.uri.edu
DEPARTMENTS www.uri.edu/acadprog.html
SPORTS www.uri.edu/student_life/athletics
CALENDAR www.uri.edu/calendar.html
CAREER CENTER www.uri.edu/career.html
STUDENT CLUBS www.uri.edu/student_life/studlif.html

Skip the brochure

- **U.R.I. MEMORIAL UNION** Entertainment comes in many shapes and sizes at the student union.

"The read of choice for URI's wired swimmers, divers, and water polo players."

Pool your resources and race to URI

Choose your pleasure: a video projection system, a pizza joint, or Wednesday night film screenings. **www.uri.edu/student_life/memu/mu.html**

- **STUDENT ENTERTAINMENT COMMITTEE** The SEC at the University of Rhode Island would like to gently remind you that since part of your tuition goes to student activities, you might as well get involved in planning how that money is spent. Concerts, speakers, and special events like off-campus trips and human bowling (now that's pretty special) are on the horizon. **www.uri.edu/student_life/sec/index.html**

- **VARSITY SWIMMING AND DIVING** URI's own version of the swimsuit edition. Wittily divided into hypertext lanes, it's the read of choice for URI's wired swimmers, divers, and water polo players. **www.uri.edu/student_life/swimming/swimhome.html**

WHAT YOU NEED TO GET IN **Application Deadline** December 15 for priority consideration; final deadline March 1 **Common App.** No **Application Fee** $30 ($45 for out-of-state applicants) **Tuition Costs** $3,004 ($10,330 out-of-state) **Room & Board** $5,410 **Need Blind** Yes **Financial Forms Deadline** March 1 with a priority given to applications received by January 1 **Undergrads Awarded Aid** 65% **Aid That Is Need-Based** 87% **Average Award of Freshman Scholarship Package** $0 **Tests Required** SAT1 or ACT **Admissions Address** Kingston, RI 02881 **Admissions Telephone** (401) 874-7000

LAST YEAR'S CLASS **Applied** 8,813 **Accepted** 6,988 **Matriculated** 1,986 **Average SAT M/V** 524/464 **Average ACT** 23 **In Top Fifth of High School Graduating Class** 38%

COLLEGE LIFE **Gender Breakdown** M 45%, F 55% **Out of State Students** 53% **From Public Schools** 87% **Ethnic Composition** White & Other 91%, Asian American 3%, Black 3%, Hispanic 2%, Native American 1% **Reside on Campus** 48% **Return as Sophomores** 75% **Total Faculty** 608 **Student Faculty Ratio** 15:1 **Fraternities (% of men participating)** 17 (17%) **Sororities (% of women participating)** 8 (14%) **Graduate Students** 3,167

Rhodes College

www.rhodes.edu

Memphis, TN · Est. 1848 · Coed · Private · 1,435 Undergrads · Urban

I need...

Admissions info adminfo@rhodes.edu
www.admissions.rhodes.edu/admissions
/default.html
Financial aid info www.admissions.rhodes.edu
/admissions/fa/fa.html

How wired is Rhodes?

Do I get email? Yes
Do I get a home page? Yes
What is the student to computer ratio? 11:1

The usual tour

DEPARTMENTS www.rhodes.edu/Default1htmls
/academicdepts.html
LIBRARY www.rhodes.edu/Default1htmls
/burrow.html
PUBLICATIONS www.rhodes.edu/default1htmls
/publications.html
STUDENT NEWSPAPER www.students.rhodes
.edu/sw
SPORTS www.rhodes.edu/default1htmls
/sports.html
CAREER CENTER tracy.stuaffairs.rhodes.edu
/default.html

Skip the brochure

• **BRITISH STUDIES AT OXFORD** Rhodes does Oxford.
Get academic credit for spending a summer
vacation abroad! (Oh yeah, there are seminars
and lectures to attend too.) **leslie.bristudies
.rhodes.edu**

Location: http://gray.music.rhodes.edu/Images/McCoy.gif

Deep in the woods of Rhodes, theatrical careers are born

• **COUNSELING AND STUDENT DEVELOPMENT CENTER**
On- and offline help for problems from eating
and drinking disorders to depression, STDs,
gender identity and anxiety attacks. The center
also offers extensive information regarding
study skills so you can get your school life
under control. **hellman.stuaffairs.rhodes.edu**

• **COLOSSUS AT RHODES** The Rhodes student-run
server offers articles and event schedules tailored to student interests, such as "Suggested
music for grubbing." If you're not familiar with
the term, a few minutes reading the related
article will give you all the context clues you
desire. **www.students.rhodes.edu**

"Rhodes at Oxford: credit for a summer abroad."

WHAT YOU NEED TO GET IN **Application Deadline** February 1 for priority consideration **Early Action Deadline** November 15
Common App. Yes **Application Fee** $40 **Tuition Costs** $16,392 **Room & Board** $5,110 **Need Blind** Yes
Financial Forms Deadline Priority given to applications received by March 1 **Undergrads Awarded Aid** 76%
Aid That Is Need-Based 60% **Average Award of Freshman Scholarship Package** $8,595 **Tests Required** SAT1
or ACT **Admissions Address** 2000 North Parkway, Memphis, TN 38112 **Admissions Telephone** (901) 726-3700

LAST YEAR'S CLASS **Applied** 2,345 **Accepted** 1,649 **Matriculated** 391 **Median Range SAT M/V** 580-680/520-630
In Top Fifth of High School Graduating Class 75% **Applied Early** 50 **Accepted Early** 43

COLLEGE LIFE **Gender Breakdown** M 44%, F 56% **Out of State Students** 74% **From Public Schools** 52% **Ethnic
Composition** White & Other 92%, Asian American 4%, Black 3%, Hispanic 1% **Foreign Students** 3% **Reside on
Campus** 78% **Return as Sophomores** 84% **Total Faculty** 151 **Student Faculty Ratio** 12:1 **Fraternities (% of men
participating)** 6 (51%) **Sororities (% of women participating)** 7 (53%) **Graduate Students** 6

Rice University

Houston, TX · Est. 1912 · Coed · Private · 2,674 Undergrads · Urban

I need...

Admissions info admi@rice.edu
riceinfo.rice.edu/RiceInfo/Courses.html
Financial aid info riceinfo.rice.edu/projects/FinAid

How wired is Rice?

Do I get email? Yes
Do I get a home page? Yes
Where? riceinfo.rice.edu/webshare_all.html
Is my dorm wired? Yes
What is the student to computer ratio? 45:1

The usual tour

CALENDAR riceinfo.rice.edu/RiceInfo/Calendars
.html
DEPARTMENTS riceinfo.rice.edu/RiceInfo
/Departments.html
LIBRARY riceinfo.rice.edu/Fondren
SPORTS riceinfo.rice.edu/projects/athletics
STUDENT NEWSPAPER riceinfo.rice.edu/projects
/thresher
STUDENT CLUBS www.ruf.rice.edu/~stact
/clubs.html

Skip the brochure

- **MARCHING OWL BAND HOME PAGE** The Rice band
doesn't march, but likes its own acronym
(MOB) too much to change its name. MOB's
specialty is as a scatter band, which means
crazy formations, crazier scripts, and music,
too. **riceinfo.rice.edu/~lynette/MOB.html**

School spirit is a hoot with the Marching Owls

- **RICE ANGLERS** Fish your way across Texas with a
small but devoted group of anglers. **www.owlnet
.rice.edu/~mpbro/fishing.html**

- **RICE OUTDOORS CLUB** Go fly a kite, climb a rock,
or hike a trail with other fans of the great outdoors. **riceinfo.rice.edu/~raksha/out/out.html**

- **RICE SPEECH AND DEBATE HOME PAGE** What's more
satisfying than winning an argument? How
about winning a competition for winning an
argument. Competitive communication is the
name of the game for the George R. Brown
Forensics Society. **riceinfo.rice.edu/~indigo/grbfs
/grbfs.html**

"Fly a kite, climb a rock, or hike a trail."

WHAT YOU NEED TO GET IN **Application Deadline** January 2 **Early Action Deadline** November 1 **Common App.** Yes
Application Fee $25 **Tuition Costs** $11,650 **Room & Board** $5,900 **Financial Forms Deadline** Rolling
Undergrads Awarded Aid 84% **Aid That Is Need-Based** 45% **Average Award of Freshman Scholarship Package**
$7,376 **Tests Required** SAT1 **Admissions Address** P.O. Box 1892, Houston, TX 77251 **Admissions Telephone**
(713) 527-4036

LAST YEAR'S CLASS **Applied** 7,935 **Accepted** 1,514 **Matriculated** 633 **Median Range SAT M/V** 665-763/592-708
In Top Quarter of High School Graduating Class 96% **Applied Early** 196 **Accepted Early** 82

COLLEGE LIFE **Gender Breakdown** M 59%, F 41% **Out of State Students** 53% **From Public Schools** 90% **Ethnic
Composition** White & Other 72%, Asian American 13%, Black 5.7%, Hispanic 8.8%, Native American 0.5%
Foreign Students 1% **Reside on Campus** 70% **Return as Sophomores** 95% **Total Faculty** 398 **Student Faculty
Ratio** 9:1 **Fraternities** none **Sororities** none **Graduate Students** 1,449

University of Richmond

Richmond, VA · Est. 1830 · Coed · Private · 3,501 Undergrads · Urban

I need...

Admissions info admissions@urich.edu
www.urich.edu/~admit
Financial aid info www.urich.edu/~admit

How wired is the University of Richmond?

Do I get email? Yes
Do I get a home page? Yes
Is my dorm wired? Yes
What is the student to computer ratio? 7:1

The usual tour

DEPARTMENTS www.urich.edu/Academic/schools
.html
SPORTS www.urich.edu/student_life.html#sports
STUDENT CLUBS www.urich.edu/student_life
.html#organs
STUDENT NEWSPAPER www.urich.edu/~collegia
/collegia.html
PUBLICATIONS www.urich.edu/student_life.html
#pubs
LIBRARY www.urich.edu/~library
CALENDAR www.urich.edu/~provost/Resources/
EventsCalendar/Events.HTML

Skip the brochure

- **BACCHUS** Drink up, but not the fruit of the vine
(or the hops). These Richmond students seek
to promote non-alcoholic fun in addition to providing safe rides for those who choose to drink
alcoholic beverages. **www.urich.edu/~bacchus**

An aerial shot of Richmond's campus

- **DEBATER'S MONTHLY** Now University of Richmond
students who like to shoot off at the mouth
can do so in print. This monthly publication,
which exists both on- and offline, is a collection of debating info, advice, and humor.
www.urich.edu/~debate/debmon.htm

- **RUSSIAN LANGUAGE CHATS HOMEPAGE** For all the
University of Richmond students who know
how to speak Russian, and even for all those
who don't. An advanced conversation group
meets for the former; a beginner's group
exists for students wanting to learn.
www.urich.edu/~russia/rus_chats.html

- **HONOR COUNCIL HOME PAGE** If you're honorable,
come and learn about the university's policy of
non-toleration. If you're not, come and read
about people who screwed up and how they
were punished. **www.urich.edu/~urhc**

WHAT YOU NEED TO GET IN **Application Deadline** February 1 **Early Action Deadline** November 15 **Common App.** Yes
Application Fee $40 **Tuition Costs** $16,570 **Room & Board** $3,595 **Need Blind** Yes **Financial Forms Deadline**
February 25 **Undergrads Awarded Aid** 60% **Aid That Is Need-Based** 38% **Average Award of Freshman
Scholarship Package** $8,500 **Tests Required** SAT1 or ACT **Admissions Address** Richmond, VA 23173
Admissions Telephone (804) 289-8640

LAST YEAR'S CLASS **Applied** 5,204 **Accepted** 2,744 **Matriculated** 797 **Median Range SAT M/V** 590-680/600-670
In Top Fifth of High School Graduating Class 77% **Applied Early** 351 **Accepted Early** 210

COLLEGE LIFE **Gender Breakdown** M 48%, F 52% **Out of State Students** 85% **From Public Schools** 73% **Ethnic
Composition** White & Other 90%, Asian American 3%, Black 5%, Hispanic 2% **Foreign Students** 2% **Reside on
Campus** 94% **Return as Sophomores** 92% **Total Faculty** 246 **Student Faculty Ratio** 11:1 **Fraternities (% of men
participating)** 10 (51%) **Sororities (% of women participating)** 8 (61%) **Graduate Students** 819

Rochester Institute of Technology

www.rit.edu

Rochester, NY · Est. 1829 · Coed · Private · 10,552 Undergrads · Urban

I need...

Admissions info admissions@rit.edu
www.isc.rit.edu/~960www
Financial aid info www.isc.rit.edu/~930www/Proj
/UGrad/UGradCat/Finaid/financial.html

How wired is RIT?

Do I get email? Yes
Do I get a home page? Yes
Is my dorm wired? Yes
What is the student to computer ratio? 10:1

FULL APPLICATION ONLINE

The usual tour

DEPARTMENTS www.isc.rit.edu/~930www/Proj
/UGrad/UGradCat/list.html
STUDENT CLUBS www.isc.rit.edu/CampusLife
/StuOrg
SPORTS www.isc.rit.edu/~934www
CALENDAR www.isc.rit.edu/~930www/Proj
/Calendar
LIBRARY wally.rit.edu
CAREER CENTER www.isc.rit.edu/~300www
/centers.html#ccdc

Skip the brochure

- **RIT AMBULANCE HOME PAGE** Who you gonna call? How about the friendly and helpful members of the local volunteer emergency medical unit? Best of all, they offer a virtual tour of the facili-

Location: http://www.it.rit.edu/~gehouse/house/libgard.html

Take a break from the books and stroll through the library garden

ties so you can get a sense of the place without actually having to go out and hurt yourself. **dumbo.isc.rit.edu/ems/rit/index.html**

- **COMMUNITY SERVICE CLUBHOUSE** One of RIT's seven special interest houses—this one's for do-gooders. **www.isc.rit.edu/~csch**

- **GEORGE EASTMAN HOUSE** The Kodak guru's house is now a museum which covers—surprise, surprise—the art, technology, and impact of photography and cinema. **www.it.rit.edu/~gehouse**

- **RIT OUTING CLUB** Club activites include backpacking, climbing, mountainbiking, caving, snowshoeing and more. **www.isc.rit.edu/~ritocwww**

WHAT YOU NEED TO GET IN Application Deadline March 1 for priority consideration; final deadline August 1 **Early Action Deadline** December 1 **Common App.** Yes **Application Fee** $40 **Tuition Costs** $15,375 **Room & Board** $6,135 **Need Blind** Yes **Financial Forms Deadline** Priority given to applications received by March 15 **Undergrads Awarded Aid** 70% **Aid That Is Need-Based** 90% **Average Award of Freshman Scholarship Package** $8,500 **Tests Required** SAT1 or ACT **Admissions Address** One Lomb Memorial Drive, Rochester, NY 14623 **Admissions Telephone** (716) 475-6631

LAST YEAR'S CLASS Applied 5,635 **Accepted** 4,294 **Matriculated** 1,647 **Median Range SAT M/V** 540-660/450-560 **In Top Fifth of High School Graduating Class** 50% **Applied Early** 610 **Accepted Early** 531

COLLEGE LIFE Gender Breakdown M 66%, F 34% **Out of State Students** 42% **From Public Schools** 85% **Ethnic Composition** White & Other 86%, Asian American 5%, Black 5%, Hispanic 3%, Native American 1% **Foreign Students** 5% **Reside on Campus** 70% **Return as Sophomores** 85% **Total Faculty** 1,100 **Student Faculty Ratio** 12:1 **Fraternities (% of men participating)** 15 (10%) **Sororities (% of women participating)** 9 (10%) **Graduate Students** 2,048

University of Rochester

www.rochester.edu

Rochester, NY · Est. 1850 · Coed · Private · 5,182 Undergrads · Urban

I need...

Admissions info admit@macmail.cc.rochester.edu
www.rochester.edu/admissions
Financial aid info help@finaid.rochester.edu
www.cc.rochester.edu/admissions/RC/tour.
html

How wired is the University of Rochester?

Do I get email? Yes
Do I get a home page? No
What is the student to computer ratio? 20:1

The usual tour

VIRTUAL TOUR www.cc.rochester.edu/admissions
/RC/tour.html
DEPARTMENTS www.rochester.edu/AcadDiv.html
LIBRARY rodent.lib.rochester.edu
STUDENT NEWSPAPER www.ct.rochester.edu
STUDENT CLUBS www.rochester.edu/sa-org/List
/index.html
SPORTS www.rochester.edu/sa-org/List/ath.html
GREEK LIFE www.rochester.edu/sa-org/List
/fratorgs.html

Skip the brochure

- **COMMONGROUND COFFEEHOUSE COMMITTEE** Coffee
without entertainment is like... well, it's bad.
The Commonground Coffeehouse Committee
fills the gap with music, comedy, and more.
www.rochester.edu/sa-org/COFFEE/index.html

- **STRONG JUGGLERS** They can juggle and make

These may be the only hot spots in chilly Rochester

people laugh; they can juggle and make people
gasp. "We do not limit ourselves. We are willing to act like fools in front of any audience."
No doubt, they often do. **www.rochester.edu/sa-org
/Jugglers/jugglers.html**

- **COALITION AGAINST SEXUAL HARASSMENT AND
ASSAULT (CASHA)** Women and men rally against
sexual harassment and assault through proactive behavior such as a Late Night Home
Program, a men's pledge to end rape, and various awareness projects. **www.rochester.edu/sa-org
/CASHA**

"We are willing to act like fools in front of any audience."

WHAT YOU NEED TO GET IN **Application Deadline** January 15 (first part) and January 31 (second part) **Early Action Deadline** November 15, but requests are considered until February 1 **Common App.** Yes **Application Fee** $50 **Tuition
Costs** $19,630 **Room & Board** $6,930 **Need Blind** Yes **Financial Forms Deadline** Priority given to
applications received by February 1 **Undergrads Awarded Aid** 89% **Aid That Is Need-Based** 85% **Average Award
of Freshman Scholarship Package** $15,540 **Tests Required** SAT1 or ACT **Admissions Address** Rochester, NY
14627 **Admissions Telephone** (716) 275-3221

LAST YEAR'S CLASS **Applied** 9,195 **Accepted** 5,608 **Matriculated** 1,227 **Median Range SAT M/V** 570-690/480-610
In Top Fifth of High School Graduating Class 78% **Applied Early** 249 **Accepted Early** 158

COLLEGE LIFE **Gender Breakdown** M 51%, F 49% **Out of State Students** 54% **Ethnic Composition** White & Other
78%, Asian American 10%, Black 8%, Hispanic 4% **Foreign Students** 9% **Reside on Campus** 78% **Return as
Sophomores** 92% **Total Faculty** 451 **Student Faculty Ratio** 12:1 **Fraternities (% of men participating)** 14 (18%)
Sororities (% of women participating) 9 (13%) **Graduate Students** 2,938

Rockford College

Rockford, IL · Est. 1847 · Coed · Private · 1,170 Undergrads · Urban

I need...

Admissions info admission@rockford.edu
www.rockford.edu/admissn/quick.htm
Financial aid info www.rockford.edu/admissn
/quick.htm#fina

How wired is Rockford?

Do I get email? Yes
Do I get a home page? Yes
Is my dorm wired? No
What is the student to computer ratio? 26:1

The usual tour

SPORTS www.rockford.edu/studserv/intram.htm
STUDENT CLUBS www.rockford.edu/studserv
/rcorgs.htm
STUDY ABROAD www.rockford.edu/regents
/regents.htm

Skip the brochure

- **S3FSIG HOME PAGE** In case you couldn't guess from the name, the members of the Science Fiction, Fact, and Fantasy Special Interest Group are a diverse lot. Join them for movies,

"Community involvement is music to the ears at Rockford."

Location: http://www.rockford.edu/images/lab1.gif

Ready and waiting to do your bidding

games, food, folks, and fun. **www.rockford.edu
/orgs/scifi/scifi.htm**

- **ROCKFORD COLLEGE COMPUTING SOCIETY**
Rockford's computer club has established a page that offers a succession of links mainly to commercial sites. It pays to think about the future. **www.rockford.edu/orgs/rccs/rccs.html**

- **ROCKFORD COLLEGE MUSIC ACADEMY** Community involvement is music to the ears at Rockford, where music instruction is offered to Rockfordites, ages six months and up. **www.rockford.edu/outrch/musicaca.htm**

- **UNCOMMON LIVES** Every two years it's time to celebrate and explore women's contributions to the arts with a week full of workshops and performances. **www.rockford.edu/outrch/uncommon.htm**

WHAT YOU NEED TO GET IN **Application Deadline** Rolling admissions **Common App.** Yes **Application Fee** $35 (fee waived with campus visit) **Tuition Costs** $14,100 **Room & Board** $4,500 **Need Blind** Yes **Financial Forms Deadline**
Priority given to applications received by April 15 **Undergrads Awarded Aid** 98% **Average Award of Freshman Scholarship Package** $4,300 **Tests Required** SAT1 or ACT (preferred) **Admissions Address** 5050 East State Street, Rockford, IL 61108-2393 **Admissions Telephone** (815) 226-4050

LAST YEAR'S CLASS **Applied** 472 **Accepted** 371 **Matriculated** 127 **Average SAT M/V** 520/506 **Average ACT** 22 **In Top Fifth of High School Graduating Class** 42%

COLLEGE LIFE **Gender Breakdown** M 31%, F 69% **Out of State Students** 18% **From Public Schools** 73% **Ethnic Composition** White & Other 89%, Asian American 2%, Black 6%, Hispanic 3% **Foreign Students** 5% **Reside on Campus** 40% **Return as Sophomores** 56% **Total Faculty** 146 **Student Faculty Ratio** 15:1 **Fraternities** none **Sororities** none **Graduate Students** 269

Rose-Hulman Institute of Technology

www.rose-hulman.edu

Terre Haute, IN · Est. 1874 · Coed · Private · 1,548 Undergrads · Big Town

I need...

Admissions info www.rose-hulman.edu/Class
/Admissions
Financial aid info www.rose-hulman.edu/Class
/Admissions/FinancialAid.html

How wired is Rose-Hulman ?

Do I get email? Yes
Do I get a home page? Yes
   Where? www.rose-hulman.edu/users.html
Is my dorm wired? Yes
What is the student to computer ratio? 2:1

The usual tour

DEPARTMENTS www.rose-hulman.edu
/Departments.html
SPORTS www.rose-hulman.edu/Class/Relations
/lans/sports/websport.htm
PUBLICATIONS www.rose-hulman.edu/Publications
.html
STUDENT NEWSPAPER www.rose-hulman.edu
/Users/groups/Thorn/HTML/index.html
CALENDAR www.rose-hulman.edu/Calendar
/calendar.html
STUDENT CLUBS www.rose-hulman.edu/People.html

Skip the brochure

- **SOLAR PHANTOM PROJECT** It's fun in the sun with
  Rose-Hulman's hot rod, a solar car designed,

Location: http://www.rose-hulman.edu/Users/groups/SolarPhantom/HTML/index.html

At Rose-Hulman, the sky's the limit—and the power supply

engineered, built, and raced by students.
**www.rose-hulman.edu/Users/groups/SolarPhantom
/HTML/index.html**

- **ROSE-HULMAN MARTIAL ARTS CLUB** R-H students
  get a kick out of Aikido, Tae Kwon-Do, and
  Kempo with training sessions and tournaments. **www.rose-hulman.edu/Users/groups/Martia
  l_Arts_Club/Public/HTML/index.html**

- **RIFLE TEAM** Not to be confused with its companion organization, the Gun Club (which is more
  concerned with shooting for shooting's sake),
  the Rifle Team doesn't just shoot. It shoots to
  win. Another way to tell them apart—the Rifle
  Team's page is the one that doesn't link to the
  NRA. **www.rose-hulman.edu/Users/groups/RifleTeam
  /Public/HTML/index.html**

WHAT YOU NEED TO GET IN **Application Deadline** December 1 for priority consideration; final deadline April 1 **Common App.** No **Application Fee** $35 **Tuition Costs** $15,600 **Room & Board** $4,700 **Financial Forms Deadline** Priority given to applications received by February 1 **Undergrads Awarded Aid** 91% **Aid That Is Need-Based** 80% **Average Award of Freshman Scholarship Package** $4,000 **Tests Required** SAT1 or ACT **Admissions Address** 5500 Wabash Avenue, Terre Haute, IN 47803 **Admissions Telephone** (812) 877-1511

LAST YEAR'S CLASS **Applied** 3,505 **Accepted** 2,200 **Matriculated** 461 **Average SAT M/V** 700/570 **Average ACT** 30 **In Top Fifth of High School Graduating Class** 93%

COLLEGE LIFE **Gender Breakdown** M 94%, F 6% **Out of State Students** 40% **From Public Schools** 73% **Ethnic Composition** White & Other 95%, Asian American 2%, Black 2%, Hispanic 1% **Foreign Students** 2% **Reside on Campus** 65% **Return as Sophomores** 90% **Total Faculty** 109 **Student Faculty Ratio** 13:1 **Fraternities (% of men participating)** 8 (44%) **Sororities** none **Graduate Students** 103

Rutgers College

New Brunswick, NJ · Est. 1969 · Coed · Public · 3,149 Undergrads · Big Town

I need...

Admissions info www.rutgers.edu/Academics /Admit/under

Financial aid info www.rutgers.edu/Services /Financial-Aid

How wired is Rutgers?

Do I get email? Yes

What is the student to computer ratio? 5:1

REQUEST APPLICATION ONLINE

The usual tour

SPORTS www.rutgers.edu/athletics

GREEK LIFE www.rutgers.edu/Academics/Admit /under/stu-life/stu-life.htm#fraternities

STUDY ABROAD www.rutgers.edu/Academics /Study_Abroad

LIBRARY www.rutgers.edu/rulib

CALENDAR www.rutgers.edu/UC/kiosk/whahapn .html

STUDENT CLUBS www.rutgers.edu/Services/stud _org

Skip the brochure

- **ABOUT RUTGERS UNIVERSITY** Rutgers: The State University of New Jersey, is composed of three campuses; Rutgers College is just one of them—the others are Camden and Newark. Founded in 1766, Rutgers is one of the country's oldest schools and accommodates more than 25,000 undergraduates. In the Garden State, big is clearly better. **www.rutgers.edu/UC /aboutru/about.html**

The Rutgers University Bookstore has a monopoly on board game mascots

- **WELCOME TO THE RUTGERS BOOKSTORE** Just like the real thing minus the long lines, scrambling for the last used texts, and haggling with the clerk at the buy-back counter. Of course, you do miss the social side of a trip to the one place every student has to go at the beginning of the semester. What you will get in the online alternative is a look at the latest deals and specials, access to the text reservation system, contests, personals, and classified ads. **www.virtual-media.com/rutgers.850/welcome.html**

- **THE DAILY TARGUM ONLINE** One of the great mysteries at Rutgers is the meaning of the word "Targum." Whatever its meaning, the student newspaper, whose inception dates back to 1866, has entered the new age of information with its online version. Enjoy access to news, sports, or entertainment, or read about the history of the paper with the inexplicable name. **www.injersey.com/Media/targum**

- -

WHAT YOU NEED TO GET IN **Application Deadline** December 15 for priority consideration **Common App.** No **Application Fee** $50 **Tuition Costs** $3,786 ($7,707 out-of-state) **Room & Board** $4,936 **Need Blind** Yes **Financial Forms Deadline** Priority given to applications received by March 1 **Undergrads Awarded Aid** 64% **Aid That Is Need-Based** 90% **Average Award of Freshman Scholarship Package** $4,973 **Tests Required** SAT1 or ACT **Admissions Address** New Brunswick, NJ 08903 **Admissions Telephone** (908) 932-3770

LAST YEAR'S CLASS **Applied** 11,208 **Accepted** 7,060 **Matriculated** 561 **Average SAT M/V** 555/532 **In Top Fifth of High School Graduating Class** 28%

COLLEGE LIFE **Gender Breakdown** M 60%, F 40% **Out of State Students** 14% **Ethnic Composition** White & Other 65%, Asian American 15%, Black 12%, Hispanic 8% **Foreign Students** 2% **Reside on Campus** 43% **Return as Sophomores** 87% **Total Faculty** 763 **Student Faculty Ratio** 18:1 **Fraternities (% of men participating)** 31 (11%) **Sororities (% of women participating)** 15 (7%)

St. Bonaventure University

St. Bonaventure, NY · Est. 1858 · Coed · Private · 1,893 Undergrads · Small Town

I need...

Admissions info admissions@sbu.edu
www.sbu.edu/prospectivestudents
/prospective_students.html
Financial aid info www.cs.sbu.edu/admiss
/financialaid.html

How wired is St. Bonaventure University?

Do I get email? Yes
Do I get a home page? Yes
Is my dorm wired? Yes
What is the student to computer ratio? 14:1

The usual tour

DEPARTMENTS www.cs.sbu.edu/departments
/dept-hmpg.html
STUDENT CLUBS www.cs.sbu.edu/admiss/stud
_org.html
SPORTS www.cs.sbu.edu/athl/index.html
VIRTUAL TOUR www.cs.sbu.edu/campus/campus
_map.html
CALENDAR www.cs.sbu.edu/acad/calendar.html

Skip the brochure

• **WSBU 88.3 FM** Bona's Best Rock. As alternative
music has become hip, even mainstream, college radio has gained prestige. Often the first
station to play and promote unsigned NY
bands, WSBU radio offers some of the only
non-corporate, non-commercial-laden material.
www.cs.sbu.edu/wsbu/wsbul.html

St. Bonaventure is an athletic adventure

• **MICROSOFT CURRICULUM DEVELOPER** On the edge,
though not the cutting edge. For those interested in cyberclasses, St. Bonaventure's has
recently started developing courseware. Some
of the participating courses are hyperlinked
here. www.cs.sbu.edu/msg/ms_grant.html

• **BONNY SPORTS** St. Bonaventure's nickname is
"Bona," and the athletic teams are the
"Bonnies." This site highlight's Bona's best
b-ballers, batters, and breaststrokers. Check
here for info on playing schedules and a list of
the Bona Backers. www.cs.sbu.edu/athl/index.html

"WSBU promotes unsigned bands and non-corporate material."

WHAT YOU NEED TO GET IN **Application Deadline** Rolling admissions; April 15 for priority consideration **Common App.**
Yes **Application Fee** $30 (waived for HEOP applicants) **Tuition Costs** $11,919 **Room & Board** $5,156 **Need
Blind** Yes **Financial Forms Deadline** Priority given to applications received by February 1 **Undergrads Awarded
Aid** 92% **Aid That Is Need-Based** 85% **Average Award of Freshman Scholarship Package** $7,217 **Tests**
SAT1 or ACT **Admissions Address** P.O. Box D, St. Bonaventure, NY 14778-2284 **Admissions Telephone** (716)
375-2400

LAST YEAR'S CLASS **Applied** 1,615 **Accepted** 1,434 **Matriculated** 548 **Average SAT M/V** 540/480 **Average ACT** 24
In Top Fifth of High School Graduating Class 44%

COLLEGE LIFE **Gender Breakdown** M 49%, F 51% **Out of State Students** 26% **From Public Schools** 71% **Ethnic
Composition** White & Other 95%, Asian American 1%, Black 2%, Hispanic 1%, Native American 1% **Foreign
Students** 2% **Reside on Campus** 78% **Return as Sophomores** 81% **Total Faculty** 138 **Student Faculty Ratio**
17:1 **Fraternities (% of men participating)** 1 (1%) **Sororities (% of women participating)** 1 (1%) **Graduate
Students** 698

St. John's College, Annapolis

www.sjca.edu

Annapolis, MD · Est. 1696 · Coed · Private · 419 Undergrads · Big Town

I need...

Admissions info admissions@sjca.edu
www.sjca.edu/admissions

Financial aid info www.sjca.edu/admissions
/finaid.html

How wired is St. John's, Annapolis?

Do I get email? Yes
Do I get a home page? Yes
Is my dorm wired? No
What is the student to computer ratio? 35:1

DOWNLOAD APPLICATION ONLINE

The usual tour

CURRICULUM www.sjca.edu/college/readlist.html
VIRTUAL TOUR www.sjca.edu/college/tour
/tour.htm
STUDENT CLUBS www.sjca.edu/admissions
/camplife.html#activities
SPORTS www.sjca.edu/admissions
/camplife.html#athletics
LIBRARY www.sjca.edu/library

Skip the brochure

- **ST JOHN'S COLLEGE LIST OF PROGRAM READINGS** If there is one aspect of St. John's that prospective students need to know, it is the curriculum—it begins with the ancient Greeks, and over a course of four years, moves into the twentieth century. This program of study calls for a commitment to the most philosophical, scientific, and literary works in Western history. www.sjca.edu/college/readlist.html

Location: http://www.sjca.edu/college/tour/aerial.htm

Aerial View of the Annapolis Campus

St. John's Campus is located in the heart of historic Annapolis. The college green (bottom) faces the city's 18th century residential district, while back campus overlooks College Creek. At the left edge of the photo is the beginning of the Georgian-style state office complex; just out of the picture to the right is the United States Naval Academy and its park-like grounds.

SJC Home Page | Beginning of Tour

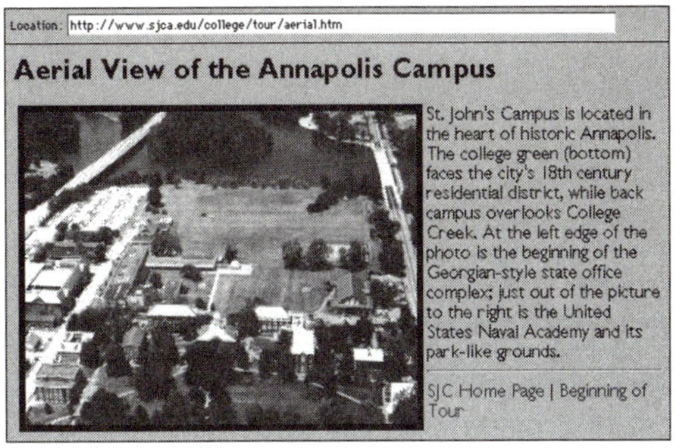

The 36 acre campus is a cozy retreat from Baltimore and Washington, D.C., only 30 miles away

- **THE MITCHELL GALLERY** Mitchell Gallery exhibition openings always include discussions inaugurated by a probing, and hopefully stimulating and interesting question. Commensurate with the Great Books Program, which is St John's curriculum of old school superstar canonical texts, the Mitchell Gallery tends to feature artists of "major stature." **www.sjca.edu/gallery/gallery.html**

- **HISTORIC ANNAPOLIS: THE VIRTUAL TOUR** Want to have a sleepover with 4,000 Navy boys? Annapolis is a charming mix of the ultra-colonial and the modern-day military. The United States Naval Academy, whose Bancroft Hall sleeps 4,000 midshipmen is there, as is the Middletown Tavern, which quenched the thirst of Benjamin Franklin and George Washington. **www.capitalonline.com/tour**

WHAT YOU NEED TO GET IN **Application Deadline** March 1 for priority consideration; final deadline Rolling Admissions **Common App.** Yes **Tuition Costs** $19,840 **Room & Board** $5,950 **Need Blind** Yes **Financial Forms Deadline** Priority given to applications received by February 15 **Undergrads Awarded Aid** 65% **Aid That Is Need-Based** 100% **Average Award of Freshman Scholarship Package** $13,305 **Tests Required** SAT1 or ACT **Admissions Address** P.O. Box 2800, Annapolis, MD 21404 **Admissions Telephone** (800) 727-9238

LAST YEAR'S CLASS **Applied** 338 **Accepted** 292 **Matriculated** 111 **Median Range SAT M/V** 530-670/560-670 **In Top Fifth of High School Graduating Class** 40%

COLLEGE LIFE **Gender Breakdown** M 52%, F 48% **Out of State Students** 88% **From Public Schools** 65% **Ethnic Composition** White & Other 90%, Asian American 3%, Black 2%, Hispanic 4%, Native American 1% **Foreign Students** 6% **Reside on Campus** 75% **Return as Sophomores** 81% **Total Faculty** 67 **Student Faculty Ratio** 8:1 **Fraternities** none **Sororities** none **Graduate Students** 94

St. John's College, Santa Fe

www.sjcsf.edu

Santa Fe, NM · Est. 1964 · Coed · Private · 379 Undergrads · Big Town

How wired is St. John's, Santa Fe?

Do I get email? Yes
Do I get a home page? Yes
Is my dorm wired? No
What is the student to computer ratio? 34:1

DOWNLOAD APPLICATION ONLINE

The usual tour

DEPARTMENTS www.sjcsf.edu/curriculum.html
VIRTUAL TOUR www.sjcsf.edu/tour.html

Skip the brochure

- **INFORMATION ABOUT THE COLLEGE** Explore the Annapolis campus's pages for a general overview of St. John's College and the Great Books Program. While the Santa Fe campus offers different programs and activities from the Annapolis campus, both constitute St. John's College. Students are welcome to spend time in either place. sjc.stjohns-nm.edu /main.html

- **STUDENT LIFE** Life and study at St. John's are definitely stylized, and seem to date from an earlier century: "At 8 p.m. on Monday and Thursday evenings, the tower bell signals the seminars to assemble. Approximately 20

WELCOME TO THE SANTA FE CAMPUS OF ST. JOHN'S COLLEGE

Location: http://sjc.stjohns-nm.edu/main.html

Ptolemy, Galileo—you do the math at St. John's

students gather with two tutors to discuss a section of a book they have all read. Throughout the session, students and tutors voice and defend their opinions. The seminar is a way of learning and reflects a way of living." **www.sjcsf.edu/stulif**

- **SEARCH AND RESCUE TEAM** Training for this group involves search and rescue techniques, outdoor leadership, rock climbing, survival skills, emergency medical care, two-way radio communications, backpacking, navigation and high altitude mountaineering. But the rescuers are good, damn good, and are asked to participate in, on average, 30 search and rescue expeditions every year. **www.sjcsf.edu/stulif**

"The Search and Rescue team is good, damn good. "

WHAT YOU NEED TO GET IN **Application Deadline** Rolling admissions; March 1 for priority consideration **Common App.** Yes **Tuition Costs** $18,520 **Room & Board** $6,055 **Need Blind** Yes **Financial Forms Deadline** Priority given to applications received by February 15 **Undergrads Awarded Aid** 85% **Aid That Is Need-Based** 100% **Average Award of Freshman Scholarship Package** $11,325 **Tests Required** SAT1 or ACT **Admissions Address** 1160 Camino Cruz Blanca, Santa Fe, NM 87501 **Admissions Telephone** (800) 332-5232

LAST YEAR'S CLASS **Applied** 286 **Accepted** 234 **Matriculated** 116 **Median Range SAT M/V** 540-670/540-650 **In Top Fifth of High School Graduating Class** 55%

COLLEGE LIFE **Gender Breakdown** M 55%, F 45% **Out of State Students** 85% **From Public Schools** 77% **Ethnic Composition** White & Other 88%, Asian American 3%, Black 1%, Hispanic 7%, Native American 1% **Foreign Students** 2% **Reside on Campus** 80% **Return as Sophomores** 80% **Total Faculty** 61 **Student Faculty Ratio** 8:1 **Fraternities** none **Sororities** none **Graduate Students** 87

St. John's University

www.stjohns.edu

Jamaica, NY · Est. 1870 · Coed · Private · 12,395 Undergrads · Urban

I need...

Admissions info www.stjohns.edu/sjuinfo
/policies/admissns.html
Financial aid info www.stjohns.edu/sjuinfo
/policies/finanaid.html

How wired is St. John's University?

Do I get email? Yes
Do I get a home page? Yes
Is my dorm wired? No
What is the student to computer ratio? 18:1

REQUEST APPLICATION ONLINE

The usual tour

DEPARTMENTS www.stjohns.edu/sjuinfo
/academic/schools
VIRTUAL TOUR www.stjohns.edu/sjuinfo/campus
Life/tours.html
LIBRARY www.stjohns.edu/sjuinfo/academic
/library.html
SPORTS www.stjohns.edu/RedStorm
STUDY ABROAD www.stjohns.edu/sjuinfo
/academic/schools/abroad
STUDENT CENTER s005.infomall.org

Skip the brochure

- **STUDY ABROAD PROGRAMS** If Queens and Staten Island start to wear on your nerves, there are other options. Maynooth (Ireland), Rome, Tokyo, and Budapest are some of the established sites of St. John's study abroad programs. **www.stjohns.edu/sjuinfo/academic /schools/abroad**

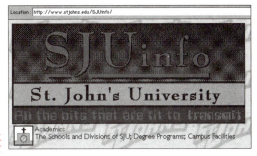

The only Division I champ school named St. John's

- **VINCENTIAN CENTER** Come all ye faithful: Since St. John's is a Catholic university, there is a strong scent of incense wafting through this Web site. The Vincentian Center has an attractive spiritual presence online that explains its divine mission. Vincent de Paul was a seventeenth century Frenchman who, after experiencing a personal conversion, dedicated himself to proselytizing and charity. The center upholds this tradition, organizing programs to bring the church closer to society. **www.stjohns .edu/vincentianctr**

"A strong scent of incense wafts through this site."

WHAT YOU NEED TO GET IN Application Deadline Rolling admissions **Common App.** No **Application Fee** $30 **Tuition Costs** $10,950 **Need Blind** Yes **Financial Forms Deadline** Priority given to applications received by April 1 **Undergrads Awarded Aid** 77% **Aid That Is Need-Based** 60% **Average Award of Freshman Scholarship Package** $7,756 **Tests Required** SAT1 (preferred) or ACT **Admissions Address** 8000 Utopia Parkway, Jamaica, NY 11439 **Admissions Telephone** (718) 990-6114

LAST YEAR'S CLASS Applied 8,297 **Accepted** 6,697 **Matriculated** 2,296 **Average SAT M/V** 510/440 **In Top Half of High School Graduating Class** 90%

COLLEGE LIFE Gender Breakdown M 46%, F 54% **Out of State Students** 4% **Ethnic Composition** White & Other 64%, Asian American 11%, Black 12%, Hispanic 12%, Native American 1% **Foreign Students** 3% **Return as Sophomores** 82% **Total Faculty** 1,001 **Student Faculty Ratio** 20:1 **Fraternities (% of men participating)** 15 (8%) **Sororities (% of women participating)** 12 (6%) **Graduate Students** 5,027

Saint Louis University

www.slu.edu

St. Louis, MO · Est. 1818 · Coed · Private · 6,123 Undergrads · Urban

I need...

Admissions info belobrs@sluvca.slu.edu
www.slu.edu/admissions/admissions.html
Financial aid info www.slu.edu/services/fin_aid

How wired is SLU?

Do I get email? Yes
Do I get a home page? No
Is my dorm wired? Yes
What is the student to computer ratio? 27:1

The usual tour

DEPARTMENTS www.slu.edu/colleges/colleges
.html
SPORTS www.slu.edu/athletics/athletics.html
LIBRARY www.slu.edu/libraries/libraries.html
PUBLICATIONS www.slu.edu/publications
/publications.html
CALENDAR www.slu.edu/info/calendar.html

Skip the brochure

• **ST. LOUIS ZOO** Widely regarded as one of the
world's premiere zoos, the St. Louis Zoo is a
great place to reconnect with wildlife. Meet
some of the animals in residence, like the new
baby orangutan, and read up about current
projects and future initiatives. **www.st-louis
.mo.us/st-louis/zoo**

• **WHAT YOU MUST SEE IN ST. LOUIS** J. Brad Hicks'
insider guide to the city not only tells you
where and when to go to see a "bazillion"

Saint Louis University, the first university established west
of the Mississippi River, in 1832

trees in bloom, but also identifies some real
hot spots like the National Coin-Op and Video
Game Museum. **www.inlink.com/~jbhicks/stl_must
_see.html**

• **ST. LOUIS UNIVERSITY NEWS** Finding something
exciting at SLU is a real challenge. Perhaps it
is easiest to check in at this page, though at
press time, there was no news. **www.slu.edu
/info/news.html**

"J. Brad Hicks knows some real hot spots like the National Coin-Op and Video Game Museum."

WHAT YOU NEED TO GET IN Application Deadline December 1 for priority consideration; final deadline August 1
Common App. No **Application Fee** $25 **Tuition Costs** $13,900 **Room & Board** $5,110 **Need Blind** Yes **Financial
Forms Deadline** Priority given to applications received by January 1 **Undergrads Awarded Aid** 84% **Aid That Is
Need-Based** 66% **Average Award of Freshman Scholarship Package** $7,850 **Tests Required** SAT1 or ACT
(preferred) **Admissions Address** 221 North Grand Boulevard, St. Louis, MO 63103-2097 **Admissions Telephone**
(314) 977-2500

LAST YEAR'S CLASS Applied 3,694 **Accepted** 3,167 **Matriculated** 1,049 **Average SAT M/V** 1157 (combined
average) **Average ACT** 25 **In Top Fifth of High School Graduating Class** 47%

COLLEGE LIFE Gender Breakdown M 47%, F 53% **Out of State Students** 44% **Ethnic Composition** White & Other
84%, Asian American 4%, Black 9%, Hispanic 2%, Native American 1% **Foreign Students** 8% **Reside on Campus**
33% **Return as Sophomores** 84% **Total Faculty** 1,196 **Student Faculty Ratio** 10:1 **Fraternities (% of men
participating)** 9 (17%) **Sororities (% of women participating)** 5 (12%) **Graduate Students** 4,596

St. Olaf College

www.stolaf.edu

Northfield, MN · Est. 1874 · Coed · Private · 2,936 Undergrads · Small Town

I need...

Admissions info www.stolaf.edu/admissions

How wired is Saint Olaf?

REQUEST APPLICATION ONLINE

Do I get email? Yes

Do I get a home page? Yes

Where? www.stolaf.edu/people

Is my dorm wired? Yes

What is the student to computer ratio? 6:1

The usual tour

DEPARTMENTS www.stolaf.edu/depts

SPORTS www.stolaf.edu/athletics

LIBRARY www.stolaf.edu/library

STUDENT CLUBS www.stolaf.edu/stulife/orgs
/#orgs

Skip the brochure

- **NORWEGIAN AMERICAN HISTORICAL ASSOCIATION**
Minnesota in general, and St. Olaf's in particular, has a substantial population of people of Norwegian descent. This group sets out to: "locate, collect, preserve and interpret the Norwegian-American part of this whole with accuracy, integrity, and liveliness. In doing so, Norwegian Americans will have an identifiable position in America's past, present, and future." **www.stolaf.edu/other/naha/naha.html**

- **INTERNATIONAL SUMMER SCHOOL** Norway, Norway, and more Norway. It seems like a joke from the Coen brothers' movie, *Fargo*, but the only

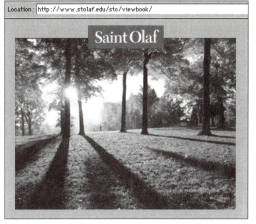

Location: http://www.stolaf.edu/sto/viewbook/

Saint Olaf

St. Olaf experiences yet another alien visitation

international programs described here are in Oslo, Norway. **www.stolaf.edu/people/iss**

- **SCHOOL NATURE AREA PROJECT** The SNAP program is an outreach program that helps schools procure natural areas and then helps develop an environmental education curriculum. If you want to make the next generation green, come here. **www.stolaf.edu/other/snap**

"The SNAP program: making the next generation green"

WHAT YOU NEED TO GET IN **Application Deadline** Rolling admissions; February 1 for priority consideration **Early Action Deadline** November 15 **Common App.** Yes **Application Fee** $25 **Tuition Costs** $15,000 **Room & Board** $3,850 **Need Blind** Yes **Financial Forms Deadline** Priority given to applications received by March 1 **Undergrads Awarded Aid** 81% **Aid That Is Need-Based** 95% **Average Award of Freshman Scholarship Package** $8,599 **Tests Required** SAT1 or ACT **Admissions Address** 1520 Saint Olaf Avenue, Northfield, MN 55057-1098 **Admissions Telephone** (507) 646-3025

LAST YEAR'S CLASS **Applied** 2,333 **Accepted** 1,736 **Matriculated** 749 **Average SAT M/V** 620/550 **Average ACT** 26 **In Top Fifth of High School Graduating Class** 69% **Applied Early** 175 **Accepted Early** 155

COLLEGE LIFE **Gender Breakdown** M 42%, F 58% **Out of State Students** 45% **Ethnic Composition** White & Other 93.7%, Asian American 4%, Black 1%, Hispanic 1%, Native American 0.3% **Foreign Students** 2% **Reside on Campus** 91% **Return as Sophomores** 84% **Total Faculty** 394 **Student Faculty Ratio** 11:1 **Fraternities** none **Sororities** none

Samford University

www.samford.edu

Birmingham, AL · Est. 1841 · Coed · Private · 3,102 Undergrads · Urban

How wired is Samford University?

Do I get email? Yes
Do I get a home page? No
Is my dorm wired? No
What is the student to computer ratio? 7:1

The usual tour

DEPARTMENTS server1.samford.edu/schools.html
STUDENT CLUBS server1.samford.edu/groups
/stuafair.html #Student Activities
GREEK LIFE server1.samford.edu/groups/dean
_stu.html #greek
CAREER CENTER server1.samford.edu/groups
/careerdv.html
LIBRARY davisweb.samford.edu

Skip the brochure

- **BEESON DIVINITY SCHOOL** Being a committed Baptist institution, Samford has its own divinity school. However, don't let the Baptist origins mislead you.Like most divinity schools, Beeson is interdenominational. Explore your faith here. **server1.samford.edu/schools/divinity.html**

- **INSTITUTE OF GENEALOGY AND HISTORICAL RESEARCH** For the past 32 years, Samford has hosted this quasi-conference on how to research your genealogy. Courses are very focused: They

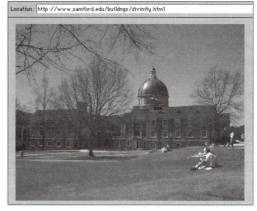

Domed buildings, gently sloping lawns, and friendly debate—yet another idyllic day at Samford University apply only to the Old South, Britain, and Ireland. **server1.samford.edu/schools/ighr/ighr.html**

- **SIGMA PHI EPSILON** This site certainly has the most grandiose graphics on the Samford page. It's linked to an essay on the "Balanced Man," which posits that men should take heed of the Ancient Greek emphasis on body and mind. One wonders whether these Sigma Phi Epsilon boys are major jocks, or just followers of Nietzsche. **www.samford.edu/groups/spe/sigep.htm**

"Are these frat boys jocks, or just followers of Nietzsche?"

WHAT YOU NEED TO GET IN **Application Deadline** December 15 for priority consideration; final deadline June 1 **Common App.** No **Application Fee** $25 **Tuition Costs** $9,070 **Room & Board** $3,930 **Need Blind** Yes **Financial Forms Deadline** Priority given to applications received by March 1 **Undergrads Awarded Aid** 77% **Aid That Is Need-Based** 85% **Average Award of Freshman Scholarship Package** $5,100 **Tests Required** SAT1 (preferred) or ACT **Admissions Address** 800 Lakeshore Drive, Birmingham, AL 35229 **Admissions Telephone** (800) 888-7218

LAST YEAR'S CLASS **Applied** 1,713 **Accepted** 1,459 **Matriculated** 647 **Average SAT M/V** 566/572 **Average ACT** 25 **In Top Fifth of High School Graduating Class** 44%

COLLEGE LIFE **Gender Breakdown** M 38%, F 62% **Out of State Students** 60% **From Public Schools** 71% **Ethnic Composition** White & Other 94.2%, Asian American 1.1%, Black 4%, Hispanic 0.5%, Native American 0.2% **Foreign Students** 1% **Reside on Campus** 59% **Return as Sophomores** 82% **Total Faculty** 314 **Student Faculty Ratio** 17:1 **Fraternities (% of men participating)** 5 (40%) **Sororities (% of women participating)** 8 (40%) **Graduate Students** 1,528

San Diego State University

www.sdsu.edu

San Diego, CA · Est. 1897 · Coed · Public · 21,957 Undergrads · Urban

I need...

Admissions info www.sdsu.edu/gettingin /#Admitinfo

Financial aid info www.sdsu.edu/gettingin

How wired is San Diego State?

Is my dorm wired? No

What is the student to computer ratio? 15:1

The usual tour

DEPARTMENTS www.sdsu.edu/academicprog /index.html

STUDENT CLUBS www.sdsu.edu/studentlife /index.html

SPORTS www.sdsu.edu/sports

LIBRARY libweb.sdsu.edu

CAREER CENTER www.sa.sdsu.edu/career/cs _homepage.html

Skip the brochure

- **SKULL AND DAGGER** Surfing is not the only non-academic activity in this neck of the beach. SDSU has a long theater tradition. Dating from 1923, this theater production group is the oldest student group on the San Diego State campus. **rohan.sdsu.edu/dept/dagger**

- **THE AZTEC EQUITY FUND** Though it may have a reputation as a party school, some folks at SDSU are serious about investments. Academic economic theories are put into

San Diego State—so beautiful outside, you may never get online

practice when real capital investments are made by this group. **rohan.sdsu.edu/dept/aef**

- **ASSOCIATED STUDENTS** This independent student-run corporation has its hands in every element of student life. Students book performers like Bush and the Cranberries to play on campus, while others run recreation and sports programs. Power-hungry applicants should take note—the AS council is the highest decision-making organization within the student government. **www.sdsu.edu/as**

"Students book performers like Bush to play on campus, others run recreation and sports programs."

WHAT YOU NEED TO GET IN **Application Deadline** Rolling admissions; November 30 for priority consideration **Common App.** No **Application Fee** $55 **Tuition Costs** $1,902 ($9,282 out-of-state) **Room & Board** $5,624 **Financial Forms Deadline** Priority given to applications received by March 2 **Undergrads Awarded Aid** 41% **Aid That Is Need-Based** 99% **Average Award of Freshman Scholarship Package** $1,500 **Tests Required** SAT1 or ACT **Admissions Address** 5300 Campanile, San Diego, CA 92182-0771 **Admissions Telephone** (619) 594-6871

LAST YEAR'S CLASS **Applied** 8,187 **Accepted** 7,319 **Matriculated** 2,151 **Average SAT M/V** 457/394 **Average ACT** 20

COLLEGE LIFE **Gender Breakdown** M 49%, F 51% **Ethnic Composition** White & Other 65%, Asian American 14%, Black 5%, Hispanic 15%, Native American 1% **Foreign Students** 11% **Reside on Campus** 8% **Return as Sophomores** 71% **Student Faculty Ratio** 19:1 **Fraternities (% of men participating)** 17 (7%) **Sororities (% of women participating)** 12 (6%) **Graduate Students** 4,195

University of San Diego

San Diego, CA · Est. 1949 · Coed · Private · 4,106 Undergrads · Urban

I need...

Admissions info admissions@acusd.edu
  gopher://pwa.acusd.edu:70/00/USDinfo
  /latestbulletin/policies/usd1cptb.txt
Financial aid info gopher://pwa.acusd.edu:70
  /11/USDinfo/usdofa

How wired is the University of San Diego?

Do I get email? Yes
Do I get a home page? Yes
Is my dorm wired? Yes
What is the student to computer ratio? 27:1

The usual tour

DEPARTMENTS www.acusd.edu/Departments
STUDENT CLUBS as.acusd.edu/as/cluborg
  /studorg.html
SPORTS as.acusd.edu/as/programs/ath.html
LIBRARY www.acusd.edu/Libraries
CAREER CENTER gopher://pwa.acusd.edu:70/11
  /USDinfo/careers

Skip the brochure

• **CAFE MOY** These days, all you need from a cyber-cafe is an audience, bad poetry, cool links, and maybe, a cup of joe to drink at your terminal. Well, Cafe Moy has all of the cyber-hallmarks and more. Just get yourself a cappucino and surf over to the cafe. **cafe.acusd.edu**

• **PRIVACY RIGHTS CLEARINGHOUSE** All netters should visit this site. With the Communications

San Diego has the typical cybercafe, complete with an audience, bad poetry, and cool links

Decency Act, a Net user's privacy, among other rights, was compromised. The program located at the University of San Diego, the Privacy Rights Clearinghouse, has posted terrific and easy-to-read explanations of the nature of online privacy. They also address other privacy issues such as credit card fraud, caller ID, and Social Security Number disclosure. **www.acusd.edu/~prc**

• **A.S. TRAFFIC COURT** Boo is the director of parking at the University of San Diego, which leads one to conclude that parking and traffic are major issues. Indeed, the school has an in house judicial system that handles campus parking issues. There are also links to pages with "cyber-lots" and "cyber trams." **as.acusd .edu/as/court.html**

WHAT YOU NEED TO GET IN **Application Deadline** Rolling admissions; January 15 for priority consideration **Common App.** No **Application Fee** $45 **Tuition Costs** $14,860 **Room & Board** $7,150 **Need Blind** Yes **Financial Forms Deadline** Priority given to applications received by February 20 **Undergrads Awarded Aid** 61% **Aid That Is Need-Based** 83% **Average Award of Freshman Scholarship Package** $9,765 **Tests Required** SAT1 (preferred) or ACT **Admissions Address** 5998 Alcala Park, San Diego, CA 92110-2492 **Admissions Telephone** (619) 260-4506

LAST YEAR'S CLASS **Applied** 3,864 **Accepted** 3,145 **Matriculated** 981 **Average SAT M/V** 550/490 **Average ACT** 25

COLLEGE LIFE **Gender Breakdown** M 43%, F 57% **Out of State Students** 32% **From Public Schools** 61% **Ethnic Composition** White & Other 72%, Asian American 10%, Black 2%, Hispanic 15%, Native American 1% **Foreign Students** 3% **Reside on Campus** 50% **Return as Sophomores** 84% **Total Faculty** 508 **Student Faculty Ratio** 18:1 **Fraternities (% of men participating)** 4 (20%) **Sororities (% of women participating)** 4 (20%) **Graduate Students** 2,310

San Francisco State University

www.sfsu.edu

San Francisco, CA · Est. 1899 · Coed · Public · 20,404 Undergrads · Urban

How wired is SFSU?

Do I get email? Yes
Do I get a home page? Yes
Is my dorm wired? Yes
What is the student to computer ratio? 21:1

REQUEST APPLICATION ONLINE

The usual tour

DEPARTMENTS www.sfsu.edu/acaddept.htm
STUDENT CLUBS www.sfsu.edu/studorg.htm
CALENDAR www.sfsu.edu/acal4.htm
CAREER CENTER www.sfsu.edu/careerop.htm
SPORTS www.sfsu.edu/~athletic

Skip the brochure

- **SFSU CINEMA DEPARTMENT** This gorgeous site is designed to bring out the inner Tarantino in everyone. The cinema department not only teaches production and animation, but also offers courses in history and criticism. Some of the student film clips are really funky.
  www.cinema.sfsu.edu

- **LYNDA'S NET NODE** If you attend SFSU, Lynda Williams could be your physics TA. She is also a self-proclaimed "Science Entertainer," meaning physics for fun, not for formulae. The soon-to-be Dr. Williams writes and performs a

Location: http://www.sfsu.edu/clickmap/castrt2.gif

SFSU—home to Lynda Williams and other members of San Francisco's creative set

"Cosmic Cabaret," a multimedia musical exploration of cosmology and modern physics.
www.physics.sfsu.edu/grad/lwilliam/lwilliam.html

- **ANIME FX** What is anime? Japanese Animation, which has had a cult following since its inception 50 years ago. Films such as the '50s *Astro Boys* and '70s *G-Force* are bonding material for this group of anime aficionados.
  www.sfsu.edu/~animefx

"Designed to bring out the inner Tarantino in everyone"

WHAT YOU NEED TO GET IN **Application Deadline** Rolling admissions; November 1 for priority consideration **Early Action Deadline** November 1-30 **Common App.** Yes **Application Fee** $55 **Tuition Costs** $5,904 **Room & Board** $5,500 **Financial Forms Deadline** May 1 **Undergrads Awarded Aid** 40% **Aid That Is Need-Based** 95% **Average Award of Freshman Scholarship Package** $3,710 **Tests Required** SAT1 or ACT **Admissions Address** 1600 Holloway Avenue, San Francisco, CA 94132 **Admissions Telephone** (415) 338-2017

LAST YEAR'S CLASS **Applied** 7,142 **Accepted** 4,765 **Matriculated** 1,690 **Average SAT M/V** 472/460 **Average ACT** 19

COLLEGE LIFE **Gender Breakdown** M 43%, F 57% **Out of State Students** 3% **From Public Schools** 77% **Ethnic Composition** White & Other 39.6%, Asian American 38.5%, Black 7.7%, Hispanic 13.3%, Native American 0.9% **Foreign Students** 2% **Reside on Campus** 5% **Return as Sophomores** 81% **Total Faculty** 1,484 **Student Faculty Ratio** 21:1 **Fraternities (% of men participating)** 12 (1%) **Sororities (% of women participating)** 9 (1%) **Graduate Students** 6,387

Santa Clara University

Santa Clara, CA · Est. 1851 · Coed · Private · 4,100 Undergrads · Urban

I need...

Admissions info ugadmissions@scu.edu
  scuish.scu.edu/SCU/Departments
  /UGAdmissions
Financial aid info scuish.scu.edu/SCU
  /Departments/StdFinSrvs

How wired is Santa Clara?

Do I get email? Yes
Do I get a home page? Yes
  Where? www-acc.scu.edu/www
  /personal_pages.html
Is my dorm wired? Yes
What is the student to computer ratio? 12:1

REQUEST APPLICATION ONLINE

The usual tour

DEPARTMENTS scuish.scu.edu/Undergraduate
  Programs.html
STUDY ABROAD scuish.scu.edu/Studies
  Abroad.html
STUDENT CLUBS www-acc.scu.edu/clubs
  /homepage.html
SPORTS scuish.scu.edu/SCU/Departments
  /UGAdmissions/Offers/AthleticsAtSCU.html

Skip the brochure

- **THE EASTSIDE PROJECT** The Eastside Project is "an experiential learning program that arranges for students each year to mingle with a diversity of low-income and underserved people on their turf." If you're interested in standing on the turf of less fortunate Santa

Location: http://scuish.scu.edu/SCU/Programs/EastsideProject/

Illustration by A. Meisner
Color by J. Grivich

Santa Clara's participants in the Eastside Project reach out to help their local community

Clarans, come here. **scuish.scu.edu/SCU /Programs/EastsideProject**

- **STUDENTS OF OBJECTIVISM** Ayn Rand, author of *Atlas Shrugged*, *The Fountainhead*, and *The Virtue of Selfishness*, among other works, was an advocate of "rational self-interest." This student group consists of fans, eager to distill and disseminate Rand's ideas. **www-acc.scu.edu/clubs/objectivism**

- **ATHLETICS** Hang out with the Broncos, just one of the sports teams you'll find in this cyber-arena. Meet the sports teams of Santa Clara University. **scuish.scu.edu/SCU/Department s/UGAdmissions/Offers/AthleticsAtSCU.html**

"Hang out with the Broncos."

WHAT YOU NEED TO GET IN **Application Deadline** January 15 **Common App.** Yes **Application Fee** $40 **Tuition Costs** $15,450 **Room & Board** $6,780 **Need Blind** Yes **Financial Forms Deadline** Priority given to applications received by February 1 **Undergrads Awarded Aid** 68% **Aid That Is Need-Based** 85% **Average Award of Freshman Scholarship Package** $10,505 **Tests Required** SAT1 (preferred) or ACT **Admissions Address** Santa Clara, CA 95053 **Admissions Telephone** (408) 554-4700

LAST YEAR'S CLASS **Applied** 4,270 **Accepted** 3,237 **Matriculated** 1,043 **Median Range SAT M/V** 540-650/450-560 **In Top Quarter of High School Graduating Class** 56%

COLLEGE LIFE **Gender Breakdown** M 48%, F 52% **Out of State Students** 34% **From Public Schools** 58% **Ethnic Composition** White & Other 61%, Asian American 21%, Black 3%, Hispanic 14%, Native American 1% **Foreign Students** 11% **Reside on Campus** 43% **Return as Sophomores** 92% **Total Faculty** 413 **Student Faculty Ratio** 15:1 **Fraternities (% of men participating)** 4 (12%) **Sororities (% of women participating)** 3 (14%) **Graduate Students** 3,554

Sarah Lawrence College www.slc.edu/college.html

Bronxville, NY · Est. 1926 · Coed · Private · 1,035 Undergrads · Suburban

I need...

Admissions info slcadmit@mail.slc.edu
www.slc.edu/admission/undergrad/first
year/1styrsteps.html
Financial aid info www.slc.edu/admission
/undergrad/firstyear/finaid.html

How wired is Sarah Lawrence?

Do I get email? Yes
Do I get a home page? Yes
Where? www.slc.edu/studspac
/studwwwp.htm
Is my dorm wired? Yes
What is the student to computer ratio? 22:1

The usual tour

DEPARTMENTS www.slc.edu/academic
/academi.htm
STUDENT CLUBS www.slc.edu/studspac
/GROUPPUB.HTM
CALENDAR www.slc.edu/colevent/news
/news.htm
STUDY ABROAD www.slc.edu/admission
/INTPROGS.HTML

Skip the brochure

• **SARAH LAWRENCE IN OXFORD** Sarah Lawrence
offers an exchange with Oxford University's
Wadham College that allows students in the
program to be considered as "associate members" of the College. Wadham is home to the
university's "liberal" bunch, with famous liter-

Express yourself at Sarah Lawrence

ary scholar and Marxist Terry Eagleton as its
figurehead. **www.wadham.ox.ac.uk/slp.html**

• **TYPICAL WEEK** This sample week's calendar provides a good outline of Sarah Lawrence's personality: lectures on nationalism and colonial-
ism, youth involvement in third world political
movements, as well as poetry readings, art
films, and readings of erotic fiction at the
Coffeehaus in the evening. **www.slc.edu
/admission/closerlook/campuscomm/typweek.html**

"Oxford University's Wadham is home to the 'liberal' bunch."

WHAT YOU NEED TO GET IN Application Deadline February 1 **Early Action Deadline** November 15 (Early Decision I) and
January 1 (Early Decision II) **Common App.** Yes **Application Fee** $45 **Tuition Costs** $21,450 **Room & Board**
$6,902 **Financial Forms Deadline** Priority given to applications received by February 1 **Undergrads Awarded Aid**
50% **Aid That Is Need-Based** 100% **Average Award of Freshman Scholarship Package** $13,641 **Tests Required**
SAT1 or ACT **Admissions Address** One Meadway, Bronxville, NY 10708 **Admissions Telephone** (914) 395-2510

LAST YEAR'S CLASS Applied 1,284 **Accepted** 755 **Matriculated** 230 **Average SAT M/V** 580/660 **Average ACT** 26
In Top Fifth of High School Graduating Class 57% **Applied Early** 81 **Accepted Early** 60

COLLEGE LIFE Gender Breakdown M 24%, F 76% **Out of State Students** 76% **From Public Schools** 60% **Ethnic
Composition** White & Other 82.4%, Asian American 4.7%, Black 6.4%, Hispanic 5.5%, Native American 1%
Foreign Students 5% **Reside on Campus** 90% **Return as Sophomores** 90% **Total Faculty** 227 **Student Faculty
Ratio** 6:1 **Fraternities** none **Sororities** none **Graduate Students** 244

Scripps College

Claremont, CA · Est. 1926 · Women · Private · 684 Undergrads · Small Town

I need...

Admissions info admofc@ad.scrippscol.edu
www.scrippscol.edu/Scripps/net/Admissions/admiss.html

Financial aid info www.scrippscol.edu/Scripps/net/Admissions/link20.html

How wired is Scripps?

Do I get email? Yes
Do I get a home page? Yes
Is my dorm wired? Yes
What is the student to computer ratio? 18:1

The usual tour

DEPARTMENTS www.scrippscol.edu/scripps/net/academics/departments.html
STUDENT CLUBS www.scrippscol.edu/scripps/net/students/student_life.html
CALENDAR www.cuc.claremont.edu/calendar.htm
LIBRARY voxlibris.claremont.edu
STUDY ABROAD www.scrippscol.edu/Scripps/net/Admissions/link12.html

Skip the brochure

- **SCRIPP'S HISTORY** The founder of Scripps College, Ellen Browning Scripps, was a renowned publisher and philanthropist of the mid-nineteenth century. She didn't believe that being a woman limited her opportunities, and neither should you. Come to this page to learn more about the woman whose checkbook helped create one of California's most inti-

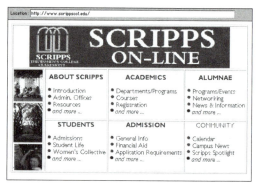

Tips for prospective Scripps students, and community news to boot

mate women-only college enviromnents.
www.scrippscol.edu/Scripps/net/Admissions/link2.html

- **HAO HUANG** Everyone should meet Dr. Huang, a much-honored Harvard and Julliard alumni and world-renowned pianist. He is an active faculty member at Scripps—that is, when he's not playing at some incredibly prestigious event or studying the performances of Billie Holiday.
www.scrippscol.edu/Scripps/net/FACULTY/huang/hao.html

> ## "Learn more about the woman whose checkbook helped create Scripps."

WHAT YOU NEED TO GET IN **Application Deadline** February 1 **Early Action Deadline** November 15 and January 1 **Common App.** Yes **Application Fee** $40 **Tuition Costs** $18,680 **Room & Board** $7,650 **Need Blind** Yes **Financial Forms Deadline** Priority given to applications received by February 1 **Undergrads Awarded Aid** 50% **Aid That Is Need-Based** 95% **Average Award of Freshman Scholarship Package** $13,617 **Tests Required** SAT1 or ACT **Admissions Address** 1030 Columbia Avenue, Claremont, CA 91711 **Admissions Telephone** (909) 621-8149

LAST YEAR'S CLASS **Applied** 914 **Accepted** 735 **Matriculated** 215 **Average SAT M/V** 590/610 **Average ACT** 25 **In Top Fifth of High School Graduating Class** 68% **Applied Early** 34 **Accepted Early** 28

COLLEGE LIFE **Out of State Students** 51% **From Public Schools** 64% **Ethnic Composition** White & Other 72%, Asian American 17%, Black 3%, Hispanic 7%, Native American 1% **Foreign Students** 4% **Reside on Campus** 92% **Return as Sophomores** 90% **Total Faculty** 73 **Student Faculty Ratio** 9:1 **Sororities** none

Seattle University

Seattle, WA · Est. 1891 · Coed · Private · 3,294 Undergrads · Urban

I need...

Admissions info admissions@seattleu.edu
www.seattleu.edu/admissions
Financial aid info financial-aid@seattleu.edu
www.seattleu.edu/admissions/finaid

How wired is Seattle University?

Do I get email? Yes
Do I get a home page? Yes
Is my dorm wired? Yes
What is the student to computer ratio? 16:1

The usual tour

DEPARTMENTS www.seattleu.edu/academics
/ugprog.htm
LIBRARY www.seattleu.edu/lemlib
CAREER CENTER www.seattleu.edu/student/cdc
CALENDAR www.seattleu.edu/new/calendar.html
STUDENT CLUBS /www.seattleu.edu/assu
/clubs.html

Skip the brochure

- **SUN ONLINE** Something's brewing at Seattle University. In this case, it's Charlie and Cindy Sullivan, Class of '89, who founded the Skagit River Brewery after graduating. Learn about other famous SU grads at this glossy online alumni mag. **www.seattleu.edu/sunonline/main.html**

- **THE SEATTLE UNIVERSITY SEAL** Become familiar with staid Seattle University, and more specifically, its official seal. The symbolic emblem's

Seattle University is one of the country's 28 Jesuit colleges or universities

evergreens make reference to Washington State and to the tree of knowledge, but other elements include wolves and seven stripes.
www.seattleu.edu/general/seal.html

- **THE JESUITS** As one of the 28 Jesuit colleges and universities in the United States, Seattle University is well-informed about the 450-year-old Jesuit community. You can be too.
www.seattleu.edu/general/jesuits.html

"Charlie and Cindy Sullivan founded the Skagit River Brewery after graduating."

WHAT YOU NEED TO GET IN **Application Deadline** February 1 for priority consideration; final deadline March 1 **Early Action Deadline** October 1 **Common App.** Yes **Application Fee** $40 **Tuition Costs** $14,265 **Room & Board** $5,283 **Need Blind** Yes **Financial Forms Deadline** Priority given to applications received by February 1 **Undergrads Awarded Aid** 63% **Aid That Is Need-Based** 82% **Average Award of Freshman Scholarship Package** $7,067 **Tests Required** SAT1 or ACT **Admissions Address** Broadway and Madison, Seattle, WA 98122-4460 **Admissions Telephone** (206) 296-5800

LAST YEAR'S CLASS **Applied** 1,863 **Accepted** 1,676 **Matriculated** 432 **Average SAT M/V** 555/556 **Average ACT** 24 **In Top Quarter of High School Graduating Class** 53%

COLLEGE LIFE **Gender Breakdown** M 43%, F 57% **Out of State Students** 41% **From Public Schools** 55% **Ethnic Composition** White & Other 75%, Asian American 18%, Black 4%, Hispanic 2%, Native American 1% **Foreign Students** 13% **Reside on Campus** 29% **Return as Sophomores** 74% **Total Faculty** 334 **Student Faculty Ratio** 14:1 **Fraternities** none **Sororities** none **Graduate Students** 2,694

Simon's Rock of Bard College

www.simons-rock.edu

Great Barrington, MA · Est. 1964 · Coed · Private · 310 Undergrads · Small Town

I need...

Admissions info admit@simons-rock.edu
www.simons-rock.edu/dept/admissions
Financial aid info 198.112.200.2/dept/academic
_affairs/catalog/Financial_Information.html

How wired is Simon's Rock?

Do I get email? Yes
Do I get a home page? Yes
Where? www.simons-rock.edu
/homepages
Is my dorm wired? No
What is the student to computer ratio? 15:1

REQUEST APPLICATION ONLINE

The usual tour

DEPARTMENTS www.simons-rock.edu/dept
/admissions/viewbook
LIBRARY www.simons-rock.edu/dept/library
STUDENT CLUBS www.simons-rock.edu/dept
/student_life/student_org.html
PUBLICATIONS plato.simons-rock.edu/dept
/student_life/llama

Skip the brochure

- **VICTORIAN ART AND SOCIAL CLASS** As far as small liberal arts colleges go, Simon's Rock's Web site falls under the rubric of "funky." Course descriptions are prominently featured, and they'll make you feel like you're in the class-

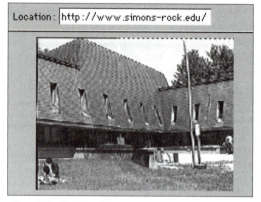

Location: http://www.simons-rock.edu/

Simon's Rock, although it resembles a Pizza Hut, is really a two-year college for young scholars

room. For example, Victorian Art and Social Class examines how art can reflect class antagonism and ideology. **www.simons-rock.edu /dept/admissions/viewbook/Div_of_Arts.html**

- **POST-DEGREE AND CAREER CENTER** Since Simon's Rock attracts young scholars ready to leave high school early, this office helps with transfers as well as the standard tasks of a career and international programs office. **www.simons -rock.edu/dept/post_degree_office**

- **SIMON'S ROCK CIVIL LIBERTIES UNION** Maintained by club member and student "Schizo," this group fights for free speech, online and off. **www .simons-rock.edu/dept/student_life/srclu/charter.html**

WHAT YOU NEED TO GET IN **Application Deadline** Rolling admissions **Common App.** No **Application Fee** $25 **Tuition Costs** $18,580 **Room & Board** $5,860 **Need Blind** Yes **Undergrads Awarded Aid** 85% **Aid That Is Need-Based** 65% **Average Award of Freshman Scholarship Package** $9,500 **Tests Required** SAT1 (preferred) or ACT **Admissions Address** 84 Alford Road, Great Barrington, MA 01230 **Admissions Telephone** (800) 235-7186

LAST YEAR'S CLASS **Applied** 381 **Accepted** 229 **Matriculated** 124 **Average SAT M/V** 600/600

COLLEGE LIFE **Gender Breakdown** M 38%, F 62% **Out of State Students** 88% **From Public Schools** 77% **Ethnic Composition** White & Other 85%, Asian American 8%, Black 4%, Hispanic 2%, Native American 1% **Foreign Students** 3% **Reside on Campus** 95% **Return as Sophomores** 68% **Total Faculty** 36 **Student Faculty Ratio** 8:1 **Fraternities** none **Sororities** none

Skidmore College

Saratoga Springs, NY · Est. 1903 · Coed · Private · 2,130 Undergrads · Big Town

www.skidmore.edu

How wired is Skidmore?

Do I get email? Yes
Do I get a home page? Yes
Is my dorm wired? Yes
What is the student to computer ratio? 7:1
Is there an online student hangout? Yes (IRC)

REQUEST APPLICATION ONLINE

The usual tour

DEPARTMENTS don.skidmore.edu/academics
SPORTS don.skidmore.edu/campus/Sports.html
CALENDAR don.skidmore.edu/campus/Calendar.html
LIBRARY don.skidmore.edu/irc/library
STUDENT CLUBS www.skidmore.edu/phonebook/sgaorgs.html
CAREER CENTER don.skidmore.edu/~adoyle

Skip the brochure

• **THOROUGHBRED NEWS** Why Thoroughbred? Because Skidmore students like to ride. When they're not saddling up, they're playing golf or tennis. Learn all about Skidmore sports here. **don.skidmore.edu/campus/Sports.html**

• **THE NOOCH OUTING CLUB** If the opening graphics of this page didn't set a comic tone, this group's

Skidmore—a New York college with a New England feel

charter would be offensive: "We, the mighty manly men of the Nooch Adventure Club, do hereby decree that we shall uphold the great achievements of our gender in all endeavors." Somewhere, Robert Bly is laughing—you may be, too. **don.skidmore.edu/~afrancis/nooch.html**

• **FROM THE GROUND UP** Associated with Habitat for Humanity, this Skidmore student group attempts to eradicate poverty and homelessness, not with charitable contributions, but with hard work. Spend your Spring Break hammering, plumbing, plastering, caulking, tiling—and helping. **don.skidmore.edu/studentorgs/fgu/index.html**

"Somewhere, Robert Bly is laughing."

WHAT YOU NEED TO GET IN **Application Deadline** February 1 **Early Action Deadline** December 1 or January 15 **Common App.** Yes **Application Fee** $45 **Tuition Costs** $20,670 **Room & Board** $6,110 **Need Blind** No **Financial Forms Deadline** February 1 **Undergrads Awarded Aid** 47% **Aid That Is Need-Based** 99% **Average Award of Freshman Scholarship Package** $13,013 **Tests Required** SAT1 or ACT **Admissions Address** Saratoga Springs, NY 12866 **Admissions Telephone** (800) 867-6007

LAST YEAR'S CLASS **Applied** 4,673 **Accepted** 3,030 **Matriculated** 610 **Average SAT M/V** 561/512 **In Top Fifth of High School Graduating Class** 27% **Applied Early** 298 **Accepted Early** 219

COLLEGE LIFE **Gender Breakdown** M 40%, F 60% **Out of State Students** 73% **From Public Schools** 60% **Ethnic Composition** White & Other 89%, Asian American 4%, Black 2%, Hispanic 5% **Foreign Students** 2% **Reside on Campus** 80% **Return as Sophomores** 88% **Total Faculty** 195 **Student Faculty Ratio** 11:1 **Fraternities** none **Sororities** none **Graduate Students** 55

Smith College

www.smith.edu

Northampton, MA · Est. 1871 · Women · Private · 2,668 Undergrads · Big Town

I need...

Admissions info admission@smith.smith.edu
www.smith.edu/dept/admission/applying.html

Financial aid info pcounselors@ais.smith.edu
www.smith.edu/dept/admission/finaid.html

How wired is Smith?

Do I get email? Yes
Do I get a home page? Yes
Is my dorm wired? Yes
What is the student to computer ratio? 11:1

REQUEST APPLICATION ONLINE

The usual tour

DEPARTMENTS www.smith.edu/dept/admission/majors.html
STUDENT CLUBS www.smith.edu/dept/admission/stuact.html
LIBRARY www.smith.edu/libraries
SPORTS www.smith.edu/dept/admission/stulife.html
CAREER CENTER www.smith.edu/cdo
VIRTUAL TOUR www.smith.edu/map/collegemap.html

Skip the brochure

- **CENTER FOR AMAZONIAN LITERATURE AND CULTURE**
Clearly an exotic and fascinating resource at Smith, the Center for Amazonian Literature and Culture focuses on the writing and culture of Brazil, Bolivia, Peru, Ecuador, Colombia and Venezuela. socsci.smith.edu/dept/calc/home.html

Smith, one of the country's premier women's colleges

- **FIVE COLLEGES** Along with Mount Holyoke, Hampshire, Amherst College, and U Mass at Amherst, Smith is a member of the Five College Consortium, a general purpose union with social, academic, and cultural features. **www.fivecolleges.edu**

- **THE SOPHIA SMITH COLLECTION** An important resource for those interested in women's history, this collection is particularly strong in the areas of birth control, middle-class family life in nineteenth- and twentieth-century New England, and the contemporary women's movement. **www.smith.edu/libraries/sscl.htm**

"The Sophia Smith Collection: an important women's history resource"

WHAT YOU NEED TO GET IN **Application Deadline** February 1 **Early Action Deadline** November 15 and January 1 **Common App.** Yes **Application Fee** $50 **Tuition Costs** $20,380 **Room & Board** $6,920 **Need Blind** No **Financial Forms Deadline** February 1 **Undergrads Awarded Aid** 52% **Aid That Is Need-Based** 100% **Average Award of Freshman Scholarship Package** $13,799 **Tests Required** SAT1 or ACT **Admissions Address** Northampton, MA 01063 **Admissions Telephone** (413) 585-2500

LAST YEAR'S CLASS **Applied** 3,334 **Accepted** 1,635 **Matriculated** 631 **Median Range SAT M/V** 573-670/550-640 **In Top Fifth of High School Graduating Class** 84% **Applied Early** 229 **Accepted Early** 146

COLLEGE LIFE **Out of State Students** 88% **From Public Schools** 67% **Ethnic Composition** White & Other 81%, Asian American 11%, Black 3%, Hispanic 4%, Native American 1% **Foreign Students** 8% **Reside on Campus** 90% **Return as Sophomores** 88% **Total Faculty** 277 **Student Faculty Ratio** 10:1 **Sororities** none **Graduate Students** 504

University of South Carolina

www.csd.scarolina.edu

Columbia, SC · Est. 1801 · Coed · Public · 15,915 Undergrads · Urban

I need...

Admissions info admissions-ugrad@sc.edu
www.sc.edu/admissions/ugrad/index.html
Financial aid info www.sc.edu/admissions/ugrad
/10finaid.html

How wired is USC?

Do I get email? Yes
Do I get a home page? No
Is my dorm wired? Yes
What is the student to computer ratio? 16:1

FULL APPLICATION ONLINE

The usual tour

DEPARTMENTS www.sc.edu/admissions/ugrad
/02majors.html
LIBRARY www.sc.edu/library
STUDENT CLUBS 129.252.184.64/0c
:/studorgs.html|
CALENDAR www.sc.edu/calendar.html
SPORTS 129.252.61.27/0c:/welcome/highlts
.html|/#athletics
VIRTUAL TOUR www.sc.edu/horseshoe/index.html

Skip the brochure

• **WORLD WAR MEMORIAL BUILDING** Founded in the late nineteenth century by the United Daughters of the Confederacy, and now dedicated to the military accomplishments of South Carolinians throughout American histo-

Gamecocks of the world unite at the USC home page

ry, this museum is one of the highlights of the Columbia campus. **www.sc.edu/uscmap/north /world_war.html**

• **SEIDOKAN AIKIDO CLUB** If yoga and meditation have failed you, there is another New Age niche to be explored. These South Carolina students are just mad about Seidokan Aikido, and serenely explain that in addition to being a potent form of self-defense, it's a "way of life through harmony with nature." **www.ece.sc.edu /organizations/seidokan**

• **SOUTH CAROLINA HISTORY** More Revolutionary War battles were fought in South Carolina than in any other state. One-fifth of the white male population of South Carolina died in the Civil War. Get to know its history. **www.state.sc. us/schist.html**

WHAT YOU NEED TO GET IN **Application Deadline** Rolling admissions; December 25 for priority consideration **Common App.** No **Application Fee** $35 **Tuition Costs** $3,378 ($8,574 out-of-state) **Room & Board** $3,674 **Need Blind** Yes **Financial Forms Deadline** Priority given to applications received by April 15 **Undergrads Awarded Aid** 60% **Aid That Is Need-Based** 90% **Average Award of Freshman Scholarship Package** $2,500 **Tests Required** SAT1 or ACT **Admissions Address** Columbia, SC 29208 **Admissions Telephone** (803) 777-7700

LAST YEAR'S CLASS **Applied** 8,793 **Accepted** 6,719 **Matriculated** 2,632 **Average SAT M/V** 529/473 **Average ACT** 22 **In Top Fifth of High School Graduating Class** 61%

COLLEGE LIFE **Gender Breakdown** M 46%, F 54% **Out of State Students** 16% **From Public Schools** 80% **Ethnic Composition** White & Other 77.9%, Asian American 3%, Black 17.8%, Hispanic 1.3% **Foreign Students** 2% **Reside on Campus** 38% **Return as Sophomores** 82% **Total Faculty** 1,261 **Student Faculty Ratio** 16:1 **Fraternities (% of men participating)** 20 (9%) **Sororities (% of women participating)** 14 (9%) **Graduate Students** 10,431

University of South Dakota, Vermillion

www.usd.edu

Vermillion, SD · Est. 1862 · Coed · Public · 5,694 Undergrads · Small Town

How wired is South Dakota, Vermillion?

Do I get email? Yes
Do I get a home page? Yes
   Where? www.usd.edu/student-life/personal
Is my dorm wired? Yes
What is the student to computer ratio? 5:1

The usual tour

DEPARTMENTS www.usd.edu/colleges
SPORTS www.usd.edu/sports.html
LIBRARY www.usd.edu/library
CAREER CENTER www.usd.edu/cdc

Skip the brochure

• **SOUTH DAKOTA PUBLIC BROADCASTING** Located in the middle of Vermillion, in the middle of South Dakota, is this terrific educational broadcast and production resource. www.usd.edu/sdpb

• **INSTITUTE OF AMERICAN INDIAN STUDIES AND THE SOUTH DAKOTA ORAL HISTORY CENTER** Most Native American history was handed down orally from generation to generation. The Oral History Center is one of the largest and most important in the country, archiving more than 5,000 recorded interviews. The Institute of

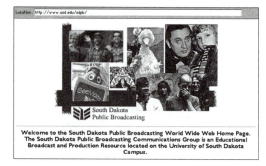

Welcome to the South Dakota Public Broadcasting World Wide Web Home Page. The South Dakota Public Broadcasting Communications Group is an Educational Broadcast and Production Resource located on the University of South Dakota Campus.

The Universy of South Dakota is home to the state's public broadcast channel

American Indians organizes academic programs and also works to recruit Native American students and faculty. www.usd.edu/~iais

• **TRACK TEAM** The University of South Dakota's track team is thrilled to be running, jumping, and throwing in the company of other Division II schools. You can email the coach from this page or just get to know the team. www.usd.edu/sports/track

"The Oral History Center is one of the largest and most important in the country."

WHAT YOU NEED TO GET IN Application Deadline Rolling admissions **Common App.** No **Application Fee** $15 **Tuition Costs** $1,648 ($4,480 out-of-state) **Room & Board** $2,572 **Need Blind** Yes **Financial Forms Deadline** Priority given to applications received by March 1 **Undergrads Awarded Aid** 84% **Aid That Is Need-Based** 84% **Average Award of Freshman Scholarship Package** $1,170 **Tests Required** SAT1 or ACT (preferred) **Admissions Address** 414 East Clark Street, Vermillion, SD 57069 **Admissions Telephone** (605) 677-5434

LAST YEAR'S CLASS Applied 2,461 **Accepted** 2,120 **Matriculated** 1,192 **Average ACT** 22 **In Top Fifth of High School Graduating Class** 32%

COLLEGE LIFE Gender Breakdown M 44%, F 56% **Out of State Students** 31% **From Public Schools** 91% **Ethnic Composition** White & Other 94.5%, Asian American 1%, Black 1%, Hispanic 1%, Native American 2.5% **Foreign Students** 1% **Reside on Campus** 34% **Return as Sophomores** 72% **Student Faculty Ratio** 17:1 **Fraternities (% of men participating)** 9 (20%) **Sororities (% of women participating)** 5 (15%) **Graduate Students** 1,635

University of South Florida

www.usf.edu

Tampa, FL · Est. 1956 · Coed · Public · 21,102 Undergrads · Urban

I need...

Admissions info www.rmit.usf.edu/enroll/admiss
/admiss.htm

How wired is USF?

Do I get email? Yes
Do I get a home page? Yes
Is my dorm wired? Yes
Is there an online student hangout? Yes

The usual tour

VIRTUAL TOUR www.usf.edu/interactive.html
SPORTS www.rmit.usf.edu/athletics/go_bulls.htm
STUDENT CLUBS ctr.usf.edu/mc_points/student
_orgs/groups.htm
DEPARTMENTS www.usf.edu/academic.html
PUBLICATIONS www.oracle.usf.edu

Skip the brochure

- **EDUCATION IN CYBERSPACE** The University of
Southern Florida offers a number of courses
online. Though the CyberEd areas are restricted to USF students, syllabi are available for
the cybercourses. **www.usf.edu/cyberspace.html**

- **VICTIM'S ADVOCACY CENTER** Caution: the following
is politically correct. Many a cultural critic has
lambasted popular American culture as glorify-
ing and celebrating victimhood. These critics
should not come here, or maybe they should,
as they might recognize the variant and insidi-
ous forms of persecution and oppression that

Location: http://arts.usf.edu/theater/thehist.html

Professor Patrick Fineli's Theater History

pervade contemporary society. USF has
attempted to make the campus as peaceful
and inclusive as possible by providing the
members of the University community with a
safe and confidential place to report hate
crimes, sexual assault, and other related
behaviors. **www.rmit.usf.edu/advocacy/victims.htm**

- **THE ORACLE** The student newspaper can be an
interesting window on a school. What does it
say about USF that the lifestyle section has
graphics of a couple in their bathing suits, a
shiny red sportscar, and a windsurfer cutting
through ocean foam? **www.oracle.usf.edu/today**

"USF offers a number of courses online."

WHAT YOU NEED TO GET IN **Application Deadline** Rolling admissions; June 1 for priority consideration **Common App.** No
Application Fee $20 **Tuition Costs** $1,860 ($6,760 out-of-state) **Room & Board** $5,290 **Need Blind** Yes
Financial Forms Deadline March 1 **Undergrads Awarded Aid** 58% **Aid That Is Need-Based** 75% **Average Award
of Freshman Scholarship Package** $1,000 **Tests Required** SAT1 or ACT **Admissions Address** 4202 East Fowler
Avenue, Tampa, FL 33620 **Admissions Telephone** (813) 974-3350

LAST YEAR'S CLASS **Applied** 7,884 **Accepted** 5,105 **Matriculated** 1,906 **Average SAT M/V** 553/492 **Average ACT**
23 **In Top Fifth of High School Graduating Class** 47%

COLLEGE LIFE **Gender Breakdown** M 45%, F 55% **Out of State Students** 12% **Ethnic Composition** White & Other
80%, Asian American 4%, Black 8%, Hispanic 8% **Foreign Students** 2% **Reside on Campus** 11% **Total Faculty**
1,504 **Student Faculty Ratio** 12:1 **Fraternities (% of men participating)** 19 (5%) **Sororities (% of women
participating)** 12 (5%) **Graduate Students** 7,046

University of the South

Sewanee, TN · Est. 1857 · Coed · Private · 1,242 Undergrads · Rural

I need...

Admissions info admiss@sewanee.edu
www.sewanee.edu/admiss.html
Financial aid info finaid@sewanee.edu
www.sewanee.edu/admiss.html

How wired is Sewanee?

Do I get email? Yes
Do I get a home page? Yes
Is my dorm wired? Yes
What is the student to computer ratio? 14:1

REQUEST APPLICATION ONLINE

The usual tour

DEPARTMENTS www.sewanee.edu/CollegeCatalog
/CollegeDepartments/00DepartmentIndex
.html
VIRTUAL TOUR www.sewanee.edu/campustour
.html
LIBRARY www.sewanee.edu/dupontlibrary/home
.html
CALENDAR www.sewanee.edu/Events.html
PUBLICATIONS www.sewanee.edu/sewaneepurple
/00PurpleHome.html

Skip the brochure

- **THE SEWANEE REVIEW** Asked about the literary journal that has featured writers such as Robert Penn Warren, Randall Jarrell, and Robert Lowell, the American poet Thomas Stearns Eliot wrote in 1952: "*The Sewanee Review* has now reached the status of an

Throw out your tie-dyes and cutoffs—students at Sewanee attend classes in formal dress

institution—by which I mean that if it came to an end, its loss would be something more than merely the loss of one good periodical: it would be a symptom of an alarming decline in the periodical world at its highest level." T.S. or B.S.? Decide for yourself. **www.sewanee.edu
/sreview/Home.html**

- **UNIVERSITY GALLERY ONLINE TOUR** The folks at the University Gallery put on an impressive show; the current exhibit, the photography of Geof Bowie, who teaches at University of the South, is staggeringly beautiful. Even if it doesn't remain the frontline exhibit, it will be archived; its worth seeing. **www.sewanee.edu/Gallery
/Frontdoor.html**

- **SEWANNEE** "Sewanee has 1 grammar school, 1 gas station, 4 eateries, a small noncommercial airport, 2 convenience markets, 6 shops,and 1 traffic light." Get the big picture about a small town. **www.sewanee.edu/sewand
midten.html**

WHAT YOU NEED TO GET IN **Application Deadline** February 1 for priority consideration **Early Action Deadline** November 15 **Common App.** Yes **Application Fee** $40 **Tuition Costs** $16,790 **Room & Board** $4,460 **Financial Forms Deadline** Priority given to applications received by March 1 **Undergrads Awarded Aid** 59% **Aid That Is Need-Based** 87% **Average Award of Freshman Scholarship Package** $9,035 **Tests Required** SAT1 or ACT **Admissions Address** 735 University Avenue, Sewanee, TN 37383-1000 **Admissions Telephone** (615) 598-1238

LAST YEAR'S CLASS **Applied** 1,864 **Accepted** 1,192 **Matriculated** 370 **Average SAT M/V** 617/570 **Average ACT** 27 **In Top Fifth of High School Graduating Class** 74% **Applied Early** 152 **Accepted Early** 121

COLLEGE LIFE **Gender Breakdown** M 50%, F 50% **Out of State Students** 82% **From Public Schools** 52% **Ethnic Composition** White & Other 97%, Asian American 0.5%, Black 2%, Hispanic 0.5% **Foreign Students** 2% **Reside on Campus** 93% **Return as Sophomores** 90% **Total Faculty** 132 **Student Faculty Ratio** 11:1 **Fraternities (% of men participating)** 18 (68%) **Sororities (% of women participating)** 7 (55%) **Graduate Students** 80

University of Southern California

Los Angeles, CA · Est. 1880 · Coed · Private · 14,962 Undergrads · Urban

I need...

Admissions info www.usc.edu/dept/admissions/undergrad
Financial aid info www.usc.edu/dept/admissions/undergrad/finaid2.html

How wired is USC?

Do I get email? Yes
Do I get a home page? Yes
Is my dorm wired? Yes
What is the student to computer ratio? 3:1

REQUEST APPLICATION ONLINE

The usual tour

STUDENT CLUBS www.usc.edu/Students/Student-Orgs.html
DEPARTMENTS www.usc.edu/Academic/Departments.html
LIBRARY www.usc.edu/Academic/Libraries.html
PUBLICATIONS www.usc.edu/Univ/USC-Online-Pubs.html
SPORTS www.usc.edu/dept/sports

Skip the brochure

• **1994 NOBEL PRIZE WINNER** If you're ever in need of some academic inspiration, check out this page, which documents the life and Nobelification of Professor George A. Olah. Olah's career has always been high-profile, but it wasn't until 1994 that he got the big N.

USC has taken to the Web with a vengeance, employing the TommyCam for a live video feed

netherrealm.usc.edu:8080/Users/cyee/USCAwardsPage/olah.html

• **TOMMYCAM** Forget virtual tours, this is live! If you're remotely interested in visiting USC, or interested in visiting USC remotely, make use of the TommyCam. **www.usc.edu/dept/TommyCam**

• **THE TELE-GARDEN** "This tele-robotic installation allows WWW users to view and interact with a remote garden filled with living plants. Members can plant, water, and monitor the progress of seedlings via the tender movements of an industrial robot arm." This site is amazing—all the pleasures of gardening without the dirt under your nails. **www.usc.edu/dept/garden**

WHAT YOU NEED TO GET IN **Application Deadline** December 15 for priority consideration; final deadline February 1 **Common App.** No **Application Fee** $55 ($45 for electronic applications) **Tuition Costs** $19,140 **Room & Board** $6,632 **Need Blind** Yes **Financial Forms Deadline** March 1 with a priority given to applications received by February 15 **Undergrads Awarded Aid** 51% **Aid That Is Need-Based** 70% **Tests Required** SAT1 or ACT **Admissions Address** University Park, Los Angeles, CA 90089-0911 **Admissions Telephone** (213) 740-1111

LAST YEAR'S CLASS **Applied** 12,642 **Accepted** 8,801 **Matriculated** 2,608 **Average SAT M/V** 601/509 **Average ACT** 25 **In Top Quarter of High School Graduating Class** 74%

COLLEGE LIFE **Gender Breakdown** M 54%, F 46% **Out of State Students** 34% **From Public Schools** 65% **Ethnic Composition** White & Other 55.7%, Asian American 22.6%, Black 6.7%, Hispanic 14.5%, Native American 0.5% **Foreign Students** 5% **Reside on Campus** 31% **Return as Sophomores** 90% **Student Faculty Ratio** 14:1 **Fraternities (% of men participating)** 26 (11%) **Sororities (% of women participating)** 16 (13%) **Graduate Students** 12,940

University of Southern Maine

www.usm.maine.edu

Gorham, ME · Est. 1878 · Coed · Public · 7,908 Undergrads · Urban

I need...

Admissions info usmadm@maine.maine.edu
www.petersons.com/sites/824800si.html
Financial aid info www.usm.maine.edu/~fin

How wired is USM?

Do I get email? Yes
Do I get a home page? Yes
What is the student to computer ratio? 30:1

The usual tour

DEPARTMENTS www.usm.maine.edu/departments.html
VIRTUAL TOUR www.usm.maine.edu/tour/tour.html
STUDENT CLUBS www.usm.maine.edu/campus.html
CALENDAR www.usm.maine.edu/news.html
LIBRARY eeunix.ee.usm.maine.edu/library
SPORTS macweb.acs.usm.maine.edu/athletics
CAREER CENTER macweb.acs.usm.maine.edu/csce

Skip the brochure

• **DR. NO'S HOME PAGE** Sometimes academics can be very strange. Nestled in the faculty pages is the home page of Dr. No, Professor of Torture. Visit this James Bond fan, and you may never look at your professors quite the same way again. **www.usm.maine.edu/staff/drno.html**

USM's planetarium has its own laser show set to the music of Pink Floyd

• **SOUTHWORTH PLANETARIUM** Stars in your eyes? This groovy site of the USM Planetarium has lots of great graphics that twinkle and sparkle. Laser shows feature the music of the Beatles, Garth Brooks, and Led Zeppelin. The Planetarium also hosts academic programs on topics like Native American astrology and navigation. **www.usm.maine.edu/~planet**

• **WPMG** This is one of the best college radio sites out there: "Our many music and cultural programs include jazz, folk, blues, underground rock, experimental radio, women's music, the avant garde, world beat, and ethnic programming from Cambodian, Native American, Irish, Middle Eastern, and other cultures around the world." **www.usm.maine.edu/~wmpg**

WHAT YOU NEED TO GET IN Application Deadline February 1 for priority consideration; final deadline August 15 **Common App.** No **Application Fee** $25 **Tuition Costs** $3,180 ($9,000 out-of-state) **Room & Board** $4,494 **Need Blind** Yes **Financial Forms Deadline** Priority given to applications received by March 1 **Undergrads Awarded Aid** 70% **Aid That Is Need-Based** 99% **Average Award of Freshman Scholarship Package** $2,100 **Tests Required** SAT1 (preferred) or ACT **Admissions Address** 37 College Avenue, Gorham, ME 04038 **Admissions Telephone** (207) 780-5670

LAST YEAR'S CLASS Applied 2,235 **Accepted** 1,737 **Matriculated** 798 **Average SAT M/V** 519/526 **In Top Fifth of High School Graduating Class** 23%

COLLEGE LIFE Gender Breakdown M 40%, F 60% **Out of State Students** 10% **Ethnic Composition** White & Other 97.5%, Asian American 0.9%, Black 0.4%, Hispanic 0.3%, Native American 0.9% **Reside on Campus** 12% **Total Faculty** 525 **Student Faculty Ratio** 15:1 **Fraternities** 4 **Sororities** 4 **Graduate Students** 1,813

Southern Methodist University

www.smu.edu

Dallas, TX · Est. 1911 · Coed · Private · 5,298 Undergrads · Urban

I need...

Admissions info www.smu.edu/smu/admission
.html
Financial aid info www.smu.edu/~ofa

How wired is SMU

Do I get email? Yes
Do I get a home page? Yes
Is my dorm wired? Yes
What is the student to computer ratio? 18:1

REQUEST APPLICATION ONLINE

The usual tour

VIRTUAL TOUR www.smu.edu/smu/photo.html
SPORTS www.smu.edu/~athletics
DEPARTMENTS www.smu.edu/~dedman/index
.html#DEPTSwww.smu.edu/~meadows/MSA
_Divisions.HTMLwww.seas.smu.edu/ugrad.html
LIBRARY www.smu.edu/~cul
CALENDAR www.smu.edu/~cul

Skip the brochure

• **FORT BURGWIN** Established in 1852, this New
Mexico fort's original function was to protect
American soldiers. The elements did what the
local indigenous population could not, leveling
the fort whose ruins now serve as the centerpiece of the SMU summer campus. More than
just archaeology is taught here: humanities,
natural and social sciences, and performing
and studio art classes are also offered.
Students live in adobes, and with Taos nearby,

SMU—one big happy family

cultural events and good food are not far off.
www.smu.edu/~smutaos

• **VOLUNTEER OPPORTUNITIES** Want to lend a hand?
See what SMU offers in altruistic ventures:
Meals on Wheels, Alternative Spring Break,
Habitat for Humanity, and Boys and Girls Club.
www.smu.edu/~vols

• **SMU'S OLYMPIANS** And you thought the guy who
sat next to you in calculus was a dork. He
wasn't. He was a bona fide Olympian. **www.smu
.edu/~athletics/olympic.html**

"Fort Burgwin now serves as the centerpiece of SMU's summer campus."

WHAT YOU NEED TO GET IN **Application Deadline** January 15 for priority consideration; final deadline April 1 **Early Action Deadline** November 1 **Common App.** Yes **Application Fee** $40 **Tuition Costs** $14,186 **Room & Board** $5,268 **Need Blind** Yes **Financial Forms Deadline** Priority given to applications received by February 1 **Undergrads Awarded Aid** 72% **Aid That Is Need-Based** 65% **Average Award of Freshman Scholarship Package** $6,788 **Tests Required** SAT1 or ACT **Admissions Address** 6422 Boaz Street, P.O. Box 296, Dallas, TX 75275 **Telephone** (214) SMU-2058

LAST YEAR'S CLASS **Applied** 3,869 **Accepted** 3,472 **Matriculated** 1,229 **Median Range SAT M/V** 940-1180 (combined) **In Top Fifth of High School Graduating Class** 53% **Applied Early** 751 **Accepted Early** 655

COLLEGE LIFE **Gender Breakdown** M 47%, F 53% **Out of State Students** 47% **From Public Schools** 68% **Ethnic Composition** White & Other 79.5%, Asian American 5.8%, Black 5.6%, Hispanic 8.5%, Native American 0.6% **Foreign Students** 3% **Reside on Campus** 45% **Return as Sophomores** 84% **Total Faculty** 581 **Student Faculty Ratio** 12:1 **Fraternities (% of men participating)** 15 (32%) **Sororities (% of women participating)** 11 (47%) **Graduate Students** 3,875

Southwestern University

www.southwestern.edu

Georgetown, TX · Est. 1840 · Coed · Private · 1,261 Undergrads · Small Town

I need...

Admissions info admission@southwestern.edu
www.southwestern.edu/admission-finaid
/adm-finaid-home.html
Financial aid info www.southwestern.edu
/admission-finaid/adm-finaid-home.html

How wired is Southwestern?

Do I get a home page? No
Is my dorm wired? No
What is the student to computer ratio? 8:1

REQUEST APPLICATION ONLINE

The usual tour

DEPARTMENTS www.southwestern.edu/academic
/academic-home.html
SPORTS www.southwestern.edu/student-life
/athletic-program.html
STUDENT CLUBS www.southwestern.edu/student
-life/org-list.html
LIBRARY www.southwestern.edu/library/library
-home.html
CALENDAR www.southwestern.edu/calendar
/master-calendar.html

"The Office of Diversity Education tries to ensure a positive college experience."

Location: http://www.southwestern.edu/academic/academic-home

The college years are a time of experimentation for many

Skip the brochure

- **DIVERSITY EDUCATION** Southwestern seems to have its heart in the right place: The Office of Diversity Education tries to ensure that all students have a positive college experience. Unfortunately, it does not succeed at making sure that all Web visitors have a good Southwestern experience—this site is somewhat perfunctory. **www.southwestern.edu/student -life/diversity-education.html**

- **STUDENT ORGANIZATIONS** Blame the administration for making this list of student organizations as dull as can be. Groups like the Spanish Acting Club and the Philosphy Club are reduced to meager one-sentence descriptions. One can only hope that the students aren't as dreary as the Web site suggests. **www.southwestern.edu/student-life/org-list.html**

WHAT YOU NEED TO GET IN **Application Deadline** January 1 for priority consideration; final deadline February 15 **Early Action Deadline** November 1 and January 1 **Common App.** Yes **Application Fee** $40 **Tuition Costs** $13,400 **Room & Board** $5,024 **Need Blind** Yes **Financial Forms Deadline** March 1 **Undergrads Awarded Aid** 73% **Aid That Is Need-Based** 74% **Average Award of Freshman Scholarship Package** $8,091 **Tests Required** SAT1 or ACT **Admissions Address** University at Maple, Georgetown, TX 78626 **Admissions Telephone** (512) 863-1200

LAST YEAR'S CLASS **Applied** 1,229 **Accepted** 928 **Matriculated** 328 **Average SAT M/V** 600/610 **Average ACT** 26 **In Top Quarter of High School Graduating Class** 81% **Applied Early** 136 **Accepted Early** 110

COLLEGE LIFE **Gender Breakdown** M 44%, F 56% **Out of State Students** 12% **From Public Schools** 87% **Ethnic Composition** White & Other 80.1%, Asian American 5.1%, Black 3%, Hispanic 11.2%, Native American 0.6% **Foreign Students** 2% **Reside on Campus** 75% **Return as Sophomores** 84% **Total Faculty** 139 **Student Faculty Ratio** 12:1 **Fraternities (% of men participating)** 4 (36%) **Sororities (% of women participating)** 4 (38%)

Spelman College

Atlanta, GA · Est. 1881 · Women · Private · 2,004 Undergrads · Urban

I need...

Admissions info fbuddy@auc.edu

How wired is Spelman?

Do I get email? Yes
Do I get a home page? No
Is my dorm wired? No

The usual tour

DEPARTMENTS www.auc.edu/academic.html

Skip the brochure

Department of History

Opening up the African-American canon

- **THE AFRICAN DIASPORA AND THE WORLD** World demographics are changing. The next century will see a proportional increase in the number of women and people of color. Does this shift the importance of Spelman's mission—to provide an excellent education for all African-American women? Maybe. **www.auc .edu/ADW.html**

- **BEARING WITNESS** Though this site has a solid essay explaining the contemporary position of women artists of color, there are, unfortunately, no graphics accompanying them. **www.auc.edu/Witness.html**

- **DEPARMENT OF HISTORY** Like many colleges and universities, Spelman's academic departments have become more interdisciplinary in recent years. The history department reflects this intellectual shift, and their program "encourages an examination of varying cultures to develop an understanding of difference, convergence, and continuity, with an emphasis on the social dimension." **www.auc .edu/History.htmll**

"The next century will see a proportional increase in the number of women and people of color."

WHAT YOU NEED TO GET IN Application Deadline February 1 **Early Action Deadline** November 15 **Common App.** Yes **Application Fee** $35 **Tuition Costs** $7,550 **Room & Board** $5,890 **Need Blind** Yes **Financial Forms Deadline** April 15 with a priority given to applications received by March 1 **Undergrads Awarded Aid** 81% **Aid That Is Need-Based** 100% **Tests Required** SAT1 or ACT **Admissions Address** 350 Spelman Lane, SW, Atlanta, GA 30314-4399 **Admissions Telephone** (404) 681-3643

LAST YEAR'S CLASS Applied 2,933 **Accepted** 1,393 **Matriculated** 481 **Average SAT M/V** 1010 (combined) **Average ACT** 23 **Applied Early** 440 **Accepted Early** 189

COLLEGE LIFE Out of State Students 78% **From Public Schools** 84% **Ethnic Composition** White & Other 1%, Black 99% **Foreign Students** 2% **Reside on Campus** 59% **Return as Sophomores** 90% **Total Faculty** 134 **Student Faculty Ratio** 14:1 **Sororities (% of women participating)** 5 (8%)

Stanford University

Stanford, CA · Est. 1891 · Coed · Private · 6,577 Undergrads · Big Town

I need...

Admissions info www-leland.stanford.edu/group
/uga/uga.html

Financial aid info www-leland.stanford.edu/group
/uga/finance.html

How wired is Stanford?

Do I get email? Yes

Do I get a home page? Yes

Where? www-leland.stanford.edu
/dir.html

Is my dorm wired? Yes

What is the student to computer ratio? 7:1

Is there an online student hangout? Yes

REQUEST APPLICATION ONLINE

The usual tour

DEPARTMENTS www-leland.stanford.edu/group
/uga/academics/fieldsofstudy.html

CALENDAR www-leland.stanford.edu/group
/uga/calendar.html

SPORTS www-athletics.stanford.edu

STUDENT CLUBS www.stanford.edu/home
/students/orgs.html

LIBRARY www-sul.stanford.edu

Skip the brochure

• **RAM'S HEAD THEATRICAL SOCIETY** The Ram's Head Society puts on traditional musicals, such as *Guys and Dolls*, and original works like *The Axe Files*, (a postmodern mystery of paranoia set at Stanford). **www-leland.stanford.edu/group /rams-head**

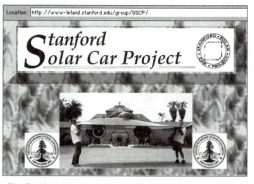

The Stanford solar car gets a lift from two club members

• **STANFORD SOLAR CAR PROJECT** Trying to strike a balance between solar panels and batteries, these Stanford undergrads design solar vehicles and race them. Solar racing is a good career move, too, as it seems to enhance any graduate's resume. **www-leland.stanford.edu /group/SSCP**

• **THE FARM ALMANAC OR HOW TO SURVIVE AT STANFORD** Stanford has already felt the wrath of alleged Unabomber Ted Kaczynski, so it makes perfect sense that the almanac has a section on mail bombs. The almanac also has information on more ephemeral threats, like earthquakes, astronomy, and bulb planting. **portfolio.stanford.edu/I04367**

"Stanford has felt the wrath of the Unabomber."

WHAT YOU NEED TO GET IN Application Deadline December 15 **Early Action Deadline** November 1 **Common App.** No **Application Fee** $50 **Tuition Costs** $20,490 **Room & Board** $7,337 **Need Blind** Yes **Financial Forms Deadline** February 1 **Undergrads Awarded Aid** 60% **Aid That Is Need-Based** 90% **Average Award of Freshman Scholarship Package** $14,253 **Tests Required** SAT1 or ACT **Admissions Address** Stanford, CA 94305 **Admissions Telephone** (415) 723-2091

LAST YEAR'S CLASS Applied 15,390 **Accepted** 2,908 **Matriculated** 1,601 **Median Range SAT M/V** 660-750/ 590-690 **In Top Fifth of High School Graduating Class** 96%

COLLEGE LIFE Gender Breakdown M 50%, F 50% **Out of State Students** 59% **From Public Schools** 67% **Ethnic Composition** White & Other 55%, Asian American 24%, Black 8%, Hispanic 12%, Native American 1% **Foreign Students** 5% **Reside on Campus** 92% **Return as Sophomores** 96% **Total Faculty** 1459 **Student Faculty Ratio** 10:1 **Fraternities (% of men participating)** 21 (10%) **Sororities (% of women participating)** 10 (10%) **Graduate Students** 7,467

Stevens Institute of Technology

Hoboken, NJ · Est. 1870 · Coed · Private · 1,313 Undergrads · Urban

I need...

Admissions info admissions@stevens-tech.edu
www.stevens-tech.edu/stevens/undergrad
/admis.html
Financial aid info attila.stevens-tech.edu/finaid
/finaid.html

How wired is Stevens Tech?

Do I get email? Yes
Do I get a home page? Yes
  Where? www.stevens-tech.edu/userhome.html
Is my dorm wired? Yes
What is the student to computer ratio? 1:1

The usual tour

DEPARTMENTS www.stevens-tech.edu/stevens
/admin/department.html
CALENDAR www.stevens-tech.edu/stevens
/admin/calendar.html
STUDENT CLUBS www.stevens-tech.edu/stevens
/clubs/activities.html
VIRTUAL TOUR www.stevens-tech.edu/stevens
/maps/maps.html
CAREER CENTER attila.stevens-tech.edu/ocs

Skip the brochure

- **HYPER DISCORDIA** This 'zine, or whatever it is, is
smart, weird, kind of manic, and definitely
interesting, which is a lot more than can be

Not all technology Web pages are fantasias of fractals

said about the rest of the Stevens Tech site.
Discordianism is a kind of skepticism popular
in hacker culture. This is a site for people who
love the Net, and are familiar, or want to be
familiar, with cyberaffect. **www.stevens-tech.edu
/~jformoso/discordians.html**

- **JERSEYWOCKY** "Twas Bergen and the Erie road/
Did Mahwah into Paterson;/ All Jersey were
the Ocean Groves/ And the Red Bank
Bayonne." So begins this spoof on Lewis
Carroll's "Jabberwocky" from *Alice in
Wonderland*. One of the more fascinating con-
tributions to a largely uninvolving Web site.
www.stevens-tech.edu/jerseywocky.html

"Hyper Discordia: kind of manic, but interesting"

WHAT YOU NEED TO GET IN **Application Deadline** March 1 **Early Action Deadline** November 1 **Common App.** Yes
Application Fee $45 **Tuition Costs** $18,200 **Room & Board** $6,400 **Need Blind** Yes **Financial Forms Deadline**
March 1 with a priority given to applications received by December 1 **Undergrads Awarded Aid** 85% **Aid That Is
Need-Based** 80% **Tests Required** SAT1 (preferred) or ACT **Admissions Address** Castle Point on Hudson,
Hoboken, NJ 07030 **Admissions Telephone** (201) 216-5194

LAST YEAR'S CLASS **Applied** 1,749 **Accepted** 1,227 **Matriculated** 403 **Average SAT M/V** 670/530 **In Top Fifth of
High School Graduating Class** 70%

COLLEGE LIFE **Gender Breakdown** M 79%, F 21% **Out of State Students** 30% **Ethnic Composition** White & Other
57%, Asian American 25%, Black 7%, Hispanic 11% **Foreign Students** 7% **Reside on Campus** 80% **Return as
Sophomores** 85% **Total Faculty** 195 **Student Faculty Ratio** 9:1 **Fraternities (% of men participating)** 10 (40%)
Sororities (% of women participating) 3 (40%) **Graduate Students** 1,326

SUNY, Albany

www.albany.edu

Albany, NY · Est. 1844 · Coed · Public · 10,953 Undergrads · Urban

I need...

Admissions info www.albany.edu/admiss/ugrad
/admiss1.html

Financial aid info www.albany.edu/admiss/ugrad
/financia.html

How wired is SUNY, Albany?

Do I get email? Yes
Do I get a home page? Yes
Is my dorm wired? Yes
What is the student to computer ratio? 22:1

REQUEST APPLICATION ONLINE

The usual tour

DEPARTMENTS www.albany.edu/colleges/college1
.html#departments
SPORTS www.albany.edu/activities/arts_sports
.html
CALENDAR www.albany.edu/catalogs_calendars
_schedules/cat_cal_sch.html
LIBRARY www.albany.edu/libcomp/libcomp.html
VIRTUAL TOUR www.albany.edu/ugrad/bulletin
/geninfo/13.html
GREEK LIFE www.albany.edu/activities/student
/affairs/greek.html

Skip the brochure

- **CROSS-COUNTRY** Are you a running junkie when
you're not surfing the Net? Check out SUNY,
Albany's cross-country teams. Find out about
the school's All-Americans and national champions, and links to other cross-country sites.
www.albany.edu/xctrack/index.html

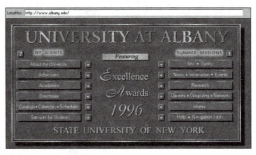

Check out Albany's feature of the week

- **NEW YORK STATE WRITERS INSTITUTE** Founded by
Albany native and Pulitzer Prize winner William
Kennedy, the New York State Writers Institute
sponsors a Summer Writers Institute at nearby
Skidmore. **www.albany.edu/writers-inst**

- **NEWS AND INFORMATION** What's new in Albany?
Find features on the New York Giants, who
train here every summer, and articles on
alums such as the one who studies huge
protozoans in the waters of the Antarctic.
www.albany.edu/pr/pr.html

"Are you a running junkie when you're not surfing the Net?"

WHAT YOU NEED TO GET IN Application Deadline November 15 for priority consideration; final deadline February 15
Early Action Deadline November 15 **Common App.** No **Application Fee** $25 **Tuition Costs** $3,400 ($8,300 out-
of-state) **Room & Board** $5,050 **Need Blind** Yes **Financial Forms Deadline** Priority given to applications received
by April 19 **Undergrads Awarded Aid** 75% **Aid That Is Need-Based** 84% **Average Award of Freshman
Scholarship Package** $2,700 **Tests Required** SAT1 (preferred) or ACT **Admissions Address** 1400 Washington
Avenue, Albany, NY 12222 **Admissions Telephone** (518) 442-5435

LAST YEAR'S CLASS Applied 14,967 **Accepted** 9,341 **Matriculated** 1,900 **Average SAT M/V** 581/500 **In Top Fifth of
High School Graduating Class** 43% **Accepted Early** 65

COLLEGE LIFE Gender Breakdown M 52%, F 48% **Out of State Students** 2% **Ethnic Composition** White & Other 75%,
Asian American 8%, Black 9%, Hispanic 7%, Native American 1% **Foreign Students** 1% **Reside on Campus** 54%
Return as Sophomores 90% **Student Faculty Ratio** 18:1 **Fraternities (% of men participating)** 29 (22%)
Sororities (% of women participating) 18 (12%) **Graduate Students** 5,090

SUNY, Binghamton

www.binghamton.edu

Binghamton, NY · Est. 1946 · Coed · Public · 9,273 Undergrads · Big Town

How wired is SUNY, Binghamton?

REQUEST APPLICATION ONLINE

Do I get email? Yes
Do I get a home page? No
Is my dorm wired? Yes

The usual tour

DEPARTMENTS www.binghamton.edu/academics
/academics.html
LIBRARY library.lib.binghamton.edu/libs.html
STUDENT CLUBS www.sa.binghamton.edu/SA
/groups.htm
CAREER CENTER cdc.adm.binghamton.edu
SPORTS www.binghamton.edu/academics
/bulletin/student_life.html#athletics
COMPUTING SERVICES www.binghamton.edu
/academics/bulletin/introduction.html
#ComputerServ

Skip the brochure

• **LITERATURE AND FOLKLORE** To some, Bob Dylan
and Arlo Guthrie are poets on a par with
Shakespeare and Milton. Binghamton's
English department, like many others around
the country, is moving toward more interdisciplinary discourse, breaking down cultural

BINGHAMTON UNIVERSITY
STATE UNIVERSITY OF NEW YORK

SUNY, Binghamton, home to CoRE and their adventure with
rats

boundaries. Although Bob and Arlo aren't on
the syllabus, students are encouraged to
explore the fields of folk song, folk religion,
and material culture. **english.adm.binghamton.edu
/under/litfolk.htm**

• **CORE** CoRE is the Computer Robotics
Engineering Special Interest Housing Module.
In other words, a bunch of wacky techies, who,
besides running some basic computer facilities, boast of taping rodents to doors. Their
home pages are linked here and tend to be
pretty cool (they are techies after all). **www.core
.binghamton.edu**

"CoRE is a bunch of wacky techies who boast of taping rodents to doors."

WHAT YOU NEED TO GET IN **Application Deadline** January 1 for priority consideration; final deadline February 15 **Early
Action Deadline** November 1 **Common App.** No **Application Fee** $30 **Tuition Costs** $3,400 ($8,300 out-of-state)
Room & Board $4,654 **Need Blind** Yes **Financial Forms Deadline** Priority given to applications received by
March 1 **Undergrads Awarded Aid** 49% **Aid That Is Need-Based** 95% **Average Award of Freshman Scholarship
Package** $3,801 **Tests Required** SAT1 or ACT **Admissions Address** P.O. Box 6000, Binghamton, NY 13902-
6000 **Admissions Telephone** (607) 777-2171

LAST YEAR'S CLASS **Applied** 16,348 **Accepted** 6,507 **Matriculated** 1,790 **Average SAT M/V** 618/608 **In Top Fifth of
High School Graduating Class** 89%

COLLEGE LIFE **Gender Breakdown** M 46%, F 54% **Out of State Students** 6% **From Public Schools** 83% **Ethnic
Composition** White & Other 69%, Asian American 17%, Black 6.5%, Hispanic 6.5%, Native American 1% **Foreign
Students** 2% **Reside on Campus** 57% **Return as Sophomores** 93% **Total Faculty** 448 **Student Faculty Ratio**
21:1 **Fraternities (% of men participating)** 21 (15%) **Sororities (% of women participating)** 14 (15%) **Graduate
Students** 2,679

SUNY, Buffalo

wings.buffalo.edu

Buffalo, NY · Est. 1846 · Coed · Public · 16,150 Undergrads · Urban

I need...

Admissions info ub_admissions@acsu.buffalo.edu
wings.buffalo.edu/provost/admissions

How wired is SUNY, Buffalo?

Do I get email? Yes
Do I get a home page? Yes
   Where? wings.buffalo.edu
   /student-life/userpages
Is my dorm wired? No
What is the student to computer ratio? 16:1

REQUEST APPLICATION ONLINE

The usual tour

DEPARTMENTS wings.buffalo.edu/academic
   /department
STUDENT CLUBS wings.buffalo.edu/student-life
   /sa/sawww/Club.html
GREEK LIFE wings.buffalo.edu/student-life
   /sa/chess
LIBRARY wings.buffalo.edu/libraries
CAREER CENTER wings.buffalo.edu/employment
   /career
SPORTS wings.buffalo.edu/sports

Skip the brochure

• **THE CHESS CLUB** Some Net critics have claimed that online games will seduce unsuspecting surfers from their responsibilities. Meet Exhibit A. In all fairness, chess has long been popular online, its not just the folks at SUNY Buffalo who are addicted. If you just can't get

A home where the University of Buffalo's Wings roam

enough, you can play and learn techniques here 24 hours a day. **wings.buffalo.edu/student-life/sa/chess**

• **PHI BETA SIGMA** This black fraternity started with three men at Howard University in 1914. There are now more than 100,000 members nationwide, all of whom subscribe to the three-pronged party line: social action, education, and bigger and better business. **wings.buffalo.edu/student-life/greeks/pbs**

• **THE SQUEAKY WHEEL** If living in a town called Buffalo sounds a little weird to begin with, you may want to delve further into the wackiness of upstate New York by checking out the Squeaky Wheel. A cutting edge arts resource that is particularly supportive of digital art, the Wheel hosts an exhibit called "Kill, Kill, Kill" and another called "That Christmas One." **www.iawd.com/sw**

WHAT YOU NEED TO GET IN **Application Deadline** Rolling admissions; November 1 for priority consideration **Early Action Deadline** November 1 **Common App.** No **Application Fee** $30 (may be waived) **Tuition Costs** $3,400 ($8300 out-of-state) **Room & Board** $5,300 **Need Blind** Yes **Financial Forms Deadline** May 1 with a priority given to applications received by March 1 **Undergrads Awarded Aid** 59% **Aid That Is Need-Based** 90% **Average Award of Freshman Scholarship Package** $1,642 **Tests Required** SAT1 or ACT **Admissions Address** Buffalo, NY 14260 **Admissions Telephone** (716) 645-6900

LAST YEAR'S CLASS **Applied** 15,461 **Accepted** 10,624 **Matriculated** 2,685 **Average SAT M/V** 591/561 **Average ACT** 25 **In Top Fifth of High School Graduating Class** 51% **Applied Early** 230 **Accepted Early** 142

COLLEGE LIFE **Gender Breakdown** M 55%, F 45% **Out of State Students** 3% **Ethnic Composition** White & Other 77%, Asian American 11%, Black 7%, Hispanic 4%, Native American 1% **Foreign Students** 2% **Reside on Campus** 23% **Return as Sophomores** 85% **Total Faculty** 1286 **Student Faculty Ratio** 14:1 **Fraternities (% of men participating)** 15 (1%) **Sororities (% of women participating)** 13 (1%) **Graduate Students** 8,343

SUNY, Stony Brook

www.sunysb.edu

Stony Brook, NY · Est. 1957 · Coed · Public · 11,485 Undergrads · Small Town

REQUEST APPLICATION ONLINE

I need...

Admissions info www.sunysb.edu/admissions/admin3.htm

How wired is SUNY, Stony Brook?

Do I get email? Yes
Do I get a home page? Yes
Is my dorm wired? Yes
What is the student to computer ratio? 30:1

The usual tour

DEPARTMENTS www.sunysb.edu/admissions/maj.htm
VIRTUAL TOUR www.cs.sunysb.edu/tour/tourhome.html
LIBRARY www.sunysb.edu/library/ldintro.htmlx
CAREER CENTER www.sunysb.edu/career
CALENDAR sbnews.sunysb.edu/inter/campcal.html
CAREER CENTER sbnews.sunysb.edu/sbnews.html

Skip the brochure

• **STONY BROOK** Stony Brook is on Long Island, the stomping grounds of the infamous Joey Buttafuoco. If your association with the area is limited to Amy Fisher, then it is time to meet a

"Stomping grounds of Joey Buttafuoco"

Arboreal bliss awaits you at SUNY Stony Brook

much more charming and hospitable Long Island. Along with Old Fields and Setauket, Stony Brook makes up the Three Village area, and this site gives an introduction to the charming scenery. **sbnews.sunysb.edu/tour/Village.html**

• **PHARMACOLOGY** While some are interested in pharmacology for recreational reasons, there are those at Stony Brook who study it. And because pharmaceuticals are also inextricably linked to the latest in medical research and environmental issues, Stony Brook's Pharmacology page outlines career and internship possibilities. **www.pharm.sunysb.edu/undergraduate**

WHAT YOU NEED TO GET IN **Application Deadline** July 10 **Common App.** No **Application Fee** $30 **Tuition Costs** $3,400 ($8,300 out-of-state) **Room & Board** $5,166 **Need Blind** Yes **Financial Forms Deadline** Priority given to applications received by March 1 **Undergrads Awarded Aid** 85% **Aid That Is Need-Based** 43% **Tests Required** SAT1 or ACT **Admissions Address** Stony Brook, NY 11794 **Admissions Telephone** (516) 632-6868

LAST YEAR'S CLASS **Applied** 13,741 **Accepted** 7,391 **Matriculated** 1,737 **Average SAT M/V** 549/456 **In Top Quarter of High School Graduating Class** 68%

COLLEGE LIFE **Gender Breakdown** M 49%, F 51% **Out of State Students** 5% **From Public Schools** 85% **Ethnic Composition** White & Other 66%, Asian American 17%, Black 10%, Hispanic 7% **Foreign Students** 4% **Reside on Campus** 55% **Return as Sophomores** 83% **Total Faculty** 1607 **Student Faculty Ratio** 17:1 **Fraternities** 15 **Sororities** 11 **Graduate Students** 6,180

SUNY College, Geneseo

Geneseo, NY · Est. 1871 · Coed · Public · 5,334 Undergrads · Small Town

I need...

Admissions info conlonj@sgenva.cc.geneseo.edu
onesun.cc.geneseo.edu/admissions
/admissions.html

Financial aid info cureton@sgenva.cc.geneseo.edu
onesun.cc.geneseo.edu/administration
/financial.html

How wired is SUNY, Geneseo?

Do I get email? Yes
Do I get a home page? Yes
Is my dorm wired? Yes
What is the student to computer ratio? 10:1

REQUEST APPLICATION ONLINE

The usual tour

DEPARTMENTS onesun.cc.geneseo.edu
/academics/academics.html
STUDENT CLUBS onesun.cc.geneseo.edu
/studentlife/studentlife.html
SPORTS onesun.cc.geneseo.edu/studentlife
/sports.html
CALENDAR onesun.cc.geneseo.edu/studentlife
/happening.html
LIBRARY 137.238.50.66
VIRTUAL TOUR mosaic.cc.geneseo.edu/campus
_map/campus_map.html

Skip the brochure

- **FIELD STUDIES** These programs are designed to
let you get out of the classroom and into the
world. Whether it's studying artifacts in

Geneseo—all the benefits of the SUNY system, with a liberal arts feel

Africa, or studying group behavior in the social
laboratory of a soup kitchen, students turn
theory into practice. **onesun.cc.geneseo.edu/first
_look/viewbook/field.html**

- **THE LAMRON** Read the student newspaper in
print or online. One recent scandal involved
the theft of the entire print run of *The Lamron*
following an editorial about female bonding
and sorority abuse. This event in turn incited a
raging free speech debate. **onesun.cc.geneseo.edu
/~lamron**

- **ALPHA OMEGA PI** Given the *Lamron* scandal (see
above), you might expect to read of strange
sorority rituals and wacky female bonding.
Instead, you'll find a site that explains the
sorority's commitment to community.
onesun.cc.geneseo.edu/~aopi

WHAT YOU NEED TO GET IN Application Deadline November for priority consideration; final deadline January 15 **Early Action Deadline** November 15 **Common App.** No **Application Fee** $30 **Tuition Costs** $3,400 ($8,300 out-of-state) **Room & Board** $4,500 **Need Blind** Yes **Financial Forms Deadline** February 15 **Undergrads Awarded Aid** 50% **Aid That Is Need-Based** 77% **Average Award of Freshman Scholarship Package** $2,065 **Tests Required** SAT1 or ACT **Admissions Address** 1 College Circle, Geneseo, NY 14454 **Admissions Telephone** (716) 245-5571

LAST YEAR'S CLASS Applied 8,934 **Accepted** 4,868 **Matriculated** 1,210 **Average SAT M/V** 608/540 **Average ACT** 26 **In Top Fifth of High School Graduating Class** 82% **Applied Early** 270 **Accepted Early** 158

COLLEGE LIFE Gender Breakdown M 36%, F 64% **Out of State Students** 2% **From Public Schools** 83% **Ethnic Composition** White & Other 88.4%, Asian American 6.2%, Black 1.6%, Hispanic 3.6%, Native American 0.2% **Reside on Campus** 61% **Return as Sophomores** 90% **Total Faculty** 327 **Student Faculty Ratio** 19:1 **Fraternities (% of men participating)** 9 (19%) **Sororities (% of women participating)** 11 (15%) **Graduate Students** 385

SUNY College, Potsdam

www.potsdam.edu

Potsdam, NY · Est. 1816 · Coed · Public· 3,584 Undergrads · Small Town

How wired is SUNY, Potsdam?

Do I get email? Yes
Do I get a home page? Yes
  Where? www.potsdam.edu/direct
  ories/Studentpages.html
Is my dorm wired? Yes
What is the student to computer ratio? 10:1

REQUEST APPLICATION ONLINE

The usual tour

DEPARTMENTS www.potsdam.edu/AcadDeptlist
  .html
SPORTS www.potsdam.edu/sports/sports.html
STUDY ABROAD www.potsdam.edu/INTRNAT
  /InternationalHP.html
STUDENT CLUBS www.potsdam.edu/DIRECTORIES
  /students/Studentorganization.pages.html
CAREER CENTER www.potsdam.edu/CAREER
  /CareerPlanningindex.html
CALENDAR www.potsdam.edu/Events.html

Skip the brochure

• **THE CRANE SCHOOL** Do two things at once: work
  on your own musical skills while learning to

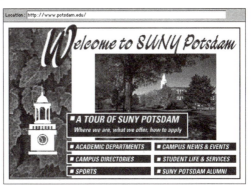

If SUNY, Potsdam's not sunny enough, take a road trip to Ottawa, only 90 miles away

teach music to others at the first school in the
country for musical education. **www.potsdam.edu
/CRANE/Crane.html**

• **THE THEATRE GUILD** The Theatre Guild teaches
  students how to mount and produce shows,
  everything from stage managing to lighting to
  costumes. The page has nice graphics, but is
  still under construction. **www.student.potsdam
  .edu/clubs/theater/thehome.htm**

• **STAR LAKE CAMPUS** Nestled in the Adirondack
  Mountains, SUNY, Potsdam has a beautiful
  satellite campus that often serves as a backdrop for environmental or leadership education. Who needs a gorgeous lake, a sauna,
  canoes, trees? You might. Star Lake even has
  a computer lab. **www.student.potsdam.edu/robarg80
  /campus.html**

WHAT YOU NEED TO GET IN Application Deadline December 1 for priority consideration; final deadline Rolling Admissions **Early Action Deadline** November 1 **Common App.** Yes **Application Fee** $30 **Tuition Costs** $3,900 ($8,800 out-of-state) **Room & Board** $4,900 **Need Blind** Yes **Undergrads Awarded Aid** 93% **Aid That Is Need-Based** 94% **Average Award of Freshman Scholarship Package** $1,400 **Tests Required** SAT1 or ACT **Admissions Address** Potsdam, NY 13676-2294 **Admissions Telephone** (315) 267-2180

LAST YEAR'S CLASS Applied 3,103 **Accepted** 2,315 **Matriculated** 665 **Average SAT M/V** 521/464 **Average ACT** 22 **In Top Fifth of High School Graduating Class** 23% **Applied Early** 64 **Accepted Early** 57

COLLEGE LIFE Gender Breakdown M 43%, F 57% **Out of State Students** 3% **From Public Schools** 80% **Ethnic Composition** White & Other 93.6%, Asian American 1%, Black 2%, Hispanic 2%, Native American 1.4% **Foreign Students** 1% **Reside on Campus** 60% **Return as Sophomores** 78% **Student Faculty Ratio** 21:1 **Fraternities (% of men participating)** 6 (10%) **Sororities (% of women participating)** 8 (15%) **Graduate Students** 518

Swarthmore College

www.cc.swarthmore.edu

Swarthmore, PA · Est. 1864 · Coed · Private · 1,353 Undergrads · Urban

I need...

Admissions info admissions@swarthmore.edu
www.cc.swarthmore.edu/Home/Admissions
/index.html

How wired is Swarthmore?

Do I get email? Yes
Do I get a home page? Yes
  Where? www.sccs.swarthmore
  .edu/studpages.html
What is the student to computer ratio? 11:1

The usual tour

DEPARTMENTS www.cc.swarthmore.edu/Home
  /Academic/index.html
LIBRARY www.swarthmore.edu/Library
VIRTUAL TOUR www.swarthmore.edu/cc/swat-tour
PUBLICATIONS www.swarthmore.edu/Home/News
  /Pubs/index.html
COMPUTER CENTER www.swarthmore.edu/cc

Skip the brochure

• **HOT AT SWAT** Swarthmore has the reputation of
being a fiercely intellectual yet hip liberal arts
college. Their Hot at Swat page should reflect
this, but the information isn't quite so thrilling
as it might be, perhaps because this page is
put out by the public relations office. Hot at
Swat is somewhat telling—Lani Guinier, the
Supreme Court nominee dissed by Bill Clinton,
received an honorary degree from Swarthmore

Look to the left, look to the right: More than 50% of
Swarthmore students find their mate here

in the spring of '96. One also learns that
Swarthmore had a record number of applicants last year. Bet you love the sound of that.
www.swarthmore.edu/Home/News/Hot/index.html

• **THE PHOENIX** If you're willing to read between
the lines, you can learn lots about Swarthmore
and its campus scandals and happenings. The
administration recently touched off a curricular
battle when it booted a course called "Wisdom
and the Healing Arts" because it didn't fit into
a specific department. Sure enough, the move
angered students who were upset that its
"interdisciplinary" nature wasn't embraced.
www.sccs.swarthmore.edu/org/phoenix/curr

WHAT YOU NEED TO GET IN Application Deadline Fall for priority consideration; final deadline January 1 **Early Action
Deadline** November 15 **Common App.** Yes **Application Fee** $50 **Tuition Costs** $20,846 **Room & Board** $7,176
Need Blind Yes **Financial Forms Deadline** early February **Aid That Is Need-Based** 97% **Average Award of
Freshman Scholarship Package** $15,685 **Tests Required** SAT1 or ACT **Admissions Address** 500 College
Avenue, Swarthmore, PA 19081 **Admissions Telephone** (610) 328-8300

LAST YEAR'S CLASS Applied 3,512 **Accepted** 1,229 **Matriculated** 352 **Average SAT M/V** 694/648 **In Top Fifth of
High School Graduating Class** 60% **Applied Early** 139 **Accepted Early** 83

COLLEGE LIFE Gender Breakdown M 48%, F 52% **Out of State Students** 89% **From Public Schools** 65% **Ethnic
Composition** White & Other 77%, Asian American 11%, Black 6%, Hispanic 5%, Native American 1% **Foreign
Students** 5% **Reside on Campus** 91% **Return as Sophomores** 96% **Student Faculty Ratio** 9:1 **Fraternities
(% of men participating)** 2 (5%) **Sororities** none

Syracuse University

Syracuse, NY · Est. 1870 · Coed · Private · 10,097 Undergrads · Urban

cwis.syr.edu

I need...

Admissions info orange@suadmin.syr.edu
cwis.syr.edu/WWW-Syr/AboutSU/Admission
.html

Financial aid info finaid@suadmin.syr.edu
sumweb.syr.edu/summon3/bulkdist
/public/web/index.htm

How wired is Syracuse University?

Do I get email? Yes
Do I get a home page? Yes
   Where? web.syr.edu
Is my dorm wired? Yes
What is the student to computer ratio? 10:1

The usual tour

DEPARTMENTS cwis.syr.edu/WWW-Syr/School
College/Academic/SUdepartments.html
STUDENT CLUBS cwis.syr.edu/WWW-Syr/Student
Activities/index.html
SPORTS cwis.syr.edu/WWW-Syr/Recreation
Sports/index.html
CALENDAR cwis.syr.edu/WWW-Syr/Calendar
Events
STUDY ABROAD sumweb.syr.edu/dipa
CAREER CENTER web.syr.edu/~clreutli/career

Skip the brochure

• **SPECIAL INTERESTS CLUB** The Licking the Lit club
may sound a bit risqué, but is in fact comprised of literary types. The page also has

You'll be seeing orange if you decide to attend Syracuse

links to descriptions of some of the more interesting clubs on campus, like the Shaped Clay
Society and the Japanese Animation Club.
students.syr.edu/student_orgs/spec-int

• **ARTS ADVENTURE** Have an adventure while sitting
in a seat watching a play? Perhaps adventure
isn't the right word, but the idea is solid
enough—this resource encourages students
to explore the local arts community by making
it easy and more economical for them to do
so. **students.syr.edu/events/artsadv/index.html**

• **SYBERCUSE** This is a terrific, graphics-rich way to
get to know the city of Syracuse. There are
links to the latest local news, weather, sports,
and cultural events. Perhaps most importantly,
Sybercuse includes a dining guide, which could
be handy for students living on a starvation
budget. **www.sybercuse.com**

WHAT YOU NEED TO GET IN **Application Deadline** February 1 for priority consideration **Early Action Deadline** November
15 **Common App.** No **Application Fee** $40 **Tuition Costs** $16,710 **Room & Board** $7,210 **Need Blind** Yes
Financial Forms Deadline February 15 **Undergrads Awarded Aid** 75% **Aid That Is Need-Based** 85% **Average
Award of Freshman Scholarship Package** $8,600 **Tests Required** SAT1 (preferred) or ACT **Admissions Address**
201 Tolley Administration Building, Syracuse, NY 13244 **Admissions Telephone** (315) 443-3611

LAST YEAR'S CLASS **Applied** 10,149 **Accepted** 6,670 **Matriculated** 2,409 **Median Range SAT M/V** 520-650/
450-570 **In Top Fifth of High School Graduating Class** 60% **Applied Early** 356 **Accepted Early** 340

COLLEGE LIFE **Gender Breakdown** M 49%, F 51% **Out of State Students** 60% **From Public Schools** 80% **Ethnic
Composition** White & Other 79%, Asian American 5%, Black 9%, Hispanic 6%, Native American 1% **Foreign
Students** 4% **Reside on Campus** 70% **Return as Sophomores** 88% **Total Faculty** 1,343 **Student Faculty Ratio**
11:1 **Fraternities (% of men participating)** 23 (16%) **Sororities (% of women participating)** 19 (25%) **Graduate
Students** 4,539

Temple University

Philadelphia, PA · Est. 1884 · Coed · Public · 20,289 Undergrads · Urban

I need...

Admissions info www.temple.edu/admissions
.html

How wired is Temple?

Do I get email? Yes
Do I get a home page? Yes
Is my dorm wired? Yes
What is the student to computer ratio? 10:1

REQUEST APPLICATION ONLINE

The usual tour

DEPARTMENTS www.temple.edu/tu.www.servers
.html#academic
STUDENT NEWSPAPER astro.ocis.temple.edu
/~kate
VIRTUAL TOUR www.temple.edu/maps
/maincampus.html
HISTORY www.temple.edu/documentation
/heritage/acres.html
LIBRARY telnet://155.247.22.70

Skip the brochure

• **TEMPLE UNIVERSITY GALLERY OF THE ARTS** This
"experimental project," overseen jointly by the
Department of Radio-Television-Film and the
Esther Boyer College of Music, houses an
eclectic array of artwork. Traditional media is
presented on the Web (such as a local
painter's works) alongside artwork created via
new media (such as an excellent MFA thesis
exhibition showcasing virtual jewelry and met-
alsmithing objects). **betty.music.temple.edu/Gallery**

Hone your graphic skills at the Graphics Media Center, a
temple of fine arts

• **FILM & MEDIA ARTS** Catch a glimpse of some of
the projects produced by the department's faculty and students, ranging from wacky films
about pop-rock survivors to 3-D animation programs. **www.temple.edu/departments/fma**

• **MEN'S GYMNASTICS** The rough and tumbling men
of Temple take to the Web with their match
results and a dashing team photo. Nice tights.
blue.temple.edu/~turoff

"See wacky films about pop-rock survivors."

WHAT YOU NEED TO GET IN **Application Deadline** Fall for priority consideration; final deadline June 15 **Common App.** No
Application Fee $30 **Tuition Costs** $5,314 ($10,096 out-of-state) **Room & Board** $3,866 **Need Blind** Yes
Financial Forms Deadline March 31 **Tests Required** SAT1 or ACT **Admissions Address** 1801 North Broad Street,
Philadelphia, PA 19122-1803 **Admissions Telephone** (215) 204-7200

LAST YEAR'S CLASS **Applied** 9,599 **Accepted** 6,247 **Matriculated** 2,575 **Average SAT M/V** 494/458 **In Top Fifth of
High School Graduating Class** 34%

COLLEGE LIFE **Gender Breakdown** M 45%, F 55% **Out of State Students** 23% **From Public Schools** 63% **Ethnic
Composition** White & Other 59.7%, Asian American 13.1%, Black 24.1%, Hispanic 2.9%, Native American 0.2%
Foreign Students 2% **Reside on Campus** 10% **Student Faculty Ratio** 12:1 **Fraternities (% of men participating)**
13 (7%) **Sororities (% of women participating)** 7 (3%) **Graduate Students** 10,476

University of Tennessee, Knoxville

www.utk.edu

Knoxville, TN · Est. 1794 · Coed · Public · 19,671 Undergrads · Urban

I need...

Admissions info funnelweb.utcc.utk.edu/vet /admstu.html

Financial aid info funnelweb.utcc.utk.edu/acct /macc/finance.html

How wired is Tennessee, Knoxville?

Do I get email? Yes

Do I get a home page? Yes

　Where? solar.rtd.utk.edu/utk-home pages

What is the student to computer ratio? 13:1

REQUEST APPLICATION ONLINE

The usual tour

DEPARTMENTS loki.ur.utk.edu/catalogs /admitme.html

LIBRARY www.lib.utk.edu

SPORTS www.utk.edu/sports/default.html

STUDENT CLUBS www.utk.edu/student

CALENDAR www.utk.edu/calendar

STUDY ABROAD utkvx1.utk.edu/~cie/Progabr.html

CAREER CENTER funnelweb.utcc.utk.edu/~career /crclit.html

GREEK LIFE funnelweb.utcc.utk.edu/~borellis /frat.html

Skip the brochure

• **THE TOASTMASTERS** While the Net allows for certain kinds of communication, as of yet it

ROD DELMONICO

Sluggers, take note: In 1995, Rod Delmonico was *Baseball America* National Coach of the Year

doesn't involve too much speech-making. This student club, part of a larger national organization, is all about talk. Students get together to evaluate delivery, content, and coherence of their toasts. **funnelweb.utcc.utk.edu/~jgrobin/uttm.html**

• **THE SMOKY MOUNTAIN FIELD SCHOOL** A joint venture between the University of Tennessee and the Great Smoky Mountains National Park has created a number of outdoor and wilderness programs. Besides hiking and backpacking excursions, there are field courses on nature sketching, landscape photography, and the study of bats, spiders, birds, forests, mosses, Native Americans (the Cherokees), and mountains (the Smokies). **web.ce.utk.edu/departments /noncredit/smoky/smoky.html**

WHAT YOU NEED TO GET IN **Application Deadline** July 1 **Common App.** No **Application Fee** $15 **Tuition Costs** $2,220 ($6,474 out-of-state) **Room & Board** $3,620 **Need Blind** Yes **Financial Forms Deadline** Priority given to applications received by February 14 **Undergrads Awarded Aid** 45% **Aid That Is Need-Based** 88% **Average Award of Freshman Scholarship Package** $2,270 **Tests Required** SAT1 or ACT **Admissions Address** 320 Student Services Building, Knoxville, TN 37996-0230 **Admissions Telephone** (423) 974-2184

LAST YEAR'S CLASS **Applied** 8,305 **Accepted** 5,977 **Matriculated** 3,506 **Average SAT M/V** 552/554 **Average ACT** 23 **In Top Fifth of High School Graduating Class** 43%

COLLEGE LIFE **Gender Breakdown** M 51%, F 49% **Out of State Students** 18% **Ethnic Composition** White & Other 89%, Asian American 4%, Black 5%, Hispanic 1%, Native American 1% **Foreign Students** 4% **Reside on Campus** 35% **Return as Sophomores** 78% **Total Faculty** 1165 **Student Faculty Ratio** 17:1 **Fraternities (% of men participating)** 26 (16%) **Sororities (% of women participating)** 19 (16%)

Tennessee Technological University

Cookeville, TN · Est. 1915 · Coed · Public · 7,158 Undergrads · Small Town

www.tntech.edu

How wired is Tennessee Tech?

Do I get email? Yes
Do I get a home page? Yes
Is my dorm wired? No
What is the student to computer ratio? 25:1

REQUEST APPLICATION ONLINE

The usual tour

DEPARTMENTS www.tntech.edu/www/acad
/depts.html
LIBRARY gopher://gopher.tntech.edu
/11gopher_root%3a%5bcampus.library%5d
STUDENT CLUBS www.tntech.edu/www/life/orgs
/index.html
CAREER CENTER www.tntech.edu/www/admin
/career/index.html
GREEK LIFE www.tntech.edu/www/life/orgs
/index.html

Skip the brochure

• **HUMAN-POWERED SUBMARINE CLUB** If you were
eager to know that human-powered sub-
marines are wet on the inside as well as on

Location: http://www.tntech.edu/www/life/orgs/sub/ttusub/torp2f3.gif

All at sea with the sub club

the outside, then this site will be a treat.
Documentation, movies, and images give you
everything you need to feel the excitement of
one of the least-known sporting events in the
water. **www.tntech.edu/www/life/orgs/sub/index.html**

• **UPPER CUMBERLAND GROTTO** Affiliated with the
National Speleological Society, this site teaches its members to cave in a safe, responsible,
and environmentally conscientious manner—
and it also provides opportunities to meet fellow cavers. **www.tntech.edu/www/life/orgs/grotto
/index.html**

• **CAMPUS CRUSADE FOR CHRIST** The campus crusade serves as a resource to college students
to help them get the most out of college life
through weekly meetings. **www.tntech
.edu/www/life/orgs/ccfc/about.html**

WHAT YOU NEED TO GET IN Application Deadline February 1 for priority consideration; final deadline August 1 **Common App.** No **Application Fee** $5 **Tuition Costs** $1,840 ($5,970 out-of-state) **Room & Board** $3,360 **Need Blind** Yes **Financial Forms Deadline** Priority given to applications received by March 15 **Undergrads Awarded Aid** 60% **Aid That Is Need-Based** 90% **Average Award of Freshman Scholarship Package** $1,100 **Tests Required** ACT **Admissions Address** Box 5006 T.T.U., Cookeville, TN 38505 **Admissions Telephone** (800) 255-8881

LAST YEAR'S CLASS Applied 2,303 **Accepted** 2,110 **Matriculated** 1,266 **Average ACT** 23 **In Top Quarter of High School Graduating Class** 55%

COLLEGE LIFE Gender Breakdown M 54%, F 46% **Out of State Students** 7% **From Public Schools** 98% **Ethnic Composition** White & Other 96%, Asian American 2%, Black 2% **Foreign Students** 3% **Reside on Campus** 40% **Return as Sophomores** 65% **Student Faculty Ratio** 20:1 **Fraternities (% of men participating)** 16 (18%) **Sororities (% of women participating)** 6 (12%) **Graduate Students** 1,008

University of Texas, Austin

Austin, TX · Est. 1883 · Coed · Public · 35,086 Undergrads · Urban

I need...

Admissions info admit@utxdp.dp.utexas.edu
www.utexas.edu/student/admissions
Financial aid info fadas@utxdp.dp.utexas.edu
www.utexas.edu/student/finaid

How wired is UT?

Do I get email? Yes
Do I get a home page? Yes
   Where? www.utexas.edu/personal
What is the student to computer ratio? 4:1

FULL APPLICATION ONLINE

The usual tour

DEPARTMENTS www.utexas.edu/dept
LIBRARY www.lib.utexas.edu
SPORTS www.utexas.edu/athletics
STUDENT CLUBS www.utexas.edu/student/orgs
CALENDAR dpweb1.dp.utexas.edu/events
CAREER CENTER www.utexas.edu/search
   /jobs.html

Skip the brochure

- **40 ACRES FEST** A huge school-sponsored shindig, complete with local bands, booths, and outdoor madness. Last year's party, organized by more than 80 students, attracted approximately 10,000 (and that's a conservative estimate). What did you expect? "Big school. Big party." **www.utexas.edu/students/forty**

- **LONGHORN SOLAR RACE CAR TEAM** The university has been involved in solar car racing since

The Bard and the Bard-inspired at UT, Austin

1988. A team of students is responsible for designing and building a really cool car, and then racing it against other environmentally-sound autos from around the country. **nesc.me.utexas.edu/~lsrct**

- **OBJECTIVIST STUDY GROUP** If reading *The Fountainhead* twelve times wasn't enough, if you've got Ayn Rand on the brain, if subjectivity represents all you abhor, why not join the Objectivist Study Group? What do these Ayn Rand zealots talk about all day? There's only one way to find out—take the plunge! **uts.cc.utexas.edu/~osg**

"40 Acres Fest: big school, big party"

WHAT YOU NEED TO GET IN **Application Deadline** February 1 for priority consideration; final deadline March 1 **Common App.** No **Application Fee** $40 **Tuition Costs** $840 ($5,130 out-of-state) **Room & Board** $4,420 **Need Blind** No **Financial Forms Deadline** Priority given to applications received by April 1 **Undergrads Awarded Aid** 53% **Aid That Is Need-Based** 44% **Average Award of Freshman Scholarship Package** $2,450 **Tests Required** SAT1 or ACT **Admissions Address** Austin, TX 78712-1157 **Admissions Telephone** (512) 475-7399

LAST YEAR'S CLASS **Applied** 14,959 **Accepted** 9,668 **Matriculated** 5,687 **Average SAT M/V** 618/599 **Average ACT** 25 **In Top Quarter of High School Graduating Class** 75%

COLLEGE LIFE **Gender Breakdown** M 51%, F 49% **Out of State Students** 6% **Ethnic Composition** White & Other 68.7%, Asian American 12%, Black 4.2%, Hispanic 14.7%, Native American 0.4% **Foreign Students** 4% **Reside on Campus** 13% **Return as Sophomores** 87% **Total Faculty** 2398 **Student Faculty Ratio** 19:1 **Fraternities of men participating)** 34 (11%) **Sororities (% of women participating)** 20 (13%) **Graduate Students** 12,819

Texas A&M University

College Station, TX · Est. 1876 · Coed · Public · 34,371 Undergrads · Big Town

www.tamu.edu

How wired is Texas A&M?

Do I get email? Yes
Do I get a home page? Yes
  Where? tamu.edu:8000/~sdd
  2252/Docs/Fun/Fun.html
What is the student to computer ratio? 17:1

REQUEST APPLICATION ONLINE

The usual tour

DEPARTMENTS www.tamu.edu/tamu_subject
/31.html
CALENDAR www.tamu.edu/calendar/calendar
.html
SPORTS www.tamu.edu/tamu_subject/1056.html
LIBRARY www.tamu.edu/tamu_subject/17.html
STUDENT CLUBS www.tamu.edu/tamu_subject
/20.html
CAREER CENTER www.tamu.edu/tamu_subject
/8.html

Skip the brochure

• **FREUDIAN SLIP** Freudian Slip is Texas A&M's
improv comedy troupe, and while the players
may not be ready for prime time, fellow students seem amused. Membership is based on
an incredibly nerve-racking audition, but it's not

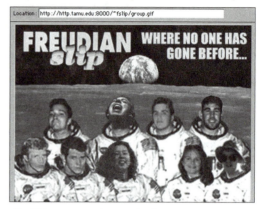

FREUDIAN slip **WHERE NO ONE HAS GONE BEFORE...**

Location: http://http.tamu.edu:8000/~fslip/group.gif

In space, no one can hear you laugh

unheard of for TAMU freshmen to join the
troupe. **http.tamu.edu:8000/~fslip**

• **TEXAS A&M FLYING CLUB** When the walls of finals
close in, students have many avenues of
escape. Witness the Flying Club, which has
more than 200 members. How many parents
are kept in the dark when Junior takes the con-
trols for the first time? **http.tamu.edu:8000/~drh0553
/flyclub.html**

• **OLD ARMY GENTLEMAN SOCIETY** Are they for real,
and if so, what kind of women do they date?
http.tamu.edu:8000/~jsh6345/olags/olags.html

"Membership is based on a nerve-racking audition."

WHAT YOU NEED TO GET IN **Application Deadline** February 1 for priority consideration; final deadline March 1 **Common
App.** No **Application Fee** $35 ($75 for international applicants) **Tuition Costs** $960 ($7,380 out-of-state) **Room
& Board** $2,639 **Financial Forms Deadline** Priority given to applications received by April 1 **Undergrads Awarded
Aid** 63% **Aid That Is Need-Based** 35% **Average Award of Freshman Scholarship Package** $2,829 **Tests
Required** SAT1 or ACT **Admissions Address** College Station, TX 77843-1265 **Admissions Telephone** (409)
845-3741

LAST YEAR'S CLASS **Applied** 15,888 **Accepted** 10,915 **Matriculated** 6,072 **Average SAT M/V** 599/575 **Average
ACT** 25 **In Top Fifth of High School Graduating Class** 77%

COLLEGE LIFE **Gender Breakdown** M 54%, F 46% **Out of State Students** 7% **Ethnic Composition** White & Other
82%, Asian American 4%, Black 3%, Hispanic 11% **Foreign Students** 2% **Reside on Campus** 28% **Return as
Sophomores** 87% **Total Faculty** 2,313 **Student Faculty Ratio** 20:1 **Fraternities (% of men participating)** 29
(9%) **Sororities (% of women participating)** 15 (12%) **Graduate Students** 7,419

Texas Christian University

www.tcu.edu

Fort Worth, TX · Est. 1873 · Coed · Private · 5,886 Undergrads · Urban

How wired is TCU?

Do I get email? Yes
Do I get a home page? Yes
Is my dorm wired? Yes
What is the student to computer ratio? 5:1

REQUEST APPLICATION ONLINE

The usual tour

VIRTUAL TOUR www.tcu.edu/tcu/tcu_tour.html
LIBRARY library.tcu.edu

Skip the brochure

- **TCU RANCH MANAGEMENT HOME PAGE** Attention all parents: The next time your son or daughter defiantly asks you, "What's a college education good for, anyway?" send them to this site. Courses like "Beef Cattle Production" and "Forage Production and Use" are combined with field trips to working ranches, livestock expositions, cattle auctions and the occasional wool and mohair company to provide a well-rounded education for anyone who wants to be head honcho on a ranch. **www.ranch.tcu.edu/ranch**

- **TCU INTENSIVE ENGLISH PROGRAM** Hola! Güten Tag! Bonjour! Howdy! Texas Christian University's Intensive English Program offers language study for international students in a number of

Location: http://beta.is.tcu.edu/pub/summer96/roundworms

All the cool protozoa go to Texas Christian University

different levels and concentrations. Accent optional. **www.iep.tcu.edu/iep/index.htm**

- **TCU'S FIGHT SONG** If this doesn't inspire you to win one for the home team, nothing will. The first URL is for the .AIFF format, the second for the .WAV format **www.tcu.edu/tcu/tcu.aiff · www.tcu.edu/tcu.tcu.wav.**

"Courses like 'Beef Cattle Production' are combined with field trips to working ranches and cattle auctions."

WHAT YOU NEED TO GET IN **Application Deadline** February 15 **Common App.** Yes **Application Fee** $30 **Tuition Costs** $9,420 **Room & Board** $3,500 **Need Blind** Yes **Financial Forms Deadline** Priority given to applications received by May 1 **Undergrads Awarded Aid** 55% **Aid That Is Need-Based** 30% **Average Award of Freshman Scholarship Package** $5,067 **Tests Required** SAT1 (preferred) or ACT **Admissions Address** 2800 South University Drive, Fort Worth, TX 76129 **Admissions Telephone** (817) 921-7490

LAST YEAR'S CLASS **Applied** 4,233 **Accepted** 3,100 **Matriculated** 1,330 **Median Range SAT M/V** 500-620/430-550 **In Top Fifth of High School Graduating Class** 45%

COLLEGE LIFE **Gender Breakdown** M 41%, F 59% **Out of State Students** 36% **From Public Schools** 88% **Ethnic Composition** White & Other 87%, Asian American 2%, Black 4%, Hispanic 6%, Native American 1% **Foreign Students** 3% **Reside on Campus** 52% **Return as Sophomores** 80% **Total Faculty** 323 **Student Faculty Ratio** 15:1 **Fraternities (% of men participating)** 12 (28%) **Sororities (% of women participating)** 14 (34%) **Graduate Students** 1,164

Trenton State College

www.trenton.edu

Ewing Township, NJ · Est. 1855 · Coed · Public · 5,965 Undergrads · Big Town

I need...

Admissions info www.trenton.edu/admin.html
Financial aid info www.trenton.edu/admin.html

How wired is Trenton State?

Do I get email? Yes
Do I get a home page? Yes
  Where? www.trenton.edu/~ssivy/webpages
  .html
Is my dorm wired? Yes
How many computers? 12:1

The usual tour

DEPARTMENTS www.trenton.edu/deptacad.html
LIBRARY www.trenton.edu/librscs.html
SPORTS www.trenton.edu/organs.html
STUDENT CLUBS www.trenton.edu/organs.html
GREEK LIFE www.trenton.edu/organs.html
STUDY ABROAD www.trenton.edu/admin.html

Skip the brochure

- **DIGITAL GALLERY** A feast for the enthusiasts of the fine arts, this digital gallery exhibits graphic design, photography and sculpture.
web1.trenton.edu/~artmain/gal/gal.html

- **AYN RAND SOCIETY** The world according to Ayn Rand is governed by reason and the pursuit of individual success. This site contains links to other Rand and Objectivism (Rand's philosophy) sites, and putatively inspirational quotations from *The Fountainhead*. **www.trenton.edu/~aynrand**

No campus is an island, even if it looks like one

- **TRENTON STATE HUMANE SOCIETY** "One unspayed female dog and her descendants can produce 4,372 puppies in just seven generations." Staggering statistics aside, the truth is that only one dog or cat in ten will find a home. Tips on choosing animals from shelters and humane links are available from this site. **159.91.15.227/~tshs**

"A feast for fine arts enthusiasts, this digital gallery exhibits graphic design, photography, and sculpture."

WHAT YOU NEED TO GET IN **Application Deadline** March 1 **Early Action Deadline** November 15 **Common App.** No **Application Fee** $50 **Tuition Costs** $3,432 ($5,994 out-of-state) **Room & Board** $5,800 **Need Blind** Yes **Financial Forms Deadline** Priority given to applications received by April 1 **Undergrads Awarded Aid** 51% **Aid That Is Need-Based** 58% **Average Award of Freshman Scholarship Package** $2,600 **Tests Required** SAT1 (preferred) or ACT **Admissions Address** Hillwood Lakes, CN 4700, Trenton, NJ 08650-4700 **Admissions Telephone** (609) 771-2131

LAST YEAR'S CLASS **Applied** 5,946 **Accepted** 2,683 **Matriculated** 1,088 **Average SAT M/V** 597/589 **In Top Fifth of High School Graduating Class** 82% **Applied Early** 465 **Accepted Early** 120

COLLEGE LIFE **Gender Breakdown** M 40%, F 60% **Out of State Students** 5% **Ethnic Composition** White & Other 83%, Asian American 5%, Black 7%, Hispanic 5% **Reside on Campus** 59% **Return as Sophomores** 92% **Total Faculty** 316 **Student Faculty Ratio** 14:1 **Fraternities (% of men participating)** 14 (19%) **Sororities (% of women participating)** 16 (19%) **Graduate Students** 1,019

Trinity College

www.trincoll.edu

Hartford, CT · Est. 1823 · Coed · Private · 1,985 Undergrads · Urban

I need...

Admissions info admissions.office@trincoll.edu
www.trincoll.edu/pubrel/facts.html
Financial aid info www.trincoll.edu/pubrel/facts
.html

How wired is Trinity?

Do I get email? Yes
Do I get a home page? Yes
   Where? www2.trincoll.edu
Is my dorm wired? Yes
What is the student to computer ratio? 13:1

REQUEST APPLICATION ONLINE

The usual tour

DEPARTMENTS www.trincoll.edu/trinity/acaddept
.html
SPORTS www.trincoll.edu/pubrel/facts.html
PUBLICATIONS /www.trincoll.edu/trinity
/pubevnt.html
CAREER CENTER www.trincoll.edu/career
STUDENT CLUBS www.trincoll.edu/trinity/student
.html

Skip the brochure

- **TRINCOLL JOURNAL** Trinity's *Trincoll Journal*
appears to be able to lay claim to the fact that
it was the Internet's first magazine. It
launched back in 1992, came to the Web in
1993 and has been appearing weekly and
impressively during the school year since.
www.trincoll.edu/tj/trincolljournal.html

There are more than three voices to be heard at Trinity

- **THE OTHER VOICE** Another somewhat edgier and
occasionally bombastic online zine has forged
an identity of its own at Trinity. Dating back to
April 1994, this pesky little sibling to the
Trincoll Journal chugs along irreverently.
www.trincoll.edu/othervoi

- **ANNUAL FIREFIGHTING ROBOT CONTEST** In just three
years, the Firefighting Robot Contest has
evolved into a competition attracting 41
teams, including a handful of Canadian
entrants. Contestants must produce a robot
capable of navigating a mock house, locating a
flame and extinguishing it before it consumes
the entire campus. **shakti.trincoll.edu
/~jhough/fire_robot/comp.html**

WHAT YOU NEED TO GET IN Application Deadline January 15 **Early Action Deadline** November 15 (Option I); February 1
(Option II) **Common App.** Yes **Application Fee** $50 **Tuition Costs** $20,650 **Room & Board** $6,120 **Financial
Forms Deadline** February 1 **Undergrads Awarded Aid** 47% **Aid That Is Need-Based** 100% **Average Award of
Freshman Scholarship Package** $14,440 **Tests Required** SAT1 or ACT **Admissions Address** Summit Street,
Hartford, CT 06016 **Admissions Telephone** (860) 297-2180

LAST YEAR'S CLASS Applied 3,054 **Accepted** 1,751 **Matriculated** 509 **Average SAT M/V** 610/630 **Average ACT** 27
In Top Fifth of High School Graduating Class 72% **Applied Early** 195 **Accepted Early** 109

COLLEGE LIFE Gender Breakdown M 50%, F 50% **Out of State Students** 81% **From Public Schools** 50% **Ethnic
Composition** White & Other 85%, Asian American 5%, Black 6%, Hispanic 4% **Foreign Students** 2% **Reside on
Campus** 92% **Return as Sophomores** 94% **Total Faculty** 248 **Student Faculty Ratio** 10:1 **Fraternities** none
Sororities none **Graduate Students** 156

Trinity University

San Antonio, TX · Est. 1869 · Coed · Private · 2,227 Undergrads · Urban

I need...

Admissions info admissions@trinity.edu
WWW.Trinity.Edu/departments/admissions
Financial aid info WWW.Trinity.Edu/departments
/admissions/faid.html

How wired is Trinity University?

Do I get email? Yes
Do I get a home page? Yes
Where? www.trinity.edu/general
_index.html
What is the student to computer ratio? 4:1

REQUEST APPLICATION ONLINE

The usual tour

LIBRARY www.trinity.edu/departments
/maddux_library/library.html
SPORTS WWW.Trinity.Edu/departments
/athletics/index.html
CAREER CENTER www.trinity.edu/~rboyles
/homepage.html

Skip the brochure

• **TRINITY UNIVERSITY ATHLETICS** The denizens of Trinity University are crazy for their Tiger teams. Whether it be a track and field event, a football or volleyball game, or even a trap and skeet shooting match, the excitement of competition pervades the campus. Adhering to the NCAA Division III philosophy of academic priority, Tiger teams are comprised of a diverse bunch of individuals. www.trinity.edu
/departments/athletics/index.html

Bright lights, big city, as seen from Trinity Hill

• **THE MUSIC DEPARTMENT** Trinity encourages students to participate in its active music department as a music major, a member of an ensemble or chorus, or a scholar of music theory or education. And the encouragement pays off. The Trinity Jazz Band has performed on television and has opened for such artists as Dizzy Gillespie and Billy Taylor. www.trinity.edu/departments/music/index.html

"The Trinity Jazz Band has opened for Dizzy Gillespie."

WHAT YOU NEED TO GET IN **Application Deadline** February 1 **Early Action Deadline** November 15 **Common App.** Yes **Application Fee** $25 **Tuition Costs** $13,500 **Room & Board** $5,545 **Financial Forms Deadline** February 1 **Undergrads Awarded Aid** 78% **Aid That Is Need-Based** 48% **Tests Required** SAT1 (preferred) or ACT **Admissions Address** 715 Stadium Drive, San Antonio, TX 78212-7200 **Admissions Telephone** (210) 736-7207

LAST YEAR'S CLASS **Applied** 2,442 **Accepted** 1,940 **Matriculated** 615 **Average SAT M/V** 639/566 **Average ACT** 28 **In Top Fifth of High School Graduating Class** 81% **Applied Early** 132 **Accepted Early** 109

COLLEGE LIFE **Gender Breakdown** M 49%, F 51% **Out of State Students** 40% **From Public Schools** 76% **Ethnic Composition** White & Other 80.6%, Asian American 8.8%, Black 1.5%, Hispanic 8.6%, Native American 0.5% **Foreign Students** 3% **Reside on Campus** 76% **Return as Sophomores** 85% **Total Faculty** 220 **Student Faculty Ratio** 11:1 **Fraternities (% of men participating)** 5 (30%) **Sororities (% of women participating)** 6 (33%) **Graduate Students** 255

Tufts University

Medford, MA · Est. 1852 · Coed · Private · 4,558 Undergrads · Urban

www.tufts.edu

How wired is Tufts University?

Do I get email? Yes
Do I get a home page? Yes
   Where? www.tufts.edu/people/student.html
Is my dorm wired? Yes
What is the student to computer ratio? 18:1

The usual tour

DEPARTMENTS www.tufts.edu/htmls/schoolcol.html
LIBRARY library.tufts.edu
STUDENT CLUBS www.tufts.edu/people/org.html
GREEK LIFE www.tufts.edu/~jholland/IFC.html

Skip the brochure

- **THE O-ZONE HOME PAGE** This student-run site promises rude language, nasty images, and ugly comments courtesy of "a small group of people living under one roof who have dedicated their lives to fulfilling their own selfish desires." **www.tufts.edu/~nherman/Omain.html**

- **PERSEUS PROJECT** Want to see the Sanctuary of Apollo at Delphi or learn all the Greek words

"Rude language, nasty images, and more..."

How better to illustrate Tufts' "Experimental College" program?

that end in *-sis*? (Now, there's a project for a really rainy day.) You're in luck. This thorough, multimedia library of information about archaic and classical Greece will help you get Hellenic. **www.perseus.tufts.edu**

- **EXPERIMENTAL COLLEGE HOME PAGE** Why settle for the usual degree when you can spice up your academic life with experimental education? **www.tufts.edu/~kriley/index.html**

- **TORN TICKET II** "Beauty And The Beastie Boys" and "A Streetcar Named K.I.T.T." are just two of the musicals you won't see performed by this student-run musical theater group. There's a lot you will see, though (more musical theater jokes, with varying amounts of good taste), both at their site and on their stage. **www.tufts.edu/as/stu-org/tornticket**

WHAT YOU NEED TO GET IN Application Deadline January 1 **Early Action Deadline** November 15 (first round); January 1 (second round) **Common App.** Yes **Application Fee** $50 **Tuition Costs** $21,402 **Room & Board** $6,540 **Financial Forms Deadline** February 1 **Undergrads Awarded Aid** 43% **Aid That Is Need-Based** 100% **Average Award of Freshman Scholarship Package** $14,800 **Tests Required** SAT1 or ACT **Admissions Address** Medford, MA 02155 **Admissions Telephone** (617) 627-3170

LAST YEAR'S CLASS Applied 8,510 **Accepted** 3,649 **Matriculated** 1,158 **Median Range SAT M/V** 610-690/600-690 **In Top Fifth of High School Graduating Class** 86% **Applied Early** 538 **Accepted Early** 319

COLLEGE LIFE Gender Breakdown M 48%, F 52% **Out of State Students** 77% **From Public Schools** 64% **Ethnic Composition** White & Other 77%, Asian American 14%, Black 4%, Hispanic 5% **Foreign Students** 8% **Reside on Campus** 80% **Return as Sophomores** 99% **Student Faculty Ratio** 13:1 **Fraternities (% of men participating)** 10 (14%) **Sororities (% of women participating)** 3 (4%) **Graduate Students** 3,539

Tulane University

New Orleans, LA · Est. 1834 · Coed · Private · 6,327 Undergrads · Urban

www.tulane.edu

I need...

Admissions info undergrad.admission@tulane.edu
www.tulane.edu/Admission.html
Financial aid info erivera@mailhost.tcs.tulane.edu
www.tulane.edu/Admission/FinancingEducation/FinancialAid.html

How wired is Tulane?

Do I get email? Yes
Is my dorm wired? Yes
What is the student to computer ratio? 13:1

REQUEST APPLICATION ONLINE

The usual tour

LIBRARY www.tulane.edu/Libraries.html
STUDENT CLUBS www.tulane.edu/StudentLife.html
SPORTS www.tulane.edu/Athletics/Athletics Home.html
CALENDAR www.tulane.edu/AboutTulane.html
DEPARTMENTS www.tulane.edu/Academics .html#3
CAREER CENTER www.tulane.edu/~csc
STUDENT NEWSPAPER www.Tulane.EDU/~tuhulla

Skip the brochure

- **THE GREEN CLUB** College may very well be your last opportunity to reinvent yourself, so why not have a go at it? The Green Club can turn you into an instant environmental activist, and the truly committed can help organize an Earth Day celebration, or work on a project at

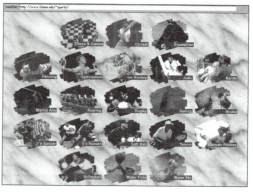

If you can hit it, move it, ride it, strike it, or swim in it, Tulane can help

the Center for Bioenvironmental Research.
www.tulane.edu/~greenclb/green.html

- **TULANE MEN AGAINST RAPE** Tulane Men Against Rape has stepped into relatively uncharted territory with the launch of their sexual assault education organization. **www.tulane.edu/~tmar**

- **TULANE MEDIA BOARD** The Tulane Media Board, comprised of students, is responsible for varied media-related institutions such as the school newspaper, the student television station, and the literary society. Members of the board allocate funds, work directly with representatives from the organizations, and plan future media projects at Tulane. Aspiring Hollywood moguls would do well to join this centralized media powerhouse. **www.tulane.edu/~media**

WHAT YOU NEED TO GET IN Application Deadline January 15 **Common App.** Yes **Application Fee** $35 **Tuition Costs** $19,700 **Room & Board** $6,314 **Need Blind** Yes **Financial Forms Deadline** Priority given to applications received by January 15 **Undergrads Awarded Aid** 53% **Aid That Is Need-Based** 55% **Average Award of Freshman Scholarship Package** $15,864 **Tests Required** SAT1 or ACT **Admissions Address** 6823 St. Charles Avenue, New Orleans, LA 70118 **Admissions Telephone** (504) 865-5731

LAST YEAR'S CLASS Applied 8,707 **Accepted** 6,324 **Matriculated** 1,239 **Average SAT M/V** 632/575 **In Top Fifth of High School Graduating Class** 79%

COLLEGE LIFE Gender Breakdown M 50%, F 50% **Out of State Students** 85% **From Public Schools** 55% **Ethnic Composition** White & Other 79.2%, Asian American 5.1%, Black 10%, Hispanic 5.3%, Native American 0.4% **Foreign Students** 4% **Reside on Campus** 62% **Return as Sophomores** 85% **Total Faculty** 627 **Student Faculty Ratio** 11:1 **Fraternities (% of men participating)** 15 (33%) **Sororities (% of women participating)** 7 (33%) **Graduate Students** 4,831

University of Tulsa

www.utulsa.edu

Tulsa, OK · Est. 1894 · Coed · Private · 3,025 Undergrads · Urban

I need...

Admissions info admission@utulsa.edu
www.utulsa.edu/Admission/AdmandReg.html
Financial aid info www.utulsa.edu/Financial
/Aid.html

How wired is University of Tulsa?

Do I get email? Yes
Do I get a home page? Yes
Is my dorm wired? Yes
What is the student to computer ratio? 6:1

The usual tour

CALENDAR www.utulsa.edu/CalendarofEvents
/JanCal.html
DEPARTMENTS www.utulsa.edu/Academic
Colleges/AcademicColleges.html
STUDENT CLUBS www.utulsa.edu/StudentLife
/CampusOrgs.html
GREEK LIFE www.utulsa.edu/StudentLife
/greeklife.html
LIBRARY www.utulsa.edu/Libraries/TULibraries
.html
SPORTS www.utulsa.edu/Athletics/Gold
Athletics.html

"The oldest private university in the state"

Welcome to The University of Tulsa, Oklahoma's oldest private university. A fully accredited university that offers programs through the doctoral level, TU currently accommodates approximately 4,400 students. At the heart of the institution's mission is the theme of international and intercultural unity.

You are only 28,800 bps away from Tulsa

Skip the brochure

- **KWGS FM89** Public radio has a home at the University of Tulsa's Kendall Hall. As the oldest FM radio station in Oklahoma, it's only appropriate that it should be located at the oldest private university in the state. **www.utulsa.edu/KWGS/Welcome.html**

- **DIALOG** The University of Tulsa's alumni magazine offers a broad perspective on the school's activities, with articles about both past and present students, organizations, administrations and policies. Check the class notes to see what past students are up to now. **www.cba.utulsa.edu/cbalum/diawin95**

- **TULSA OVERVIEW** Tulsa, Okla.: it's not just a city, it's a way of life. Or at least that's what the university would have you believe. Here, Tulsa is described as sophisticated and sunny, a place of great music and fine food. **www.utulsa.edu/CityofTulsa/Tulsa.html**

WHAT YOU NEED TO GET IN **Application Deadline** Rolling admissions; February for priority consideration **Common App.** Yes **Application Fee** $25 (waived if application is presented at campus visit) **Tuition Costs** $12,300 **Room & Board** $4,100 **Need Blind** Yes **Financial Forms Deadline** Priority given to applications received by April 1 **Undergrads Awarded Aid** 71% **Aid That Is Need-Based** 70% **Average Award of Freshman Scholarship Package** $6,358 **Tests Required** SAT1 or ACT **Admissions Address** 600 South College Avenue, Tulsa, OK 74104 **Admissions Telephone** (918) 631-2307

LAST YEAR'S CLASS **Applied** 1,808 **Accepted** 1,476 **Matriculated** 545 **Average SAT M/V** 582/537 **Average ACT** 25 **In Top Fifth of High School Graduating Class** 59%

COLLEGE LIFE **Gender Breakdown** M 46%, F 54% **Out of State Students** 33% **From Public Schools** 85% **Ethnic Composition** White & Other 82%, Asian American 2%, Black 7%, Hispanic 3%, Native American 6% **Foreign Students** 10% **Reside on Campus** 39% **Return as Sophomores** 75% **Total Faculty** 405 **Student Faculty Ratio** 11:1 **Fraternities (% of men participating)** 7 (23%) **Sororities (% of women participating)** 7 (21%) **Graduate Students** 1,361

Union College

Schenectady, NY · Est. 1795 · Coed · Private · 2,120 Undergrads · Suburban

I need...

Admissions info admissions@union.edu
apollo.union.edu/ADM/Admissions.html
Financial aid info apollo.union.edu/ADM
/FinancialAidFastFacts.html

How wired is Union?

Do I get email? Yes
Do I get a home page? Yes
What is the student to computer ratio? 12:1

PARTIAL APPLICATION ONLINE

The usual tour

VIRTUAL TOUR apollo.union.edu/ADM/Walking
TourOfUnion.html
DEPARTMENTS www.union.edu/academics
/Academics.html
STUDENT CLUBS virtual.union.edu/~sg/clubs.html
CAREER CENTER virtual.union.edu/~vu
CALENDAR apollo.union.edu/EVENTS/Events.html
LIBRARY apollo.union.edu/EVENTS/Events.html

Skip the brochure

• **VIRTUAL U** This nicely decorated site is home to a
number of Union's online projects. Some are
just home pages, but others are more sophisticated. There's even corporate-sponsored material—some students are working on a virtual
museum with General Electric. **virtual.union.edu/~vu**

• **CONCORDIENSIS** Reading the student newspaper,
the *Concordiensis*, one is struck by the inordi-
nate number of articles relating to

Welcome To Union College
Schenectady, New York

Union has been in the education game since 1795 and
counts among its graduates President Chester Arthur
fraternities and sororities. Could this school
be Greek-centric? For those looking beyond
chapter houses and pledges, the site also
links to *The New York Times.* **virtual.union.edu
/~concordy/index.html**

• **PHOTO GALLERY** Get a sense of the New
England-like charm of Schenectady from this
site, which even includes a picture of Chester
Alan Arthur (sources say he was a 19th century President of the United States who graduated from Union). **apollo.union.edu/cgi-bin/gallery?IG**

"Union students are working on a virtual museum with General Electric."

WHAT YOU NEED TO GET IN **Application Deadline** February 1 **Early Action Deadline** December 1 (Option I), February 1
(Option II) **Common App.** Yes **Application Fee** $50 **Tuition Costs** $20,805 **Room & Board** $6,330 **Need Blind**
Yes **Financial Forms Deadline** February 1 **Undergrads Awarded Aid** 57% **Aid That Is Need-Based** 99% **Average
Award of Freshman Scholarship Package** $13,000 **Tests Required** ACT **Admissions Address** Schenectady, NY
12308 **Admissions Telephone** (518) 388-6112

LAST YEAR'S CLASS **Applied** 3,550 **Accepted** 1,845 **Matriculated** 515 **Average SAT M/V** 637/533 **Average ACT** 27
In Top Fifth of High School Graduating Class 75% **Applied Early** 208 **Accepted Early** 163

COLLEGE LIFE **Gender Breakdown** M 54%, F 46% **Out of State Students** 50% **From Public Schools** 73% **Ethnic
Composition** White & Other 88%, Asian American 6%, Black 3%, Hispanic 3% **Foreign Students** 2% **Reside on
Campus** 80% **Return as Sophomores** 95% **Total Faculty** 198 **Student Faculty Ratio** 12:1 **Fraternities (% of men
participating)** 14 (37%) **Sororities (% of women participating)** 4 (25%) **Graduate Students** 391

U.S. Air Force Academy

www.usafa.af.mil

USAF Academy, CO · Est. 1954 · Coed · Public · 4,117 Undergrads · Urban

I need...

Admissions info %rr%usafa@sc4199.usafa.af.mil
www.usafa.af.mil/rr/adms.html

How wired is the Academy?

Do I get email? Yes
What is the student to computer ratio? 20:1

REQUEST APPLICATION ONLINE

The usual tour

SPORTS www.usafa.af.mil/ah/ah-home.html
CAREER CENTER www.usafa.af.mil/dfbl/dfblc
/counsel.htm#voc

Skip the brochure

• **LANCE SIJAN AND JOE ROSS** This page is harrowing, giving the separate fates of two United States Air Force Academy alums. Both served in Vietnam, and both died mysterious deaths (in fact, the status of Joe Ross was changed in 1975 from Missing in Action to Killed in

"Visit this page to honor two brave Americans and get an unromanticized version of soldiers' lives."

Location: http://www.usafa.af.mil/usafa-orgs.html

US Air Force Academy Units

Don't try this at home

Action). It is worth visiting this page just to honor these brave Americans and to get an unromanticized version of the lives, and deaths, of soldiers. **www.usafa.af.mil/rr/history /histl.htm**

• **UNITED STATES AIR FORCE CHAPEL** In the armed forces, religion can take on a new resonance: "As modern airmen brush wings with infinity there is an increasing awareness of an ordered universe, a Divine Designer. The limitless vistas of the space age challenge man's spritual resources as well as his technology." Learn how to fly with God as your co-pilot. **www.usafa.af.mil/hc/chapwww.htm**

• **PIKE'S PEAK** Pike's Peak is the gorgeous backdrop to the United States Air Force Academy. Live images of the peak, via video camera, are available here. **www.softronics.com/peak _cam.html**

WHAT YOU NEED TO GET IN **Application Deadline** January 31 **Common App.** No **Application Fee** $0 **Tuition Costs, Room & Board** $0 (all U.S. Academies offer full tuition for accepted students) **Tests Required** SAT1 or ACT **Admissions Address** HQ USAFA/QII, 2304 Cadet Drive, Suite 300, USAF Academy, CO 80840-5025 **Admissions Telephone** (719) 472-2520

LAST YEAR'S CLASS **Applied** 8,538 **Accepted** 1,839 **Matriculated** 1,340 **Average SAT M/V** 661/635 **In Top Fifth of High School Graduating Class** 89%

COLLEGE LIFE **Gender Breakdown** M 85%, F 15% **Out of State Students** 96% **From Public Schools** 70% **Ethnic Composition** White & Other 82%, Asian American 4%, Black 6%, Hispanic 7%, Native American 1% **Foreign Students** 1% **Reside on Campus** 100% **Return as Sophomores** 90% **Student Faculty Ratio** 8:1 **Fraternities** none **Sororities** none

U.S. Coast Guard Academy

www.dot.gov/dotinfo/uscg/hq/uscga/uscga.html

New London, CT · Est. 1876 · Coed · Public · 862 Undergrads · Big Town

I need...

Admissions info uscgatr@dcseq.uscga.edu
www.dot.gov/dotinfo/uscg/hq/uscga
/admit.htm

How wired is the Coast Guard Academy?

Do I get email? Yes
What is the student to computer ratio? 7:1

REQUEST APPLICATION ONLINE

The usual tour

DEPARTMENTS www.dot.gov/dotinfo
/uscg/hq/uscga/academic.htm
SPORTS www.dot.gov/dotinfo/uscg/hq/uscga
/athletic.htm
STUDENT CLUBS www.dot.gov/dotinfo/uscg/hq
/uscga/extra.htm

Skip the brochure

- **FOURTH CLASS SUMMER** No, you won't be doing some cushy internship in the air-conditioned office of a new media company. You will be suffering. "The first summer is the toughest. Emphasis is on intense military indoctrination and physical training. Courses are taken in all phases of military activity and you are tested regularly for physical fitness (it's a good idea to arrive in top-notch shape). There's even a math review for those who need it. The highlight of the summer is a one-week training

Location: http://www.dot.gov/dotinfo/uscg/hq/uscga/academic.htm

The U.S. Coast Guard—sailing the high seas

cruise aboard the academy's beautiful training ship *Eagle*." All in all, this is an experience you simply can't get anywhere else. **www.dot.gov /dotinfo/uscg/hq/uscga/military.htm**

- **COAST GUARD HOME PAGE** On an average day the U.S. Coast Guard will board 90 large vessels for port safety checks; process 120 seaman's documents; seize 209 pounds of marijuana and 170 pounds of cocaine worth $9.2 million; conduct 120 law enforcement boardings; investigate 17 marine accidents; inspect 64 commercial vessels; save 14 lives; assist 328 people in distress; save $2,490,000 in property; service 150 aids to navigation; and interdict 176 illegal migrants. Somehow, they manage to keep busy. **www.dot.gov/dotinfo/uscg /welcome.html**

WHAT YOU NEED TO GET IN **Application Deadline** December 15 **Common App.** No **Application Fee** $0 **Tuition Costs, Room & Board** $0 (all U.S. Academies offer full tuition for accepted students) **Tests Required** SAT1 or ACT **Admissions Address** 15 Mohegan Avenue, New London, CT 06320-4195 **Admissions Telephone** (203) 444-8501

LAST YEAR'S CLASS **Applied** 2,009 **Accepted** 433 **Matriculated** 243 **Average SAT M/V** 639/552 **In Top Quarter of High School Graduating Class** 98%

COLLEGE LIFE **Gender Breakdown** M 76%, F 24% **Out of State Students** 93% **Ethnic Composition** White & Other 81%, Asian American 7%, Black 5%, Hispanic 6%, Native American 1% **Foreign Students** 2% **Reside on Campus** 100% **Return as Sophomores** 85% **Student Faculty Ratio** 10:1 **Fraternities** none **Sororities** none

U.S. Military Academy (West Point)

www.usma.edu

West Point, NY · Est. 1802 · Coed · Public · 3,973 Undergrads · Small Town

I need...

Admissions info 8opa@sunams.usma.army.mil
www.usma.edu/Admissions
Financial aid info yw5879@sunams.usma.army
.mil

How wired is West Point?

Do I get email? Yes
Do I get a home page? No
Is my dorm wired? Yes
What is the student to computer ratio? 7:1

The usual tour

SPORTS www.usma.edu/Athletics
DEPARTMENTS www.dean.usma.edu/dean/docs
/dpts.htm
VIRTUAL TOUR www.usma.edu/USMA_Tour

Skip the brochure

- **DEPARTMENT OF MILITARY INSTRUCTION HOME PAGE**
You might be disappointed to learn that none of the information here is classified. Nevertheless, you can learn about the "transformation process" that cadets undergo, or about the two sub-componenets of the Department of Military Instruction: Military Science and Military Training. **www.dmi.usma.edu**

- **ASSOCIATION OF GRADUATES** Once a cadet, always a cadet. The Association of Graduates keeps

Office of the Dean of the Academic Board

Welcome to the Web page for the U.S. Military Academy Office of the Dean. Though we make every effort to ensure information presented here is complete and correct, this page is not an official publication of the USMA.

The mission of the United States Military Academy is to educate and train the Corps of cadets so that each graduate shall have the attributes essential to professional growth throughout a career as an officer of the Regular Army and to inspire each to a lifetime of service to the nation.

Click on the image for an AVI of the graduation hat toss.

West Point's proud servants keep the patriotic faith

alumni in touch with each other and also with the institution through newsletters, class pages, and activity announcements.
www.aog.usma.edu

"You might be disappointed to learn that none of the information here is classified."

WHAT YOU NEED TO GET IN **Application Deadline** December 1 for priority consideration; final deadline March 21 **Early Action Deadline** October 25 **Common App.** No **Application Fee** $0 **Tuition Costs, Room & Board** $0 (all U.S. Academies offer full tuition for accepted students) **Tests Required** SAT1 or ACT **Admissions Address** West Point, NY 10996 **Admissions Telephone** (914) 938-4041

LAST YEAR'S CLASS **Applied** 12,429 **Accepted** 1,634 **Matriculated** 1,187 **Average SAT M/V** 652/556 **Average ACT** 28 **In Top Fifth of High School Graduating Class** 79% **Applied Early** 1,664 **Accepted Early** 548

COLLEGE LIFE **Gender Breakdown** M 88%, F 12% **Out of State Students** 92% **From Public Schools** 86% **Ethnic Composition** White & Other 83.5%, Asian American 5%, Black 7%, Hispanic 4%, Native American 0.5% **Foreign Students** 1% **Reside on Campus** 100% **Return as Sophomores** 97% **Total Faculty** 529 **Student Faculty Ratio** 12:1 **Fraternities** none **Sororities** none

U.S. Naval Academy

www.nadn.navy.mil

Annapolis, MD · Est. 1845 · Coed · Public · 4,040 Undergrads · Big Town

I need...

Admissions info www.nadn.navy.mil/Admissions
Financial aid info www.nadn.navy.mil/Admissions
/cg-05.html

How wired is the Naval Academy?

Do I get email? Yes
Do I get a home page? No
Is my dorm wired? Yes
What is the student to computer ratio? 9:1

The usual tour

DEPARTMENTS www.nadn.navy.mil/departments
.html
LIBRARY www.nadn.navy.mil/Library
SPORTS www.nadn.navy.mil/AthDept
HISTORY www.nadn.navy.mil/VirtualTour/150
years
STUDENT NEWSPAPER www.dcmilitary.com
/trident.htm
RESEARCH www.nadn.navy.mil/AcResearch

Skip the brochure

• **NAVAL ACADEMY BAND** These guys and gals would
have no problem winning a battle of the
bands. If their musical talents give out, they
can always revert to other skills, like how to
defend themselves in hand-to-hand combat, or
if need be, wield a bassoon in any number of
ways that will strike fear into the opposition.
www.nadn.navy.mil/USNABand

Location: http://www.nadn.navy.mil/or1.html

Service Academies

Critical to Our Future

By Admiral Charles R. Larson, U.S. Navy

The U.S. Navy has weathered many recent storms

• **F-14 TOMCAT** The Navy certainly knows its
recruiting, and while business is primarily
afloat, it gets the testosterone pumping. Here
find encyclopedic coverage of the F-14 Tomcat,
the Navy's standard carrier-based fighter. It's a
toy shop for the *Top Gun* set. **www.nadn.navy.mil
/f-14.html#description**

• **U.S. NAVAL ACADEMY MUSEUM** Learn about the role
the Navy has played in the nation's history
whether at war or in peacetime, on the high
seas or in Tailhook hearings. Its collection and
documentation appear to be excellent and the
museum is free to boot, as is the entire education. **www.nadn.navy.mil/Museum**

"It's a toy shop for the *Top Gun* set."

WHAT YOU NEED TO GET IN **Application Deadline** March 1 **Common App.** No **Application Fee** $0 **Tuition Costs, Room &
Board** $0 (all U.S. Academies offer full tuition for accepted students) **Tests Required** SAT1 (preferred) or ACT
Admissions Address Leahy Hall, Annapolis, MD 21402-5018 **Admissions Telephone** (410) 293-4361

LAST YEAR'S CLASS **Applied** 10,422 **Accepted** 1,474 **Matriculated** 1,165 **Average SAT M/V** 657/562 **In Top Fifth of
High School Graduating Class** 78%

COLLEGE LIFE **Gender Breakdown** M 87%, F 13% **Out of State Students** 96% **From Public Schools** 67% **Ethnic
Composition** White & Other 82%, Asian American 4%, Black 7%, Hispanic 6%, Native American 1% **Foreign
Students** 1% **Reside on Campus** 100% **Return as Sophomores** 86% **Total Faculty** 498 **Student Faculty Ratio**
7:1 **Fraternities** none **Sororities** none

Ursinus College

Collegeville, PA · Est. 1869 · Coed · Private · 1,245 Undergrads · Rural

I need...

Admissions info admissions@ursinus.edu
www.ursinus.edu/admissions-form-test.html
Financial aid info www.ursinus.edu/catalog
/ucmnu1d.html

How wired is Ursinus College?

Do I get email? Yes
Do I get a home page? Yes
What is the student to computer ratio? 8:1

The usual tour

DEPARTMENTS www.ursinus.edu/about/about
.html
LIBRARY www.ursinus.edu/myrin/lib_resources
.html
PUBLICATIONS www.ursinus.edu/ucwwwpub.html
DEPARTMENTS www.ursinus.edu/about/about
.html
STUDENT CLUBS www.ursinus.edu/catalog/uccat2
.html#Organizations
CALENDAR www.ursinus.edu/catalog/uccat12
.html
SPORTS www.ursinus.edu/catalog/uccat2.html
#Athletics

Skip the brochure

- **THE POSTMODERN PROGRAMME** Hypertext—a post-modern form of communication, or what? Then again, as Hans Bertens observes, "Although the omnipresence of the postmodern and its advocates would seem to suggest otherwise,

Only in a place called Collegeville would you find Ursinus

not everybody subscribes to the view that language constitutes, rather than represents, reality." Got that? Welcome to Semiotics Online 101. **acad.ursinus.edu/~rrichter**

- **THE LIBERAL STUDIES PROGRAM** This text essay explains the liberal studies program, which consists of the tripartite Core, Study in Depth, and Explorations stages. This is the heartfelt Ursinus way of explaining a core curriculum, a major, and opportunities for studying abroad. **www.ursinus.edu/catalog/uccat6.html#Liberal**

- **ATHLETICS** Ursinus may not be a Division I champion, but does offer a wide variety of sports: football, basketball, soccer, wrestling, swimming, cross country, golf, baseball, track, tennis, field hockey, softball, lacrosse, gymnastics, and volleyball. Sadly, Utimate Frisbee and Street Luge are not big favorites. **www.ursinus.edu/catalog/uccat2.html#Athletics**

WHAT YOU NEED TO GET IN Application Deadline February 15 **Early Action Deadline** January 15 **Common App.** Yes
Application Fee $30 **Tuition Costs** $15,650 **Room & Board** $5,160 **Need Blind** Yes **Financial Forms Deadline**
Priority given to applications received by February 15 **Undergrads Awarded Aid** 75% **Aid That Is Need-Based** 85%
Average Award of Freshman Scholarship Package $10,100 **Tests Required** SAT1 (preferred) or ACT
Admissions Address Box 1000 Main Street, Collegeville, PA 19426 **Admissions Telephone** (610) 409-3200

LAST YEAR'S CLASS Applied 1,486 **Accepted** 1,206 **Matriculated** 317 **Median Range SAT M/V** 520-640/460-550
In Top Fifth of High School Graduating Class 64% **Applied Early** 62 **Accepted Early** 51

COLLEGE LIFE Gender Breakdown M 48%, F 52% **Out of State Students** 37% **From Public Schools** 76% **Ethnic
Composition** White & Other 90%, Asian American 4%, Black 4%, Hispanic 2% **Foreign Students** 3% **Reside on
Campus** 88% **Return as Sophomores** 93% **Total Faculty** 135 **Student Faculty Ratio** 12:1 **Fraternities (% of men
participating)** 9 (55%) **Sororities (% of women participating)** 5 (50%)

University of Utah

Salt Lake City, UT · Est. 1850 · Coed · Public · 21,756 Undergrads · Urban

I need...

Admissions info cmahone@ssb1.saff.utah.edu
   www.saff.utah.edu/admiss
Financial aid info wclark@ssb2.saff.utah.edu
   www.saff.utah.edu/finance

How wired is the U of U?

Do I get email? Yes
Do I get a home page? Yes
What is the student to computer ratio? 7:1

The usual tour

DEPARTMENTS www.utah.edu/HTML_Docs/UofU
   _List.html
STUDENT CLUBS www.utah.edu/HTML_Docs/UofU
   _List.html#Orgs_and_Clubs
LIBRARY www.lib.utah.edu
CALENDAR www.utah.edu/HTML_Docs/Calendars
   .html
PUBLICATIONS gopher://gopher.cc.utah.edu/11
   /General%20Campus%20Information/Campus
   %20Newsletters

Skip the brochure

• **THE ASSOCIATED STUDENTS OF THE UNIVERSITY OF UTAH** Modeled after the U.S. Government, campus heads are divided into three branches: Executive, Legislative, and Judicial. This may seem like a bureaucratic nightmare to some, but take it from these powermongers—omnipotence is addictive. **www.asuu.utah.edu**

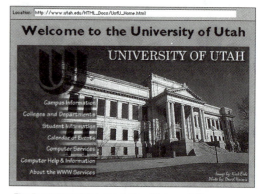

The Rocky Mountains and stellar ski slopes influence U of U students' class schedules

• **OUTDOOR RECREATION PROGRAM** Sure, the Mormon Tabernacle is pretty, but why matriculate in Utah if you don't take advantage of the great outdoors? That's the attitude of the school's Outdoor Recreation Program. Participants have the opportunity to camp in the desert, experience the thrills of river kayaking, and hike through Zion National Park. **gopher://gopher.utah.edu:70/00/General%20Campus %20Information/Outdoor%20Recreation**

• **CRITICAL MASS** Don a cloak, unsheath your dagger, and head for the Magical Forest, where faeries dance and elfin folk cast mysterious spells. Critical Mass began as a science fiction and fantasy reading club, but has developed into a haven for role-play fans and fanatics alike. Escapism, thy name is Elfquest! **www.cc.utah.edu/~jch9478/Mass.html**

WHAT YOU NEED TO GET IN **Application Deadline** February 15 for priority consideration; final deadline July 1 **Common App.** No **Application Fee** $30 **Tuition Costs** $2,508 ($7,707 out-of-state) **Room & Board** $6,318 **Financial Forms Deadline** Priority given to applications received by February 15 **Undergrads Awarded Aid** 55% **Aid That Is Need-Based** 80% **Average Award of Freshman Scholarship Package** $1,241 **Tests Required** SAT1 or ACT (preferred) **Admissions Address** 110 Park, Salt Lake City, UT 84112 **Admissions Telephone** (801) 581-7281

LAST YEAR'S CLASS **Applied** 6,093 **Accepted** 5,418 **Matriculated** 2,728 **Average SAT M/V** 559/501 **Average ACT** 24

COLLEGE LIFE **Gender Breakdown** M 54%, F 46% **Out of State Students** 17% **From Public Schools** 94% **Ethnic Composition** White & Other 92%, Asian American 3%, Black 1%, Hispanic 3%, Native American 1% **Foreign Students** 5% **Reside on Campus** 10% **Return as Sophomores** 62% **Total Faculty** 3,414 **Student Faculty Ratio** 14:1 **Fraternities (% of men participating)** 8 (3%) **Sororities (% of women participating)** 6 (3%) **Graduate Students** 5,054

Vanderbilt University

Nashville, TN · Est. 1873 · Coed · Private · 5,792 Undergrads · Urban

I need...

Admissions info admissions@vanderbilt.edu
www.vanderbilt.edu/Admissions
Financial aid info askfinad@uansv2.vanderbilt.edu
www.vanderbilt.edu/FinancialAid/finhome.htm

How wired is Vanderbilt?

Do I get email? Yes
Do I get a home page? Yes
Is my dorm wired? Yes
What is the student to computer ratio? 14:1

REQUEST APPLICATION ONLINE

The usual tour

SPORTS www.vanderbilt.edu/Athletics
/commodores.html
LIBRARY www.library.vanderbilt.edu
CAREER CENTER www.vanderbilt.edu/career
ARMY ROTC www.vanderbilt.edu/Army
/DEFAULT.HTM
PUBLICATIONS www.vanderbilt.edu/Versus
/Versus.htm
DEBATE CLUB www.vanderbilt.edu/DebateTeam
/deb.htm

Skip the brochure

• **THE ALTERNATIVE BREAK CONNECTION** Students at Vanderbilt party all year, so rather than take a spring break to the Bahamas, some choose to participate in the Alternative Break Program. Students work on a variety of short-term projects for community agencies and learn about issues such as literacy, poverty, racism, and

Come smell the magnolia blossoms on Vanderbilt's campus

homelessness. **www.vanderbilt.edu/breakaway /altbreak.html**

• **CHRYSALIS** "Building community between Vanderbilt's students and Nashville's homeless persons," Chrysalis proves that college students don't have to live in a vacuum, even at a relatively conservative university. Club projects include service at a soup kitchen, community outreach, and the unique Meals on Heels program, wherein club members and homeless individuals join forces to distribute "kits" to people living on the streets. **www.vuse .vanderbilt.edu/~staianac/chryhome.htm**

• **VANDERBILT UNIVERSITY COLLEGE REPUBLICANS** This organization has taken to the Internet like an elephant to the savannah, providing members and interested parties with links to pages on Clinton humor and abortion. **www.vanderbilt .edu/VUCR**

WHAT YOU NEED TO GET IN Application Deadline January 15 for priority consideration **Early Action Deadline** November 1 **Common App.** Yes **Application Fee** $50 **Tuition Costs** $19,920 **Room & Board** $7,088 **Need Blind** Yes **Financial Forms Deadline** Priority given to applications received by February 15 **Undergrads Awarded Aid** 53% **Aid That Is Need-Based** 62% **Average Award of Freshman Scholarship Package** $13,200 **Tests Required** SAT1 (preferred) or ACT **Admissions Address** 2305 West End Avenue, Nashville, TN 37203-1700 **Admissions Telephone** (615) 322-2561

LAST YEAR'S CLASS Applied 8,878 **Accepted** 5,153 **Matriculated** 1,539 **Average SAT M/V** 660/640 **Average ACT** 28 **In Top Fifth of High School Graduating Class** 52% **Applied Early** 323 **Accepted Early** 167

COLLEGE LIFE Gender Breakdown M 54%, F 46% **Out of State Students** 91% **From Public Schools** 59% **Ethnic Composition** White & Other 85%, Asian American 7%, Black 4%, Hispanic 3%, Native American 1% **Foreign Students** 1% **Reside on Campus** 86% **Return as Sophomores** 92% **Total Faculty** 790 **Student Faculty Ratio** 8:1 **Fraternities (% of men participating)** 17 (38%) **Sororities (% of women participating)** 12 (50%) **Graduate Students** 4,282

Vassar College

www.vassar.edu

Poughkeepsie, NY · Est. 1861 · Coed · Private · 2,344 Undergrads · Big Town

How wired is Vassar?

Do I get email? Yes
Do I get a home page? Yes
Is my dorm wired? Yes
What is the student to computer ratio? 18:1

The usual tour

LIBRARY iberia.vassar.edu/vcl/index.html
SPORTS www.vassar.edu/Athletes.html
DEPARTMENTS www.vassar.edu/Departments
.html
HISTORY www.vassar.edu/MatthewInfo.html

Skip the brochure

- **SCOOP** International travel and study is a major area of emphasis at Vassar, reveals *Scoop*. Last year, a group of 44 students traveled to

"Vassar's musical library houses 90 instruments, some dating back to ancient Egypt. "

Mind-blowing ideas flow from the Vassar fountain of knowledge

Vietnam with history professor Robert Brigham. Activities included boat rides and a roundtable discussion with Vietnamese students. Other students won presigious scholarships to continue their studies after graduation at venues at home and abroad. [No water buffalo were slaughtered in the making of this Web site.] **www.vassar.edu/Observatory.html**

- **MUSIC LIBRARY HOMEPAGE** Vassar's music library houses not only the expected collection of books, periodicals, scores, and sound recordings, but also a museum of "musical treasures" which includes 90 musical instruments, some dating back to ancient Egypt. A selection from this collection can be viewed in a virtual tour. **openweb.vassar.edu/library/music /MusLibHomepage.html**

WHAT YOU NEED TO GET IN Application Deadline Fall for priority consideration; final deadline January 1 **Early Action Deadline** December 15 and January 15 **Common App.** Yes **Application Fee** $60 **Tuition Costs** $20,840 **Room & Board** $6,310 **Need Blind** Yes **Financial Forms Deadline** January 1 **Undergrads Awarded Aid** 62% **Aid That Is Need-Based** 100% **Average Award of Freshman Scholarship Package** $15,201 **Tests Required** SAT1 (preferred) or ACT **Admissions Address** Raymond Avenue, Poughkeepsie, NY 12601 **Admissions Telephone** (914) 437-7300

LAST YEAR'S CLASS Applied 3,943 **Accepted** 1,906 **Matriculated** 636 **Average SAT M/V** 657/616 **Average ACT** 29 **In Top Fifth of High School Graduating Class** 80% **Applied Early** 251 **Accepted Early** 155

COLLEGE LIFE Gender Breakdown M 37%, F 63% **Out of State Students** 64% **From Public Schools** 60% **Ethnic Composition** White & Other 80%, Asian American 9%, Black 6%, Hispanic 5% **Foreign Students** 3% **Reside on Campus** 98% **Return as Sophomores** 93% **Student Faculty Ratio** 11:1 **Fraternities** none **Sororities** none **Graduate Students** 2

University of Vermont

Burlington, VT · Est. 1791 · Coed · Public · 7,539 Undergrads · Big Town

I need...

Admissions info admadm@sis-em.uvm.edu
  www.uvm.edu/aboutuvm/Information.html
Financial aid info www.uvm.edu/aboutuvm
  /FinancialAid.html

How wired is UVM?

Do I get email? Yes
Do I get a home page? Yes
Is my dorm wired? Yes
What is the student to computer ratio? 13:1

REQUEST APPLICATION ONLINE

The usual tour

LIBRARY sageunix.uvm.edu
SPORTS www.uvm.edu/~sportspr/sportshome
  .html
STUDENT CLUBS www.uvm.edu/uvmarts.html
GREEK LIFE www.uvm.edu/%7edosa/studact
  /#lead
STUDENT NEWSPAPER moose.uvm.edu/%7ecynic
  /index.html
OFFICE OF RADIATION SAFETY www.uvm.edu
  /~radsafe

Skip the brochure

- **EXPERIMENTAL MUSIC PROGRAM** "Get involved!"
your parents always say, but here's one club
you may not want to tell them about: the
Experimental Music Program, a communal liv-
ing-based nod to the sixties. Cook alongside
your housemate, the tambourine player; shower outside with an orchestra-level oboist; or be

The University of Vermont
Arts, Activities, Athletics, and Events

- The University of Vermont Calendar of Events
- UVMToday: Announcements, Marketplaces, Soapboxes
- The George Bishop Lane Artist Series
- Artsfest 96: Dreamers, Iconoclasts, Mavericks...Artists. months of groundbreaking

UVM Campus Green, January 3, 1996

Sunscreen, swimsuits, and beach towels are optional

lulled to sleep by the dulcet strains of your
neighbor's alternative/noise-based drumming.
www.uvm.edu/~music/emp/index.html#explain

- **THE OUTING CLUB** In Vermont, the weather man-
dates snow skiing, but no one's complaining.
Students afraid to brave the sub-zero tempera-
tures of Killington can scale indoor climbing
walls in climate-controlled bliss. **www.uvm.edu
/~outside**

- **TAE KWON-DO** Martial arts training may not
seem like the New England extracurricular pursuit of choice, but that hasn't stopped UVM
students from learning Tae kwon-do. The truly
dedicated can choose to kick together and live
together—imagine the battles for the TV
remote. **wired.uvm.edu/lnl/programs/groupa/tkd**

WHAT YOU NEED TO GET IN **Application Deadline** February 1 **Early Action Deadline** November 1 **Common App.** No
Application Fee $50 **Tuition Costs** $6,732 ($16,824 out-of-state) **Room & Board** $5,096 **Financial Forms
Deadline** Priority given to applications received by March 1 **Undergrads Awarded Aid** 58% **Aid That Is Need-
Based** 98% **Average Award of Freshman Scholarship Package** $4,027 **Tests Required** SAT1 (preferred) or ACT
Admissions Address 194 South Prospect Street, Burlington, VT 05405-3596 **Admissions Telephone** (802)
656-3370

LAST YEAR'S CLASS **Applied** 7,979 **Accepted** 6,498 **Matriculated** 1,889 **Average SAT M/V** 545/482 **In Top Fifth of
High School Graduating Class** 36% **Applied Early** 228 **Accepted Early** 142

COLLEGE LIFE **Gender Breakdown** M 46%, F 54% **Out of State Students** 57% **Ethnic Composition** White & Other
96%, Asian American 2%, Black 1%, Hispanic 1% **Foreign Students** 1% **Reside on Campus** 45% **Return as
Sophomores** 85% **Total Faculty** 859 **Student Faculty Ratio** 15:1 **Fraternities (% of men participating)** 14 (10%)
Sororities (% of women participating) 6 (8%) **Graduate Students** 1,195

Villanova University

www.vill.edu

Villanova, PA · Est. 1842 · Coed · Private · 7,643 Undergrads · Suburban

I need...

Admissions info gotovu@ucis.vill.edu
www.vill.edu/admin/admissio
Financial aid info www.vill.edu/admin/finaid
/home page.htm

How wired is Villanova?

Do I get email? Yes
Do I get a home page? No
Is my dorm wired? Yes
What is the student to computer ratio? 3:1

The usual tour

STUDENT CLUBS www.vill.edu/studlife/organ
/home page.htm
LIBRARY www.vill.edu/admin/library/index.htm
SPORTS www.vill.edu/admin/sports/home page
.htm
STUDY ABROAD www.vill.edu/admin/intrstud
/home page.htm
GREEK LIFE www.vill.edu/studlife/organ/greek
/home page.htm
CAMPUS MINISTRY www.vill.edu/admin/ministry
/home page.htm

Skip the brochure

- **THE INDIAN STUDENTS' ASSOCIATION** One of the most active student organizations on campus, the Indian Students' association is dedicated to bringing "the multi-faceted, dynamic face of India to Villanova." **www.ece.vill.edu/~senthil /visa**

222 acres of suburban Philadelphia delight

- **THE BLUE KEY SOCIETY** Undergraduates who love Villanova enjoy showing it off to prospective students and their parents. Members of the Blue Key Society act as a welcoming and information resource, giving tours and arranging dorm stays for high school seniors with an interest in the school. **www.vill.edu/studlife /organ/service/home page.htm**

- **VILLANOVA STUDENT SECURITY SERVICES** Because two student bodies are better than one, volunteers accompany lone student pedestrians as they lurch home from late night parties and caffeine-infused study sessions. **www.vill.edu /studlife/organ/service/home page.htm**

"The Blue Key Society gives tours and arranges dorm stays."

WHAT YOU NEED TO GET IN Application Deadline December 1 for priority consideration; final deadline January 15 **Early Action Deadline** December 1 **Common App.** No **Application Fee** $45 **Tuition Costs** $17,500 **Room & Board** $6,300 **Need Blind** Yes **Financial Forms Deadline** Priority given to applications received by March 15 **Undergrads Awarded Aid** 67% **Aid That Is Need-Based** 70% **Average Award of Freshman Scholarship Package** $13,170 **Tests Required** SAT1 (preferred) or ACT **Admissions Address** 800 Lancaster Avenue, Villanova, PA 19085 **Admissions Telephone** (610) 519-4000

LAST YEAR'S CLASS Applied 7,976 **Accepted** 5,864 **Matriculated** 1,669 **Median Range SAT M/V** 593-688/476-575 **In Top Fifth of High School Graduating Class** 57% **Applied Early** 1,716 **Accepted Early** 1,450

COLLEGE LIFE Gender Breakdown M 50%, F 50% **Out of State Students** 70% **From Public Schools** 49% **Ethnic Composition** White & Other 92%, Asian American 3%, Black 2%, Hispanic 2%, Native American 1% **Foreign Students** 1% **Reside on Campus** 62% **Return as Sophomores** 93% **Total Faculty** 726 **Student Faculty Ratio** 13:1 **Fraternities (% of men participating)** 14 (29%) **Sororities (% of women participating)** 8 (48%) **Graduate Students** 2,499

University of Virginia

www.virginia.edu

Charlottesville, VA · Est. 1819 · Coed · Public · 11,949 Undergrads · Big Town

I need...

Admissions info undergrad-admission@virginia.edu
www.virginia.edu/~admiss/ugadmiss/home
.shtml
Financial aid info faid@virginia.edu
minerva.acc.Virginia.EDU/~finaid

How wired is UVA?

Do I get email? Yes
Do I get a home page? Yes
Is my dorm wired? Yes
What is the student to computer ratio? 13:1

DOWNLOAD APPLICATION ONLINE

The usual tour

DEPARTMENTS www.virginia.edu/schools.html
VIRTUAL TOUR minerva.acc.Virginia.EDU
/~urelat/Tours/walking/walking.html
CALENDAR www.virginia.edu/~regist/oregpage
/calendar.html
SPORTS athletic.virginia.edu/uva/uva.ath
LIBRARY www.lib.virginia.edu

Skip the brochure

• **THE LAWN TOUR** On his gravestone, Thomas
Jefferson claimed the University of Virginia as
one of his proudest achievements, along with
authoring the Declaration of Independence and
Virginia's statute on religious freedom, of
course. Here you can embark on an interactive
tour of Jefferson's original academic village.
www.virginia.edu/~finearts/Lawntour/Welcome.html

Location: http://faraday.clas.Virginia.EDU/~en2k/wr1.htm

The University of Virginia's Women's Rugby Club

UVA women take Olivia Newton-John's paean "(Let's Get)
Physical" to heart

• **ACADEMICAL VILLAGE PEOPLE** These kids do a lot
more than just harmonize. You've got to
admire a group that makes Play-Doh mush-
rooms and convinces people to eat them; imi-
tates the touchtone course registration system; and sidelines as a men's a cappella
group. **minerva.acc.Virginia.EDU/~acadvil**

• **DIGITAL MEDIA AND MUSIC CENTER** The digital age
is in full swing at the University of Virginia's
Digital Media and Music Center. Video and
audio are manipulated into multimedia presentations. Visit the gallery to see current works,
including MIDI music files of student composi-
tions and a Web-based library exhibit about
the burning of the rotunda in 1895.
www.lib.Virginia.EDU/dmmc

WHAT YOU NEED TO GET IN Application Deadline December 1 for priority consideration; final deadline January 2 **Early
Action Deadline** November 1 **Common App.** No **Application Fee** $40 **Tuition Costs** $4,620 ($14,406
out-of-state) **Room & Board** $3,962 **Need Blind** Yes **Financial Forms Deadline** Priority given to applications
received by March 1 **Undergrads Awarded Aid** 38% **Aid That Is Need-Based** 95% **Average Award of Freshman
Scholarship Package** $5,950 **Tests Required** SAT1 (preferred) or ACT **Admissions Address** P.O. Box 9017,
Charlottesville, VA 22906 **Admissions Telephone** 804 982-3200

LAST YEAR'S CLASS Applied 15,578 **Accepted** 5,713 **Matriculated** 2,876 **Average SAT M/V** 651/576 **In Top Fifth of
High School Graduating Class** 56% **Applied Early** 1663 **Accepted Early** 731

COLLEGE LIFE Gender Breakdown M 47%, F 53% **Out of State Students** 35% **From Public Schools** 77% **Ethnic
Composition** White & Other 77%, Asian American 10%, Black 11%, Hispanic 2% **Foreign Students** 2% **Reside on
Campus** 48% **Return as Sophomores** 97% **Total Faculty** 1,082 **Student Faculty Ratio** 11:1 **Fraternities (% of
men participating)** 39 (30%) **Sororities (% of women participating)** 22 (30%) **Graduate Students** 6,106

Virginia Military Institute

www.vmi.edu

I need...

Admissions info Admissions@VAX.VMI.edu
www.vmi.edu/~admis/admissns.htm
Financial aid info golden@VMI.edu

How wired is VMI?

Do I get email? Yes
Do I get a home page? No
Is my dorm wired? No
What is the student to computer ratio? 11:1

REQUEST APPLICATION ONLINE

The usual tour

SPORTS www.vmi.edu/~pr/vmi_sports.html
LIBRARY www.vmi.edu/~wwwhtml/library.html
PUBLICATIONS www.vmi.edu/~dean/bulletin.html
CAREER CENTER www.vmi.edu/~jobs/jobs.htm
STUDY ABROAD www.vmi.edu/~chem/fswinfot
.html

Skip the brochure

• **VMI NEWS AND EVENTS** The very latest on the battle raging over the admission of female cadets to the VMI. Read the Supreme Court decision handed down June 26, 1996, and the reactions of the VMI administration. **www.vmi.edu/~pr/vmi_news.html**

• **THE GENERAL EDUCATION PILOT PROGRAM** In an attempt to address the need for a more interdisciplinary curriculum, VMI has sponsored the Integrated Pilot Program, involving students and faculty from all departments. A recent

Young men have been developing strong bonds at VMI for more than 150 years

endeavor of the program, the Mark Twain Project, probed *A Connecticut Yankee in King Arthur's Court* from a historical, technical, and literary perspective. **www.vmi.edu/~gen /program.html**

• **THE VMI ARCHIVES** The old boy network of VMI depends upon a well-documented connection to the past. The archives serve this purpose mightily, containing photographs and manuscripts of cadets dating back to the Civil War. Now, it's possible to search the images and text of the archives online. **www.vmi.edu/~archtml /index.html**

"The latest on female cadets at the VMI."

WHAT YOU NEED TO GET IN **Application Deadline** November 15 for priority consideration; final deadline April 1 **Early Action Deadline** November 15 **Common App.** No **Application Fee** $25 **Tuition Costs** $3,655 ($10,120 out-of-state) **Room & Board** $3,435 **Need Blind** Yes **Financial Forms Deadline** April 1 with a priority given to applications received by March 1 **Undergrads Awarded Aid** 63% **Aid That Is Need-Based** 38% **Average Award of Freshman Scholarship Package** $7,462 **Tests Required** SAT1 or ACT **Admissions Address** Lexington, VA 24450 **Admissions Telephone** (540) 464-7211

LAST YEAR'S CLASS **Applied** 902 **Accepted** 717 **Matriculated** 409 **Average SAT M/V** 536/484 **Average ACT** 22 **In Top Quarter of High School Graduating Class** 40% **Applied Early** 135 **Accepted Early** 117

COLLEGE LIFE **Out of State Students** 36% **From Public Schools** 71% **Ethnic Composition** White & Other 87%, Asian American 3%, Black 7%, Hispanic 2%, Native American 1% **Foreign Students** 3% **Reside on Campus** 100% **Return as Sophomores** 75% **Total Faculty** 115 **Student Faculty Ratio** 12:1 **Fraternities** none

Virginia Polytechnic Institute and State University

www.vt.edu

Blacksburg, VA · Est. 1872 · Coed · Public · 19,496 Undergrads · Big Town

I need...

Admissions info vtadmiss@vt.edu
www.vt.edu/admissions.html
Financial aid info finaid@vtvml.cc.vt.edu
wwwfinaid.es.vt.edu

How wired is Virginia Tech?

Do I get email? Yes
Do I get a home page? Yes
Is my dorm wired? Yes
What is the student to computer ratio? 1:1

FULL APPLICATION ONLINE

The usual tour

LIBRARY www.lib.vt.edu
STUDENT CLUBS www.vt.edu/studorgs.html
SPORTS www.uusa.vt.edu/recsprt/extramur.htm
CAREER CENTER www.career.vt.edu
STUDENT NEWSPAPER www.vt.edu/studmedia.html

Skip the brochure

- **VTTV** You won't find these videos on MTV, or even cable access. VTTV is an entirely student-run broadcasting station, putting Tabitha Soren and Kurt Loder to shame. Star in the campus soap opera, host a talk show, direct an infomercial, win friends, and influence people! Come on—you know you've been dying for a piece of the spotlight! **www.comm.vt.edu/vttv**

Location: http://video.cs.vt.edu:90/~dhoang/vrml/

The Virtual Reality Library of Virginia Tech

(The Newman Library)

The Virtual Reality Library of Virginia Tech is a user-friendly application to assist the user in locating books, newspapers, periodicals, and other various resources of Newman Library. In addition, the software provides the user virtual tours of the library and connections to MARIAN and Virginia Tech Library System (VTLS); a search system for library catalog data.

Virginia Tech goes virtual

- **SILHOUETTE** The student literary magazine proves that one side of the brain doesn't always have to battle the other. In between lab experiments, multi-faceted students can fly away on the magical wings of poesy. **athena.english.vt.edu/silhouette/index.html**

- **WOMEN'S CENTER** Funded by the Provost's Office, the Women's Center addresses the sexual harassment, recruitment, and equality issues. The Women's Center welcomes student and faculty volunteers, and recently celebrated its 75th anniversary. **www.vt.edu:I0021/women/WomensCenter.html**

WHAT YOU NEED TO GET IN **Application Deadline** December 1 for priority consideration; final deadline February 1 **Early Action Deadline** November 1 **Common App.** Yes **Application Fee** $20 ($10 before December 1) **Tuition Costs** $3,500 ($10,152 out-of-state) **Room & Board** $3250 **Need Blind** Yes **Financial Forms Deadline** Priority given to applications received by March 1 **Undergrads Awarded Aid** 69% **Aid That Is Need-Based** 47% **Average Award of Freshman Scholarship Package** $3,578 **Tests Required** SAT1 (preferred) or ACT **Admissions Address** Blacksburg, VA 24061-0202 **Admissions Telephone** (540) 231-6267

LAST YEAR'S CLASS **Applied** 14,779 **Accepted** 11,662 **Matriculated** 4,708 **Median Range SAT M/V** 510-640/440-540 **In Top Fifth of High School Graduating Class** 60% **Applied Early** 1,300 **Accepted Early** 800

COLLEGE LIFE **Gender Breakdown** M 59%, F 41% **Out of State Students** 26% **Ethnic Composition** White & Other 86%, Asian American 7%, Black 5%, Hispanic 2% **Foreign Students** 1% **Reside on Campus** 43% **Return as Sophomores** 87% **Total Faculty** 1,915 **Student Faculty Ratio** 17:1 **Fraternities (% of men participating)** 33 (13%) **Sororities (% of women participating)** 16 (17%) **Graduate Students** 3,861

Wabash College

www.wabash.edu

Crawfordsville, IN · Est. 1832 · Men · Private · 803 Undergrads · Small Town

How wired is Wabash?

Do I get email? Yes
Do I get a home page? Yes
Is my dorm wired? Yes
What is the student to computer ratio? 8:1

The usual tour

VIRTUAL TOUR www.wabash.edu/admis/campus
DEPARTMENTS www.wabash.edu/scholar.sys
/wwww/pages/depart/dospage.html
CALENDAR www.wabash.edu/scholar.sys
/wwww/info/wcevents.htm
LIBRARY telnet://maple.palni.edu
VIEWBOOK www.wabash.edu/admis/viewbook
.htm
ALUMNI www.wabash.edu/pages/alumni

Skip the brochure

• **ALUMNI BULLETIN BOARD** Alumni notes aren't about checking up on your friends and classmates; they're a family affair. Wabash graduates can report in here and bring all up to date. A class of '93 grad wrote: "Hello everyone! I'm happy to report that my wife of 2½ years is expecting a baby in the summer of '96. This is Sam's second but my first. Our daughter, Jackie, 5, is happy to be a 'big sis

Location: http://www.wabash.edu/admis/lab1.jpg

A Wabash professor introduces a student to the concept of "round"

ter' but [not] really too clear on the concept yet." [Names have been changed to protect the expectant.] **www.wabash.edu/pages/alumni/bulletin.html**

• **GENDER ISSUES COMMITTEE HOME PAGE** What used to be the Women's Studies Coordinating Committee is now the Gender Issues Committee, a group that encompasses two subcommittees: Gender Studies and the Status of Women. Did you follow all that? If so, skip right down and browse through descriptions of past committee programs, including a forum on the men's movement and a discussion of court cases involving paternity. If not, you may want to read the committee's mission statement over and over again. **www.wabash.edu/Gender/home.htm**

WHAT YOU NEED TO GET IN **Application Deadline** December 1 for priority consideration; final deadline March 1 **Common App.** Yes **Application Fee** $27.50 **Tuition Costs** $14,525 **Room & Board** $4,150 **Need Blind** Yes **Financial Forms Deadline** Priority given to applications received by February 15 **Undergrads Awarded Aid** 93% **Aid That Is Need-Based** 62% **Average Award of Freshman Scholarship Package** $10,780 **Tests Required** SAT1 (preferred) or ACT **Admissions Address** P.O. Box 352, Crawfordsville, IN 47933-0352 **Admissions Telephone** (317) 361-6225

LAST YEAR'S CLASS **Applied** 779 **Accepted** 611 **Matriculated** 227 **Median Range SAT M/V** 550-650/540-640 **In Top Fifth of High School Graduating Class** 56%

COLLEGE LIFE **Out of State Students** 26% **From Public Schools** 92% **Ethnic Composition** White & Other 88%, Asian American 4%, Black 4%, Hispanic 3%, Native American 1% **Foreign Students** 5% **Reside on Campus** 94% **Return as Sophomores** 84% **Total Faculty** 76 **Student Faculty Ratio** 10:1 **Fraternities (% of men participating)** 10 (75%)

Wake Forest University

Winston-Salem, NC · Est. 1834 · Coed · Private · 3,853 Undergrads · Urban

www.wfu.edu

I need...

Admissions info wakeinfo@wfu.edu
www.wfu.edu/campus-vis

How wired is Wake Forest?

Do I get email? Yes
Do I get a home page? Yes
   Where? www.wfu.edu/users
Is my dorm wired? Yes
What is the student to computer ratio? 24:1

DOWNLOAD APPLICATION ONLINE

The usual tour

VIRTUAL TOUR www.wfu.edu/campus-vis/maps.html
STUDENT NEWSPAPER www.ogb.wfu.edu
CALENDAR www.wfu.edu/Information-Desk/Wake
   -Forest-events-calendar
SPORTS www.wfu.edu/Sports
LIBRARY www.wfu.edu/Library
STUDENT CLUBS www.wfu.edu/Student
   -organizations
DEPARTMENTS www.wfu.edu/Academic
   -departments

Skip the brochure

• **WFU KARATE CLUB** Students unleash their aggression with reverse crescent kicks, tornado kicks, and back punches. In doing so, they manage to earn themselves a rainbow of belt colors. **www.wfu.edu/~forsyth/karate.htm**

• **WAKE RADIO** Wake up, Winston-Salem, it's Wake Forest's one and only alternative radio station.

Wake Forest's Winston-Salem campus: building by numbers

You'll find a concert calendar for the area and *The Wavelength*, WAKE Radio's newsletter "devoted to music and the 'alternative' lifestyle." **www.wfu.edu/Student-organizations/WAKE-Radio**

• **WAKE FOREST WOMEN'S GOLF** Look out for those Demon Deacon divots! The women's golf team hits it long and hard in national and international tournaments, while individual players earn distinction through their performances in the NCAA Championship. **www.wfu.edu/Sports/wg/WFAWGOPEN.HTML**

• **WAKE FOREST UNIVERSITY STORES** It's never too early to sport a WFU shirt, boxer shorts, umbrella, or hat. **www.wfu.edu/Administrative-offices/University-Stores.**

WHAT YOU NEED TO GET IN **Application Deadline** January 15 **Early Action Deadline** November 15 **Common App.** Yes **Application Fee** $25 **Tuition Costs** $18,500 **Room & Board** $5,200 **Need Blind** Yes **Financial Forms Deadline** Priority given to applications received by May 15 **Undergrads Awarded Aid** 66% **Aid That Is Need-Based** 42% **Average Award of Freshman Scholarship Package** $8,339 **Tests Required** SAT1 **Admissions Address** Box 7305 Reynolda Station, Winston-Salem, NC 27109 **Admissions Telephone** (910) 759-5201

LAST YEAR'S CLASS **Applied** 6,342 **Accepted** 2,710 **Matriculated** 966 **Median Range SAT M/V** 630-700/500-600 **In Top Fifth of High School Graduating Class** 71%

COLLEGE LIFE **Gender Breakdown** M 50%, F 50% **Out of State Students** 74% **From Public Schools** 77% **Ethnic Composition** White & Other 89.7%, Asian American 2%, Black 7.3%, Hispanic 1% **Foreign Students** 2% **Reside on Campus** 81% **Return as Sophomores** 93% **Total Faculty** 327 **Student Faculty Ratio** 13:1 **Fraternities (% of men participating)** 15 (42%) **Sororities (% of women participating)** 10 (51%) **Graduate Students** 1,955

University of Washington
www.washington.edu

Seattle, WA · Est. 1861 · Coed · Public · 24,838 Undergrads · Urban

I need...

Admissions info askuwadm@u.washington.edu
www.washington.edu/home/admissions
.html

How wired is UW?

Do I get email? Yes
Do I get a home page? Yes
Is my dorm wired? Yes
What is the student to computer ratio? 21:1

REQUEST APPLICATION ONLINE

The usual tour

VIRTUAL TOUR www.washington.edu/home/tour
CALENDAR www.washington.edu/home/uwin
/services/calendar/TableOfContents0.html
LIBRARY www.lib.washington.edu
DEPARTMENTS www.washington.edu/home
/departments/departments.html
UW BULLETIN GENERAL CATALOG www.washington
.edu/home/catalog/catalogTOC.html
SPORTS www.washington.edu/home/catalog
/university/intercolleg_ath.html

Skip the brochure

• **UNIVERSITY OF WASHINGTON: A PICTORIAL HISTORY**
When the Union was on the brink of a civil war,
some enterprising people in the new territory
of Washington energetically embarked on a
mission to build a university. The cornerstone
was laid on May 20, 1861 and six months
later classes began with about 30 students.
www.washington.edu/home/historical

Location: http://www.washington.edu/home/imagemaps/ctourmap.map?242,2

But it doesn't look grungy: Seattle's U of Washington

• **UNIVERSITY OF WASHINGTON HOMEPAGE** See what
life on campus really looks like with a near-live
camera shot and description as you enter the
UW site. When we visited, the temperature
was 64 degrees, winds were at 3 knots from
the west with gusts to 8 knots, the moon was
waning gibbous, and eight students were
exchanging meaningful conversation in the
courtyard. **www.washington.edu**

• **NEW STUDENT ORIENTATION** Find out what you're
getting yourself into. When can you move into
the residence halls? When can you take your
placement test? Where is the HUB, McMahon,
Haggett, and Schmitz? Options for orientation
include overnight, two-day, community service,
and outdoor versions. **weber.u.washington.edu
/~newstdnt/nsohome.html**

WHAT YOU NEED TO GET IN Application Deadline February 1 for priority consideration **Common App.** No **Application Fee**
$35 **Tuition Costs** $2,875 ($8,599 out-of-state) **Room & Board** $5,118 **Need Blind** Yes **Financial Forms
Deadline** Priority given to applications received by February 28 **Undergrads Awarded Aid** 43% **Aid That Is
Need-Based** 76% **Average Award of Freshman Scholarship Package** $3,962 **Tests Required** SAT1 or ACT
Admissions Address 1400 N.E. Campus Parkway, Seattle, WA 98195 **Admissions Telephone** (206) 543-9686

LAST YEAR'S CLASS Applied 12,527 **Accepted** 8,107 **Matriculated** 3,701 **In Top Tenth of High School Graduating
Class** 40%

COLLEGE LIFE Gender Breakdown M 50%, F 50% **Out of State Students** 15% **Ethnic Composition** White & Other
72%, Asian American 20%, Black 3%, Hispanic 4%, Native American 1% **Foreign Students** 2% **Reside on
Campus** 15% **Return as Sophomores** 91% **Student Faculty Ratio** 11:1 **Fraternities (% of men participating)** 30
(16%) **Sororities (% of women participating)** 18 (16%) **Graduate Students** 9,158

Washington and Lee University

www.wlu.edu

Lexington, VA · Est. 1749 · Coed · Private · 1,620 Undergrads · Small Town

How wired is Washington and Lee?

Do I get email? Yes
Do I get a home page? Yes
Is my dorm wired? Yes
What is the student to computer ratio? 8:1

REQUEST APPLICATION ONLINE

The usual tour

DEPARTMENTS www.wlu.edu/~hblackme/sum95
/acadepts3.html
LIBRARY www.wlu.edu/~hblackme/sum95
/lib1.html
CALENDAR www.wlu.edu/~hblackme/sum95
/calsched.html
CAREER CENTER www.wlu.edu/~career/home.html
STUDENT CLUBS www.wlu.edu/~hblackme/sum95
/stud.html

Skip the brochure

- **THE TRIDENT** This glamorously designed digital student newspaper has, among other features, a nice interactive "Opinions" slot in which readers get to vote on issues of the day. **www.wlu.edu/~trident**

- **W & L FILM SOCIETY** An active, if not necessarily

Location: http://liberty.uc.wlu.edu/~trident/

THE TRIDENT
MAY 29, 1996

Senior arrested
Second arrest of a W&L senior this month for a felony drug possession raises concern in the Dean of Students office.

Panhel plans KD's arrival
They know KD's coming, now they just need to plan.

by RACHAEL BARLOW

Washington & Lee's *Trident* takes its news, views, and grievances to the Web

inspired, society which at the time of this writing was looking for help planning a film festival with a presidential theme. **liberty.uc.wlu.edu/~dgrefe/filmsoc/filmsoc.html**

- **W & L DANCE** Since there isn't much dancing going on at Washington and Lee, this page does what it can to compensate. It's more successful as a page of links to other dance sites. **www.wlu.edu/~dance**

- **G&L** The school's Gay, Lesbian and Bisexual Group gets kudos for having big pictures of American President number one and the Good General on their page. There's advice for students who aren't sure they are ready to come out, as well as general info about G&L. Gay collegians of all stripes will love the picture of a Southern Georgian building with rainbow columns. **www.wlu.edu/~aechrist/gnl.html**

WHAT YOU NEED TO GET IN **Application Deadline** January 15 **Early Action Deadline** December 1 **Common App.** Yes **Application Fee** $40 **Tuition Costs** $15,280 **Room & Board** $4,610 **Need Blind** Yes **Financial Forms Deadline** January 19 **Undergrads Awarded Aid** 52% **Aid That Is Need-Based** 75% **Average Award of Freshman Scholarship Package** $10,540 **Tests Required** SAT1 or ACT **Admissions Address** Lexington, VA 24450 **Admissions Telephone** (540) 463-8710

LAST YEAR'S CLASS **Applied** 3,446 **Accepted** 1,074 **Matriculated** 435 **Median Range SAT M/V** 630-710/570-660 **In Top Fifth of High School Graduating Class** 91% **Applied Early** 374 **Accepted Early** 170

COLLEGE LIFE **Gender Breakdown** M 59%, F 41% **Out of State Students** 88% **From Public Schools** 67% **Ethnic Composition** White & Other 95%, Asian American 1%, Black 3%, Hispanic 1% **Foreign Students** 2% **Reside on Campus** 61% **Return as Sophomores** 92% **Total Faculty** 141 **Student Faculty Ratio** 11:1 **Fraternities (% of men participating)** 15 (80%) **Sororities (% of women participating)** 4 (65%) **Graduate Students** 375

Washington State University

www.wsu.edu

Pullman, WA · Est. 1890 · Coed · Public · 16,237 Undergrads · Small Town

I need...

Admissions info admiss@wsu.edu
www.wsu.edu/Enrolling.html
Financial aid info www.wsu.edu/FINAID/fafbase
.htm

How wired is WSU?

Do I get email? Yes
Do I get a home page? Yes
Is my dorm wired? Yes
What is the student to computer ratio? 3:1

The usual tour

DEPARTMENTS www.wsu.edu:8080/~libarts/dept
.html
LIBRARY www.wsulibs.wsu.edu
STUDENT CLUBS www.wsu.edu:8080/~stu_aff/stu
_orgs.html
SPORTS www.eecs.wsu.edu/sports
CALENDAR 134.121.31.99/spr_cal.txt
PUBLICATIONS www.wsu.edu/Directory
Publications.html
CAREER CENTER www.wsu.edu/carserv/cs-home2
.html

"Virtual WSU attests to the school's commitment to the online medium."

Ask Butch

Butch, the school mascot, relaxes between extensive Q&A with prospectives

Skip the brochure

- **VIRTUAL WSU** WSU offers an impressive array of resources on its Web site. Virtual WSU attests to the school's commitment to the entire medium and points to its continued and substantial involvement. **www.wsu.edu:8001/vwsu/vwsu.html**

- **ASK BUTCH** Butch, the school mascot, strikes a sexy cougar pose, awaiting email queries from prospective students. **www.wsu.edu/NIS/Ask Butch.html**

- **WSU CREAMERY** Washington State's Creamery has helped the school become a leader in agricultural research and education. For example, the Creamery has advanced methods of cheese packing by leaps and bounds. Read about the cheesy things that have come to pass or even order some dairy products of your own. **www.wsu.edu:8080/~creamery**

WHAT YOU NEED TO GET IN **Application Deadline** May 1 for priority consideration; final deadline August 1 **Common App.** No **Application Fee** $35 **Tuition Costs** $3,142 ($9,758 out-of-state) **Room & Board** $4,900 **Financial Forms Deadline** Priority given to applications received by March 1 **Undergrads Awarded Aid** 62% **Aid That Is Need-Based** 57% **Average Award of Freshman Scholarship Package** $3,936 **Tests Required** SAT1 or ACT **Admissions Address** 342 French Administration Building, Pullman, WA 99164-1036 **Admissions Telephone** (509) 335-5586

LAST YEAR'S CLASS **Applied** 7,308 **Accepted** 6,337 **Matriculated** 2,530 **Median Range SAT M/V** 420-570/370-490 **In Top Fifth of High School Graduating Class** 63%

COLLEGE LIFE **Gender Breakdown** M 52%, F 48% **Out of State Students** 13% **Ethnic Composition** White & Other 88%, Asian American 5%, Black 2%, Hispanic 3%, Native American 2% **Foreign Students** 6% **Reside on Campus** 42% **Return as Sophomores** 82% **Total Faculty** 950 **Student Faculty Ratio** 17:1 **Fraternities (% of men participating)** 26 (17%) **Sororities (% of women participating)** 14 (16%) **Graduate Students** 3,334

Washington University

www.wustl.edu

St. Louis, MO · Est. 1853 · Coed · Private · 5,964 Undergrads · Urban

I need...

Admissions info admission@wustl.edu
admission.wustl.edu/admission
Financial aid info cf6000.wustl.edu/~admis/app
/wuadfa2.html

How wired is Wash. U?

Do I get email? Yes
Do I get a home page? Yes
What is the student to computer ratio? 6:1

FULL APPLICATION ONLINE

Meet me in St. Louis, Louis: Brookings Hall, the former administrative center for the World's Fair

The usual tour

VIRTUAL TOUR library.wustl.edu/~spec/archives
/tour
SPORTS rescomp.wustl.edu/Athletics
CALENDAR cf6000.wustl.edu/calendar/events
/v1.1
LIBRARY library.wustl.edu
DEPARTMENTS www.wustl.edu/wu_schools
CAREER CENTER www.wustl.edu/careers

Skip the brochure

• **FILMBOARD THIS WEEK** What's playing at
Washington U? Everything from *Babe* to *Bye,
Bye Birdie*, *Leaving Las Vegas* to *Raising
Arizona*, *Twelve Monkeys* to *The Muppet Movie*.
At Filmboard, students run the show and admission is $3 for the first flick, and $2 for every
subsequent screening. nimue.wustl.edu/~film

• **BEARINGS** What the freshman bear really needs
to know, from school policies and procedures

to more crucial information like the coolest
clubs in St. Louis and the best (and cheapest)
Chinese take-out in the area. **rescomp.wustl.edu
/~su/bearings**

• **THE 1996 PRESIDENTIAL DEBATE AT WASHINGTON
UNIVERSITY** Get all the dirt on the first face-off
between Bob and Bill in September at
Washington University's Athletic Complex Field
House. **library.wustl.edu/~spec/archives/debate96**

"Get the dirt on the first face-off between Bob and Bill in September at Washington University."

WHAT YOU NEED TO GET IN **Application Deadline** January 15 **Early Action Deadline** January 1 **Common App.** No
Application Fee $50 **Tuition Costs** $20,000 **Room & Board** $6,210 **Need Blind** No **Financial Forms Deadline**
February 15 **Undergrads Awarded Aid** 51% **Aid That Is Need-Based** 88% **Average Award of Freshman
Scholarship Package** $12,600 **Tests Required** SAT1 or ACT **Admissions Address** One Brookings Drive, Box
1089, St. Louis, MO 63130 **Admissions Telephone** (314) 935-6000

LAST YEAR'S CLASS **Applied** 9,380 **Accepted** 5,262 **Matriculated** 1,184 **Median Range SAT M/V** 610-710/500-620
In Top Fifth of High School Graduating Class 88% **Applied Early** 417 **Accepted Early** 236

COLLEGE LIFE **Gender Breakdown** M 51%, F 49% **Out of State Students** 86% **From Public Schools** 65% **Ethnic
Composition** White & Other 78.5%, Asian American 14%, Black 5%, Hispanic 2%, Native American 0.5% **Foreign
Students** 5% **Reside on Campus** 60% **Return as Sophomores** 93% **Total Faculty** 992 **Student Faculty Ratio** 6:1
Fraternities (% of men participating) 11 (25%) **Sororities (% of women participating)** 6 (25%) **Graduate
Students** 5,518

Wellesley College

www.wellesley.edu

Wellesley, MA · Est. 1870 · Women · Private · 2,253 Undergrads · Big Town

I need...

Admissions info www.wellesley.edu/PublicAffairs
/VirtualGuide/admission.html

How wired is Wellesley?

Do I get email? Yes
Do I get a home page? Yes
Is my dorm wired? Yes
What is the student to computer ratio? 15:1

The usual tour

VIRTUAL TOUR www.wellesley.edu/PublicAffairs
/VirtualGuide/tour.html
DEPARTMENTS www.wellesley.edu/Academic
/academic.html
LIBRARY www.wellesley.edu/Library/library-menu
.html
STUDY ABROAD www.wellesley.edu/StAbroad
/contents.html
CALENDAR www.wellesley.edu/Registrar/calendar
_outline.html

Skip the brochure

• **WELLESLEY IN AIX-EN-PROVENCE** *Le pouvoir du croissants!* Aix, pronounced "eeks," has been home to Wellesley women abroad for more than 20 years. Aix-en-Provence is a gorgeous French town, famous for its Gallo-Roman ruins and Romanesque churches. The university has an excellent reputation, particularly in literature, history and linguistics. **www.wellesley .edu/Aix/wellesley-in-aix.html**

Wellesley counts among its many prominent alumnae a certain Hillary Rodham Clinton

• **VIRTUAL MEMORY MUSEUM** Exhibits from the Davis Museum don't die and go to art heaven—they go here. Rodin, Matisse, and Klimt participate in the exhibit "Modern Hieroglyphs." There are also two very cool photo exhibits. **www.wellesley.edu/DavisMuseum/www virtual.html**

• **STONE CENTER** Eating disorders, gender/sexual identity, and self-esteem are just some of the issues addressed in counseling sessions at the Stone Center, which is committed to the psychological well-being of Wellesley students. **www.wellesley.edu/Counseling/stone_home.html**

• **PRESERVATION** Entertainment and edification converge with these cartoons illustrating "The Daunting Dangers To Our Library Books." The message seems to be, do unto your library books as you would have others do unto you. **www.wellesley.edu/Library/Preserv/cartoonl.html**

WHAT YOU NEED TO GET IN **Application Deadline** January 1 for priority consideration; final deadline January 15 **Early Action Deadline** November 1 **Common App.** Yes **Application Fee** $50 **Tuition Costs** $20,174 **Room & Board** $6,416 **Need Blind** Yes **Financial Forms Deadline** February 1 **Undergrads Awarded Aid** 55% **Aid That Is Need-Based** 100% **Average Award of Freshman Scholarship Package** $15,000 **Tests Required** SAT1 or ACT **Admissions Address** Wellesley, MA 02181 **Admissions Telephone** (617) 283-2270

LAST YEAR'S CLASS **Applied** 3,411 **Accepted** 1,344 **Matriculated** 585 **Average SAT M/V** 651/618 **In Top Fifth of High School Graduating Class** 97% **Applied Early** 176 **Accepted Early** 90

COLLEGE LIFE **Out of State Students** 85% **From Public Schools** 64% **Ethnic Composition** White & Other 62.2%, Asian American 24.6%, Black 6.5%, Hispanic 5.7%, Native American 1% **Foreign Students** 9% **Reside on Campus** 98% **Return as Sophomores** 97% **Total Faculty** 314 **Student Faculty Ratio** 10:1 **Sororities** none

Wesleyan University

Middletown, CT · Est. 1831 · Coed · Private · 2,733 Undergrads · Big Town

Admissions info www-admiss@wesleyan.edu
www.admiss.wesleyan.edu
Financial aid info www-admiss@wesleyan.edu
www.admiss.wesleyan.edu/finaid.html

How wired is Wesleyan?

Do I get email? Yes
Do I get a home page? Yes
   Where? www.con.wesleyan.edu
Is my dorm wired? Yes
What is the student to computer ratio? 9:1

The usual tour

DEPARTMENTS www.wesleyan.edu/home
/departments.html
CALENDAR www.wesleyan.edu/events/home.html
STUDENT CLUBS www.con.wesleyan.edu/stud
group.html
CAREER CENTER www.alumni.wesleyan.edu/CPC
.html

Skip the brochure

- **DAVID TUDOR'S COOKBOOK** If you're hungry and tired of text pages, this is for you. It's not clear what David Tudor's connection to Wesleyan University is, but it doesn't matter. His handwritten cookbook makes a really cool electronic facsimile. lo-cal.music.wesleyan.edu :8000/cookbook.html

- **E3** stands for three big E's: Earth, Equality and

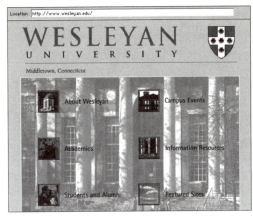

Wesleyan's strong tradition carries on

Education. One of the distinguishing aims of this group is its emphasis on fighting environmental racism, i.e. the way that the poor are often subject to environmental hazards that richer populations aren't. This group has good intentions and fascinating projects. **www.con .wesleyan.edu/groups/e3/home page.htm**

- **THE MERKIN** They say it best: "Expect in the future a virtual Webcarnival of Merkin articles, pictures, links, and downloadable abstraxia to brighten your day and possibly dampen your pants. We want you to leave here thinking, 'Hey, I thought: conservatives are squares, but I guess believing in liberty, nationalism, and free markets and being hip are not mutually exclusive after all.'" **www.con.wesleyan.edu /~cbays/Merkin.html**

WHAT YOU NEED TO GET IN **Application Deadline** January 1 for priority consideration **Early Action Deadline** November 15 **Common App.** Yes **Application Fee** $55 **Tuition Costs** $20,130 **Room & Board** $5,810 **Need Blind** Yes **Financial Forms Deadline** February 1 **Undergrads Awarded Aid** 49% **Aid That Is Need-Based** 100% **Average Award of Freshman Scholarship Package** $13,993 **Tests Required** SAT1 or ACT **Admissions Address** Middletown, CT 06459 **Admissions Telephone** (203) 685-3000

LAST YEAR'S CLASS **Applied** 5,482 **Accepted** 1,955 **Matriculated** 727 **Average SAT M/V** 660/600 **Average ACT** 29 **In Top Fifth of High School Graduating Class** 85% **Applied Early** 518 **Accepted Early** 261

COLLEGE LIFE **Gender Breakdown** M 47%, F 53% **Out of State Students** 92% **From Public Schools** 59% **Ethnic Composition** White & Other 72.9%, Asian American 11%, Black 9%, Hispanic 7%, Native American 0.1% **Foreign Students** 4% **Reside on Campus** 95% **Return as Sophomores** 93% **Total Faculty** 329 **Student Faculty Ratio** 11:1 **Fraternities (% of men participating)** 9 (10%) **Sororities (% of women participating)** 4 (2%) **Graduate Students** 537

Whitman College

Walla Walla, WA · Est. 1859 · Coed · Private · 1,370 Undergrads · Small Town

I need...

Admissions info admission@whitman.edu
www.whitman.edu/info.html
Financial aid info fox@whitman.edu
www.whitman.edu/Departments/Admission
/FinAid/aid1.html

How wired is Whitman?

Do I get email? Yes
Do I get a home page? Yes
   Where? www.whitman.edu/Students/students
   .html
Is my dorm wired? Yes
What is the student to computer ratio? 14:1

The usual tour

VIRTUAL TOUR www.whitman.edu/tour/tourlist.html
STUDENT CLUBS www.whitman.edu/org.html
DEPARTMENTS www.whitman.edu/Departments
   /Admission/majlist.html
SPORTS www.whitman.edu/Departments/News
   /Sports/athletics.html

Skip the brochure

- **INTERNATIONAL CLUB** One of the coolest
resources a school can have is its student
body. And if students hail from the four cor-
ners of the world, even better. Whitman has an
especially global and Web-friendly bunch of
students. The group not only tries to promote
intercultural exchange, but also aims to

at Whitman College.

Whitman at Walla Walla: The city they liked so much they named it twice

help international students adapt to life in
Walla Walla. **www.whitman.edu/~mitkovm/isfc.html**

- **WALLA WALLA, WASHINGTON** What does "Walla
Walla" mean? It's a Native American name
meaning "many waters" or "small, rapid,
streams." Many diverse tribes, including the
Nez Perce, Cayuse, Yakama, and Umatilla, and
even the Walla Walla, roamed this beautiful
region of the Pacific Northwest. Now a thriving
small community, and home of Whitman
College, Walla Walla has more than 300 days
of sunshine per year, local vineyards, and fantastic outdoor beauty and recreation possibilities. **www.bmi.net/wwchamb**

"Whitman: an especially global and Web-friendly bunch of students"

WHAT YOU NEED TO GET IN Application Deadline February 1 **Early Action Deadline** November 15 or January 1 **Common App.** Yes **Application Fee** $45 **Tuition Costs** $18,650 **Room & Board** $5,420 **Need Blind** Yes **Financial Forms Deadline** February 15 **Undergrads Awarded Aid** 87% **Aid That Is Need-Based** 69% **Average Award of Freshman Scholarship Package** $8,052 **Tests Required** SAT1 (preferred) or ACT **Admissions Address** 345 Boyer Avenue, Walla Walla, WA 99362 **Admissions Telephone** (509) 527-5176

LAST YEAR'S CLASS Applied 1,993 **Accepted** 1,030 **Matriculated** 373 **Average SAT M/V** 650/640 **Average ACT** 28 **In Top Fifth of High School Graduating Class** 79% **Applied Early** 126 **Accepted Early** 120

COLLEGE LIFE Gender Breakdown M 49%, F 51% **Out of State Students** 60% **From Public Schools** 70% **Ethnic Composition** White & Other 89%, Asian American 7%, Black 1%, Hispanic 2%, Native American 1% **Foreign Students** 2% **Reside on Campus** 77% **Return as Sophomores** 86% **Total Faculty** 177 **Student Faculty Ratio** 11:1 **Fraternities (% of men participating)** 4 (15%) **Sororities (% of women participating)** 5 (19%)

Whittier College

www.whittier.edu

Whittier, CA · Est. 1887 · Coed · Private · 1,330 Undergrads · Urban

How wired is Whittier?

Do I get email? Yes
Do I get a home page? Yes
Where? www.whittier.edu/www
/student_org.html
Is my dorm wired? Yes
What is the student to computer ratio? 9:1

The usual tour

DEPARTMENTS www.whittier.edu/www/catalog
/fac_life.html
LIBRARY www.whittier.edu/www/html/libmedia
.html
STUDENT CLUBS www.whittier.edu/www/student
_org.html
CAREER CENTER www.whittier.edu/www/student
_serv.html#cs

Skip the brochure

- **LANCER SOCIETY HOMEPAGE** It's not clear what the glue of the Lancer bond is, but it is blindingly clear that Lancers like to throw Mona Kai parties and that they want their parties to be celebrated by the poobahs of hedonism: "In 1969, *Playboy* rated Mona Kai the fourth best college party in the United States. Subsequent years

The first day of a legendary Mona Kai party

saw *Playboy* discontinue college rating scales. It is assumed by many, including the Lancers, if the ratings scale still existed, Mona Kai would still be up near the top!" **www.whittier.edu/lancers /welcome.html**

- **THE FAIRCHILD AERIAL PHOTOGRAPHY COLLECTION** From the top, looking down. Whittier College hosts one of the three largest aerial photography collections in the United States. Most of the photos were taken in the '50s and are of the American West. **keck.whittier.edu/Fairchild.html**

- **THE QUAKER CAMPUS ONLINE** This cyber-rag gives the lowdown on campus, profiling students, reporting the latest campus drama. Unsurprisingly, the archive includes an article on the huge Mona Kai bacchanal, sponsored by the omnifestive Lancer society. **www.whittier .edu/qc/index.html**

WHAT YOU NEED TO GET IN **Application Deadline** Rolling admissions; February 15 for priority consideration **Early Action Deadline** December 5 **Common App.** Yes **Application Fee** $35 **Tuition Costs** $17,800 **Room & Board** $6,047 **Need Blind** Yes **Financial Forms Deadline** Priority given to applications received by February 15 **Undergrads Awarded Aid** 81% **Aid That Is Need-Based** 88% **Average Award of Freshman Scholarship Package** $10,767 **Tests Required** SAT1 or ACT **Admissions Address** 13406 East Philadelphia Street, Whittier, CA 90608 **Admissions Telephone** (310) 907-4238

LAST YEAR'S CLASS **Applied** 1,896 **Accepted** 1,254 **Matriculated** 336 **Average SAT M/V** 493/450 **Average ACT** 22 **In Top Fifth of High School Graduating Class** 38% **Applied Early** 38 **Accepted Early** 37

COLLEGE LIFE **Gender Breakdown** M 45%, F 55% **Out of State Students** 30% **From Public Schools** 68% **Ethnic Composition** White & Other 55%, Asian American 10%, Black 5%, Hispanic 29%, Native American 1% **Foreign Students** 3% **Reside on Campus** 62% **Return as Sophomores** 72% **Total Faculty** 88 **Student Faculty Ratio** 14:1 **Fraternities (% of men participating)** 4 (17%) **Sororities (% of women participating)** 5 (24%) **Graduate Students** 836

Widener University

Chester, PA · Est. 1821 · Coed · Private · 2,364 Undergrads · Urban

I need...

Admissions info www.widener.edu/widener3.2
.html

Financial aid info www.widener.edu/widener3.2a
.html

How wired is Widener?

Do I get a home page? No
Is my dorm wired? No
What is the student to computer ratio? 10:1

The usual tour

DEPARTMENTS www.widener.edu/widener4.1.html
STUDENT CLUBS www.widener.edu/widener5.4
.html
SPORTS www.widener.edu/widener5.3.html
PUBLICATIONS www.widener.edu/widener5.4.html
#anchor1104430

Skip the brochure

- **FLASH** This is a somewhat strange site, as it
appears to be a collection of unlinked articles.
In fact, it's a quasi-showcase of the Widener
faculty. A psychology professor is featured in a
piece about eating disorders, and an economics instructor contributes a piece on the
Telecommunications Bill. **www.widener.edu
/widener6.4.html**

- **TIP SHEET** Somebody give the Widener publicist
a pat on the back. The only substantial sites
on the school's page publicize the Widener

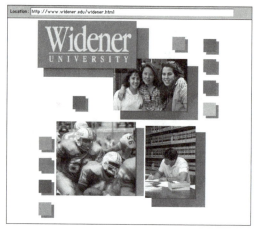

Widener students at work and at play

faculty. This site is full of story ideas and contact numbers for arranging interviews. A great
place to get some helpful scoop before applying. **www.widener.edu/widener6.2.html**

"A great place to get some helpful scoop before applying."

WHAT YOU NEED TO GET IN **Application Deadline** April 1 **Common App.** Yes **Application Fee** $25 **Tuition Costs** $13,560
Room & Board $5,910 **Need Blind** Yes **Financial Forms Deadline** Priority given to applications received by
March 1 **Undergrads Awarded Aid** 78% **Aid That Is Need-Based** 71% **Average Award of Freshman Scholarship
Package** $5,778 **Tests Required** SAT1 (preferred) or ACT **Admissions Address** One University Place, Chester, PA
19013 **Admissions Telephone** (610) 499-4126

LAST YEAR'S CLASS **Applied** 2,030 **Accepted** 1,170 **Matriculated** 492 **Average SAT M/V** 492/471 **In Top Fifth of
High School Graduating Class** 32%

COLLEGE LIFE **Gender Breakdown** M 53%, F 47% **Out of State Students** 48% **From Public Schools** 52% **Ethnic
Composition** White & Other 82.7%, Asian American 3.4%, Black 11.2%, Hispanic 2.2%, Native American 0.5%
Foreign Students 5% **Reside on Campus** 60% **Return as Sophomores** 77% **Total Faculty** 202 **Student Faculty
Ratio** 12:1 **Fraternities (% of men participating)** 8 (28%) **Sororities (% of women participating)** 4 (18%)
Graduate Students 2,230

College of William and Mary

www.wm.edu

Williamsburg, VA · Est. 1693 · Coed · Public · 5,480 Undergrads · Small Town

I need...

Admissions info ccharr@facstaff.wm.edu
www.wm.edu/admission.html
Financial aid info Dadeib@facstaff.wm.edu
warthog.cc.wm.edu/OSFA

How wired is William and Mary ?

Do I get email? Yes
Do I get a home page? No
Is my dorm wired? Yes
What is the student to computer ratio? 16:1

The usual tour

VIRTUAL TOUR www.ctown.com/colleges/wima
/wima.htm
DEPARTMENTS www.ctown.com/colleges/wima
/wima.htm
CALENDAR warthog.cc.wm.edu/CAL/academic
STUDENT CLUBS warthog.cc.wm.edu/SO
CAREER CENTER www.wm.edu/csrv/career
/career.html

Skip the brochure

• **JUMP! MAGAZINE** This online magazine has lots
of spirit and the articles seem well written and
suited to college students. One article playfully
recounts a summer internship at CNN's fashion program *Style with Elsa Klensch*. "So from
gallery openings to the Fashion Cafe, we ate
and drank for free and oh so fabulously...."
Another tells of having a mental disorder in

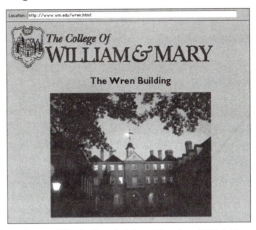

William and Mary's Wren Building, dating from 1694, is the
oldest academic structure in use in America

college, "Following a tumultuous first semester
of my freshman year, I was diagnosed with
unipolar disorder, a condition more commonly
known as depression. I found every single day
to be a taxing ordeal, since virtually every
aspect of my life was marred by a struggle for
sanity." warthog.cc.wm
.edu/SO/JUMP

• **WCWM** "The Giant Sucking Sound From the
South." They shouldn't be so self-deprecating.
This college radio station, like some of its
cousins, is responsible for giving airplay to the
music that commercial radio won't. Check out
the charts, and see how alterna-literate you
are. warthog.cc.wm.edu/SO/WCWM/wcwmstickers.html

WHAT YOU NEED TO GET IN Application Deadline January 15 **Early Action Deadline** November 1 **Common App.** No
Application Fee $40 **Tuition Costs** $2,890 ($12,900 out-of-state) **Room & Board** $4,470 **Financial Forms
Deadline** Priority given to applications received by February 15 **Undergrads Awarded Aid** 53% **Aid That Is
Need-Based** 91% **Average Award of Freshman Scholarship Package** $3,300 **Tests Required** SAT1 or ACT
Admissions Address Williamsburg, VA 23187-8795 **Admissions Telephone** (804) 221-4223

LAST YEAR'S CLASS Applied 6,802 **Accepted** 3,333 **Matriculated** 1,373 **Average SAT M/V** 639/656 **Average ACT**
29 **In Top Fifth of High School Graduating Class** 90% **Applied Early** 621 **Accepted Early** 401

COLLEGE LIFE Gender Breakdown M 42%, F 58% **Out of State Students** 33% **From Public Schools** 82% **Ethnic
Composition** White & Other 85%, Asian American 7%, Black 6%, Hispanic 2% **Foreign Students** 2% **Reside on
Campus** 75% **Return as Sophomores** 92% **Total Faculty** 537 **Student Faculty Ratio** 13:1 **Fraternities (% of men
participating)** 16 (44%) **Sororities (% of women participating)** 12 (42%) **Graduate Students** 2,229

William Jewell College

www.jewell.edu

Liberty, MO · Est. 1849 · Coed · Private · 1,250 Undergrads · Urban

I need...

Admissions info admission@william.jewell.edu
www.jewell.edu/admission
Financial aid info admission@william.jewell.edu
www.jewell.edu/admission/fnaid.html

How wired is William Jewell?

Do I get email? Yes
Do I get a home page? Yes
Is my dorm wired? Yes
What is the student to computer ratio? 11:1

REQUEST APPLICATION ONLINE

The usual tour

DEPARTMENTS www.jewell.edu/admission/majors
.html
STUDENT CLUBS www.jewell.edu/admission
/camorg.html
SPORTS www.jewell.edu/sports
LIBRARY www.jewell.edu/Curr
CALENDAR www.jewell.edu/pr/cal.htm

Skip the brochure

• **COLLEGE COMMUNITY FOR CULTURAL UNITY** Every
'90s college student will be exposed to diversity issues. William Jewell's site offers an index
of links to multicultural sites on the Web. Great
resources such as Diverse World and the
National MultiCultural Institute are at your fin-
gertips. www.jewell.edu/students/organizations/cccu

• **CHRISTIAN STUDENT MINISTRIES** Besides being the
umbrella group for all religious affiliations on

The World Campus

William Jewell College is an independent, undergraduate liberal arts college situated in the Kansas City suburban town of Liberty, Missouri. Founded in 1849, the College has a long-established reputation for excellence and for its overseas studies programs with Oxford, Cambridge and other university centers. At Jewell, our approach to education is *world class*.

ABOUT JEWELL | BREAKING NEWS | ALUMNI CONNECTION | CALENDAR OF EVENTS | STUDENT CATALOG | OFFICE OF ADMISSION

About Jewell | Breaking News | Alumni Connection | Calendar | Student Catalog | Admission | Gallery

They can call it anything they want, but it's still in Liberty, Mo.

campus, the CSM also places "shepherds"
(students) in the dorms to provide spiritual
and personal counseling to any student who
desires it. CSM also sponsors Thrill On the
Hill, a fun and exciting event during orientation
week in which students play games and
dance around. In general, "It's a BLAST."
www.jewell.edu/students/organizations/csm

• **KWJC** Howard Stern definitely does not get airplay here. KWJC Radio is the non-commercial
station sponsored by the University.
Programming consists of contemporary
Christian music, classical music, sports,
news, and public affairs shows. **kwjc.jewell.edu**

"Howard Stern definitely does not get airplay at KWJC Radio."

WHAT YOU NEED TO GET IN Application Deadline March 15 **Common App.** Yes **Application Fee** $25 **Tuition Costs**
$11,130 **Room & Board** $3,270 **Need Blind** Yes **Financial Forms Deadline** Priority given to applications
received by March 1 **Undergrads Awarded Aid** 96% **Aid That Is Need-Based** 47% **Average Award of Freshman
Scholarship Package** $5,631 **Tests Required** SAT1 or ACT **Admissions Address** 500 College Hill, Liberty, MO
64068 **Admissions Telephone** (800) 753-7009

LAST YEAR'S CLASS Applied 708 **Accepted** 598 **Matriculated** 279 **Average SAT M/V** 580/600 **Average ACT** 24
In Top Fifth of High School Graduating Class 54%

COLLEGE LIFE Gender Breakdown M 40%, F 60% **Out of State Students** 27% **From Public Schools** 97% **Ethnic
Composition** White & Other 95%, Asian American 1%, Black 2%, Hispanic 1%, Native American 1% **Foreign
Students** 2% **Return as Sophomores** 88% **Total Faculty** 155 **Student Faculty Ratio** 13:1 **Fraternities (% of men
participating)** 4 (40%) **Sororities (% of women participating)** 4 (50%)

Williams College

www.williams.edu

Williamstown, MA · Est. 1793 · Coed · Private · 1,982 Undergrads · Small Town

I need...

Admissions info admissions@williams.edu
www.williams.edu:803/Admissions
/admissions_index.html
Financial aid info www.williams.edu:803
/Admissions/finaid_script.html

How wired is Williams?

Do I get email? Yes
Do I get a home page? Yes
Where? wso.williams.edu/students
Is my dorm wired? Yes
What is the student to computer ratio? 13:1

The usual tour

SPORTS www.williams.edu:803/OPI/.test/sports
info.html
DEPARTMENTS www.williams.edu/depts.html
STUDENT CLUBS wso.williams.edu/orgs
LIBRARY www.williams.edu:803/library/library
.www/wcl.html
CALENDAR gopher://otis.cc.williams.edu:708
/11/calendars
CAREER CENTER www_occ.williams.edu

Skip the brochure

• **WILLIAMS STUDENTS ONLINE** If colleges could
dance they'd be following the lead of Williams.
WSO is the best college site we've seen, with
hip design and links to everything you'd ever
need to know. It has forums, mailing lists,

Web-wise Williams is at the head of the class

campus bulletin boards, online magazines, a
chat group, and more. **wso.williams.edu**

• **PROSPECTIVE STUDENTS CORRESPONDENCE PROJECT**
A great idea for Purple Cow wannabes, this is
the place to come for questions on the
Williams experience. Current students have vol-
unteered their time and email addresses
and are yours for the grilling. **www.williams.edu
:803/Admissions/firstyear/firstyear.html**

• **WILLIAMS HEALTH CENTER** No question about this
one; the health center's site is in a class of its
own. While decidedly less aesthetically appealing than WSO, its resources and candor on the
real issues facing students are impressive.
wso.williams.edu/peerh

"Current students are yours for the grilling."

WHAT YOU NEED TO GET IN **Application Deadline** January 1 **Early Action Deadline** November 15 **Common App.** Yes
Application Fee $50 (may be waived) **Tuition Costs** $20,639 **Room & Board** $5,990 **Need Blind** Yes **Financial
Forms Deadline** Priority given to applications received by February 1 **Undergrads Awarded Aid** 50% **Aid That Is
Need-Based** 100% **Average Award of Freshman Scholarship Package** $15,500 **Tests Required** SAT1 or ACT
Admissions Address Williamstown, MA 01267 **Admissions Telephone** (413) 597-2211

LAST YEAR'S CLASS **Applied** 4,996 **Accepted** 1,300 **Matriculated** 525 **Median Range SAT M/V** 660-740/600-710
In Top Fifth of High School Graduating Class 95% **Applied Early** 416 **Accepted Early** 189

COLLEGE LIFE **Gender Breakdown** M 51%, F 49% **Out of State Students** 87% **From Public Schools** 57% **Ethnic
Composition** White & Other 76%, Asian American 11%, Black 6%, Hispanic 7% **Foreign Students** 3% **Reside on
Campus** 96% **Return as Sophomores** 96% **Total Faculty** 237 **Student Faculty Ratio** 11:1 **Fraternities** none
Sororities none **Graduate Students** 52

University of Wisconsin, Madison

www.wisc.edu

Madison, WI · Est. 1848 · Coed · Public · 26,207 Undergrads · Urban

The UW-Madison Campus-Wide Information System

How wired is UW, Madison?

Do I get email? Yes
Do I get a home page? No
Is my dorm wired? Yes
What is the student to computer ratio? 9:1

The usual tour

DEPARTMENTS www.wisc.edu/wiscinfo/prostudy
.html
CALENDAR gopher://gopher.adp.wisc.edu:70
/11/.browse/.METACACCA
STUDENT CLUBS www.stdorg.wisc.edu/soo.html
LIBRARY www.library.wisc.edu
SPORTS gopher://gopher.adp.wisc.edu:3000
/7?athletics

Skip the brochure

- **UNIVERSITY OF WISCONSIN MADISON BALLROOM DANCE ASSOCIATION** Besides the online dance program generator, there's a lot to see here: links, information pages on the club, sched-

UW, Madison's Web site is intellectually stimulating, visually drab. Sounds like some dates we've had ules, and a music database. A whirlwind of info, it's enough to send a person spinning. Maybe that's the point. **phenom.physics.wisc.edu/~fosdal/UWMBDA**

- **MADISON BY NIGHT** "Do you want to live forever?" Decide before coming to this page, which isn't about cryonics or infrared goggles, but about role-playing games. **www.cs.wisc.edu/~desmet/mbn**

- **INTERNATIONAL SOCIALIST ORGANIZATION** While some college students are content just to drink beer and study in the ivory tower, these student activists "believe that most of the problems in the world today are directly caused or perpetuated by the capitalist mode of production, including: racism, sexism, environmental destruction, war, hunger, poverty, homelessness, and homophobia." Abhor capitalism with them. **physservl.physics.wisc.edu/~dwright/iso**

WHAT YOU NEED TO GET IN **Application Deadline** February 1 **Common App.** No **Application Fee** $28 **Tuition Costs** $2,730 ($9,050 out-of-state) **Room & Board** $4,520 **Need Blind** Yes **Financial Forms Deadline** Priority given to applications received by March 1 **Undergrads Awarded Aid** 41% **Aid That Is Need-Based** 90% **Average Award of Freshman Scholarship Package** $2,900 **Tests Required** SAT1 or ACT **Admissions Address** 750 University Avenue, Madison, WI 53706 **Admissions Telephone** (608) 262-3961

LAST YEAR'S CLASS **Applied** 16,403 **Accepted** 11,719 **Matriculated** 5,164 **Average SAT M/V** 630/610 **Average ACT** 27 **In Top Fifth of High School Graduating Class** 80%

COLLEGE LIFE **Gender Breakdown** M 49%, F 51% **Out of State Students** 36% **From Public Schools** 67% **Ethnic Composition** White & Other 90%, Asian American 4%, Black 3%, Hispanic 3% **Foreign Students** 5% **Reside on Campus** 40% **Return as Sophomores** 97% **Student Faculty Ratio** 12:1 **Fraternities (% of men participating)** 34 (14%) **Sororities (% of women participating)** 17 (14%) **Graduate Students** 11,932

University of Wisconsin, Milwaukee

www.uwm.edu

Milwaukee, WI · Est. 1885 · Coed · Public · 17,667 Undergrads · Urban

I need...

Admissions info www.des.uwm.edu/des/admiss
/index.html-ssi
Financial aid info www.des.uwm.edu/viewbook
/OPT10-3.HTM

How wired is UW, Milwaukee?

Do I get email? Yes
Do I get a home page? Yes
Is my dorm wired? Yes
What is the student to computer ratio? 25:1

The usual tour

DEPARTMENTS id.csd.uwm.edu/UWM/Depart
ments/Dept.html
SPORTS www.uwm.edu/Dept/Athletics
CAREER CENTER www.uwm.edu/Dept/CDC
LIBRARY www.uwm.edu/Dept/Library
PUBLICATIONS www.uwm.edu/Dept/News
_Publications

Skip the brochure

• **CENTER FOR GREAT LAKE STUDIES** "Water is important." This center focuses on the bodies of
water local to the Milwaukee area and is filled
to the brim with H_2O truisms. **www.uwm.edu/Dept
/CGLS**

• **CENTER FOR 20TH CENTURY STUDIES** Although this
site might seem a little pedantic and preten-

UW, Milwaukee: set back from the shores of Lake Michigan

tious, it has its redeeming qualities. Devoted
to studying new fields like mass culture, experimental arts and film, multiculturalism, and
gay and lesbian theory, this funky center
attracts lots of academic superstars from
around the globe for conferences like "Public/
Private Matters" and "Materializing Culture."
www.uwm.edu/Dept/20th

• **MCC** The Midwestern Collegiate Conference is
a consortium of schools in Division I of the
NCAA. This page serves the nine participating
schools, and is a good site for those who follow college baseball, basketball, golf, tennis,
and softball. **www.indy.net/~whancock/mcchome.html**

"This funky center attracts academic superstars."

WHAT YOU NEED TO GET IN **Application Deadline** Rolling admissions; June 30 for priority consideration **Common App.**
No **Application Fee** $28 **Tuition Costs** $2,966 ($9,402 out-of-state) **Room & Board** $3,565 **Need Blind** Yes
Financial Forms Deadline Priority given to applications received by March 1 **Undergrads Awarded Aid** 47%
Aid That Is Need-Based 90% **Average Award of Freshman Scholarship Package** $2,816 **Tests Required** SAT1
or ACT (preferred) **Admissions Address** P.O. Box 749, Milwaukee, WI 53201-0749 **Admissions Telephone** (414)
229-3800

LAST YEAR'S CLASS **Applied** 4,741 **Accepted** 3,608 **Matriculated** 1,988 **Average ACT** 22 **In Top Fifth of High School
Graduating Class** 21%

COLLEGE LIFE **Gender Breakdown** M 46%, F 54% **Out of State Students** 4% **Ethnic Composition** White & Other 84%,
Asian American 2%, Black 9%, Hispanic 4%, Native American 1% **Foreign Students** 2% **Reside on Campus** 8%
Return as Sophomores 68% **Student Faculty Ratio** 18:1 **Fraternities** 8 **Sororities** 4 **Graduate Students** 4,675

Wittenberg University

Springfield, OH · Est. 1845 · Coed · Private · 2,075 Undergrads · Big Town

I need...

Admissions info admission@wittenberg.edu
www.wittenberg.edu/admit
Financial aid info www.wittenberg.edu/admit
/finaid

How wired is Wittenberg?

Do I get email? Yes
What is the student to computer ratio? 10:1

FULL APPLICATION ONLINE

The usual tour

DEPARTMENTS www.wittenberg.edu/academics
LIBRARY www.wittenberg.edu/lib
VIRTUAL TOUR www.wittenberg.edu/admit/tour
/index.shtml
STUDENT CLUBS www.wittenberg.edu/witt/wuss

Skip the brochure

- **WITTENBERG UNIVERSITY SPELEOLOGICAL SOCIETY**
Though it is the only student club online, the Speleological Society makes up for the dearth of cyber-literates at Wittenberg by being extra-cool. These students are into caves—and they're literally into them, with trips scheduled regularly. Their page introduces speleology and explains what these folks look for when they crawl into dark and narrow spaces.
www.wittenberg.edu/witt/wuss

- **SPRINGFIELD, OHIO** Could this Springfield be the Springfield of *The Simpsons*? There seem to

Wittenberg's dramatists in *Waiting for Godot*. For all we know, they're still waiting

be some parallels: suburban size, one big company. D'oh! **www.wittenberg.edu/area /springfield.shtml**

- **DEPARTMENT OF THEATRE AND DANCE** The Theatre and Dance page highlights the faculty of the program as well as the respectable production calendar for the current academic year, which features major works by well-known dramatists and choreographers. The gallery offers a chance to see Wittenberg students in action, with photos from past performances.
www.wittenberg.edu/academics/thdn/index.shtml

- **SPORTS SHORTS** No, it's not a list of vertically-challenged Wittenberg athletes. Instead, it's a quick way to stay abreast of the current sports scene. **www.wittenberg.edu/news/athletics/spshorts .shtml**

WHAT YOU NEED TO GET IN **Application Deadline** January 15 for priority consideration; final deadline March 15 **Early Action Deadline** December 15 **Common App.** Yes **Application Fee** $40 **Tuition Costs** $17,360 **Room & Board** $4,718 **Need Blind** Yes **Financial Forms Deadline** Priority given to applications received by March 15 **Undergrads Awarded Aid** 70% **Aid That Is Need-Based** 85% **Average Award of Freshman Scholarship Package** $10,500 **Tests Required** SAT1 or ACT **Admissions Address** P.O. Box 720, Springfield, OH 45501 **Admissions Telephone** (800) 677-7558

LAST YEAR'S CLASS **Applied** 2,344 **Accepted** 2,013 **Matriculated** 626 **Average SAT M/V** 590/600 **Average ACT** 25 **In Top Fifth of High School Graduating Class** 62% **Applied Early** 45 **Accepted Early** 40

COLLEGE LIFE **Gender Breakdown** M 47%, F 53% **Out of State Students** 44% **From Public Schools** 80% **Ethnic Composition** White & Other 89%, Asian American 3%, Black 7%, Hispanic 1% **Foreign Students** 5% **Reside on Campus** 98% **Return as Sophomores** 84% **Student Faculty Ratio** 14:1 **Fraternities (% of men participating)** 5 (20%) **Sororities (% of women participating)** 6 (40%)

Wofford College

Spartanburg, SC · Est. 1854 · Coed · Private · 1,115 Undergrads · Suburban

www.wofford.edu

How wired is Wofford?

Do I get email? Yes
Do I get a home page? Yes
Is my dorm wired? No
What is the student to computer ratio? 14:1

The usual tour

DEPARTMENTS www.wofford.edu/www
/departments/departments.htm
CALENDAR www.wofford.edu/www/registrar
/calendars.htm
SPORTS www.wofford.edu/www/athletics.htm
LIBRARY gopher://truth.wofford.edu:70
/11gopher_root%3A%5Blibrary%5D
STUDY ABROAD gopher://truth.wofford.edu:70
/00gopher_root%3A%5Bdepts.other_prog
rams_and_opportunities%5Dforeign_study.txt

"'In 1864—trustees invest the endowment in Confederate currency.' Smart move?"

A Wofford student: "Old Main is part of us, and we are part of it"

Skip the brochure

- **WOFFORD HISTORY** "In 1864—trustees invest virtually all of the college's endowment in Confederate currency, bonds, and other soon-to-be-worthless securities." Smart move? The official College History gopher offers up some interesting moments from Wofford's past. **gopher://gopher.wofford.edu:70/00gopher_root%3A% 5Binfo.history%5Dchronology.**

- **WOFFORD OVERVIEW** According to this essay, "Wofford is a classical campus with beautiful, historic buildings surrounded by magnolias, dogwoods, azaleas, and towering oak trees. Its center is the majestic Main Building, erected between 1851 and 1854." Unfortunately, all you'll see is a single photo. **www.wofford.edu /www/overview.html**

WHAT YOU NEED TO GET IN Application Deadline December 1 for priority consideration; final deadline February 1 **Common App.** Yes **Application Fee** $25 **Tuition Costs** $14,370 **Room & Board** $4,185 **Need Blind** Yes **Financial Forms Deadline** Priority given to applications received by March 15 **Undergrads Awarded Aid** 76% **Aid That Is Need-Based** 51% **Average Award of Freshman Scholarship Package** $7,597 **Tests Required** SAT1 or ACT **Admissions Address** 429 North Church Street, Spartanburg, SC 29303-3663 **Admissions Telephone** (864) 597-4130

LAST YEAR'S CLASS Applied 1,134 **Accepted** 989 **Matriculated** 286 **Average SAT M/V** 577/528 **Average ACT** 26 **In Top Fifth of High School Graduating Class** 70%

COLLEGE LIFE Gender Breakdown M 55%, F 45% **Out of State Students** 38% **From Public Schools** 79% **Ethnic Composition** White & Other 91%, Asian American 2%, Black 6.2%, Hispanic 0.5%, Native American 0.3% **Foreign Students** 1% **Reside on Campus** 82% **Return as Sophomores** 88% **Total Faculty** 93 **Student Faculty Ratio** 15:1 **Fraternities (% of men participating)** 8 (52%) **Sororities (% of women participating)** 3 (58%)

The College of Wooster

Wooster, OH · Est. 1866 · Coed · Private · 1,669 Undergrads · Small Town

I need...

Admissions info admissions@acs.wooster.edu
www.wooster.edu/admissions
Financial aid info www.wooster.edu/admissions
/defaultfaid.html

How wired is The College of Wooster?

Do I get email? Yes
Do I get a home page? Yes
Where? pages.wooster.edu
Is my dorm wired? Yes
What is the student to computer ratio? 11:1

The usual tour

DEPARTMENTS www.wooster.edu/programs
/programs.html
SPORTS www.wooster.edu/athletics
PUBLICATIONS www.wooster.edu/admissions
/defaultpubs.html
LIBRARY www.wooster.edu/library/index.html
STUDENT CLUBS www.wooster.edu/inside
/inside.html

Skip the brochure

- **COW JUGGLERS** College students juggle different parts of life: social, academic, athletic, family, professional. These students take this process of integration to a new level: they actually juggle. The site links to online juggling resources—you *can* learn to juggle online. But is it possible to juggle and click a mouse at

Wooster students do their best to keep their many activities aloft

the same time? Don't have a cow, man.
www.wooster.edu/cowjugglers/jugglingindex.html

- **FACULTY HOME PAGE** If Mark Weaver's page is any indication of the teaching at the College of Wooster, then students are in good hands. He teaches the very '90s combination of Poli- Sci and Women's Studies, and he's so devoted to the cause that he named one of his dogs Foucault. pages.wooster.edu/mweaver

- **SCOT PIPERS** Although the Presbyterian Church no longer has formal ties to the College of Wooster, it once owned the school. The Scot Pipers are just a bunch of people who like to wear kilts and play the bagpipes, but the group associates itself with Wooster's Presbyterian heritage. www.wooster.edu/pipers/pipers.html

---

WHAT YOU NEED TO GET IN **Application Deadline** February 15 for priority consideration **Early Action Deadline** December 1 and January 15 **Common App.** Yes **Application Fee** $35 **Tuition Costs** $18,380 **Room & Board** $4,850 **Financial Forms Deadline** Priority given to applications received by February 15 **Undergrads Awarded Aid** 87% **Aid That Is Need-Based** 88% **Average Award of Freshman Scholarship Package** $10,700 **Tests Required** SAT1 or ACT **Admissions Address** Wooster, OH 44691 **Admissions Telephone** (330) 263-2322

LAST YEAR'S CLASS **Applied** 1,823 **Accepted** 1,629 **Matriculated** 512 **Average SAT M/V** 590/538 **Average ACT** 25 **In Top Fifth of High School Graduating Class** 53% **Applied Early** 106 **Accepted Early** 100

COLLEGE LIFE **Gender Breakdown** M 48%, F 52% **Out of State Students** 50% **From Public Schools** 70% **Ethnic Composition** White & Other 93%, Asian American 1.2%, Black 5%, Hispanic 0.7%, Native American 0.1% **Foreign Students** 9% **Reside on Campus** 93% **Return as Sophomores** 85% **Total Faculty** 175 **Student Faculty Ratio** 12:1 **Fraternities (% of men participating)** 8 (20%) **Sororities (% of women participating)** 8 (15%)

Worcester Polytechnic Institute www.wpi.edu

Worcester, MA· Est. 1865 · Coed · Private · 2,573 Undergrads · Urban

I need...

Admissions info admissions@wpi.edu
www.wpi.edu/Admin/Depts/AO
Financial aid info mjcurley@jake.wpi.edu
www.wpi.edu/Admin/Depts/FA/Freshmen

How wired is WPI?

Do I get email? Yes
Do I get a home page? Yes
  Where? www.wpi.edu/Campus/students.html
Is my dorm wired? Yes
What is the student to computer ratio? 3:1

The usual tour

VIRTUAL TOUR www.wpi.edu/Visitors/Tour/index
.html
STUDENT CLUBS www.wpi.edu/Campus/student
-groups.html
SPORTS www.wpi.edu/Campus/student-groups
.html#sports
DEPARTMENTS www.wpi.edu/Academics/Depts|
/index.html
GREEK LIFE www.wpi.edu/Campus/student-groups
.html#greek
LIBRARY www.wpi.edu/Academics/IMS/Library
PUBLICATIONS www.wpi.edu/AboutUs/Pubs

Skip the brochure

• **LENS AND LIGHTS** The members of Lens and
Lights will be the first to inform you that they're
not your ordinary audio-visual club: "We don't

Location: http://www.wpi.edu/Visitors/Tour/Images/boynton.gif

Boynton Hall was named for John Boynton, whose gift of $100,000 started the WPI ball rolling

do overheads or slide projectors." Instead,
they're into heavier—or at least more technically advanced—machinery such as sound systems and movie projectors. **www.wpi.edu/~lnl**

• **WPI AUTOCROSS CLUB** Feeling racy? Try this:
"Autocrossing is a form of motorsports featuring one car at a time, racing against the clock
on a tight, twisty course." Check it out at a
parking lot near you. **www.wpi.edu/~autox**

• **SOCIAL COMMITTEE** Who says that techies don't
know how to have fun? The social committee
offers entertainment of all kinds, from films and
coffeehouses to big-name bands and comedians. The group hasn't lost touch with its geeky
roots; their motto is Entertainment for the
Mundane College Campus, or $E=mc^2$. **www.wpi
.edu/~soccomm**

WHAT YOU NEED TO GET IN **Application Deadline** February 15 **Common App.** yes **Application Fee** $40 (refundable for Early Decision applicants; may be waived) **Tuition Costs** $17,860 **Room & Board** $5,940 **Need Blind** yes **Financial Forms Deadline** April 1 with a priority given to applications received by March 1 **Undergrads Awarded Aid** 80% **Aid That Is Need-Based** 98% **Average Award of Freshman Scholarship Package** $7,960 **Tests Required** SAT1 or ACT **Admissions Address** 100 Institute Road, Worcester, 01609 MA **Admissions Telephone** (508) 831-5286

LAST YEAR'S CLASS **Applied** 2,480 **Accepted** 2,112 **Matriculated** 589 **Median Range SAT M/V** 610-700/490-590 **Average ACT** 29 **In Top Fifth of High School Graduating Class** 70%

COLLEGE LIFE **Gender Breakdown** M 79%, F 21% **Out of State Students** 58% **From Public Schools** 78% **Ethnic Composition** White & Other 91%, Asian American 6%, Black 1%, Hispanic 2% **Foreign Students** 7% **Reside on Campus** 50% **Return as Sophomores** 90% **Total Faculty** 251 **Student Faculty Ratio** 12:1 **Fraternities (% of men participating)** 12 (38%) **Sororities (% of women participating)** 2 (40%) **Graduate Students** 753

University of Wyoming

www.uwyo.edu

Laramie, WY · Est. 1886 · Coed · Public · 8,805 Undergrads · Big Town

How wired is U Wyoming?

Do I get email? Yes
Do I get a home page? Yes
Is my dorm wired? Yes
What is the student to computer ratio? 17:1

REQUEST APPLICATION ONLINE

The usual tour

DEPARTMENTS WWW.uwyo.edu/OM/UNIREL/HTM /MAJORS.HTM

SPORTS www.uwyo.edu/om/unirel/htm/athlete .htm

CALENDAR www.uwyo.edu/OM/UNIREL/HTM /ACTIVE.HTM

STUDENT CLUBS www.uwyo.edu/asa/r&r/stuserv .htm

LIBRARY www.uwyo.edu/Lib/coe.htm

Skip the brochure

- **CAMPUS LIBERTARIANS** Check out the principles of some of the youngest members of the third-largest and fastest-growing political party in the United States. **www.uwyo.edu/asa/sorg/libertar**

- **LARAMIE, WYOMING** Situated at 7,200 feet, the University of Wyoming has the highest students in the United States. The town of

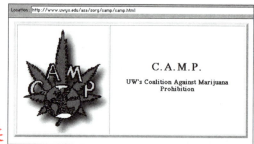

C.A.M.P.

UW's Coalition Against Marijuana Prohibition

Legalize it. So goes the slogan of UW's hemp advocates

Laramie, host to the university, has a population of 27,000. Much of the recreation that takes place in Laramie depends on its wilderness resources, so you should come here expecting to see the great outdoors. **www.uwyo. edu/wyoming/laramie/default.html**

- **COALITION AGAINST MARIJUANA PROHIBITION** It's already been established that students at University of Wyoming are high. Well, some want to get higher. Part of the growing American lobby to decriminalize marijuana and use hemp for industrial and medical purposes, this group aims to "high"-ten awareness about this much contested plant. **www.uwyo.edu /asa/sorg/camp/camp.html**

"Laramie, situated at 7,200 feet, has the highest students in the U.S."

WHAT YOU NEED TO GET IN **Application Deadline** March 1 for priority consideration; final deadline August 10 **Common App.** No **Application Fee** $30 **Tuition Costs** $2,144 ($6,872 out-of-state) **Room & Board** $3,986 **Financial Forms Deadline** Priority given to applications received by March 1 **Undergrads Awarded Aid** 65% **Aid That Is Need-Based** 53% **Average Award of Freshman Scholarship Package** $1,200 **Tests Required** SAT1 or ACT **Admissions Address** Laramie, WY 82071 **Admissions Telephone** (307) 766-5160

LAST YEAR'S CLASS **Applied** 2,079 **Accepted** 1,970 **Matriculated** 1,284 **Average ACT** 23 **In Top Fifth of High School Graduating Class** 44%

COLLEGE LIFE **Gender Breakdown** M 49%, F 51% **Out of State Students** 35% **Ethnic Composition** White & Other 92%, Asian American 1%, Black 1%, Hispanic 5%, Native American 1% **Foreign Students** 1% **Reside on Campus** 48% **Return as Sophomores** 72% **Total Faculty** 710 **Student Faculty Ratio** 15:1 **Fraternities (% of men participating)** 12 (10%) **Sororities (% of women participating)** 4 (9%) **Graduate Students** 2,556

Yale University

New Haven, CT · Est. 1701 · Coed · Private · 5,326 Undergrads · Urban

I need...

Admissions info admissions_receptionist@qm.yale.edu
www.yale.edu/admit/info.html
Financial aid info finaid@qm.yale.edu
www.yale.edu/admit/info.html

How wired is Yale?

Do I get email? Yes
Do I get a home page? Yes
Where? www.yale.edu/gallery
Is my dorm wired? Yes
What is the student to computer ratio? 13:1

The usual tour

VIRTUAL TOUR pantheon.cis.yale.edu/~ykchou/MainMenu.html
SPORTS www.yale.edu/athletic
PUBLICATIONS www.yale.edu/yaleinfo/publications.html
STUDENT CLUBS www.yale.edu/yaleinfo/studentorgs.html
LIBRARY www.library.yale.edu
DEPARTMENTS www.yale.edu/yaleinfo/depts.html

Skip the brochure

- **NADINE** This irreverent magazine—a heady mix of bombast, music coverage, and light social commentary—wishes it were a band, or so it claims. **pantheon.cis.yale.edu/~tpole/nadine/home_page.html**

A typical college green scene: Students study, sun, and sleep

- **YALE CHILDREN'S THEATER** Keeping in touch with their inner children, Yalies perform theater for, with, and by little ones. **pantheon.cis.yale.edu/~anise/yct.html**

- **YALE LGBT COOPERATIVE** Yale's cooperative is sure to be one of the most active (and interactive) organizations in the gay, lesbian, bisexual, and transgendered world. In addition to event information and announcements, be sure to check out The Yale Out List, which flings the closet door wide open. **www.yale.edu/lgb**

- **YALE BALLROOM DANCE CLUB** On top of their academic excellence, Yale students compete nationally in ballroom dancing. This site includes a how-to guide and a list of upcoming events **pantheon.cis.yale.edu/~vlahovic/yaleballroom.html**

WHAT YOU NEED TO GET IN **Application Deadline** December 31 **Early Action Deadline** November 1 **Common App.** No **Application Fee** $65 (may be waived in cases of economic hardship) **Tuition Costs** $22,200 **Room & Board** $6,680 **Financial Forms Deadline** February 1 **Undergrads Awarded Aid** 53% **Average Award of Freshman Scholarship Package** $12,624 **Tests Required** SAT1 or ACT **Admissions Address** 208234 Yale Station, New Haven, CT 06520-8234 **Admissions Telephone** (203) 432-1900

LAST YEAR'S CLASS **Applied** 12,620 **Accepted** 2,522 **Matriculated** 1,364 **Median Range SAT M/V** 680-760/620-710 **Applied Early** 1,590 **Accepted Early** 518

COLLEGE LIFE **Gender Breakdown** M 51%, F 49% **Out of State Students** 94% **From Public Schools** 57% **Ethnic Composition** White & Other 67.1%, Asian American 16.9%, Black 9.1%, Hispanic 6.9% **Foreign Students** 4% **Reside on Campus** 86% **Return as Sophomores** 98% **Graduate Students** 5,660

Appendices

Internet Providers

by region and state

National

America Online
800-827-6364 (vox)

Arrownet
517-371-7100 (vox)

AT&T WorldNet
800-967-5363 (vox)

CompuServe
800-848-8199 (vox)

Delphi
800-695-4005 (vox)

EarthLink Network
800-395-8425 (vox)

GEnie
800-638-9636 (vox)

Internet Express
800-592-1240 (vox)

HoloNet
510-704-0160 (vox)

Hypercon
800-652-2590 (vox)

IBM Global Network
800-775-5808 (vox)

IPSnet
407-426-8782 (vox)

NETCOM On-Line Communications Services
800-501-8649/408-554-8649 (vox)

NovaLink Interactive
800-274-2814 (vox)

Prodigy
800-776-3449 (vox)

Questar Microsystems
206-487-2627 (vox)

UUNET Technologies
800-488-6384 (vox)

The WELL
415-332-9200 (vox)

ZONE One Network Exchange
212-824-4000 (vox)

Alabama

Cheney Communications Company
800-CHENEY-1 (vox)

Community Internet Connect, Inc.
205-722-0199 (vox)

db Technology
205-556-9020 (vox)

interQuest
205-464-8280 (vox)

The Matrix
205-251-9347 (vox)

Renaissance Internet Services
205-535-2113 (vox)

Scott Network Services, Inc.
205-987-5889 (vox)

TECH-COMM Inc.
205-250-8053

WSNetwork Communications Services, Inc.
800-463-8750/334-263-5505 (vox)

Alaska

Corcom, Inc.
907-563-1191 (vox)

Internet Alaska
907-562-4638 (vox)

MicroNet Communications
907-333-8663 (vox)

Arizona

Arizona Macintosh Users' Group
602-553-8966 (vox)

Crossroads Communications
602-813-9040 (vox)

Evergreen Internet
602-926-4500 (vox)

GetNet International, Inc.
602-943-3119

Internet Direct of Utah, Inc.
602-274-0100 (vox)

Opus One
602-324-0494 (vox)

NETWEST Communications, Inc.
602-948-5052

Primenet
800-463-8386/602-870-1010 (vox)

RTD Systems & Networking, Inc.
520-318-0696 (vox)

Systems Solutions Inc.
602-955-5566 (vox)

Arkansas

AR - Internet Partners of America
800-785-4091 ext 0 (vox)

Aristotle Internet Access
501-374-4638 (vox)

Cloverleaf Technologies
800-830-9677/903-832-1367 (vox)

IntelliNet
800-290-7677 (vox)

world lynx
501-562-8297 (vox)

YourNET
501-988 9432

California

Access InfoSystems
707-422-1034 (vox)

Aimnet Information Services
408-567-3800(vox)

CC NET
800-CC-NET4U/510-988-0680 (vox)

QuickNet
714-895-3075 (vox)

CONNECTnet Internet Network Services
619-450-0254 (vox)

CRL
415-837-5300 (vox)

CTS Network Services
619-637-3637 (vox)

Cybergate Information Services
209-486-4283 (vox)

Delta Internet Services
714-778-0370 (vox)

DigiLink Network Services
310-542-7421 (vox)

Direct Net Access Inc.
510-649-6110 (vox)

Directnet
213-383-3144 (vox)

EarthLink Network, Inc.
213-644-9500 (vox)

Electriciti
619-338-9000 (vox)

HoloNet Information Access
510-704-0160 (vox)

Infoserv Connections
408-335-5600 (vox)

INTERNEX
408-496-5466 (vox)

ISP Networks
408-653-0100 (vox)

KAIWAN Internet
714-638-2139 (vox)

LanMinds, Inc.
510-843-6389 (vox)

Lightside, Inc.
818-858-9261 (vox)

LineX Communications
415-455-1650 (vox)

NetGate Communications
408-565-9601 (vox)

Northcoast Internet
707-443-8696 (vox)

Primenet
800-463-8386/602-395-1010 (vox)

QuakeNet
415-655-6607 (vox)

Scruz-Net
800-319-5555/408-457-5050 (vox)

Sierra-Net
702-832-6911 (vox)

South Valley Internet
408-683-4533 (vox)

ViaNet Communications
415-903-2242 (vox)

The WELL
415-332-4335 (vox)

West Coast Online
707-586-3060 (vox)

WombatNet
415-462-8800 (vox)

zNET
619-755-7772 (vox)

Colorado

Colorado SuperNet, Inc.
303-296-8202 (vox)

Community News Service, Inc.
719-592-1240 (vox)

CSDC, Inc.
303-665-8053 (vox)

ENVISIONET, Inc.
303-770-2408 (vox)

Indra's Net, Inc.
303-546-9151 (vox)

Old Colorado City Communications
719-528-5849 (vox)

Rocky Mountain Internet
800-900-7644 (vox)

Stonehenge Internet Communications
800-786-4638 (vox)

Internet Providers

Connecticut

CONNIX
203-349-7059 (vox)

CallNet Information Services, Inc.
203-389-7130 (vox)

Futuris Networks, Inc.
203-359-8868 (vox)

I-2000, Inc.
516-867-6379 (vox)

LocalNet of Fairfield County
203-452-3535 (vox)

Mindport Internet Services, Inc.
203 892-2081 (vox)

NECAnet, Inc.
203-429-2035 (vox)

NETAXIS
203-969-0618 (vox)

Paradigm Communications
203-250-7397 (vox)

Delaware

Business Data Systems, Inc.
302-674-2840 (vox)

DCANet
302-654-1019 (vox)

DelNet Internet Delaware
302-737-1001 (vox)

iNET Communications
302-454-1780 (vox)

The Magnetic Page
302-651-9753 (vox)

SSNet, Inc.
302-378-1386 (vox)

District of Columbia

CAPCON Library Network
202-331-5771 (vox)

CharmNet
410-558-3900 (vox)

Genuine Computing Resources
703-878-4680 (vox)

Internet Online, Inc.
301-652-4468 (vox)

usNet, Inc.
301-572-5926 (vox)

Florida

CocoNet Corporation
813-540-2626 (vox)

CyberGate, Inc.
305-428-4283 (vox)

IDS
401-885-6855/800-IDS-1680 (vox)

The EmiNet Domain
407-731-0222 (vox)

Florida Online
407-635-8888/800-676-2599 (vox)

InternetU
407-952-8487 (vox)

MagicNet, Inc.
407-657-2202 (vox)

MetroLink Internet Services
407-726-6707 (vox)

PacketWorks, Inc.
813-446-8826 (vox)

Polaris Network, Inc.
904-878-9745 (vox)

PSS InterNet Services
904-253-7100/800-463-8499 (vox)

SymNet
904-222-8555 (vox)

Georgia

Connect Atlanta
770-475-0980 (vox)

CyberNet Communications
770-518-5711 (vox)

Future Services
770-978-1175 (vox)

Hargray Telephone-Interstar
803-686-5000 (vox)

Homenet Communications, Inc.
912-329-8638 (vox)

Internet Atlanta
404-410-9000 (vox)

LightSpeed Data Links, Inc.
706-321-1261 (vox)

MindSpring
404-888-0725 (vox)

Znet
706-722-2175 (vox)

Prometheus Information Network Group, Inc. PING)
800-746-4835 (vox)

Hawaii

1st Source, Inc.
808-521-3472 (vox)

FLEX INFORMATION NET-WORK
808-732-8849 (vox)

Hawaii OnLine
808-533-6981/800-291-5951 (vox)

hula.net
808-524-7717 (vox)

Inter-Pacific Networks
808-935-5550 (vox)

LavaNet, Inc.
808-545-5282 (vox)

Pacific Information Exchange, Inc.
808-596-7494 (vox)

Sense Networking
408-335-9400 (vox)

Idaho

Atlas BBS
800-ATLAS-WEB (vox)

DMI Computers / DMI Computer Graphics
208-664-1340 Coeur d'Alene, Id-
208-345-8555 Boise, Id-(vox)

First Step Research
208-882-8869 (vox)

Idaho Computer Services, Inc.
208-734-2245 (vox)

Micron Internet Services
208-368-5400 (vox)

Primenet
800-463-8386/602-870-1010 (vox)

SRVnet, Inc.
208-524-6237 (vox)

Tribune Internet Services
208-743-9411 (vox)

Illinois

American Information Systems
708-413-8400/312-255-8500 (vox)

Allied Access, Inc.
800-463-8366 (vox)

InterAccess Co.
800-967-1580 (vox)

Open Business Systems, Inc.
708-250-0260 (vox)

Ripco Communications, Inc.
312-477-6210 (vox)

Tezcatlipoca, Inc.
312-850-0181 (vox)

WorldWide Access
708-367-1870 (vox)

Indiana

Evansville Online
812-479-1700 (vox)

HolliCom Internet Services
317-883-4500 (vox)

IgLou Internet ServiceS
800-436-4456 (vox)

IQuest Network Services
317-259-5050 (vox)

Metropolitan Data Networks Limited
317-449-0539 (vox)

Net Direct
317-251-5252 (vox)

World Connection Services
812-479-1700 (vox)

Iowa

Cedar Rapids Public Library
319-398-5123 (vox)

Des Moines Internet, Inc.
515-270-9191 (vox)

Nishna Net, Inc
800-223-3911 (vox)

The Online Pitstop
402-293-0384 BBS-- (vox)

Kansas

DATABANK, Inc.
800-200-8985/913-842-6699 (vox)

Interstate Networking Corporation
816-472-4949 (vox)

Primenet
800-463-8386/602-870-1010 (vox)

SouthWind Internet Access, Inc.
316-263-7963 (vox)

Kentucky

BluegrassNet
502-589-INET 4638-(vox)

IgLou Internet ServiceS
800-436-4456 (vox)

The Louisville Connection
502-241-3878 (vox)

South Central Rural Telephone Co-op Inc.
502-678-8281 (vox)

Louisiana

AccessCom Internet Providers
504-887-0022 (vox)

The Big Easy
800-819-4847 (vox)/504-821-2700

Communique Inc.
504-527-6200 (vox)

Cyberlink
504-277-4186 (vox)

Greater New Orleans FreeNet
504-529-5576 (vox)

I-Link Ltd
800-454-6599 (vox)

Internet Providers

JAMNet Internet Services, Inc.
504-361-3492 (vox)

Light House Computer Services
504-879-2888 (vox)

NEOSOFT
800-438-6367/713-968-5800 (vox)

North Shore Internet
504-867-8008 (vox)

Maine

AcadiaNet
207-288-5959 (vox)

Agate Internet
207-947-8248 (vox)

Biddeford Internet
207-286-3265 (vox)

Internet Maine Inc.
207-780-0416 (vox)

The Maine InternetWorks, Inc.
207-453-4000

Maryland

CAPCON Library Network
202-331-5771 (vox)

CharmNet
410-558-3900 (vox)

FredNet
301-631-5300 (vox)

Genuine Computing Resources
703-878-4680 (vox)

Internet Interstate
301-652-4468 (vox)

jaguNET Access Services
410-931-3157 (vox)

Softaid Internet Services Inc.
410-290-7763 (vox)

usNet, Inc.
301-572-5926 (vox)

Massachusetts

CENTnet, Inc.
508-454-5688/617-492-6079 (vox)

FOURnet Information Network
508-291-2900 (vox)

The Internet Access Company
617-276-7200 (vox)

intuitive information, inc.
508-342-1100 (vox)

Mallard Electronics, Inc.
413-732-0214 (vox)

North Shore Access
617-593-3110 (vox)

Pioneer Global
617-375-0200 (vox)

ShaysNet.COM
413-772-2923 (vox)

StarNet Internet Access Advanced Communication Systems, Inc.)
508-922-8238 (vox)

TerraNet, Inc.
617-450-9000 (vox)

UltraNet Communications, Inc.
800-763-8111/508-229-8400 (vox)

Wilder Systems, Inc.
617-933-8810 (vox)

The World
617-739-0202 (vox)

Michigan

Alliance Network, Inc.
800-767-4654 (vox)

Branch Information Services
313-741-4442 (vox)

Dale Information Services
616-527-4747 (vox)

EagleQuest, Inc.
810-650-4700 (vox)

Grand Rapids Freenet
616-224-7020 (vox)

ICNET / Innovative Concepts
313-998-0090 (vox)

Internet Services of Michigan
517-548-1400 (vox)

Isthmus Corporation
313-973-2100 (vox)

Msen, Inc.
313-998-4562 (vox)

Novagate Communications Corp.
616-847-0910

RustNet, Inc.
810-650-6812 (vox)

Minnesota

InforMNs
612-638-8786 (vox)

Internet Connections, Inc.
507-625-7320 (vox)

Red River Net
701-232-2227 (vox)

StarNet Communications, Inc.
612-941-9177 (vox)

Mississippi

ARIS Technology, Inc.
601-324-7638 (vox)

Datasync Internet Services
601-872-0001 (vox)

Hub City Access
601-268-9176 (vox)

Southwind Technologies, Inc.
601-374-6510 (vox)

Missouri

AccuNet, Inc.
816-246-9094 (vox)

Allied Access, Inc.
800-463-8366 (vox)

Basenet-Access U.S
618-244-4187 (vox)

Cybergate L.L.C.
-314-214-1013 (vox)

Green Hills Telephone-Rain
816-644-2000, 800-675-1440 (vox)

Midwest Internet
618-529-7271 (vox)

Q-Networks, Inc QNI)
816-795-1000 (vox)

THOUGHTPORT
314-474-6870 (vox)

Montana

Intermountain Internet Corp.
800-966-3930 (vox)

Kootenet
406-293-2778 (vox)

Montana Online
406-721-4952 (vox)

Netrix Internet System Design, Inc.
406-257-4638 (vox)

Nebraska

Internet Nebraska
402-434-8680 (vox)

Lincoln Telephone Company (Navix)
402-436-4959 (vox)

Nebraska On-Ramp
402-339-6366 (vox)

New Conclusions, Inc.
402-593-9800 (vox)

Omaha Free-Net
402-559-5866

Nevada

Great Basin Internet Services
702-348-7299 (vox)

InterMind
702-878-6111 (vox)

NevadaNet
702-784-4827 (vox)

Sierra-Net
702-831-3353 (vox)

wizard.com
702-871-4461 (vox)

New Hampshire

Blue Fin Systems
603-433-2223 (vox)

CyberPort, LLC
603-542-5833 (vox)

Destek
603-635-7263 (vox)

info@millcomm.com
603-635-3857 (vox)

MV Communications, Inc.
603-429-2223 (vox)

NETIS Public Access Internet
603-437-1811 (vox)

North Country Internet Access
603-752-1250 (vox)

New Jersey

Carroll-Net
201-488-1332 (vox)

Castle Network, Inc.
800-577-9449/908-548-8881 (vox)

The Connection
201-435-4414 (vox)

I-2000, Inc.
516-867-6379 (vox)

INTAC Access Corporation
800-504-6822 (vox)

InterCom Online
212-714-7183 (vox)

Internet For 'U'
800-638-9291 (vox)

Internet Online Services
201-928-1000 EXT.226 (vox)

K2NE Software
609-893-0673 (vox)

New Jersey Computer Connection
609-896-2799 (vox)

New York Net
718-776-6811 (vox)

NIC - Neighborhood Internet Connection
201-934-1445 (vox)

Planet Access Networks
201-691-4704 (vox)

Internet Providers

New Mexico

Community Internet Access
505-863-2424 (vox)

CyberPort Station
505-324-6400 (vox)

Southwest Cyberport
505-293-5967/505-271-0009 (vox)

ZyNet SouthWest
505-343-8846 (vox)

New York

Computer Solutions by Hawkinson
914-473-0844 (vox)

Creative Data Consultants SILLY.COM)
718-229-0489 EXT.23 (vox)

E-Znet, Inc.
716-262-2485 (vox)

East Greenwich, Rhode Island
401-885-6855 (vox)

Echo Communications Group
212-255-3839 (vox)

escape.com - Kazan Corp
212-888-8780 (vox)

I-2000, Inc.
516-867-6379 (vox)

Ingress Communications Inc.
212-268-1100 EXT. 105 (vox)

INTAC Access Corporation
800-504-6822 (vox)

InterCom Online
212-714-7183 (vox)

The Internet Channel
212-243-5200 (vox)

Internet For 'U'
800-638-9291 (vox)

Internet Online Services
201-928-1000 EXT.226 (vox)

Interport Communications Corp.
212-989-1128 (vox)

LI Net, Inc.
516-265-0997 (vox)
Maestro
212-240-9600 (vox)

Mnematics, Incorporated
914-359-4546 (vox)

Moran Communications
716-639-1254 (vox)

Network Internet Services
516-543-0234 (vox)

New York Net
718-776-6811 (vox)

NY WEBB, Inc.
800-458-4660 (vox)

NYSERNet
315-453-2912 EXT.294/286 (vox)

Panix
212-741-4400 (vox)

PHANTOM MindVox)
212-989-2418 (vox)

The Pipeline Network
800-341-6487 (vox)

ServiceTech
716-546-6908 (vox)

TZ-Link
914-353-5443 (vox)

Wizvax Communications
518-273-4325 (vox)

North Carolina

SunBelt.Net
803-328-1500 (vox)

Vnet Internet Access
800-377-3282/704-334-3282 (vox)

North Dakota

Corporate Communications
701-277-0011 (vox)

Dakota Central Telecommunications Cooperative
701-652-3184

Red River Net
701-232-2227 (vox)

Ohio

APK Net, Ltd
216-241-7166

The Dayton Network Access Company
513-237-6868 (vox)

EriNet
513-436-1700 (vox)

Exchange Network Services, Inc.
216-615-9400 (vox)

IgLou Internet ServiceS
800-436-4456 (vox)

Infinite Systems
614-268-9941 (vox)

Internet Access Cincinnati
513-887-8877 (vox)

New Age Consulting Service
216-524-8414 (vox)

Oarnet
800-627-8101 EXT.217/614-728-8100 (vox)

Oklahoma

Galaxy Star Systems
918-835-3655 (vox)

InterConnect Online
405-949-1800 (vox)

Internet Oklahoma
405-721-1580 (vox)

OKNET, The Tulsa SuperNet, Black Gold BBS
918-481-5899, 800-221-6478 (vox)

Questar Network Services, Inc.
405-848-3228 (vox)

Oregon

Data Research Group, Inc.
503-465-3282 (vox)

Europa
503-222-9508 (vox)

Hevanet Communications
503-228-3520 (vox)

Open Door Networks, Inc.
503-488-4127 (vox)

Structured Network Systems, Inc.
800-881-0962/503-656-3530 (vox)

Teleport, Inc.
503-223-4245 (vox)

Transport Logic
503-243-1940 (vox)

Pennsylvania

City-Net
412-481-5406 (vox)

King of Prussia, PA Internet Services
610-337-9994 (vox)

Microserve
800-380-4638/717-821-5964 (vox)

OASIS
610-439-8560 (vox)

PREPnet
412-268-7870 (vox)

PSCNET
412-268-4960 (vox)

SSNet, Inc.
302-378-1386 (vox)

Telerama Public Access
412-481-3505 (vox)

YOU TOOLS Corporation
610-954-5910 (vox)

Rhode Island

Aquidneck Web Inc.
401-841-5WWW (vox)

brainiac services, inc
401-539-9050 (vox)

IDS World Network
401-885-6855 (vox)

Log On America
401-453-6100 (vox)/401-459-6200

South Carolina

A World of Difference, Inc.
803-769-4488 (vox)

Global Vision Inc.
803-241-0901 (vox)

SIMS, Inc.
803-762-4956 (vox)

South Carolina SuperNet
803-748-1207 (vox)

SunBelt.Net
803-328-1500 (vox)

South Dakota

Dakota Internet Services, Inc.
605-371-1962 (vox)

Internet Services of the Black Hills, Inc.
605-642-2244 (vox)

RapidNet LLC
605-341-3283 (vox)

SoDak Net
605-582-2549 (vox)

Tennessee

The Edge
615-726-8700 (vox)

GoldSword Systems
615-691-6498 (vox)

ISDN-Net Inc.
615-377-7672 (vox)

Magibox Incorporated
901-452-7555 (vox)

Preferred Internet Services
615-323-1142 (vox)

The Telalink Corporation
615-321-9100 (vox)

The Tri-Cities Connection
615-378-5355 (vox)

Texas

The Black Box
713-480-2684 (vox)

Cloverleaf Technologies
903-832-1367 (vox)

Electrotex,Inc.
800-460-1801/713-526-3456 (vox)

I-Link Ltd
800-454-6599 (vox)

Internet Providers

Illuminati Online
512-462-0999 (vox)

Internet Access of El Paso
915-533-1525 (vox)

Internet Connect Services
512-572-9987 (vox)

NEOSOFT
800-438-6367 (vox)

Real/Time Communications, Inc.
512-451-0046 (vox)

Sesquinet
713-527-4988 (vox)

@sig.net
512-306-0700 (vox)

Texas Metronet, Inc.
214-705-2900 (vox)

USiS
713-682-1666 (vox)

Zilker Internet Park, Inc.
512-206-3850 (vox)

Utah

ArosNet, Inc.
801-532-2767 (vox)

CacheNET
801-753-2199 (vox)

DATABANK, Inc.
913-842-6699 (vox)

Fibernet Corporation
801-223-9939 (vox)

Utah Wired
801-532-1117 (vox)

XMission
801-539-0852 (vox)

Vermont

SoVerNet
802-463-2111 (vox)

TGF Technologies, Inc.
802-862-2030 (vox)

Virginia

CAPCON Library Network
202-331-5771 (vox)

CharmNet
410-558-3900 (vox)

CLARK
410-254-3900 (vox)
DATABANK, Inc.
913-842-6699 (vox)

Genine Computing Resources
703-878-4680 (vox)

Internet Interstate
301-652-4468 (vox)

usNet, Inc.
301-572-5926 (vox)

Widomaker Communication Service
804-253-7621 (vox)

Washington

Eskimo North
206-361-1161 (vox)

Halcyon
800-539-3505/206-455-3505 (vox)

Internetworks, Inc.
206-576-7147 (vox)

Network Access Services
206-733-9279 (vox)

Northwest NEXUS
206-455-3505 (vox)

Olympus Net
360-385-0464 (vox)

Pacific Rim Network, Inc.
360-650-0442 (vox)

Pacifier Computers
206-254-3886 (vox)

Seanet Online Services
206-343-7828 (vox)

SenseMedia
408-335-9400 (vox)

Skagit On-Line Services
360-755-0190 (vox)

Structured Network Systems, Inc.
800-881-0962/503-656-3530 (vox)

Teleport, Inc.
503-223-4245 (vox)

Transport Logic
503-243-1940 (vox)

WLN
800-342-5956/360-923-4000 (vox)

West Virginia

CityNet Corporation
304-342-5700 (vox)

MountainNet, Inc.
304-594-9075, 800-846-1458 (vox)

WVNET
304-293-5192 (vox)

Wisconsin

Exec-PC, Inc.
800-393-2721/414-789-4200 (vox)

FullFeed Communications
608-246-4239 (vox)

MIX Communications
414-351-1868 (vox)

NetNet, Inc.
414-499-1339 (vox)

WiscNet
608-265-7661 (vox)

Wyoming

CoffeyNet
307-234-5443 (vox)

WAVE Communications Inc
307-674-4925 (vox)

wyoming.com
800-996-4638/307-332-3030 (vox)

Canada

CCI Networks
403-450-6787 (vox)

Information Gateway
613-592-5619 (vox)

Sunshine Net, Inc.
604-886-4120 (vox)

Alberta

Alberta SuperNet, Inc.
403-441-3663 (vox)

Internet North
403-873-5975 (vox)

Spots InterConnect, Inc
403-571-SPOT 7768-(vox)

British Columbia

auroraNET, Inc.
604-294-4357 x101 (vox)

Cyberstore Systems, Inc.
604-482-3400 (vox)

Newfoundland

Atlantic Connect Inc.
902-429-0222, 800-661-0222 (vox)

NLnet
709-737-4555 (vox)

Nova Scotia

Internet Passport Services
902-INT-ERNET 468-3763-(vox)

North Shore Internet Service
902-928-0565 (vox)

Ontario

9 To 5 Communications
416-363-9100 (vox)

DataBridge
905-940-1885 (vox)

Inforamp, Inc. —Ontario
416-363-9100 (vox)

Québec

Accent Internet
514-737-6077, 800-920-SURF (vox)

ClicNet Telecommunications, Inc.
418-686-CLIC 2542-(vox)

CyberPlus Technologies Inc.
613-749-8598 (vox)

Saskatchewan

Stonefield Systems Group Inc.
306-586-3341 (vox)

@	Separates the **userid** and **domain name** of an Internet address. Pronounced "at."
anonymous FTP	Method of logging in to public file archives over the **Internet**. Enter "anonymous" when prompted for a **userid**. See **FTP**.
Archie	A program that lets you search **Internet FTP** archives worldwide by file name. One variant is called **Veronica**.
ASCII	A basic text format readable by most computers. The acronym stands for American Standard Code for Information Interchange.
bandwidth	The data transmission capacity of a network. Used colloquially to refer to the "size" of the Net; some information transmittals (e.g., multitudes of graphic files) are considered to be a "waste of bandwidth."
baud	The speed at which signals are sent by a **modem**, measured by the number of changes per second in the signals during transmission. A baud rate of 1,200, for example, would indicate 1,200 signal changes in one second. Baud rate is often confused with **bits per second (bps)**.
BBS	"Bulletin-board system." Once referred to stand-alone desktop computers with a single modem that answered the phone, but can now be as complicated and inter-connected as a commercial service.
binary transfer	A file transfer between two computers that preserves binary data—used for all non-text files.
bits per second (bps)	The data-transfer rate between two **modems**. The higher the bps, the higher the speed of the transfer.
bounced message	An **email** message "returned to sender," usually because of an address error.
bye	A log-off command, like "quit" and "exit."
carrier signal	The squeaking noise that modems use to maintain a connection. See also **hand-shake**.
cd	"Change directory." A command used, for example, at an **FTP** site to move from a directory to a subdirectory.
cdup	"Change directory up." Can be used at an **FTP** site to move from a subdirectory to its parent directory. Also **chdirup**.
chdirup	See **cdup**.
client	A computer that connects to a more powerful computer (see **server**) for complex tasks.
commercial service	General term for large online services (e.g., America Online, CompuServe, Prodigy, GEnie).
compression	Shrinkage of computer files to conserve storage space and reduce transfer times. Special utility programs, available for most platforms (including DOS, Mac, and

	Amiga), perform the compression and decompression.
cracker	A person who maliciously breaks into a computer system in order to steal files or disrupt system activities.
dial-up access	Computer connection made over standard telephone lines.
dir	"Directory." A command used to display the contents of the current directory.
domain name	The worded address of an **IP number** on the **Internet**, in the form of domain subsets separated by periods. The full address of an **Internet** user is **userid@domain name**.
email	"Electronic mail."
emoticon	See **smiley**.
FAQ	"Frequently asked questions." A file of questions and answers compiled for **Usenet newsgroups**, **mailing lists**, and games to reduce repeated posts about commonplace subjects.
file transfer	Transfer of a file from one computer to another over a network.
finger	A program that provides information about a user who is logged into your local system or on a remote computer on the Internet. Generally invoked by typing "finger" and the person's **userid**.
flame	A violent and usually *ad hominem* attack against another person in a **newsgroup** or message area.
flame war	A back-and-forth series of **flames**.
Free-Net	A community-based network that provides free access to the **Internet**, usually to local residents, and often includes its own forums and news.
freeware	Free software. Not to be confused with **shareware**.
FTP	"File transfer protocol." The standard used to transfer files between computers.
get	An **FTP** command that transfers single files from the **FTP** site to your local directory. The command is followed by a file name; typing "get file.name" would transfer only that file. Also see **mget**.
GIF	Common file format for pictures first popularized by CompuServe, standing for "graphics interchange format." Pronounced with a hard *g*.
gopher	A menu-based guide to directories on the **Internet**, usually organized by subject.
GUI	"Graphical user interface" with windows and point-and-click capability, as opposed to a command-line interface with typed-out instructions.
hacker	A computer enthusiast who enjoys exploring computer systems and programs, sometimes to the point of obsession. Not to be confused with **cracker**.
handle	The name a user wishes to be known by; a user's handle may differ significantly from his or her real name or **userid**.
handshake	The squawking noise at the beginning of a computer connection when two modems settle on a protocol for exchanging information.
Home Page	The main **World Wide Web** site for a particular group or organization.
hqx	File suffix for a BinHex file, a common format for transmitting Macintosh binary files over the **Internet**.
hypertext	An easy method of retrieving information by choosing highlighted words in a text on the screen. The words link to documents with related subject matter.
IC	"In character." A game player who is IC is acting as his or her **character**'s persona.
Internet	The largest network of computer networks in the world, easily recognizable by the format of Internet **email** addresses: **userid**@host.

Internet provider   Wholesale or retail reseller of access to the **Internet**. YPN is one example.

IP connection   Full-fledged link to the **Internet**. See **SLIP**, **PPP**, and **TCP/IP**.

IP number   The unique number that determines the ultimate **Internet** identity of an **IP connection**.

IRC   "**Internet** relay chat." A service that allows **real-time** conversations between multiple users on a variety of subject-oriented channels.

jpeg   Common compressed format for picture files. Pronounced "jay-peg."

ls   "List." A command that provides simplified directory information at **FTP** sites and other directories. It lists only file names for the directory, not file sizes or dates.

lurkers   Regular readers of messages online who never post.

lynx   A popular text-based **Web browser**.

mailing list   Group discussion distributed through **email**. Many mailing lists are administered through listserv.

mget   An **FTP** command that transfers multiple files from the **FTP** site to your local directory. The command is followed by a list of file names separated by spaces, sometimes in combination with an asterisk used as a wild card. Typing "mget b*" would transfer all files in the directory beginning with the letter *b*. Also see **get**.

Net, the   A colloquial term that is often used to refer to the entirety of cyberspace: the **Internet**, the **commercial services**, **BBSs**, etc.

netiquette   The rules of cyberspace civility. Usually applied to the **Internet**, where manners are enforced exclusively by fellow users.

newbie   A newcomer to the **Net**, to a game, or to a discussion. Also called fluxer.

newsgroups   The **Usenet** message areas, organized by subject.

newsreader   Software program for reading **Usenet newsgroups** on the **Internet**.

port number   A number that follows a **telnet** address. The number connects a user to a particular application on the telnet site. LambdaMOO, for example, is at port 8888 of lambda.parc.xerox.com (lambda.parc.xerox.com 8888).

posting   The sending of a message to a **newsgroup**, bulletin board, or other public message area. The message itself is called a **post**.

pwd   A command used at an **FTP** site to display the name of the current directory on your screen.

real-time   The **Net** term for "live," as in "live broadcast." Real-time connections include **IRC** and **MUD**s.

remote machine   Any computer on the **Internet** reached with a program such as **FTP** or **telnet**. The machine making the connection is called the home, or local, machine.

RL   "Real life."

server   A software program, or the computer running the program, that allows other computers, called **clients**, to share its resources.

shareware   Free software, distributed over the **Net** with a request from the programmer for voluntary payment.

sig   Short for **signature**.

signature   A file added to the end of **email** messages or **Usenet** posts that contains personal information—usually your name, email address, postal address, and telephone number. **Netiquette** dictates that signatures, or **sigs**, should be no longer than four or five lines.

SLIP and PPP   "Serial line **Internet** protocol" and "point-to-point protocol." Connecting by

SLIP or PPP actually puts a computer on the Internet, which offers a number of advantages over regular **dial-up**. A SLIP or PPP connection can support a graphical **Web browser** (such as Mosaic), and allows for multiple connections at the same time. Requires special software and a SLIP or PPP service provider.

smiley	Text used to indicate emotion, humor, or irony in electronic messages—best understood if viewed sideways. Also called an **emoticon**. The most common smileys are :-) and :-(
snail mail	The paper mail the U.S. Postal Service delivers. The forerunner of **email**.
spam	The posting of the same article to multiple **newsgroups** (usually every possible one) regardless of the appropriateness of the topic (e.g., "Make Money Fast").
sysop	"System operator." The person who owns and/or manages a **BBS** or other **Net** site.
TCP/IP	The "transmission control protocol" and the "**Internet** protocol." The basis of a full-fledged Internet connection. See **IP Connection**, **PPP**, and **SLIP**. Pronounced "T-C-P-I-P."
telnet	An **Internet** program that allows you to log into other Internet-connected computers.
terminal emulator	A program or utility that allows a computer to communicate in a foreign or non-standard **terminal mode**.
terminal mode	The software standard a computer uses for text communication—for example, ANSI for PCs and **VT-100** for UNIX.
thread	Posted **newsgroup** message with a series of replies. Threaded **newsreaders** organize replies under the original subject.
timeout	The break in communication that occurs when two computers are talking and one takes so long to respond that the other gives up.
URL	"Uniform resource locator." The **World Wide Web** address of a resource on the **Internet**.
Usenet	A collection of networks and computer systems that exchange messages, organized by subject in **newsgroups**.
userid	The unique name (often eight characters or less) given to a user on a system for his or her account. The complete address, which can be used for **email** or **fingering**, is a userid followed by the @ sign and the **domain name** (e.g., Bill Clinton's address is president@whitehouse.gov).
Veronica	See **Archie**.
VT-100 emulation	Widely used terminal protocol for formatting full screens of text over computer connections.
WAIS	"Wide area information server." A system that searches through database indexes around the **Internet**, using keywords.
Web browser	A **client** program designed to interact with **World Wide Web servers** on the **Internet** for the purpose of viewing **Web pages**.
Web page	A **hypertext** document that is part of the **World Wide Web** and that can incorporate graphics, sounds, and links to other **Web pages**, **FTP** sites, **gophers**, and a variety of other **Internet** resources.
World Wide Web	A **hypertext**-based navigation system that lets you browse through a variety of linked **Net** resources, including **Usenet newsgroups** and **FTP**, **telnet**, and **gopher** sites, without typing commands. Also known as WWW and the Web.
zip	File-compression standard in the DOS and Windows worlds.

NetCollege Honor Roll

These schools passed the NetCollege exam with flying colors. They've fully embraced the Net, making it easier for you to get to know the school and to use the Web to apply, download or request additional information.

The Head of the Class: These schools received Wired ratings of five out of five for their A+ Web sites.

Amherst College
Bates College
Drexel University
Duke University
University of Florida
Harvard University
University of Illinois, Urbana-Champaign
Iowa State University
Johns Hopkins University
University of Maine

Massachusetts Institute of Technology
University of Mississippi
University of New Hampshire
New Jersey Institute of Technology
University of New Mexico
New York University
University of North Carolina, Chapel Hill
University of Notre Dame
University of Oregon
University of Pennsylvania
Princeton University
Rensselaer Polytechnic Institute

San Francisco State University
University of Southern California
University of Tennessee, Knoxville
University of Texas, Austin
Trinity College
University of Virginia
Washington and Lee University
Washington State University
Wesleyan University
Whitman College
College of William and Mary
Williams College
Worcester Polytechnic Institute
University of Wyoming

You can apply to these schools entirely online. Some will even waive their application fee.

FULL APPLICATION ONLINE

University of Arizona
Baylor University
Beloit College
University of Cincinnati
University of Delaware

George Mason University
Georgia Institute of Technology
Kansas State University
University of Minnesota, Twin Cities
Mississippi State University
University of Mississippi
Nazareth College of Rochester
New Jersey Institute of Technology
University of New Orleans
Northeastern University
Occidental College
Oklahoma State University

Purdue University
Rochester Institute of Technology
University of South Carolina
University of Texas, Austin
Virginia Polytechnic Institute and State University
Washington University
Whittier College
Wittenberg University
Worcester Polytechnic Institute

You can fill out most of the application online at these schools; you'll only need to follow up through snail mail with a few answers and the essay.

PARTIAL APPLICATION ONLINE

Case Western University
Davidson College
Hampden-Sydney College

You can download the application from these schools to print and fill out at home.

Brigham Young University
Bucknell University
Carnegie Mellon University
Emerson College

University of Florida
Gettysburg College
Humboldt State University
Indiana University, Bloomington
Kent State University
Kenyon College
University of Maryland, College Park
University of Massachusetts, Amherst
Michigan State University
Middlebury College
University of Missouri, Rolla

New Mexico Institute of Mining
   and Technology
University of North Carolina,
   Chapel Hill
University of Notre Dame
Pennsylvania State University
St. John's College, Annapolis
St. John's College, Santa Fe
Sarah Lawrence College
University of Virginia
Wake Forest University

If you want more information and an application, these schools let you request them online. They will send them to you by mail.

Adelphi University
Brandeis University
California State University, Long
   Beach
California State University, Los
   Angeles
Denison University
University of Denver
DePaul University
DePauw University
Drew University
Drury College
East Carolina University
Emory University
University of Evansville
Farleigh Dickinson University
Florida International University
Furman University
Grinnell College
Hampshire College
Harvey Mudd College
Haverford College
Hillsdale College
Hobart and William Smith Colleges
Howard University
Illinois College
University of Illinois, Chicago

University of Kansas
Lafayette College
Lehigh University
Macalester College
Marlboro College
Miami University
Michigan Technological University
University of Missouri, Columbia
University of Montana
Morehouse College
University of Nevada, Las Vegas
University of North Dakota
Ohio Wesleyan University
Oregon State University
University of Oregon
University of Pennsylvania
University of Pittsburgh
Pitzer College
Pomona College
Princeton University
University of Rhode Island
Rutgers College
St. John's University
Saint Louis University
St. Olaf University
San Diego State University
San Francisco State University
Santa Clara University
Seattle University
Simon's Rock College
Skidmore College
Smith College
University of the South
University of Southern California

University of Southern Maine
Southern Methodist University
Southwestern University
Stanford University
SUNY, Albany
SUNY, Binghamton
SUNY, Buffalo
SUNY, Stony Brook
SUNY, Geneseo
SUNY, Potsdam
Swarthmore College
Temple University
Tennessee Technological University
University of Tennessee, Knoxville
Texas A&M University
Texas Christian University
Trinity College
Trinity University
Tulane University
University of Tulsa
United States Air Force Academy
United States Coast Guard
   Academy
United States Military Academy
   (West Point)
United States Naval Academy
Ursinus College
Vanderbilt University
University of Vermont
Virginia Military Institute
Washington and Lee University
University of Washington
William Jewell College
University of Wyoming

Colleges by state

Alabama
University of Alabama
Auburn University
Birmingham-Southern College
Samford University

Alaska
University of Alaska, Fairbanks

Arizona
University of Arizona

Arkansas
University of Arkansas, Fayetteville
Hendrix College

California
California Institute of Technology
California State University, Fresno
California State University,
  Hayward
California State University, Long
  Beach
California State University, Los
  Angeles
California State University,
  Sacramento
University of California, Berkeley
University of California, Davis
University of California, Irvine
University of California, Los
  Angeles
University of California, Riverside
University of California, San Diego
University of California, Santa
  Barbara
University of California, Santa Cruz
Claremont McKenna College
Harvey Mudd College
Humboldt State University
Mills College
Occidental College
Pitzer College
Pomona College
San Diego State University
University of San Diego
San Francisco State University
Santa Clara University

Scripps College
University of Southern California
Stanford University
Whittier College

Colorado
Colorado College
Colorado School of Mines
University of Colorado, Boulder
University of Denver
United States Air Force Academy

Connecticut
Connecticut College
University of Connecticut
Trinity College
United States Coast Guard
  Academy
Wesleyan University
Yale University

Delaware
University of Delaware

District of Columbia
The American University
The Catholic University of America
George Washington University
Georgetown University
Howard University

Florida
Florida International University
Florida State University
University of Florida
University of Miami
New College of the University of
  South Florida
University of South Florida

Georgia
Agnes Scott College
Emory University
Georgia Institute of Technology
Georgia State University
University of Georgia
Mercer University
Morehouse College

Spelman College

Hawaii
University of Hawaii, Manoa

Illinois
University of Chicago
DePaul University
Illinois College
Illinois Institute of Technology
University of Illinois, Chicago
University of Illinois, Urbana-
  Champaign
Lake Forest College
Loyola University, Chicago
Northwestern University
Rockford College

Indiana
Ball State University
DePauw University
Earlham College
University of Evansville
Hanover College
Indiana University, Bloomington
University of Notre Dame
Purdue University
Rose-Hulman Institute of Technology
Wabash College

Iowa
Central College
Drake University
Grinnell College
Iowa State University
University of Iowa

Kansas
Benedictine College
Kansas State University
University of Kansas

Kentucky
University of Kentucky
University of Louisville

Louisiana
Louisiana State University

University of New Orleans
Tulane University

Maine
Bates College
Bowdoin College
Colby College
University of Maine
University of Southern Maine

Maryland
University of Maryland,
    College Park
St. John's College, Annapolis
Johns Hopkins University
United States Naval Academy

Massachusetts
Amherst College
Assumption College
Babson College
Boston College
Boston University
Brandeis University
Clark University
Emerson College
Hampshire College
Harvard University
College of the Holy Cross
Massachusetts Institute of
    Technology
University of Massachusetts,
    Amherst
University of Massachusetts, Boston
Mount Holyoke College
Northeastern University
Simon's Rock of Bard College
Smith College
Tufts University
Wellesley College
Williams College
Worcester Polytechnic Institute

Michigan
Hillsdale College
Kalamazoo College
Lawrence Technological University
Michigan State University
Michigan Technological University
University of Michigan, Ann Arbor

Minnesota
Carleton College
Macalester College
University of Minnesota, Twin Cities
Saint Olaf College

Mississippi
Millsaps College
University of Mississippi
Mississippi State University

Missouri
Drury College
University of Missouri, Columbia
University of Missouri, Rolla
Saint Louis University
Washington University
William Jewell College

Montana
University of Montana

Nebraska
Creighton University
University of Nebraska, Lincoln

Nevada
University of Nevada, Las Vegas

New Hampshire
Dartmouth College
University of New Hampshire
New Hampshire College

New Jersey
Drew University
Fairleigh Dickinson University
New Jersey Institute of Technology
Princeton University
Rutgers College
Stevens Institute of Technology
Trenton State College

New Mexico
New Mexico Institute of Mining
    and Technology
University of New Mexico
St. John's College, Santa Fe

New York
Adelphi University
Alfred University
Bard College

Barnard College
Canisius College
City University of New York,
    Brooklyn College
Clarkson University
Colgate University
Columbia University
Cooper Union
Cornell University
Eugene Lang College of the New
    School for Social Research
Fordham University
Hamilton College
Hartwick College
Hobart and William Smith Colleges
Hofstra University
LeMoyne College
Long Island University, C.W. Post
    Campus
Nazareth College of Rochester
New York University
Rensselaer Polytechnic Institute
Rochester Institute of Technology
University of Rochester
St. Bonaventure University
St. John's University
Sarah Lawrence College
Skidmore College
SUNY, Albany
SUNY, Binghamton
SUNY, Buffalo
SUNY, Stony Brook
SUNY College, Geneseo
SUNY College, Potsdam
Syracuse University
Union College
United States Military Academy
    (West Point)
Vassar College

North Carolina
Davidson College
Duke University
East Carolina University
Guilford College
Lenoir-Rhyne College
University of North Carolina,
    Chapel Hill
North Carolina State University
Wake Forest University

North Dakota
University of North Dakota

Colleges by State

Ohio
Antioch College
Case Western Reserve University
University of Cincinnati
Denison University
Kent State University
Kenyon College
Miami University
Oberlin College
Ohio State University
Ohio University
Ohio Wesleyan University
Wittenberg University
The College of Wooster

Oklahoma
Oklahoma State University
University of Tulsa

Oregon
Lewis & Clark College
Oregon State University
University of Oregon
Reed College

Pennsylvania
Allegheny College
Bryn Mawr College
Bucknell University
Carnegie Mellon University
Dickinson College
Drexel University
Duquesne University
Franklin & Marshall College
Gettysburg College
Haverford College
Lafayette College
LaSalle University
Lehigh University
Pennsylvania State University
University of Pennsylvania
University of Pittsburgh
Swarthmore College
Temple University
Ursinus College
Villanova University
Widener University

Rhode Island
Brown University
Providence College
Rhode Island School of Design
University of Rhode Island

South Carolina
Clemson University
Furman University
University of South Carolina
Wofford College

South Dakota
University of South Dakota, Vermillion

Tennessee
Fisk University
Rhodes College
University of the South
University of Tennessee, Knoxville
Tennessee Technological University
Vanderbilt University

Texas
Austin College
Baylor University
University of Dallas
University of Houston
Rice University
Southern Methodist University
Southwestern University
Texas A&M University, College Station
University of Texas, Austin
Texas Christian University
Trinity University

Utah
Brigham Young University
University of Utah

Vermont
Bennington College
Marlboro College
Middlebury College
University of Vermont

Virginia
George Mason University
Hampden-Sydney College
James Madison University
Mary Washington College
University of Richmond
University of Virginia
Virginia Military Institute
Virginia Polytechnic Institute and State University
Washington and Lee University
College of William and Mary

Washington
Evergreen State College
Seattle University
Washington State University
University of Washington
Whitman College

Wisconsin
Beloit College
Marquette University
University of Wisconsin, Madison
University of Wisconsin, Milwaukee

Wyoming
University of Wyoming

Canada
Concordia University
McGill University

Index

A

alcohol
  See **health/safety**
A. Magazine, 68
ABACI's College Financial Aid Software, 36
Abortion and Reproduction Rights Internet Resources, 66
ACADEM, 32
Academic Counseling Services, Inc., 27
Academic Scholarship Consultants, 46
Academic Scholarship Services, 46
Academic South, The, 28
Acquaintance Rape, 77
activism, 64-66
  community service, 64-65
  environmentalism, 65
  feminism, 65
  homeless organizations, 65
  reproductive rights, 66
  sexual identity, 66
Adelphi University, 88
Adult Student Survival Guide, 73
Adventures in Education, 40
AFAM-L, 67
Afro-American Culture & Arts Forum, 67
AFRONET Junior Posse, 68
Agnes Scott College, 89
Aid For College, 46
Air Force ROTC, 50
Alcohol, Drugs, Cigarettes & Recovery, 76
ALD College Basketball Site, 59
Alfred University, dir005
Allegheny College, 93
Alliance to Save Student Aid, The, 54
Allsport's Free College Sports Recruiting and Scholarship Service, 48
alt.activism.d, 64

alt.art.colleges, 28
alt.college.food, 81
alt.college.fraternities, 62
alt.college.sororities, 62
alt.flame.roommate, 81
alt.folklore.college, 81
alt.fraternity.sorority, 62
alt.sex.first-time, 74
alt.society.generation-x, 81
Alternative Higher Education Network, The, 28
Alumni and Alumnae, 26
Amarillo's ACE Scholarship Program, 49
American Association of University Women, 73
American Express University: The Money Pit, 41
American Indian College Fund, 71
American Revolution Summer Study Program at Trinity College in Oxford, England, 83
American Student Assistance Home Page, 42
American University, The, 94
Americana Funding, 46
Amerispan Unlimited, 83
Amherst College, 95
Amnesty International Online, 64
Antioch College, 96
applications, 30-32
  common, 31-32
  essays, 30-31
  software, 26, 32
ApplyWeb, 31
Armenian Students' Association of America, 47
ASA-L, 68
Asian Student Connection, 68
Asian-American Clubs, 69
Asian-American Studies Center, 69
assault/rape
  See **health & safety**
Associated Western Universities

Incorporated, 28
Association of Jesuit Colleges and Universities, 28
Assumption College, 99
athletics, 58-61
  baseball, 59
  basketball, 59
  crew, 60
  football, 60
  hockey, 60
  NCAA, 58
  soccer, 61
  volleyball, 61
  women's sports, 61
Auburn University, 100
Austin College, 101

B

Babson College, 102
Bacchus, 76
Ball State University, 103
Bard College, 104
Barnard College, 105
Bates College, 106
Baylor in Africa 1996, 83
Baylor University, 107
Be Real, Get In, 30
Beloit College, 108
Benedictine College, 109
Bennington College, 110
BiAct-L, 66
Birchwood Scholarship Services, 46
Birmingham-Southern College, 111
bisexuality, 72-73
  See also multiculturalism
Black Collegian, The, 68
Black Excel: The College Help Network, 47
Black Voices, 68
Boston College, 112
Boston University, 113
Bowdoin College, 114

Index

Index

N

O

P

Index

Index

Wolff New Media

Wolff New Media is one of the leading providers of information about the Net and the emerging Net culture. The company's NetBooks Series, presently at 16 titles—*NetGuide, NetGames, NetChat, NetMoney, NetTrek, NetSports, NetTech, NetMusic, Fodor's NetTravel, NetTaxes, NetJobs, NetVote, NetMarketing, NetDoctor, NetStudy,* and *NetCollege*—will expand to more than 25 titles in 1996. This will include *NetKids, NetSpy, NetSci-Fi, NetShopping,* and *NetScreen.* The entire NetBooks Series (to date) is now available on the companion Web site YPN—Your Personal Net (http://www.ypn.com). And *Net Guide*—"the *TV Guide*® to Cyberspace," according to *Wired* magazine editor Louis Rossetto—is now a monthly magazine published by CMP Publications.

The company was founded in 1988 by journalist Michael Wolff to bring together writers, editors, and graphic designers to create editorially and visually compelling information products in books, magazines, and new media. Among the company's other projects are *Where We Stand—Can America Make It in the Global Race for Wealth, Health, and Happiness?* (Bantam Books), one of the most graphically complex information books ever to be wholly created and produced by means of desktop-publishing technology, and *Made in America?*, a four-part PBS series on global competitiveness, hosted by Labor Secretary Robert B. Reich.

The company frequently acts as a consultant to other information companies, including WGBH, Boston's educational television station; CMP Publications; and Time Warner, which it has advised on the development of Time's online business and the launch of its Web site, Pathfinder.

Notes

Notes

Notes

Notes

Who are the most influential Asian Americans in the U.S.?

Who are the Asians making waves in Corporate America, in Cyberspace, in Hollywood?

What are the issues, challenges, and opportunities that face America's fastest-growing ethnic group?

Turn to A. Magazine for the answers! From politics to pop culture, from trends to technology, from our disparate past to our promising future, we'll take you inside Asian America in every issue. The hottest writers. The timeliest topics. Stunning design and photography. Get them all, six times a year, direct to your door.

GET A FREE PREVIEW COPY OF A. MAGAZINE, AND START YOUR NO-OBLIGATION TRIAL SUBSCRIPTION! USE THE COUPON BELOW OR CALL 1-800-346-0085 X 477 AND MENTION CODE MNB961.

If after getting your free copy, you don't like what you read, simply call us toll-free, or write "cancel" on your invoice and you'll owe absolutely nothing — the free issue is yours to keep. Otherwise, you'll receive six more issues of A. Magazine — a full year — for the low rate of $11 — 25% less than the regular subscription rate, and 38% lower than the newsstand price

"A. Magazine captures the life and times of Asian America, and gives them what they want — widely acclaimed editorial covering trends, leaders, culture, and style."
— *Inside Media* magazine.

The College
Admissions Process
STARTS HERE

↓

CollegeBound.NET

A STUDENT'S
INTERACTIVE GUIDE
TO COLLEGE LIFE

http://www.cbnet.com/collegebound

COMING SEPTEMBER 9TH, 1996

Fun, Frolic & Figure Out The College Fuss!

* Bang Your Brain For Bucks
* Interactive Stuff
* Contests Galore
* On-line Recruiter
* Campus Tours à la CB.NET
* CB Student of the Year Contest
* Student Corner Café

...The Best Bet on the Net for Teens

http://www.cbnet.com/collegebound